Blackstone's Statutes on

PROPERTY LAW

Blackstone's Statutes on

PROPERTY LAW

Fourth Edition

Edited by

Meryl Thomas BA, LLM

Senior Lecturer in Law, University of Central England

First published in Great Britain 1989 by Blackstone Press Limited, 9–15 Aldine Street, London W12 8AW. Telephone 0181–740 2277

First edition 1989
Reprinted 1991
Reprinted 1992
Reprinted 1993
Second edition 1994
Third edition 1995
Fourth edition 1996
Reprinted 1997

ISBN: 1 85431 563 3

British Library Cataloguing in Publication Data
A CIP catalogue record for this book is available from the British Library

Typeset by Style Photosetting Ltd, Mayfield, East Sussex
Printed in Great Britain by Ashford Colour Press, Gosport, Hants

CONTENTS

EDITOR'S PREFACE

Blackstone's Statutes on Property Law seeks primarily to provide a convenient and concise collection of statutes which is suitable for use by all students who are studying land law, trusts, succession and conveyancing. The statutes have been edited so as to remove the extraneous sections that are rarely referred to by the student and to provide only the essential text of the statute.

Despite careful editing, however, about two-thirds of the book comprises the edited text of the 1925 property legislation (viz the Settled Land Act, the Trustee Act, the Law of Property Act, the Land Registration Act and the Administration of Estates Act), although the Settled Land Act 1925 is at a fraction of its original length, a decision which reflects the lack of importance given to settled land not only in the teaching of land law at universities and colleges these days but also in society generally. The remaining one third of the book consists primarily of the post 1925 property legislation which has developed out of the 1925 legislation. There has been a plethora of new legislation in the area of landlord and tenant law in recent years, but very little of it is reproduced in this book, since it is the opinion of the editor that this topic is not within the realms of 'traditional property law' and merits consideration in a separate book.

The statutes are printed in chronological order with any subsequent amendments incorporated in the appropriate place in the statute and indicated by means of a square bracket only. The amending statute is not printed separately and any repealed provisions are deleted (with the exception of a few sections of the Law of Property Act 1925 which are printed in italics). In all but a few cases no note or reference is made of the amending statute. For the most part where complete sections and subsections are repealed no note is made of the fact and the section is merely omitted from the text although in parts this is indicated by three dots in square brackets. Any editing in a section or a subsection by the editor is indicated by three dots without a square bracket. The title of the statute, the marginal notes referring to the relevant section and the material parts of the section are included in the text but there are no references to preambles, headings, provisions or the commencement of the statute, extent and citation, or references to previous law. Provisions relating to Scotland or Northern Ireland have largely been omitted.

The present text has been updated to include material which received the Royal Assent in the 1995–96 Parliamentary session. Therefore the Family Law Act 1996 and the Trusts of Land and Appointment of Trustees Act 1996 are included. In addition the Law Reform (Succession) Act 1995, which had not received Royal Assent at the time of publication of the third edition, has been incorporated into the body of the statutes to which it relates.

Finally I would like to thank those at Blackstone Press who were always available to give me help whenever I needed it.

Meryl Thomas
September 1996

PRESCRIPTION ACT 1832
(1832, c.71)

1. Claims to right of common and other profits à prendre, not to be defeated after thirty years enjoyment by merely showing the commencement; after sixty years enjoyment the right to be absolute, unless had by consent or agreement
No claim which may be lawfully made at the common law, by custom, prescription, or grant, to any right of common or other profit or benefit to be taken and enjoyed from or upon any land of our sovereign lord the King, [...] or any land being parcel of the duchy of Lancaster or of the duchy of Cornwall, or of any ecclesiastical or lay person, or body corporate, except such matters and things as are herein specially provided for, and except tithes, rent, and services, shall, where such right, profit, or benefit shall have been actually taken and enjoyed by any person claiming right thereto without interruption for the full period of thirty years, be defeated or destroyed by showing only that such right, profit, or benefit was first taken or enjoyed at any time prior to such period of thirty years, but nevertheless such claim may be defeated in any other way by which the same is now liable to be defeated; and when such right, profit, or benefit shall have been so taken and enjoyed as aforesaid for the full period of sixty years, the right thereto shall be deemed absolute and indefeasible, unless it shall appear that the same was taken and enjoyed by some consent or agreement expressly made or given for that purpose by deed or writing.

2. In claims of right of way or other easement the periods to be twenty years and forty years
No claim which may be lawfully made at the common law, by custom, prescription, or grant, to any way or other easement, or to any watercourse, or the use of any water, to be enjoyed or derived upon, over, or from any land or water of our said lord the King, [...] or being parcel of the duchy of Lancaster or of the duchy of Cornwall, or being the property of any ecclesiastical or lay person, or body corporate, when such way or other matter as herein last before mentioned shall have been actually enjoyed by any person claiming right thereto without interruption for the full period of twenty years, shall be defeated or destroyed by showing only that such way or other matter was first enjoyed at any time prior to such period of twenty years, but nevertheless such claim may be defeated in any other way by which the same is now liable to be defeated; and where such way or other matter as herein last before mentioned shall have been so enjoyed as aforesaid for the full period of forty years, the right thereto shall be deemed absolute and indefeasible, unless it shall appear that the same was enjoyed by some consent or agreement expressly given or made for that purpose by deed or writing.

3. Claim to the use of light enjoyed for 20 years
When the access and use of light to and for any dwelling house, workshop, or other building shall have been actually enjoyed therewith for the full period of twenty years without interruption, the right thereto shall be deemed absolute and indefeasible, any local usage or custom to the contrary notwithstanding, unless it shall appear that the same was enjoyed by some consent or agreement expressly made or given for that purpose by deed or writing.

4. Before mentioned periods to be deemed those next before suits
Each of the respective periods of years herein-before mentioned shall be deemed and taken to be the period next before some suit or action wherein the claim or matter to which such period may relate shall have been or shall be brought into question and that no act or other matter shall be deemed to be an interruption, within the meaning of this statute, unless the same shall have been or shall be submitted to or acquiesced in for one year after the party interrupted shall have had or shall have notice thereof, and of the person making or authorizing the same to be made.

5. In actions on the case, the claimant may allege his right generally, as at present. In pleas to trespass and certain other pleadings, the period mentioned in this Act may be alleged. Exceptions, etc. to be replied to specially

In all actions upon the case and other pleadings, wherein the party claiming may now by law allege his right generally, without averring the existence of such right from time immemorial, such general allegation shall still be deemed sufficient, and if the same shall be denied all and every the matters in this Act mentioned and provided, which shall be applicable to the case, shall be admissible in evidence to sustain or rebut such allegation; and that in all pleadings to actions of trespass, and in all other pleadings wherein before the passing of this Act it would have been necessary to allege the right to have existed from time immemorial, it shall be sufficient to allege the enjoyment thereof as of right by the occupiers of the tenement in respect whereof the same is claimed for and during such of the periods mentioned in this Act as may be applicable to the case, and without claiming in the name or right of the owner of the fee, as is now usually done; and if the other party shall intend to rely on any proviso, exception, incapacity, disability, contract, agreement, or other matter herein-before mentioned, or on any cause or matter of fact or of law not inconsistent with the simple fact of enjoyment, the same shall be specially alleged and set forth in answer to the allegation of the party claiming, and shall not be received in evidence on any general traverse or denial of such allegation.

6. Presumption to be allowed in claims herein provided for

In the several cases mentioned in and provided for by this Act, no presumption shall be allowed or made in favour or support of any claim, upon proof of the exercise or enjoyment of the right or matter claimed for any less period of time or number of years than for such period or number mentioned in this Act as may be applicable to the case and to the nature of the claim.

7. Proviso for infants, etc.

Provided also, that the time during which any person otherwise capable of resisting any claim to any of the matters before mentioned shall have been or shall be an infant, idiot, non compos mentis, feme covert, or tenant for life, or during which any action or suit shall have been pending, and which shall have been diligently prosecuted, until abated by the death of any party or parties thereto, shall be excluded in the computation of the periods herein-before mentioned, except only in cases where the right or claim is hereby declared to be absolute and indefeasible.

8. What time to be excluded in computing the term of forty years appointed by this Act

Provided always, that when any land or water upon, over, or from which any such way or other convenient watercourse or use of water shall have been or shall be enjoyed or derived hath been or shall be held under or by virtue of any term of life, or any term of years exceeding three years from the granting thereof, the time of the enjoyment of any such way or other matter as herein last before mentioned, during the continuance of such terms, shall be excluded in the computation of the said period of forty years, in case the claim shall within three years next after the end or sooner determination of such term be resisted by any person entitled to any reversion expectant on the determination thereof.

WILLS ACT 1837
(1837, c. 26)

1. Meaning of certain words in this Act

The words and expressions herein-after mentioned, which in their ordinary signification have a more confined or a different meaning, shall in this Act, except where the nature of the provision or the context of the Act shall exclude such construction, be interpreted as follows; (that is to say,) the word 'will' shall extend to a testament, and to a codicil, and to an appointment by will or by writing in the nature of a will in exercise of a power [and also to an appointment by will of a guardian of a child] [. . .] and to any other testamentary disposition; and the words 'real estate' shall extend to manors, advowsons, messuages, lands, tithes, rents, and hereditaments, [. . .] whether corporeal, incorporeal, or personal, [. . .] and to any estate, right, or interest (other than a chattel interest) therein; and the words 'personal estate' shall extend to leasehold estates and other chattels real, and also to monies, shares of government and other funds, securities for money (not being real estates), debts, choses in action, rights, credits, goods, and all other property whatsoever which by law devolves upon the executor or administrator, and to any share or interest therein; and every word importing the singular number only shall extend and be applied to several persons or things as well as one person or thing; and every word importing the masculine gender only shall extend and be applied to a female as well as a male.

3. All property may be disposed of by will

It shall be lawful for every person to devise, bequeath, or dispose of, by his will executed in manner herein-after required, all real estate and all personal estate which he shall be entitled to, either at law or in equity, at the time of his death, and which, if not so devised, bequeathed, or disposed of, would devolve [. . .] upon his executor or administrator; and the power hereby given shall extend [. . .] to all contingent, executory or other future interests in any real or personal estate, whether the testator may or may not be ascertained as the person or one of the persons in whom the same respectively may become vested, and whether he may be entitled thereto under the instrument by which the same respectively were created, or under any disposition thereof by deed or will, and also to all rights of entry for conditions broken, and other rights of entry; and also to such of the same estates, interests, and rights respectively, and other real and personal estate, as the testator may be entitled to at the time of his death, notwithstanding that he may become entitled to the same subsequently to the execution of his will.

7. No will of a person under age valid

No will made by any person under the age of [eighteen years] shall be valid.

[9. Signing and attestation of wills

No will shall be valid unless—

(a) it is in writing, and signed by the testator, or by some other person in his presence and by his direction; and

(b) it appears that the testator intended by his signature to give effect to the will; and

(c) the signature is made or acknowledged by the testator in the presence of two or more witnesses present at the same time; and

(d) each witness either—

(i) attests and signs the will; or

(ii) acknowledges his signature in the presence of the testator (but not necessarily in the presence of any other witness) but no form of attestation shall be necessary.]

10. Appointments by will to be executed like other wills, and to be valid, although other required solemnities are not observed

No appointment made by will, in exercise of any power, shall be valid, unless the same be executed in manner herein-before required; and every will executed in manner hereinbefore required shall, so far as respects the execution and attestation thereof, be a valid execution of a power of appointment by will, notwithstanding it shall have been expressly required that a will made in exercise of such power should be executed with some additional or other form of execution or solemnity.

11. Soldiers and mariners wills excepted

Provided always, that any soldier being in actual military service, or any mariner or seaman being at sea, may dispose of his personal estate as he might have done before the making of this Act.

13. Publication of will not be requisite

Every will executed in manner herein-before required shall be valid without any other publication thereof.

14. Will not to be void on account of incompetency of attesting witness

If any person who shall attest the execution of a will shall at the time of the execution thereof or at any time afterwards be incompetent to be admitted a witness to prove the execution thereof, such will shall not on that account be invalid.

15. Gifts to an attesting witness to be void

If any person shall attest the execution of any will to whom or to whose wife or husband any beneficial devise, legacy, estate, interest, gift, or appointment, of or affecting any real or personal estate (other than and except charges and directions for the payment of any debt or debts), shall be thereby given or made, such devise, legacy, estate, interest, gift, or appointment shall, so far only as concerns such person attesting the execution of such will, or the wife or husband of such person, or any person claiming under such person or wife or husband, be utterly null and void, and such person so attesting shall be admitted as a witness to prove the execution of such will, or to prove the validity or invalidity thereof, notwithstanding such devise, legacy, estate, interest, gift, or appointment mentioned in such will.

16. Creditor attesting to be admitted a witness

In case by any will any real or personal estate shall be charged with any debt or debts, and any creditor, or the wife or husband of any creditor, whose debt is so charged, shall attest the execution of such will, such creditor notwithstanding such charge shall be admitted a witness to prove the execution of such will, or to prove the validity or invalidity thereof.

17. Executor shall be admitted a witness

No person shall, on account of his being an executor of a will, be incompetent to be admitted a witness to prove the execution of such will, or a witness to prove the validity or invalidity thereof.

[18. Wills to be revoked by marriage, except in certain cases

(1) Subject to subsections (2) to (4) below, a will shall be revoked by the testator's marriage.

(2) A disposition in a will in exercise of a power of appointment shall take effect notwithstanding the testator's subsequent marriage unless the property so appointed would in default of appointment pass to his personal representatives.

(3) Where it appears from a will that at the time it was made the testator was expecting to be married to a particular person and that he intended that the will should not be revoked by the marriage, the will shall not be revoked by his marriage to that person.

(4) Where it appears from a will that at the time it was made the testator was expecting to be married to a particular person and that he intended that a disposition in the will should not be revoked by his marriage to that person—

(a) that disposition shall take effect notwithstanding the marriage; and

(b) any other disposition in the will shall take effect also, unless it appears from the will that the testator intended the disposition to be revoked by the marriage.]

[18A. Effect of dissolution or annulment of marriage on wills

(1) Where, after a testator has made a will, [an order or decree] of a court [of civil jurisdiction in England and Wales] dissolves or annuls his marriage [or his marriage is dissolved or annulled and the divorce or annulment is entitled to recognition in England and Wales by virtue of Part 11 of the Family Law Act 1986]—

[(a) provisions of the will appointing executors or trustees or conferring a power of appointment, if they appoint or confer the power on the former spouse, shall take effect as if the former spouse had died on the date on which the marriage is dissolved or annulled, and

(b) any property which, or an interest in which, is devised or bequeathed to the former spouse shall pass as if the former spouse had died on that date.]

(2) Subsection (1)(b) above is without prejudice to any right of the former spouse under the Inheritance (Provision for Family and Dependants) Act 1975.

Note: Sections 18A(1)(a) and 18A(1)(b) were substituted by the Law Reform (Succession) Act 1995.

19. No will to be revoked by presumption

No will shall be revoked by any presumption of an intention on the ground of an alteration in circumstances.

20. No will to be revoked but by another will or codicil, or by a writing executed like a will, or by destruction

No will or codicil, or any part thereof, shall be revoked otherwise than as aforesaid, or by another will or codicil executed in manner herein-before required, or by some writing declaring an intention to revoke the same, and executed in the manner in which a will is herein-before required to be executed, or by the burning, tearing, or otherwise destroying the same by the testator, or by some person in his presence and by his direction, with the intention of revoking the same.

21. No alteration in a will shall have any effect unless executed as a will

No obliteration, interlineation, or other alteration made in any will after the execution thereof shall be valid or have any effect, except so far as the words or effect of the will before such alteration shall not be apparent, unless such alteration shall be executed in like manner as herein-before is required for the execution of the will; but the will, with such alteration as part thereof, shall be deemed to be duly executed if the signature of the testator and the subscription of the witnesses be made in the margin or on some other part of the will opposite or near to such alteration, or at the foot or end of or opposite to a memorandum referring to such alteration, and written at the end or some other part of the will.

22. No will revoked to be revived otherwise than by Re-execution or a Codicil to revive it

No will or codicil, or any part thereof, which shall be in any manner revoked, shall be revived otherwise than by the re-execution thereof, or by a codicil executed in manner herein-before required and showing an intention to revive the same; and when any will or codicil which shall be partly revoked, and afterwards wholly revoked, shall be revived, such revival shall not extend to so much thereof as shall have been revoked before the revocation of the whole thereof, unless an intention to the contrary shall be shown.

23. A devise not to be rendered inoperative by any subsequent conveyance or act

No conveyance or other Act made or done subsequently to the execution of a will of or relating to any real or personal estate therein comprised, except an act by which such will shall be revoked as aforesaid, shall prevent the operation of the will with respect to such estate or interest in such real or personal estate as the testator shall have power to dispose of by will at the time of his death.

24. A will shall be construed to speak from the death of the testator
Every will shall be construed, with reference to the real estate and personal estate comprised in it, to speak and take effect as if it had been executed immediately before the death of the testator, unless a contrary intention shall appear by the will.

25. Residuary devise shall include estates comprised in lapsed and void devises
Unless a contrary intention shall appear by the will, such real estate or interest therein as shall be comprised or intended to be comprised in any devise in such will contained, which shall fail or be void by reason of the death of the devisee in the lifetime of the testator, or by reason of such devise being contrary to law or otherwise incapable of taking effect shall be included in the residuary devise (if any) contained in such will.

26. A general devise of the testator's lands shall include copyhold and leasehold as well as freehold lands
A devise of the land of the testator, or of the land of the testator in any place or in the occupation of any person mentioned in his will, or otherwise described in a general manner, and any other general devise which would describe a [. . .] leasehold estate if the testator had no freehold estate which could be described by it, shall be construed to include the [. . .] leasehold estates of the testator, or his [. . .] leasehold estates, or any of them, to which such description shall extend, as the case may be, as well as freehold estates, unless a contrary intention shall appear by the will.

27. A general gift shall include estates over which the testator has a general power of appointment
A general devise of the real estate of the testator, or of the real estate of the testator in any place or in the occupation of any person mentioned in his will, or otherwise described in a general manner, shall be construed to include any real estate, or any real estate to which such description shall extend (as the case may be), which he may have power to appoint in any manner he may think proper, and shall operate as an execution of such power, unless a contrary intention shall appear by the will; and in like manner a bequest of the personal estate of the testator, or any bequest of personal property described in a general manner, shall be construed to include any personal estate, or any personal estate to which such description shall extend (as the case may be), which he may have power to appoint in any manner he may think proper, and shall operate as an execution of such power, unless a contrary intention shall appear by the will.

28. A devise without any words of limitation shall be construed to pass as free
Where any real estate shall be devised to any person without any words of limitation, such devise shall be construed to pass the fee simple, or other the whole estate or interest which the testator had power to dispose of by will in such real estate, unless a contrary intention shall appear by the will.

29. The words 'die without issue,' or 'die without leaving issue,' shall be construed to mean die without issue living at the death
In any devise or bequest of a real or personal estate the words 'die without issue,' or 'die without leaving issue,' or 'have no issue,' or any other words which may import either a want or failure of issue of any person in his lifetime or at the time of his death, or an indefinite failure of his issue, shall be construed to mean a want or failure of issue in the lifetime or at the time of the death of such person, and not an indefinite failure of his issue, unless a contrary intention shall appear by the will, by reason of such person having a prior estate tail, or of a preceding gift, being, without any implication arising from such words, a limitation of an estate tail to such person or issue, or otherwise: Provided, that this Act shall not extend to cases where such words as aforesaid import

if no issue described in a preceding gift shall be born, or if there shall be no issue who shall live to attain the age or otherwise answer the description required for obtaining a vested estate by a preceding gift to such issue.

30. No devise to trustees or executors, except for a term or a presentation to a church, shall pass a chattel interest
Where any real estate (other than or not being a presentation to a church) shall be devised to any trustee or executor, such devise shall be construed to pass the fee simple or other the whole estate or interest which the testator had power to dispose of by will in such real estate, unless a definite term of years, absolute or determinable, or an estate of freehold, shall thereby be given to him expressly or by implication.

31. Trustees under an unlimited devise, where the trust may endure beyond the life of a person beneficially entitled for life, shall take the fee
Where any real estate shall be devised to a trustee, without any express limitation of the estate to be taken by such trustee, and the beneficial interest in such real estate, or in the surplus rents and profits thereof, shall not be given to any person for life, or such beneficial interest shall be given to any person for life, but the purposes of the trust may continue beyond the life of such person, such devise shall be construed to vest in such trustee the fee simple, or other the whole legal estate which the testator had power to dispose of by will in such real estate, and not an estate determinable when the purposes of the trust shall be satisfied.

32. Devises of estates tail shall not lapse
Where any person to whom any real estate shall be devised for an estate tail [or an estate in quasi entail] shall die in the lifetime of the testator leaving issue who would be inheritable under such entail, and any such issue shall be living at the time of the death of the testator, such devise shall not lapse, but shall take effect as if the death of such person had happened immediately after the death of the testator, unless a contrary intention shall appear by the will.

[33. Gifts to children or other issue who leave issue living at the testator's death shall not lapse
(1) Where—
(a) a will contains a devise or bequest to a child or remote descendant of the testator; and
(b) the intended beneficiary dies before the testator, leaving issue; and
(c) issue of the intended beneficiary are living at the testator's death,
then, unless a contrary intention appears by the will, the devise or bequest shall take effect as a devise or bequest to the issue living at the testator's death.
(2) Where—
(a) a will contains a devise or bequest to a class of person consisting of children or remoter descendants of the testator; and
(b) a member of the class dies before the testator, leaving issue; and
(c) issue of that member are living at the testator's death, then, unless a contrary intention appears by the will, the devise or bequest shall take effect as if the class included the issue of its deceased member living at the testator's death.
(3) Issue shall take under this section through all degrees, according to their stock, in equal shares if more than one, any gift or share which their parent would have taken and so that no issue shall take whose parent is living at the testator's death and that no issue shall take whose parent is living at the testator's death and so capable of taking.
(4) For the purposes of this section
(a) the illegitimacy of any person is to be disregarded; and
(b) a person conceived before the testator's death and born living thereafter is to be taken to have been living at the testator's death.]

34. Act not to extend to wills made before 1838, nor to estates pur autre vie of persons who die before 1838

This Act shall not extend to any will made before the first day of January one thousand eight hundred and thirty-eight, and every will re-executed or republished, or revived by any codicil, shall for the purposes of this Act be deemed to have been made at the time at which the same shall be so re-executed, republished or revived; and this Act shall not extend to any estate pur autre vie of any person who shall die before the first day of January one thousand eight hundred and thirty-eight.

COMMON LAW PROCEDURE ACT 1852
(1852, c. 76)

210. Proceedings in ejectment by landlord for nonpayment of rent

In all cases between landlord and tenant, as often as it shall happen that one half year's rent shall be in arrear, and the landlord or lessor, to whom the same is due, hath right by law to re-enter for the nonpayment thereof, such landlord or lessor shall and may, without any formal demand or re-entry, serve a writ in ejectment for the recovery of the demised premises, [. . .] which service [. . .] shall stand in the place and stead of a demand and re-entry; and in case of judgment against the defendant for nonappearance, if it shall be made appear to the court where the said action is depending, by affidavit, or be proved upon the trial in case the defendant appears, that half a year's rent was due before the said writ was served, and that no sufficient distress was to be found on the demised premises, countervailing the arrears then due, and that the lessor had power to re-enter, then and in every such case the lessor shall recover judgment and execution, in the same manner as if the rent in arrear had been legally demanded, and a re-entry made and in case the lessee or his assignee, or other person claiming or deriving under the said lease, shall permit and suffer judgment to be had and recovered on such trial in ejectment, and execution to be executed thereon, without paying the rent and arrears, together with full costs, and without proceeding for relief in equity within six months after such execution executed, then in such case the said lessee, his assignee, and all other persons claiming and deriving under the said lease, shall be barred and foreclosed from all relief or remedy in law or equity, other than by bringing error for reversal of such judgment, in case the same shall be erroneous; and the said landlord or lessor shall from thenceforth hold the said demised premises discharged from such lease; [. . .], provided that nothing herein contained shall extend to bar the right of any mortgagee of such lease, or any part thereof, who shall not be in possession, so as such mortgagee shall and do, within six months after such judgment obtained and execution executed pay all rent in arrear, and all costs and damages sustained by such lessor or person entitled to the remainder or reversion as aforesaid, and perform all the covenants and agreements which, on the part and behalf of the first lessee, are and ought to be performed.

211. Lessee proceeding in equity not to have injunction or relief without payment of rent and costs

In case the said lessee, his assignee, or other person claiming any right, title, or interest, in law or equity, of, in, or to the said lease, shall, within the time aforesaid, proceed for relief in any court of equity, such person shall not have or continue any injunction against the proceedings at law on such ejectment, unless he does or shall, within forty days next after a full and perfect answer shall be made by the claimant in such ejectment, bring into court, and lodge with the proper officer such sum and sums of money as the lessor or landlord shall in his answer swear to be due and in arrear over and above all just allowances, and also the costs taxed in the said suit, there to remain till the hearing of the cause, or to be paid out to the lessor or landlord on good security, subject to the decree of the court; and in case such proceedings for relief in equity shall be taken within the time aforesaid, and after execution is executed, the lessor or landlord shall be accountable only for so much and no more as he shall really and bona fide, without fraud, deceit, or wilful neglect, make of the demised premises from the time of his entering into the actual possession thereof; and if what shall be so made by the lessor or landlord happen to be less than the rent reserved on the said lease, then the said lessee or his assignee, before he shall be restored to his possession, shall pay such lessor or landlord, what the money so by him made fell short of the reserved rent for the time such lessor or landlord held the said lands.

212. Tenant paying all rent with costs, proceedings to cease
If the tenant or his assignee do or shall, at any time before the trial in such ejectment, pay or tender to the lessor or landlord, his executors or administrators, or his or their attorney in that cause, or pay into the court where the same cause is depending, all the rent and arrears, together with the costs, then and in such case, all further proceedings on the said ejectment shall cease and be discontinued; and if such lessee, his executors, administrators, or assigns, shall, upon such proceedings as aforesaid, be relieved in equity, he and they shall have, hold, and enjoy the demised lands, according to the lease thereof made, without any new lease.

WILLS (SOLDIERS AND SAILORS) ACT 1918
(1918, c. 58)

1. Explanation of s. 11 of 7 Will. 4 & 1 Vict. c. 26. 1837 c. 26
In order to remove doubts as to the construction of the Wills Act 1837, it is hereby declared and enacted that section eleven of that Act authorises and always has authorised any soldier being in actual military service, or any mariner or seaman being at sea, to dispose of his personal estate as he might have done before the passing of that Act, though under the age of [eighteen years].

2. Extension of s. 11 of Wills Act, 1837
Section eleven of the Wills Act, 1837, shall extend to any member of His Majesty's naval or marine forces not only when he is at sea but also when he is so circumstanced that if he were a soldier he would be in actual military service within the meaning of that section.

3. Validity of testamentary dispositions of real property made by soldiers and sailors
(1) A testamentary disposition of any real estate in England or Ireland made by a person to whom section eleven of the Wills Act 1837, applies, and who dies after the passing of this Act, shall, notwithstanding that the person making the disposition was at the time of making it under [eighteen years] of age or that the disposition has not been made in such manner or form as was at the passing of this Act required by law, be valid in any case where the person making the disposition was of such age and the disposition has been made in such manner and form that if the disposition had been a disposition of personal estate made by such a person domiciled in England or Ireland it would have been valid.

4. Power to appoint testamentary guardians
Where any person dies after the passing of this Act having made a will which is, or which, if it had been a disposition of property, would have been rendered valid by section eleven of the Wills Act, 1837, any appointment contained in that will of any person as guardian of the infant children of the testator shall be of full force and effect.

5. Short title and interpretation

(2) For the purposes of section eleven of the Wills Act, 1837, and this Act the expression 'soldier' includes a member of the Air Force, and references in this Act to the said section eleven include a reference to that section as explained and extended by this Act.

LAW OF PROPERTY ACT 1922
(1922, c. 16)

145. Conversion of perpetually renewable leaseholds

For the purpose of converting perpetually renewable leases and underleases (not being an interest in perpetually renewable copyhold land enfranchised by Part V. of this Act, but including a perpetually renewable underlease derived out of an interest in perpetually renewable copyhold land) into long terms, for preventing the creation of perpetually renewable leasehold interests and for providing for the interests of the persons affected, the provisions contained in the Fifteenth Schedule to this Act shall have effect.

FIFTEENTH SCHEDULE
PROVISIONS RELATING TO PERPETUALLY RENEWABLE LEASES AND UNDERLEASES

1. Conversion of perpetually renewable leases into long terms

(1) Land comprised in a perpetually renewable lease which was subsisting at the commencement of this Act shall, by virtue of this Act, vest in the person who at such commencement was entitled to such lease, for a term of two thousand years, to be calculated from the date at which the existing term or interest commenced, at the rent and subject to the lessees' covenants and conditions (if any) which under the lease would have been payable or enforceable during the subsistence of such term or interest.

(2) The rent, covenants and conditions (if any) shall (subject to the express provisions of this Act to the contrary) be payable and enforceable during the susbsistence of the term created by this Act; and that term shall take effect in substitution for the term or interest created by the lease, and be subject to the like power of re-entry (if any) and other provisions which affected the term or interest created by the lease, but without any right of renewal.

2. Conversion of perpetually renewable underleases into long terms

(1) Land comprised in any underlease, which at the commencement of this Act was perpetually renewable and was derived out of a head term affected by this Act, shall, by virtue of this Act, vest in the person who at such commencement was entitled to the subterm or interest for a term of two thousand years less one day, to be calculated from the date at which the head term created by this Act commenced, at the rent and subject to the underlessee's covenants and conditions (if any) which under the underlease would have been payable or enforceable during the subsistence of such subterm or interest.

(2) The rent, covenants and conditions (if any) shall (subject to the express provisions of this Act to the contrary) be payable and enforceable during the subsistance of the subterm created by this Act; and that subterm shall take effect in substitution for the subterm or interest created by the underlease, and be subject to the like power of re-entry (if any) and other provisions which affected the subterm or interest created by the underlease, but without any right of renewal.

(3) The foregoing provisions of this section shall also apply to any perpetually renewable subterm or interest which, at the commencement of this Act, was derived out of any other subterm or interest, but so that in every case the subterm created by

this Act shall be one day less in duration than the derivative term created by this Act, out of which it takes effect.

5. Dispositions purporting to create perpetually renewable leaseholds
A grant, after the commencement of this Act, of a term, subterm, or other leasehold interest with a covenant or obligation for perpetual renewal, which would have been valid if this Part of this Act had not been passed, shall (subject to the express provisions of this Act) take effect as a demise for a term of two thousand years or in the case of a subdemise for a term less in duration by one day than the term out of which it is derived, to commence from the date fixed for the commencement of the term, subterm, or other interest, and in every case free from any obligation for renewal or for payment of any fines, fees, costs, or other money in respect of renewal.

SETTLED LAND ACT 1925
(1925, c. 18)

PART 1
GENERAL PRELIMINARY PROVISIONS

Settlements and Settled Land

1. What constitutes a settlement
(1) Any deed, will, agreement for a settlement or other agreement, Act of Parliament, or other instrument, or any number of instruments, whether made or passed before or after, or partly before and partly after, the commencement of this Act, under or by virtue of which instrument or instruments any land, after the commencement of this Act, stands for the time being—

(i) limited in trust for any persons by way of succession; or

(ii) limited in trust for any person in possession—

(a) for an entailed interest whether or not capable of being barred or defeated;

(b) for an estate in fee simple or for a term of years absolute subject to an executory limitation, gift, or disposition over on failure of his issue or in any other event;

(c) for a base or determinable fee [(other than a fee which is a fee simple absolute by virtue of section 7 of the Law of Property Act 1925)] or any corresponding interest in leasehold land;

(d) being an infant, for an estate in fee simple or for a term of years absolute; or

(iii) limited in trust for any person for an estate in fee simple or for a term of years absolute contingently on the happening of any event; or

(iv) [. . .]

(v) charged, whether voluntarily or in consideration of marriage or by way of family arrangement, and whether immediately or after an interval, with the payment of any rentcharge for the life of any person, or any less period, or of any capital, annual, or periodical sums for the portions, advancement, maintenance, or otherwise for the benefit of any persons, with or without any terms of years for securing or raising the same; creates or is for the purposes of this Act a settlement and is in this Act referred to as a settlement, or as the settlement, as the case requires:

Provided that, where land is the subject of a compound settlement, references in this Act to the settlement shall be construed as meaning such compound settlement, unless the context otherwise requires.

(2) Where an infant is beneficially entitled to land for an estate in fee simple or for a term of years absolute and by reason of an intestacy or otherwise there is no instrument under which the interest of the infant arises or is acquired, a settlement shall be deemed to have been made by the intestate, or by the person whose interest the infant has acquired.

(3) An infant shall be deemed to be entitled in possession notwithstanding any subsisting right of dower[1] (not assigned by metes and bounds) affecting the land, and such a right of dower shall be deemed to be an interest comprised in the subject of the settlement and coming to the dowress under or by virtue of the settlement.

Where dower has been assigned by metes and bounds, the letters of administration or probate granted in respect of the estate of the husband of the dowress shall be deemed a settlement made by the husband.

(4) An estate or interest not disposed of by a settlement and remaining in or reverting to the settlor, or any person deriving title under him, is for the purposes of this Act an estate or interest comprised in the subject of the settlement and coming to the settlor or such person under or by virtue of the settlement.

(5) Where—

(a) a settlement creates an entailed interest which is incapable of being barred or defeated, or a base or determinable fee, whether or not the reversion or right of reverter is in the Crown, or any corresponding interest in leasehold land; or

(b) the subject of a settlement is an entailed interest, or a base or determinable fee, whether or not the reversion or right of reverter is in the Crown, or any corresponding interest in leasehold land;

the reversion or right of reverter upon the cesser of the interest so created or settled shall be deemed to be an interest comprised in the subject of the settlement, and limited by the settlement.

(6) Subsections (4) and (5) of this section bind the Crown.

[(7) This section does not apply to land held upon trust for sale.]

Note

[1]See Administration of Estates Act 1925, ss. 45(1)(c) and 51(2).

2. What is settled land

Land which is or is deemed to be the subject of a settlement is for the purposes of this Act settled land, and is in relation to the settlement referred to in this Act as the settled land.

3. Duration of settlements

Land [which has been subject to a settlement which is a settlement for the purposes of this Act] shall be deemed for the purposes of this Act to remain and be settled land, and the settlement shall be deemed to be a subsisting settlement for the purposes of this Act so long as—

(a) any limitation, charge, or power of charging under the settlement subsists, or is capable of being exercised; or

(b) the person who, if of full age, would be entitled as beneficial owner to have that land vested in him for a legal estate is an infant.

4. Authorised method of settling land inter vivos

(1) Every settlement of a legal estate in land inter vivos shall, save as in this Act otherwise provided, be effected by two deeds, namely, a vesting deed and a trust instrument and if effected in any other way shall not operate to transfer or create a legal estate.

(2) By the vesting deed the land shall be conveyed to the tenant for life or statutory owner (and if more than one as joint tenants) for the legal estate the subject of the intended settlement:

Provided that, where such legal estate is already vested in the tenant for life or statutory owner, it shall be sufficient, without any other conveyance, if the vesting deed declares that the land is vested in him for that estate.

(3) The trust instrument shall—

(a) declare the trusts affecting the settled land;

(b) appoint or constitute trustees of the settlement,

(c) contain the power, if any, to appoint new trustees of the settlement;

(d) set out, either expressly or by reference, any powers intended to be conferred by the settlement in extension of those conferred by this Act;

(e) bear any ad valorem stamp duty which may be payable (whether by virtue of the vesting deed or otherwise) in respect of the settlement.

5. Contents of vesting deeds

(1) Every vesting deed for giving effect to a settlement or for conveying settled land to a tenant for life or statutory owner during the subsistence of the settlement (in this Act referred to as a 'principle vesting deed') shall contain the following statements and particulars, namely:—

(a) A description, either specific or general, of the settled land;

(b) A statement that the settled land is vested in the person or persons to whom it is conveyed or in whom it is declared to be vested upon the trusts from time to time affecting the settled land;

(c) The names of the persons who are the trustees of the settlement;

(d) Any additional or larger powers conferred by the trust instrument relating to the settled land which by virtue of this Act operate and are exercisable as if conferred by this Act on a tenant for life;

(e) The name of any person for the time being entitled under the trust instrument to appoint new trustees of the settlement.

(2) The statements or particulars required by this section may be incorporated by reference to an existing vesting instrument, and, where there is a settlement subsisting at the commencement of this Act, by reference to that settlement and to any instrument whereby land has been conveyed to the uses or upon the trusts of that settlement, but not (save as last aforesaid) by reference to a trust instrument nor by reference to a disentailing deed.

(3) A principal vesting deed shall not be invalidated by reason only of any error in any of the statements or particulars by this Act required to be contained therein.

6. Procedure in the case of settlements by will

Where a settlement is created by the will of an estate owner who dies after the commencement of this Act—

(a) the will is for the purposes of this Act a trust instrument; and

(b) the personal representatives of the testator shall hold the settled land on trust, if and when required so to do, to convey it to the person who, under the will, or by virtue of this Act, is the tenant for life or statutory owner, and, if more than one, as joint tenants.

7. Procedure on change of ownership

(1) If, on the death of a tenant for life or statutory owner, or of the survivor of two or more tenants for life or statutory owners, in whom the settled land was vested, the land remains settled land, his personal representatives shall hold the settled land on trust, if and when required so to do, to convey it to the person who under the trust instrument or by virtue of this Act becomes the tenant for life or statutory owner and, if more than one, as joint tenants.

(2) If a person by reason of attaining full age becomes a tenant for life for the purposes of this Act of settled land, he shall be entitled to require the trustees of the settlement, personal representatives, or other persons in whom the settled land is vested, to convey the land to him.

(3) If a person who, when of full age, will together with another person or other persons constitute the tenant for life for the purposes of this Act of settled land attains that age, he shall be entitled to require the tenant for life, trustees of the settlement, personal representatives or other persons in whom the settled land is vested to convey the land to him and the other person or persons who together with him constitute the tenant for life as joint tenants.

(4) If by reason of forfeiture, surrender, or otherwise the estate owner of any settled land ceases to have the statutory powers of a tenant for life and the land remains settled land, he shall be bound forthwith to convey the settled land to the person who under the trust instrument, or by virtue of this Act, becomes the tenant for life or statutory owner and, if more than one, as joint tenants.

(5) If any person of full age becomes absolutely entitled to the settled land (whether beneficially, or as a personal representative, or as [trustee of land], or otherwise) free from all limitations, powers, and charges taking effect under the settlement, he shall be entitled to require the trustees of the settlement, personal representatives, or other persons in whom the settled land is vested, to convey the land to him, and if more persons than one being of full age become so entitled to the settled land they shall be entitled to require such persons as aforesaid to convey the land to them as joint tenants.

8. Mode and costs of conveyance, and saving of rights of personal representatives and equitable chargees

(1) A conveyance by personal representatives under either of the last two preceding sections may be made by an assent in writing signed by them which shall operate as a conveyance.

(2) Every conveyance under either of the last two preceding sections shall be made at the cost of the trust estate.

(3) The obligations to convey settled land imposed by the last two preceding sections are subject and without prejudice—

(a) where the settlement is created by a will, to the rights and powers of the personal representatives for purposes of administration; and

(b) in any case, to the person on whom the obligation is imposed being satisfied that provision has been or will be made for the payment of any unpaid death duties in respect of the land or any interest therein from which he is accountable, and any interest and costs in respect of such duties, or that he is otherwise effectually indemnified against such duties, interest and costs.

(4) Where the land is or remains settled land a conveyance under either of the last two preceding sections shall—

(a) if by deed, be a principal vesting deed; and

(b) if by an assent, be a vesting assent, which shall contain the like statements and particulars as are required by this Act in the case of a principle vesting deed.

(5) Nothing contained in either of the last two preceding sections affects the right of personal representatives to transfer or create such legal estates to take effect in priority to a conveyance under either of those sections as may be required for giving effect to the obligations imposed on them by statute.

(6) A conveyance under either of the last two preceding sections, if made by deed, may contain a reservation to the person conveying of a term of years absolute in the land conveyed, upon trusts for indemnifying him against any unpaid death duties in respect of the land conveyed or any interest therein, and any interest and costs in respect of such duties.

(7) Nothing contained in either of the last two preceding sections affects any right which a person entitled to an equitable charge for securing money actually raised, and affecting the whole estate the subject of the settlement, may have to require effect to be given thereto by a legal mortgage, before the execution of a conveyance under either of those sections.

9. Procedure in the case of settlements and of instruments deemed to be trust instruments

(1) Each of the following settlements or instruments shall for the purposes of this Act be deemed to be a trust instrument, and any reference to a trust instrument contained in this Act shall apply thereto, namely:—

(i) An instrument executed, or, in case of a will, coming into operation, after the commencement of this Act which by virtue of this Act is deemed to be a settlement;

(ii) A settlement which by virtue of this Act is deemed to have been made by any person after the commencement of this Act;

(iii) An instrument inter vivos intended to create a settlement of a legal estate in land which is executed after the commencement of this Act, and does not comply with the requirements of this Act with respect to the method of effecting such a settlement; and

(iv) A settlement made after the commencement of this Act (including a settlement by the will of a person who dies after such commencement) of any of the following interests—

(a) an equitable interest in land which is capable, when in possession, of subsisting at law; or

(b) an entailed interest; or

(c) a base or determinable fee or any corresponding interest in leasehold land, but only if and when the interest settled takes effect free from all equitable interests and powers under every prior settlement (if any).

(2) As soon as practicable after a settlement, or an instrument which for the purposes of this Act is deemed to be a trust instrument, takes effect as such, the trustees of the settlement may, and on the request of the tenant for life or statutory owner shall, execute a principal vesting deed, containing the proper statements and particulars, declaring that the legal estate in the settled land shall vest or is vested in the person or persons therein named, being the tenant for life or statutory owner, and including themselves if they are the statutory owners, and such deed shall, unless the legal estate is already so vested, operate to convey or vest the legal estate in the settled land to or in the person or persons aforesaid and, if more than one, as joint tenants.

(3) If there are no trustees of the settlement, then (in default of a person able and willing to appoint such trustees) an application under this Act shall be made to the court for the appointment of such trustees.

(4) The provisions of the last preceding section with reference to a conveyance shall apply, so far as they are applicable, to a principal vesting deed under this section.

10. Procedure on acquisition of land to be made subject to a settlement

(1) Where after the commencement of this Act land is acquired with capital money arising under this Act or in exchange for settled land, or a rentcharge is reserved on a grant of settled land, the land shall be conveyed to, and the rentcharge shall by virtue of this Act become vested in, the tenant for life or statutory owner, and such conveyance or grant is in this Act referred to as a subsidiary vesting deed:

Provided that, where an instrument is subsisting at the commencement of this Act, or is made or comes into operation after such commencement, by virtue of which any money or securities are liable under this Act, or the Acts which it replaces, or under a trust or direction contained in the instrument, to be invested in the purchase of land to be conveyed so as to become settled land, but at the commencement of this Act, or when such instrument is made or comes into operation after such commencement, as the case may be, there is no land in respect of which a principal vesting deed is capable of being executed, the first deed after the commencement of this Act by which any land is acquired as aforesaid shall be a principal vesting deed and shall be framed accordingly.

(2) A subsidiary vesting deed executed on the acquisition of land to be made subject to a settlement shall contain the following statements and particulars, namely—

(a) particulars of the last or only principal vesting instrument affecting land subject to the settlement;

(b) a statement that the land conveyed is to be held upon and subject to the same trusts and powers as the land comprised in such last or only principal vesting instrument;

(c) the names of the persons who are the trustees of the settlement;

(d) the name of any person for the time being entitled to appoint new trustees of the settlement.

(3) A subsidiary vesting deed reserving a rentcharge on a grant of settled land shall contain the following statements and particulars—

(a) a statement that the rentcharge is vested in the grantor and is subject to the settlement which, immediately before the grant, was subsisting with respect to the land out of which it was reserved;

(b) particulars of the last or only principal vesting instrument affecting such land.

(4) A subsidiary vesting deed shall not be invalidated by reason only of any error in any of the statements or particulars by this Act required to be contained herein.

(5) The acquisition of the land shall not operate to increase or multiply charges or powers of charging.

11. As to contracts for the settlement of land

(1) A contract made or other liability created or arising after the commencement of this Act for the settlement of land—

(i) by or on the part of an estate owner; or

(ii) by a person entitled to—

(a) an equitable interest which is capable when in possession of subsisting at law; or

(b) an entailed interest; or

(c) a base or determinable fee or any corresponding interest in leasehold land;

shall, but in cases under paragraph (ii) only if and when the interest of the person entitled takes effect free from all equitable interests and powers under every prior settlement, if any, be deemed an estate contract within the meaning of the Land Charges Act, 1925,[1] and may be registered as a land charge accordingly, and effect shall be given thereto by a vesting deed and a trust instrument in accordance with this Act.

(2) A contract made or other liability created or arising before the commencement of this Act to make a settlement of land shall be deemed to be sufficiently complied with if effect is given thereto by a vesting deed and a trust instrument in accordance with this Act.

Note

[1]Now the Land Charges Act 1972.

12. Power to make vesting orders as to settled land

(1) if—

(a) any person who is bound under this Part of this Act to execute a conveyance, vesting deed or vesting assent or in whom settled land is wrongly vested refuses or neglects to execute the requisite conveyance, vesting deed or vesting assent within one month after demand in writing; or

(b) any such person is outside the United Kingdom, or cannot be found, or it is not known whether he is alive or dead; or

(c) for any reason the court is satisfied that the conveyance, vesting deed or vesting assent cannot be executed, or cannot be executed without undue delay or expense; the court may, on the application of any person interested, make an order vesting the settled land in the tenant for life or statutory owner or person, if any, of full age absolutely entitled (whether beneficially or as personal representative or trustee for sale or otherwise), and, if the land remains settled land, the provisions of this Act relating to a principal vesting deed or a subsidiary vesting deed, as the case may be, shall apply to any order so made and every such order shall contain the like statements and particulars.

(2) No stamp duty shall be payable in respect of a vesting order made in place of a vesting or other assent.

13. Dispositions not to take effect until vesting instrument is made

Where a tenant for life or statutory owner has become entitled to have a principal vesting deed or a vesting assent executed in his favour, then until a vesting instrument is executed or made pursuant to this Act in respect of the settled land, any purported disposition thereof inter vivos by any person, other than a personal representative (not being a disposition which he has power to make in right of his equitable interests or powers under a trust instrument), shall not take effect except in favour of a purchaser of a legal estate [without notice of such tenant for life or statutory owner having become so entitled as aforesaid.] but, save as aforesaid, shall operate only as a contract for valuable consideration to carry out the transaction after the requisite vesting instrument has been executed or made, and a purchaser of a legal estate shall not be concerned with such disposition unless the contract is registered as a land charge.

[Nothing in this section affects the creation or transfer of a legal estate by virtue of an order of the court or the Minister or other competent authority.]

Enforcement of Equitable Interests and Powers against Estate Owner and discharge on termination of Settlement

16. Enforcement of equitable interests and powers against estate owner

(1) All equitable interests and powers in or over settled land (whether created before or after the date of any vesting instrument affecting the legal estate) shall be enforceable against the estate owner in whom the settled land is vested (but in the case of personal representatives without prejudice to their rights and powers for purposes of administration) in manner following (that is to say):—

(i) The estate owner shall stand possessed of the settled land and the income thereof upon such trusts and subject to such powers and provisions as may be requisite for giving effect to the equitable interests and powers affecting the settled land or the income thereof of which he has notice according to their respective priorities:

(ii) Where any person of full age becomes entitled to require a legal estate in the settled land to be vested in him in priority to the settlement, by reason of a right of reverter, statutory or otherwise, or an equitable right of entry taking effect, or on the ground that his interest ought no longer to be capable of being over-reached under the powers of this Act, the estate owner shall be bound, if so requested in writing, to transfer or create such legal estate as may be required for giving legal effect to the rights of the person so entitled;

(iii) Where—

(a) any principal sum is required to be raised on the security of the settled land, by virtue of any trust, or by reason of the exercise of an equitable power affecting the settled land, or by any person or persons who under the settlement is or are entitled or together entitled to or has or have a general power of appointment over the settled land, whether subject to any equitable charges or powers of charging subsisting under the settlement or not; or

(b) the settled land is subject to any equitable charge for securing money actually raised and affecting the whole estate the subject of the settlement; the estate owner shall be bound, if so requested in writing, to create such legal estate or charge by way of legal mortgage as may be required for raising the money or giving legal effect to the equitable charge:

Provided that, so long as the settlement remains subsisting, any legal estate or charge by way of legal mortgage so created shall take effect and shall be expressed to take effect subject to any equitable charges or powers of charging subsisting under the settlement which have priority to the interests or powers of the person or persons by or on behalf of whom the money is required to be raised or legal effect is required to be given to the equitable charge, unless the persons entitled to the prior charges or entitled to exercise the powers consent in writing to the same being postponed, but it shall not be necessary for such consent to be expressed in the instrument creating such legal estate or charge by way of legal mortgage.

(2) Where a mortgage or charge is expressed to be made by an estate owner pursuant to this section, then, in favour of the mortgagee or chargee and persons deriving title under him, the same shall take effect in priority to all the trusts of the settlement and all equitable interests and powers subsisting or to arise under the settlement except those to which it is expressly made subject, and shall so take effect, whether the mortgagee or chargee has notice of any such trusts, interests, or powers, or not, and the mortgagee or chargee shall not be concerned to see that a case had arisen to authorise the mortgage or charge, or that no more money than was wanted was raised.

(3) Nothing contained in paragraph (iii) of subsection (1) of this section affects the power conferred by this Act on a tenant for life of raising money by mortgage or of directing capital money to be applied in discharge of incumbrances.

(4) Effect may be given by means of a legal mortgage to an agreement for a mortgage, or a charge or lien, whether or not arising by operation of law, if the agreement charge or lien ought to have priority over the settlement.

(5) Save as hereinbefore expressly provided, no legal estate shall, so long as the settlement is subsisting, be transferred or created by the estate owner for giving effect to any equitable interest or power under the settlement.

(6) If a question arises or a doubt is entertained whether any and what legal estate ought to be transferred or created pursuant to this section, an application may be made to the court for directions as hereinafter provided.

(7) If an estate owner refuses or neglects for one month after demand in writing to transfer or create any such legal estate, or if by reason of his being outside the United Kingdom, or being unable to be found, or by reason of the dissolution of a corporation, or for any other reason, the court is satisfied that the transaction cannot otherwise be effected, or cannot be effected without undue delay or expense, the court may, on the application of any person interested, make a vesting order transferring or creating the requisite legal estate.

(8) This section does not affect a purchaser of a legal estate taking free from any equitable interest or power.

17. Deed of discharge on termination of settlement

(1) Where the estate owner of any settled land holds the land free from all equitable interests and powers under a trust instrument, the persons who in the last or only principal vesting instrument or the last or only endorsement on or annex thereto are declared to be the trustees of the settlement or the survivors of them shall, save as hereinafter mentioned, be bound to execute, at the cost of the trust estate, a deed declaring that they are discharged from the trust so far as regards that land:

Provided that, if the trustees have notice of any derivative settlement [trust of land] or equitable charge affecting such land, they shall not execute a deed of discharge until—

(a) in the case of a derivative settlement, or [trust of land], a vesting instrument or a conveyance has been executed or made for giving effect thereto; and

(b) in the case of an equitable charge, they are satisfied that the charge is or will be secured by a legal mortgage, or is protected by registration as a land charge, or by deposit of the documents of title, or that the owner thereof consents to the execution of the deed of discharge.

Where the land is affected by a derivative settlement or [trust of land], the deed of discharge shall contain a statement that the land is settled land by virtue of such vesting instrument as aforesaid and the trust instrument therein referred to, or is [subject to a trust of land] by virtue of such conveyance as aforesaid, as the case may require.

(2) If, in the circumstances mentioned in subsection (1) of this section and when the conditions therein mentioned have been complied with, the trustees of a settlement on being requested to execute a deed of discharge—

(a) by the estate owner; or

(b) by a person interested under, or by the trustees of, a derivative settlement; or

(c) by the trustees of [land] ;

refuse to do so, or if for any reason the discharge cannot be effected without undue delay or expense, the estate owner, person interested, or trustees may apply to the court for an order discharging the first mentioned trustees as respects the whole or any part of the settled land, and the court may make such order as it may think fit.

(3) Where a deed or order of discharge contains no statement to the contrary, a purchaser of a legal estate in the land to which the deed or order relates shall be entitled to assume that the land has ceased to be settled land, and is not subject to [a trust of land].

Restrictions on dispositions of Settled Land where Trustees have not been Discharged

18. Restrictions on dispositions of settled land where trustees have not been discharged

(1) Where land is the subject of a vesting instrument and the trustees of the settlement have not been discharged under this Act, then—

(a) any disposition by the tenant for life or statutory owner of the land, other than a disposition authorised by this Act or any other statute, or made in pursuance of any additional or larger powers mentioned in the vesting instrument, shall be void, except for the purpose of conveying or creating such equitable interests as he has power, in right of his equitable interests and powers under the trust instrument, to convey or create; and

(b) if any capital money is payable in respect of a transaction, a conveyance to a purchaser of the land shall only take effect under this Act if the capital money is paid to or by the direction of the trustees of the settlement or into court; and

(c) notwithstanding anything to the contrary in the vesting instrument, or the trust instrument, capital money shall not, except where the trustee is a trust corporation, be paid to or by the direction of fewer persons than two as trustees of the settlement.

(2) The restrictions imposed by this section do not affect—

(a) the right of a personal representative in whom the settled land may be vested to convey or deal with the land for the purposes of administration;

(b) the right of a person of full age who has become absolutely entitled (whether beneficially or as [trustee of land] or personal representative or otherwise) to the settled land, free from all limitations, powers, and charges taking effect under the trust instrument, to require the land to be conveyed to him;

(c) the power of the tenant for life, statutory owner, or personal representative in whom the settled land is vested to transfer or create such legal estates, to take effect in priority to the settlement, as may be required for giving effect to any obligations imposed on him by statute, but where any capital money is raised or received in respect of the transaction the money shall be paid to or by the direction of the trustees of the settlement or in accordance with an order of the court.

Tenants for Life and Persons with Powers of Tenant for Life

19. Who is tenant for life

(1) The person of full age who is for the time being beneficially entitled under a settlement to possession of settled land for his life is for the purposes of this Act the tenant for life of that land and the tenant for life under that settlement.

(2) If in any case there are two or more persons of full age so entitled as joint tenants, they together constitute the tenant for life for the purposes of this Act.

(3) If in any case there are two or more persons so entitled as joint tenants and they are not of full age, such one or more of them as is or are for the time being of full age is or (if more than one) together constitute the tenant for life for the purposes of this Act, but this subsection does not affect the beneficial interests of such of them as are not for the time being of full age.

(4) A person being tenant for life within the foregoing definitions shall be deemed to be such notwithstanding that, under the settlement or otherwise, the settled land, or his estate or interest therein, is incumbered or charged in any manner or to any extent, and notwithstanding any assignment by operation of law or otherwise of his estate or interest under the settlement, whether before or after it came into possession, other than an assurance which extinguishes that estate or interest.

20. Other limited owners having powers of tenant for life

(1) Each of the following persons being of full age shall, when his estate or interest is in possession, have the powers of a tenant for life under this Act, (namely):—

(i) A tenant in tail, including a tenant in tail after possibility of issue extinct, and a tenant in tail who is by Act of Parliament restrained from barring or defeating his estate tail, and although the reversion is in the Crown, but not including such a tenant in tail where the land in respect whereof he is so restrained was purchased with money provided by Parliament in consideration of public services;

(ii) A person entitled to land for an estate in fee simple or for a term of years absolute with or subject to, in any of such cases, an executory limitation, gift, or disposition over on failure of his issue or in any other event;

(iii) A person entitled to a base or determinable fee, although the reversion or right of reverter is in the Crown, or to any corresponding interest in leasehold land;

(iv) A tenant for years determinable on life, not holding merely under a lease at a rent;

(v) A tenant for the life of another, not holding merely under a lease at a rent;

(vi) A tenant for his own or any other life, or for years determinable on life, whose estate is liable to cease in any event during that life, whether by expiration of the estate, or by conditional limitation, or otherwise, or to be defeated by an executory limitation, gift, or disposition over, or is subject to a trust for accumulation of income for any purpose;

(vii) A tenant by the curtesy;[1]

(viii) A person entitled to the income of land under a trust or direction for payment thereof to him during his own or any other life, whether or not subject to expenses of management or to a trust for accumulation of income for any purpose, or until sale of the land, or until forfeiture, cesser or determination by any means of his interest therein, unless the land is subject to [a trust of land];

(ix) A person beneficially entitled to land for an estate in fee simple or for a term of years absolute subject to any estates, interests, charges, or powers of charging, subsisting or capable of being exercised under a settlement;

(x) [. . .]

(2) In every such case as is mentioned in subsection (1) of this section, the provisions of this Act referring to a tenant for life, either as conferring powers on him or otherwise, shall extend to each of the persons aforesaid, and any reference in this Act to death as regards a tenant for life shall, where necessary, be deemed to refer to the determination by death or otherwise of the estate or interest of the person on whom the powers of a tenant for life are conferred by this section.

(3) For the purposes of this Act the estate or interest of a tenant by the curtesy shall be deemed to be an estate or interest arising under a settlement made by his wife.

(4) Where the reversion or right of reverter or other reversionary right is in the Crown, the exercise by a person on whom the powers of a tenant for life are conferred by this section of his powers under this Act, binds the Crown.

Note

[1]See Administration of Estates Act 1925, ss. 45(1)(b), (2), 51(2).

21. Absolute owners subject to certain interests to have the powers of tenant for life

(1) Where a person of full age is beneficially entitled in possession to a legal estate subject to any equitable interests or powers, then, for the purpose of overreaching such interests or powers, he may, notwithstanding any stipulation to the contrary, by deed (which shall have effect as a principal vesting deed within the meaning of this Act) declare that the legal estate is vested in him on trust to give effect to all equitable interests and powers affecting the legal estate, and that deed shall be executed by two or more individuals approved or appointed by the court or a trust corporation, who shall be stated to be the trustees of the settlement for the purposes of this Act.

Thereupon so long as any of the equitable interests and powers are subsisting the following provisions shall have effect:—

(a) The person so entitled as aforesaid and each of his successors in title being an estate owner shall have the powers of a tenant for life and the land shall be deemed to be settled land;

(b) The instrument (if any) under which his estate arises or is acquired, and the instrument (if any) under which the equitable interests or powers are subsisting or capable of taking effect shall be deemed to be the trust instrument:

Provided that where there is no such instrument as last aforesaid then a deed (which shall take effect as a trust instrument) shall be executed contemporaneously with the vesting deed, and shall declare the trusts affecting the land;

(c) The persons stated in the principal vesting deed to be the trustees of the settlement for the purposes of this Act shall also be the trustees of the trust instrument for those purposes; and

(d) Capital money arising on any disposition of the land shall be paid to or by the direction of the trustees of the settlement or into court, and shall be applicable towards discharging or providing for payment in due order of any principal money payable in respect of such interests or charges as are overreached by such disposition, and until so applied shall be invested or applied as capital money under the trust instrument, and the income thereof shall be applied as the income of such capital money, and be liable for keeping down in due order any annual or periodical sum which may be overreached by the disposition.

(2) The following equitable interests and powers are excepted from the operation of subsection (1) of this section, namely—

(i) an equitable interest protected by a deposit of documents relating to the legal estate affected;

(ii) the benefit of a covenant or agreement restrictive of the user of land;

(iii) an easement, liberty or privilege over or affecting land and being merely an equitable interest;

(iv) the benefit of a contract to convey or create a legal estate, including a contract conferring either expressly or by statutory implication a valid option of purchase, a right of preemption, or any other like right;

(v) any equitable interest protected by registration under the Land Charges Act, 1925,[1] other than—

(a) an annuity within the meaning of Part II of that Act;

(b) a limited owner's charge or a general equitable charge within the meaning of that Act.

(3) Subject to the powers conferred by this Act on a tenant for life, nothing contained in this section shall deprive an equitable chargee of any of his rights or of his remedies for enforcing those rights.

Note
[1]Now the Land Charges Act 1972.

23. Powers of trustees, etc. when there is no tenant for life

(1) Where under a settlement there is no tenant for life nor, independently of this section, a person having by virtue of this Act the powers of a tenant for life then—

(a) any person of full age on whom such powers are by the settlement expressed to be conferred; and

(b) in any other case the trustees of the settlement; shall have the powers of a tenant for life under this Act.

(2) This section applies to trustees of settlements of land purchased with money provided by Parliament in consideration of public services where the tenant in tail is restrained from barring or defeating his estate tail, except that, if the tenant in tail is of full age and capacity, the powers shall not be exercised without his consent, but a purchaser shall not be concerned to see or inquire whether such consent has been given.

24. As to a tenant for life who has parted with his interest

(1) If it is shown to the satisfaction of the court that a tenant for life, who has by reason of bankruptcy, assignment, incumbrance, or otherwise ceased in the opinion of the court to have a substantial interest in his estate or interest in the settled land or any part thereof, has unreasonably refused to exercise any of the powers conferred on him by this Act, or consents to an order under this section, the court may, on the application of any person interested in the settled land or the part thereof affected, make an order authorising the trustees of the settlement, to exercise in the name and on behalf of the tenant for life, any of the powers of a tenant for life under this Act, in relation to the settled land or the part thereof affected, either generally and in such manner and for such period as the court may think fit, or in a particular instance, and the court may by the order direct that any documents of title in the possession of the tenant for life relating to the settled land be delivered to the trustees of the settlement.

(2) While any such order is in force, the tenant for life shall not, in relation to the settled land or the part thereof affected, exercise any of the powers thereby authorised to be exercised in his name and on his behalf, but no person dealing with the tenant for life shall be affected by any such order, unless the order is for the time being registered as an order affecting land.

(3) An order may be made under this section at any time after the estate or interest of the tenant for life under the settlement has taken effect in possession, and notwithstanding that he disposed thereof when it was an estate or interest in remainder or reversion.

26. Infants, how to be affected

(1) Where an infant is beneficially entitled in possession to land for an estate in fee simple or for a term of years absolute or would if of full age be a tenant for life of or have the powers of a tenant for life over settled land, then, during the minority of the infant—

(a) if the settled land is vested in a personal representative, the personal representative, until a principal vesting instrument has been executed pursuant to the provisions of this Act; and

(b) in every other case, the trustees of the settlement;

shall have, in reference to the settled land and capital money, all the powers conferred by this Act and the settlement on a tenant for life, and on the trustees of the settlement.

(2) If the settled land is vested in a personal representative, then, if and when during the minority the infant, if of full age, would have been entitled to have the legal estate

in the settled land conveyed to or otherwise vested in him pursuant to the provisions of this Act, a principal vesting instrument shall, if the trustees of the settlement so require, be executed, at the cost of the trust estate, for vesting the legal estate in themselves, and in the meantime the personal representatives shall, during the minority, give effect to the directions of the trustees of the settlement, and shall not be concerned with the propriety of any conveyance directed to be made by those trustees if the conveyance appears to be a proper conveyance under the powers conferred by this Act or by the settlement, and the capital money, if any, arising under the conveyance is paid to or by the direction of the trustees of the settlement or into court, but a purchaser dealing with the personal representative and paying the capital money, if any, to him shall not be concerned to see that the money is paid to trustees of the settlement or into court, or to inquire whether the personal representative is liable to give effect to any such directions, or whether any such directions have been given.

(3) Subsection (2) of this section applies whether the infant becomes entitled before or after the commencement of this Act, and has effect during successive minorities until a person of full age becomes entitled to require the settled land to be vested in him.

(4) This section does not apply where an infant is beneficially entitled in possession to land for an estate in fee simple or for a term of years absolute jointly with a person of full age (for which case provision is made in the Law of Property Act, 1925), but it applies to two or more infants entitled as aforesaid jointly, until one of them attains full age.

(5) This section does not apply where an infant would, if of full age, constitute the tenant for life or have the powers of a tenant for life together with another person of full age, but it applies to two or more infants who would, if all of them were of full age, together constitute the tenant for life or have the powers of a tenant for life, until one of them attains full age.

(6) Nothing in this section affects prejudicially any beneficial interests of an infant.

Trustees of Settlement

30. Who are trustees for purposes of Act

(1) Subject to the provisions of this Act, the following persons are trustees of a settlement for the purposes of this Act, and are in this Act referred to as the 'trustees of the settlement' or 'trustees of a settlement,' namely—

(i) the persons, if any, who are for the time being under the settlement, trustees with power of sale of the settled land (subject or not to the consent of any person), or with power of consent to or approval of the exercise of such a power of sale, or if there are no such persons; then

(ii) the persons, if any, for the time being, who are by the settlement declared to be trustees thereof for the purposes of the Settled Land Acts, 1882 to 1890, or any of them, or this Act, or if there are no such persons; then

(iii) the persons, if any, who are for the time being under the settlement trustees with [a power or duty to sell] any other land comprised in the settlement and subject to the same limitations as the land to be sold or otherwise dealt with, or with power of consent to or approval of the exercise of such power of sale, or, if there are no such persons; then

(iv) the persons, if any, who are for the time being under the settlement trustees with [a future power or duty to sell] the settled land, or with power of consent to or approval of the exercise of such a future power of sale, and whether the power [or duty] takes effect in all events or not, or, if there are no such persons; then

(v) the persons, if any, appointed by deed to be trustees of the settlement by all the persons who at the date of the deed were together able, by virtue of their beneficial interests or by the exercise of an equitable power, to dispose of the settled land in equity for the whole estate the subject of the settlement.

(2) Paragraphs (i), (iii) and (iv) of the last preceding subsection take effect in like manner as if the powers therein referred to had not by this Act been made exercisable by the tenant for life or statutory owner.

(3) Where a settlement is created by will, or a settlement has arisen by the effect of an intestacy, and apart from this subsection there would be no trustees for the purposes of this Act of such settlement, then the personal representatives of the deceased shall, until other trustees are appointed, be by virtue of this Act the trustees of the settlement, but where there is a sole personal representative, not being a trust corporation, it shall be obligatory on him to appoint an additional trustee to act with him for the purposes of this Act, and the provisions of the Trustee Act, 1925, relating to the appointment of new trustees and the vesting of trust property shall apply accordingly.

31. As to trustees of compound settlements

(1) Persons who are for the time being trustees for the purposes of this Act of an instrument which is a settlement, or is deemed to be a subsisting settlement for the purposes of this Act, shall be the trustees for the purposes of this Act of any settlement constituted by that instrument and any instruments subsequent in date or operation.

Where there are trustees for the purposes of this Act of the instrument under which there is a tenant for life or statutory owner but there are no trustees for those purposes of a prior instrument, being one of the instruments by which a compound settlement is constituted, those trustees shall, unless and until trustees are appointed of the prior instrument or of the compound settlement, be the trustees for the purposes of this Act of the compound settlement.]

(2) This section applies to instruments coming into operation before as well as after the commencement of this Act, but shall have effect without prejudice to any appointment made by the court before such commencement of trustees of a settlement constituted by more than one instrument, and to the power of the court in any case after such commencement to make any such appointment, and where any such appointment has been made before such commencement or is made thereafter this section shall not apply or shall cease to apply to the settlement consisting of the instruments to which the appointment relates.

34. Appointment of trustees by court

(1) If at any time there are no trustees of a settlement, or where in any other case it is expedient, for the purposes of this Act, that new trustees of a settlement be appointed, the court may, if it thinks fit, on the application of the tenant for life, statutory owner, or of any other person having, under the settlement, an estate or interest in the settled land, in possession, remainder or otherwise, or, in the case of an infant, of his testamentary or other guardian or next friend, appoint fit persons to be trustees of the settlement.

(2) The persons so appointed, and the survivors and survivor of them, while continuing to be trustees or trustee, and, until the appointment of new trustees, the personal representatives or representative for the time being of the last surviving or continuing trustee, shall become and be the trustees or trustee of the settlement.

35. Procedure on appointment of new trustees

(1) Whenever a new trustee for the purposes of this Act is appointed of a trust instrument or a trustee thereof for the purposes aforesaid is discharged from the trust without a new trustee being appointed, a deed shall be executed supplemental to the last or only principal vesting instrument containing a declaration that the persons therein named, being the persons who after such appointment or discharge, as the case may be, are the trustees of the trust instrument for the purposes aforesaid, are the trustees of the settlement for those purposes; and a memorandum shall be endorsed on or annexed to the last or only principal vesting instrument in accordance with the Trustee Act, 1925.

(2) Every such deed as aforesaid shall, if the trustee was appointed or discharged by the court, be executed by such person as the court may direct, and, in any other case, shall be executed by—

(i) the person, if any, named in the principal vesting instrument as the person for the time being entitled to appoint new trustees of the settlement, or if no person is so named, or the person is dead or unable or unwilling to act, the persons who if the principal vesting instrument had been the only instrument constituting the settlement would have had power to appoint new trustees thereof;

(ii) the persons named in the deed of declaration as the trustees of the settlement; and

(iii) any trustee who is discharged as aforesaid or retires.

(3) A statement contained in any such deed of declaration as is mentioned in this section to the effect that the person named in the principal vesting instrument as the person for the time being entitled to appoint new trustees of the settlement is unable or unwilling to act, or that a trustee has remained outside the United Kingdom for more than twelve months, or refuses or is unfit to act, or is incapable of acting, shall in favour of a purchaser of a legal estate be conclusive evidence of the matter stated.

Provisions as to Undivided Shares

36. Undivided shares to take effect behind a [trust of land]

(1) If and when, after the commencement of this Act, settled land is held in trust for persons entitled in possession under a trust instrument in undivided shares, the trustees of the settlement (if the settled land is not already vested in them) may require the estate owner in whom the settled land is vested (but in the case of a personal representative subject to his rights and powers for purposes of administration), at the cost of the trust estate, to convey the land to them, or assent to the land vesting in them as joint tenants, and in the meantime the land shall be held on the same trusts as would have been applicable thereto if it had been so conveyed to or vested in the trustees.

(2) If and when the settled land so held in trust in undivided shares is or becomes vested in the trustees of the settlement, the land shall be held by them (subject to any incumbrances affecting the settled land which are secured by a legal mortgage, but freed from any incumbrances affecting the undivided shares or not secured as aforesaid, and from any interests, powers and charges subsisting under the trust instrument which have priority to the trust for the persons entitled to the undivided shares) [in trust for the persons interested in the land].

(3) If the estate owner refuses or neglects for one month after demand in writing to convey the settled land so held in trust in undivided shares in manner aforesaid, or if by reason of his being outside the United Kingdom or being unable to be found, or by reason of the dissolution of a corporation, or for any other reason, the court is satisfied that the conveyance cannot otherwise be made, or cannot be made without undue delay or expense, the court may, on the application of the trustees of the settlement, make an order vesting the settled land in them [in trust for the persons interested in the land].

(4) An undivided share in land shall not be capable of being created except under a trust instrument or under the Law of Property Act, 1925, and shall then only take effect behind a [trust of land].

(5) Nothing in this section affects the priority inter se of any incumbrances whether affecting the entirety of the land or an undivided share.

[(6) In subsections (2) and (3) of this section references to the persons interested in the land include persons interested as trustees or personal representatives (as well as persons beneficially interested).]

(7) The provisions of this section bind the Crown.

PART II
POWERS OF A TENANT FOR LIFE

Sale and Exchange

38. Powers of sale and exchange

A tenant for life—

(i) May sell the settled land, or any part thereof, or any easement, right or privilege of any kind over or in relation to the land; and

(ii) [. . .]

(iii) May make an exchange of the settled land, or any part thereof, or of any easement, right, or privilege of any kind, whether or not newly created, over or in relation to the settled land, or any part thereof, for other land, or for any easement, right or privilege of any kind, whether or not newly created, over or in relation to other land, including an exchange in consideration of money paid for equality of exchange.

39. Regulations respecting sales

(1) Save as hereinafter provided every sale shall be made for the best consideration in money that can reasonably be obtained.

(2) A sale may be made in consideration wholly or partially of a perpetual rent, or a terminable rent consisting of principal and interest combined, payable yearly or half yearly to be secured upon the land sold, or the land to which the easement, right or privilege sold is to be annexed in enjoyment or an adequate part thereof.

In the case of a terminable rent, the conveyance shall distinguish the part attributable to principal and that attributable to interest, and the part attributable to principal shall be capital money arising under this Act:

Provided that, unless the part of the terminable rent attributable to interest varies according to the amount of the principal repaid, the trustees of the settlement shall, during the subsistence of the rent, accumulate the income of the said capital money in the way of compound interest by investing it and the resulting income thereof in securities authorised for the investment of capital money and shall add the accumulations to capital.

(3) The rent to be reserved on any such sale shall be the best rent that can reasonably be obtained, regard being had to any money paid as part of the consideration, or laid out, or to be laid out, for the benefit of the settled land, and generally to the circumstances of the case, but a peppercorn rent, or a nominal or other rent less than the rent ultimately payable, may be made payable during any period not exceeding five years from the date of the conveyance.

(4)–(7) . . .

40. Regulations respecting exchanges

(1) Save as in the Part of this Act provided, every exchange shall be made for the best consideration in land or in land and money that can reasonably be obtained.

(2) An exchange may be made subject to any stipulations respecting title, or evidence of title, or other things.

(3) Settled land in England or Wales shall not be given in exchange for land out of England and Wales.

Leasing Powers

41. Power to lease for ordinary or building or mining or forestry purposes

A tenant for life may lease the settled land, or any part thereof, or any easement, right, or privilege of any kind over or in relation to the land, for any purpose whatever, whether involving waste or not, for any term not exceeding—

(i) In case of a building lease, nine hundred and ninety-nine years;

(ii) In case of a mining lease, one hundred years;
(iii) In case of a forestry lease, nine hundred and ninety-nine years;
(iv) In case of any other lease, fifty years.

42. Regulations respecting leases generally

(1) Save as hereinafter provided, every lease—

(i) shall be by deed, and be made to take effect in possession not later than twelve months after its date, or in reversion after an existing lease having not more than seven years to run at the date of the new lease;

(ii) shall reserve the best rent that can reasonably be obtained, regard being had to any fine taken, and to any money laid out or to be laid out for the benefit of the settled land, and generally to the circumstances of the case;

(iii) shall contain a covenant by the lessee for payment of the rent, and a condition of re-entry on the rent not being paid within a time therein specified not exceeding thirty days.

(2) A counterpart of every lease shall be executed by the lessee and delivered to the tenant for life or statutory owner, of which execution and delivery the execution of the lease by the tenant for life or statutory owner shall be sufficient evidence.

(3) . . .

(4) A fine received on the grant of a lease under any power conferred by this Act shall be deemed to be capital money arising under this Act.

(5) A lease at the best rent that can be reasonably obtained without fine, and whereby the lessee is not exempted from punishment for waste, may be made—

(i) Where the term does not exceed twenty-one years—

(a) without any notice of an intention to make the lease having been given under this Act; and

(b) notwithstanding that there are no trustees of the settlement; and

(ii) Where the term does not extend beyond three years from the date of the writing, by any writing under hand only containing an agreement instead of a covenant by the lessee for payment of rent.

Miscellaneous Powers

49. Power on dispositions to impose restrictions and make reservations and stipulations

(1) On a sale or other disposition or dealing under the powers of this Act—

(a) any easement, right, or privilege of any kind may be reserved or granted over or in relation to the settled land or any part thereof or other land, including the land disposed of, and, in the case of an exchange, the land taken in exchange; and

(b) any restriction with respect to building on or other user of land, or with respect to mines and minerals, or with respect to or for the purpose of the more beneficial working thereof, or with respect to any other thing, may be imposed and made binding, as far as the law permits, by covenant, condition or otherwise, on the tenant for life or statutory owner and the settled land or any part thereof, or on the other party and any land disposed of to him; and

(c) the whole or any part of any capital or annual sum (and in the case of an annual sum whether temporary or perpetual) charged on or payable out of the land disposed of, or any part thereof, and other land subject to the settlement, may as between the tenant for life or statutory owner and his successors in title, and the other party and persons deriving title under or in succession to him (but without prejudice to the rights of the person entitled to such capital or annual sum) be charged exclusively on the land disposed of, or any part thereof, or such other land as aforesaid, or any part thereof, in exoneration of the rest of the land on or out of which such capital or annual sum is charged or payable.

51. Power to grant options

(1) A tenant for life may at any time, either with or without consideration, grant by writing an option to purchase or take a lease of the settled land, or any part thereof, or any easement, right, or privilege over or in relation to the same at a price or rent fixed at the time of the granting of the option.

. . .

54. Power to grant water rights to statutory bodies

. . .

55. Power to grant land for public and charitable purposes

. . .

56. Dedication for streets, open spaces, etc.

. . .

57. Provision of land for small dwellings, small holdings and dwellings for working classes

. . .

59. Power to vary leases and grants and to give licences and consents

. . .

60. Power to apportion rents

. . .

63. Power to complete predecessor's contracts

A tenant for life may make any disposition which is necessary or proper for giving effect to a contract entered into by a predecessor in title, and which if made by that predecessor would have been valid as against his successors in title.

64. General power for the tenant for life to effect any transaction under an order of the court

(1) Any transaction affecting or concerning the settled land, or any part thereof, or any other land (not being a transaction otherwise authorised by this Act, or by the settlement) which in the opinion of the court would be for the benefit of the settled land, or any part thereof, or the persons interested under the settlement, may, under an order of the court, be effected by a tenant for life, if it is one which could have been validly effected by an absolute owner.

(2) In this section 'transaction' includes any sale [. . .] exchange, assurance, grant, lease, surrender, reconveyance, release, reservation, or other disposition, and any purchase or other acquisition, and any covenant, contract, or option, and any application of capital money [. . .] and any compromise or other dealing, or arrangement; [. . .] and 'effected' has the meaning appropriate to the particular transaction; and the references to land include references to restrictions and burdens affecting land.

Provisions as to special classes of property

65. Power to dispose of mansion

. . .

66. Cutting and sale of timber, and capitalisation of part of proceeds

. . .

67. Sale and purchase of heirlooms under order of court

. . .

Dealings as between tenants for life and the estate

68. Provision enabling dealings with tenant for life

(1) In the manner mentioned and subject to the provisions contained in this section—

(a) a sale, grant, lease, mortgage, charge or other disposition of settled land, or of any easement, right, or privilege over the same may be made to the tenant for life; or

(b) capital money may be advanced on mortgage to him; or

(c) a purchase may be made from him of land to be made subject to the limitations of the settlement; or

(d) an exchange may be made with him of settled land for other land; and

(e) any such disposition, advance, purchase, or exchange as aforesaid may be made to, from, or with any persons of whom the tenant for life is one.

(2) In every such case the trustees of the settlement shall, in addition to their powers as trustees, have all the powers of a tenant for life in reference to negotiating and completing the transaction, and shall have power to enforce any covenants by the tenant for life, or, where the tenant for life is himself one of the trustees, then the other or others of them shall have such power, and the said powers of a tenant for life may be exercised by the trustees of the settlement in the name and on behalf of the tenant for life.

(3) This section applies, notwithstanding that the tenant for life is one of the trustees of the settlement, or that an order has been made authorising the trustees to act on his behalf, or that he is [suffering from mental disorder] but does not apply to dealings with any body of persons which includes a trustee of the settlement, not being the tenant for life, unless the transaction is either previously or subsequently approved by the court.

Raising of Money

71. Power to raise money by mortgage

(1) Where money is required for any of the following purposes namely:—

(i) Discharging an incumbrance on the settled land or part thereof;

(ii) paying for any improvement authorised by this Act or by the settlement;

(iii) Equality of exchange:

(iv) [. . .]

(v) [. . .]

(vi) Redeeming a compensation rentcharge in respect of the extinguishment of manorial incidents and affecting the settled land;

(vii) Commuting any additional rent made payable on the conversion of a perpetually renewable leasehold interest into a long term;

(viii) Satisfying any claims for compensation on the conversion of a perpetually renewable leasehold interest into a long term by any officer, solicitor, or other agent of the lessor in respect of fees or remuneration which would have been payable by the lessee or under-lessee on any renewal;

(ix) Payment of the costs of any transaction authorised by this section or either of the two last preceding sections,

the tenant for life may raise the money so required, on the security of the settled land, or of any part thereof, by a legal mortgage, and the money so raised shall be capital money for that purpose, and may be paid or applied accordingly.

(2) 'Incumbrance' in this section does not include any annual sum payable only during a life or lives or during a term of years absolute or determinable.

(3) The restrictions imposed by this Part of this Act on the leasing powers of a tenant for life do not apply in relation to a mortgage term created under this Act.

Conveyance

72. Completion of transactions by conveyance

(1) On a sale, exchange, lease, mortgage, charge, or other disposition, the tenant for life may, as regards land sold, given in exchange, leased, mortgaged, charged, or otherwise disposed of, or intended so to be, or as regards easements or other rights or privileges sold, given in exchange, leased, mortgaged, or otherwise disposed of, or intended so to be, effect the transaction by deed to the extent of the estate or interest vested or declared to be vested in him by the last or only vesting instrument affecting the settled land or any less estate or interest, in the manner requisite for giving effect to the sale, exchange, lease, mortgage charge, or other disposition, but so that a mortgage shall be effected by the creation of a term of years absolute in the settled land or by charge by way of legal mortgage, and not otherwise.

(2) Such a deed, to the extent and in the manner to and in which it is expressed or intended to operate and can operate under this Act, is effectual to pass the land conveyed, or the easements, rights, privileges or other interests created, discharged from all the limitations, powers, and provisions of the settlement, and from all estates, interests, and charges subsisting or to arise thereunder, but subject to and with the exception of—

(i) all legal estates and charges by way of legal mortgage having priority to the settlement; and

(ii) all legal estates and charges by way of legal mortgage which have been conveyed or created for securing money actually raised at the date of the deed; and

(iii) all leases and grants at fee-farm rents or otherwise, and all grants of easements, rights of common, or other rights or privileges which—

(a) were before the date of the deed granted or made for value in money or money's worth, or agreed so to be, by the tenant for life or statutory owner, or by any of his predecessors in title, or any trustees for them, under the settlement, or under any statutory power, or are at that date otherwise binding on the successors in title of the tenant for life or statutory owner; and

(b) are at the date of the deed protected by registration under the Land Charges Act, 1925,[1] if capable of registration thereunder.

(3) Notwithstanding registration under the Land Charges Act, 1925,[1] of—

(a) an annuity within the meaning of Part II. of that Act;

(b) a limited owner's charge or a general equitable charge within the meaning of that Act;

a disposition under this Act operates to overreach such annuity or charge which shall, according to its priority, take effect as if limited by the settlement.

(4) . . .

Note

[1]Now the Land Charges Act 1972.

PART III
INVESTMENT OR OTHER APPLICATION OF CAPITAL MONEY

73. Modes of investment or application

(1) Capital money arising under this Act, subject to payment of claims properly payable thereout and to the application thereof for any special authorised object for which the capital money was raised, shall, when received, be invested or otherwise applied wholly in one, or partly in one and partly in another or others, of the following modes (namely):—

(i) In investment in Government securities, or in other securities in which the trustees of the settlement are by the settlement or by law authorised to invest trust money of the settlement, with power to vary the investment into or for any other such securities;

(ii) In discharge, purchase, or redemption of incumbrances affecting the whole estate the subject of the settlement, or of [. . .] rentcharge in lieu of tithe,' Crown rent, chief rent, or quit rent, charged on or payable out of the settled land, or of any charge in respect of an improvement created on a holding under the [Agricultural Holdings Act 1986] or any similar previous enactment;

(iii) In payment for any improvement authorised by this Act;

(iv) In payment as for an improvement authorised by this Act of any money expended and costs incurred by a landlord under or in pursuance of the [Agricultural Holdings Act, 1986] or any similar previous enactment, or under custom or agreement or otherwise, in or about the execution of any improvement comprised in [Schedule 7] of the said Agricultural Holdings Act;

(v) In payment for equality of exchange of settled land;

(vi) [. . .]

(vii) [. . .]

(viii) In redemption of any compensation rentcharge created in respect of the extinguishment of manorial incidents, and affecting the settled land;

(ix) In commuting any additional rent made payable on the conversion of a perpetually renewable leasehold interest into a long term, and in satisfying any claim for compensation on such conversion by any officer, solicitor, or other agent of the lessor in respect of fees or remuneration which would have been payable by the lessee or under-lessee on any renewal;

(x) In purchase of the freehold reversion in fee of any part of the settled land, being leasehold land held for years;

(xi) In purchase of land in fee simple, or of leasehold land held for sixty years or more unexpired at the time of purchase, subject or not to any exception or reservation of or in respect of mines or minerals therein, or of or in respect of rights or powers relative to the working of mines or minerals therein, or in other land;

(xii) In purchase either in fee simple, or for a term of sixty years or more, of mines and minerals convenient to be held or worked with the settled land, or of any easement, right or privilege convenient to be held with the settled land for mining or other purposes;

(xiii) In redemption of an improvement rentcharge, that is to say, a rentcharge (temporary or permanent) created, whether before or after the commencement of this Act, in pursuance of any Act of Parliament, with the object of paying off any money advanced for defraying the expenses of an improvement of any kind authorised by Part I. of the Third Schedule to this Act;

(xiv) In the purchase, with the leave of the court, of any leasehold interest where the immediate reversion is settled land, so as to merge the leasehold interest (unless the court otherwise directs) in the reversion, and notwithstanding that the leasehold interest may have less than sixty years to run;

(xv) In payment of the costs and expenses of all plans, surveys, and schemes, including schemes under the Town Planning Act, 1925, or any similar previous enactment, made with a view to, or in connexion with the improvement or development of the settled land, or any part thereof, or the exercise of any statutory powers, and of all negotiations entered into by the tenant for life with a view to the exercise of any of the said powers, notwithstanding that such negotiations may prove abortive, and in payment of the costs and expenses of opposing any such proposed scheme as aforesaid affecting the settled land, whether or not the scheme is made;

(xvi) [1]In the purchase of an annuity charged under section four of the Tithe Act, 1918, on the settled land or any part thereof, or in the discharge of such part of any such annuity as does not represent interest;

(xvii) In payment to a local or other authority of such sum as may be agreed in consideration of such authority taking over and becoming liable to repair a private road on the settled land or a road for the maintenance whereof a tenant for life is liable ratione tenurae;

(xviii) In financing any person who may have agreed to take a lease or grant for building purposes of the settled land, or any part thereof, by making advances to him in the usual manner on the security of an equitable mortgage of his building agreement;

(xix) In payment to any person becoming absolutely entitled or empowered to give an absolute discharge;

(xx) In payment of costs, charges, and expenses of or incidental to the exercise of any of the powers, or the execution of any of the provisions of this Act including the costs and expenses incidental to any of the matters referred to in this section;

(xxi) In any other mode authorised by the settlement with respect to money produced by the sale of the settled land.

(2) Notwithstanding anything in this section capital money arising under this Act from settled land in England or Wales shall not be applied in the purchase of land out of England and Wales, unless the settlement expressly authorises the same.

Note

[1]See Tithe Act 1936, ss. 1, 30.

75. Regulations respecting investment, devolution, and income of securities, etc.

(1) Capital money arising under this Act shall, in order to its being invested or applied as aforesaid, be paid either to the trustees of the settlement or into court at the option of the tenant for life, and shall be invested or applied by the trustees, or under the direction of the court, as the case may be, accordingly.

(2) The investment or other application by the trustees shall be made according to the direction of the tenant for life, and in default thereof according to the discretion of the trustees, but in the last-mentioned case subject to any consent required or direction given by the settlement with respect to the investment or other application by the trustees of trust money of the settlement, and any investment shall be in the names or under the control of the trustees.

(3) The investment or other application under the direction of the court shall be made on the application of the tenant for life, or of the trustees.

(4) Any investment or other application shall not during the subsistence of the beneficial interest of the tenant for life be altered without his consent.

(5) Capital money arising under this Act while remaining uninvested or unapplied, and securities on which an investment of any such capital money is made shall for all purposes of disposition, transmission and devolution be treated as land, and shall be held for and go to the same persons successively, in the same manner and for and on the same estates, interests, and trusts, as the land wherefrom the money arises would, if not disposed of, have been held and have gone under the settlement.

(6) The income of those securities shall be paid or applied as the income of that land, if not disposed of, would have been payable or applicable under the settlement.

(7) Those securities may be converted into money, which shall be capital money arising under this Act.

(8) All or any part of any capital money paid into court may, if the court thinks fit, be at any time paid out to the trustees of the settlement.

77. Application of money in hands of trustees under powers of settlement

Where—

(a) under any instrument coming into operation either before or after the commencement of this Act money is in the hands of trustees, and is liable to be laid out in the purchase of land to be made subject to the trust declared by the instrument; or

(b) under any instrument coming in to operation after the commencement of this act money or securities or the proceeds of sale of any property is or are held by trustees on trusts creating entailed interests therein;

then, in addition to such powers of dealing therewith as the trustees have independently of this Act, they may, at the option of the tenant for life, invest or apply the money securities or proceeds as if they were capital money arising under this Act.

78. Provision as to personal estate settled by reference to capital money, or on trusts corresponding with the limitations of land

(1) Where money or securities or the proceeds of sale of any property is or are by any instrument coming into operation either before or after the commencement of this Act directed to be held on trusts declared by reference to capital money arising under this Act from land settled by that instrument or any other instrument, the money securities or proceeds shall be held on the like trusts as if the same had been or represented money which had actually arisen under this Act from the settled land.

[This subsection operates without prejudice to the rights of any person claiming under a disposition for valuable consideration of any such money securities or proceeds, made before the commencement of this Act.]

(2) Where money or securities or the proceeds of sale of any property is or are by any instrument coming into operation after the commencement of this Act directed to be held on the same trusts as, or on trusts corresponding as nearly as may be with the limitations of land settled by that instrument or any other instrument, the money, securities or proceeds shall be held on the like trusts as if the same had been or represented capital money arising under this Act from the settled land.

(3) Such money, securities, or proceeds of sale shall be paid or transferred to or retained by the trustees of the settlement of the settled land, or paid or transferred into court, and invested or applied accordingly.

(4) Where the settled land includes freehold land, the money, securities, or proceeds of sale aforesaid shall be held on the like trusts as if the same had been or represented capital money arising from the freehold land.

(5) This section has effect notwithstanding any direction in the instrument creating the trust that the trust property is not to vest absolutely in any tenant in tail or in tail male or in tail female under the limitations of the settled land who dies under a specified age, or before the happening of a specified event, but, save as aforesaid, has effect with any variations and subject to any contrary intention expressed in the instrument creating the trust.

79. Application of money paid for lease or reversion

Where capital money arising under this Act is purchase-money paid in respect of—

(a) a lease for years; or

(b) any other estate or interest in land less than the fee simple; or

(c) a reversion dependent on any such lease, estate, or interest;

the trustees of the settlement or the court, as the case may be, and in the case of the court on the application of any party interested in that money, may, notwithstanding anything in this Act, require and cause the same to be laid out, invested, accumulated, and paid in such manner as, in the judgment of the trustees or of the court, as the case may be, will give to the parties interested in that money the like benefit therefrom as they might lawfully have had from the lease, estate, interest, or reversion in respect whereof the money was paid, or as near thereto as may be.

80. As to money received by way of damages for breach of covenant

(1) Money, not being rent, received by way of damages or compensation for breach of any covenant by a lessee or grantee contained in any lease or grant of settled land shall, unless in any case the court on the application of the tenant for life or the trustees

of the settlement otherwise directs, be deemed to be capital money arising under this Act, and shall be paid to or retained by the trustees of the settlement, or paid into court, and invested or applied, accordingly.

(2) In addition to the other modes in which capital money may be applied under this Act or the settlement, money so received as aforesaid or any part thereof may, if the circumstances permit, be applied at any time within twelve months after such receipt, or such extended period as the court may allow, in or towards payment of the costs of making good in whole or in part the breach of covenant in respect of which it was so received, or the consequences thereof, and the trustees of the settlement, if they think fit, may require any money so received or any part thereof to be so applied.

(3) In the application of any such money in or towards payment of the cost of making good any such breach or the consequences of any such breach as aforesaid, the work required to be done for the purpose shall be deemed to be an improvement authorised by Part 1. of the Third Schedule to this Act.

(4) This section does not apply to money received by way of damages or compensation for the breach of a covenant to repay to the lessor or grantor money laid out or expended by him, or to any case in which if the money received were applied in making good the breach of covenant or the consequences thereof such application would not enure for the benefit of the settled land, or any buildings thereon.

(5) . . .

(6) The provisions of this section apply only if and as far as a contrary intention is not expressed in the settlement, and have effect subject to the terms of the settlement, and to any provisions therein contained, but a contrary intention shall not be deemed to be expressed merely by words negativing impeachment for waste.

81. As to capital arising otherwise than under the Act

Any money which after the commencement of this Act arises from settled land otherwise than under this Act, as well as any money or securities in the names or under the control of the tenant for life or the trustees of the settlement, being or representing money which had arisen before the commencement of this Act from the settled land otherwise than under the Settled Land Acts, 1882 to 1890, and which ought, as between the persons interested in the settled land, to be or to have been treated as capital, shall (without prejudice to any other statutory provisions affecting the same) be deemed to be or to represent capital money arising under this Act, and shall be paid or transferred to or retained by the trustees of the settlement, or paid or transferred into court, and invested or applied, accordingly.

PART IV
IMPROVEMENTS

Improvements with Capital Money

83. Description of improvements authorised by Act

Improvements authorised by this Act are the making or execution on, or in connexion with, and for the benefit of settled land, of any of the works mentioned in the Third Schedule to this Act, or of any works for any of the purposes mentioned in that Schedule, and any operation incident to or necessary or proper in the execution of any of those works, or necessary or proper for carrying into effect any of those purposes, or for securing the full benefit of any of those works or purposes.

84. Mode of application of capital money

Capital money arising under this Act may be applied in or towards payment for any improvement authorised by this Act or by the settlement, without any scheme for the execution of the improvement being first submitted for approval to, or approved by, the trustees of the settlement or the court.

(2) . . .

Sundry Provisions as to Improvements

86. Concurrence in improvements

The tenant for life may join or concur with any other person interested in executing any improvement authorised by this Act, or in contributing to the cost thereof.

87. Court may order payment for improvements executed

The court may, in any case where it appears proper, make an order directing or authorising capital money to be applied in or towards payment for any improvement authorised by the Settled Land Acts, 1882 to 1890, or this Act, notwithstanding that a scheme was not, before the execution of the improvement, submitted for approval, as required by the Settled Land Act, 1882, to the trustees of the settlement or to the court, and notwithstanding that no capital money is immediately available for the purpose.

88. Obligation on tenant for life and successors to maintain, insure, etc.

(1) The tenant for life, and each of his successors in title having under the trust instrument a limited estate or interest only in the settled land, shall, during such period, if any, as the Minister by certificate in any case prescribes, maintain and repair, at his own expense, every improvement executed under the foregoing provisions of this Act or the enactments replaced thereby, and where a building or work in its nature insurable against damage by fire is comprised in the improvement, shall at his own expense insure and keep insured the improvement in such amount, if any, as the Minister by certificate in any case prescribes.

(2) The tenant for life, or any of his successors as aforesaid, shall not cut down or knowingly permit to be cut down, except in proper thinning, any trees planted as an improvement under the foregoing provisions of this Act, or under the enactments replaced by those provisions.

(3) The tenant for life, and each of his successors as aforesaid, shall from time to time, if required by the Minister on or without the application of any person having under the trust instrument any estate or interest in the settled land in possession, remainder, or otherwise, report to the Minister the state of every improvement executed under this Act, and the fact and particulars of fire insurance, if any.

(4) The Minister may vary any certificate made by him under this section in such manner or to such extent as circumstances appear to him to require, but not so as to increase the liabilities of the tenant for life, or any of his successors as aforesaid.

(5) If the tenant for life, or any of his successors as aforesaid, fails in any respect to comply with the requisitions of this section, or does any act in contravention thereof, any person having, under the trust instrument, any estate or interest in the settled land in possession, remainder, or reversion, shall have a right of action, in respect of that default or act, against the tenant for life; and the estate of the tenant for life, after his death, shall be liable to make good to the persons entitled under the trust instrument any damages occasioned by that default or act.

(6) Where in connexion with any improvement an improvement rent charge, as hereinbefore defined, has been created, and that rentcharge has been redeemed out of capital money, this section shall apply to the improvement as if it had been an improvement executed under this Act.

89. Protection as regards waste in execution and repair of improvements

The tenant for life, and each of his successors in title having, under the trust instrument, a limited estate or interest only in the settled land, and all persons employed by or under contract with the tenant for life or any such successor, may from time to time enter on the settled land, and, without impeachment of waste by any remainderman or reversioner, thereon execute any improvement authorised by this Act, or inspect, maintain, and repair the same, and for the purposes thereof do, make, and use on the settled land, all acts, works and conveniences proper for the execution, maintenance, repair, and use thereof, and get and work freestone, limestone, clay, sand, and other substances, and make tramways and other ways, and burn and make bricks, tiles, and other things, and cut down and use timber and other trees not planted or left standing for shelter or ornament.

PART V
MISCELLANEOUS PROVISIONS

90. Power for tenant for life to enter into contracts

(1) A tenant for life—

(i) may contract to make any sale, exchange, mortgage, charge or other disposition authorised by this Act; and

(ii) may vary or rescind, with or without consideration, the contract in the like cases and manner in which, if he were absolute owner of the settled land, he might lawfully vary or rescind the same, but so that the contract as varied be in conformity with this Act; and

(iii) may contract to make any lease, and in making the lease may vary the terms, with or without consideration, but so that the lease be in conformity with this Act; and

(iv) may accept a surrender of a contract for a lease or a grant in fee simple at a rent, in like manner and on the like terms in and on which he might accept a surrender of a lease or a regrant, and thereupon may make a new or other contract for or relative to a lease or leases, or a grant or grants in fee simple at a rent, in like manner and on the like terms in and on which he might make a new or other lease or grant, or new or other leases or grants, where a lease or a grant in fee simple at a rent had been executed; and

(v) may enter into a contract for or relating to the execution of any improvement authorised by this Act, and may vary or rescind any such contract; and

(vi) may in any other case, enter into a contract to do any act for carrying into effect any of the purposes of this Act, and may vary or rescind any such contract.

(2) Every contract, including a contract arising by reason of the exercise of an option, shall be binding on and shall enure for the benefit of the settled land, and shall be enforceable against and by every successor in title for the time being of the tenant for life, or statutory owner, and may be carried into effect by any such successor, but so that it may be varied or rescinded by any such successor, in the like case and manner, if any, as if it had been made by himself.

(3) The court may, on the application of the tenant for life, or statutory owner, or of any such successor as aforesaid, or of any person interested in any contract, give directions respecting the enforcing, carrying into effect, varying, or rescinding thereof.

(4) A preliminary contract under this Act for or relating to a lease, and a contract conferring an option, shall not form part of the title or evidence of the title of any person to the lease, or to the benefit thereof, or to the land the subject of the option.

(5) All money, not being rent, received on the exercise by the tenant for life or statutory owner of the powers conferred by subsection (1) of this section, shall, unless the court on an application made within six months after the receipt of the money, or within such further time as the court may in special circumstances allow, otherwise directs, be capital money arising under this Act.

PART VI
GENERAL PROVISIONS AS TO TRUSTEES

94. Number of trustees to act

(1) Notwithstanding anything in this Act, capital money arising under this Act shall not be paid to fewer than two persons as trustees of a settlement, unless the trustee is a trust corporation.

(2) Subject as aforesaid the provisions of this Act referring to the trustees of a settlement apply to the surviving or continuing trustees or trustee of the settlement for the time being.

95. Trustees' receipts
The receipt or direction in writing of or by the trustees of the settlement, or where a sole trustee is a trust corporation, of or by that trustee, or of or by the personal representatives of the last surviving or continuing trustee, for or relating to any money or securities, paid or transferred to or by the direction of the trustees, trustee, or representatives, as the case may be, effectually discharges the payer or transferor therefrom, and from being bound to see to the application or being answerable for any loss or misapplication thereof, and, in case of a mortgagee or other person advancing money, from being concerned to see that any money advanced by him is wanted for any purpose of this Act, or that no more than is wanted is raised.

96. Protection of each trustee individually
Each person who is for the time being a trustee of a settlement is answerable for what he actually receives only, notwithstanding his signing any receipts for conformity, and in respect of his own acts, receipts, and defaults only, and is not answerable in respect of those of any other trustee, or of any banker, broker, or other person, or for the insufficiency or deficiency of any securities, or for any loss not happening through his own wilful default.

97. Protection of trustees generally
The trustees of a settlement, or any of them—

(a) are not liable for giving any consent, or for not making, bringing, taking, or doing any such application, action, proceeding, or thing, as they might make, bring, take, or do; and

(b) in case of a purchase of land with capital money arising under this Act, or of an exchange, lease, or other disposition, are not liable for adopting any contract made by the tenant for life or statutory owner, or bound to inquire as to the propriety of the purchase, exchange, lease, or other disposition, or answerable as regards any price, consideration, or fine; and

(c) are not liable to see to or answerable for the investigation of the title, or answerable for a conveyance of land, if the conveyance purports to convey the land in the proper mode; and

(d) are not liable in respect of purchase-money paid by them by the direction of the tenant for life or statutory owner to any person joining in the conveyance as a conveying party, or as giving a receipt for the purchase-money, or in any other character, or in respect of any other money paid by them by the direction of the tenant for life or statutory owner on the purchase, exchange, lease, or other disposition.

98. Protection of trustees in particular cases

(1) Where the tenant for life or statutory owner directs capital money to be invested on any authorised security or investment, the trustees of the settlement shall not be liable for the acts of any agent employed by the tenant for life or statutory owner in connexion with the transaction, or for not employing a separate agent in or about the valuation of the subject of the security or the investigation of the title thereto, or for the form of the security or of any deed conveying the subject thereof to the trustees.

(2) The trustees of the settlement shall not be liable for paying or applying any capital money by the direction of the tenant for life or statutory owner for any authorised purpose.

(3) The trustees of the settlement shall not be liable in any way on account of any vesting instrument or other documents of title relating to the settled land, other than securities for capital money, being placed in the possession of the tenant for life or statutory owner:

Provided that where, if the settlement were not disclosed, it would appear that the tenant for life had a general power of appointment over, or was absolutely and beneficially entitled to the settled land, the trustees of the settlement shall, before they deliver the documents to him, require that notice of the last or only principal vesting instrument be written on one of the documents under which the tenant for life acquired his title, and may, if the documents are not in their possession, require such notice to be written as aforesaid, but, in the latter case, they shall not be liable in any way for not requiring the notice to be written.

(4) This section applies to dealings and matters effected before as well as after the commencement of this Act.

99. Indemnities to personal representatives and others

Personal representatives, trustees, or other persons who have in good faith, pursuant to this Act, executed a vesting deed, assent, or other conveyance of the settled land, or a deed of discharge of trustees, shall be absolutely discharged from all liability in respect of the equitable interests and powers taking effect under the settlement, and shall be entitled to be kept indemnified at the cost of the trust estate from all liabilities affecting the settled land, but the person to whom the settled land is conveyed (not being a purchaser taking free therefrom) shall hold the settled land upon the trusts, if any, affecting the same.

100. Trustees' reimbursements

The trustees of a settlement may reimburse themselves or pay and discharge out of the trust property all expenses properly incurred by them.

101. Notice to trustees

(1) Save as otherwise expressly provided by this Act, a tenant for life or statutory owner, when intending to make a sale, exchange, lease, mortgage, or charge or to grant an option—

(a) shall give notice of his intention in that behalf to each of the trustees of the settlement, by posting registered letters, containing the notice, addressed to the trustees severally, each at his usual or last known place of abode in the United Kingdom; and

(b) shall give a like notice to the solicitor for the trustees, if any such solicitor is known to the tenant for life or statutory owner, by posting a registered letter, containing the notice, addressed to the solicitor at his place of business in the United Kingdom;

every letter under this section being posted not less than one month before the making or granting by the tenant for life or statutory owner of the sale, exchange, lease, mortgage, charge, or option, or of a contract for the same:

Provided that a notice under this section shall not be valid unless at the date thereof the trustee is a trust corporation, or the number of trustees is not less than two.

(2) The notice required by this section of intention to make a sale, exchange, or lease, or to grant an option, may be notice of a general intention in that behalf.

(3) The tenant for life or statutory owner is, upon request by a trustee of the settlement, to furnish to him such particulars and information as may reasonably be required by him from time to time with reference to sales, exchanges, or leases effected, or in progress, or immediately intended.

(4) Any trustee, by writing under his hand, may waive notice either in any particular case, or generally, and may accept less than one months' notice.

(5) A person dealing in good faith with the tenant for life is not concerned to inquire respecting the giving of any such notice as is required by this section.

102. Management of land during minority or pending contingency

(1) If and as long as any person who is entitled to a beneficial interest in possession affecting land is an infant, the trustees appointed for this purpose by the settlement, or if there are none so appointed, then the trustees of the settlement, unless the settlement

or the order of the court whereby they or their predecessors in office were appointed to be such trustees expressly provides to the contrary, or if there are none, then any persons appointed as trustees for this purpose by the court on the application of a guardian or next friend of the infant, may enter into and continue in possession of the land on behalf of the infant, and in every such case the subsequent provisions of this section shall apply.

(2) The trustees shall manage or superintend the management of the land, with full power—

(a) to fell timber or cut underwood from time to time in the usual course for sale, or for repairs or otherwise; and

(b) to erect, pull down, rebuild, and repair houses, and other buildings and erections; and

(c) to continue the working of mines, minerals, and quarries which have usually been worked; and

(d) to drain or otherwise improve the land or any part thereof; and

(e) to insure against loss by fire; and

(f) to make allowances to and arrangements with tenants and others; and

(g) to determine tenancies, and to accept surrenders of leases and tenancies; and

(h) generally to deal with the land in a proper and due course of management;

but so that, where the infant is impeachable for waste, the trustees shall not commit waste, and shall cut timber on the same terms only, and subject to the same restrictions, on and subject to which the infant could, if of full age, cut the same.

(3) The trustees may from time to time, out of the income of the land, including the produce of the sale of timber and underwood, pay the expenses incurred in the management, or in the exercise of any power conferred by this section, or otherwise in relation to the land, and all outgoings not payable by any tenant or other person, and shall keep down any annual sum, and the interest of any principal sum, charged on the land.

(4) This section has effect subject to an express appointment by the settlement, or the court, of trustees for the purposes of this section or of any enactment replaced by this section.

(5) Where any person is contingently entitled to land, this section shall, subject to any prior interests or charges affecting that land, apply until his interest vests, or, if his interest vests during his minority, until he attains the age of [eighteen years].

This subsection applies only where a person becomes contingently entitled under an instrument coming into operation after the commencement of this Act.

(6) This section applies only if and as far as a contrary intention is not expressed in the instrument, if any, under which the interest of the infant or person contingently entitled as aforesaid arises, and has effect subject to the terms of that instrument and to the provisions therein contained.

PART VII
RESTRICTIONS, SAVINGS, AND PROTECTION OF PURCHASERS

103. Legal estate in settled land not to vest in trustee in bankruptcy of estate owner

[For the purpose of determining, where the estate owner of any settled land is bankrupt, whether the legal estate in the settled land is comprised in, or is capable of being claimed for, the bankrupt's estate, the legal estate in the settled land shall be deemed not to vest in the] estate owner unless and until the estate owner becomes absolutely and beneficially entitled to the settled land free from all limitations, powers, and charges taking effect under the settlement.

104. Powers not assignable, and contract not to exercise powers void

(1) The powers under this Act of a tenant for life are not capable of assignment or release, and do not pass to a person as being, by operation of law or otherwise, an

assignee of a tenant for life, and remain exercisable by the tenant for life after and nothwithstanding any assignment, by operation of law or otherwise, of his estate or interest under the settlement.

This subsection applies notwithstanding that the estate or interest of the tenant for life under the settlement was not in possession when the assignment was made or took effect by operation of law.

(2) A contract by a tenant for life not to exercise his powers under this Act or any of them shall be void.

(3) Where an assignment for value for the estate or interest of the tenant for life was made before the commencement of this Act, this section shall operate without prejudice to the rights of the assignee, and in that case the assignee's rights shall not be affected without his consent, except that—

(a) unless the assignee is actually in possession of the settled land or the part thereof affected, his consent shall not be requisite for the making of leases thereof by the tenant for life or statutory owner, provided the leases are made at the best rent that can reasonably be obtained, without fine, and in other respects are in conformity with this Act; and

(b) the consent of the assignee shall not be required to an investment of capital money for the time being affected by the assignment in securities authorised by statute for the investment of trust money.

(4) Where such an assignment for value is made or comes into operation after the commencement of this Act, the consent of the assignee shall not be requisite for the exercise by the tenant for life of any of the powers conferred by this Act:

provided that—

(a) the assignee shall be entitled to the same or the like estate or interest in or charge on the land, money, or securities for the time being representing the land, money, or securities comprised in the assignment, as he had by virtue of the assignment in the last-mentioned land, money, or securities; and

(b) if the assignment so provides, or if it takes effect by operation of the law of bankruptcy, and after notice thereof to the trustees of the settlement, no investment or application of capital money for the time being affected by the assignment shall be made without the consent of the assignee, except an investment in securities authorised by statute for the investment of trust money; and

(c) notice of the intended transaction shall, unless the assignment otherwise provides, be given to the assignee, but a purchaser shall not be concerned to see or inquire whether such notice has been given.

(5) Where such an assignment for value was made before the commencement of this Act, then on the exercise by the tenant for life after such commencement of any of the powers conferred by this Act—

(a) a purchaser shall not be concerned to see or inquire whether the consent of the assignee has been obtained; and

(b) the provisions of paragraph (a) of the last subsection shall apply for the benefit of the assignee.

(6) A trustee or personal representative who is an assignee for value shall have power to consent to the exercise by the tenant for life of his powers under this Act, or to any such investment or application of capital money as aforesaid, and to bind by such consent all persons interested in the trust estate, or the estate of the testator or intestate.

(7) If by the original assignment, or by any subsequent disposition, the estate or interest assigned or created by the original assignment, or any part thereof, or any derivative interest is settled on persons in succession, whether subject to any prior charge or not, and there is no trustee or personal representative in whom the entirety of the estate or interest so settled is vested, then the person for the time being entitled in possession under the limitations of that settlement, whether as trustee or beneficiary,

or who would, if of full age, be so entitled, and notwithstanding any charge or incumbrance subsisting or to arise under such settlement, shall have power to consent to the exercise by the tenant for life of his powers under this Act, or to any such investment or application of capital money as aforesaid, and to bind by such consent all persons interested or to become interested under such settlement.

(8) Where an assignee for value, or any person who has power to consent as aforesaid under this section, is an infant, the consent may be given on his behalf by his parents or parent or testamentary or other guardian in the order named.

(9) The court shall have power to authorise any person interested under any assignment to consent to the exercise by the tenant for life of his powers under this Act, or to any such investment or application of capital money as aforesaid, on behalf of himself and all other persons interested, or who may become interested under such assignment.

(10) An assignment by operation of the law of bankruptcy, where the assignment comes into operation after the commencement of this Act, shall be deemed to be an assignment for value for the purposes of this section.

(11) An instrument whereby a tenant for life, in consideration of marriage or as part or by way of any family arrangement, not being a security for payment of money advanced, makes an assignment of or creates a charge upon his estate or interest under the settlement is to be deemed one of the instruments creating the settlement, and not an assignment for value for the purposes of this section:

Provided that this subsection shall not have effect with respect to any disposition made before the eighteenth day of August eighteen hundred and ninety, if inconsistent with the nature or terms of the disposition.

(12) This section extends to assignments made or coming into operation before or after commencement of this Act, and in this section 'assignment' includes assignment by way of mortgage, and any partial or qualified assignment, and any charge or incumbrance, 'assignee' has a corresponding meaning, and 'assignee for value' includes persons deriving title under the original assignee.

105. Effect of surrender of life estate to the next remainderman

(1) Where the estate or interest of a tenant for life under the settlement has been or is absolutely assured with intent to extinguish the same, either before or after the commencement of this Act, to the person next entitled in remainder or reversion under the settlement, then, [. . .] the statutory powers of the tenant for life under this Act shall, in reference to the property affected by the assurance, and notwithstanding the provisions of the last preceding section, cease to be exercisable by him, and the statutory powers shall thenceforth become exercisable as if he were dead, but without prejudice to any incumbrance affecting the estate or interest assured, and to the rights to which any incumbrancer would have been entitled if those powers had remained exercisable by the tenant for life.

This subsection applies whether or not any term of years or charge intervenes, or the estate of the remainderman or reversioner is liable to be defeated, and whether or not the estate or interest of the tenant for life under the settlement was in possession at the date of the assurance.

This subsection does not prejudice anything done by the tenant for life before the commencement of this Act, in exercise of any power operating under the Settled Land Acts, 1882 to 1890, or, unless the assurance provides to the contrary, operate to accelerate any such intervening term of years or charge as aforesaid.

(2) In this section 'assurance' means any surrender, conveyance, assignment or appointment under a power (whether vested in any person solely, or jointly in two or more persons) which operates in equity to extinguish the estate or interest of the tenant for life, and 'assured' has a corresponding meaning.

106. Prohibition or limitation against exercise of powers void, and provision against forfeiture

(1) If in a settlement, will, assurance, or other instrument executed or made before or after, or partly before and partly after, the commencement of this Act a provision is inserted—

(a) purporting or attempting, by way of direction, declaration, or otherwise, to forbid a tenant for life or statutory owner to exercise any power under this Act, or his right to require the settled land to be vested in him; or

(b) attempting, or tending, or intended, by a limitation, gift, or disposition over of settled land, or by a limitation, gift, or disposition of other real or any personal property, or by the imposition of any condition, or by forfeiture, or in any other manner whatever, to prohibit or prevent him from exercising, or to induce him to abstain from exercising or to put him into a position inconsistent with his exercising, any power under this Act, or his right to require the settled land to be vested in him; that provision, as far as it purports, or attempts, or tends, or is intended to have, or would or might have, the operation aforesaid, shall be deemed to be void.

(2) For the purposes of this section an estate or interest limited to continue so long only as a person abstains from exercising any such power or right as aforesaid shall be and take effect as an estate or interest to continue for the period for which it would continue if that person were to abstain from exercising the power or right, discharged from liability to determination or cesser by or on his exercising the same.

(3) Notwithstanding anything in a settlement, the exercise by the tenant for life or statutory owner of any power under this Act shall not occasion a forfeiture.

107. Tenant for life trustee for all parties interested

(1) A tenant for life or statutory owner shall, in exercising any power under this Act, have regard to the interests of all parties entitled under the settlement, and shall, in relation to the exercise thereof by him, be deemed to be in the position and to have the duties and liabilities of a trustee for those parties.

(2) The provision by a tenant for life or statutory owner, at his own expense, of dwellings available for the working classes on any settled land shall not be deemed to be an injury to any interest in reversion or remainder in that land, but such provision shall not be made by a tenant for life or statutory owner without the previous approval in writing of the trustees of the settlement.

108. Saving for and exercise of other powers

(1) Nothing in this Act shall take away, abridge, or prejudicially affect any power for the time being subsisting under a settlement, or by statute or otherwise, exercisable by a tenant for life, or (save as hereinafter provided) by trustees with his consent, or on his request, or by his direction, or otherwise, and the powers given by this Act are cumulative.

(2) In case of conflict between the provisions of a settlement and the provisions of this Act, relative to any matter in respect whereof the tenant for life or statutory owner exercises or contracts or intends to exercise any power under this Act, the provisions of this Act shall prevail; and, notwithstanding anything in the settlement, any power (not being merely a power of revocation or appointment) relating to the settled land thereby conferred on the trustees of the settlement or other persons exercisable for any purpose, whether or not provided for in this Act, shall, after the commencement of this Act, be exercisable by the tenant for life or statutory owner as if it were an additional power conferred on the tenant for life within the next following section of this Act and not otherwise.

(3) If a question arises or a doubt is entertained respecting any matter within this section, the tenant for life or statutory owner, or the trustees of the settlement, or any other person interested, under the settlement may apply to the court for its decision thereon, and the court may make such order respecting the matter as the court thinks fit.

109. Saving for additional or larger powers under settlement

(1) Nothing in this Act precludes a settlor from conferring on the tenant for life, or (save as provided by the last preceding section) on the trustees of the settlement, any powers additional to or larger than those conferred by this Act.

(2) Any additional or larger powers so conferred shall, as far as may be, notwithstanding anything in this Act, operate and be exercisable in the like manner, and with all the like incidents, effects, and consequences, as if they were conferred by this Act, and, if relating to the settled land, as if they were conferred by this Act on a tenant for life.

110. Protection of purchasers, etc.

(1) On a sale, exchange, lease, mortgage, charge, or other disposition, a purchaser dealing in good faith with a tenant for life or statutory owner shall, as against all parties entitled under the settlement, be conclusively taken to have given the best price, consideration, or rent as the case may require, that could reasonably be obtained by the tenant for life or statutory owner, and to have complied with all the requisitions of this Act.

(2) A purchaser of a legal estate in settled land shall not, except as hereby expressly provided, be bound or entitled to call for the production of the trust instrument or any information concerning that instrument or any ad valorem stamp duty thereon, and whether or not he has notice of its contents he shall, save as hereinafter provided, be bound and entitled if the last or only principal vesting instrument contains the statements and particulars required by this Act to assume that—

(a) the person in whom the land is by the said instrument vested or declared to be vested is the tenant for life or statutory owner and has all the powers of a tenant for life under this Act, including such additional or larger powers, if any, as are therein mentioned;

(b) the persons by the said instrument stated to be the trustees of the settlement, or their successors appearing to be duly appointed, are the properly constituted trustees of the settlement;

(c) the statements and particulars required by this Act and contained (expressly or by reference) in the said instrument were correct at the date thereof;

(d) the statements contained in any deed executed in accordance with this Act declaring who are the trustees of the settlement for the purposes of this Act are correct;

(e) the statements contained in any deed of discharge, executed in accordance with this Act, are correct:

Provided that, as regards the first vesting instrument executed for the purpose of giving effect to—

(a) a settlement subsisting at the commencement of this Act; or

(b) an instrument which by virtue of this Act is deemed to be a settlement; or

(c) a settlement which by virtue of this Act is deemed to have been made by any person after the commencement of this Act; or

(d) an instrument inter vivos intended to create a settlement of a legal estate in land which is executed after the commencement of this Act and does not comply with the requirements of this Act with respect to the method of effecting such a settlement;

a purchaser shall be concerned to see—

(i) that the land disposed of to him is comprised in such settlement or instrument;

(ii) that the person in whom the settled land is by such vesting instrument vested, or
declared to be vested, is the person in whom it ought to be vested as tenant for life or statutory owner

(iii) that the persons thereby stated to be the trustees of the settlement are the properly constituted trustees of the settlement.

(3) A purchaser of a legal estate in settled land from a personal representative shall be entitled to act on the following assumptions:—

(i) If the capital money, if any, payable in respect of the transaction is paid to the personal representative, that such representative is acting under his statutory or other powers and requires the money for purposes of administration;

(ii) If such capital money is, by the direction of the personal representative, paid to persons who are stated to be the trustees of a settlement, that such persons are the duly constituted trustees of the settlement for the purposes of this Act, and that the personal representative is acting under his statutory powers during a minority;

(iii) In any other case, that the personal representative is acting under his statutory or other powers.

(4) Where no capital money arises under a transaction, a disposition by a tenant for life or statutory owner shall, in favour of a purchaser of a legal estate, have effect under this Act notwithstanding that at the date of the transaction there are no trustees of the settlement.

(5) If a conveyance of or an assent relating to land formerly subject to a vesting instrument does not state who are the trustees of the settlement for the purposes of this Act, a purchaser of a legal estate shall be bound and entitled to act on the assumption that the person in whom the land was thereby vested was entitled to the land free from all limitations, powers, and charges taking effect under that settlement, absolutely and beneficially, or, if so expressed in the conveyance or assent, as personal representative, or [trustee of land] or otherwise, and that every statement of fact in such conveyance or assent is correct.

111. Purchaser of beneficial interest of tenant for life to have remedies of a legal owner

Where—

(a) at the commencement of this Act the legal beneficial interest of a tenant for life under a settlement is vested in a purchaser; or

(b) after the commencement of this Act a tenant for life conveys or deals with his beneficial interest in possession in favour of a purchaser, and the interest so conveyed or created would, but for the restrictions imposed by statute on the creation of legal estates, have been a legal interest,

the purchaser shall (without prejudice to the powers conferred by this Act on the tenant for life) have and may exercise all the same rights and remedies as he would have had or have been entitled to exercise if the interest had remained or been a legal interest and the reversion, if any, on any leases or tenancies derived out of the settled land had been vested in him:

Provided that, where the conveyance or dealing is effected after the commencement of this Act, the purchaser shall not be entitled to the possession of the documents of title relating to the settled land, but shall have the same rights with respect thereto as if the tenant for life had given to him a statutory acknowledgement of his right to production and delivery of copies thereof, and a statutory undertaking for the safe custody thereof.

The tenant for life shall not deliver any such documents to a purchaser of his beneficial interest, who is not also a purchaser of the whole of the settled land to which such documents relate.

112. Exercise of powers; limitation of provisions, etc.

(1) Where a power of sale, exchange, leasing, mortgaging, charging, or other power is exercised by a tenant for life, or statutory owner or by the trustees of a settlement, he and they may respectively execute, make, and do all deeds, instruments, and things necessary or proper in that behalf.

(2) Where any provision in this Act refers to sale, purchase, exchange, mortgaging, charging, leasing, or other disposition or dealing, or to any power, consent, payment,

receipt, deed, assurance, contract, expenses, act, or transaction, it shall (unless the contrary appears) be construed as extending only to sales, purchases, exchanges, mortgages, charges, leases, dispositions, dealings, powers, consents, payments, receipts, deeds, assurances, contracts, expenses, acts, and transactions under this Act.

PART IX
SUPPLEMENTARY PROVISIONS

117. Definitions

(1) In this Act, unless the context otherwise requires, the following expressions have the meanings hereby assigned to them respectively, that is to say:—

(i) 'Building purposes' include the erecting and the improving of, and the adding to, and the repairing of buildings; and a 'building lease' is a lease for any building purposes or purposes connected therewith;

(ii) 'Capital money arising under this Act' means capital money arising under the powers and provisions of this Act or the Acts replaced by this Act, and receivable for the trusts and purposes of the settlement and includes securities representing capital money;

(iii) 'Death duty' means estate duty and every other duty leviable or payable on death;

(iv) 'Determinable fee' means a fee determinable whether by limitation or condition;

(v) 'Disposition' and 'conveyance' include a mortgage, charge by way of legal mortgage, lease, assent, vesting declaration, vesting instrument, disclaimer, release and every other assurance of property or of an interest therein by any instrument, except a will, and 'dispose of' and 'convey' have corresponding meanings;

(vi) 'Dower' includes 'freebench';

(vii) 'Hereditaments' mean real property which on an intestacy might before the commencement of this Act have devolved on an heir;

(viii) 'Instrument' does not include a statute unless the statute creates a settlement;

(ix) 'Land' includes land of any tenure, and mines and minerals whether or not held apart from the surface, buildings or parts of buildings (whether the division is horizontal, vertical or made in any other way) and other corporeal hereditaments, also a manor, an advowson, and a rent and other incorporeal hereditaments, and an easement, right, privilege, or benefit in, over, or derived from land, and any estate or interest in land [, but does not (except in the phrase 'trust of land') include] an undivided share in land;

(x) 'Lease' includes an agreement for a lease, and 'forestry lease' means a lease to the Forestry Commissioners for any purpose for which they are authorised to acquire land by the Forestry Act, 1919;

(xi) 'Legal mortgage' means a mortgage by demise or subdemise or a charge by way of legal mortgage, and 'legal mortgagee' has a corresponding meaning; 'legal estate' means an estate interest or charge in or over land (subsisting or created at law) which is by statute authorised to subsist or to be created at law; and 'equitable interests' mean all other interests and charges in or over land or in the proceeds of sale thereof; an equitable interest 'capable of subsisting at law' means such an equitable interest as could validly subsist at law, if clothed with the legal estate; and 'estate owner' means the owner of a legal estate;

(xii) 'Limitation' includes a trust, and 'trust' includes an implied or constructive trust;

(xiii) [. . .]

(xiv) 'Manor' includes lordship, and reputed manor or lordship; and 'manorial incident' has the same meaning as in the Law of Property Act, 1922;[1]

(xv) 'Mines and minerals' mean mines and minerals whether already opened or in work or not, and include all minerals and substances in, on, or under the land, obtainable by underground or by surface working; and 'mining purposes' include the sinking and searching for, winning, working, getting, making merchantable, smelting or otherwise converting or working for the purposes of any manufacture, carrying away, and disposing of mines and minerals, in or under the settled land, or any other land, and the erection of buildings, and the execution of engineering and other works suitable for those purposes; and a 'mining lease' is a lease for any mining purposes or purposes connected therewith, and includes a grant or licence for any mining purposes,

(xvi) 'Minister' means the [Minister of Agriculture, Fisheries and Food];

(xvii) 'Notice' includes constructive notice;

(xviii) 'personal representative' means the executor, original or by representation, or administrator, for the time being of a deceased person, and where there are special personal representatives for the purposes of settled land means those personal representatives;

(xix) 'Possession' includes receipt of rents and profits, or the right to receive the same, if any; and 'income' includes rents and profits;

(xx) 'property' includes any thing in action, and any interest in real or personal property;

(xxi) 'purchaser' means a purchaser in good faith for value, and includes a lessee, mortgagee or other person who in good faith acquires an interest in settled land for value; and in reference to a legal estate includes a chargee by way of legal mortgage;

(xxii) 'Rent' includes yearly or other rent, and toll, duty, royalty, or other reservation, by the acre, or the ton, or otherwise; and, in relation to rent, 'payment' includes delivery; and 'fine' includes premium or fore-gift, and any payment, consideration, or benefit in the nature of a fine, premium, or fore-gift;

(xxiii) 'Securities' include stocks, funds, and shares;

(xxiv) 'Settled land' includes land which is deemed to be settled land; 'settlement' includes an instrument or instruments which under this Act or the Acts which it replaces is or are deemed to be or which together constitute a settlement, and a settlement which is deemed to have been made by any person or to be subsisting for the purposes of this Act; 'a settlement subsisting at the commencement of this Act' includes a settlement created by virtue of this Act immediately on the commencement thereof; and 'trustees of the settlement' mean the trustees thereof for the purposes of this Act howsoever appointed or constituted;

(xxv) 'Small dwellings' mean dwelling-houses of a rateable value not exceeding one hundred pounds per annum;

(xxvi) 'Statutory owner' means the trustees of the settlement or other persons who, during a minority, or at any other time when there is no tenant for life, have the powers of a tenant for life under this Act, but does not include the trustees of the settlement, where by virtue of an order of the court or otherwise the trustees have power to convey the settled land in the name of the tenant for life;

(xxvii) 'Steward' includes deputy steward, or other proper officer, of a manor;

(xxviii) 'Tenant for life' includes a person (not being a statutory owner) who has the powers of a tenant for life under this Act, and also (where the context requires) one of two or more persons who together constitute the tenant for life, or have the powers of a tenant for life, and 'tenant in tail' includes a person entitled to an entailed interest in any property; and 'entailed interest' has the same meaning as in the Law of Property Act, 1925;

(xxix) A 'term of years absolute' means a term of years, taking effect either in possession or in reversion, with or without impeachment for waste, whether at a rent or not and whether subject or not to another legal estate, and whether certain or liable to determination by notice, re-entry, operation of law, or by a provision for cesser on redemption, or in any other event (other than the dropping of a life, or the determination of a determinable life interest), but does not include any term of years determinable with life or lives or with the cesser of a determinable life interest, nor, if created after the commencement of this Act, a term of years which is not expressed to take effect in possession within twenty-one years after the creation thereof where required by statute to take effect within that period; and in this definition the expression 'term of years' includes a term for less than a year, or for a year or years and a fraction of a year or from year to year;

(xxx) 'Trust corporation' means the Public Trustee or a corporation either appointed by the court in any particular case to be a trustee or entitled by rules made under subsection (3) of section four of the Public Trustee Act, 1906, to act as custodian trustee, and 'trust for sale' [has the same meaning] as in the Law of Property Act, 1925;

(xxxi) In relation to settled land 'vesting deed' or 'vesting order' means the instrument whereby settled land is conveyed to or vested or declared to be vested in a tenant for life or statutory owner, 'vesting assent' means the instrument whereby a personal representative, after the death of a tenant for life or statutory owner, or the survivor of two or more tenants for life or statutory owners, vests settled land in a person entitled as tenant for life or statutory owner; 'vesting instrument' means a vesting deed, a vesting assent or, where the land affected remains settled land, a vesting order 'principal vesting instrument' includes any vesting instrument other than a subsidiary vesting deed; and 'trust instrument' means the instrument whereby the trusts of the settled land are declared, and includes any two or more such instruments and a settlement or instrument which is deemed to be a trust instrument,

(xxxii) 'United Kingdom' means Great Britain and Northern Ireland;

(xxxiii) 'Will' includes codicil.

[(1A) Any reference in this Act to money, securities or proceeds of sale being paid or transferred into court shall be construed as referring to the money, securities or proceeds being paid or transferred into the Supreme Court or any other court that has jurisdiction, and any reference in this Act to the court, in a context referring to the investment or application of money, securities or proceeds of sale paid or transferred into court, shall be construed, in the case of money, securities or proceeds paid or transferred into the Supreme Court, as referring to the High Court, and, in the case of money, securities or proceeds paid or transferred into another court, as referring to that other court.]

(2) Where an equitable interest in or power over property arises by statute or operation of law, references to the 'creation' of an interest or power include any interest or power so arising.

(3) Reference to registration under the Land Charges Act, 1925,2 apply to any registration made under any statute which is by the Land Charges Act, 1925,[2] to have effect as if the registration had been made under that Act.

Notes

[1]All manorial incidents have now been extinguished, Law of Property Act 1922, Part VI.

[2]Now the Land Charges Act 1972.

119. Repeals, savings, and construction

(1) [. . .] without prejudice to the provisions of section thirty-eight of the Interpretation Act, 1889.[1]

(a) Nothing in this repeal shall affect the validity or legality of any dealing in land or other transaction completed before the commencement of this Act, or any title or right acquired or appointment made before the commencement of this Act, but, subject as aforesaid, this Act shall, except where otherwise expressly provided, apply to and in respect of settlements and other instruments whether made or coming into operation before or after the commencement of this Act;

(b) Nothing in this repeal shall affect any rules, orders, or other instruments made under any enactment so repealed, but all such rules, orders and instruments shall continue in force as if made under the corresponding enactment in this Act;

(c) References in any document to any enactment repealed by this Act shall be construed as reference to this Act or the corresponding enactment in this Act.

(2) References in any statute to the Settled Estates Act, 1877, and to any enactment which it replaced shall be construed as references to this Act.

(3) This Act, as respects registered land, takes effect subject to the provisions of the Land Registration Act, 1925.

Note

[1]Now the Interpretation Act 1978, ss. 16(1), 17(2).

THIRD SCHEDULE

PART I

IMPROVEMENTS, THE COSTS OF WHICH ARE NOT LIABLE TO BE REPLACED BY INSTALMENTS

(i) Drainage, including the straightening, widening, or deepening of drains, streams, and watercourses:

(ii) Bridges:

(iii) Irrigation; warping:

(iv) Drains, pipes, and machinery for supply and distribution of sewage as manure:

(v) Embanking or weiring from a river or lake, or from the sea, or a tidal water.

(vi) Groynes; sea walls; defences against water:

(vii) Inclosing; straightening of fences; re-division of fields:

(viii) Reclamation; dry warping:

(ix) Farm roads; private roads; roads or streets in villages or towns:

(x) Clearing; trenching; planting:

(xi) Cottages for labourers, farm-servants, and artisans, employed on the settled land or not:

(xii) Farmhouses, offices, and outbuildings, and other buildings for farm purposes:

(xiii) Saw-mills, scutch-mills, and other mills, water-wheels, engine-houses, and kilns, which will increase the value of the settled land for agricultural purposes or as woodland or otherwise:

(xiv) Reservoirs, tanks, conduits, watercourses, pipes, wells, ponds, shafts, dams, weirs, sluices, and other works and machinery for supply and distribution of water for agricultural, manufacturing, or other purposes, or for domestic or other consumption:

(xv) Tramways; railways; canals; docks:

(xvi) Jetties, piers, and landing places on rivers, lakes, the sea or tidal waters, for facilitating transport of persons and of agricultural stock and produce, and of manure and other things required for agricultural purposes, and of minerals, and of things required for mining purposes:

(xvii) Markets and market-places:

(xviii) Streets, roads, paths, squares, gardens, or other open spaces for the use, gratuitously or on payment, of the public or of individuals, or for dedication to the public, the same being necessary or proper in connexion with the conversion of land into building land:

(xix) Sewers, drains, watercourses, pipe-making, fencing, paving, brick-making, tile-making, and other works necessary or proper in connexion with any of the objects aforesaid:

(xx) Trial pits for mines, and other preliminary works necessary or proper in connexion with development of mines:

(xxi) Reconstruction, enlargement, or improvement of any of those works:

(xxii) The provision of small dwellings, either by means of building new buildings or by means of the reconstruction, enlargement, or improvement of existing buildings, if that provision of small dwellings is, in the opinion of the court, not injurious to the settled land or is agreed to by the tenant for life and the trustees of the settlement:

(xxiii) Additions to or alterations in buildings reasonably necessary or proper to enable the same to be let:

(xxiv) Erection of buildings in substitution for buildings within an urban sanitary district taken by a local or other public authority, or for buildings taken under compulsory powers, but so that no more money be expended than the amount received for the buildings taken and the site thereof:

(xxv) The rebuilding of the principal mansion house on the settled land: provided that the sum to be applied under this head shall not exceed one-half of the annual rental of the settled land.

PART II
IMPROVEMENTS, THE COSTS OF WHICH THE TRUSTEES OF THE SETTLEMENT OR THE COURT MAY REQUIRE TO BE REPLACED BY INSTALMENTS

(i) Residential houses for land or mineral agents, managers, clerks, bailiffs, woodmen, gamekeepers and other persons employed on the settled land, or in connexion with the management or development thereof:

(ii) Any offices, workshops and other buildings of a permanent nature required in connexion with the management or development of the settled land or any part thereof:

(iii) The erection and building of dwelling houses, shops, buildings for religious, educational, literary, scientific, or public purposes, market places, market houses, places of amusement and entertainment, gasworks, electric light or power works, or any other works necessary or proper in connexion with the development of the settled land, or any part thereof as a building estate:

(iv) Restoration or reconstruction of buildings damaged or destroyed by dry rot:

(v) Structural additions to or alterations in buildings reasonably required, whether the buildings are intended to be let or not, or are already let:

(vi) Boring for water and other preliminary works in connexion therewith.

PART III
IMPROVEMENTS, THE COSTS OF WHICH THE TRUSTEES OF THE SETTLEMENT AND THE COURT MUST REQUIRE TO BE REPLACED BY INSTALMENTS

(i) Heating, hydraulic or electric power apparatus for buildings, and engines, pumps, lifts, rams, boilers, flues, and other works required or used in connexion therewith:

(ii) Engine houses, engines, gasometers, dynamos, accumulators, cables, pipes, wiring, switchboards, plant and other works required for the installation of electric, gas, or other artificial light, in connexion with any principal mansion house, or other house or buildings; but not electric lamps, gas fittings, or decorative fittings required in any such house or building:

(iii) Steam rollers, traction engines, motor lorries and moveable machinery for farming or other purposes.

TRUSTEE ACT 1925
(1925, c. 19)

PART I
INVESTMENTS

2. Purchase at a premium of redeemable stocks; change of character of investment

(1) A trustee may under the powers of this Act invest in any of the securities mentioned or referred to in section one of this Act,[1] notwithstanding that the same may be redeemable, and that the price exceeds the redemption value.

(2) A trustee may retain until redemption any redeemable stock, fund, or security which may have been purchased in accordance with the powers of this Act, or any statute replaced by this Act.

Note

[1]References to s. 1 of this Act (except in s.69(2)) are to be construed as references to s. 1 of the Trustee Investments Act 1961.

3. Discretion of trustees

Every power conferred by the preceding sections shall be exercised according to the discretion of the trustee, but subject to any consent or direction required by the instrument, if any, creating the trust or by statute with respect to the investment of the trust funds.

4. Power to retain investment which has ceased to be authorised

A trustee shall not be liable for breach of trust by reason only of his continuing to hold an investment which has ceased to be an investment authorised by the trust instrument or by the general law.

5. Enlargement of powers of investment

(1) A trustee having power to invest in real securities may invest and shall be deemed always to have had power to invest—

(a) [. . .]

(b) on any charge, or upon mortgage of any charge made under the Improvement of Land Act, 1864.

(2) A trustee having power to invest in real securities may accept the security in the form of a charge by way of legal mortgage, and may, in exercise of the statutory power, convert an existing mortgage into a charge by way of legal mortgage.

(3) A trustee having power to invest in the mortgages or bonds of any railway company or of any other description of company may invest in the debenture stock of a railway company or such other company as aforesaid.

(4)–(6) [. . .]

6. Power to invest in land subject to drainage charges

A trustee having power to invest in the purchase of land or on mortgage of land may invest in the purchase or on mortgage of any land notwithstanding the same is charged with [. . .] an absolute order made under the Improvement of Land Act, 1864, unless the terms of the trust expressly provide that the land to be purchased or taken in mortgage shall not be subject to any such prior charge.

7. Investment in bearer securities

(1) A trustee may, unless expressly prohibited by the instrument creating the trust, retain or invest in securities payable to bearer which, if not so payable, would have been authorised investments:

Provided that securities to bearer retained or taken as an investment by a trustee (not being a trust corporation) shall, until sold, be deposited by him for safe custody and collection of income with a banker or banking company.

A direction that investments shall be retained or made in the name of a trustee shall not, for the purposes of this subsection, be deemed to be such an express prohibition as aforesaid.

(2) A trustee shall not be responsible for any loss incurred by reason of such deposit, and any sum payable in respect of such deposit and collection shall be paid out of the income of the trust property.

8. Loans and investments by trustees not chargeable as breaches of trust

(1) A trustee lending money on the security of any property on which he can properly lend shall not be chargeable with breach of trust by reason only of the

proportion borne by the amount of the loan to the value of the property at the time when the loan was made if it appears to the court—

(a) that in making the loan the trustee was acting upon a report as to the value of the property made by a person whom he reasonably believed to be an able practical surveyor or valuer instructed and employed independently of any owner of the property, whether such surveyor or valuer carried on business in the locality where the property is situated or elsewhere; and

(b) that the amount of the loan does not exceed two third parts of the value of the property as stated in the report; and

(c) that the loan was made under the advice of the surveyor or valuer expressed in the report.

(2) A trustee lending money on the security of any leasehold property shall not be chargeable with breach of trust only upon the ground that in making such loan he dispensed either wholly or partly with the production or investigation of the lessor's title.

(3) A trustee shall not be chargeable with breach of trust only upon the ground that in effecting the purchase, or in lending money upon the security, of any property he has accepted a shorter title than the title which a purchaser is, in the absence of a special contract, entitled to require, if in the opinion of the court the title accepted be such as a person acting with prudence and caution would have accepted.

(4) This section applies to transfers of existing securities as well as to new securities and to investments made before as well as after the commencement of this Act.

9. Liability for loss by reason of improper investment

(1) Where a trustee improperly advances trust money on a mortgage security which would at the time of the investment be a proper investment in all respects for a smaller sum than is actually advanced thereon, the security shall be deemed an authorised investment for the smaller sum, and the trustee shall only be liable to make good the sum advanced in excess thereof with interest.

(2) This section applies to investments made before as well as after the commencement of this Act.

10. Powers supplementary to powers of investment

(1) Trustees lending money on the security of any property on which they can lawfully lend may contract that such money shall not be called in during any period not exceeding seven years from the time when the loan was made, provided interest be paid within a specified time not exceeding thirty days after every half-yearly or other day on which it becomes due, and provided there be no breach of any covenant by the mortgagor contained in the instrument of mortgage or charge for the maintenance and protection of the property.

(2) On a sale of land for an estate in fee simple or for a term having at least five hundred years to run [. . .] by a tenant for life or statutory owner, [. . .] the tenant for life or statutory owner on behalf of the trustees of the settlement, may, where the proceeds are liable to be invested, contract that the payment of any part, not exceeding two-thirds, of the purchase money shall be secured by a charge by way of legal mortgage or a mortgage by demise or subdemise for a term of at least five hundred years (less a nominal reversion when by sub-demise), of the land sold, with or without the security of any other property, such charge or mortgage, if any buildings are comprised in the mortgage, to contain a covenant by the mortgagor to keep them insured against loss or damage by fire to the full value thereof.

[. . .] [T]he trustees of the settlement shall be bound to give effect to such contract made by the tenant for life or statutory owner.

(3) Where any securities of a company are subject to a trust, the trustees may concur in any scheme or arrangement—

(a) for the reconstruction of the company;

(b) for the sale of all or any part of the property and undertaking of the company to another company

[(bb) for the acquisition of the securities of the company, or of control thereof, by another company]

(c) for the amalgamation of the company with another company;

(d) for the release, modification, or variation of any rights, privileges or liabilities attached to the securities or any of them;

in like manner as if they were entitled to such securities beneficially, with power to accept any securities of any denomination or description of the reconstructed or purchasing or new company in lieu of or in exchange for all or any of the first-mentioned securities; and the trustees shall not be responsible for any loss occasioned by any act or thing so done in good faith, and may retain any securities so accepted as aforesaid for any period for which they could have properly retained the original securities.

(4) If any conditional or preferential right to subscribe for any securities in any company is offered to trustees in respect of any holding in such company, they may as to all or any of such securities, either exercise such right and apply capital money subject to the trust in payment of the consideration, or renounce such right, or assign for the best consideration that can be reasonably obtained the benefit of such right or the title thereto to any person, including any beneficiary under the trust, without being responsible for any loss occasioned by any act or thing so done by them in good faith:

Provided that the consideration for any such assignment shall be held as capital money of the trust.

(5) The powers conferred by this section shall be exercisable subject to the consent of any person whose consent to a change of investment is required by law or by the instrument, if any, creating the trust.

(6) Where the loan referred to in subsection (1), or the sale referred to in subsection (2), of this section is made under the order of the court, the powers conferred by those subsections respectively shall apply only if and as far as the court may by order direct.

11. Power to deposit money at bank and to pay calls

(1) Trustees may, pending the negotiation and preparation of any mortgage or charge, or during any other time while an investment is being sought for, pay any trust money into a bank to a deposit or other account, and all interest, if any, payable in respect thereof shall be applied as income.

(2) Trustees may apply capital money subject to a trust in payment of the calls on any shares subject to the same trust.

PART II
GENERAL POWERS OF TRUSTEES AND PERSONAL REPRESENTATIVES

General Powers

12. Power of trustees for sale to sell by auction, etc.

(1) Where [a trustee has a duty or power to sell property], he may sell or concur with any other person in selling all or any part of the property, either subject to prior charges or not, and either together or in lots, by public auction or by private contract, subject to any such conditions respecting title or evidence of title or other matter as the Trustee thinks fit, with power to vary any contract for sale, and to buy in at any auction, or to rescind any contract for sale and to re-sell, without being answerable for any loss.

(2) A trust or power to sell or dispose of land includes a [duty] or power to sell or dispose of part thereof, whether the division is horizontal, vertical, or made in any other way.

(3) This section does not enable an express power to sell settled land to be exercised where the power is not vested in the tenant for life or statutory owner.

13. Power to sell subject to depreciatory conditions

(1) No sale made by a trustee shall be impeached by any beneficiary upon the ground that any of the conditions subject to which the sale was made have been unnecessarily depreciatory, unless it also appears that the consideration for the sale was thereby rendered inadequate.

(2) No sale made by a trustee shall, after the execution of the conveyance, be impeached as against the purchaser upon the ground that any of the conditions subject to which the sale was made may have been unnecessarily depreciatory, unless it appears that the purchaser was acting in collusion with the trustee at the time when the contract for sale was made.

(3) No purchaser, upon any sale made by a trustee, shall be at liberty to make any objection against the title upon any of the grounds aforesaid.

(4) This section applies to sales made before or after the commencement of this Act.

14. Power of trustees to give receipts

(1) The receipt in writing of a trustee for any money, securities, or other personal property or effects payable, transferable, or deliverable to him under any trust or power shall be a sufficient discharge to the person paying, transferring, or delivering the same and shall effectually exonerate him from seeing to the application or being answerable for any loss or misapplication thereof.

(2) This section does not, except where the trustee is a trust corporation, enable a sole trustee to give a valid receipt for—

[(a) proceeds of sale or other capital money arising under a trust of land;]

(b) capital money arising under the Settled Land Act, 1925.

(3) This section applies notwithstanding anything to the contrary in the instrument, if any, creating the trust.

15. Power to compound liabilities

A personal representative, or two or more trustees acting together, or, subject to the restrictions imposed in regard to receipts by a sole trustee not being a trust corporation, a sole acting trustee where by the instrument, if any, creating the trust, or by statute, a sole trustee is authorised to execute the trusts and powers reposed in him, may, if and as he or they think fit—

(a) accept any property, real or personal, before the time at which it is made transferable or payable; or

(b) sever and apportion any blended trust funds or property; or

(c) pay or allow any debt or claim on any evidence that he or they think sufficient; or

(d) accept any composition or any security, real or personal, for any debt or for any property, real or personal claimed; or

(e) allow any time of payment of any debt; or

(f) compromise, compound, abandon, submit to arbitration, or otherwise settle any debt, account, claim, or thing whatever relating to the testator's or intestate's estate or to the trust;

and for any of those purposes may enter into, give, execute, and do such agreements, instruments of composition or arrangement, releases, and other things as to him or them seem expedient, without being responsible for any loss occasioned by any act or thing so done by him or them in good faith.

16. Power to raise money by sale, mortgage, etc.

(1) Where trustees are authorised by the instrument, if any, creating the trustor by law to pay or apply capital money subject to the trust for any purpose or in any manner, they shall have and shall be deemed always to have had power to raise the money required by sale, conversion, calling in, or mortgage of all or any part of the trust property for the time being in possession.

(2) This section applies notwithstanding anything to the contrary contained in the instrument, if any, creating the trust, but does not apply to trustees of property held for charitable purposes, or to trustees of a settlement for the purposes of the Settled Land Act, 1925, not being also the statutory owners.

17. Protection to purchasers and mortgagees dealing with trustees

No purchaser or mortgagee, paying or advancing money on a sale or mortgage purporting to be made under any trust or power vested in trustees, shall be concerned to see that such money is wanted, or that no more than is wanted is raised, or otherwise as to the application thereof.

18. Devolution of powers or trusts

(1) Where a power or trust is given to or imposed on two or more trustees jointly, the same may be exercised or performed by the survivors or survivor of them for the time being.

(2) Until the appointment of new trustees, the personal representatives or representative for the time being of a sole trustee, or, where there were two or more trustees of the last surviving or continuing trustee, shall be capable of exercising or performing any power or trust which was given to, or capable of being exercised by, the sole or last surviving or continuing trustee, or other the trustees or trustee for the time being of the trust.

(3) This section takes effect subject to the restrictions imposed in regard to receipts by a sole trustee, not being a trust corporation.

(4) In this section 'personal representative' does not include an executor who has renounced or has not proved.

19. Power to insure

(1) A trustee may insure [any personal property against loss or damage] to any amount, including the amount of any insurance already on foot, not exceeding three fourth parts of the full value of the [. . .] property, and pay the premiums for such insurance out of the income thereof or out of the income of any other property subject to the same trusts without obtaining the consent of any person who may be entitled wholly or partly to such income.

(2) This section does not apply to any [personal] property which a trustee is bound forthwith to convey absolutely to any beneficiary upon being requested to do so.

20. Application of insurance money where policy kept up under any trust, power or obligation

(1) Money receivable by trustees or any beneficiary under a policy of insurance against the loss or damage of any property subject to a trust or to a settlement within the meaning of the Settled Land Act, 1925, whether by fire or otherwise, shall, where the policy has been kept up under any trust in that behalf or under any power statutory or otherwise, or in performance of any covenant or of any obligation statutory or otherwise, or by a tenant for life impeachable for waste, be capital money for the purposes of the trust or settlement, as the case may be.

(2) If any such money is receivable by any person, other than the trustees of the trust or settlement, that person shall use his best endeavours to recover and receive the money, and shall pay the net residue thereof, after discharging any costs of recovering and receiving it, to the trustees of the trust or settlement, or, if there are no trustees capable of giving a discharge therefor, into court.

(3) Any such money—

(a) if it was receivable in respect of settled land within the meaning of the Settled Land Act, 1925, or any building or works thereon, shall be deemed to be capital money arising under that Act from the settled land, and shall be invested or applied by the trustees, or, if in court, under the direction of the court, accordingly;

(b) if it was receivable in respect of personal chattels settled as heirlooms within the meaning of the Settled Land Act, 1925, shall be deemed to be capital money arising under that Act, and shall be applicable by the trustees, or, if in court, under the direction of the court, in like manner as provided by that Act with respect to money arising by a sale of chattels settled as heirlooms as aforesaid;

(c) if it was receivable in respect of [land subject to a trust of land or personal property held on trust for sale], shall be held upon the trusts and subject to the powers and provisions applicable to money arising by a sale under such trust;

(d) in any other case, shall be held upon trusts corresponding as nearly as may be with the trusts affecting the property in respect of which it was payable.

(4) Such money, or any part thereof, may also be applied by the trustees, or, if in court, under the direction of the court, in rebuilding, reinstating, replacing, or repairing the property lost or damaged, but any such application by the trustees shall be subject to the consent of any person whose consent is required by the instrument, if any, creating the trust to the investment of money subject to the trust, and, in the case of money which is deemed to be capital money arising under the Settled Land Act, 1925, be subject to the provisions of that Act with respect to the application of capital money by the trustees of the settlement.

(5) Nothing contained in this section prejudices or affects the right of any person to require any such money or any part thereof to be applied in rebuilding, reinstating, or repairing the property lost or damaged, or the rights of any mortgagee, lessor, or lessee, whether under any statute or otherwise.

(6) This section applies to policies effected either before or after the commencement of this Act, but only to money received after such commencement.

21. Deposit of documents for safe custody

Trustees may deposit any documents held by them relating to the trust, or to the trust property, with any banker or banking company or any other company whose business includes the undertaking of the safe custody of documents, and any sum payable in respect of such deposit shall be paid out of the income of the trust property.

22. Reversionary interests, valuations and audit

(1) Where trust property includes any share or interest in property not vested in the trustees, or the proceeds of the sale of any such property, or any other thing in action, the trustees on the same falling into possession, or becoming payable or transferable may—

(a) agree or ascertain the amount or value thereof or any part thereof in such manner as they may think fit;

(b) accept in or towards satisfaction thereof, at the market or current value, or upon any valuation or estimate of value which they may think fit, any authorised investments;

(c) allow any deductions for duties, costs, charges and expenses which they may think proper or reasonable;

(d) execute any release in respect of the premises so as effectually to discharge all accountable parties from all liability in respect of any matters coming within the scope of such release;

without being responsible in any such case for any loss occasioned by any act or thing so done by them in good faith.

(2) The trustees shall not be under any obligation and shall not be chargeable with any breach of trust by reason of any omission—

(a) to place any distringas notice or apply for any stop or other like order upon any securities or other property out of or on which such share or interest or other thing in action as aforesaid is derived, payable or charged; or

(b) to take any proceedings on account of any act, default, or neglect on the part of the persons in whom such securities or other property or any of them or any part thereof are for the time being, or had at any time been, vested; unless and until required in writing so to do by some person, or the guardian of some person, beneficially interested under the trust, and unless also due provision is made to their satisfaction for payment of the costs of any proceedings required to be taken:

Provided that nothing in this subsection shall relieve the trustees of the obligation to get in and obtain payment or transfer of such share or interest or other thing in action on the same falling into possession.

(3) Trustees may, for the purpose of giving effect to the trust, or any of the provisions of the instrument, if any, creating the trust or of any statute, from time to time (by duly qualified agents) ascertain and fix the value of any trust property in such manner as they think proper, and any valuation so made in good faith shall be binding upon all persons interested under the trust.

(4) Trustees may, in their absolute discretion, from time to time, but not more than once in every three years unless the nature of the trust or any special dealings with the trust property make a more frequent exercise of the right reasonable, cause the accounts of the trust property to be examined or audited by an independent accountant, and shall, for that purpose, produce such vouchers and give such information to him as he may require; and the costs of such examination or audit, including the fee of the auditor, shall be paid out of the capital or income of the trust property, or partly in one way and partly in the other, as the trustees, in their absolute discretion, think fit, but, in default of any direction by the trustees to the contrary in any special case, costs attributable to capital shall be borne by capital and those attributable to income by income.

23. Power to employ agents

(1) Trustees or personal representatives may, instead of acting personally, employ and pay an agent, whether a solicitor, banker, stockbroker, or other person, to transact any business or do any act required to be transacted or done in the execution of the trust, or the administration of the testator's or intestate's estate, including the receipt and payment of money, and shall be entitled to be allowed and paid all charges and expenses so incurred, and shall not be responsible for the default of any such agent if employed in good faith.

(2) Trustees or personal representatives may appoint any person to act as their agent or attorney for the purpose of selling, converting, collecting, getting in, and executing and perfecting insurances of, or managing or cultivating, or otherwise administering any property, real or personal, moveable or immoveable, subject to the trust or forming part of the testator's or intestate's estate, in any place outside the United Kingdom or executing or exercising any discretion or trust or power vested in them in relation to any such property, with such ancillary powers, and with and subject to such provisions and restrictions as they may think fit, including a power to appoint substitutes, and shall not, by reason only of their having made such appointment, be responsible for any loss arising thereby.

(3) Without prejudice to such general power of appointing agents as aforesaid—

(a) A trustee may appoint a solicitor to be his agent to receive and give a discharge for any money or valuable consideration or property receivable by the trustee under the trust, by permitting the solicitor to have the custody of, and to produce, a deed having in the body thereof or endorsed thereon a receipt for such money or valuable consideration or property, the deed being executed, or the endorsed receipt being signed, by the person entitled to give a receipt for that consideration;

(b) A trustee shall not be chargeable with breach of trust by reason only of his having made or concurred in making any such appointment; and the production of any such deed by the solicitor shall have the same statutory validity and effect as if the person appointing the solicitor had not been a trustee;

(c) A trustee may appoint a banker or solicitor to be his agent to receive and give a discharge for any money payable to the trustee under or by virtue of a policy of insurance, by permitting the banker or solicitor to have the custody of and to produce the policy of insurance with a receipt signed by the trustee, and a trustee shall not be chargeable with a breach of trust by reason only of his having made or concurred in making any such appointment:

Provided that nothing in this subsection shall exempt a trustee from any liability which he would have incurred if this Act and any enactment replaced by this Act had not been passed, in case he permits any such money, valuable consideration, or property to remain in the hands or under the control of the banker or solicitor for a period longer than is reasonably necessary to enable the banker or solicitor, as the case may be, to pay or transfer the same to the trustee.

This subsection applies whether the money or valuable consideration or property was or is received before or after the commencement of this Act.

24. Power to concur with others

Where an undivided share in [any] property, is subject to a trust, or forms part of the estate of a testator or intestate, the trustees or personal representatives may (without prejudice to the [trust] affecting the entirety of the land and the powers of the [trustees] in reference thereto) execute or exercise any [duty or] power vested in them in relation to such share in conjunction with the persons entitled to or having power in that behalf over the other share or shares, and notwithstanding that any one or more of the trustees or personal representatives may be entitled to or interested in any such other share, either in his or their own right or in a fiduciary capacity.

25. Power to delegate trusts during absence abroad

[(1) Notwithstanding any rule of law or equity to the contrary, a trustee may, by power of attorney, delegate for a period not exceeding twelve months the execution or exercise of all or any of the trusts, powers and discretions vested in him as trustee either alone or jointly with any other person or persons.

(2) The persons who may be donees of a power of attorney under this section include a trust corporation but not (unless a trust corporation) the only other co-trustee of the donor of the power.

(3) An instrument creating a power of attorney under this section shall be attested by at least one witness.

(4) Before or within seven days after giving a power of attorney under this section the donor shall give written notice thereof (specifying the date on which the power comes into operation and its duration, the donee of the power, the reason why the power is given and, where some only are delegated, the trusts, powers and discretions delegated) to—

(a) each person (other than himself), if any, who under any instrument creating the trust has power (whether alone or jointly) to appoint a new trustee; and

(b) each of the other trustees, if any; but failure to comply with this subsection shall not, in favour of a person dealing with the donee of the power, invalidate any act done or instrument executed by the donee.

(5) The donor of a power of attorney given under this section shall be liable for the acts or defaults of the donee in the same manner as if they were the acts or defaults of the donor.]

[(6) For the purpose of executing or exercising the trusts or powers delegated to him, the donee may exercise any of the powers conferred on the donor as trustee by statute or by the instrument creating the trust, including power, for the purpose of the transfer of any inscribed stock, himself to delegate to an attorney power to transfer but not including the power of delegation conferred by this section.]

[(7) The fact that it appears from any power of attorney given under this section, or from any evidence required for the purposes of any such power of attorney or otherwise, that in dealing with any stock the donee of the power is acting in the execution of a trust shall not be deemed for any purpose to affect any person in whose books the stock is inscribed or registered with any notice of the trust.]

[(8) This section applies to a personal representative, tenant for life and statutory owner as it applies to a trustee except that subsection (4) shall apply as if it required the notice there mentioned to be given—

(a) in the case of a personal representative, to each of the other personal representatives, if any, except any executor who has renounced probate;

(b) in the case of a tenant for life, to the trustees of the settlement and to each person, if any, who together with the person giving the notice constitutes the tenant for life;

(c) in the case of a statutory owner, to each of the persons if any, who together with the person giving the notice constitute the statutory owner and, in the case of a statutory owner by virtue of section 23(1)(a) of the Settled Land Act 1925, to the trustees of the settlement.]

Indemnities

26. Protection against liability in respect of rents and convenants

(1) Where a personal representative or trustee liable as such for—

(a) any rent, covenant, or agreement reserved by or contained in any lease; or

(b) any rent, covenant or agreement payable under or contained in any grant made in consideration of a rentcharge; or

(c) any indemnity given in respect of any rent, covenant or agreement referred to in either of the foregoing paragraphs;

satisfies all liabilities under the lease or grant [which may have accrued and been claimed] up to the date of the conveyance hereinafter mentioned, and, where necessary, sets apart a sufficient fund to answer any future claim that may be made in respect of any fixed and ascertained sum which the lessee or grantee agreed to lay out on the property demised or granted, although the period for laying out the same may not have arrived, then and in any such case the personal representative or trustee may convey the property demised or granted to a purchaser, legatee, devisee, or other person entitled to call for a conveyance thereof and thereafter—

(i) he may distribute the residuary real and personal estate of the deceased testator or intestate, or, as the case may be, the trust estate (other than the fund, if any, set apart as aforesaid) to or amongst the persons entitled thereto, without appropriating any part, or any further part, as the case may be, of the estate of the deceased or of the trust estate to meet any future liability under the said lease or grant;

(ii) notwithstanding such distribution, he shall not be personally liable in respect of any subsequent claim under the said lease or grant.

[(1A) Where a personal representative or trustee has as such entered into, or may as such be required to enter into, an authorised guarantee agreement with respect to any lease comprised in the estate of a deceased testator or intestate or a trust estate (and, in a case where he has entered into such an agreement, he has satisfied all liabilities under it which may have accrued and been claimed up to the date of distribution)—

(a) he may distribute the residuary real and personal estate of the deceased testator or intestate, or the trust estate, to or amongst the persons entitled thereto—

(i) without appropriating any part of the estate of the deceased, or the trust estate, to meet any future liability (or, as the case may be, any liability) under any such agreement, and

(ii) notwithstanding any potential liability of his to enter into any such agreement; and

(b) notwithstanding such distribution, he shall not be personally liable in respect of any subsequent claim (or, as the case may be, any claim) under any such agreement.

In this subsection 'authorised guarantee agreement' has the same meaning as in the Landlord and Tenant (Covenants) Act 1995.]

(2) This section operates without prejudice to the right of the lessor or grantor, or the persons deriving title under the lessor or grantor, to follow the assets of the deceased or the trust property into the hands of the persons amongst whom the same may have been respectively distributed, and applies notwithstanding anything to the contrary in the will or other instrument, if any, creating the trust.

(3) In this section 'lease' includes an underlease and an agreement for a lease or underlease and any instrument giving any such indemnity as aforesaid or varying the liabilities under the lease; 'grant' applies to a grant whether the rent is created by limititation, grant, reservation or otherwise, and includes an agreement for a grant and any instrument giving any such indemnity as aforesaid or varying the liabilities under the grant; 'lessee' and 'grantee' include persons respectively deriving title under them.

Note: Section 26(1A) was inserted by The Landlord and Tenants (Covenants) Act 1995.

27. Protection by means of advertisements

(1) With a view to the conveyance to or distribution among the persons entitled to any real or personal property, the trustees of a settlement [trustees of land, trustees for sale of personal property] or personal representatives, may give notice by advertisement in the Gazette, and [in a newspaper circulating in the district in which the land is situated] and such other like notices, including notices elsewhere than in England and Wales, as would, in any special case, have been directed by a court of competent jurisdiction in an action for administration, of their intention to make such conveyance or distribution as aforesaid, and requiring any person interested to send to the trustees or personal representatives within the time, not being less than two months, fixed in the notice or, where more than one notice is given, in the last of the notices, particulars of his claim in respect of the property or any part thereof to which the notice relates.

(2) At the expiration of the time fixed by the notice the trustees or personal representatives may convey or distribute the property or any part thereof to which the notice relates, to or among the persons entitled thereto, having regard only to the claims, whether formal or not, of which the trustees or personal representatives then had notice and shall not, as respects the property so conveyed or distributed, be liable to any person of whose claim the trustees or personal representatives have not had notice at the time of conveyance or distribution; but nothing in this section—

(a) prejudices the right of any person to follow the property, or any property representing the same, into the hands of any person, other than a purchaser, who may have received it; or

(b) frees the trustees or personal representatives from any obligation to make searches or obtain official certificates of search similar to those which an intending purchaser would be advised to make or obtain.

(3) This section applies notwithstanding anything to the contrary in the will or other instrument, if any, creating the trust.

28. Protection in regard to notice

A trustee or personal representative acting for the purposes of more than one trust or estate shall not, in the absence of fraud, be affected by notice of any instrument, matter, fact or thing in relation to any particular trust or estate if he has obtained notice thereof merely by reason of his acting or having acted for the purposes of another trust or estate.

30. Implied indemnity of trustees

(1) A trustee shall be chargeable only for money and securities actually received by him notwithstanding his signing any receipt for the sake of conformity, and shall be answerable and accountable only for his own acts, receipts, neglects, or defaults, and not for those of any other trustee, nor for any banker, broker, or other person with whom any trust money or securities may be deposited, nor for the insufficiency or

deficiency of any securities, nor for any other loss, unless the same happens through his own wilful default.

(2) A trustee may reimburse himself or pay or discharge out of the trust premises all expenses incurred in or about the execution of the trusts or powers.

Maintenance, Advancement and Protective Trusts

31. Power to apply income for maintenance and to accumulate surplus income during a minority

(1) Where any property is held by trustees in trust for any person for any interest whatsoever, whether vested or contingent, then, subject to any prior interests or charges affecting that property—

(i) during the infancy of any such person, if his interest so long continues, the trustees may, at their sole discretion, pay to his parent or guardian, if any, or otherwise apply for or towards his maintenance, education, or benefit, the whole or such part, if any, of the income of that property as may, in all the circumstances, be reasonable, whether or not there is—

(a) any other fund applicable to the same purpose: or

(b) any person bound by law to provide for his maintenance or education; and

(ii) if such person on attaining the age of [eighteen years] has not a vested interest in such income, the trustees shall thenceforth pay the income of that property and of any accretion thereto under subsection (2) of this section to him, until he either attains a vested interest therein or dies, or until failure of his interest:

Provided that, in deciding whether the whole or any part of the income of the property is during a minority to be paid or applied for the purposes aforesaid, the trustees shall have regard to the age of the infant and his requirements and generally to the circumstances of the case, and in particular to what other income, if any, is applicable for the same purposes; and where trustees have notice that the income of more than one fund is applicable for those purposes, then, so far as practicable, unless the entire income of the funds is paid or applied as aforesaid or the court otherwise directs, a proportionate part only of the income of each fund shall be so paid or applied.

(2) During the infancy of any such person, if his interest so long continues, the trustees shall accumulate all the residue of that income in the way of compound interest by investing the same and the resulting income thereof from time to time in authorised investments, and shall hold those accumulations as follows:—

(i) If any such person—

(a) attains the age of [eighteen years], or marries under that age, and his interest in such income during his infancy or until his marriage is a vested interest or;

(b) on attaining the age of [eighteen years] or on marriage under that age becomes entitled to the property from which such income arose in fee simple, absolute or determinable, or absolutely, or for an entailed interest;

the trustees shall hold the accumulations in trust for such person absolutely, but without prejudice to any provision with respect thereto contained in any settlement by him made under any statutory powers during his infancy, and so that the receipt of such person after marriage, and though still an infant shall be a good discharge, and

(ii) In any other case the trustees shall, notwithstanding that such person had a vested interest in such income, hold the accumulations as an accretion to the capital of the property from which such accumulations arose, and as one fund with such capital for all purposes, and so that, if such property is settled land, such accumulations shall be held upon the same trusts as if the same were capital money arising therefrom; but the trustees may, at any time during the infancy of such person if his interest so long continues, apply those accumulations, or any part thereof, as if they were income arising in the then current year.

(3) This section applies in the case of a contingent interest only if the limitation or trust carries the intermediate income of the property, but it applies to a future or contingent legacy by the parent of, or a person standing in loco parentis to, the legatee, if and for such period as, under the general law, the legacy carries interest for the maintenance of the legatee, and in any such case as last aforesaid the rate of interest shall (if the income available is sufficient, and subject to any rules of court to the contrary) be five pounds per centum per annum.

(4) This section applies to a vested annuity in like manner as if the annuity were the income of property held by trustees in trust to pay the income thereof to the annuitant for the same period for which the annuity is payable, save that in any case accumulations made during the infancy of the annuitant shall be held in trust for the annuitant or his personal representatives absolutely.

(5) This section does not apply where the instrument, if any, under which the interest arises came into operation before the commencement of this Act.

32. Power of advancement

(1) Trustees may at any time or times pay or apply any capital money subject to a trust, for the advancement or benefit, in such manner as they may, in their absolute discretion, think fit, of any person entitled to the capital of the trust property or of any share thereof, whether absolutely or contingently on his attaining any specified age or on the occurrence of any other event, or subject to a gift over on his death under any specified age or on the occurrence of any other event, and whether in possession or in remainder or reversion, and such payment or application may be made notwithstanding that the interest of such person is liable to be defeated by the exercise of a power of appointment or revocation, or to be diminished by the increase of the class to which he belongs:

Provided that—

(a) the money so paid or applied for the advancement or benefit of any person shall not exceed altogether in amount one-half of the presumptive or vested share or interest of that person in the trust property; and

(b) if that person is or becomes absolutely and indefeasibly entitled to a share in the trust property the money so paid or applied shall be brought into account as part of such share; and

(c) no such payment or application shall be made so as to prejudice any person entitled to any prior life or other interest, whether vested or contingent, in the money paid or applied unless such person is in existence and of full age and consents in writing to such payment or application.

[(2) This section does not apply to capital money arising under the Settled Land Act 1925.]

(3) This section does not apply to trusts constituted or created before the commencement of this Act.

33. Protective trusts

(1) Where any income, including an annuity or other periodical income payment, is directed to be held on protective trusts for the benefit of any person (in this section called 'the principal beneficiary') for the period of his life or for any less period, then, during that period (in this section called the 'trust period') the said income shall, without prejudice to any prior interest, be held on the following trusts, namely:—

(i) Upon trust for the principal beneficiary during the trust period or until he, whether before or after the termination of any prior interest, does or attempts to do or suffers any act or thing, or until any event happens, other than an advance under any statutory or express power, whereby, if the said income were payable during the trust period to the principal beneficiary absolutely during that period, he would be deprived of the right to receive the same or any part thereof, in any of which cases, as well as on the termination of the trust period, whichever first happens, this trust of the said income shall fail or determine;

(ii) If the trust aforesaid fails or determines during the subsistence of the trust period, then, during the residue of that period, the said income shall be held upon trust for the application thereof for the maintenance or support, or otherwise for the benefit, of all or any one or more exclusively of the other or others of the following persons (that is to say)—

(a) the principal beneficiary and his or her wife or husband, if any, and his or her children or more remote issue, if any; or

(b) if there is no wife or husband or issue of the principal beneficiary in existence, the principal beneficiary and the persons who would, if he were actually dead, be entitled to the trust property or the income thereof or to the annuity fund, if any, or arrears of the annuity, as the case may be;

as the trustees in their absolute discretion, without being liable to account for the exercise of such discretion, think fit.

(2) This section does not apply to trusts coming into operation before the commencement of this Act, and has effect subject to any variation of the implied trusts aforesaid contained in the instrument creating the trust.

(3) Nothing in this section operates to validate any trust which would, if contained in the instrument creating the trust, be liable to be set aside.

[(4) In relation to the dispositions mentioned in section 19(1) of the Family Law Reform Act 1987, this section shall have effect as if any reference (however expressed) to any relationship between two persons were construed in accordance with section 1 of that Act.]

PART III
APPOINTMENT AND DISCHARGE OF TRUSTEES

34. Limitation of the number of trustees

(1) Where, at the commencement of this Act, there are more than four trustees of a settlement of land, or more than four trustees holding land on trust for sale, no new trustees shall (except where as a result of the appointment the number is reduced to four or less) be capable of being appointed until the number is reduced to less than four, and thereafter the number shall not be increased beyond four.

(2) In the case of settlements and dispositions [creating trusts of land] made or coming into operation after the commencement of this Act—

(a) the number of trustees thereof shall not in any case exceed four, and where more than four persons are named as such trustees, the four first named (who are able and willing to act) shall alone be the trustees, and the other persons named shall not be trustees unless appointed on the occurrence of a vacancy;

(b) the number of the trustees shall not be increased beyond four.

(3) This section only applies to settlements and dispositions of land, and the restrictions imposed on the number of trustees do not apply—

(a) in the case of land vested in trustees for charitable, ecclesiastical, or public purposes; or

(b) where the net proceeds of the sale of the land are held for like purposes; or

(c) to the trustees of a term of years absolute limited by a settlement on trusts for raising money, or of a like term created under the statutory remedies relating to annual sums charged on land.

35. Appointments of trustees of settlements and [trustees of land]

[(1) Appointments of new trustees of land and of new trustees of any trust of the proceeds of sale of the land shall, subject to any order of the court, be effected by separate instruments, but in such manner as to secure that the same persons become trustees of land and trustees of the trust of the proceeds of sale.]

(2) Where new trustees of a settlement are appointed, a memorandum of the names and addresses of the persons who are for the time being the trustees thereof for the purposes of the Settled Land Act, 1925, shall be endorsed on or annexed to the last or only principal vesting instrument by or on behalf of the trustees of the settlement, and such vesting instrument shall, for that purpose, be produced by the person having the possession thereof to the trustees of the settlement when so required.

[(3) Where new trustees of land are appointed, a memorandum of the persons who are for the time being the trustees of the land shall be endorsed on or annexed to the conveyance by which the land was vested in trustees of land; and that conveyance shall be produced to the persons who are for the time being the trustees of the land by the person in possession of it in order for that to be done when the trustees require its production.]

(4) This section applies only to settlements and dispositions of land.

36. Power of appointing new or additional trustees

(1) Where a trustee, either original or substituted, and whether appointed by a court or otherwise, is dead, or remains out of the United Kingdom for more than twelve months, or desires to be discharged from all or any of the trusts or powers reposed in or conferred on him, or refuses or is unfit to act therein, or in incapable of acting therein, or is an infant, then, subject to the restrictions imposed by this Act on the number of trustees,—

(a) the person or persons nominated for the purpose of appointing new trustees by the instrument, if any, creating the trust; or

(b) if there is no such person, or no such person able and willing to act, then the surviving or continuing trustees or trustee for the time being, or the personal representatives of the last surviving or continuing trustee;

may, by writing, appoint one or more other persons (whether or not being the persons exercising the power) to be a trustee or trustees in the place of the trustee so deceased remaining out of the United Kingdom, desiring to be discharged, refusing, or being unfit or being incapable, or being an infant, as aforesaid.

(2) Where a trustee has been removed under a power contained in the instrument creating the trust, a new trustee or new trustees may be appointed in the place of the trustee who is removed, as if he were dead, or, in the case of a corporation, as if the corporation desired to be discharged from the trust, and the provisions of this section shall apply accordingly, but subject to the restrictions imposed by this Act on the number of trustees.

(3) Where a corporation being a trustee is or has been dissolved, either before or after the commencement of this Act, then, for the purposes of this section and of any enactment replaced thereby, the corporation shall be deemed to be and to have been from the date of the dissolution incapable of acting in the trusts or powers reposed in or conferred on the corporation.

(4) The power of appointment given by subsection (1) of this section or any similar previous enactment to the personal representatives of last surviving or continuing trustee shall be and shall be deemed always to have been exercisable by the executors for the time being (whether original or by representation) of such surviving or continuing trustee who have proved the will of their testator or by the administrators for the time being of such trustee without the concurrence of any executor who has renounced or has not proved.

(5) But a sole or last surviving executor intending to renounce, or all the executors where they all intend to renounce, shall have and shall be deemed always to have had power, at any time before renouncing probate, to exercise the power of appointment given by this section, or by any similar previous enactment, if willing to act for that purpose and without thereby accepting the office of executor.

[(6) Where, in the case of any trust, there are not more than three trustees—]

(a) the person or persons nominated for the purpose of appointing new trustees by the instrument, if any, creating the trust; or

(b) if there is no such person, or no such person able and willing to act, then the trustee or trustees for the time being;

may, by writing, appoint another person or other persons to be an additional trustee or additional trustees, but it shall not be obligatory to appoint any additional trustee, unless the instrument, if any, creating the trust, or any statutory enactment provides to the contrary, nor shall the number of trustees be increased beyond four by virtue of any such appointment.

(7) Every new trustee appointed under this section as well before as after all the trust property becomes by law, or by assurance, or otherwise, vested in him, shall have the same powers, authorities, and discretions, and may in all respects act as if he had been originally appointed a trustee by the instrument, if any, creating the trust.

(8) The provisions of this section relating to a trustee who is dead include the case of a person nominated trustee in a will but dying before the testator, and those relative to a continuing trustee include a refusing or retiring trustee, if willing to act in the execution of the provisions of this section.

[(9) Where a trustee is incapable, by reason of mental disorder within the meaning of [the Mental Health Act 1983] of exercising his functions as trustee and is also entitled in possession to some beneficial interest in the trust property, no appointment of a new trustee in his place shall be made by virtue of paragraph (b) of subsection (1) of this section unless leave to make the appointment has been given by the authority having jurisdiction under [Part VII of the Mental Health Act 1983].]

37. Supplemental provisions as to appointment of trustees

(1) On the appointment of a trustee for the whole or any part of trust property—

(a) the number of trustees may, subject to the restrictions imposed by this Act on the number of trustees, be increased; and

(b) a separate set of trustees, not exceeding four, may be appointed for any part of the trust property held on trusts distinct from those relating to any other part or parts of the trust property, notwithstanding that no new trustees or trustee are or is to be appointed for other parts of the trust property, and any existing trustee may be appointed or remain one of such separate set of trustees, or, if only one trustee was originally appointed, then, save as hereinafter provided, one separate trustee may be so appointed; and

(c) it shall not be obligatory, save as hereinafter provided, to appoint more than one new trustee where only one trustee was originally appointed, or to fill up the original number of trustees where more than two trustees were originally appointed, but, except where only one trustee was originally appointed, and a sole trustee when appointed will be able to give valid receipts for all capital money, a trustee shall not be discharged from his trust unless there will be either a trust corporation or at least two [persons] to act as trustees to perform the trust; and

(d) any assurance or thing requisite for vesting the trust property, or any part thereof, in a sole trustee, or jointly in the persons who are the trustees, shall be executed or done.

(2) Nothing in this Act shall authorise the appointment of a sole trustee, not being a trust corporation, where the trustee, when appointed, would not be able to give valid receipts for all capital money arising under the trust.

38. Evidence as to a vacancy in a trust

(1) A statement, contained in any instrument coming into operation after the commencement of this Act by which a new trustee is appointed for any purpose connected with land, to the effect that a trustee has remained out of the United

Kingdom for more than twelve months or refuses or is unfit to act, or is incapable of acting, or that he is not entitled to a beneficial interest in the trust property in possession, shall, in favour of a purchaser of a legal estate, be conclusive evidence of the matter stated.

(2) In favour of such purchaser any appointment of a new trustee depending on that statement, and any vesting declaration, express or implied, consequent on the appointment, shall be valid.

39. Retirement of trustee without a new appointment

(1) Where a trustee is desirous of being discharged from the trust, and after this discharge there will be either a trust corporation or at least two [persons] to act as trustees to perform the trust, then, if such trustee as aforesaid by deed declares that he is desirous of being discharged from the trust, and if his co-trustees and such other person, if any, as is empowered to appoint trustees, by deed consent to the discharge of the trustee, and to the vesting in the co-trustees alone of the trust property, the trustee desirous of being discharged shall be deemed to have retired from the trust, and shall, by the deed, be discharged therefrom under this Act, without any new trustee being appointed in his place.

(2) Any assurance or thing requisite for vesting the trust property in the continuing trustees alone shall be executed or done.

40. Vesting of trust property in new or continuing trustees

(1) Where by a deed a new trustee is appointed to perform any trust, then—

(a) if the deed contains a declaration by the appointor to the effect that any estate or interest in any land subject to the trust, or in any chattel so subject, or the right to recover or receive any debt or other thing in action so subject, shall vest in the persons who by virtue of the deed become or are the trustees for performing the trust, the deed shall operate, without any conveyance or assignment, to vest in those persons as joint tenants and for the purposes of the trust the estate interest or right to which the declaration relates; and

(b) if the deed is made after the commencement of this Act and does not contain such a declaration, the deed shall, subject to any express provision to the contrary therein contained, operate as if it had contained such a declaration by the appointor extending to all the estates interests and rights with respect to which a declaration could have been made.

(2) Where by a deed a retiring trustee is discharged under [section 39 of this Act or section 19 of the Trusts of Land and Appointment of Trustees Act 1996] without a new trustee being appointed, then—

(a) if the deed contains such a declaration as aforesaid by the retiring and continuing trustees, and by the other person, if any, empowered to appoint trustees, the deed shall, without any conveyance or assignment, operate to vest in the continuing trustees alone, as joint tenants, and for the purposes of the trust, the estate, interest, or right to which the declaration relates; and

(b) if the deed is made after the commencement of this Act and does not contain such a declaration, the deed shall, subject to any express provision to the contrary therein contained, operate as if it had contained such a declaration by such persons as aforesaid extending to all the estates, interests and rights with respect to which a declaration could have been made.

(3) An express vesting declaration, whether made before or after the commencement of this Act, shall, notwithstanding that the estate, interest or right to be vested is not expressly referred to, and provided that the other statutory requirements were or are complied with, operate and be deemed always to have operated (but without prejudice to any express provision to the contrary contained in the deed of appointment or discharge) to vest in the persons respectively referred to in subsections (1) and (2)

of this section, as the case may require, such estates, interests and rights as are capable of being and ought to be vested in those persons.

(4) This section does not extend—

(a) to land conveyed by way of mortgage for securing money subject to the trust, except land conveyed on trust for securing debentures or debenture stock;

(b) to land held under a lease which contains any covenant, condition or agreement against assignment or disposing of the land without licence or consent, unless, prior to the execution of the deed containing expressly or impliedly the vesting declaration, the requisite licence or consent has been obtained, or unless, by virtue of any statute or rule of law, the vesting declaration, express or implied, would not operate as a breach of covenant or give rise to a forfeiture;

(c) to any share, stock, annuity or property which is only transferable in books kept by a company or other body, or in manner directed by or under an Act of Parliament.

In this subsection 'lease' includes an underlease and an agreement for a lease or underlease.

(5) For purposes of registration of the deed in any registry, the person or persons making the declaration expressly or impliedly, shall be deemed the conveying party or parties, and the conveyance shall be deemed to be made by him or them under a power conferred by this Act.

(6) This section applies to deeds of appointment or discharge executed on or after the first day of January, eighteen hundred and eighty-two.

PART IV
POWERS OF THE COURT
Appointment of new Trustees

41. Power of court to appoint new trustees

(1) The court may, whenever it is expedient to appoint a new trustee or new trustees, and it is found inexpedient difficult or impracticable so to do without the assistance of the court, make an order appointing a new trustee or new trustees either in substitution for or in addition to any existing trustees, or although there is no existing trustee.

In particular and without prejudice to the generality of the foregoing provision, the court may make an order appointing a new trustee in substitution for a trustee who [. . .] is [incapable, by reason of mental disorder within the meaning of [the Mental Health Act 1983] of exercising his functions as trustee], or is a bankrupt, or is a corporation which is in liquidation or has been dissolved.

(2) The power conferred by this section may, in the case of a deed of arrangement within the meaning of the Deeds of Arrangement Act, 1914, be exercised either by the High Court or by the court having jurisdiction in the bankruptcy in the district in which the debtor resided or carried on business at the date of the execution of the deed.

(3) An order under this section, and any consequential vesting order or conveyance, shall not operate further or otherwise as a discharge to any former or continuing trustee than an appointment of new trustees under any power for that purpose contained in any instrument would have operated.

(4) Nothing in this section gives power to appoint an executor or administrator.

42. Power to authorise remuneration

Where the court appoints a corporation, other than the Public Trustee, to be a trustee either solely or jointly with another person, the court may authorise the corporation to charge such remuneration for its services as trustee as the court may think fit.

43. Powers of new trustee appointed by the court

Every trustee appointed by a court of competent jurisdiction shall, as well before as after the trust property becomes by law, or by assurance, or otherwise, vested in him, have the same powers, authorities, and discretions, and may in all respects act as if he had been originally appointed a trustee by the instrument, if any, creating the trust.

Vesting Orders

44. Vesting orders of land

In any of the following cases, namely:—

(i) Where the court appoints or has appointed a trustee, or where a trustee has been appointed out of court under any statutory or express power;

(ii) Where a trustee entitled to or possessed of any land or interest therein, whether by way of mortgage or otherwise, or entitled to a contingent right therein, either solely or jointly with any other person—

(a) is under disability; or

(b) is out of the jurisdiction of the High Court; or

(c) cannot be found, or, being a corporation, has been dissolved.

(iii) Where it is uncertain who was the survivor of two or more trustees jointly entitled to or possessed of any interest in land;

(iv) Where it is uncertain whether the last trustee known to have been entitled to or possessed of any interest in land is living or dead;

(v) Where there is no personal representative of a deceased trustee who was entitled to or possessed of any interest in land, or where it is uncertain who is the personal representative of a deceased trustee who was entitled to or possessed of any interest in land;

(vi) Where a trustee jointly or solely entitled to or possessed of any interest in land, or entitled to a contingent right therein, has been required, by or on behalf of a person entitled to require a conveyance of the land or interest or a release of the right, to convey the land or interest or to release the right, and has wilfully refused or neglected to convey the land or interest or release the right for twenty-eight days after the date of the requirement;

(vii) Where land or any interest therein is vested in a trustee whether by way of mortgage or otherwise, and it appears to the court to be expedient; the court may make an order (in this Act called a vesting order) vesting the land or interest therein in any such person in any such manner and for any such estate or interest as the court may direct, or releasing or disposing of the contingent right to such person as the court may direct:

Provided that—

(a) Where the order is consequential on the appointment of a trustee the land or interest therein shall be vested for such estate as the court may direct in the persons who on the appointment are the trustees; and

(b) Where the order relates to a trustee entitled or formerly entitled jointly with another person, and such trustee is under disability or out of the jurisdiction of the High Court or cannot be found, or being a corporation has been dissolved, the land interest or right shall be vested in such other person who remains entitled, either alone or with any other person the court may appoint.

45. Orders as to contingent rights of unborn persons

Where any interest in land is subject to a contingent right in an unborn person or class of unborn persons who, on coming into existence would, in respect thereof, become entitled to or possessed of that interest on any trust, the court may make an order releasing the land or interest therein from the contingent right, or may make an order vesting in any person the estate or interest to or of which the unborn person or class of unborn persons would, on coming into existence, be entitled or possessed in the land.

46. Vesting order in place of conveyance by infant mortgagee

Where any person entitled to or possessed of any interest in land, or entitled to a contingent right in land, by way of security for money, is an infant, the court may make an order vesting or releasing or disposing of the interest in the land or the right in like manner as in the case of a trustee under disability.

47. Vesting order consequential on order for sale or mortgage of land
Where any court gives a judgment or makes an order directing the sale or mortgage of any land, every person who is entitled to or possessed of any interest in the land, or entitled to a contingent right therein, and is a party to the action or proceeding in which the judgment or order is given or made or is otherwise bound by the judgment or order, shall be deemed to be so entitled or possessed, as the case may be, as a trustee for the purpose of this Act, and the court may, if it thinks expedient, make an order vesting the land or any part thereof for such estate or interest as that court thinks fit in the purchaser or mortgagee or in any other person:

Provided that, in the case of a legal mortgage, the estate to be vested in the mortgagee shall be a term of years absolute.

48. Vesting order consequential on judgment for specific performance, etc.
Where a judgment is given for the specific performance of a contract concerning any interest in land, or for sale or exchange of any interest in land, or generally where any judgment is given for the conveyance of any interest in land either in cases arising out of the doctrine of election or otherwise, the court may declare—

(a) that any of the parties to the action are trustees of any interest in the land or any part thereof within the meaning of this Act; or

(b) that the interests of unborn persons who might claim under any party to the action, or under the will or voluntary settlement of any deceased person who was during his lifetime a party to the contract or transaction concerning which the judgment is given, are the interests of persons who, on coming into existence, would be trustees within the meaning of this Act;

and thereupon the court may make a vesting order relating to the rights of those persons, born and unborn, as if they had been trustees.

49. Effect of vesting order
A vesting order under any of the foregoing provisions shall in the case of a vesting order consequential on the appointment of a trustee, have the same effect—

(a) as if the persons who before the appointment were the trustees, if any, had duly executed all proper conveyances of the land for such estate or interest as the court directs; or

(b) if there is no such person, or no such person of full capacity, as if such person had existed and been of full capacity and had duly executed all proper conveyances of the land for such estate or interest as the court directs: and shall in every other case have the same effect as if the trustee or other person or description or class of persons to whose rights or supposed rights the said provisions respectively relate had been an ascertained and existing person of full capacity, and had executed a conveyance or release to the effect intended by the order.

50. Power to appoint person to convey
In all cases where a vesting order can be made under any of the foregoing provisions, the court may, if it is more convenient, appoint a person to convey the land or any interest therein or release the contingent right, and a conveyance or release by that person in conformity with the order shall have the same effect as an order under the appropriate provision.

51. Vesting orders as to stock and things in action
(1) In any of the following cases, namely:—

(i) Where the court appoints or has appointed a trustee, or where a trustee has been appointed out of court under any statutory or express power;

(ii) Where a trustee entitled, whether by way of mortgage or otherwise, alone or jointly with another person to stock or to a thing in action—

(a) is under disability; or

(b) is out of the jurisdiction of the High Court; or

(c) cannot be found, or, being a corporation, has been dissolved; or

(d) neglects or refuses to transfer stock or receive the dividends or income thereof, or to sue for or recover a thing in action, according to the direction of the person absolutely entitled thereto for twenty-eight days next after a request in writing has been made to him by the person so entitled; or

(e) neglects or refuses to transfer stock or receive the dividends or income thereof, or to sue for or recover a thing in action for twenty-eight days next after an order of the court for that purpose has been served on him;

(iii) Where it is uncertain whether a trustee entitled alone or jointly with another person to stock or to a thing in action is alive or dead;

(iv) Where stock is standing in the name of a deceased person whose personal representative is under disability;

(v) Where stock or a thing in action is vested in a trustee whether by way of mortgage or otherwise and it appears to the court to be expedient; the court may make an order vesting the right to transfer or call for a transfer of stock, or to receive the dividends or income thereof, or to sue for or recover the thing in action, in any such person as the court may appoint:

Provided that—

(a) Where the order is consequential on the appointment of a trustee, the right shall be vested in the persons who, on the appointment, are the trustees; and

(b) Where the person whose right is dealt with by the order was entitled jointly with another person, the right shall be vested in that last-mentioned person either alone or jointly with any other person whom the court may appoint.

(2) In all cases where a vesting order can be made under this section, the court may, if it is more convenient, appoint some proper person to make or join in making the transfer:

Provided that the person appointed to make or join in making a transfer of stock shall be some proper officer of the bank, or the company or society whose stock is to be transferred.

(3) The person in whom the right to transfer or call for the transfer of any stock is vested by an order of the court under this Act, may transfer the stock to himself or any other person, according to the order, and the Bank of England and all other companies shall obey every order under this section according to its tenor.

(4) After notice in writing of an order under this section it shall not be lawful for the Bank of England or any other company to transfer any stock to which the order relates or to pay any dividends thereon except in accordance with the order.

(5) The court may make declarations and give directions concerning the manner in which the right to transfer any stock or thing in action vested under the provisions of this Act is to be exercised.

(6) The provisions of this Act as to vesting orders shall apply to shares in ships registered under the [Merchant Shipping Act 1995] as if they were stock.

52. Vesting orders of charity property

The powers conferred by this Act as to vesting orders may be exercised for vesting any interest in land, stock, or thing in action in any trustee of a charity or society over which the court would have jurisdiction upon action duly instituted, whether the appointment of the trustee was made by instrument under a power or by the court under its general or statutory jurisdiction.

53. Vesting orders in relation to infant's beneficial interests
Where an infant is beneficially entitled to any property the court may, with a view to the application of the capital or income thereof for the maintenance, education, or benefit of the infant, make an order—

(a) appointing a person to convey such property; or

(b) in the case of stock, or a thing in action, vesting in any person the right to transfer or call for a transfer of such stock, or to receive the dividends or income thereof, or to sue for and recover such thing in action, upon such terms as the court may think fit.

[54. Jurisdiction in regard to mental patients

(1) Subject to the provisions of this section, the authority having jurisdiction under [Part VII of the Mental Health Act 1983] shall not have power to make any order, or give any direction or authority, in relation to a patient who is a trustee if the High Court has power under this Act to make an order to the like effect.

(2) Where a patient is a trustee and a receiver appointed by the said authority is acting for him or an application for the appointment of a receiver has been made but not determined, then, except as respects a trust which is subject to an order for administration made by the High Court, the said authority shall have concurrent jurisdiction with the High Court in relation to—

(a) mortgaged property of which the patient has become a trustee merely by reason of the mortgage having been paid off;

(b) matters consequent on the making of provision by the said authority for the exercise of a power of appointing trustees or retiring from a trust;

(c) matters consequent on the making of provision by the said authority for the carrying out of any contract entered into by the patient;

(d) property to some interest in which the patient is beneficially entided but which, or some interest in which, is held by the patient under an express, implied or constructive trust.

The Lord Chancellor may make rules with respect to the exercise of the jurisdiction referred to in this subsection.

(3) In this section 'patient' means a patient as defined by [section 94 of the Mental Health Act 1983], or a person as to whom powers are [exercisable under section 98 of that Act and have been exercised under that section or under section 104 of the Mental Health Act 1959].]

55. Orders made upon certain allegations to be conclusive evidence
Where a vesting order is made as to any land under this Act or under [Part VII of the Mental Health Act 1983], as amended by any subsequent enactment, or under any Act relating to lunacy in Northern Ireland, founded on an allegation of any of the following matters namely—

(a) the personal incapacity of a trustee or mortgage; or

(b) that a trustee or mortgagee or the personal representative of or other person deriving title under a trustee or mortgagee is out of the jurisdiction of the High Court or cannot be found, or being a corporation has been dissolved; or

(c) that it is uncertain which of two or more trustees, or which of two or more persons interested in a mortgage, was the survivor, or

(d) that it is uncertain whether the last trustee or the personal representative of or other person deriving title under a trustee or mortgagee, or the last surviving person interested in a mortgage is living or dead; or

(e) that any trustee or mortgagee has died intestate without leaving a person beneficially interested under the intestacy or has died and it is not known who is his personal representative or the person interested;

the fact that the order has been so made shall be conclusive evidence of the matter so alleged in any court upon any question as to the validity of the order; but this section does not prevent the court from directing a reconveyance or surrender or the payment of costs occasioned by any such order if improperly obtained.

Jurisdiction to make other Orders

57. Power of court to authorise dealings with trust property

(1) Where in the management or administration of any property vested in trustees, any sale, lease, mortgage, surrender, release, or other disposition, or any purchase, investment, acquisition, expenditure or other transaction, is in the opinion of the court expedient, but the same cannot be effected by reason of the absence of any power for that purpose vested in the trustees by the trust instrument, if any, or by law, the court may by order confer upon the trustees, either generally or in any particular instance, the necessary power for the purpose, on such terms, and subject to such provisions and conditions, if any, as the court may think fit and may direct in what manner any money authorised to be expended, and the costs of any transaction, are to be paid or borne as between capital and income.

(2) The court may, from time to time, rescind or vary any order made under this section, or may make any new or further order.

(3) An application to the court under this section may be made by the trustees, or by any of them, or by any person beneficially interested under the trust.

(4) This section does not apply to trustees of a settlement for the purposes of the Settled Land Act, 1925.

58. Persons entitled to apply for orders

(1) An order under this Act for the appointment of a new trustee or concerning any interest in land, stock, or thing in action subject to a trust, may be made on the application of any person beneficially interested in the land, stock, or thing in action, whether under disability or not, or on the application of any person duly appointed trustee thereof.

(2) An order under this Act concerning any interest in land, stock, or thing in action subject to a mortgage may be made on the application of any person beneficially interested in the equity of redemption, whether under disability or not, or of any person interested in the money secured by the mortgage.

59. Power to give judgment in absence of a trustee

Where in any action the court is satisfied that diligent search has been made for any person who, in the character of trustee, is made a defendant in any action, to serve him with a process of the court, and that he cannot be found, the court may hear and determine the action and give judgment therein against that person in his character of a trustee as if he had been duly served, or had entered an appearance in the action, and had also appeared by his counsel and solicitor at the hearing, but without prejudice to any interest he may have in the matters in question in the action in any other character.

60. Power to charge costs on trust estate

The court may order the costs and expenses of and incident to any application for an order appointing a new trustee, or for a vesting order, or of and incident to any such order, or any conveyance or transfer in pursuance thereof, to be raised and paid out of the property in respect whereof the same is made, or out of the income thereof, or to be borne and paid in such manner and by such persons as to the court may seem just.

61. Power to relieve trustee from personal liability

If it appears to the court that a trustee, whether appointed by the court or otherwise, is or may be personally liable for any breach of trust, whether the transaction alleged to be a breach of trust occurred before or after the commencement of this Act, but has acted honestly and reasonably, and ought fairly to be excused for the breach of trust and for omitting to obtain the directions of the court in the matter in which he committed such breach, then the court may relieve him either wholly or partly from personal liability for the same.

62. Power to make beneficiary indemnify for breach of trust

(1) Where a trustee commits a breach of trust at the instigation or request or with the consent in writing of a beneficiary, the court may, if it thinks fit [. . .] make such order as to the court seems just, for impounding all or any part of the interest of the beneficiary in the trust estate by way of indemnity to the trustee or persons claiming through him.

(2) This section applies to breaches of trust committed as well before as after the commencement of this Act.

Payment into Court

63. Payment into court by trustees

(1) Trustees, or the majority of trustees, having in their hands or under their control money or securities belonging to a trust, may pay the same into court [. . .] .

(2) The receipt or certificate of the proper officer shall be a sufficient discharge to trustees for the money or securities so paid into court.

(3) Where money or securities are vested in any persons as trustees, and the majority are desirous of paying the same into court, but the concurrence of the other or others cannot be obtained, the court may order the payment into court to be made by the majority without the concurrence of the other or others.

(4) Where any such money or securities are deposited with any banker, broker, or other depositary, the court may order payment or delivery of the money or securities to the majority of the trustees for the purpose of payment into court.

(5) Every transfer payment and delivery made in pursuance of any such order shall be valid and take effect as if the same had been made on the authority or by the act of all the persons entitled to the money and securities so transferred, paid, or delivered.

PART V
GENERAL PROVISIONS

64. Application of Act to Settled Land Act Trustees

(1) All the powers and provisions contained in this Act with reference to the appointment of new trustees, and the discharge and retirement of trustees, apply to and include trustees for the purposes of the Settled Land Act, 1925, and trustees for the purpose of the management of land during a minority, whether such trustees are appointed by the court or by the settlement, or under provisions contained in any instrument.

(2) Where, either before or after the commencement of this Act, trustees of a settlement have been appointed by the court for the purposes of the Settled Land Acts, 1882 to 1890, or of the Settled Land Act, 1925, then, after the commencement of this Act—

(a) the person or persons nominated for the purpose of appointing new trustees by the instrument, if any, creating the settlement, though no trustees for the purposes of the said Acts were thereby appointed; or

(b) if there is no such person, or no such person able and willing to act, the surviving or continuing trustees or trustee for the time being for the purposes of the said Acts, or the personal representatives of the last surviving or continuing trustee for those purposes, shall have the powers conferred by this Act to appoint new or additional trustees of the settlement for the purposes of the said Acts.

(3) Appointments of new trustees for the purposes of the said Acts made or expressed to be made before the commencement of this Act by the trustees or trustee or personal representatives referred to in paragraph (b) of the last preceding subsection

or by the persons referred to in paragraph (a) of that subsection are, without prejudice to any order of the court made before such commencement, hereby confirmed.

66. Indemnity to banks, etc.

This Act, and every order purporting to be made under this Act, shall be a complete indemnity to the Bank of England, and to all persons for any acts done pursuant thereto, and it shall not be necessary for the Bank or for any person to inquire concerning the propriety of the order, or whether the court by which the order was made had jurisdiction to make it.

67. Jurisdiction of the 'court'

(1) In this Act 'the court' means the High Court, [. . .], or the county court, where those courts respectively have jurisdiction.[1]

(2) The procedure under this Act in, [. . .] county courts shall be in accordance with the Acts and rules regulating the procedure of those courts.

Note

[1]See County Courts Act 1984, s. 148(1), Sched. 2, Pt. I as to the jurisdiction of the County Court with regard to this Act

68. Definitions

In this Act, unless the context otherwise requires, the following expressions have the meanings hereby assigned to them respectively, that is to say: —

(1) 'Authorised investments' mean investments authorised by the instrument, if any, creating the trust for the investment of money subject to the trust, or by law;

(2) 'Contingent right' as applied to land includes a contingent or executory interest, a possibility coupled with an interest, whether the object of the gift or limitation of the interest, or possibility is or is not ascertained, also a right of entry, whether immediate or future, and whether vested or contingent;

(3) 'Convey' and 'conveyance' as applied to any person include the execution by that person of every necessary or suitable assurance (including an assent) for conveying, assigning, appointing, surrendering, or otherwise transferring or disposing of land whereof he is seised or possessed, or wherein he is entitled to a contingent right, either for his whole estate or for any less estate, together with the performance of all formalities required by law for the validity of the conveyance; 'sale' includes an exchange;

(4) 'Gazette' means the London Gazette;

(5) 'Instrument' includes Act of Parliament;

(6) 'Land' includes land of any tenure, and mines and minerals, whether or not severed from the surface, buildings or parts of buildings, whether the division is horizontal, vertical or made in any other way, and other corporeal hereditaments; also a manor, an advowson, and a rent and other incorporeal hereditaments, and an easement, right, privilege, or benefit in, over, or derived from land [. . .]; and in this definition 'mines and minerals' include any strata or seam of minerals or substances in or under any land, and powers of working and getting the same [. . .]; and 'hereditaments' mean real property which under an intestacy occurring before the commencement of this Act might have devolved on an heir;

(7) 'Mortgage' and 'mortgagee' include a charge or chargee by way of legal mortgage, and relate to every estate and interest regarded in equity as merely a security for money, and every person deriving title under the original mortgagee;

(8) [. . .]

(9) 'Personal representative' means the executor, original or by representation, or administrator for the time being of a deceased person;

(10) 'Possession' includes receipt of rents and profits or the right to receive the same, if any; 'income' includes rents and profits; and 'possessed' applies to receipt of income of and to any vested estate less than a life interest in possession or in expectancy in any land;

(11) 'Property' includes real and personal property, and any estate share and interest in any property, real or personal, and any debt, and any thing in action, and any other right or interest, whether in possession or not;

(12) 'Rights' include estates and interests;

(13) 'Securities' include stocks, funds, and shares; [. . .] and 'securities payable to bearer' include securities transferable by delivery or by delivery and endorsement;

(14) 'Stock' includes fully paid up shares, and so far as relates to vesting orders made by the court under this Act, includes any fund, annuity, or security transferable in books kept by any company or society, or by instrument of transfer either alone or accompanied by other formalities, and any share of interest therein;

(15) 'Tenant for life,' 'statutory owner,' 'settled land,' 'settlement,' 'trust instrument,' 'trustees of the settlement' [. . .] 'term of years absolute' and 'vesting instrument' have the same meanings as in the Settled Land Act, 1925, and 'entailed interest' has the same meaning as in the Law of Property Act, 1925;

(16) 'Transfer' in relation to stock or securities, includes the performance and execution of every deed, power of attorney, act, and thing on the part of the transferor to effect and complete the title in the transferee;

(17) 'Trust' does not include the duties incident to an estate conveyed by way of mortgage, but with this exception the expressions 'trust' and 'trustee' extend to implied and constructive trusts, and to cases where the trustee has a beneficial interest in the trust property, and to the duties incident to the office of a personal representative, and 'trustee' where the context admits, includes a personal representative, and 'new trustee' includes an additional trustee;

(18) 'Trust corporation' means the Public Trustee or a corporation either appointed by the court in any particular case to be a trustee, or entitled by rules made under subsection (3) of section four of the Public Trustee Act, 1906, to act as custodian trustee;

(19) 'Trust for sale' in relation to land means an immediate [. . .] trust for sale, whether or not exercisable at the request or with the consent of any person [. . .];

(20) 'United Kingdom' means Great Britain and Northern Ireland.

[(2) Any reference in this Act to paying money or securities into court shall be construed as referring to paying the money or transferring or depositing the securities into or in the Supreme Court or into or in any other court that has jurisdiction, and any reference in this Act to payment of money or securities into court shall be construed—

(a) with reference to an order of the High Court, as referring to payment of the money or transfer or deposit of the securities into or in the Supreme Court; and

(b) with reference to an order of any other court, as referring to payment of the money or transfer or deposit of the securities into or in that court.]

69. Application of Act

(1) This Act, except where otherwise expressly provided, applies to trusts including, so far as this Act applies thereto, executorships and administratorships constituted or created either before or after the commencement of this Act.

(2) The powers conferred by this Act on trustees are in addition to the powers conferred by the instrument, if any, creating the trust, but those powers, unless otherwise stated, apply if and so far only as a contrary intention is not expressed in the instrument, if any, creating the trust, and have effect subject to the terms of that instrument.

(3) [. . .]

70. Enactments repealed

[. . .] without prejudice to the provisions of section thirty-eight of the Interpretation Act, 1889:

(a) Nothing in this repeal shall affect any vesting order or appointment made or other thing done under any enactment so repealed, and any order or appointment so made may be revoked or varied in like manner as if it had been made under this Act;

(b) References in any document to any enactment repealed by this Act shall be construed as references to this Act or to the corresponding enactment in this Act.

LAW OF PROPERTY ACT 1925
(1925, c. 20)

PART I
GENERAL PRINCIPLES AS TO LEGAL ESTATES, EQUITABLE INTERESTS AND POWERS

1. Legal estates and equitable interests

(1) The only estates in land which are capable of subsisting or of being conveyed or created at law are—

(a) An estate in fee simple absolute in possession;

(b) A term of years absolute.

(2) The only interests or charges in or over land which are capable of subsisting or of being conveyed or created at law are—

(a) An easement, right, or privilege in or over land for an interest equivalent to an estate in fee simple absolute in possession or a term of years absolute;

(b) A rentcharge in possession issuing out of or charged on land being either perpetual or for a term of years absolute;

(c) A charge by way of legal mortgage;

(d) [. . .] and any other similar charge on land which is not created by an instrument;

(e) Rights of entry exercisable over or in respect of a legal term of years absolute, or annexed, for any purpose, to a legal rentcharge.

(3) All other estates, interests, and charges in or over land take effect as equitable interests.

(4) The estates, interests, and charges which under this section are authorised to subsist or to be conveyed or created at law are (when subsisting or conveyed or created at law) in this Act referred to as 'legal estates', and have the same incidents as legal estates subsisting at the commencement of this Act; and the owner of a legal estate is referred to as an estate owner' and his legal estate is referred to as his estate.

(5) A legal estate may subsist concurrently with or subject to any other legal estate in the same land in like manner as it could have done before the commencement of this Act.

(6) A legal estate is not capable of subsisting or of being created in an undivided share in land or of being held by an infant.

(7) Every power of appointment over, or power to convey or charge land or any interest therein, whether created by a statute or other instrument or implied by law, and whether created before or after the commencement of this Act (not being a power vested in a legal mortgagee or an estate owner in right of his estate and exercisable by him or by another person in his name and on his behalf), operates only in equity.

(8) Estates, interests, and charges in or over land which are not legal estates are in this Act referred to as 'equitable interests,' and powers which by this Act are to operate in equity only are in this Act referred to as 'equitable powers.'

(9) The provisions in any statute or other instrument requiring land to be conveyed to uses shall take effect as directions that the land shall (subject to creating or reserving thereout any legal estate authorised by this Act which may be required) be conveyed to a person of full age upon the requisite trusts.

(10) The repeal of the Statute of Uses (as amended) does not affect the operation thereof in regard to dealings taking effect before the commencement of this Act.

2. Conveyances overreaching certain equitable interests and powers

(1) A conveyance to a purchaser of a legal estate in land shall overreach any equitable interest or power affecting that estate, whether or not he has notice thereof, if—

(i) the conveyance is made under the powers conferred by the Settled Land Act 1925, or any additional powers conferred by a settlement, and the equitable interest or power is capable of being overreached thereby, and the statutory requirements respecting the payment of capital money arising under the settlement are complied with;

(ii) the conveyance is made by [trustees of land] and the equitable interest or power is at the date of the conveyance capable of being overreached by such trustees under the provisions of subsection (2) of this section or independently of that subsection, and [the requirements of section 27 of this Act respecting the payment of capital money arising on such a conveyance] are complied with;

(iii) the conveyance is made by a mortgagee or personal representative in the exercise of his paramount powers, and the equitable interest or power is capable of being overreached by such conveyance, and any capital money arising from the transaction is paid to the mortgagee or personal representative;

(iv) the conveyance is made under an order of the court and the equitable interest or power is bound by such order, and any capital money arising from the transaction is paid into, or in accordance with the order of, the court.

[(1A) An equitable interest in land subject to a trust of land which remains in, or is to revert to, the settlor shall (subject to any contrary intention) be overreached by the conveyance if it would be so overreached were it an interest under the trust.]

(2) [Where the legal estate affected is subject to [a trust of land], then if at the date of a conveyance made after the commencement of this Act [by the trustees], the trustees (whether original or substituted) are either]—

(a) two or more individuals approved or appointed by the court or the successors in office of the individuals so approved or appointed; or

(b) a trust corporation,

[any equitable interest or power having priority [to the trust] shall, notwithstanding any stipulation to the contrary, be overreached by the conveyance, and shall, according to its priority, take effect as if created or arising by means of a primary trust affecting the proceeds of sale and the income of the land until sale.

(3) The following equitable interests and powers are excepted from the operation of subsection (2) of this section, namely—

(i) Equitable interest protected by a deposit of documents relating to the legal estate affected;

(ii) The benefit of any covenant or agreement restrictive of the user of land;

(iii) Any easement, liberty, or privilege over or affecting land and being merely an equitable interest (in this Act referred to as an 'equitable easement');

(iv) The benefit of any contract (in this Act referred to as an 'estate contract') to convey or create a legal estate, including a contract conferring either expressly or by statutory implication a valid option to purchase, a right of preemption, or any other like right;

(v) Any equitable interest protected by registration under the Land Charges Act, 1925,[1] other than—

(a) an annuity within the meaning of Part II. of that Act;

(b) a limited owner's charge or a general equitable charge within the meaning of that Act.

(4) Subject to the protection afforded by this section to the purchaser of a legal estate, nothing contained in this section shall deprive a person entitled to an equitable charge of any of his rights or remedies for enforcing the same.

(5) So far as regards the following interests, created before the commencement of this Act (which accordingly are not within the provisions of the Land Charges Act, 1925[1]), namely—

(a) the benefit of any covenant or agreement restrictive of the user of the land;

(b) any equitable easement;

(c) the interest under a puisne mortgage within the meaning of the Land Charges Act, 1925,[1] unless and until acquired under a transfer made after the commencement of this Act;

(d) the benefit of an estate contract, unless and until the same is acquired under a conveyance made after the commencement of this Act; a purchaser of a legal estate shall only take subject thereto if he has notice thereof, and the same are not overreached under the provisions contained or in the manner referred to in this section.

Note
[1]Now the Land Charges Act 1972.

3. Manner of giving effect to equitable interests and powers

(1) All equitable interests and powers in or over land shall be enforceable against the estate owner of the legal estate affected in manner following (that is to say):—

(a) Where the legal estate affected is settled land, the tenant for life or statutory owner shall be bound to give effect to the equitable interests and powers in manner provided by the Settled Land Act, 1925;

(b) [. . .]

(c) [In any other case], the estate owner shall be bound to give effect to the equitable interests and powers affecting his estate of which he has notice according to their respective priorities. This provision does not affect the priority or powers of a legal mortgagee, or the powers of personal representatives for purposes of administration.

(2) [. . .]

(3) Where, by reason [. . .] of an equitable right of entry taking effect, or for any other reason, a person becomes entitled to require a legal estate to be vested in him, then and in any such case the estate owner whose estate is affected shall be bound to convey or create such legal estate as the case may require.

(4) If any question arises whether any and what legal estate ought to be transferred or created as aforesaid, any person interested may apply to the court for directions in the manner provided by this Act.

(5) If the [. . .] estate owners refuse or neglect for one month after demand to transfer or create any such legal estate, or if by reason of their being out of the United Kingdom or being unable to be found, or by reason of the dissolution of a corporation, or for any other reason, the court is satisfied that the transaction cannot otherwise be effected, or cannot be effected without undue delay or expense, the court may, on the application of any person interested, make a vesting order transferring or creating a legal estate in the manner provided by this Act.

(6) This section does not affect a purchaser of a legal estate taking free from an equitable interest or power.

[(7) The county court has jurisdiction under this section where the land which is to be dealt with in the court does not exceed the county court limit in capital value or net annual value for rating.]

4. Creation and disposition of equitable interests

(1) Interests in land validly created or arising after the commencement of this Act, which are not capable of subsisting as legal estates, shall take effect as equitable interests,

and, save as otherwise expressly provided by statute, interests in land which under the Statute of Uses or otherwise could before the commencement of this Act have been created as legal interests, shall be capable of being created as equitable interests:

Provided that, after the commencement of this Act (and save as hereinafter expressly enacted), an equitable interest in land shall only be capable of being validly created in any case in which an equivalent equitable interest in property real or personal could have been validly created before such commencement.

(2) All rights and interests in land may be disposed of, including—

(a) a contingent, executory or future equitable interest in any land, or a possibility coupled with an interest in any land, whether or not the object of the gift or limitation of such interest or possibility be ascertained;

(b) a right of entry, into or upon land whether immediate or future, and whether vested or contingent.

(3) All rights of entry affecting a legal estate which are exercisable on condition broken or for any other reason may after the commencement of this Act, be made exercisable by any person and the persons deriving title under him, but, in regard to an estate in fee simple (not being a rentcharge held for a legal estate) only within the period authorised by the rule relating to perpetuities.

5. Satisfied terms, whether created out of freehold or leasehold land to cease

(1) Where the purposes of a term of years created or limited at any time out of freehold land, become satisfied either before or after the commencement of this Act (whether or not that term either by express declaration or by construction of law becomes attendant upon the freehold reversion) it shall merge in the reversion expectant thereon and shall cease accordingly.

(2) Where the purposes of a term of years created or limited, at any time, out of leasehold land, become satisfied after the commencement of this Act, that term shall merge in the reversion expectant thereon and shall cease accordingly.

(3) Where the purposes are satisfied only as respects part of the land comprised in a term, this section shall have effect as if a separate term had been created in regard to that part of the land.

6. Saving of lessors' and lessees' covenants

(1) Nothing in this Part of this Act affects prejudicially the right to enforce any lessor's or lessee's covenants, agreements or conditions (including a valid option to purchase or right of preemption over the reversion), contained in any such instrument as is in this section mentioned, the benefit or burden of which runs with the reversion or the term.

(2) This section applies where the covenant, agreement or condition is contained in any instrument—

(a) creating a term of years absolute, or

(b) varying the rights of the lessor or lessee under the instrument creating the term.

7. Saving of certain legal estates and statutory powers

(1) A fee simple which, by virtue of the Lands Clauses Acts, [. . .] or any similar statute, is liable to be divested, is for the purposes of this Act a fee simple absolute, and remains liable to be divested as if this Act had not been passed, [and a fee simple subject to a legal or equitable right of entry or re-entry is for the purposes of this Act a fee simple absolute].

(2) A fee simple vested in a corporation which is liable to determine by reason of the dissolution of the corporation is, for the purposes of this Act, a fee simple absolute.

(3) The provisions of—

(a) [. . .]

(b) the Friendly Societies Act 1896, in regard to land to which that Act applies;

(c) any other statutes conferring special facilities or prescribing special modes (whether by way of registered memorial or otherwise) for disposing of or acquiring land, or providing for the vesting (by conveyance or otherwise) of the land in trustees or any person, or the holder for the time being of an office or any corporation sole or aggregate (including the Crown);

shall remain in full force.

[. . .]

(4) Where any such power for disposing of or creating a legal state is exercisable by a person who is not the estate owner, the power shall, when practicable, be exercised in the name and on behalf of the estate owner.

8. Saving of certain legal powers to lease

(1) All leases or tenancies at a rent for a term of years absolute authorised to be granted by a mortgagor or mortgagee or by the Settled Land Act, 1925, or any other statute (whether or not extended by any instrument) may be granted in the name and on behalf of the estate owner by the person empowered to grant the same, whether being an estate owner or not, with the same effect and priority as if this Part of this Act had not been passed; but this section does not (except as respects the usual qualified covenant for quiet enjoyment) authorise any person granting a lease in the name of an estate owner to impose any personal liability on him.

(2) Where a rentcharge is held for a legal estate, the owner thereof may under the statutory power or under any corresponding power, create a legal term of years absolute for securing or compelling payment of the same; but in other cases terms created under any such power shall, unless and until the estate owner of the land charged gives legal effect to the transaction, take effect only as equitable interests.

9. Vesting orders and dispositions of legal estates operating as conveyances by an estate owner

(1) Every such order, declaration, or conveyance as is hereinafter mentioned, namely—

(a) every vesting order made by any court or other competent authority;

(b) every vesting declaration (express or implied) under any statutory power;

(c) every vesting instrument made by the trustees of a settlement or other persons under the provisions of the Settled Land Act, 1925;

(d) every conveyance by a person appointed for the purpose under an order of the court or authorised under any statutory power to convey in the name or on behalf of an estate owner;

(e) every conveyance made under any power reserved or conferred by this Act, which is made or executed for the purpose of vesting, conveying, or creating a legal estate, shall operate to convey or create the legal estate disposed of in like manner as if the same had been a conveyance executed by the estate owner of the legal estate to which the order, declaration, vesting instrument, or conveyance relates.

(2) Where the order, declaration, or conveyance is made in favour of a purchaser, the provisions of this Act relating to a conveyance of a legal estate to a purchaser shall apply thereto.

(3) The provisions of the Trustee Act, 1925, relating to vesting orders and orders appointing a person to convey shall apply to all vesting orders authorised to be made by this Part of this Act.

10. Title to be shown to legal estates

(1) Where title is shown to a legal estate in land, it shall be deemed not necessary or proper to include in the abstract of title an instrument relating only to interests or

powers which will be overreached by the conveyance of the estate to which title is being shown; but nothing in this Part of this Act affects the liability of any person to disclose an equitable interest or power which will not be so overreached, or to furnish an abstract of any instrument creating or affecting the same.

(2) A solicitor delivering an abstract framed in accordance with this Part of this Act shall not incur any liability on account of an omission to include therein an instrument which, under this section, is to be deemed not necessary or proper to be included, nor shall any liability be implied by reason of the inclusion of any such instrument.

12. Limitation and Prescription Acts

Nothing in this Part of this Act affects the operation of any statute, or of the general law for the limitation of actions or proceedings relating to land or with reference to the acquisition of easements or rights over or in respect of land.

13. Effect of possession of documents

This Act shall not prejudicially affect the right or interest of any person arising out of or consequent on the possession by him of any documents relating to a legal estate in land, nor affect any question arising out of or consequent upon any omission to obtain or any other absence of possession by any person of any documents relating to a legal estate in land.

14. Interests of persons in possession

This Part of this Act shall not prejudicially affect the interest of any person in possession or in actual occupation of land to which he may be entitled in right of such possession or occupation.

15. Presumption that parties are of full age

The persons expressed to be parties to any conveyance shall, until the contrary is proved, be presumed to be of full age at the date thereof.

Infants and Lunatics

20. Infants not to be appointed trustees

The appointment of an infant to be a trustee in relation to any settlement or trust shall be void, but without prejudice to the power to appoint a new trustee to fill the vacancy.

21. Receipts by married infants

A married infant shall have power to give valid receipts for all income (including statutory accumulations of income made during the minority) to which the infant may be entitled in like manner as if the infant were of full age.

[22. Conveyances on behalf of persons suffering from mental disorder and as to land held by them [in trust]

(1) Where a legal estate in land (whether settled or not) is vested in a person suffering from mental disorder, either solely or jointly with any other person or persons, his receiver or (if no receiver is acting for him) any person authorised in that behalf shall, under an order of the authority having jurisdiction under [Part VII of the Mental Health Act, 1983,] or of the court, or under any statutory power, make or concur in making all requisite dispositions for conveying or creating a legal estate in his name and on his behalf.

(2) If land [subject to a trust of land] is vested, either solely or jointly with any other person or persons, in a person who is incapable, by reason of mental disorder, of exercising his functions as trustee, a new trustee shall be appointed in the place of that person, or he shall be otherwise discharged from the trust, before the legal estate is dealt with [by the trustees].]

Dispositions on Trust for Sale

[*Trusts of land*]

[24. Appointment of trustees of land

(1) The persons having power to appoint new trustees of land shall be bound to appoint the same persons (if any) who are for the time being trustees of any trust of the proceeds of sale of the land.

(2) A purchaser shall not be concerned to see that subsection (1) of this section has been complied with.

(3) This section applies whether the trust of land and the trust of proceeds of sale are created, or arise, before or after the commencement of this Act.]

27. Purchaser not to be concerned with the trusts of the proceeds of sale which are to be paid to two or more trustees or to a trust corporation

[(1) A purchaser of a legal estate from trustees of land shall not be concerned with the trusts affecting the land, the net income of the land or the proçeeds of sale of the land whether or not those trusts are declared by the same instrument as that by which the trust of land is created.]

[(2) Notwithstanding anything to the contrary in the instrument (if any) creating a [trust] of land or in [any trust affecting the net proceeds of sale of the land if it is sold], the proceeds of sale or other capital money shall not be paid to or applied by the direction of fewer than two persons as [trustees], except where the trustee is a trust corporation, but this subsection does not affect the right of a sole personal representative as such to give valid receipts for, or direct the application of, proceeds of sale or other capital money, nor, except where capital money arises on the transaction, render it necessary to have more than one trustee.]

31. Trust [. . .] of mortgaged property where right of redemption is barred

(1) Where any property, vested in trustees by way of security, becomes, by virtue of the statutes of limitation, or of an order for foreclosure or otherwise, discharged from the right of redemption, it shall be held by them [. . .] [in trust—

(a) to apply the income from the property in the same manner as interest paid on the mortgage debt would have been applicable; and

(b) if the property is sold, to apply the net proceeds of sale, after payment of costs and expenses, in the same manner as repayment of the mortgage debt would have been applicable.]

(2) [Subsection (1) of this section] operates without prejudice to any rule of law relating to the apportionment of capital and income between tenant for life and remainderman.

(3) [. . .]

[(4) Where—

(a) the mortgage money is capital money for the purposes of the Settled Land Act 1925;

(b) land other than any forming the whole or part of the property mentioned in subsection (1) of this section is, or is deemed to be, subject to the settlement; and

(c) the tenant for life or statutory owner requires the trustees to execute with respect to land forming the whole or part of that property a vesting deed such as would have been required in relation to the land if it had been acquired and purchased with capital money,

the trustees shall execute such a vesting deed.]

(5) This section applies whether the right of redemption was discharged before or after the first day of January, nineteen hundred and twelve, but has effect without prejudice to any dealings or arrangements made before that date.

33. Application of Part I. to personal representatives

The provisions of this Part of this Act relating to [trustees of land] apply to personal representatives holding [land in trust], but without prejudice to their rights and powers for purposes of administration.

Undivided Shares and Joint Ownership

34. Effect of future dispositions to tenants in common

(1) An undivided share in land shall not be capable of being created except as provided by the Settled Land Act, 1925, or as hereinafter mentioned.

(2) Where, after the commencement of this Act, land is expressed to be conveyed to any persons in undivided shares and those persons are of full age, the conveyance shall (notwithstanding anything to the contrary in this Act) operate as if the land had been expressed to be conveyed to the grantees, or, if there are more than four grantees, to the four first named in the conveyance, as joint tenants [in trust for the persons interested in the land]:

Provided that, where the conveyance is made by way of mortgage the land shall vest in the grantees or such four of them as aforesaid for a term of years absolute (as provided by this Act) as joint tenants subject to cesser on redemption in like manner as if the mortgage money had belonged to them on a joint account, but without prejudice to the beneficial interests in the mortgage money and interest.

(3) A devise bequest or testamentary appointment, coming into operation after the commencement of this Act, of land to two or more persons in undivided shares shall operate as a devise bequest or appointment of the land [. . .] to the personal representatives of the testator, and [. . .] (but without prejudice to the rights and powers of the personal representatives for purposes of administration) [in trust for the persons interested in the land].

[(3A) In subsections (2) and (3) of this section references to the persons interested in the land include persons interested as trustees or personal representatives (as well as persons beneficially interested).]

36. Joint tenancies

(1) Where a legal estate (not being settled land) is beneficially limited to or held in trust for any persons as joint tenants, the same shall be held [in trust] in like manner as if the persons beneficially entitled were tenants in common, but not so as to sever their joint tenancy in equity.

(2) No severance of a joint tenancy of a legal estate, so as to create a tenancy in common in land, shall be permissible, whether by operation of law or otherwise, but this subsection does not affect the right of a joint tenant to release his interest to the other joint tenants, or the right to sever a joint tenancy in an equitable interest whether or not the legal estate is vested in the joint tenants:

Provided that, where a legal estate (not being settled land) is vested in joint tenants beneficially, and any tenant desires to sever the joint tenancy in equity, he shall give to the other joint tenants a notice in writing of such desire or do such other acts or things as would, in the case of personal estate, have been effectual to sever the tenancy in equity, and thereupon [the land shall be held in trust on terms] which would have been requisite for giving effect to the beneficial interests if there had been an actual severance.

[Nothing in this Act affects the right of a survivor of joint tenants, who is solely and beneficially interested, to deal with his legal estate as if it were not held [in trust].]

(3) Without prejudice to the right of a joint tenant to release his interest to the other joint tenants no severance of a mortgage term or trust estate, so as to create a tenancy in common, shall be permissable.

37. Rights of husband and wife
A husband and wife shall, for all purposes of acquisition of any interest in property, under a disposition made or coming into operation after the commencement of this Act, be treated as two persons.

38. Party structures
(1) Where under a disposition or other arrangement which, if a holding in undivided shares had been permissible, would have created a tenancy in common, a wall or other structure is or is expressed to be made a party wall or structure, that structure shall be and remain severed vertically as between the respective owners, and the owner of each part shall have such rights to support and user over the rest of the structure as may be requisite for conferring rights corresponding to those which would have subsisted if a valid tenancy in common had been created.
(2) Any person interested may, in case of dispute, apply to the court for an order declaring the rights and interests under this section of the persons interested in any such party structure, and the court may make such order as it thinks fit.

Transitional Provisions

39. Transitional provisions in First Schedule
For the purpose of effecting the transition from the law existing prior to the commencement of the Law of Property Act, 1922, to the law enacted by that Act (as amended), the provisions set out in the First Schedule to this Act shall have effect—
(1) for converting existing legal estates, interests and charges not capable under the said Act of taking effect as legal interests into equitable interests;
(2) for discharging, getting in or vesting outstanding legal estates;
(3) for making provision with respect to legal estates vested in infants;
(4) for subjecting land held in undivided shares to [trusts];
(5) for dealing with party structures and open spaces held in common;
(6) for converting tenancies by entireties into joint tenancies;
(7) for converting existing freehold mortgages into mortgages by demise;
(8) for converting existing leasehold mortgages into mortgages by sub-demise.

PART II
CONTRACTS, CONVEYANCES AND OTHER INSTRUMENTS

Contracts

40. Contracts for sale, of land to be in writing etc.
(1) No action may be brought upon any contract for the sale or other disposition of land or any interest in land, unless the agreement upon which such action is brought, or some memorandum or note thereof, is in writing, and signed by the party to be charged or by some other person thereunder by him lawfully authorised.
(2) This section applies to contracts whether made before or after the commencement of this Act and does not affect the law relating to past performance or sales by the court.

Note: Repealed by the Law of Property (Miscellaneous Provisions) Act 1989, s. 2.

41. Stipulations not of the essence of a contract
Stipulations in a contract, as to time or otherwise, which according to rules of equity are not deemed to be or to have become of the essence of the contract, are also construed and have effect at law in accordance with the same rules.

42. Provisions as to contracts
(1) A stipulation that a purchaser of a legal estate in land shall accept a title made with the concurrence of any person entitled to an equitable interest shall be void, if a title can be made discharged from the equitable interest without such concurrence—

(a) under a [trust of land]; or
(b) under this Act, or the Settled Land Act, 1925, or any other statute.

(2) A stipulation that a purchaser of a legal estate in land shall pay or contribute towards the costs of or incidental to—

(a) obtaining a vesting order, or the appointment of trustees of a settlement, or the appointment of trustees of a conveyance on trust for sale; or

(b) the preparation stamping or execution of a conveyance on trust for sale, or of a vesting instrument for bringing into force the provisions of the Settled Land Act, 1925; shall be void.

(3) A stipulation contained in any contract for the sale or exchange of land made after the commencement of this Act, to the effect that an outstanding legal estate is to be traced or got in by or at the expense of a purchaser or that no objection is to be taken on account of an outstanding legal estate, shall be void.

(4) If the subject matter of any contract for the sale or exchange of land—

(i) is a mortgage term and the vendor has power to convey the fee simple in the land, or, in the case of a mortgage of a term of years absolute, the leasehold reversion affected by the mortgage, the contract shall be deemed to extend to the fee simple in the land or such leasehold reversion;

(ii) is an equitable interest capable of subsisting as a legal estate, and the vendor has power to vest such legal estate in himself or in the purchaser or to require the same to be so vested, the contract shall be deemed to extend to such legal estate;

(iii) is an entailed interest in possession and the vendor has power to vest in himself or in the purchaser the fee simple in the land, (or, if the entailed interest is an interest in a term of years absolute, such term,) or to require the same to be so vested, the contract shall be deemed to extend to the fee simple in the land or the term of years absolute.

(5) This section does not affect the right of a mortgagee of leasehold land to sell his mortgage term only if he is unable to convey or vest the leasehold reversion expectant thereon.

(6) [. . .]

(7) Where a purchaser has power to acquire land compulsorily, and a contract, whether by virtue of a notice to treat or otherwise, is subsisting under which title can be made without payment of the compensation money into court, title shall be made in that way unless the purchaser, to avoid expense or delay or for any special reason, considers it expedient that the money should be paid into court.

(8) A vendor shall not have any power to rescind a contract by reason only of the enforcement of any right under this section.

(9) This section only applies in favour of a purchaser for money or money's worth.

43. Rights protected by registration

(1) Where a purchaser of a legal estate is entitled to acquire the same discharged from an equitable interest which is protected by registration as a pending action, annuity, writ, order, deed of arrangement or land charge, and which will not be overreached by the conveyance to him, he may notwithstanding any stipulation to the contrary, require—

(a) that the registration shall be cancelled; or

(b) that the person entitled to the equitable interest shall concur in the conveyance; and in either case free of expense to the purchaser.

(2) Where the registration cannot be cancelled or the person entitled to the equitable interest refuses to concur in the conveyance, this section does not affect the right of any person to rescind the contract.

44. Statutory commencements of title

(1) After the commencement of this Act thirty years[1] shall be substituted for forty years as the period of commencement of title which a purchaser of land may require;

nevertheless earlier title than thirty years may be required in cases similar to those in which earlier title than forty years might immediately before the commencement of this Act be required.

(2) Under a contract to grant or assign a term of years, whether derived or to be derived out of freehold or leasehold land, the intended lessee or assign shall not be entitled to call for the title to the freehold.

(3) Under a contract to sell and assign a term of years derived out of a leasehold interest in land, the intended assign shall not have the right to call for the title to the leasehold reversion.

(4) On a contract to grant a lease for a term of years to be derived out of a leasehold interest, with a leasehold reversion, the intended lessee shall not have the right to call for the title to that reversion.

(5) Where by reason of any of the three last preceding subsections, an intending lessee or assign is not entitled to call for the title to the freehold or to a leasehold reversion, as the case may be, he shall not, where the contract is made after the commencement of this Act, be deemed to be affected with notice of any matter or thing of which, if he had contracted that such title should be furnished, he might have had notice.

(6) Where land of copyhold or customary tenure has been converted into freehold by enfranchisement, then, under a contract to sell and convey the freehold, the purchaser shall not have the right to call for the title to make the enfranchisement.

(7) Where the manorial incidents formerly affecting any land have been extinguished, then, under a contract to sell and convey the freehold, the purchaser shall not have the right to call for the title of the person entering into any compensation agreement or giving a receipt for the compensation money to enter into such agreement or to give such receipt, and shall not be deemed to be affected with notice of any matter or thing of which, if he had contracted that such title should be furnished, he might have had notice.

(8) A purchaser shall not be deemed to be or ever to have been affected with notice of any matter or thing of which, if he had investigated the title or made enquiries in regard to matters prior to the period of commencement of title fixed by this Act, or by any other statute, or by any rule of law, he might have had notice, unless he actually makes such investigation or enquiries.

(9) Where a lease whether made before or after the commencement of this Act, is made under a power contained in a settlement, will, Act of Parliament, or other instrument, any preliminary contract for or relating to the lease shall not, for the purpose of the deduction of title to an intended assign, form part of the title, or evidence of the title, to the lease.

(10) This section, save where otherwise expressly provided, applies to contracts for sale whether made before or after the commencement of this Act, and applies to contracts for exchange in like manner as to contracts for sale, save that it applies only to contracts for exchange made after such commencement.

(11) This section applies only if and so far as a contrary intention is not expressed in the contract.

Note

[1]This section applies to contracts made after 1969, as if 15 years were specified instead of 30 years as the period of commencement of title which may be required.

45. Other statutory conditions of sale

(1) A purchaser of any property shall not—

(a) require the production, or any abstract or copy, of any deed, will, or other document, dated or made before the time prescribed by law, or stipulated, for the commencement of the title, even though the same creates a power subsequently exercised by an instrument abstracted in the abstract furnished to the purchaser; or

(b) require any information, or make any requisition, objection, or inquiry, with respect to any such deed, will, or document, or the title prior to that time, notwithstanding that any such deed, will, or other document, or that prior title, is recited, agreed to be produced, or noticed;

and he shall assume, unless the contrary appears, that the recitals, contained in the abstracted instruments, of any deed, will, or other document, forming part of that prior title, are correct, and give all the material contents of the deed, will, or other document so recited, and that every document so recited was duly executed by all necessary parties, and perfected, if and as required, by fine, recovery, acknowledgment, inrolment, or otherwise:

Provided that this subsection shall not deprive a purchaser of the right to require the production, or an abstract or copy of—

(i) any power of attorney under which any abstracted document is executed; or

(ii) any document creating or disposing of an interest, power or obligation which is not shown to have ceased or expired, and subject to which any part of the property is disposed of by an abstracted document; or

(iii) any document creating any limitation or trust by reference to which any part of the property is disposed of by an abstracted document.

(2) Where land sold is held by lease (other than an under-lease), the purchaser shall assume, unless the contrary appears, that the lease was duly granted; and, on production of the receipt for the last payment due for rent under the lease before the date of actual completion of the purchase, he shall assume, unless the contrary appears, that all the covenants and provisions of the lease have been duly performed and observed up to the date of actual completion of the purchase.

(3) Where land sold is held by under-lease, the purchaser shall assume, unless the contrary appears, that the under-lease and every superior lease were duly granted; and, on production of the receipt for the last payment due for rent under the under-lease before the date of actual completion of the purchase, he shall assume, unless the contrary appears, that all the covenants and provisions of the under-lease have been duly performed and observed up to the date of actual completion of the purchase, and further that all rent due under every superior lease, and all the covenants and provisions of every superior lease, have been paid and duly performed and observed up to that date.

(4) On a sale of any property, the following expenses shall be borne by the purchaser where he requires them to be incurred for the purpose of verifying the abstract or any other purpose, that is to say—

(a) the expenses of the production and inspection of all Acts of Parliament, inclosure awards, records, proceedings of courts, court rolls, deeds, wills, probates, letters of administration, and other documents, not in the possession of the vendor or his mortgagee or trustee, and the expenses of all journeys incidental to such production or inspection; and

(b) the expenses of searching for, procuring, making, verifying, and producing all certificates, declarations, evidences, and information not in the possession of the vendor or his mortgagee or trustee, and all attested, stamped, office, or other copies or abstracts of, or extracts from, any Acts of Parliament or other documents aforesaid, not in the possession of the vendor or his mortgagee or trustee,

and where the vendor or his mortgagee or trustee retains possession of any document, the expenses of making any copy thereof, attested or unattested, which a purchaser requires to be delivered to him, shall be borne by that purchaser.

(5) On a sale of any property in lots, a purchaser of two or more lots, held wholly or partly under the same title, shall not have a right to more than one abstract of the common title, except at his own expense.

(6) Recitals, statements, and descriptions of facts, matters, and parties contained in deeds, instruments, Acts of Parliament, or statutory declarations, twenty years old

at the date of the contract, shall, unless and except so far as they may be proved to be inaccurate, be taken to be sufficient evidence of the truth of such facts, matters, and descriptions.

(7) The inability of a vendor to furnish a purchaser with an acknowledgment of his right to production and delivery of copies of documents of title or with a legal covenant to produce and furnish copies of documents of title shall not be an objection to title in case the purchaser will, on the completion of the contract, have an equitable right to the production of such documents.

(8) Such acknowledgments of the right of production or covenants for production and such undertakings or covenants for safe custody of documents as the purchaser can and does require shall be furnished or made at his expense, and the vendor shall bear the expense of perusal and execution on behalf of and by himself, and on behalf of and by necessary parties other than the purchaser.

(9) A vendor shall be entitled to retain documents of title where—

(a) he retains any part of the land to which the documents relate; or

(b) the document consists of a trust instrument or other instrument creating a trust which is still subsisting, or an instrument relating to the appointment or discharge of a trustee of a subsisting trust.

(10) This section applies to contracts for sale made before or after the commencement of this Act, and applies to contracts for exchange in like manner as to contracts for sale, except that it applies only to contracts for exchange made after such commencement:

Provided that this section shall apply subject to any stipulation or contrary intention expressed in the contract.

(11) Nothing in this section shall be construed as binding a purchaser to complete his purchase in any case where, on a contract made independently of this section, and containing stipulations similar to the provisions of this section, or any of them, specific performance of the contract would not be enforced against him by the court.

46. Forms of contracts and conditions of sale

The Lord Chancellor may from time to time prescribe and publish forms of contracts and conditions of sale of land, and the forms so prescribed shall, subject to any modification, or any stipulation or intention to the contrary, expressed in the correspondence, apply to contracts by correspondence, and may, but only by express reference thereto, be made to apply to any other cases for which the forms are made available.

47. Application of insurance money on completion of a sale or exchange

(1) Where after the date of any contract for sale or exchange of property, money becomes payable under any policy of insurance maintained by the vendor in respect of any damage to or destruction of property included in the contract, the money shall, on completion of the contract, be held or receivable by the vendor on behalf of the purchaser and paid by the vendor to the purchaser on completion of the sale or exchange, or so soon thereafter as the same shall be received by the vendor.

(2) This section applies only to contracts made after the commencement of this Act, and has effect subject to—

(a) any stipulation to the contrary contained in the contract,

(b) any requisite consents of the insurers,

(c) the payment by the purchaser of the proportionate part of the premium from the date of the contract.

(3) This section applies to a sale or exchange by an order of the court, as if—

(a) for references to the 'vendor' there were substituted references to the 'person bound by the order';

(b) for the reference to the completion of the contract there were substituted a reference to the payment of the purchase or equality money (if any) into court;

(c) for the reference to the date of the contract there were substituted a reference to the time when the contract becomes binding.

48. Stipulations preventing a purchaser, lessee, or underlessee from employing his own solicitor to be void

(1) Any stipulation made on the sale of any interest in land after the commencement of this Act to the effect that the conveyance to, or the registration of the title of, the purchaser shall be prepared or carried out at the expense of the purchaser by a solicitor appointed by or acting for the vendor, and any stipulation which might restrict a purchaser in the selection of a solicitor to act on his behalf in relation to any interest in land agreed to be purchased, shall be void; and, if a sale is effected by demise or subdemise, then, for the purposes of this subsection, the instrument required for giving effect to the transaction shall be deemed to be a conveyance:

Provided that nothing in this subsection shall affect any right reserved to a vendor to furnish a form of conveyance to a purchaser from which the draft can be prepared, or to charge a reasonable fee therefor, or, where a perpetual rentcharge is to be reserved as the only consideration in money or money's worth, the right of a vendor to stipulate that the draft conveyance is to be prepared by his solicitor at the expense of the purchaser.

(2) Any covenant or stipulation contained in, or entered into with reference to any lease or underlease made before or after the commencement of this Act—

(a) whereby the right of preparing, at the expense of a purchaser, any conveyance of the estate or interest of the lessee or underlessee in the demised premises or in any part thereof, or of otherwise carrying out, at the expense of the purchaser, any dealing with such estate or interest, is expressed to be reserved to or vested in the lessor or underlessor or his solicitor; or

(b) which in any way restricts the right of the purchaser to have such conveyance carried out on his behalf by a solicitor appointed by him; shall be void:

Provided that, where any covenant or stipulation is rendered void by this subsection, there shall be implied in lieu thereof a covenant or stipulation that the lessee or underlessee shall register with the lessor or his solicitor within six months from the date thereof, or as soon after the expiration of that period as may be practicable, all conveyances and devolutions (including probates or letters of administration) affecting the lease or under-lease and pay a fee of one guinea in respect of each registration, and the power of entry (if any) on breach of any convenant contained in the lease or underlease shall apply and extend to the breach of any covenant so to be implied.

(3) Save where a sale is effected by demise or sub-demise, this section does not affect the law relating to the preparation of a lease or underlease or the draft thereof.

(4) In this section 'lease' and 'underlease' include any agreement therefor or other tenancy, and 'lessee' and 'underlessee' and 'lessor' and 'underlessor' have corresponding meanings.

49. Applications to the court by vendor and purchaser

(1) A vendor or purchaser of any interest in land, or their representatives respectively, may apply in a summary way to the court, in respect of any requisitions or objections, or any claim for compensation, or any other question arising out of or connected with the contract (not being a question affecting the existence or validity of the contract), and the court may make such order upon the application as to the court may appear just, and may order how and by whom all or any of the costs of and incident to the application are to be borne and paid.

(2) Where the court refuses to grant specific performance of a contract, or in any action for the return of a deposit, the court may, if it thinks fit, order the repayment of any deposit.

(3) This section applies to a contract for the sale or exchange of any interest in land.

[(4) The county court has jurisdiction under this section where land which is to be dealt with in the court does not exceed [£30,000] in capital value [. . .].]

50. Discharge of incumbrances by the court on sales or exchanges

(1) Where land subject to any incumbrance, whether immediately realisable or payable or not, is sold or exchanged by the court, or out of court, the court may, if it thinks fit, on the application of any party to the sale or exchange, direct or allow payment into court of such sum as is hereinafter mentioned, that is to say—

(a) in the case of an annual sum charged on the land, or of a capital sum charged on a determinable interest in the land, the sum to be paid into court shall be of such amount as, when invested in Government securities, the court considers will be sufficient, by means of the dividends thereof, to keep down or otherwise provide for that charge; and

(b) in any other case of capital money charged on the land, the sum to be paid into court shall be of an amount sufficient to meet the incumbrance and any interest due thereon;

but in either case there shall also be paid into court such additional amount as the court considers will be sufficient to meet the contingency of further costs, expenses and interest, and any other contingency, except depreciation of investments, not exceeding one-tenth part of the original amount to be paid in, unless the court for special reason thinks fit to require a larger additional amount.

(2) Thereupon, the court may, if it thinks fit, and either after or without any notice to the incumbrancer, as the court thinks fit, declare the land to be freed from the incumbrance, and make any order for conveyance, or vesting order, proper for giving effect to the sale or exchange, and give directions for the retention and investment of the money in court and for the payment or application of the income thereof.

(3) The court may declare all other land, if any, affected by the incumbrance (besides the land sold or exchanged) to be freed from the incumbrance, and this power may be exercised either after or without notice to the incumbrancer, and notwithstanding that on a previous occasion an order, relating to the same incumbrance, has been made by the court which was confined to the land then sold or exchanged.

(4) On any application under this section the court may, if it thinks fit, as respects any vendor or purchaser, dispense with the service of any notice which would otherwise be required to be served on the vendor or purchaser.

(5) After notice served on the persons interested in or entitled to the money or fund in court, the court may direct payment or transfer thereof to the persons entitled to receive or give a discharge for the same, and generally may give directions respecting the application or distribution of the capital or income thereof.

(6) This section applies to sales or exchanges whether made before or after the commencement of this Act, and to incumbrances whether created by statute or otherwise.

51. Lands lie in grant only

(1) All lands and all interests therein lie in grant and are incapable of being conveyed by livery or livery and seisin, or by feoffment, or by bargain and sale; and a conveyance of an interest in land may operate to pass the possession or right to possession thereof, without actual entry, but subject to all prior rights thereto.

(2) The use of the word grant is not necessary to convey land or to create any interest therein.

52. Conveyances to be by deed

(1) All conveyances of land or of any interest therein are void for the purpose of conveying or creating a legal estate unless made by deed.

(2) This section does not apply to—

(a) assents by a personal representative;

(b) disclaimers made in accordance with [sections 178 to 180 or sections 315 to 319 of the Insolvency Act 1986] or not required to be evidenced in writing;

(c) surrenders by operation of law, including surrenders which may, by law, be effected without writing;

(d) leases or tenancies or other assurances not required by law to be made in writing;

(e) receipts [other than those falling within section 115 below];

(f) vesting orders of the court or other competent authority;

(g) conveyances taking effect by operation of law.

53. Instruments required to be in writing

(1) Subject to the provision hereinafter contained with respect to the creation of interests in land by parol—

(a) no interest in land can be created or disposed of except by writing signed by the person creating or conveying the same, or by his agent thereunto lawfully authorised in writing, or by will, or by operation of law;

(b) a declaration of trust respecting any land or any interest therein must be manifested and proved by some writing signed by some person who is able to declare such trust or by his will;

(c) a disposition of an equitable interest or trust subsisting at the time of the disposition, must be in writing signed by the person disposing of the same, or by his agent thereunto lawfully authorised in writing or by will.

(2) This section does not affect the creation or operation of resulting, implied or constructive trusts.

54. Creation of interests in land by parol

(1) All interests in land created by parol and not put in writing and signed by the persons so creating the same, or by their agents thereunto lawfully authorised in writing, have, notwithstanding any consideration having been given for the same, the force and effect of interests at will only.

(2) Nothing in the foregoing provisions of this Part of this Act shall affect the creation by parol of leases taking effect in possession for a term not exceeding three years (whether or not the lessee is given power to extend the term) at the best rent which can be reasonably obtained without taking a fine.

55. Savings in regard to last two sections

Nothing in the last two foregoing sections shall—

(a) invalidate dispositions by will; or

(b) affect any interest validly created before the commencement of this Act; or

(c) affect the right to acquire an interest in land by virtue of taking possession; or

(d) affect the operation of the law relating to part performance.

56. Persons taking who are not parties and as to indentures

(1) A person may take an immediate or other interest in land or other property, or the benefit of any condition, right of entry, covenant or agreement over or respecting land or other property, although he may not be named as a party to the conveyance or other instrument.

(2) A deed between parties, to effect its objects, has the effect of an indenture though not indented or expressed to be an indenture.

57. Description of deeds

Any deed, whether or not being an indenture, may be described (at the commencement thereof or otherwise) as a deed simply, or as a conveyance, deed of exchange, vesting deed, trust instrument, settlement, mortgage, charge, transfer of mortgage, appointment, lease or otherwise according to the nature of the transaction intended to be effected.

58. Provisions as to supplemental instruments

Any instrument (whether executed before or after the commencement of this Act) expressed to be supplemental to a previous instrument, shall, as far as may be, be read and have effect as if the supplemental instrument contained a full recital of the previous instrument, but this section does not operate to give any right to an abstract or production of any such previous instrument, and a purchaser may accept the same evidence that the previous instrument does not affect the title as if it had merely been mentioned in the supplemental instrument.

59. Conditions and certain covenants not implied

(1) An exchange or other conveyance of land made by deed after the first day of October, eighteen hundred and forty-five, does not imply any condition in law.

(2) The word 'give' or 'grant' does not in a deed made after the date last aforesaid, imply any covenant in law, save where otherwise provided by statute.

60. Abolition of technicalities in regard to conveyances and deeds

(1) A conveyance of freehold land to any person without words of limitation, or any equivalent expression, shall pass to the grantee the fee simple or other the whole interest which the grantor had power to convey in such land, unless a contrary intention appears in the conveyance.

(2) A conveyance of freehold land to a corporation sole by his corporate designation without the word 'successors' shall pass to the corporation the fee simple or other the whole interest which the grantor had power to convey in such land, unless a contrary intention appears in the conveyance.

(3) In a voluntary conveyance a resulting trust for the grantor shall not be implied merely by reason that the property is not expressed to be conveyed for the use or benefit of the grantee.

(4) The foregoing provisions of this section apply only to conveyances and deeds executed after the commencement of this Act:

Provided that in a deed executed after the thirty-first day of December, eighteen hundred and eighty-one, it is sufficient—

(a) In the limitation of an estate in fee simple, to use the words 'in fee simple,' without the word 'heirs';

[. . .]

61. Construction of expressions used in deeds and other instruments

In all deeds, contracts, wills, orders and other instruments executed, made or coming into operation after the commencement of this Act, unless the context otherwise requires—

(a) 'Month' means calendar month;
(b) 'Person' includes a corporation;
(c) The singular includes the plural and vice versa;
(d) The masculine includes the feminine and vice versa.

62. General words implied in conveyances

(1) A conveyance of land shall be deemed to include and shall by virtue of this Act operate to convey, with the land, all buildings, erections, fixtures, commons, hedges, ditches, fences, ways, waters, water-courses, liberties, privileges, easements, rights, and advantages whatsoever, appertaining or reputed to appertain to the land, or any part thereof, or, at the time of conveyance, demised, occupied, or enjoyed with, or reputed or known as part or parcel of or appurtenant to the land or any part thereof.

(2) A conveyance of land, having houses or other buildings thereon, shall be deemed to include and shall by virtue of this Act operate to convey, with the land,

houses, or other buildings, all outhouses, erections, fixtures, cellars, areas, courts, courtyards, cisterns, sewers, gutters, drains, ways, passages, lights, water-courses, liberties, privileges, easements, rights, and advantages whatsoever, appertaining or reputed to appertain to the land, houses, or other buildings conveyed, or any of them, or any part thereof, or, at the time of conveyance, demised, occupied, or enjoyed with, or reputed or known as part or parcel of or appurtenant to, the land, houses, or other buildings conveyed, or any of them, or any part thereof.

(3) A conveyance of a manor shall be deemed to include and shall by virtue of this Act operate to convey, with the manor, all pastures, feedings, wastes, warrens, commons, mines, minerals, quarries, furzes, trees, woods, underwoods, coppices, and the ground and soil thereof, fishings, fisheries, fowlings, courts leet, courts baron, and other courts, view of frankpledge and all that to view of frankpledge doth belong, mills, mulctures, customs, tolls, duties, reliefs, heriots, fines, sums of money, amerciaments, waifs, estrays, chief-rents, quitrents, rentscharge, rents seck, rents of assize, fee farm rents, services, royalties jurisdictions, franchises, liberties, privileges, easements, profits, advantages, rights, emoluments, and hereditaments whatsoever, to the manor appertaining or reputed to appertain, or, at the time of conveyance, demised, occupied, or enjoyed with the same, or reputed or known as part, parcel, or member thereof.

For the purposes of this subsection the right to compensation for manorial incidents on the extinguishment thereof shall be deemed to be a right appertaining to the manor.

(4) This section applies only if and as far as a contrary intention is not expressed in the conveyance, and has effect subject to the terms of the conveyance and to the provisions therein contained.

(5) This section shall not be construed as giving to any person a better title to any property, right, or thing in this section mentioned than the title which the conveyance gives to him to the land or manor expressed to be conveyed, or as conveying to him any property, right, or thing in this section mentioned, further or otherwise than as the same could have been conveyed to him by the conveying parties.

(6) This section applies to conveyances made after the thirty-first day of December, eighteen hundred and eighty-one.

63. All estate clause implied

(1) Every conveyance is effectual to pass all the estate, right, title, interest, claim, and demand which the conveying parties respectively have, in, to, or on the property conveyed, or expressed or intended so to be, or which they respectively have power to convey in, to, or on the same.

(2) This section applies only if and as far as a contrary intention is not expressed in the conveyance, and has effect subject to the terms of the conveyance and to the provisions therein contained.

(3) This section applies to conveyances made after the thirty-first day of December, eighteen hundred and eighty-one.

64. Production and safe custody of documents

(1) Where a person retains possession of documents, and gives to another an acknowledgment in writing of the right of that other to production of those documents, and to delivery of copies thereof (in this section called an acknowledgment), that acknowledgment shall have effect as in this section provided.

(2) An acknowledgment shall bind the documents to which it relates in the possession or under the control of the person who retains them, and in the possession or under the control of every other person having possession or control thereof from time to time, but shall bind each individual possessor or person as long only as he has possession or control thereof; and every person so having possession or control from time to time shall be bound specifically to perform the obligations imposed under this section by an acknowledgment, unless prevented from so doing by fire or other inevitable accident.

(3) The obligations imposed under this section by an acknowledgment are to be performed from time to time at the request in writing of the person to whom an acknowledgment is given, or of any person, not being a lessee at a rent, having or claiming any estate, interest, or right through or under that person, or otherwise becoming through or under that person interested in or affected by the terms of any document to which the acknowledgment relates.

(4) The obligations imposed under this section by an acknowledgment are—

(i) An obligation to produce the documents or any of them at all reasonable times for the purpose of inspection, and of comparison with abstracts or copies thereof, by the person entitled to request production or by any person by him authorised in writing; and

(ii) An obligation to produce the documents or any of them at any trial, hearing, or examination in any court, or in the execution of any commission, or elsewhere in the United Kingdom, on any occasion on which production may properly be required, for proving or supporting the title or claim of the person entitled to request production, or for any other purpose relative to that title or claim; and

(iii) An obligation to deliver to the person entitled to request the same true copies or extracts, attested or unattested, of or from the documents or any of them.

(5) All costs and expenses of or incidental to the specific performance of any obligation imposed under this section by an acknowledgment shall be paid by the person requesting performance.

(6) An acknowledgment shall not confer any right to damages for loss or destruction of, or injury to, the documents to which it relates, from whatever cause arising.

(7) Any person claiming to be entitled to the benefit of an acknowledgment may apply to the court for an order directing the production of the documents to which it relates, or any of them, or the delivery of copies of or extracts from those documents or any of them to him, or some person on his behalf; and the court may, if it thinks fit, order production, or production and delivery, accordingly, and may give directions respecting the time, place, terms, and mode of production or delivery, and may make such order as it thinks fit respecting the costs of the application, or any other matter connected with the application.

(8) An acknowledgment shall by virtue of this Act satisfy any liability to give a covenant for production and delivery of copies of or extracts from documents.

(9) Where a person retains possession of documents and gives to another an undertaking in writing for safe custody thereof, that undertaking shall impose on the person giving it, and on every person having possession or control of the documents from time to time, but on each individual possessor or person as long only as he has possession or control thereof, an obligation to keep the documents safe, whole, uncancelled, and undefaced, unless prevented from so doing by fire or other inevitable accident.

(10) Any person claiming to be entitled to the benefit of such an undertaking may apply to the court to assess damages for any loss or destruction of, or injury to, the documents or any of them, and the court may, if it thinks fit, direct an inquiry respecting the amount of damages, and order payment thereof by the person liable, and may make such order as it thinks fit respecting the costs of the application, or any other matter connected with the application.

(11) An undertaking for safe custody of documents shall by virtue of this Act satisfy any liability to give a covenant for safe custody of documents.

(12) The rights conferred by an acknowledgment or an undertaking under this section shall be in addition to all such other rights relative to the production, or inspection, or the obtaining of copies of documents, as are not, by virtue of this Act, satisfied by the giving of the acknowledgment or undertaking, and shall have effect subject to the terms of the acknowledgment or undertaking, and to any provisions therein contained.

(13) This section applies only if and as far as a contrary intention is not expressed in the acknowledgment or undertaking.

(14) This section applies to an acknowledgment or undertaking given, or a liability respecting documents incurred, after the thirty-first day of December, eighteen hundred and eighty-one.

65. Reservation of legal estates

(1) A reservation of a legal estate shall operate at law without any execution of the conveyance by the grantee of the legal estate out of which the reservation is made, or any regrant by him, so as to create the legal estate reserved, and so as to vest the same in possession in the person (whether being the grantor or not) for whose benefit the reservation is made.

(2) A conveyance of a legal estate expressed to be made subject to another legal estate not in existence immediately before the date of the conveyance, shall operate as a reservation, unless a contrary intention appears.

(3) This section applies only to reservations made after the commencement of this Act.

66. Confirmation of past transactions

(1) A deed containing a declaration by the estate owner that his estate shall go and devolve in such a manner as may be requisite for confirming any interests intended to affect his estate and capable under this Act of subsisting as legal estates which, at some prior date, were expressed to have been transferred or created, and any dealings therewith which would have been legal if those interests had been legally and validly transferred or created, shall, to the extent of the estate of the estate owner, but without prejudice to the restrictions imposed by this Act in the case of mortgages, operate to give legal effect to the interests so expressed to have been transferred or created and to the subsequent dealings aforesaid.

(2) The powers conferred by this section may be exercised by a tenant for life or statutory owner, [trustee of land] or a personal representative (being in each case an estate owner) as well as by an absolute owner, but if exercised by any person, other than an absolute owner, only with the leave of the court.

(3) This section applies only to deeds containing such a declaration as aforesaid if executed after the commencement of this Act.

[(4) The county court has jurisdiction under this section where the land which is to be dealt with in the court does not exceed [£30,000] in capital value [. . .].]

67. Receipt in deed sufficient

(1) A receipt for consideration money or securities in the body of a deed shall be a sufficient discharge for the same to the person paying or delivering the same, without any further receipt for the same being indorsed on the deed.

(2) This section applies to deeds executed after the thirty-first day of December, eighteen hundred and eighty-one.

68. Receipt in deed or indorsed evidence

(1) A receipt for consideration money or other consideration in the body of a deed or indorsed thereon shall, in favour of a subsequent purchaser, not having notice that the money or other consideration thereby acknowledged to be received was not in fact paid or given, wholly or in part, be sufficient evidence of the payment or giving of the whole amount thereof.

(2) This section applies to deeds executed after the thirty-first day of December, eighteen hundred and eighty-one.

69. Receipt in deed or indorsed authority for payment to solicitor

(1) Where a solicitor produces a deed, having in the body thereof or indorsed thereon a receipt for consideration money or other consideration, the deed being

executed, or the indorsed receipt being signed, by the person entitled to give a receipt for that consideration, the deed shall be a sufficient authority to the person liable to pay or give the same for his paying or giving the same to the solicitor, without the solicitor producing any separate or other direction or authority in that behalf from the person who executed or signed the deed or receipt.

(2) This section applies whether the consideration was paid or given before or after the commencement of this Act.

70. Partial release of security from rentcharge

(1) A release from a rentcharge of part of the land charged therewith does not extinguish the whole rentcharge, but operates only to bar the right to recover any part of the rentcharge out of the land released, without prejudice to the rights of any persons interested in the land remaining unreleased, and not concurring in or confirming the release.

(2) This section applies to releases made after the twelfth day of August, eighteen hundred and fifty-nine.

71. Release of part of land affected from a judgment

(1) A release from a judgment (including any writ or order imposing a charge) or part of any land charged therewith does not affect the validity of the judgment as respects any land not specifically released.

(2) This section operates without prejudice to the rights of any persons interested in the property remaining unreleased and not concurring in or confirming the release.

(3) This section applies to releases made after the twelfth day of August, eighteen hundred and fifty-nine.

72. Conveyances by a person to himself, etc.

(1) In conveyances made after the twelfth day of August, eighteen hundred and fifty-nine, personal property, including chattels real, may be conveyed by a person to himself jointly with another person by the like means by which it might be conveyed by him to another person.

(2) In conveyances made after the thirty-first day of December, eighteen hundred and eighty-one, freehold land, or a thing in action, may be conveyed by a person to himself jointly with another person, by the like means by which it might be conveyed by him to another person; and may, in like manner, be conveyed by a husband to his wife, and by a wife to her husband, alone or jointly with another person.

(3) After the commencement of this Act a person may convey land to or vest land in himself.

(4) Two or more persons (whether or not being trustees or personal representatives) may convey, and shall be deemed always to have been capable of conveying, any property vested in them to any one or more of themselves in like manner as they could have conveyed such property to a third party; provided that if the persons in whose favour the conveyance is made are, by reason of any fiduciary relationship or otherwise, precluded from validly carrying out the transaction, the conveyance shall be liable to be set aside.

[73. Execution of deeds by an individual

Repealed by the Law of Property (Miscellaneous Provisions) Act 1989, section 4.]

74. Execution of instruments by or on behalf of corporations

(1) In favour of a purchaser a deed shall be deemed to have been duly executed by a corporation aggregate if its seal be affixed thereto in the presence of and attested by its clerk, secretary or other permanent officer or his deputy, and a member of the board of directors, council or other governing body of the corporation, and where a seal purporting to be the seal of a corporation has been affixed to a deed, attested by persons

purporting to be persons holding such offices as aforesaid, the deed shall be deemed to have been executed in accordance with the requirements of this section, and to have taken effect accordingly.

(2) The board of directors, council or other governing body of a corporation aggregate may, by resolution or otherwise, appoint an agent either generally or in any particular case, to execute on behalf of the corporation any agreement or other instrument [which is not a deed] in relation to any matter within the powers of the corporation.

(3) Where a person is authorised under a power of attorney or under any statutory or other power to convey any interest in property in the name or on behalf of a corporation sole or aggregate, he may as attorney execute the conveyance by signing the name of the corporation in the presence of at least one witness, [. . .] and such execution shall take effect and be valid in like manner as if the corporation had executed the conveyance.

(4) Where a corporation aggregate is authorised under a power of attorney or under any statutory or other power to convey any interest in property in the name or on behalf of any other person (including another corporation), an officer appointed for that purpose by the board of directors, council or other governing body of the corporation by resolution or otherwise, may execute the deed or other instrument in the name of such other person; and where an instrument appears to be executed by an officer so appointed, then in favour of a purchaser the instrument shall be deemed to have been executed by an officer duly authorised.

(5) The foregoing provisions of this section apply to transactions wherever effected, but only to deeds and instruments executed after the commencement of this Act, except that, in the case of powers or appointments of an agent or officer, they apply whether the power was conferred or the appointment was made before or after the commencement of this Act or by this Act.

(6) Notwithstanding anything contained in this section, any mode of execution or attestation authorised by law or by practice or by the statute, charter, memorandum or articles, deed of settlement or other instrument constituting the corporation or regulating the affairs thereof, shall (in addition to the modes authorised by this section) be as effectual as if this section had not been passed.

75. Rights of purchaser as to execution

(1) On a sale, the purchaser shall not be entitled to require that the conveyance to him be executed in his presence, or in that of his solicitor, as such; but shall be entitled to have, at his own cost, the execution of the conveyance attested by some person appointed by him, who may, if he thinks fit, be his solicitor.

(2) This section applies to sales made after the thirty-first day of December, eighteen hundred and eighty-one.

Covenants

76. Covenants for title

(1) In a conveyance there shall, in the several cases in this section mentioned, be deemed to be included, and there shall in those several cases, by virtue of this Act, be implied, a covenant to the effect in this section stated, by the person or by each person who conveys, as far as regards the subject-matter or share of subject-matter expressed to be conveyed by him, with the person, if one, to whom the conveyance is made, or with the persons jointly, if more than one, to whom the conveyance is made as joint tenants, or with each of the persons, if more than one, to whom the conveyance is (when the law permits) made as tenants in common, that is to say:

(A) In a conveyance for valuable consideration, other than a mortgage, a covenant by a person who conveys and is expressed to convey as beneficial owner in the terms set out in Part I. of the Second Schedule to this Act;

(B) In a conveyance of leasehold property for valuable consideration, other than a mortgage, a further covenant by a person who conveys and is expressed to convey as beneficial owner in the terms set out in Part II. of the Second Schedule to this Act;

(C) In a conveyance by way of mortgage (including a charge) a covenant by a person who conveys or charges and is expressed to convey or charge as beneficial owner in the terms set out in Part III. of the Second Schedule to this Act;

(D) In a conveyance by way of mortgage (including a charge) of freehold property subject to a rent or of leasehold property, a further covenant by a person who conveys or charges and is expressed to convey or charge as beneficial owner in the terms set out in Part IV. of the Second Schedule to this Act;

(E) In a conveyance by way of settlement, a covenant by a person who conveys and is expressed to convey as settlor in the terms set out in Part V. of the Second Schedule to this Act;

(F) In any conveyance, a covenant by every person who conveys and is expressed to convey as trustee or mortgagee, or as personal representative of a deceased person, [. . .] or under an order of the court, in the terms set out in Part VI. of the Second Schedule to this Act, which covenant shall be deemed to extend to every such person's own acts only, and may be implied in an assent by a personal representative in like manner as in a conveyance by deed.

(2) Where in a conveyance it is expressed that by direction of a person expressed to direct as beneficial owner another person conveys, then, for the purposes of this section, the person giving the direction, whether he conveys and is expressed to convey as beneficial owner or not, shall be deemed to convey and to be expressed to convey as beneficial owner the subject-matter so conveyed by his direction; and a covenant on his part shall be implied accordingly.

(3) Where a wife conveys and is expressed to convey as beneficial owner, and the husband also conveys and is expressed to convey as beneficial owner, then, for the purposes of this section, the wife shall be deemed to convey and to be expressed to convey by direction of the husband, as beneficial owner; and, in addition to the covenant implied on the part of the wife, there shall also be implied, first, a covenant on the part of the husband as the person giving that direction, and secondly, a covenant on the part of the husband in the same terms as the covenant implied on the part of the wife.

(4) Where in a conveyance a person conveying is not expressed to convey as beneficial owner, or as settlor, or as trustee, or as mortgagee, or as personal representative of a deceased person, [. . .] or under an order of the court, or by direction of a person as beneficial owner, no covenant on the part of the person conveying shall be, by virtue of this section, implied in the conveyance.

(5) In this section a conveyance does not include a demise by way of lease at a rent, but does include a charge and 'convey' has a corresponding meaning.

(6) The benefit of a covenant implied as aforesaid shall be annexed and incident to, and shall go with, the estate or interest of the implied covenantee, and shall be capable of being enforced by every person in whom that estate or interest is, for the whole or any part thereof, from time to time vested.

(7) A covenant implied as aforesaid may be varied or extended by a deed or an assent, and, as so varied or extended, shall, as far as may be, operate in the like manner, and with all the like incidents, effects, and consequences, as if such variations or extensions were directed in this section to be implied.

(8) This section applies to conveyances made after the thirty-first day of December, eighteen hundred and eighty-one, but only to assents by a personal representative made after the commencement of this Act.

Note: See section 10, Law of Property (Miscellaneous Provisions) Act 1994.

77. Implied covenants in conveyances subject to rents

(1) In addition to the covenants implied under [Part I of the Law of Property (Miscellaneous Provisions) Act 1994], there shall in the several cases in this section mentioned, be deemed to be included and implied, a covenant to the effect in this section stated, by and with such persons as are hereinafter mentioned, that is to say:—

(A) In a conveyance for valuable consideration, other than a mortgage, of the entirety of the land affected by a rentcharge, a covenant by the grantee or joint and several covenants by the grantees, if more than one, with the conveying parties and with each of them, if more than one, in the terms set out in Part VII. of the Second Schedule to this Act. Where a rentcharge has been apportioned in respect of any land, with the consent of the owner of the rentcharge, the covenants in this paragraph shall be implied in the conveyance of that land in like manner as if the apportioned rentcharge were the rentcharge referred to, and the document creating the rentcharge related solely to that land:

(B) In a conveyance for valuable consideration, other than a mortgage, of part of land affected by a rentcharge, subject to a part of that rentcharge which has been or is by that conveyance apportioned (but in either case without the consent of the owner of the rentcharge) in respect of the land conveyed:—

(i) A covenant by the grantee of the land or joint and several covenants by the grantees, if more than one, with the conveying parties and with each of them, if more than one, in the terms set out in paragraph (i) of Part VIII. of the Second Schedule to this Act;

(ii) A covenant by a person who conveys or is expressed to convey as beneficial owner, or joint and several covenants by the persons who so convey or are expressed to so convey, if at the date of the conveyance any part of the land affected by such rentcharge is retained, with the grantees of the land and with each of them (if more than one) in the terms set out in paragraph (ii) of Part VIII. of the Second Schedule to this Act:

(C) In a conveyance for valuable consideration, other than a mortgage, of the entirety of the land comprised in a lease, for the residue of the term or interest created by the lease, a covenant by the assignee or joint and several covenants by the assignees (if more than one) with the conveying parties and with each of them (if more than one) in the terms set out in Part IX. of the Second Schedule to this Act. Where a rent has been apportioned in respect of any land, with the consent of the lessor, the covenants in this paragraph shall be implied in the conveyance of that land in like manner as if the apportioned rent were the original rent reserved, and the lease related solely to that land:

(D) In a conveyance for valuable consideration, other than a mortgage, of part of the land comprised in a lease, for the residue of the term or interest created by the lease, subject to a part of the rent which has been or is by the conveyance apportioned (but in either case without the consent of the lessor) in respect of the land conveyed:—

Note: The subsections in italics apply to tenancies created before the Landlord and Tenant (Covenants) Act 1995 came into force.

(i) A covenant by the assignee of the land, or joint and several covenants by the assignees, if more than one, with the conveying parties and with each of them, if more than one, in the terms set out in paragraph (i) of Part X. of the Second Schedule to this Act;

(ii) A covenant by a person who conveys or is expressed to convey as beneficial owner, or joint and several covenants by the persons who so convey or are expressed to so convey, if at the date of the conveyance any part of the land comprised in the lease is retained, with the assignees of the land and with each of them (if more than one) in the terms set out in paragraph (ii) of Part X. of the Second Schedule to this Act.

(2) Where in a conveyance for valuable consideration, other than a mortgage, part of land affected by a rentcharge, or part of land comprised in a lease is, without the consent of the owner of the rentcharge or of the lessor, as the case may be, expressed to be conveyed—

(i) subject to or charged with the entire rent — then paragraph (B)(i) or (D)(i) of the last subsection, as the case may require, shall have effect as if the entire rent were the apportioned rent; or

(ii) discharged or exonerated from the entire rent — then paragraph (B)(ii) or (D)(ii) of the last subsection, as the case may require, shall have effect as if the entire rent were the balance of the rent, and the words 'other than the covenant to pay the entire rent' had been omitted.

Note: The subsection in italics applies to tenancies created before the Landlord and Tenant (Covenants) Act 1995 came into force.

[(2) Where in a conveyance for valuable consideration, other than a mortgage, part of land affected by a rentcharge is, without the consent of the owner of the rentcharge, expressed to be conveyed subject to or charged with the entire rent, paragraph (B)(i) of subsection (1) of this section shall apply as if, in paragraph (i) of Part VII of the Second Schedule to this Act—

(a) any reference to the apportioned rent were to the entire rent; and

(b) the words '(other than the covenant to pay the entire rent)' were omitted.

(2A) Where in a conveyance for valuable consideration, other than a mortgage, part of land affected by a rentcharge is, without the consent of the owner of the rentcharge, expressed to be conveyed discharged or exonerated from the entire rent, paragraph (B)(ii) of subsection (1) of this section shall apply as if, in paragraph (ii) of Part VIII of the Second Schedule to this Act—

(a) any reference to the balance of the rent were to the entire rent; and

(b) the words ', other than the covenant to pay the entire rent,' were omitted.]

(3) In this section 'conveyance' does not include a demise by way of lease at a rent.

(4) Any convenant which would be implied under this section by reason of a person conveying or being expressed to convey as beneficial owner may, by express reference to this section, be implied, with or without variation, in a conveyance, whether or not for valuable consideration, by a person who conveys or is expressed to convey as settlor, or as trustee, or as mortgagee, or as personal representative of a deceased person, or under an order of the court.

(5) The benefit of a covenant implied as aforesaid shall be annexed and incident to, and shall go with, the estate or interest of the implied covenantee, and shall be capable of being enforced by every person in whom that estate or interest is, for the whole or any part thereof, from time to time vested.

(6) A covenant implied as aforesaid may be varied or extended by deed, and, as so varied or extended, shall, as far as may be, operate in the like manner, and with all the like incidents, effects and consequences, as if such variations or extensions were directed in this section to be implied.

(7) In particular any covenant implied under this section may be extended by providing that—

(a) the land conveyed; or

(b) the part of the land affected by the rentcharge which remains vested in the covenantor; or

(c) the part of the land demised which remains vested in the covenantor; shall, as the case may require, stand charged with the payment of all money which may become payable under the implied covenant.

Note: The subsection in italics applies to tenancies created before the Landlord and Tenant (Covenants) Act 1995 came into force.

(8) This section applies only to conveyances made after the commencement of this Act.

78. Benefit of covenants relating to land

(1) A covenant relating to any land of the covenantee shall be deemed to be made with the covenantee and his successors in title and the persons deriving title under him or them, and shall have effect as if such successors and other persons were expressed.

For the purposes of this subsection in connexion with covenants restrictive of the user of land 'successors in title' shall be deemed to include the owners and occupiers for the time being of the land of the covenantee intended to be benefited.

(2) This section applies to covenants made after the commencement of this Act, but the repeal of section fifty-eight of the Conveyancing Act, 1881, does not affect the operation of covenants to which that section applied.

79. Burden of covenants relating to land

(1) A covenant relating to any land of a covenantor or capable of being bound by him, shall, unless a contrary intention is expressed, be deemed to be made by the covenantor on behalf of himself his successors in title and the persons deriving title under him or them, and, subject as aforesaid, shall have effect as if such successors and other persons were expressed.

This subsection extends to a covenant to do some act relating to the land, notwithstanding that the subject-matter may not be in existence when the covenant is made.

(2) For the purposes of this section in connexion with covenants restrictive of the user of land 'successors in title' shall be deemed to include the owners and occupiers for the time being of such land.

(3) This section applies only to covenants made after the commencement of this Act.

Note: Does not apply to tenancies created after the Landlord and Tenant (Covenants) Act 1995 comes into force.

80. Covenants binding land

(1) A covenant and a bond and an obligation or contract [made under seal after 31st December 1881 but before the coming into force of section 1 of the Law of Property (Miscellaneous Provisions) Act 1989 or executed as a deed in accordance with that section after its coming into force] binds the real estate as well as the personal estate of the person making the same if and so far as a contrary intention is not expressed in the covenant, bond, obligation, or contract.

This subsection extends to a covenant implied by virtue of this Act.

(2) Every covenant running with the land, whether entered into before or after the commencement of this Act, shall take effect in accordance with any statutory enactment affecting the devolution of the land, and accordingly the benefit or burden of every such covenant shall vest in or bind the persons who by virtue of any such enactment or otherwise succeed to the title of the covenantee or the covenantor, as the case may be.

(3) The benefit of a covenant relating to land entered into after the commencement of this Act may be made to run with the land without the use of any technical expression if the covenant is of such a nature that the benefit could have been made to run with the land before the commencement of this Act.

(4) For the purposes of this section, a covenant runs with the land when the benefit or burden of it, whether at law or in equity, passes to the successors in title of the covenantee or the covenantor, as the case may be.

81. Effect of covenant with two or more jointly

(1) A covenant, and a contract under seal, and a bond or obligation under seal, made with two or more jointly, to pay money or to make a conveyance, or to do any other act, to them or for their benefit, shall be deemed to include, and shall, by virtue of this Act, imply, an obligation to do the act to, or for the benefit of, the survivor or survivors of them, and to, or for the benefit of, any other person to whom the right to sue on the covenant, contract, bond, or obligation devolves, and where made after the commencement of this Act shall be construed as being also made with each of them.

(2) This section extends to a covenant implied by virtue of this Act.

(3) This section applies only if and as far as a contrary intention is not expressed in the covenant, contract, bond, or obligation, and has effect subject to the covenant, contract, bond, or obligation, and to the provisions therein contained.

(4) Except as otherwise expressly provided, this section applies to a covenant, contract, bond, or obligation made or implied after the thirty-first day of December, eighteen hundred and eighty-one.

[(5) In its application to instruments made after the coming into force of section 1 of the Law of Property (Miscellaneous Provisions) Act 1989 subsection (1) above shall have effect as if the words 'under seal, and a bond or obligation under seal,' there were substituted the words 'bond or obligation executed as a deed in accordance with section 1 of the Law of Property (Miscellaneous Provisions) Act 1989'.]

82. Covenants and agreements entered into by a person with himself and another or others

(1) Any covenant, whether express or implied, or agreement entered into by a person with himself and one or more other persons shall be construed and be capable of being enforced in like manner as if the covenant or agreement had been entered into with the other person or persons alone.

(2) This section applies to covenants or agreements entered into before or after the commencement of this Act, and to covenants implied by statute in the case of a person who conveys or is expressed to convey to himself and one or more other persons, but without prejudice to any order of the court made before such commencement.

83. Construction of implied covenants

In the construction of a covenant or proviso, or other provision, implied in a deed or assent by virtue of this Act, words importing the singular or plural number, or the masculine gender, shall be read as also importing the plural or singular number, or as extending to females, as the case may require.

84. Power to discharge or modify restrictive covenants affecting land

(1) [the Lands Tribunal] shall (without prejudice to any concurrent jurisdiction of the court) have power from time to time, on the application of any person interested in any freehold land affected by any restriction arising under covenant or otherwise as to the user thereof or the building thereon, by order wholly or partially to discharge or modify any such restriction [. . .] on being satisfied—

(a) that by reason of changes in the character of the property or the neighbourhood or other circumstances of the case which [the Lands Tribunal] may deem material, the restriction ought to be deemed obsolete, or

[(aa) that [in a case falling within subsection (lA) below] the continued existence thereof would impede [some reasonable user] of the land for public or private purposes [. . .] or, as the case may be, would unless modified so impede such user; or]

(b) that the persons of full age and capacity for the time being or from time to time entitled to the benefit of the restriction, whether in respect of estates in fee simple or any lesser estates or interests in the property to which the benefit of the restriction is annexed, have agreed, either expressly or by implication, by their acts or omissions, to the same being discharged or modified; or

(c) that the proposed discharge or modification will not injure the persons entitled to the benefit of the restriction:

[and an order discharging or modifying a restriction under this subsection may direct the applicant to pay to any person entitled to the benefit of the restriction such sum by way of consideration as the Tribunal may think it just to award under one, but not both, of the following heads, that is to say, either—

(i) a sum to make up for any loss or disadvantage suffered by that person in consequence of the discharge or modification; or

(ii) a sum to make up for any effect which the restriction had, at the time when it was imposed, in reducing the consideration then received for the land affected by it.]

[(1A) Subsection (1) (aa) above authorises the discharge or modification of a restriction by reference to its impeding some reasonable user of land in any case in which the Lands Tribunal is satisfied that the restriction, in impeding that user, either—

(a) does not secure to persons entitled to the benefit of it any practical benefits of substantial value or advantage to them; or

(b) is contrary to the public interest;

and that money will be an adequate compensation for the loss or disadvantage (if any) which any such person will suffer from the discharge or modification.]

[(1B) In determining whether a case is one falling within subsection (1A) above, and in determining whether (in any such case or otherwise) a restriction ought to be discharged or modified, the Lands Tribunal shall take into account the development plan and any declared or ascertainable pattern for the grant or refusal of planning permissions in the relevant areas, as well as the period at which and context in which the restriction was created or imposed and any other material circumstances.]

[(1C) It is hereby declared that the power conferred by this section to modify a restriction includes power to add such further provisions restricting the user of or the building on the land affected as appear to the Lands Tribunal to be reasonable in view of the relaxation of the existing provisions, and as may be accepted by the applicant; and the Lands Tribunal may accordingly refuse to modify a restriction without some such addition.]

(2) The court shall have power on the application of any person interested—

(a) To declare whether or not in any particular case any freehold land is [or would in any given event be] affected by a restriction imposed by any instrument; or

(b) To declare what, upon the true construction of any instrument purporting to impose a restriction, is the nature and extent of the restriction thereby imposed and whether the same is [or would in any given event be] enforceable and if so by whom. [Neither subsections (7) and (11) of this section nor, unless the contrary is expressed, any later enactment providing for this section not to apply to any restrictions shall affect the operation of this subsection or the operation for purposes of this subsection of any other provisions of this section.]

(3) [The Lands Tribunal] shall, before making any order under this section, direct such enquiries, if any, to be made of any [government department or] local authority, and such notices, if any, whether by way of advertisement or otherwise, to be given to such of the persons who appear to be entitled to the benefit of the restriction intended to be discharged, modified, or dealt with as, having regard to any enquiries notices or other proceedings previously made, given or taken, [the Lands Tribunal] may think fit.

[(3A) On an application to the Lands Tribunal under this section the Lands Tribunal shall give any necessary directions as to the persons who are or are not to be admitted (as appearing to be entitled to the benefit of the restriction) to oppose the application, and no appeal shall lie against any such direction; but rules under the Lands Tribunal Act 1949 shall make provision whereby, in cases in which there arises on such an application (whether or not in connection with the admission of persons to oppose) any such question as is referred to in subsection (2)(a) or (b) of this section, the proceedings on the application can and, if the rules so provide, shall be suspended to enable the decision of the court to be obtained on that question by an application under that subsection, or by means of a case stated by the Lands Tribunal, or otherwise, as may be provided by those rules or by rules of court.]

(4) [. . .]

(5) Any order made under this section shall be binding on all persons, whether ascertained or of full age or capacity or not, then entitled or thereafter capable of becoming entitled to the benefit of any restriction, which is thereby discharged,

modified, or dealt with, and whether such persons are parties to the proceedings or have been served with notice or not [. . .]

(6) An order may be made under this section notwithstanding that any instrument which is alleged to impose the restriction intended to be discharged, modified, or dealt with, may not have been produced to the court or [the Lands Tribunal], and the court or [the Lands Tribunal] may act on such evidence of that instrument as it may think sufficient.

(7) This section applies to restrictions whether subsisting at the commencement of this Act or imposed thereafter, but this section does not apply where the restriction was imposed on the occasion of a disposition made gratuitously or for a nominal consideration for public purposes.

(8) This section applies whether the land affected by the restrictions is registered or not, but, in the case of registered land, the Land Registrar shall give effect on the register to any order under this section [in accordance with the Land Registration Act, 1925].

(9) Where any proceedings by action or otherwise are taken to enforce a restrictive covenant, any person against whom the proceedings are taken, may in such proceedings apply to the court for an order giving leave to apply to [the Lands Tribunal] under this section, and staying the proceedings in the meantime.

(10) [. . .]

(11) This section does not apply to restrictions imposed by the Commissioners of Works under any statutory power for the protection of any Royal Park or Garden or to restrictions of a like character imposed upon the occasion of any enfranchisement effected before the commencement of this Act in any manor vested in His Majesty in right of the Crown or the Duchy on Lancaster, nor [subject to subsection (11A) below] to restrictions created or imposed—

(a) for Naval, Military or Air Force purposes,

[(b) for civil aviation purposes under the powers of the Air Navigation Act, 1920 or of section 19 or 23 of the Civil Aviation Act 1949 or of sections 30 or 41 of the Civil Aviation Act 1982.]

[(11A) Subsection (11) of this section—

(a) shall exclude the application of this section to a restriction falling within subsection (11)(a), and not created or imposed in connection with the use of any land as an aerodrome, only so long as the restriction is enforceable by or on behalf of the Crown; and

(b) shall exclude the application of this section to a restriction falling within subsection (11)(b), or created or imposed in connection with the use of any land as an aerodrome, only so long as the restriction is enforceable by or on behalf of the Crown or any public or international authority.]

(12) Where a term of more than [forty] years is created in land (whether before or after the commencement of this Act) this section shall, after the expiration of [twenty-five] years of the term, apply to restrictions affecting such leasehold land in like manner as it would have applied had the land been freehold:

Providing that this subsection shall not apply to mining leases.

PART III
MORTGAGES, RENTCHARGES, AND POWERS OF ATTORNEY

85. Mode of mortgaging freeholds

(1) A mortgage of an estate in fee simple shall only be capable of being effected at law either by a demise for a term of years absolute, subject to a provision for cesser on redemption, or by a charge by deed expressed to be by way of legal mortgage:

Provided that a first mortgagee shall have the same right to the possession of documents as if his security included the fee simple.

(2) Any purported conveyance of an estate in fee simple by way of mortgage made after the commencement of this Act shall (to the extent of the estate of the mortgagor) operate as a demise of the land to the mortgagee for a term of years absolute, without impeachment for waste, but subject to cesser on redemption, in manner following, namely:—

(a) A first or only mortgagee shall take a term of three thousand years from the date of the mortgage:

(b) A second or subsequent mortgagee shall take a term (commencing from the date of the mortgage) one day longer than the term vested in the first or other mortgagee whose security ranks immediately before that of such second or subsequent mortgagee:

and, in this subsection, any such purported conveyance as aforesaid includes an absolute conveyance with a deed of defeasance and any other assurance which, but for this subsection, would operate in effect to vest the fee simple in a mortgagee subject to redemption.

(3) This section applies whether or not the land is registered under the Land Registration Act, 1925, or the mortgage is expressed to be made by way of trust for sale or otherwise.

(4) Without prejudice to the provisions of this Act respecting legal and equitable powers, every power to mortgage or to lend money on mortgage of an estate in fee simple shall be construed as a power to mortgage the estate for a term of years absolute, without impeachment for waste, or by a charge by way of legal mortgage or to lend on such security.

86. Mode of mortgaging leaseholds

(1) A mortgage of a term of years absolute shall only be capable of being effected at law either by a subdemise for a term of years absolute, less by one day at least than the term vested in the mortgagor, and subject to a provision for cesser on redemption, or by a charge by deed expressed to be by way of legal mortgage; and where a licence to subdemise by way of mortgage is required, such licence shall not be unreasonably refused:

Provided that a first mortgagee shall have the same right to the possession of documents as if his security had been effected by assignment.

(2) Any purported assignment of a term of years absolute by way of mortgage made after the commencement of this Act shall (to the extent of the estate of the mortgagor) operate as a subdemise of the leasehold land to the mortgagee for a term of years absolute, but subject to cesser on redemption, in manner following, namely:—

(a) The term to be taken by a first or only mortgagee shall be ten days less than the term expressed to be assigned:

(b) The term to be taken by a second or subsequent mortgagee shall be one day longer than the term vested in the first or other mortgagee whose security ranks immediately before that of the second or subsequent mortgagee, if the length of the last mentioned term permits, and in any case for a term less by one day at least than the term expressed to be assigned:

and, in this subsection, any such purported assignment as aforesaid includes an absolute assignment with a deed of defeasance and any other assurance which, but for this subsection, would operate in effect to vest the term of the mortgagor in a mortgagee subject to redemption.

(3) This section applies whether or not the land is registered under the Land Registration Act, 1925, or the mortgage is made by way of sub-mortgage of a term of years absolute, or is expressed to be by way of trust for sale or otherwise.

(4) Without prejudice to the provisions of this Act respecting legal and equitable powers, every power to mortgage for or to lend money on mortgage of a term of years absolute by way of assignment shall be construed as a power to mortgage the term by

subdemise for a term of years absolute or by a charge by way of legal mortgage, or to lend on such security.

87. Charges by way of legal mortgage

(1) Where a legal mortgage of land is created by a charge by deed expressed to be by way of legal mortgage, the mortgagee shall have the same protection, powers and remedies (including the right to take proceedings to obtain possession from the occupiers and the persons in receipt of rents and profits, or any of them) as if—

(a) where the mortgage is a mortgage of an estate in fee simple, a mortgage term for three thousand years without impeachment of waste had been thereby created in favour of the mortgagee; and

(b) where the mortgage is a mortgage of a term of years absolute, a sub-term less by one day than the term vested in the mortgagor had been thereby created in favour of the mortgagee.

(2) Where an estate vested in a mortgagee immediately before the commencement of this Act has by virtue of this Act been converted into a term of years absolute or sub-term, the mortgagee may, by a declaration in writing to that effect signed by him, convert the mortgage into a charge by way of legal mortgage, and in that case the mortgage term shall be extinguished in the inheritance or in the head term as the case may be, and the mortgagee shall have the same protection, powers and remedies (including the right to take proceedings to obtain possession from the occupiers and the persons in receipt of rents and profits or any of them) as if the mortgage term or sub-term had remained subsisting.

The power conferred by this subsection may be exercised by a mortgagee notwithstanding that he is a trustee or personal representative.

(3) Such declaration shall not affect the priority of the mortgagee or his right to retain possession of documents, nor affect his title to or right over any fixtures or chattels personal comprised in the mortgage.

88. Realisation of freehold mortgages

(1) Where an estate in fee simple has been mortgaged by the creation of a term of years absolute limited thereout or by a charge by way of legal mortgage and the mortgagee sells under his statutory or express power of sale—

(a) the conveyance by him shall operate to vest in the purchaser the fee simple in the land conveyed subject to any legal mortgage having priority to the mortgage in right of which the sale is made and to any money thereby secured, and thereupon;

(b) the mortgage term or the charge by way of legal mortgage and any subsequent mortgage term or charges shall merge or be extinguished as respects the land conveyed; and such conveyance may, as respects the fee simple, be made in the name of the estate owner in whom it is vested.

(2) Where any such mortgagee obtains an order for foreclosure absolute, the order shall operate to vest the fee simple in him (subject to any legal mortgage having priority to the mortgage in right of which the foreclosure is obtained and to any money thereby secured), and thereupon the mortgage term, if any, shall thereby be merged in the fee simple, and any subsequent mortgage term or charge by way of legal mortgage bound by the order shall thereupon be extinguished.

(3) Where any such mortgagee acquires a title under the Limitation Acts, he, or the persons deriving title under him, may enlarge the mortgage term into a fee simple under the statutory power for that purpose discharged from any legal mortgage affected by the title so acquired, or in the case of a chargee by way of legal mortgage may by deed declare that the fee simple is vested in him discharged as aforesaid, and the same shall vest accordingly.

(4) Where the mortgage includes fixtures or chattels personal any statutory power of sale and any right to foreclose or take possession shall extend to the absolute or other interest therein affected by the charge.

(5) In the case of a sub-mortgage by subdemise of a long term (less a nominal period) itself limited out of an estate in fee simple, the foregoing provisions of this section shall operate as if the derivative term, if any, created by the sub-mortgage had been limited out of the fee simple, and so as to enlarge the principal term and extinguish the derivative term created by the sub-mortgage as aforesaid, and to enable the sub-mortgagee to convey the fee simple or acquire it by foreclosure, enlargement, or otherwise as aforesaid.

(6) This section applies to a mortgage whether created before or after the commencement of this Act, and to a mortgage term created by this Act, but does not operate to confer a better title to the fee simple than would have been acquired if the same had been conveyed by the mortgage (being a valid mortgage) and the restrictions imposed by this Act in regard to the effect and creation of mortgages were not in force, and all prior mortgages (if any) not being merely equitable charges had been created by demise or by charge by way of legal mortgage.

89. Realisation of leasehold mortgages

(1) Where a term of years absolute has been mortgaged by the creation of another term of years absolute limited thereout or by a charge by way of legal mortgage and the mortgagee sells under his statutory or express power of sale,—

(a) the conveyance by him shall operate to convey to the purchaser not only the mortgage term, if any, but also (unless expressly excepted with the leave of the court) the leasehold reversion affected by the mortgage, subject to any legal mortgage having priority to the mortgage in right of which the sale is made and to any money thereby secured, and thereupon

(b) the mortgage term, or the charge by way of legal mortgage and any subsequent mortgage term or charge, shall merge in such leasehold reversion or be extinguished unless excepted as aforesaid;

and such conveyance may, as respects the leasehold reversion, be made in the name of the estate owner in whom it is vested.

Where a licence to assign is required on a sale by a mortgagee, such licence shall not be unreasonably refused.

(2) Where any such mortgagee obtains an order for foreclosure absolute, the order shall, unless it otherwise provides, operate (without giving rise to a forfeiture for want of a licence to assign) to vest the leasehold reversion affected by the mortgage and any subsequent mortgage term in him, subject to any legal mortgage having priority to the mortgage in right of which the foreclosure is obtained and to any money thereby secured, and thereupon the mortgage term and any subsequent mortgage term or charge by way of legal mortgage bound by the order shall, subject to any express provision to the contrary contained in the order, merge in such leasehold reversion or be extinguished.

(3) Where any such mortgagee acquires a title under the Limitation Acts, he, or the persons deriving title under him, may by deed declare that the leasehold reversion affected by the mortgage and any mortgage term affected by the title so acquired shall vest in him, free from any right of redemption which is barred, and the same shall (without giving rise to a forfeiture for want of a licence to assign) vest accordingly, and thereupon the mortgage term, if any, and any other mortgage term or charge by way of legal mortgage affected by the title so acquired shall, subject to any express provision to the contrary contained in the deed, merge in such leasehold reversion or be extinguished.

(4) Where the mortgage includes fixtures or chattels personal, any statutory power of sale and any right to foreclose or take possession shall extend to the absolute or other interest therein affected by the charge.

(5) In the case of a sub-mortgage by subdemise of a term (less a nominal period) itself limited out of a leasehold reversion, the foregoing provisions of this section shall

operate as if the derivative term created by the sub-mortgage had been limited out of the leasehold reversion, and so as (subject as aforesaid) to merge the principal mortgage term therein as well as the derivative term created by the sub-mortgage and to enable the sub-mortgagee to convey the leasehold reversion or acquire it by foreclosure, vesting, or otherwise as aforesaid.

(6) This section takes effect without prejudice to any incumbrance or trust affecting the leasehold reversion which has priority over the mortgage in right of which the sale, foreclosure, or title is made or acquired, and applies to a mortgage whether executed before or after the commencement of this Act, and to a mortgage term created by this Act, but does not apply where the mortgage term does not comprise the whole of the land included in the leasehold reversion unless the rent (if any) payable in respect of that reversion has been apportioned as respects the land affected, or the rent is of no money value or no rent is reserved, and unless the lessee's covenants and conditions (if any) have been apportioned, either expressly or by implication, as respects the land affected.

[In this subsection references to an apportionment include an equitable apportionment made without the consent of the lessor.]

[(7) The county court has jurisdiction under this section where the amount owing in respect of the mortgage or charge at the commencement of the proceedings does not exceed [£30,000].]

90. Realisation of equitable charges by the court

(1) Where an order for sale is made by the court in reference to an equitable mortgage on land (not secured by a legal term of years absolute or by a charge by way of legal mortgage) the court may, in favour of a purchaser, make a vesting order conveying the land or may appoint a person to convey the land or create and vest in the mortgagee a legal term of years absolute to enable him to carry out the sale, as the case may require, in like manner as if the mortgage had been created by deed by way of legal mortgage pursuant to this Act, but without prejudice to any incumbrance having priority to the equitable mortgage unless the incumbrancer consents to the sale.

(2) This section applies to equitable mortgages made or arising before or after the commencement of this Act, but not to a mortgage which has been overreached under the powers conferred by this Act or otherwise.

91. Sale of mortgaged property in action for redemption or foreclosure

(1) Any person entitled to redeem mortgaged property may have a judgment or order for sale instead of for redemption in an action brought by him either for redemption alone, or for sale alone, or for sale or redemption in the alternative.

(2) In any action, whether for foreclosure, or for redemption, or for sale, or for the raising and payment in any manner of mortgage money, the court, on the request of the mortgagee, or of any person interested either in the mortgage money or in the right of redemption, and, notwithstanding that—

(a) any other person dissents; or

(b) the mortgagee or any person so interested does not appear in the action;

and without allowing any time for redemption or for payment of any mortgage money, may direct a sale of the mortgaged property, on such terms as it thinks fit, including the deposit in court of a reasonable sum fixed by the court to meet the expenses of sale and to secure performance of the terms.

(3) But, in an action brought by a person interested in the right of redemption and seeking a sale, the court may, on the application of any defendant, direct the plaintiff to give such security for costs as the court thinks fit, and may give the conduct of the sale to any defendant, and may give such directions as it thinks fit respecting the costs of the defendants or any of them.

(4) In any case within this section the court may, if it thinks fit, direct a sale without previously determining the priorities of incumbrancers.

(5) This section applies to actions brought either before or after the commencement of this Act.

(6) In this section 'mortgaged property' includes the estate or interest which a mortgagee would have had power to convey if the statutory power of sale were applicable.

(7) For the purposes of this section the court may, in favour of a purchaser, make a vesting order conveying the mortgaged property, or appoint a person to do so, subject or not to any incumbrance, as the court may think fit; or, in the case of an equitable mortgage, may create and vest a mortgage term in the mortgagee to enable him to carry out the sale as if the mortgage had been made by deed by way of legal mortgage.

[(8) The county court has jurisdiction under this section where the amount owing in respect of the mortgage or charge at the commencement of the proceedings does not exceed [£30,000].]

92. Power to authorise land and minerals to be dealt with separately

(1) Where a mortgagee's power of sale in regard to land has become exercisable but does not extend to the purposes mentioned in this section, the court may, on his application, authorise him and the persons deriving title under him to dispose—

(a) of the land, with an exception or reservation of all or any mines and minerals, and with or without rights and powers of or incidental to the working, getting or carrying away of minerals; or

(b) of all or any mines and minerals, with or without the said rights or powers separately from the land;

and thenceforth the powers so conferred shall have effect as if the same were contained in the mortgage.

[(2) The county court has jurisdiction under this section where the amount owing in respect of the mortgage or charge at the commencement of the proceedings does not exceed [£30,000].]

93. Restriction on consolidation of mortgages

(1) A mortgagor seeking to redeem any one mortgage is entitled to do so without paying any money due under any separate mortgage made by him, or by any person through whom he claims, solely on property other than that comprised in the mortgage which he seeks to redeem.

This subsection applies only if and as far as a contrary intention is not expressed in the mortgage deeds or one of them.

(2) This section does not apply where all the mortgages were made before the first day of January, eighteen hundred and eight-two.

(3) Save as aforesaid, nothing in this Act, in reference to mortgages, affects any right of consolidation or renders inoperative a stipulation in relation to any mortgage made before or after the commencement of this Act reserving a right to consolidate.

94. Tacking and further advances

(1) After the commencement of this Act, a prior mortgagee shall have a right to make further advances to rank in priority to subsequent mortgages (whether legal or equitable)—

(a) if an arrangement has been made to that effect with the subsequent mortgagees, or

(b) if he had no notice of such subsequent mortgages at the time when the further advance was made by him; or

(c) whether or not he had such notice as aforesaid, where the mortgage imposes an obligation on him to make such further advances.

This subsection applies whether or not the prior mortgage was made expressly for securing further advances.

(2) In relation to the making of further advances after the commencement of this Act a mortgagee shall not be deemed to have notice of a mortgage merely by reason that it was registered as a land charge [. . .], if it was not so registered at the [time when the original mortgage was created] or when the last search (if any) by or on behalf of the mortgagee was made, whichever last happened.

This subsection only applies where the prior mortgage was made expressly for securing a current account or other further advances.

(3) Save in regard to the making of further advances as aforesaid, the right to tack is hereby abolished:

Provided that nothing in this Act shall affect any priority acquired before the commencement of this Act by tacking, or in respect of further advances made without notice of a subsequent incumbrance or by arrangement with the subsequent incumbrancer.

(4) This section applies to mortgages of land made before or after the commencement of this Act, but not to charges registered under the Land Registration Act, 1925, or any enactment replaced by that Act.

95. Obligation to transfer instead of re-conveying, and as to right to take possession

(1) Where a mortgagor in entitled to redeem, then subject to compliance with the terms on compliance with which he would be entitled to require a reconveyance or surrender, he shall be entitled to require the mortgagee, instead of re-conveying or surrendering, to assign the mortgage debt and convey the mortgaged property to any third person, as the mortgagor directs; and the mortgagee shall be bound to assign and convey accordingly.

(2) The rights conferred by this section belong to and are capable of being enforced by each incumbrancer, or by the mortgagor, notwithstanding any intermediate incumbrance; but a requisition of an incumbrancer prevails over a requisition of the mortgagor, and, as between incumbrancers, a requisition of a prior incumbrancer prevails over a requisition of a subsequent incumbrancer.

(3) The foregoing provisions of this section do not apply in the case of a mortgagee being or having been in possession.

(4) Nothing in this Act affects prejudicially the right of a mortgagee of land whether or not his charge is secured by a legal term of years absolute to take possession of the land, but the taking of possession by the mortgagee does not convert any legal estate of the mortgagor into an equitable interest.

(5) This section applies to mortgages made either before or after the commencement of this Act, and takes effect notwithstanding any stipulation to the contrary.

96. Regulations respecting inspection, production and delivery of documents, and priorities

(1) A mortgagor, as long as his right to redeem subsists, shall be entitled from time to time, at reasonable times, on his request, and at his own cost, and on payment of the mortgagee's costs and expenses in this behalf, to inspect and make copies or abstracts of or extracts from the documents of title relating to the mortgaged property in the custody or power of the mortgagee.

This section applies to mortgages made after the thirty-first day of December, eighteen hundred and eighty-one, and takes effect notwithstanding any stipulation to the contrary.

(2) A mortgagee, whose mortgage is surrendered or otherwise extinguished, shall not be liable on account of delivering documents of title in his possession to the person not having the best right thereto, unless he has notice of the right or claim of a person having a better right, whether by virtue of a right to require a surrender or reconveyance or otherwise.

[In this sub-section notice does not include notice implied by reason of registration under the Land Charges Act, 1925, [. . .].]

97. Priorities as between puisne mortgages

Every mortgage affecting a legal estate in land made after the commencement of this Act, whether legal or equitable (not being a mortgage protected by the deposit of documents relating to the legal estate affected) shall rank according to its date of registration as a land charge pursuant to the Land Charges Act, 1925.

This subsection does not apply [to mortgages or charges to which the Land Charges Act [1972] does not apply by virtue of section [14(3)] of that Act (which excludes certain land charges created by instruments necessitating registration under the Land Registration Act 1925), or] to mortgages or charges of registered land [. . .].

98. Actions for possession by mortgagors

(1) A mortgagor for the time being entitled to the possession or receipt of the rents and profits of any land, as to which the mortgagee has not given notice of his intention to take possession or to enter into the receipt of the rents and profits thereof, may sue for such possession, or for the recovery of such rents or profits, or to prevent or recover damages in respect of any trespass or other wrong relative thereto, in his own name only, unless the cause of action arises upon a lease or other contract made by him jointly with any other person.

(2) This section does not prejudice the power of a mortgagor independently of this section to take proceedings in his own name only, either in right of any legal estate vested in him or otherwise.

(3) This section applies whether the mortgage was made before or after the commencement of this Act.

99. Leasing powers of mortgagor and mortgagee in possession

(1) A mortgagor of land while in possession shall, as against every incumbrancer, have power to make from time to time any such lease of the mortgaged land, or any part thereof, as is by this section authorised.

(2) A mortgagee of land while in possession shall, as against all prior incumbrancers, if any, and as against the mortgagor, have power to make from time to time any such lease as aforesaid.

(3) The leases which this section authorises are—

(i) agricultural or occupation leases for any term not exceeding twenty-one years, or, in the case of a mortgage made after the commencement of this Act, fifty years; and

(ii) building leases for any term not exceeding ninety-nine years, or, in the case of a mortgage made after the commencement of this Act, nine hundred and ninety-nine years.

(4) Every person making a lease under this section may execute and do all assurances and things necessary or proper in that behalf.

(5) Every such lease shall be made to take effect in possession not later than twelve months after its date.

(6) Every such lease shall reserve the best rent that can reasonably be obtained, regard being had to the circumstances of the case, but without any fine being taken.

(7) Every such lease shall contain a covenant by the lessee for payment of the rent, and condition of re-entry on the rent not being paid within a time therein specified not exceeding thirty days.

(8) A counterpart of every such lease shall be executed by the lessee and delivered to the lessor, of which execution and delivery the execution of the lease by the lessor shall, in favour of the lessee and all persons deriving title under him, be sufficient evidence.

(9) Every such building lease shall be made in consideration of the lessee, or some person by whose direction the lease is granted, having erected, or agreeing to erect

within not more than five years from the date of the lease, buildings, new or additional, or having improved or repaired buildings, or agreeing to improve or repair buildings within that time, or having executed, or agreeing to execute within that time, on the land leased, an improvement for or in connexion with building purposes.

(10) In any such building lease a peppercorn rent, or a nominal or other rent less than the rent ultimately payable, may be made payable for the first five years, or any less part of the term.

(11) In case of a lease by the mortgagor, he shall, within one month after making the lease, deliver to the mortgagee, or, where there are more than one, to the mortgagee first in priority, a counterpart of the lease duly executed by the lessee, but the lessee shall not be concerned to see that this provision is complied with.

(12) A contract to make or accept a lease under this section may be enforced by or against every person on whom the lease if granted would be binding.

(13) [Subject to subsection 13A below] this section applies only if and as far as a contrary intention is not expressed by the mortgagor and mortgagee in the mortgage deed, or otherwise in writing, and has effect subject to the terms of the mortgage deed or of any such writing and to the provisions therein contained.

[(13A) Subection 13 of this section—

(a) shall not enable the application of any provision of this section to be excluded or restricted in relation to any mortgage of agricultural land made after 1st March 1984 but before 1st September 1995; and

(b) shall not enable the power to grant a lease of any agricultural holding to which, by virtue of section 4 of the Agricultural Tenancies Act 1995, the Agricultural Holdings Act 1986 will apply, to be excluded or restricted in relation to any mortgage of agricultural land made on or after 1st September 1995.

(13B) In subsection (13A) of this section—

'agricultural holding' has the same meaning as in the Agricultural Holdings Act 1986; and

'agricultural land' has the same meaning as in the Agricultural Act 1947.]

(14) The mortgagor and mortgagee may, by agreement in writing, whether or not contained in the mortgage deed, reserve to or confer on the mortgagor or the mortgagee, or both, any further or other powers of leasing or having reference to leasing; and any further or other powers so reserved or conferred shall be exercisable, as far as may be, as if they were conferred by this Act, and with all the like incidents, effects, and consequences:

Provided that the powers so reserved or conferred shall not prejudicially affect the rights of any mortgagee interested under any other mortgage subsisting at the date of the agreement, unless that mortgagee joins in or adopts the agreement.

(15) Nothing in this Act shall be construed to enable a mortgagor or mortgagee to make a lease for any longer term or on any other conditions than such as could have been granted or imposed by the mortgagor, with the concurrence of all the incumbrancers, if this Act and the enactments replaced by this section had not been passed:

Provided that, in the case of a mortgage of leasehold land, a lease granted under this section shall reserve a reversion of not less than one day.

(16) Subject as aforesaid, this section applies to any mortgage made after the thirty-first day of December, eighteen hundred and eighty-one, but the provisions thereof, or any of them, may, by agreement in writing made after that date between mortgagor and mortgagee, be applied to a mortgage made before that date, so nevertheless that any such agreement shall not prejudicially affect any right or interest of any mortgagee not joining in or adopting the agreement.

(17) The provisions of this section referring to a lease shall be construed to extend and apply, as far as circumstances admit, to any letting, and to an agreement, whether in writing or not, for leasing or letting.

(18) For the purposes of this section 'mortgagor' does not include an incumbrancer deriving title under the original mortgagor.

(19) The powers of leasing conferred by this section shall, after a receiver of the income of the mortgaged property or any part thereof has been appointed by a mortgagee under his statutory power, and so long as the receiver acts, be exercisable by such mortgagee instead of by the mortgagor, as respects any land affected by the receivership, in like manner as if such mortgagee were in possession of the land, and the mortgagee may, by writing, delegate any of such powers to the receiver.

100. Powers of mortgagor and mortgagee in possession to accept surrenders of leases

(1) For the purpose only of enabling a lease authorised under the last preceding section, or under any agreement made pursuant to that section, or by the mortgage deed (in this section referred to as an authorised lease) to be granted, a mortgagor of land while in possession shall, as against every incumbrancer, have, by virtue of this Act, power to accept from time to time a surrender of any lease of the mortgaged land or any part thereof comprised in the lease, with or without an exception of or in respect of all or any of the mines and minerals therein, and, on a surrender of the lease so far as it comprises part only of the land or mines and minerals leased, the rent may be apportioned.

(2) For the same purpose, a mortgagee of land while in possession shall, as against all prior or other incumbrancers, if any, and as against the mortgagor, have, by virtue of this Act, power to accept from time to time any such surrender as aforesaid.

(3) On a surrender of part only of the land or mines and minerals leased, the original lease may be varied, provided that the lease when varied would have been valid as an authorised lease if granted by the person accepting the surrender; and, on a surrender and the making of a new or other lease, whether for the same or for any extended or other term, and whether subject or not to the same or to any other covenants, provisions, or conditions, the value of the lessee's interest in the lease surrendered may, subject to the provisions of this section, be taken into account in the determination of the amount of the rent to be reserved, and of the nature of the covenants, provisions and conditions to be inserted in the new or other lease.

(4) Where any consideration for the surrender, other than an agreement to accept an authorised lease, is given by or on behalf of the lessee to or on behalf of the person accepting the surrender, nothing in this section authorises a surrender to a mortgagor without the consent of the incumbrancers, or authorises a surrender to a second or subsequent incumbrancer without the consent of every prior incumbrancer.

(5) No surrender shall, by virtue of this section, be rendered valid unless:—

(a) An authorised lease is granted of the whole of the land or mines and minerals comprised in the surrender to take effect in possession immediately or within one month after the date of the surrender; and

(b) The term certain or other interest granted by the new lease is not less in duration than the unexpired term or interest which would have been subsisting under the original lease if that lease had not been surrendered; and

(c) Where the whole of the land mines and minerals originally leased has been surrendered, the rent reserved by the new lease is not less than the rent which would have been payable under the original lease if it had not been surrendered; or where part only of the land or mines and minerals has been surrendered, the aggregate rents respectively remaining payable or reserved under the original lease and new lease are not less than the rent which would have been payable under the original lease if no partial surrender had been accepted.

(6) A contract to make or accept a surrender under this section may be enforced by or against every person on whom the surrender, if completed, would be binding.

(7) This section applies only if and as far as a contrary intention is not expressed by the mortgagor and mortgagee in the mortgage deed, or otherwise in writing, and shall have effect subject to the terms of the mortgage deed or of any such writing and to the provisions therein contained.

(8) This section applies to a mortgage made after the thirty-first day of December, nineteen hundred and eleven, but the provisions of this section, or any of them, may, by agreement in writing made after that date, between mortgagor and mortgagee, be applied to a mortgage made before that date, so nevertheless that any such agreement shall not prejudicially affect any right or interest of any mortgagee not joining in or adopting the agreement.

(9) The provisions of this section referring to a lease shall be construed to extend and apply, as far as circumstances admit, to any letting, and to an agreement, whether in writing or not, for leasing or letting.

(10) The mortgagor and mortgagee may, by agreement in writing, whether or not contained in the mortgage deed, reserve or confer on the mortgagor or mortgagee, or both, any further or other powers relating to the surrender of leases; and any further or other powers so conferred or reserved shall be exercisable, as far as may be, as if they were conferred by this Act, and with all the like incidents, effects and consequences:

Provided that the powers so reserved or conferred shall not prejudicially affect the rights of any mortgagee interested under any other mortgage subsisting at the date of the agreement, unless that mortgagee joins in or adopts the agreement.

(11) Nothing in this section operates to enable a mortgagor or mortgagee to accept a surrender which could not have been accepted by the mortgagor with the concurrence of all the incumbrancers if this Act and the enactments replaced by this section had not been passed.

(12) For the purposes of this section 'mortgagor' does not include an incumbrancer deriving title under the original mortgagor.

(13) The powers of accepting surrenders conferred by this section shall, after a receiver of the income of the mortgaged property or any part thereof has been appointed by the mortgagee, under the statutory power, and so long as the receiver acts, be exercisable by such mortgagee instead of by the mortgagor, as respects any land affected by the receivership, in like manner as if such mortgagee were in possession of the land; and the mortgagee may, by writing, delegate any of such powers to the receiver.

101. Powers incident to estate or interest of mortgagee

(1) A mortgagee, where the mortgage is made by deed, shall, by virtue of this Act, have the following powers, to the like extent as if they had been in terms conferred by the mortgage deed, but not further (namely):

(i) A power, when the mortgage money has become due, to sell, or to concur with any other person in selling, the mortgaged property, or any part thereof, either subject to prior charges or not, and either together or in lots, by public auction or by private contract, subject to such conditions respecting title, or evidence of title, or other matter, as the mortgagee thinks fit, with power to vary any contract for sale, and to buy in at an auction, or to rescind any contract for sale, and to re-sell, without being answerable for any loss occasioned thereby; and

(ii) A power, at any time after the date of the mortgage deed, to insure and keep insured against loss or damage by fire any building, or any effects or property of an insurable nature, whether affixed to the freehold or not, being or forming part of the property which or an estate or interest wherein is mortgaged, and the premiums paid for any such insurance shall be a charge on the mortgaged property or estate or interest, in addition to the mortgage money, and with the same priority, and with interest at the same rate, as the mortgage money; and

(iii) A power, when the mortgage money has become due, to appoint a receiver of the income of the mortgaged property, or any part thereof; or, if the mortgaged property consists of an interest in income, or of a rentcharge or an annual or other periodical sum, a receiver of that property or any part thereof; and

(iv) A power, while the mortgagee is in possession, to cut and sell timber and other trees ripe for cutting, and not planted or left standing for shelter or ornament, or to contract for any such cutting and sale, to be completed within any time not exceeding twelve months from the making of the contract.

(2) Where the mortgage deed is executed after the thirty-first day of December, nineteen hundred and eleven, the power of sale aforesaid includes the following powers as incident thereto (namely):—

(i) A power to impose or reserve or make binding, as far as the law permits, by covenant, condition, or otherwise, on the unsold part of the mortgaged property or any part thereof, or on the purchaser and any property sold, any restriction or reservation with respect to building on or other user of land, or with respect to mines and minerals, or for the purpose of the more beneficial working thereof, or with respect to any other thing:

(ii) A power to sell the mortgaged property, or any part thereof, or all or any mines and minerals apart from the surface:—

(a) With or without a grant or reservation of rights of way, rights of water, easements, rights, and privileges for or connected with building or other purposes in relation to the property remaining in mortgage or any part thereof, or to any property sold: and

(b) With or without an exception or reservation of all or any of the mines and minerals in or under the mortgaged property, and with or without a grant or reservation of powers or working, wayleaves, or rights of way, rights of water and drainage and other powers, easements, rights, and privileges for or connected with mining purposes in relation to the property remaining unsold or any part thereof, or to any property sold: and

(c) With or without covenants by the purchaser to expend money on the land sold.

(3) The provisions of this Act relating to the foregoing powers, comprised either in this section, or in any other section regulating the exercise of those powers, may be varied or extended by the mortgage deed, and, as so varied or extended, shall, as far as may be, operate in the like manner and with all the like incidents, effects, and consequences, as if such variations or extensions were contained in this Act.

(4) This section applies only if and as far as a contrary intention is not expressed in the mortgage deed, and has effect subject to the terms of the mortgage deed and to the provisions therein contained.

(5) Save as otherwise provided, this section applies where the mortgage deed is executed after the thirty-first day of December, eighteen hundred and eighty-one.

(6) The power of sale conferred by this section includes such power of selling the estate in fee simple or any leasehold reversion as is conferred by the provisions of this Act relating to the realisation of mortgages.

102. Provision as to mortgages of undivided shares in land

(1) A person who was before the commencement of this Act a mortgagee of an undivided share in land shall have the same power to sell his [interest under the trust to which the land is subject], as, independently of this Act, he would have had in regard to the share in the land; and shall also have a right to require the [trustees] in whom the land is vested to account to him for the income attributable to that share or to appoint a receiver to receive the same from such trustees corresponding to the right which, independently of this Act, he would have had to take possession or to appoint a receiver of the rents and profits attributable to the same share.

(2) The powers conferred by this section are exercisable by the persons deriving title under such mortgagee.

103. Regulation of exercise of power of sale

A mortgagee shall not exercise the power of sale conferred by this Act unless and until—

(i) Notice requiring payment of the mortgage money has been served on the mortgagor or one of two or more mortgagors, and default has been made in payment of the mortgage money, or of part thereof, for three months after such service; or

(ii) Some interest under the mortgage is in arrear and unpaid for two months after becoming due; or

(iii) There has been a breach of some provision contained in the mortgage deed or in this Act, or in an enactment replaced by this Act, and on the part of the mortgagor, or of some person concurring in making the mortgage, to be observed or performed, other than and besides a covenant for payment of the mortgage money or interest thereon.

104. Conveyance on sale

(1) A mortgagee exercising the power of sale conferred by this Act shall have power, by deed, to convey the property sold, for such estate and interest therein as he is by this Act authorised to sell or convey or may be the subject of the mortgage, freed from all estates, interests, and rights to which the mortgage has priority, but subject to all estates, interests, and rights which have priority to the mortgage.

(2) Where a conveyance is made in exercise of the power of sale conferred by this Act, or any enactment replaced by this Act, the title of the purchaser shall not be impeachable on the ground—

(a) that no case had arisen to authorise the sale; or

(b) that due notice was not given; or

(c) where the mortgage is made after the commencement of this Act, that leave of the court, when so required, was not obtained; or

(d) whether the mortgage was made before or after such commencement, that the power was otherwise improperly or irregularly exercised; and a purchaser is not, either before or on conveyance, concerned to see or inquire whether a case has arisen to authorise the sale, or due notice has been given, or the power is otherwise properly and regularly exercised; but any person damnified by an unauthorised, or improper, or irregular exercise of the power shall have his remedy in damages against the person exercising the power.

(3) A conveyance on sale by a mortgagee, made after the commencement of this Act, shall be deemed to have been made in exercise of the power of sale conferred by this Act unless a contrary intention appears.

105. Application of proceeds of sale

The money which is received by the mortgagee, arising from the sale, after discharge of prior incumbrances to which the sale is not made subject, if any, or after payment into court under this Act of a sum to meet any prior incumbrance, shall be held by him in trust to be applied by him, first, in payment of all costs, charges, and expenses properly incurred by him as incident to the sale or any attempted sale, or otherwise; and secondly, in discharge of the mortgage money, interest, and costs, and other money, if any, due under the mortgage; and the residue of the money so received shall be paid to the person entitled to the mortgaged property, or authorised to give receipts for the proceeds of the sale thereof.

106. Provisions as to exercise of power of sale

(1) The power of sale conferred by this Act may be exercised by any person for the time being entitled to receive and give a discharge for the mortgage money.

(2) The power of sale conferred by this Act does not affect the right of foreclosure.

(3) The mortgagee shall not be answerable for any involuntary loss happening in or about the exercise or execution of the power of sale conferred by this Act, or of any trust connected therewith, or, where the mortgage is executed after the thirty-first day of December, nineteen hundred and eleven, of any power or provision contained in the mortgage deed.

(4) At any time after the power of sale conferred by this Act has become exercisable the person entitled to exercise the power may demand and recover from any person, other than a person having in the mortgaged property an estate, interest, or right in priority to the mortgage, all the deeds and documents relating to the property, or to the title thereto, which a purchaser under the power of sale would be entitled to demand and recover from him.

107. Mortgagee's receipts, discharges, etc.

(1) The receipt in writing of a mortgagee shall be a sufficient discharge for any money arising under the power of sale conferred by this Act, or for any money or securities comprised in his mortgage, or arising thereunder; and a person paying or transferring the same to the mortgagee shall not be concerned to inquire whether any money remains due under the mortgage.

(2) Money received by a mortgagee under his mortgage or from the proceeds of securities comprised in his mortgage shall be applied in like manner as in this Act directed respecting money received by him arising from a sale under the power of sale conferred by this Act, but with this variation, that the costs, charges, and expenses payable shall include the costs, charges, and expenses properly incurred of recovering and receiving the money or securities, and of conversion of securities into money, instead of those incident to sale.

108. Amount and application of insurance money

(1) The amount of an insurance effected by a mortgagee against loss or damage by fire under the power in that behalf conferred by this Act shall not exceed the amount specified in the mortgage deed, or, if no amount is therein specified, two third parts of the amount that would be required, in case of total destruction, to restore the property insured.

(2) An insurance shall not, under the power conferred by this Act, be effected by a mortgagee in any of the following cases (namely):

(i) Where there is a declaration in the mortgage deed that no insurance is required:

(ii) Where an insurance is kept up by or on behalf of the mortgagor in accordance with the mortgage deed:

(iii) Where the mortgage deed contains no stipulation respecting insurance, and an insurance is kept up by or on behalf of the mortgagor with the consent of the mortgagee to the amount to which the mortgagee is by this Act authorised to insure.

(3) All money received on an insurance of mortgaged property against loss or damage by fire or otherwise effected under this Act, or any enactment replaced by this Act, or on an insurance for the maintenance of which the mortgagor is liable under the mortgage deed, shall, if the mortgagee so requires, be applied by the mortgagor in making good the loss or damage in respect of which the money is received.

(4) Without prejudice to any obligation to the contrary imposed by law, or by special contract, a mortgagee may require that all money received on an insurance of mortgaged property against loss or damage by fire or otherwise effected under this Act, or any enactment replaced by this Act, or on an insurance for the maintenance of which the mortgagor is liable under the mortgage deed, be applied in or towards the discharge of the mortgage money.

109. Appointment, powers, remuneration and duties of receiver

(1) A mortgagee entitled to appoint a receiver under the power in that behalf conferred by this Act shall not appoint a receiver until he has become entitled to exercise the power of sale conferred by this Act, but may then, by writing under his hand, appoint such person as he thinks fit to be receiver.

(2) A receiver appointed under the powers conferred by this Act, or any enactment replaced by this Act, shall be deemed to be the agent of the mortgagor; and the mortgagor shall be solely responsible for the receiver's acts or defaults unless the mortgage deed otherwise provides.

(3) The receiver shall have power to demand and recover all the income of which he is appointed receiver, by action, distress, or otherwise, in the name either of the mortgagor or of the mortgagee, to the full extent of the estate or interest which the mortgagor could dispose of, and to give effectual receipts accordingly for the same, and to exercise any powers which may have been delegated to him by the mortgagee pursuant to this Act.

(4) A person paying money to the receiver shall not be concerned to inquire whether any case has happened to authorise the receiver to act.

(5) The receiver may be removed, and a new receiver may be appointed, from time to time by the mortgagee by writing under his hand.

(6) The receiver shall be entitled to retain out of any money received by him, for his remuneration, and in satisfaction of all costs, charges, and expenses incurred by him as receiver, a commission at such rate, not exceeding five per centum on the gross amount of all money received, as is specified in his appointment, and if no rate is so specified, then at the rate of five per centum on that gross amount, or at such other rate as the court thinks fit to allow, on application made by him for that purpose.

(7) The receiver shall, if so directed in writing by the mortgagee, insure to the extent, if any, to which the mortgagee might have insured and keep insured against loss or damage by fire, out of the money received by him, any building, effects, or property comprised in the mortgage, whether affixed to the freehold or not, being of an insurable nature.

(8) Subject to the provisions of this Act as to the application of insurance money, the receiver shall apply all money received by him as follows, namely:

(i) In discharge of all rents, taxes, rates, and outgoings whatever affecting the mortgaged property; and

(ii) In keeping down all annual sums or other payments, and the interest on all principal sums, having priority to the mortgage in right whereof he is receiver; and

(iii) In payment of his commission, and of the premiums on fire, life, or other insurances, if any, properly payable under the mortgage deed or under this Act, and the cost of executing necessary or proper repairs directed in writing by the mortgagee; and

(iv) In payment of the interest accruing due in respect of any principal money due under the mortgage; and

(v) In or towards discharge of the principal money if so directed in writing by the mortgagee;

and shall pay the residue, if any, of the money received by him to the person who, but for the possession of the receiver, would have been entitled to receive the income of which he is appointed receiver, or who is otherwise entitled to the mortgaged property.

110. Effect of bankruptcy of the mortgagor on the power to sell or appoint a receiver

(1) Where the statutory or express power for a mortgagee either to sell or to appoint a receiver is made exercisable by reason of the mortgagor [. . .] being adjudged a bankrupt, such power shall not be exercised only on account of the [. . .] adjudication, without the leave of the court.

(2) This section applies only where the mortgage deed is executed after the commencement of this Act; [. . .].

111. Effect of advance on joint account

(1) Where—

(a) in a mortgage, or an obligation for payment of money, or a transfer of a mortgage or of such an obligation, the sum, or any part of the sum, advanced or owing is expressed to be advanced by or owing to more persons than one out of money, or as money, belonging to them on a joint account; or

(b) a mortgage, or such an obligation, or such a transfer is made to more persons than one, jointly;

the mortgage money, or other money or money's worth, for the time being due to those persons on the mortgage or obligation, shall, as between them and the mortgagor or obligor, be deemed to be and remain money or money's worth belonging to those persons on a joint account; and the receipt in writing of the survivors or last survivor of them, or of the personal representative of the last survivor, shall be a complete discharge for all money or money's worth for the time being due, notwithstanding any notice to the payer of a severance of the joint account.

(2) This section applies if and so far as a contrary intention is not expressed in the mortgage, obligation, or transfer, and has effect subject to the terms of the mortgage, obligation, or transfer, and to the provisions therein contained.

(3) This section applies to any mortgage obligation or transfer made after the thirty-first day of December, eighteen hundred and eighty-one.

112. Notice of trusts on transfer of mortgage

(1) Where, on the transfer of a mortgage, the stamp duty, if payable according to the amount of the debt transferred, would exceed the sum of ten shillings, a purchaser shall not, by reason only of the transfer bearing a ten-shilling stamp, whether adjudicated or not, be deemed to have or to have had notice of any trust, or that the transfer was made for effectuating the discharge of a trustee or the appointment of a new trustee.

(2) This section applies to transfers made before as well as after the commencement of this Act.

113. Notice of trusts affecting mortgage debts

(1) A person dealing in good faith with a mortgagee, or with the mortgagor if the mortgage has been discharged released or postponed as to the whole or any part of the mortgaged property, shall not be concerned with any trust at any time affecting the mortgage money or the income thereof, whether or not he has notice of the trust, and may assume unless the contrary is expressly stated in the instruments relating to the mortgage—

(a) that the mortgagees (if more than one) are or were entitled to the mortgage money on a joint account; and

(b) that the mortgagee has or had power to give valid receipts for the purchase money or mortgage money and the income thereof (including any arrears of interest) and to release or postpone the priority of the mortgage debt or any part thereof or to deal with the same or the mortgaged property or any part thereof; without investigating the equitable title to the mortgage debt or the appointment or discharge of trustees in reference thereto.

(2) This section applies to mortgages made before or after the commencement of this Act, but only as respects dealings effected after such commencement.

(3) This section does not affect the liability of any person in whom the mortgage debt is vested for the purposes of any trust to give effect to that trust.

114. Transfers of mortgages

(1) A deed executed by a mortgagee purporting to transfer his mortgage or the benefit thereof shall, unless a contrary intention is therein expressed, and subject to any provisions therein contained, operate to transfer to the transferee—

(a) the right to demand, sue for, recover, and give receipts for, the mortgage money or the unpaid part thereof, and the interest then due, if any, and thenceforth to become due thereon; and

(b) the benefit of all securities for the same, and the benefit of and the right to sue on all covenants with the mortgagee, and the right to exercise all powers of the mortgagee; and

(c) all the estate and interest in the mortgaged property then vested in the mortgagee subject to redemption or cesser, but as to such estate and interest subject to the right of redemption then subsisting.

(2) In this section 'transferee' includes his personal representatives and assigns.

(3) A transfer of mortgage may be made in the form contained in the Third Schedule to this Act with such variations and additions, if any, as the circumstances may require.

(4) This section applies, whether the mortgage transferred was made before or after the commencement of this Act, but applies only to transfers made after the commencement of this Act.

(5) This section does not extend to a transfer of a bill of sale of chattels by way of security.

115. Reconveyances of mortgages by endorsed receipts

(1) A receipt endorsed on, written at the foot of, or annexed to, a mortgage for all money thereby secured, which states the name of the person who pays the money and is executed by the chargee by way of legal mortgage or the person in whom the mortgaged property is vested and who is legally entitled to give a receipt for the mortgage money shall operate, without any reconveyance, surrender, or release—

(a) Where a mortgage takes effect by demise or subdemise, as a surrender of the term, so as to determine the term or merge the same in the reversion immediately expectant thereon;

(b) Where the mortgage does not take effect by demise or subdemise, as a reconveyance thereof to the extent of the interest which is the subject matter of the mortgage, to the person who immediately before the execution of the receipt was entitled to the equity of redemption;

and in either case, as a discharge of the mortgaged property from all principal money and interest secured by, and from all claims under the mortgage, but without prejudice to any term or other interest which is paramount to the estate or interest of the mortgagee or other person in whom the mortgaged property was vested.

(2) Provided that, where by the receipt the money appears to have been paid by a person who is not entitled to the immediate equity of redemption, the receipt shall operate as if the benefit of the mortgage had by deed been transferred to him; unless—

(a) it is otherwise expressly provided; or

(b) the mortgage is paid off out of capital money, or other money in the hands of a personal representative or trustee properly applicable for the discharge of the mortgage, and it is not expressly provided that the receipt is to operate as a transfer.

(3) Nothing in this section confers on a mortgagor a right to keep alive a mortgage paid off by him, so as to affect prejudicially any subsequent incumbrancer; and where there is no right to keep the mortgage alive, the receipt does not operate as a transfer.

(4) This section does not affect the right of any person to require a reassignment, surrender, release, or transfer to be executed in lieu of a receipt.

(5) A receipt may be given in the form contained in the Third Schedule to this Act with such variations and additions, if any, as may be deemed expedient [. . .]

(6) In a receipt given under this section the same covenants shall be implied as if the person who executes the receipt had by deed been expressed to convey the property as mortgagee, subject to any interest which is paramount to the mortgage.

(7) Where the mortgage consists of a mortgage and a further charge or of more than one deed, it shall be sufficient for the purposes of this section, if the receipt refers either to all the deeds whereby the mortgage money is secured or to the aggregate amount of the mortgage money thereby secured and for the time being owing, and is endorsed on, written at the foot of, or annexed to, one of the mortgage deeds.

(8) This section applies to the discharge of a charge by way of legal mortgage, and to the discharge of a mortgage, whether made by way of statutory mortgage or not, executed before or after the commencement of this Act, but only as respects discharges effected after such commencement.

(9) The provisions of this section relating to the operation of a receipt shall (in substitution for the like statutory provisions relating to receipts given by or on behalf of a building [. . .] society) apply to the discharge of a mortgage made to any such society, provided that the receipt is executed in the manner required by the statute relating to the society [. . .]

(10) This section does not apply to the discharge of a charge or incumbrance registered under the Land Registration Act, 1925.

(11) In this section 'mortgaged property' means the property remaining subject to the mortgage at the date of the receipt.

116. Cesser of mortgage terms

Without prejudice to the right of a tenant for life or other person having only a limited interest in the equity of redemption to require a mortgage to be kept alive by transfer or otherwise, a mortgage term shall, when the money secured by the mortgage has been discharged, become a satisfied term and shall cease.

117. Forms of statutory legal charges

(1) As a special form of charge by way of legal mortgage, a mortgage of freehold or leasehold land may be made by a deed expressed to be made by way of statutory mortgage, being in one of the forms (Nos. 1 or 4) set out in the Fourth Schedule to this Act, with such variations and additions, if any, as circumstances may require, and if so made the provisions of this section shall apply thereto.

(2) There shall be deemed to be included, and there shall by virtue of this Act be implied, in such a mortgage deed—

First, a covenant with the mortgagee by the person therein expressed to charge as mortgagor to the effect following, namely:

That the mortgagor will, on the stated day, pay to the mortgagee the stated mortgage money, with interest thereon in the meantime at the stated rate, and will thereafter, if and as long as the mortgage money or any part thereof remains unpaid, pay to the mortgagee (as well after as before any judgment is obtained under the mortgage) interest thereon, or on the unpaid part thereof, at the stated rate, by equal half-yearly payments the first thereof to be made at the end of six months from the day stated for payment of the mortgage money:

Secondly, a provision to the following effect (namely):

That if the mortgagor on the stated day pays to the mortgagee the stated mortgage money, with interest thereon in the meantime at the stated rate, the mortgagee at any time thereafter, at the request and cost of the mortgagor, shall discharge the mortgaged property or transfer the benefit of the mortgage as the mortgagor may direct.

This subsection applies to a mortgage deed made under section twenty-six of the Conveyancing Act, 1881, with a substitution of a reference to 'the person therein expressed to convey as mortgagor' for the reference in this subsection to 'the person therein expressed to charge as mortgagor.'

118. Forms of statutory transfers of legal charges

(1) A transfer of a statutory mortgage may be made by a deed expressed to be made by way of statutory transfer of mortgage, being in such one of the three forms (Nos. 2,

3 or 4) set out in the Fourth Schedule to this Act as may be appropriate to the case with such variations and additions, if any, as circumstances may require, and if so made the provisions of this section shall apply thereto.

(2) In whichever of those three forms the deed of transfer is made, it shall have effect as follows (namely):—

(i) There shall become vested in the person to whom the benefit of the mortgage is expressed to be transferred (who, with his personal representatives and assigns, is in this section designated the transferee), the right to demand, sue for, recover, and give receipts for the mortgage money, or the unpaid part thereof, and the interest then due, if any, and thenceforth to become due thereon, and the benefit of all securities for the same, and the benefit of and the right to sue on all covenants with the mortgagee, and the right to exercise all powers of the mortgagee:

(ii) All the term and interest, if any, subject to redemption, of the mortgagee in the mortgaged land shall vest in the transferee, subject to redemption.

(3) If a covenantor joins in the deed of transfer, there shall also be deemed to be included, and there shall by virtue of this Act be implied therein, a covenant with the transferee by the person expressed to join therein as covenantor to the effect following (namely):

That the covenantor will, on the next of the days by the mortgage deed fixed for payment of interest pay to the transferee the stated mortgage money, or so much thereof as then remains unpaid, with interest thereon, or on the unpaid part thereof, in the meantime, at the rate stated in the mortgage deed; and will thereafter, as long as the mortgage money or any part thereof remains unpaid, pay to the transferee interest on that sum, or the unpaid part thereof, at the same rate, on the successive days by the mortgage deed fixed for payment of interest.

(4) If the deed of transfer is made in the Form No. 4, it shall, by virtue of this Act, operate not only as a statutory transfer of mortgage, but also as a statutory mortgage, and the provisions of this section shall have effect in relation thereto accordingly; but it shall not be liable to any increased stamp duty by reason only of it being designated a mortgage.

(5) This section applies to the transfer of a statutory mortgage created under any enactment replaced by this Act.

119. Implied covenants, joint and several

In a deed of statutory mortgage, or of statutory transfer of mortgage, where more persons than one are expressed to convey or charge as mortgagors, or to join as covenantors, the implied covenant on their part shall be deemed to be a joint and several covenant by them; and where there are more mortgagees or more transferees than one, the implied covenant with them shall be deemed to be a covenant with them jointly, unless the amount secured is expressed to be secured to them in shares or distinct sums, in which latter case the implied covenant with them shall be deemed to be a covenant with each severally in respect of the share or distinct sum secured to him.

120. Form of discharge of statutory mortgage or charge

A statutory mortgage may be surrendered or discharged by a receipt in the form (No. 5) set out in the Fourth Schedule to this Act with such variations and additions, if any, as circumstances may require.

Rentcharges

121. Remedies for the recovery of annual sums charged on land

(1) Where a person is entitled to receive out of any land, or out of the income of any land, any annual sum, payable half-yearly or otherwise, whether charged on the land or on the income of the land, and whether by way of rentcharge of otherwise not being

rent incident to a reversion, then, subject and without prejudice to all estates, interests, and rights having priority to the annual sum, the person entitled to receive the annual sum shall have such remedies for recovering and compelling payment thereof as are described in this section, as far as those remedies might have been conferred by the instrument under which the annual sum arises, but not further.

(2) If at any time the annual sum or any part thereof is unpaid for twenty-one days next after the time appointed for any payment in respect thereof, the person entitled to receive the annual sum may enter into and distrain on the land charged or any part thereof, and dispose according to law of any distress found, to the intent that thereby or otherwise the annual sum and all arrears thereof, and all costs and expenses occasioned by non-payment thereof, may be fully paid.

(3) If at any time the annual sum or any part thereof is unpaid for forty days next after the time appointed for any payment in respect thereof, then, although no legal demand has been made for payment thereof, the person entitled to receive the annual sum may enter into possession of and hold the land charged or any part thereof, and take the income thereof, until thereby or otherwise the annual sum and all arrears thereof due at the time of his entry, or afterwards becoming due during his continuance in possession, and all costs and expenses occasioned by nonpayment of the annual sum, are fully paid; and such possession when taken shall be without impeachment of waste.

(4) In the like case the person entitled to the annual sum, whether taking possession or not, may also by deed demise the land charged, or any part thereof, to a trustee for a term of years, with or without impeachment of waste, on trust, by all or any of the means hereinafter mentioned, or by any other reasonable means, to raise and pay the annual sum and all arrears thereof due or to become due, and all costs and expenses occasioned by nonpayment of the annual sum, or incurred in compelling or obtaining payment thereof, or otherwise relating thereto, including the costs of the preparation and execution of the deed of demise, and the costs of the execution of the trusts of that deed:

Provided that this subsection shall not authorise the creation of a legal term of years absolute after the commencement of this Act, save where the annual sum is a rentcharge held for a legal estate.

The surplus, if any, of the money raised, or of the income received, under the trusts of the deed shall be paid to the person for the time being entitled to the land therein comprised in reversion immediately expectant on the term thereby created.

The means by which such annual sum, arrears, costs, and expenses may be raised includes—

(a) the creation of a legal mortgage or a sale (effected by assignment or subdemise) of the term created in the land charged or any part thereof,

(b) the receipt of the income of the land comprised in the term.

(5) This section applies only if and as far as a contrary intention is not expressed in the instrument under which the annual sum arises, and has effect subject to the terms of that instrument and to the provisions therein contained.

(6) The rule of law relating to perpetuities does not apply to any powers or remedies conferred by this section [. . .]

(7) . . .

122. Creation of rentcharges charged on another rentcharge and remedies for recovery thereof

(1) A rentcharge or other annual sum (not being rent incident to a reversion) payable half yearly or otherwise may be granted, reserved, charged or created out of or on another rentcharge or annual sum (not being rent incident to a reversion) charged on or payable out of land or on or out of the income of land, in like manner as the same could have been made to issue out of land.

(2) If at any time the annual sum so created or any part thereof is unpaid for twenty-one days next after the time appointed for any payment in respect thereof, the person entitled to receive the annual sum shall (without prejudice to any prior interest or charge) have power to appoint a receiver of the annual sum charged or any part thereof, and the provisions of this Act relating to the appointment, powers, remuneration and duties of a receiver, shall apply in like manner as if such person were a mortgagee entitled to exercise the power of sale conferred by this Act, and the annual sum charged were the mortgaged property and the person entitled thereto were the mortgagor.

(3) The power to appoint a receiver conferred by this section shall (where the annual sum is charged on a rentcharge) take effect in substitution for the remedies conferred, in the case of annual sums charged on land, by the last preceding section, but subsection (6) of that section shall apply and have effect as if herein re-enacted and in terms made applicable to the powers conferred by this section.

(4) This section applies to annual sums expressed to be created before as well as after the commencement of this Act, and, but without prejudice to any order of the court made before the commencement of this Act, operates to confirm any annual sum which would have been validly created if this section had been in force.

PART IV
EQUITABLE INTERESTS AND THINGS IN ACTION

[. . .]

130. [. . .] [E]ntailed interests in real and personal property

(1) [. . .]

(2) [. . .]

(3) [. . .]

(4) In default of and subject to the execution of a disentailing assurance or the exercise of the testamentary power conferred by this Act, an entailed interest (to the extent of the property affected) shall devolve as an equitable interest, from time to time, upon the persons who would have been successively entitled thereto as the heirs of the body (either generally or of a particular class) of the tenant in tail or other person, or as tenant by the curtesy, if the entailed interest had, before the commencement of this Act, been limited in respect of freehold land governed by the general law in force immediately before such commencement, and such law had remained unaffected.

(5) Where personal chattels are settled without reference to settled land on trusts creating entailed interests therein, the trustees, with the consent of the usufructuary for the time being if of full age, may sell the chattels or any of them, and the net proceeds of any such sale shall be held in trust for and shall go to the same persons successively, in the same manner and for the same interests, as the chattels sold would have been held and gone if they had not been sold, and the income of investments representing such proceeds of sale shall be applied accordingly.

(6) [. . .]

(7) In this Act where the context so admits 'entailed interest' includes an estate tail (now made to take effect as an equitable interest) created before the commencement of this Act.

131. Abolition of the rule in Shelley's case

Where by any instrument coming into operation after the commencement of this Act an interest in any property is expressed to be given to the heir or heirs or issue or any particular heir or any class of the heirs or issue of any person in words which, [(and paragraph 5 of Schedule 1 of the Trusts of Land and Appointment of Trustees Act 1996)] would, under the rule of law known as the Rule in Shelley's case, have operated to give to that person an interest in fee simple or an entailed interest, such words shall operate in equity as words of purchase and not of limitation, and shall be construed and have effect accordingly, and in the case of an interest in any property expressed to be given to an heir or heirs or any particular heir or class of heirs, the same person or persons shall take as would in the case of freehold land have answered that description under the general law in force before the commencement of this Act.

132. As to heirs taking by purchase

(1) A limitation of real or personal property in favour of the heir, either general or special, of a deceased person which, if limited in respect of freehold land before the commencement of this Act, would have conferred on the heir an estate in the land by purchase, shall operate to confer a corresponding equitable interest in the property on the person who would, if the general law in force immediately before such commencement had remained unaffected, have answered the description of the heir, either general or special, of the deceased in respect of his freehold land, either at the death of the deceased or at the time named in the limitation, as the case may require.

(2) This section applies whether the deceased person dies before or after the commencement of this Act, but only applies to limitations or trusts created by an instrument coming into operation after such commencement.

134. Restriction on executory limitations

(1) Where there is a person entitled to—

(a) an equitable interest in land for an estate in fee simple or for any less interest not being an entailed interest, or

(b) any interest in other property, not being an entailed interest,

with an executory limitation over on default or failure of all or any of his issue, whether within or at any specified period or time or not, that executory limitation shall be or become void and incapable of taking effect, if and as soon as there is living any issue who has attained [the age of eighteen years] of the class on default or failure whereof the limitation over was to take effect.

(2) This section applies where the executory limitation is contained in an instrument coming into operation after the thirty-first day of December, eighteen hundred and eighty-two, save that, as regards instruments coming into operation before the commencement of this Act, it only applies to limitations of land for an estate in fee, or for a term of years absolute or determinable on life, or for a term of life.

135. Equitable waste

An equitable interest for life without impeachment of waste does not confer upon the tenant for life any right to commit waste of the description known as equitable waste, unless an intention to confer such right expressly appears by the instrument creating such equitable interest.

136. Legal assignments of things in action

(1) Any absolute assignment by writing under the hand of the assignor (not purporting to be by way of charge only) of any debt or other legal thing in action, of which express notice in writing has been given to the debtor, trustee or other person from whom the assignor would have been entitled to claim such debt or thing in action, is effectual in law (subject to equities having priority over the right of the assignee) to pass and transfer from the date of such notice—

(a) the legal right to such debt or thing in action;

(b) all legal and other remedies for the same; and

(c) the power to give a good discharge for the same without the concurrence of the assignor:

Provided that, if the debtor, trustee or other person liable in respect of such debt or thing in action has notice—

(a) that the assignment is disputed by the assignor or any person claiming under him; or

(b) of any other opposing or conflicting claims to such debt or thing in action;

he may, if he thinks fit, either call upon the persons making claim thereto to interplead concerning the same, or pay the debt or other thing in action into court under the provisions of the Trustee Act, 1925.

(2) This section does not affect the provisions of the Policies of Assurance Act, 1867.

[(3) The county court has jurisdiction (including power to receive payments of money or securities into court) under the proviso to subsection (1) of this section where the amount or value of the debt or thing in action does not exceed [£30,000].]

137. Dealings with life interests, reversions and other equitable interests

(1) The law applicable to dealings with equitable things in action which regulates the priority of competing interests therein, shall, as respects dealings with equitable interests in land, capital money, and securities representing capital money effected after the commencement of this Act, apply to and regulate the priority of competing interests therein.

This subsection applies whether or not the money or securities are in court.

(2) (i) In the case of a dealing with an equitable interest in settled land, capital money or securities representing capital money, the persons to be served with notice of the dealing shall be the trustees of the settlement; and where the equitable interest is created by a derivative or subsidiary settlement, the persons to be served with notice shall be the trustees of that settlement.

(ii) In the case of a dealing with an equitable interest in [land subject to a trust of land, or the proceeds of the sale of such land, the persons to be served with notice shall be the trustees.]

(iii) In any other case the person to be served with notice of a dealing with an equitable interest in land shall be the estate owner of the land affected.

The persons on whom notice is served pursuant to this subsection shall be affected thereby in the same manner as if they had been trustees of personal property out of which the equitable interest was created or arose.

This subsection does not apply where the money or securities are in court.

(3) A notice, otherwise than in writing, given to, or received by, a trustee after the commencement of this Act as respects any dealing with an equitable interest in real or personal property, shall not affect the priority of competing claims of purchasers in that equitable interest.

(4) Where, as respects any dealing with an equitable interest in real or personal property—

(a) the trustees are not persons to whom a valid notice of the dealing can be given; or

(b) there are no trustees to whom a notice can be given; or

(c) for any other reason a valid notice cannot be served, or cannot be served without unreasonable cost or delay;

a purchaser may at his own cost require that—

(i) a memorandum of the dealing be endorsed, written on or permanently annexed to the instrument creating the trust;

(ii) the instrument be produced to him by the person having the possession or custody thereof to prove that a sufficient memorandum has been placed thereon or annexed thereto.

Such memorandum shall, as respects priorities, operate in like manner as if notice in writing of the dealing had been given to trustees duly qualified to receive the notice at the time when the memorandum is placed on or annexed to the instrument creating the trust.

(5) Where the property affected is settled land, the memorandum shall be placed on or annexed to the trust instrument and not the vesting instrument.

Where the property affected is land [subject to a trust of land], the memorandum shall be placed on or annexed to the instrument whereby the equitable interest is created.

(6) Where the trust is created by statute or by operation of law, or in any other case where there is no instrument whereby the trusts are declared, the instrument under which the equitable interest is acquired or which is evidence of the devolution thereof shall, for the purposes of this section, be deemed the instrument creating the trust.

In particular, where the trust arises by reason of an intestacy, the letters of administration or probate in force when the dealing was effected shall be deemed such instrument.

(7) Nothing in this section affects any priority acquired before the commencement of this Act.

(8) Where a notice in writing of a dealing with an equitable interest in real or personal property has been served on a trustee under this section, the trustees from time to time of the property affected shall be entitled to the custody of the notice, and the notice shall be delivered to them by any person who for the time being may have the custody thereof; and subject to the payment of costs, any person interested in the equitable interest may require production of the notice.

(9) The liability of the estate owner of the legal estate affected to produce documents and furnish information to persons entitled to equitable interests therein shall correspond to the liability of a trustee for sale to produce documents and furnish information to persons entitled to equitable interests in the proceeds of sale of the land.

(10) This section does not apply until a trust has been created, and in this section 'dealing' includes a disposition by operation of law.

138. Power to nominate a trust corporation to receive notices

(1) By any settlement or other instrument creating a trust, a trust corporation may be nominated to whom notices of dealings affecting real or personal property may be given, whether or not under the foregoing section, and in default of such nomination the trustees (if any) of the instrument, or the court on the application of any person interested, may make the nomination.

(2) The person having the possession or custody of any instrument on which notices under that section may be endorsed shall cause the name of the trust corporation to whom notices may be given to be endorsed upon that instrument.

(3) Notice given to any trust corporation whose name is so endorsed shall operate in the same way as a notice or endorsement under the foregoing section.

(4) Where a trust corporation is acting for the purposes of this section a notice given to a trustee of the trust instrument of a dealing relating to the trust property shall forthwith be delivered or sent by post by the trustee to the trust corporation, and until received by the corporation shall not affect any priority.

(5) A trust corporation shall not be nominated for the purposes of this section—

(a) unless that corporation consents to act; or

(b) where that corporation has any beneficial interest in or charge upon the trust property; or

(c) where a trust corporation is acting as the trustee or one of the trustees of the instrument creating the trust.

(6) Where a trust corporation acting for the purposes of this section becomes entitled to any beneficial interest in or charge upon the trust property, another trust corporation shall be nominated in its place and all documents relating to notices affecting the trust shall be delivered to the corporation so nominated.

(7) A trust corporation acting for the purposes of this section shall be bound to keep a separate register of notices of dealings in respect of each equitable interest and shall enter therein—

(a) the date of the notice;
(b) the name of the person giving the notice;
(c) short particulars of the equitable interest intended to be affected; and
(d) short particulars of the effect of the dealing if mentioned in the notice.

(8) The trust corporation may, before making any entry in the register, require the applicant to pay a fee not exceeding the prescribed fee.

(9) Subject to the payment of a fee not exceeding the prescribed fee, the trust corporation shall permit any person who would, if the corporation had been the trustee of the trust instrument, have been entitled to inspect notices served on the trustee, to inspect and take copies of the register and any notices held by the corporation.

(10) Subject to the payment by the applicant of a fee not exceeding the prescribed fee, the trust corporation shall reply to all inquiries respecting notices received by the corporation in like manner and in the same circumstances as if the corporation had been the trustee of the trust instrument.

(11) In this section 'prescribed fee' means the fee prescribed by the Treasury, with the sanction of the Lord Chancellor, in cases where the Public Trustee acts as a trust corporation for the purposes of this section.

PART V
LEASES AND TENANCIES

139. Effect of extinguishment of reversion

(1) Where a reversion expectant on a lease of land is surrendered or merged, the estate or interest which as against the lessee for the time being confers the next vested right to the land, shall be deemed the reversion for the purpose of preserving the same incidents and obligations as would have affected the original reversion had there been no surrender or merger thereof.

(2) This section applies to surrenders or mergers effected after the first day of October, eighteen hundred and forty-five.

140. Apportionment of conditions on severance

(1) Notwithstanding the severance by conveyance, surrender, or otherwise of the reversionary estate in any land comprised in a lease, and notwithstanding the avoidance or cesser in any other manner of the term granted by a lease as to part only of the land comprised therein, every condition or right of re-entry, and every other condition contained in the lease, shall be apportioned, and shall remain annexed to the severed parts of the reversionary estate as severed, and shall be in force with respect to the term whereon each severed part is reversionary, or the term in the part of the land as to which the term has not been surrendered, or has not been avoided or has not otherwise ceased, in like manner as if the land comprised in each severed part, or the land as to which the term remains subsisting, as the case may be, had alone originally been comprised in the lease.

(2) In this section 'right of re-entry' includes a right to determine the lease by notice to quit or otherwise; but where the notice is served by a person entitled to a severed part of the reversion so that it extends to part only of the land demised, the lessee may within one month determine the lease in regard to the rest of the land by giving to the owner of the reversionary estate therein a counter notice expiring at the same time as the original notice.

(3) This section applies to leases made before or after the commencement of this Act and whether the severance of the reversionary estate or the partial avoidance or cesser of the term was effected before or after such commencement:

Provided that, where the lease was made before the first day of January eighteen hundred and eighty-two nothing in this section shall affect the operation of a severance of the reversionary estate or partial avoidance or cesser of the term which was effected before the commencement of this Act.

141. Rent and benefit of lessee's covenants to run with the reversion

(1) Rent reserved by a lease, and the benefit of every covenant or provision therein contained, having reference to the subject-matter thereof, and on the lessee's part to be observed or performed, and every condition of re-entry and other condition therein contained, shall be annexed and incident to and shall go with the reversionary estate in the land, or in any part thereof, immediately expectant on the term granted by the lease, notwithstanding severance of that reversionary estate, and without prejudice to any liability affecting a covenantor or his estate.

(2) Any such rent, covenant or provision shall be capable of being recovered, received, enforced, and taken advantage of, by the person from time to time entitled, subject to the term, to the income of the whole or any part, as the case may require, of the land leased.

(3) Where that person becomes entitled by conveyance or otherwise, such rent, covenant or provision may be recovered, received, enforced or taken advantage of by him notwithstanding that he becomes so entitled after the condition of re-entry of forfeiture has become enforceable, but this subsection does not render enforceable any condition of re-entry or other condition waived or released before such person becomes entitled as aforesaid.

(4) This section applies to leases made before or after the commencement of this Act, but does not affect the operation of—

(a) any severance of the reversionary estate; or

(b) any acquisition by conveyance or otherwise of the right to receive or enforce any rent covenant or provision;

effected before the commencement of this Act.

Note: Does not apply to tenancies created after the Landlord and Tenant (Covenants) Act 1995 comes into force.

142. Obligation of lessor's covenants to run with reversion

(1) The obligation under a condition or of a covenant entered into by a lessor with reference to the subject-matter of the lease shall, if and as far as the lessor has power to bind the reversionary estate immediately expectant on the term granted by the lease, be annexed and incident to and shall go with that reversionary estate, or the several parts thereof, notwithstanding severance of that reversionary estate, and may be taken advantage of and enforced by the person in whom the term is from time to time vested by conveyance, devolution in law, or otherwise; and, if and as far as the lessor has power to bind the person from time to time entitled to that reversionary estate, the obligation aforesaid may be taken advantage of and enforced against any person so entitled.

(2) This section applies to leases made before or after the commencement of this Act, whether the severance of the reversionary estate was effected before or after such commencement:

Provided that, where the lease was made before the first day of January eighteen hundred and eighty-two, nothing in this section shall affect the operation of any severance of the reversionary estate effected before such commencement.

This section takes effect without prejudice to any liability affecting a covenantor or his estate.

Note: Does not apply to tenancies created after the Landlord and Tenant (Covenants) Act 1995 comes into force.

143. Effect of licences granted to lessees

(1) Where a licence is granted to a lessee to do any act, the licence, unless otherwise expressed, extends only—

(a) to the permission actually given; or

(b) to the specific breach of any provision or covenant referred to; or

(c) to any other matter thereby specifically authorised to be done; and the licence does not prevent any proceeding for any subsequent breach unless otherwise specified in the licence.

(2) Notwithstanding any such licence—

(a) All rights under covenants and powers of re-entry contained in the lease remain in full force and are available as against any subsequent breach of covenant, condition or other matter not specifically authorised or waived, in the same manner as if no licence had been granted; and

(b) The condition or right of entry remains in force in all respects as if the licence had not been granted, save in respect of the particular matter authorised to be done.

(3) Where in any lease there is a power or condition of re-entry on the lessee assigning, subletting or doing any other specified act without a licence, and a licence is granted—

(a) to any one or two or more lessees to do any act, or to deal with his equitable share or interest; or

(b) to any lessee, or to any one of two or more lessees to assign or underlet part only of the property, or to do any act in respect of part only of the property; the licence does not operate to extinguish the right of entry in case of any breach of covenant or condition by the co-lessees of the other shares or interests in the property, or by the lessee or lessees of the rest of the property (as the case may be) in respect of such shares or interests or remaining property, but the right of entry remains in force in respect of the shares, interests or property not the subject of the licence.

This subsection does not authorise the grant after the commencement of this Act of a licence to create an undivided share in a legal estate.

(4) This section applies to licences granted after the thirteenth day of August, eighteen hundred and fifty-nine.

144. No fine to be exacted for licence to assign

In all leases containing a covenant, condition, or agreement against assigning, underletting, or parting with the possession, or disposing of the land or property leased without licence or consent, such covenant, condition, or agreement shall, unless the lease contains an express provision to the contrary, be deemed to be subject to a proviso to the effect that no fine or sum of money in the nature of a fine shall be payable for or in respect of such licence or consent; but this proviso does not preclude the right to require the payment of a reasonable sum in respect of any legal or other expense incurred in relation to such licence or consent.

145. Lessee to give notice of ejectment to lessor

Every lessee to whom there is delivered any writ for the recovery of premises demised to or held by him, or to whose knowledge any such writ comes, shall forthwith give notice thereof to his lessor or his bailiff or receiver, and, if he fails so to do, he shall be liable to forfeit to the person of whom he holds the premises an amount equal to the value of three years' improved or rack rent of the premises, to be recovered by action in any court having jurisdiction in respect of claims for such an amount.

146. Restrictions on and relief against forfeiture of leases and underleases

(1) A right of re-entry or forfeiture under any proviso or stipulation in a lease for a breach of any covenant or condition in the lease shall not be enforceable, by action or otherwise, unless and until the lessor serves on the lessee a notice—

(a) specifying the particular breach complained of; and

(b) if the breach is capable of remedy, requiring the lessee to remedy the breach; and

(c) in any case, requiring the lessee to make compensation in money for the breach; and the lessee fails, within a reasonable time thereafter, to remedy the breach, if it is capable of remedy, and to make reasonable compensation in money, to the satisfaction of the lessor, for the breach.

(2) Where a lessor is proceeding, by action or otherwise, to enforce such a right of re-entry or forfeiture, the lessee may, in the lessor's action, if any, or in any action brought by himself, apply to the court for relief; and the court may grant or refuse relief, as the court, having regard to the proceedings and conduct of the parties under the foregoing provisions of this section, and to all the other circumstances, thinks fit; and in case of relief may grant it on such terms, if any, as to costs, expenses, damages, compensation, penalty, or otherwise, including the granting of an injunction to restrain any like breach in the future, as the court, in the circumstances of each case, thinks fit.

(3) A lessor shall be entitled to recover as a debt due to him from a lessee, and in addition to damages (if any), all reasonable costs and expenses properly incurred by the lessor in the employment of a solicitor and surveyor or valuer, or otherwise, in reference to any breach giving rise to a right of re-entry or forfeiture which, at the request of the lessee, is waived by the lessor, or from which the lessee is relieved, under the provisions of this Act.

(4) Where a lessor is proceeding by action or otherwise to enforce a right of re-entry or forfeiture under any covenant, proviso, or stipulation in a lease, or for non-payment of rent, the court may, on application by any person claiming as under-lessee any estate or interest in the property comprised in the lease or any part thereof, either in the lessor's action (if any) or in any action brought by such person for that purpose, make an order vesting, for the whole term of the lease or any less term, the property comprised in the lease or any part thereof in any person entitled as under-lessee to any estate or interest in such property upon such conditions as to execution of any deed or other document, payment of rent, costs, expenses, damages, compensation, giving security, or otherwise, as the court in the circumstances of each case may think fit, but in no case shall any such under-lessee be entitted to require a lease to be granted to him for any longer than he had under his original sub-lease.

(5) For the purposes of this section—

(a) 'Lease' includes an original or derivative under-lease; also an agreement for a lease where the lessee has become entitted to have his lease granted; also a grant at a fee arm rent, or securing a rent by condition;

(b) 'Lessee' includes an original or derivative under-lessee, and the persons deriving title under a lessee; also a grantee under any such grant as aforesaid and the persons deriving title under him;

(c) 'Lessor' includes an original or derivative under-lessor, and the persons deriving title under a lessor; also a person making such grant as aforesaid and the persons deriving title under him;

(d) 'Under-lease' includes an agreement for an under-lease where the under-lessee has become entitled to have his under-lease granted;

(e) 'Under-lessee' includes any person deriving title under an under-lessee.

(6) This section applies although the proviso or stipulation under which the right of re-entry or forfeiture accrues is inserted in the lease in pursuance of the directions of any Act of Parliament.

(7) For the purposes of this section a lease limited to continue as long only as the lessee abstains from committing a breach of covenant shall be and take effect as a lease to continue for any longer term for which it could subsist, but determinable by a proviso for re-entry on such a breach.

(8) This section does not extend—

(i) To a covenant or condition against assigning, underletting, parting with the possession, or disposing of the land leased where the breach occurred before the commencement of this Act; or

(ii) In the case of a mining lease, to a covenant or condition for allowing the lessor to have access to or inspect books, accounts, records, weighing machines or other things, or to enter or inspect the mine or the workings thereof.

(9) This section does not apply to a condition for forfeiture on the bankruptcy of the lessee or on taking in execution of the lessee's interest if contained in a lease of—

(a) Agricultural or pastoral land;

(b) Mines or minerals;

(c) A house used or intended to be used as a public-house or beershop;

(d) A house let as a dwelling-house, with the use of any furniture, books, works of art, or other chattels not being in the nature of fixtures;

(e) Any property with respect to which the personal qualifications of the tenant are of importance for the preservation of the value or character of the property, or on the ground of neighbourhood to the lessor, or to any person holding under him.

(10) Where a condition of forfeiture on the bankruptcy of the lessee or on taking in execution of the lessee's interest is contained in any lease, other than a lease of any of the classes mentioned in the last sub-section, then—

(a) if the lessee's interest is sold within one year from the bankruptcy or taking in execution, this section applies to the forfeiture condition aforesaid;

(b) if the lessee's interest is not sold before the expiration of that year, this section only applies to the forfeiture condition aforesaid during the first year from the date of the bankruptcy or taking in execution.

(11) This section does not, save as otherwise mentioned, affect the law relating to re-entry or forfeiture or relief in case of non-payment of rent.

(12) This section has effect notwithstanding any stipulation to the contrary.

[(13) The county court has jurisdiction under this section [. . .].]

147. Relief against notice to effect decorative repairs

(1) After a notice is served on a lessee relating to the internal decorative repairs to a house or other building, he may apply to the court for relief, and if, having regard to all the circumstances of the case (including in particular the length of the lessee's term or interest remaining unexpired), the court is satisfied that the notice is unreasonable, it may, by order, wholly or partially relieve the lessee from liability for such repairs.

(2) This section does not apply:—

(i) where the liability arises under an express covenant or agreement to put the property in a decorative state of repair and the covenant or agreement has never been performed;

(ii) to any matter necessary or proper—

(a) for putting or keeping the property in a sanitary condition, or

(b) for the maintenance or preservation of the structure;

(iii) to any statutory liability to keep a house in all respects reasonably fit for human habitation;

(iv) to any covenant or stipulation to yield up the house or other building in a specified state of repair at the end of the term.

(3) In this section 'lease' includes an underlease and an agreement for a lease, and 'lessee' has a corresponding meaning and includes any person liable to effect the repairs.

(4) This section applies whether the notice is served before or after the commencement of this Act, and has effect notwithstanding any stipulation to the contrary.

[(5) The county court has jurisdiction under this section [. . .].]

148. Waiver of a covenant in a lease

(1) Where any actual waiver by a lessor or the persons deriving title under him of the benefit of any covenant or condition in any lease is proved to have taken place in any particular instance, such waiver shall not be deemed to extend to any instance, or to any breach of covenant or condition save that to which such waiver specially relates, nor operate as a general waiver of the benefit of any such covenant or condition.

(2) This section applies unless a contrary intention appears and extends to waivers effected after the twenty-third day of July, eighteen hundred and sixty.

149. Abolition of interesse termini, and as to reversionary leases and leases for lives

(1) The doctrine of interesse termini is hereby abolished.

(2) As from the commencement of this Act all terms of years absolute shall, whether the interest is created before or after such commencement, be capable of taking effect at law or in equity, according to the estate interest or powers of the grantor, from the date fixed for commencement of the term, without actual entry.

(3) A term, at a rent or granted in consideration of a fine, limited after the commencement of this Act to take effect more than twenty-one years from the date of the instrument purporting to create it, shall be void, and any contract made after such commencement to create such a term shall likewise be void; but this subsection does not apply to any term taking effect in equity under a settlement, or created out of an equitable interest under a settlement, or under an equitable power for mortgage, indemnity or other like purposes.

(4) Nothing in subsections (1) and (2) of this section prejudicially affects the right of any person to recover any rent or to enforce or take advantage of any covenants or conditions, or, as respects terms or interests created before the commencement of this Act, operates to vary any statutory or other obligations imposed in respect of such terms or interests.

(5) Nothing in this Act affects the rule of law that a legal term, whether or not being a mortgage term, may be created to take effect in reversion expectant on a longer term, which rule is hereby confirmed.

(6) Any lease or underlease, at a rent, or in consideration of a fine, for life or lives or for any term of years determinable with life or lives, or on the marriage of the lessee, or any contract therefor, made before or after the commencement of this Act, or created by virtue of Part V. of the Law of Property Act, 1922, shall take effect as a lease, underlease or contract therefor, for a term of ninety years determinable after the death or marriage (as the case may be) of the original lessee, or of the survivor of the original lessees, by at least one month's notice in writing given to determine the same on one of the quarter days applicable to the tenancy, either by the lessor or the persons deriving title under him, to the person entitled to the leasehold interest, or if no such person is in existence by affixing the same to the premises, or by the lessee or other persons in whom the leasehold interest is vested to the lessor or the persons deriving title under him:

Provided that—

(a) this subsection shall not apply to any term taking effect in equity under a settlement or created out of an equitable interest under a settlement for mortgage, indemnity, or other like purposes;

(b) the person in whom the leasehold interest is vested by virtue of Part V. of the Law of Property Act, 1922, shall, for the purposes of this subsection, be deemed an original lessee;

(c) if the lease, underlease, or contract therefor is made determinable on the dropping of the lives of persons other than or besides the lessees, then the notice shall be capable of being served after the death of any person or of the survivor of any persons (whether or not including the lessees) on the cesser of whose life or lives the lease, underlease, or contract is made determinable, instead of after the death of the original lessee or of the survivor of the original lessees;

(d) if there are no quarter days specially applicable to the tenancy, notice may be given to determine the tenancy on one of the usual quarter days.

150. Surrender of a lease, without prejudice to underleases with a view to the grant of a new lease

(1) A lease may be surrendered with a view to the acceptance of a new lease in place thereof, without a surrender of any under-lease derived thereout.

(2) A new lease may be granted and accepted, in place of any lease so surrendered, without any such surrender of an under-lease as aforesaid, and the new lease operates as if all under-leases derived out of the surrendered lease had been surrendered before the surrender of that lease was effected.

(3) The lessee under the new lease and any person deriving title under him is entitled to the same rights and remedies in respect of the rent reserved by and the covenants, agreements and conditions contained in any under-lease as if the original lease had not been surrendered but was or remained vested in him.

(4) Each under-lessee and any person deriving title under him is entitled to hold and enjoy the land comprised in his under-lease (subject to the payment of any rent reserved by and to the observance of the covenants agreements and conditions contained in the under-lease) as if the lease out of which the under-lease was derived had not been surrendered.

(5) The lessor granting the new lease and any person deriving title under him is entitled to the same remedies, by distress or entry in and upon the land comprised in any such under-lease for rent reserved by or for breach of any covenant, agreement or condition contained in the new lease (so far only as the rents reserved by or the covenants, agreements or conditions contained in the new lease do not exceed or impose greater burdens than those reserved by or contained in the original lease out of which the under-lease is derived) as he would have had—

(a) If the original lease had remained on foot; or

(b) If a new under-lease derived out of the new lease had been granted to the under—lessee or a person deriving title under him; as the case may require.

(6) This section does not affect the powers of the court to give relief against forfeiture.

151. Provision as to attornments by tenants

(1) Where land is subject to a lease—

(a) the conveyance of a reversion in the land expectant on the determination of the lease; or

(b) the creation or conveyance of a rentcharge to issue or issuing out of the land; shall be valid without any attorrnment of the lessee:

Nothing in this subsection—

(i) affects the validity of any payment of rent by the lessee to the person making the conveyance or grant before notice of the conveyance or grant is given to him by the person entitled thereunder; or

(ii) renders the lessee liable for any breach of covenant to pay rent, on account of his failure to pay rent to the person entitled under the conveyance or grant before such notice is given to the lessee.

(2) An attornment by the lessee in respect of any land to a person claiming to be entitled to the interest in the land of the lessor, if made without the consent of the lessor, shall be void.

This subsection does not apply to an attornment—

(a) made pursuant to a judgment of a court of competent jurisdiction; or

(b) to a mortgagee, by a lessee holding under a lease from the mortgagor where the right of redemption is barred; or

(c) to any other person rightfully deriving title under the lessor.

152. Leases invalidated by reason of non-compliance with terms of powers under which they are granted

(1) Where in the intended exercise of any power of leasing, whether conferred by an Act of Parliament or any other instrument, a lease (in this section referred to as an invalid lease) is granted, which by reason of any failure to comply with the terms of the power is invalid, then—

(a) as against the person entitled after the determination of the interest of the grantor to the reversion; or

(b) as against any other person who, subject to any lease properly granted under the power, would have been entitled to the land comprised in the lease, the lease, if it was made in good faith, and the lessee has entered, thereunder, shall take effect in equity as a contract for the grant, at the request of the lessee, of a valid lease under the power, of like effect as the invalid lease, subject to such variations as may be necessary in order to comply with the terms of the power:

Provided that a lessee under an invalid lease shall not, by virtue of any such implied contract, be entitled to obtain a variation of the lease if the other persons who would have been bound by the contract are willing and able to confirm the lease without variation.

(2) Where a lease granted in the intended exercise of such a power is invalid by reason of the grantor not having power to grant the lease at the date thereof, but the grantor's interest in the land comprised therein continues after the time when he might, in the exercise of the power, have properly granted a lease in the like terms, the lease shall take effect as a valid lease in like manner as if it had been granted at that time.

(3) Where during the continuance of the possession taken under an invalid lease the person for the time being entitled, subject to such possession, to the land comprised therein or to the rents and profits thereof, is able to confirm the lease without variation, the lessee, or other person who would have been bound by the lease had it been valid, shall, at the request of the person so able to confirm the lease, be bound to accept a confirmation thereof, and thereupon the lease shall have effect and be deemed to have had effect as a valid lease from the grant thereof.

Configuration under this subsection may be by a memorandum in writing signed by or on behalf of the persons respectively confirming and accepting the confirmation of the lease.

(4) Where a receipt or a memorandum in writing confirming an invalid lease is, upon or before the acceptance of the rent thereunder, signed by or on behalf of the person accepting the rent, that acceptance shall, as against that person, be deemed to be a confirmation of the lease.

(5) The foregoing provisions of this section do not affect prejudicially—

(a) any right of action or other right or remedy to which, but for those provisions or any enactment replaced by those provisions, the lessee named in an invalid lease would or might have been entitled under any covenant on the part of the grantor for title or quiet enjoyment contained therein or implied thereby; or

(b) any right of re-entry or other right or remedy to which, but for those provisions or any enactment replaced thereby, the grantor or other person for the time being entitled to the reversion expectant on the termination of the lease, would or might have been entitled by reason of any breach of the covenants, conditions or provisions contained in the lease and binding on the lessee.

(6) Where a valid power of leasing is vested in or may be exercised by a person who grants a lease which, by reason of the determination of the interest of the grantor or

otherwise, cannot have effect and continuance according to the terms thereof independently of the power, the lease shall for the purposes of this section be deemed to have been granted in the intended exercise of the power although the power is not referred to in the lease.

(7) This section does not apply to a lease of land held on charitable, ecclesiastical or public trusts.

(8) This section takes effect without prejudice to the provision in this Act for the grant of leases in the name and on behalf of the estate owner of the land affected.

153. Enlargement of residue of long terms into fee simple estates

(1) Where a residue unexpired of not less than two hundred years of a term, which, as originally created, was for not less than three hundred years, is subsisting in land, whether being the whole land originally comprised in the term, or part only thereof,—

(a) without any trust or right of redemption affecting the term in favour of the freeholder, or other person entitled in reversion expectant on the term; and

(b) without any rent, or with merely a peppercorn rent or other rent having no money value, incident to the reversion, or having had a rent, not being merely a peppercorn rent or other rent having no money value, originally so incident, which subsequently has been released or has become barred by lapse of time, or has in any other way ceased to be payable;

the term may be enlarged into a fee simple in the manner, and subject to the restrictions in this section provided.

(2) This section applies to and includes every such term as aforesaid whenever created, whether or not having the freehold as the immediate reversion thereon; but does not apply to—

(i) Any term liable to be determined by re-entry for condition broken; or

(ii) Any term created by subdemise out of a superior term, itself incapable of being enlarged into fee simple.

(3) This section extends to mortgage terms, where the right of redemption is barred.

(4) A rent not exceeding the yearly sum of one pound which has not been collected or paid for a continuous period of twenty years or upwards shall, for the purposes of this section, be deemed to have ceased to be payable:

Provided that, of the said period, at least five years must have elapsed after the commencement of this Act.

(5) Where a rent incident to a reversion expectant on a term to which this section applies is deemed to have ceased to be payable for the purposes aforesaid, no claim for such rent or for any arrears thereof shall be capable of being enforced.

(6) Each of the following persons, namely—

(i) Any person beneficially entitled in right of the term, whether subject to any incumbrance or not, to possession of any land comprised in the term, and, in the case of a married woman without the concurrence of her husband, whether or not she is entitled for her separate use or as her separate property, [. . .];

(ii) Any person being in receipt of income as trustee, in right of the term, or having the term vested in him [as a trustee of land], whether subject to any incumbrance or not;

(iii) Any person in whom, as personal representative of any deceased person, the term is vested, whether subject to any incumbrance or not; shall, so far as regards the land to which he is entitled, or in which he is interested in right of the term, in any such character as aforesaid, have power by deed to declare to the effect that, from and after the execution of the deed, the term shall be enlarged into a fee simple.

(7) Thereupon, by virtue of the deed and of this Act, the term shall become and be enlarged accordingly, and the person in whom the term was previously vested shall acquire and have in the land a fee simple instead of the term.

(8) The estate in fee simple so acquired by enlargement shall be subject to all the same trusts, powers, executory limitations over, rights, and equities, and to all the same covenants and provisions relating to user and enjoyment, and to all the same obligations of every kind, as the term would have been subject to if it had not been so enlarged.

(9) But where—

(a) any land so held for the residue of a term has been settled in trust by reference to other land, being freehold land, so as to go along with that other land, or, in the case of settlements coming into operation before the commencement of this Act, so as to go along with that other land as far as the law permits; and

(b) at the time of enlargement, the ultimate beneficial interest in the term, whether subject to any subsisting particular estate or not, has not become absolutely and indefeasibly vested in any person, free from charges or powers of charging created by a settlement; the estate in fee simple acquired as aforesaid shall, without prejudice to any conveyance for value previously made by a person having a contingent or defeasible interest in the term, be liable to be, and shall be, conveyed by means of a subsidiary vesting instrument and settled in like manner as the other land, being freehold land, aforesaid, and until so conveyed and settled shall devolve beneficially as if it had been so conveyed and settled.

(10) The estate in fee simple so acquired shall, whether the term was originally created without impeachment of waste or not, include the fee simple in all mines and minerals which at the time of enlargement have not been severed in right or in fact, or have not been severed or reserved by an inclosure Act or award.

154. Application of Part V. to existing leases

This Part of this Act, except where otherwise expressly provided, applies to leases created before or after the commencement of this Act, and 'lease' includes an under-lease or other tenancy.

PART VI
POWERS

155. Release of powers simply collateral

A person to whom any power, whether coupled with an interest or not, is given may by deed release, or contract not to exercise, the power.

156. Disclaimer of power

(1) A person to whom any power, whether coupled with an interest or not, is given may by deed disclaim the power, and, after disclaimer, shall not be capable of exercising or joining in the exercise of the power.

(2) On such disclaimer, the power may be exercised by the other person or persons or the survivor or survivors of the other persons, to whom the power is given, unless the contrary is expressed in the instrument creating the power.

157. Protection of purchasers claiming under certain void appointments

(1) An instrument purporting to exercise a power of appointment over property, which, in default of and subject to any appointment, is held in trust for a class or number of persons of whom the appointee is one, shall not (save as hereinafter provided) be void on the ground of fraud on the power as against a purchaser in good faith:

Provided that, if the interest appointed exceeds, in amount or value, the interest in such property to which immediately before the execution of the instrument the appointee was presumptively entitled under the trust in default of appointment, having regard to any advances made in his favour and to any hotchpot provision, the protection afforded by this section to a purchaser shall not extend to such excess.

(2) In this section 'a purchaser in good faith' means a person dealing with an appointee of the age of not less than twenty-five years for valuable consideration in

money or money's worth, and without notice of the fraud, or of any circumstances from which, if reasonable inquiries had been made, the fraud might have been discovered.

(3) Persons deriving title under any purchaser entitled to the benefit of this section shall be entitled to the like benefit.

(4) This section applies only to dealings effected after the commencement of this Act.

158. Validation of appointments where objects are excluded or take illusory shares

(1) No appointment made in exercise of any power to appoint any property among two or more objects shall be invalid on the ground that—

(a) an unsubstantial, illusory, or nominal share only is appointed to or left unappointed to devolve upon any one or more of the objects of the power; or

(b) any object of the power is thereby altogether excluded; but every such appointment shall be valid notwithstanding that any one or more of the objects is not thereby, or in default of appointment, to take any share in the property.

(2) This section does not affect any provision in the instrument creating the power which declares the amount of any share from which any object of the power is not to be excluded.

(3) This section applies to appointments made before or after the commencement of this Act.

159. Execution of powers not testamentary

(1) A deed executed in the presence of and attested by two or more witnesses (in the manner in which deeds are ordinarily executed and attested) is so far as respects the execution and attestation thereof, a valid execution of a power of appointment by deed or by any instrument in writing, not testamentary, notwithstanding that it is expressly required that a deed or instrument in writing, made in exercise of the power, is to be executed or attested with some additional or other form of execution or attestation or solemnity.

(2) This section does not operate to defeat any direction in the instrument creating the power that—

(a) the consent of any particular person is to be necessary to a valid execution;

(b) in order to give validity to any appointment, any act is to be performed having no relation to the mode of executing and attesting the instrument.

(3) This section does not prevent the donee of a power from executing it in accordance with the power by writing, or otherwise than by an instrument executed and attested as a deed; and where a power is so executed this section does not apply.

(4) This section applies to appointments by deed made after the thirteenth day of August, eighteen hundred and fifty-nine.

160. Application of Part VI. to existing powers

This Part of this Act applies to powers created or arising either before or after the commencement of this Act.

PART VII
PERPETUITIES AND ACCUMULATIONS

Perpetuities

161. Abolition of the double possibility rule

(1) The rule of law prohibiting the limitation, after a life interest to an unborn person, of an interest in land to the unborn child or other issue of an unborn person is hereby abolished, but without prejudice to any other rule relating to perpetuities.

(2) This section only applies to limitations or trusts created by an instrument coming into operation after the commencement of this Act.

162. Restrictions on the perpetuity rule

(1) For removing doubts, it is hereby declared that the rule of law relating to perpetuities does not apply and shall be deemed never to have applied—

(a) To any power to distrain on or to take possession of land or the income thereof given by way of indemnity against a rent, whether charged upon or payable in respect of any part of that land or not; or

(b) To any rentcharge created only as an indemnity against another rentcharge, although the indemnity rentcharge may only arise or become payable on breach of a condition or stipulation; or

(c) To any power, whether exercisable on breach of a condition or stipulation or not, to retain or withhold payment of any instalment of a rentcharge as an indemnity against another rentcharge; or

(d) To any grant, exception, or reservation of any right of entry on, or user of, the surface of land or of any easements, rights, or privileges over or under land for the purpose of—

(i) winning, working, inspecting, measuring, converting, manufacturing, carrying away, and disposing of mines and minerals;

(ii) inspecting, grubbing up, felling and carrying away timber and other trees, and the tops and lops thereof;

(iii) executing repairs, alterations, or additions to any adjoining land, or the buildings and erections thereon;

(iv) constructing, laying down, altering, repairing, renewing, cleansing, and maintaining sewers, watercourses, cesspools, gutters, drains, water-pipes, gas-pipes, electric wires or cables or other like works.

(2) This section applies to instruments coming into operation before or after the commencement of this Act.

163. Validation of certain gifts void for remoteness[1]

(1) Where in a will, settlement or other instrument the absolute vesting either of capital or income of property, or the ascertainment of a beneficiary or class of beneficiaries, is made to depend on the attainment by the beneficiary or members of the class of an age exceeding twenty-one years, and thereby the gift to that beneficiary or class or any member thereof, or any gift over, remainder, executory limitation, or trust arising on the total or partial failure of the original gift, is, or but for this section would be, rendered void for remoteness, the will, settlement, or other instrument shall take effect for the purposes of such gift, gift over, remainder, executory limitation, or trust as if the absolute vesting or ascertainment aforesaid had been made to depend on the beneficiary or member of the class attaining the age of twenty-one years, and that age shall be substituted for the age stated in the will, settlement, or other instrument.

(2) This section applies to any instrument executed after the commencement of this Act and to any testamentary appointment (whether made in exercise of a general or special power), devise, or bequest contained in the will of a person dying after such commencement, whether the will is made before or after such commencement.

(3) This section applies without prejudice to any provision whereby the absolute vesting or ascertainment is also made to depend on the marriage of any person, or any other event which may occur before the age stated in the will, settlement, or other instrument attained.

Note

[1]Repealed in respect of instruments taking effect after 15 July 1964 by the Perpetuities and Accumulations Act.

Accumulations

164. General restrictions on accumulation of income

(1) No person may by any instrument or otherwise settle or dispose of any property in such manner that the income thereof shall, save as hereinafter mentioned, be wholly or partially accumulated for any longer period than one of the following, namely:—

(a) the life of the grantor or settlor; or

(b) a term of twenty-one years from the death of the grantor, settlor or testator; or

(c) the duration of the minority or respective minorities of any person or persons living or en ventre sa mere at the death of the grantor, settlor or testator; or

(d) the duration of the minority or respective minorities only of any person or persons who under the limitations of the instrument directing the accumulations would, for the time being, if of full age, be entitled to the income directed to be accumulated.

In every case where any accumulation is directed otherwise than as aforesaid, the direction shall (save as hereinafter mentioned) be void; and the income of the property directed to be accumulated shall, so long as the same is directed to be accumulated contrary to this section, go to and be received by the person or persons who would have been entitled thereto if such accumulation had not been directed.

(2) This section does not extend to any provision—

(i) for payment of the debts of any grantor, settlor, testator or other person;

(ii) for raising portions for—

(a) any child, children or remoter issue of any grantor, settlor or testator; or

(b) any child, children or remoter issue of a person taking any interest under any settlement or other disposition directing the accumulations or to whom any interest is thereby limited;

(iii) respecting the accumulation of the produce of timber or wood;

and accordingly such provisions may be made as if no statutory restrictions on accumulation of income had been imposed.

(3) The restrictions imposed by this section apply to instruments made on or after the twenty-eighth day of July, eighteen hundred, but in the case of wills only where the testator was living and of testamentary capacity after the end of one year from that date.

165. Qualification of restrictions on accumulation

Where accumulations of surplus income are made during a minority under any statutory power or under the general law, the period for which such accumulations are made is not (whether the trust was created or the accumulations were made before or after the commencement of this Act) to be taken into account in determining the periods for which accumulations are permitted to be made by the last preceding section, and accordingly an express trust for accumulation for any other permitted period shall not be deemed to have been invalidated or become invalid, by reason of accumulations also having been made as aforesaid during such minority.

166. Restriction on accumulation for the purchase of land

(1) No person may settle or dispose of any property in such manner that the income thereof shall be wholly or partially accumulated for the purchase of land only, for any longer period than the duration of the minority or respective minorities of any person or persons who, under the limitations of the instrument directing the accumulation, would for the time being, if of full age, be entitled to the income so directed to be accumulated.

(2) This section does not, nor do the enactments which it replaces, apply to accumulations to be held as capital money for the purposes of the Settled Land Act, 1925, or the enactments replaced by that Act, whether or not the accumulations are primarily liable to be laid out in the purchase of land.

(3) This section applies to settlements and dispositions made after the twenty-seventh day of June eighteen hundred and ninety-two.

PART IX
VOIDABLE DISPOSITIONS

173. Voluntary disposition of land how far voidable as against purchasers

(1) Every voluntary disposition of land made with intent to defraud a subsequent purchaser is voidable at the instance of that purchaser.

(2) For the purposes of this section, no voluntary disposition, whenever made, shall be deemed to have been made with intent to defraud by reason only that a subsequent conveyance for valuable consideration was made, if such subsequent conveyance was made after the twenty-eighth day of June, eighteen hundred and ninety-three.

174. Acquisitions of reversions at an under value

(1) No acquisition made in good faith, without fraud or unfair dealing, of any reversionary interest in real or personal property, for money or money's worth, shall be liable to be opened or set aside merely on the ground of under value.

In this subsection 'reversionary interest' includes an expectancy or possibility.

(2) This section does not affect the jurisdiction of the court to set aside or modify unconscionable bargains.

PART X
WILLS

175. Contingent and future testamentary gifts to carry the intermediate income

(1) A contingent or future specific devise or bequest of property, whether real or personal, and a contingent residuary devise of freehold land, and a specific or residuary devise of freehold land to trustees upon trust for persons whose interests are contingent or executory shall, subject to the statutory provisions relating to accumulations, carry the intermediate income of that property from the death of the testator, except so far as such income, or any part thereof, may be otherwise expressly disposed of.

(2) This section applies only to wills coming into operation after the commencement of this Act.

176. Power for tenant in tail in possession to dispose of property by specific devise or bequest

(1) A tenant in tail of full age shall have power to dispose by will, by means of a devise or bequest referring specifically either to the property or to the instrument under which it was acquired or to entailed property generally—

(a) of all property of which he is tenant in tail in possession at his death; and

(b) of money (including the proceeds of property directed to be sold) subject to be invested in the purchase of property, of which if it had been so invested he would have been tenant in tail in possession at his death;

in like manner as if, after barring the entail, he had been tenant in fee-simple or absolute owner thereof for an equitable interest at his death, but, subject to and in default of any such disposition by will, such property shall devolve in the same manner as if this section had not been passed.

(2) This section applies to entailed interests authorised to be created by this Act as well as to estates tail created before the commencement of this Act, but does not extend to a tenant in tail who is by statute restrained from barring or defeating his estate tail, whether the land or property in respect whereof he is so restrained was purchased with money provided by Parliament in consideration of public services or not, or to a tenant in tail after possibility of issue extinct, and does not render any interest which is not disposed of by the will of the tenant in tail liable for his debts or other liabilities.

(3) In this section 'tenant in tail' includes an owner of a base fee in possession who has power to enlarge the base fee into a fee-simple without the concurrence of any other person.

(4) This section only applies to wills executed after the commencement of this Act, or confirmed or republished by codicil executed after such commencement.

PART XI
MISCELLANEOUS

184. Presumption of survivorship in regard to claims to property

In all cases where, after the commencement of this Act, two or more persons have died in circumstances rendering it uncertain which of them survived the other or others, such deaths shall (subject to any order of the court), for all purposes affecting the title to property, be presumed to have occurred in order of seniority, and accordingly the younger shall be deemed to have survived the elder.

185. Merger

There is no merger by operation of law only of any estate the beneficial interest in which would not be deemed to be merged or extinguished in equity.

186. Rights of preemption capable of release

All statutory and other rights of preemption affecting a legal estate shall be and be deemed always to have been capable of release, and unless released shall remain in force as equitable interests only.

187. Legal easements

(1) Where an easement, right or privilege for a legal estate is created, it shall enure for the benefit of the land to which it is intended to be annexed.

(2) Nothing in this Act affects the right of a person to acquire, hold or exercise an easement, right or privilege over or in relation to land for a legal estate in common with any other person, or the power of creating or conveying such an easement right or privilege.

188. Power to direct division of chattels

(1) Where any chattels belong to persons in undivided shares, the persons interested in a moiety or upwards may apply to the court for an order for division of the chattels or any of them, according to a valuation or otherwise, and the court may make such order and give any consequential directions as it thinks fit.

(2) . . .

189. Indemnities against rents

(1) A power of distress given by way of indemnity against a rent or any part thereof payable in respect of any land, or against the breach of any covenant or condition in relation to land, is not and shall not be deemed ever to have been a bill of sale within the meaning of the Bills of Sale Acts, 1878 and 1882, as amended by any subsequent enactment.

(2) The benefit of all covenants and powers given by way of indemnity against a rent or any part thereof payable in respect of land, or against the breach of any covenant or condition in relation to land, is and shall be deemed always to have been annexed to the land to which the indemnity is intended to relate, and may be enforced by the estate owner for the time being of the whole or any part of that land, notwithstanding that the benefit may not have been expressly apportioned or assigned to him or to any of his predecessors in title.

Redemption and Apportionment of Rents, etc.

190. Equitable apportionment of rents and remedies for non-payment or breach of covenant

(1) Where in a conveyance for valuable consideration, other than a mortgage, or part of land which is affected by a rentcharge, such rentcharge or a part thereof is, without the consent of the owner thereof, expressed to be—

(a) charged exclusively on the land conveyed or any part thereof in exoneration of the land retained or other land; or

(b) charged exclusively on the land retained or any part thereof in exoneration of the land conveyed or other land; or

(c) apportioned between the land conveyed or any part thereof, and the land retained by the grantor or any part thereof;

then, without prejudice to the rights of the owner of the rentcharge, such charge or apportionment shall be binding as between the grantor and the grantee under the conveyance and their respective successors in title.

(2) Where—

(a) any default is made in payment of the whole or part of a rentcharge by the person who, by reason of such charge or apportionment as aforesaid, is liable to pay the same; or

(b) any breach occurs of any of the covenants (other than in the case of an apportionment the covenant to pay the entire rentcharge) or conditions contained in the deed or other document creating the rentcharge, so far as the same relate to the land retained or conveyed, as the case may be;

the owner for the time being of any other land affected by the entire rentcharge who—

(i) pays or is required to pay the whole or part of the rentcharge which ought to have been paid by the defaulter aforesaid; or

(ii) incurs any costs, damages or expenses by reason of the breach of covenant or condition aforesaid,

may enter into and distrain on the land in respect of which the default or breach is made or occurs, or any part of that land, and dispose according to law of any distress found, and may also take possession of the income of the same land until, by means of such distress and receipt of income or otherwise the whole or part of the rentcharge (charged or apportioned as aforesaid) so unpaid and all costs, damages and expenses incurred by reason of the non-payment thereof or of the breach of the said covenants and conditions, are fully paid or satisfied.

(3) Where in a conveyance for valuable consideration, other than a mortgage, of part of land comprised in a lease, for the residue of the term or interest created by the lease, the rent reserved by such lease or a part thereof is, without the consent of the lessor, expressed to be—

(a) charged exclusively on the land conveyed or any part thereof in exoneration of the land retained by the assignor or other land; or

(b) charged exclusively on the land retained by the assignor or any part thereof in exoneration of the land conveyed or other land; or

(c) appportioned between the land conveyed or any part thereof and the land retained by the assignor or any part thereof;

then, without prejudice to the rights of the lessor, such charge or apportionment shall be binding as between the assignor and the assignee under the conveyance and their respective successors in title.

(4) Where—

(a) any default is made in payment of the whole or part of a rent by the person who, by reason of such charge or apportionment as aforesaid, is liable to pay the same; or

(b) any breach occurs of any of the lessee's covenants (other than in the case of an apportionment the covenant to pay the entire rent) or conditions contained in the lease, so far as the same relate to the land retained or conveyed, as the case may be; the lessee for the time being of any other land comprised in the lease, in whom, as respects that land, the residue of the term or interest created by the lease is vested, who—

(i) pays or is required to pay the whole or part of the rent which ought to have been paid by the defaulter aforesaid; or

(ii) incurs any costs, damages or expenses by reason of the breach of covenant or condition aforesaid;

may enter into and distrain on the land comprised in the lease in respect of which the default or breach is made or occurs, or any part of that land, and dispose according to law of any distress found, and may also take possession of the income of the same land until (so long as the term or interest created by the lease is subsisting) by means of such distress and receipt of income or otherwise, the whole or part of the rent (charged or apportioned as aforesaid) so unpaid and all costs, damages and expenses incurred by reason of the non-payment thereof or of the breach of the said covenants and conditions, are fully paid or satisfied.

(5) The remedies conferred by this section take effect so far only as they might have been conferred by the conveyance whereby the rent or any part thereof is expressed to be charged or apportioned as aforesaid, but a trustee, personal representative, mortgagee or other person in a fiduciary position has, and shall be deemed always to have had, power to confer the same or like remedies.

(6) This section applies only if and so far as a contrary intention is not expressed in the conveyance whereby the rent or any part thereof is expressed to be charged or apportioned as aforesaid, and takes effect subject to the terms of that conveyance and to the provisions therein contained.

(7) The remedies conferred by this section apply only where the conveyance whereby the rent or any part thereof is expressed to be charged or apportioned is made after the commencement of this Act, and do not apply where the rent is charged exclusively as aforesaid or legally apportioned with the consent of the owner or lessor.

(8) The rule of law relating to perpetuities does not affect the powers or remedies conferred by this section or any like powers or remedies expressly conferred, before or after the commencement of this Act, by an instrument.

Commons and Waste Lands

193. Rights of the public over commons and waste lands

(1) Members of the public shall, subject as hereinafter provided, have rights of access for air and exercise to any land which is a metropolitan common within the meaning of the Metropolitan Commons Acts, 1866 to 1898, or manorial waste, or a common which is wholly or partly situated within [an area which immediately before 1st April 1974 was] a borough or urban district, and to any land which at the commencement of this Act is subject to rights of common and to which this section may from time to time be applied in manner hereinafter provided:

Provided that—

(a) such rights of access shall be subject to any Act, scheme, or provisional order for the regulation of the land, and to any byelaw, regulation or order made thereunder or under any other statutory authority; and

(b) the Minister shall, on the application of any person entitled as lord of the manor or otherwise to the soil of the land, or entitled to any commonable rights affecting the land, impose such limitations on and conditions as to the exercise of the rights of access or as to the extent of the land to be affected as, in the opinion of the Minister, are necessary or desirable for preventing any estate, right or interest of a profitable or beneficial nature in, over, or affecting the land from being injuriously affected, or for protecting any object of historical interest and, where any such limitations or conditions are so imposed, the rights of access shall be subject thereto; and

(c) such rights of access shall not include any right to draw or drive upon the land a carriage, cart, caravan, truck, or other vehicle, or to camp or light any fire thereon; and

(d) the rights of access shall cease to apply—

(i) to any land over which the commonable rights are extinguished under any statutory provision;

(ii) to any land over which the commonable rights are otherwise extinguished if the council of the county [or county borough] in which the land is situated by resolution assent to its exclusion from the operation of this section, and the resolution is approved by the Minister.

(2) The lord of the manor or other person entitled to the soil of any land subject to rights of common may by deed, revocable or irrevocable, declare that this section shall apply to the land, and upon such deed being deposited with the Minister the land shall, so long as the deed remains operative, be land to which this section applies.

194. Restrictions on inclosure of commons

(1) The erection of any building or fence, or the construction of any other work, whereby access to land to which this section applies is prevented or impeded, shall not be lawful unless the consent of the Minister thereto is obtained, and in giving or withholding his consent the Minister shall have regard to the same considerations and shall, if necessary, hold the same inquiries as are directed by the Commons Act, 1876, to be taken into consideration and held by the Minister before forming an opinion whether an application under the Inclosure Acts, 1845 to 1882, shall be acceded to or not.

(2) Where any building or fence is erected, or any other work constructed without such consent as is required by this section, the county court within whose jurisdiction the land is situated, shall, on an application being made by the council of any county [. . .] or district concerned, or by the lord of the manor or any other person interested in the common, have power to make an order for the removal of the work, and the restoration of the land to the condition in which it was before the work was erected or constructed, but any such order shall be subject to the like appeal as an order made under section thirty of the Commons Act, 1876.

(3) This section applies to any land which at the commencement of this Act is subject to rights of common:

Provided that this section shall cease to apply—

(a) to any land over which the rights of common are extinguished under any statutory provision

(b) to any land over which the rights of common are otherwise extinguished, if the council of the county [. . .] [or metropolitan district] in which the land is situated by resolution assent to its exclusion from the operation of this section and the resolution is approved by the Minister.

(4) This section does not apply to any building or fence erected or work constructed if specially authorised by Act of Parliament, or in pursuance of an Act of Parliament or Order having the force of an Act, or if lawfully erected or constructed in connexion with the taking or working of minerals in or under any land to which the section is otherwise applicable, or to any [telecommunication apparatus installed for the purposes of a telecommunications code system].

Judgments, etc. affecting Land

195. Equitable charges in right of judgment debt, etc.

(1)—(3) [. . .]

(4) A recognisance, on behalf of the Crown or otherwise, whether entered into before or after the commencement of this Act, and an inquisition finding a debt due to the Crown, and any obligation or speciality made to or in favour of the Crown, whatever may have been its date, shall not operate as a charge on any interest in land, or on the unpaid purchase money for any land, unless or until a writ or order, for the purpose of enforcing it, is registered in the register of writs and orders at the Land Registry.

(5) [. . .]

198. Registration under the Land Charges Act, 1925, to be notice

(1) The registration of any instrument or matter [in any register kept under the Land Charges Act 1972 or any local land charges register], shall be deemed to constitute

actual notice of such instrument or matter, and of the fact of such registration, to all persons and for all purposes connected with the land affected, as from the date of registration or other prescribed date and so long as the registration continues in force.

(2) This section operates without prejudice to the provisions of this Act respecting the making of further advances by a mortgagee, and applies only to instruments and matters required or authorised to be registered [in any such register].

199. Restrictions on constructive notice

(1) A purchaser shall not be prejudicially affected by notice of—

(i) any instrument or matter capable of registration under the provisions of the Land Charges Act, 1925, or any enactment which it replaces, which is void or not enforceable as against him under that Act or enactment, by reason of the non-registration thereof;

(ii) any other instrument or matter or any fact or thing unless—

(a) it is within his own knowledge, or would have come to his knowledge if such inquiries and inspections had been made as ought reasonably to have been made by him; or

(b) in the same transaction with respect to which a question of notice to the purchaser arises, it has come to the knowledge of his counsel, as such, or of his solicitor or other agent, as such, or would have come to the knowledge of his solicitor or other agent, as such, if such inquiries and inspections had been made as ought reasonably to have been made by the solicitor or other agent.

(2) Paragraph (ii) of the last subsection shall not exempt a purchaser from any liability under, or any obligation to perform or observe, any covenant, condition, provision, or restriction contained in any instrument under which his title is derived, mediately or immediately; and such liability or obligation may be enforced in the same manner and to the same extent as if that paragraph had not been enacted.

(3) A purchaser shall not by reason of anything in this section be affected by notice in any case where he would not have been so affected if this section had not been enacted.

(4) This section applies to purchases made either before or after the commencement of this Act.

200. Notice of restrictive covenants and easements

(1) Where land having a common title with other land is disposed of to a purchaser (other than a lessee or a mortgagee) who does not hold or obtain possession of the documents forming the common title, such purchaser, notwithstanding any stipulation to the contrary, may require that a memorandum giving notice of any provision contained in the disposition to him restrictive of user of, or giving rights over, any other land comprised in the common title, shall, where practicable, be written or indorsed on, or, where impracticable, be permanently annexed to some one document selected by the purchaser but retained in the possession or power of the person who makes the disposition, and being or forming part of the common title.

(2) The title of any person omitting to require an indorsement to be made or a memorandum to be annexed shall not, by reason only of this enactment, be prejudiced or affected by the omission.

(3) This section does not apply to dispositions of registered land.

(4) Nothing in this section affects the obligation to register a land charge in respect of—

(a) any restrictive covenant or agreement affecting freehold land; or
(b) any estate contract; or
(c) any equitable easement, liberty or privilege.

PART XII
CONSTRUCTION, JURISDICTION, AND GENERAL PROVISIONS

201. Provisions of Act to apply to incorporeal hereditaments

(1) The provisions of this Act relating to freehold land apply to manors, reputed manors, lordships, advowsons, [. . .] perpetual rentcharges, and other incorporeal hereditaments, subject only to the qualifications necessarily arising by reason of the inherent nature of the hereditament affected.

(2) This Act does not affect the special restrictions imposed on dealing with advowsons by the Benefices Act, 1898, or any other statute or measure, nor affect the limitation of, or authorise any disposition to be made of, a title or dignity of honour which in its nature is inalienable.

(3) [. . .]

202. Provisions as to enfranchisement of copyholds, etc.

For giving effect to this Act, the enfranchisement of copyhold land, and the conversion into long terms of perpetually renewable leaseholds, and of leases for lives and of leases for years terminable with life or lives or on marriage, effected by the Law of Property Act, 1922, as amended by any subsequent enactment, shall be deemed to have been effected immediately before the commencement of this Act.

205. General definitions

(1) In this Act unless the context otherwise requires, the following expressions have the meanings hereby assigned to them respectively, that is to say:—

(i) 'Bankruptcy' includes liquidation by arrangement; also in relation to a corporation means the winding up thereof;

(ii) 'Conveyance' includes a mortgage, charge, lease, assent, vesting declaration, vesting instrument, disclaimer, release and every other assurance of property or of an interest therein by any instrument, except a will; 'convey' has a corresponding meaning; and 'disposition' includes a conveyance and also a devise, bequest, or an appointment of property contained in a will; and 'dispose of' has a corresponding meaning;

(iii) 'Building purposes' include the erecting and improving of, and the adding to, and the repairing of buildings; and a 'building lease' is a lease for building purposes or purposes connected therewith;

[(iii A) 'the county court limit', in relation to any enactment contained in this Act, means the amount for the time being specified by an Order in Council under section 145 of the County Courts Act 1984 as the county court limit for the purposes of that enactment (or, where no such Order in Council has been made, the corresponding limit specified by Order in Council under section 192 of the County Courts Act 1959);]

(iv) 'Death duty' means estate duty [. . .] and every other duty reviable or payable on a death;

(v) 'Estate owner' means the owner of a legal estate, but an infant is not capable of being an estate owner;

(vi) 'Gazette' means the London Gazette;

(vii) 'Incumbrance' includes a legal or equitable mortgage and a trust for securing money, and a lien, and a charge of a portion, annuity, or other capital or annual sum; and 'incumbrancer' has a meaning corresponding with that of incumbrance, and includes every person entitled to the benefit of an incumbrance, or to require payment or discharge thereof;

(viii) 'Instrument' does not include a statute, unless the statute creates a settlement;

(ix) 'Land' includes land of any tenure, and mines and minerals, whether or not held apart from the surface, buildings or parts of buildings (whether the division is horizontal, vertical or made in any other way) and other corporeal hereditaments, also a manor, an advowson, and a rent and other incorporeal hereditaments, and an easement, right, privilege, or benefit in, over, or derived from land; [. . .] and 'mines and minerals' include any strata or seam of minerals or substances in or under any land, and powers of working and getting the same, [. . .] and 'manor' includes a lordship, and reputed manor or lordship; and 'hereditament' means any real property which on an intestacy occurring before the commencement of this Act might have devolved upon an heir;

(x) 'Legal estates' mean the estates, interests and charges, in or over land (subsisting or created at law) which are by this Act authorised to subsist or to be created as legal estates; 'equitable interests' means all the other interests and charges in or over land, [. . .] an equitable interest 'capable of subsisting as a legal estate' means such as could validly subsist or be created as a legal estate under this Act;

(xi) 'Legal powers' include the powers vested in a chargee by way of legal mortgage or in an estate owner under which a legal estate can be transferred or created; and 'equitable powers' mean all the powers in or over land under which equitable interests or powers only can be transferred or created;

(xii) 'Limitation Acts' mean the Real Property Limitation Acts, 1833, 1837 and 1874, and 'limitation' includes a trust;

[(xiii) 'Mental disorder' has the meaning assigned to it by [section one of the Mental Health Act, 1983], and 'receiver', in relation to a person suffering from mental disorder, means a receiver appointed for that person under [Part VIII of the Mental Health Act 1959 or Part VII of the said Act of 1983];]

(xiv) A 'mining lease' means a lease for mining purposes, that is, the searching for, winning, working, getting, making merchantable, carrying away, or disposing of mines and minerals, or purposes connected therewith, and includes a grant or licence for mining purposes;

(xv) 'Minister'[1] means the 'Minister of Agriculture and Fisheries and Food';

(xvi) 'Mortgage' includes any charge or lien on any property for securing money or money's worth; 'legal mortgage' means a mortgage by demise or subdemise or a charge by way of legal mortgage and 'legal mortgagee' has a corresponding meaning; 'mortgage money' means money or money's worth secured by a mortgage; 'mortgagor' includes any person from time to time deriving title under the original mortgagor or entitled to redeem a mortgage according to his estate interest or right in the mortgaged property; 'mortgagee' includes a chargee by way of legal mortgage and any person from time to time deriving title under the original mortgagee; and 'mortgagee in possession' is, for the purposes of this Act, a mortgagee who, in right of the mortgage, has entered into and is in possession of the mortgaged property; and 'right of redemption' includes an option to repurchase only if the option in effect creates a right of redemption;

(xvii) 'Notice' includes constructive notice;

(xviii) 'Personal representative' means the executor, original or by representa—tion, or administrator for the time being of a deceased person, and as regards any liability for the payment of death duties includes any person who takes possession of or intermeddles with the property of a deceased person without the authority of the personal representatives or the court;

(xix) 'Possession' includes receipt of rents and profits or the right to receive the same, if any; and 'income' includes rents and profits;

(xx) 'Property' includes any thing in action, and any interest in real or personal property;

(xxi) 'Purchaser' means a purchaser in good faith for valuable consideration and includes a lessee, mortgagee or other person who for valuable consideration acquires an interest in property except that in Part I of this Act and elsewhere where so expressly provided 'purchaser' only means a person who acquires an interest in or charge on property for money or money's worth; and in reference to a legal estate includes a chargee by way of legal mortgage; and where the context so requires 'purchaser' includes an intending purchaser; 'purchase' has a meaning corresponding with that of 'purchaser'; and 'valuable consideration' includes marriage but does not include a nominal consideration in money;

(xxii) 'Registered land' has the same meaning as in the Land Registration Act, 1925, and 'Land Registrar' means the Chief Land Registrar under that Act;

(xxiii) 'Rent' includes a rent service or a rentcharge, or other rent, toll, duty, royalty, or annual or periodical payment in money or money's worth, reserved or issuing out of or charged upon land, but does not include mortgage interest; 'rentcharge' includes a fee farm rent; 'fine' includes a premium or foregift and any payment, consideration, or benefit in the nature of a fine, premium or foregift; 'lessor' includes an underlessor and a person deriving title under a lessor or underlessor; and 'lessee' includes an underlessee and a person deriving title under a lessee or underlessee, and 'lease' includes an underlease or other tenancy;

(xxiv) 'Sale' includes an extinguishment of manorial incidents, but in other respects means a sale properly so called;

(xxv) 'Securities' include stocks, funds and shares;

(xxvi) 'Tenant for life,' 'statutory owner,' 'settled land,' 'settlement,' 'vesting deed,' 'subsidiary vesting deed,' 'vesting order,' 'vesting instrument,' 'trust instrument,' 'capital money,' and 'trustees of the settlement' have the same meanings as in the Settled Land Act, 1925;

(xxvii) 'Term of years absolute' means a term of years (taking effect either in possession or in reversion whether or not at a rent) with or without impeachment for waste, subject or not to another legal estate, and either certain or liable to determination by notice, re-entry, operation of law, or by a provision for cesser on redemption, or in any other event (other than the dropping of a life, or the determination of a determinable life interest); but does not include any term of years determinable with life or lives or with the cesser of a determinable life interest, nor, if created after the commencement of this Act, a term of years which is not expressed to take effect in possession within twenty-one years after the creation thereof where required by this Act to take effect within that period; and in this definition the expression 'term of years' includes a term for less than a year, or for a year or years and a fraction of a year or from year to year;

(xxviii) 'Trust Corporation' means the Public Trustee or a corporation either appointed by the court in any particular case to be a trustee or entitled by rules made under subsection (3) of section four of the Public Trustee Act, 1906, to act as custodian trustee;

(xxix) 'Trust for sale,' in relation to land, means an immediate [. . .] trust for sale, whether or not exercisable at the request or with the consent of any person [. . .]; 'trustees for sale' mean the persons (including a personal representative) holding land on trust for sale [. . .];

(xxx) 'United Kingdom' means Great Britain and Northern Ireland;

(xxxi) 'Will' includes codicil.

[(1A) Any reference in this Act to money being paid into court shall be construed as referring to the money being paid into the Supreme Court or any other court that has jurisdiction, and any reference in this Act to the court, in a context referring to the investment or application of money paid into court, shall be construed, in the case of money paid into the Supreme Court, as referring to the High Court, and in the case of money paid into another court, as referring to that other court.]

(2) Where an equitable interest in or power over property arises by statute or operation of law, references to the creation of an interest or power include references to any interest or power so arising.

(3) References to registration under the Land Charges Act, 1925, apply to any registration made under any other statute which is by the Land Charges Act, 1925, to have effect as if the registration had been made under that Act.

Note

[1]This definition does not apply to sections 192–4. The Minister in these sections refers to the Secretary of State for the Environment and the Secretary of State for Wales.

207. Repeals as respects England and Wales

[. . .] without prejudice to the provisions of section thirty-eight of the Interpretation Act, 1889:—

(a) Nothing in this repeal shall affect the validity or legality of any dealing in property or other transaction completed before the commencement of this Act, or any title or right acquired or appointment made before such commencement, but, subject as aforesaid, this Act shall, except where otherwise expressly provided, apply to and in respect of instruments whether made or coming into operation before or after such commencement:

(b) Nothing in this repeal shall affect any rules, orders, or other instruments made under any enactment so repealed, but all such rules, orders and instruments shall continue in force as if made under the corresponding enactment in this Act:

(c) References in any document to any enactment repealed by this Act shall be construed as references to this Act or to the corresponding enactment in this Act.

208. Application to the Crown

(1) Nothing in this Act shall be construed as rendering any property of the Crown subject to distress, or liable to be taken or disposed of by means of any distress.

(2) This Act shall not in any manner (save as otherwise expressly provided and except so far as it relates to undivided shares, joint ownership, leases for lives or leases for years terminable with life or marriage) affect or alter the descent, devolution or tenure or the nature of the estates and interests of or in any land for the time being vested in His Majesty either in right of the Crown or of the Duchy of Lancaster or of or in any land for the time being belonging to the Duchy of Cornwall and held in right or in respect of the said Duchy, but so nevertheless that, after the commencement of this Act, no estates, interests or charges in or over any such lands as aforesaid shall be conveyed or created, except such estates, interests or charges as are capable under this Act of subsisting or of being conveyed or created.

(3) Subject as aforesaid the provisions of this Act bind the Crown.

SCHEDULES

Section 39

FIRST SCHEDULE
TRANSITIONAL PROVISIONS
PART I
CONVERSION OF CERTAIN EXISTING LEGAL ESTATES INTO EQUITABLE INTERESTS

All estates, interests and charges in or over land, including fees determinable whether by limitation or condition, which immediately before the commencement of this Act were estates, interests or charges, subsisting at law, or capable of taking effect as such, but which by virtue of Part I. of this Act are not capable of taking effect as legal estates, shall as from the commencement of this Act be converted into equitable interests, and shall not fail by reason of being so converted into equitable interests either in the land or in the proceeds of sale thereof, nor shall the priority of any such estate, charge or interest over other equitable interests be affected.

PART II
VESTING OF LEGAL ESTATES

1. Where the purposes of a term of years, created or limited out of leasehold land, are satisfied at the commencement of this Act, that term shall merge in the reversion expectant thereon and shall cease accordingly; but where the term was vested in the owner of the reversion, the merger and cesser shall take effect without prejudice to any protection which would have been afforded to the owner for the time being of that reversion had the term remained subsisting.

Where the purposes are satisifed only as respects part of the land comprised in a term, this provision has effect as if a separate term had been created in regard to that part of the land.

2. Where immediately after the commencement of this Act any owner of a legal estate is entitled, subject or not to the payment of the costs of tracing the title and of conveyance, to require any other legal estate in the same land to be surrendered, released or conveyed to him so as to merge or be extinguished, the last-mentioned estate shall by virtue of this Part of this Schedule be extinguished, but without prejudice to any protection which would have been afforded to him had that estate remained subsisting.

3. Where immediately after the commencement of this Act any person is entitled, subject or not to the payment of the costs of tracing the title and of conveyance, to require any legal estate (not vested in trustees for sale) to be conveyed to or otherwise vested in him, such legal estate shall, by virtue of this Part of this Schedule, vest in manner hereinafter provided.

[The divesting of a legal estate by virtue of this paragraph shall not, where the person from whom the estate is so divested was a trustee, operate to prevent the legal estate being conveyed, or a legal estate being created, by him in favour of a purchaser for money or money's worth, if the purchaser has no notice of the trust and if the documents of title relating to the estate divested are produced by the trustee or by persons deriving title under him.]

This paragraph shall (without prejudice to any claim, in respect of fines, fees, and other customary payments) apply to a person who, under a surrender or any disposition having the effect of a surrender, or under a covenant to surrender or otherwise, was, immediately before the commencement of this Act, entitled to require a legal customary estate of inheritance to be vested in him, or who, immediately after such commencement becomes entitled to enfranchised land.

4. Any person who, immediately after the commencement of this Act, is entitled to an equitable interest capable of subsisting as a legal estate which has priority over any legal estate in the same land, shall be deemed to be entitled for the foregoing purposes to require a legal estate to be vested in him for an interest of a like nature not exceeding in extent or duration the equitable interest:

Provided that this paragraph shall not—

(a) apply where the equitable interest is capable of being overreached by virtue of a subsisting trust for sale or a settlement;

(b) operate to prevent such person from acquiring any other legal estate under this Part of this Schedule to which he may be entitled.

5. For the purposes of this Part of this Schedule, a tenant for life, statutory owner or personal representative, shall be deemed to be entitled to require to be vested in him any legal estate in settled land (whether or not vested in the Crown) which he is, by the Settled Land Act, 1925, given power to convey.

6. Under the provisions of this Part of this Schedule, the legal estate affected (namely, any estate which a person is entitled to require to be vested in him as aforesaid) shall vest as follows:—

(a) Where at the commencement of this Act land is subject to a mortgage (not being an equitable charge unsecured by any estate), the legal estate affected shall vest in accordance with the provisions relating to mortgages contained in this Schedule;

(b) Where the land is at the commencement or by virtue of this Act or any Act coming into operation at the same time subject or is by virtue of any statute made subject to a trust for sale, the legal estate affected shall vest in the trustees for sale (including personal representatives holding land on trust for sale) but subject to any mortgage term subsisting or created by this Act;

(c) Where at the commencement of this Act or by virtue of any statute coming into operation at the same time the land is settled land, the legal estate affected shall vest in the tenant for life or statutory owner entitled under the Settled Land Act, 1925, to require a vesting deed to be executed in his favour, or in the personal representative, if any, in whom the land may be vested or the Public Trustee, as the case may require but subject to any mortgage term subsisting or created by this Act;

(d) In any case to which the foregoing sub-paragraphs do not apply the legal estate affected shall vest in the person of full age who, immediately after the commencement of this Act, is entitled (subject or not to the payment of costs and any customary payments) to require the legal estate to be vested in him, but subject to any mortgage term subsisting or created by this Act.

7. Nothing in this Part of this Schedule shall operate—

(a) To vest in a mortgagee of a term of years absolute any nominal leasehold reversion which is held in trust for him subject to redemption; or

(b) To vest in a mortgagee any legal estate except a term of years absolute; or

(c) To vest in a person entitled to a leasehold interest, as respects such interest, any legal estate except a term of years absolute; or

(d) To vest in a person entitled to a rentcharge (either perpetual or held for a term of years absolute) as respects such rentcharge, any legal estate except a legal estate in the rentcharge; or

(e) To vest in a person entitled to an easement, right or privilege with reference thereto, any legal estate except a legal estate in the easement, right or privilege; or

(f) To vest any legal estate in a person for an undivided share, or

(g) To vest any legal estate in an infant; or

(h) To affect prejudicially the priority of any mortgage or other incumbrance or interest subsisting at the commencement of this Act; or

(i) To render invalid any limitation or trust which would have been capable of taking effect as an equitable limitation or trust; or

(j) To vest in a purchaser or his personal representatives any legal estate which he has contracted to acquire and in regard to which a contract, including an agreement to create a legal mortgage, is pending at the commencement of this Act, although the consideration may have been paid or satisfied and the title accepted, or to render unnecessary the conveyance of such estate; or

(k) To vest in the managing trustees or committee of management of a charity any legal estate vested in the Official Trustee of Charity Lands; or

(l) To vest in any person any legal estate which failed to pass to him by reason of his omission to be registered as proprietor under the Land Transfer Acts, 1875 and 1897, until brought into operation by virtue of the Land Registration Act, 1925.

[(m) To vest in any person any legal estate affected by any rent covenants or conditions if, before any proceedings are commenced in respect of the rent covenants or conditions, and before any conveyance of the legal estate or dealing therewith inter vivos is effected, he or his personal representatives disclaim it in writing signed by him or them.]

8. Any legal estate acquired by virtue of this Part of this Schedule shall be held upon the trusts and subject to the powers, provisions, rents, covenants, conditions, rights of

redemption (as respects terms of years absolute) and other rights, burdens and obligations, if any, upon or subject to which the estate acquired ought to be held.

9. No stamp duty shall become payable by reason only of any vesting surrender or release effected by this Schedule.

PART III
PROVISIONS AS TO LEGAL ESTATE VESTED IN INFANT

1. Where immediately before the commencement of this Act a legal estate in land is vested in one or more infants beneficially, or where immediately after the commencement of this Act a legal estate in land would by virtue of this Act have become vested in one or more infants beneficially if he or they had been of full age, the legal estate shall vest in the manner provided by the Settled Land Act, 1925.

2. Where immediately before the commencement of this Act a legal estate in land is vested in an infant jointly with one or more other persons of full age beneficially, the legal estate shall by virtue of this Act vest in that other person or those other persons on the statutory trusts, but not so as to sever any joint tenancy in the net proceeds of sale or in the rents and profits until sale:

Provided that, if by virtue of this paragraph the legal estate becomes vested in one person as trustee, then, if no other person is able and willing to do so, the parents or parent, testamentary or other guardian of the infant, if respectively able and willing to act, (in the order named) may, and at the request of any person interested shall (subject to the costs being provided for) by writing appoint an additional trustee and thereupon by virtue of this Act the legal estate shall vest in the additional trustee and existing trustee as joint tenants.

3. Where, immediately before the commencement of this Act, a legal estate in land is vested solely in an infant as a personal representative, or a trustee of a settlement, or on trust for sale or on any other trust, or by way of mortgage, or where immediately after the commencement of this Act a legal estate in land would by virtue of any provision of this Act or otherwise have been so vested if the infant were of full age, the legal estate and the mortgage debt (if any) and interest thereon shall, by virtue of this Act, vest in the Public Trustee, pending the appointment of trustees as hereinafter provided—

(a) as to the land, upon the trusts, and subject to the equities affecting the same (but in the case of a mortgage estate for a term of years absolute in accordance with this Act); and

(b) as to the mortgage debt and interest, upon such trusts as may be requisite for giving effect to the rights (if any) of the infant or other persons beneficially interested therein:

Provided that—

(i) The Public Trustee shall not be entitled to act in the trust, or charge any fee, or be liable in any manner, unless and until requested in writing to act by or on behalf of the persons interested in the land or the income thereof, or in the mortgage debt or interest thereon (as the case may be), which request may be made on behalf of the infant by his parents or parent, or testamentary or other guardian (in the order named), and those persons may, in the order aforesaid (if no other person is able and willing to do so) appoint new trustees in the place of the Public Trustee, and thereupon by virtue of this Act the land or term and mortgage money shall vest in the trustees so appointed upon the trusts and subject to the equities aforesaid: Provided that the Public Trustee may, before he accepts the trust, but subject to the payment of his costs, convey to a person of full age who becomes entitled;

(ii) After the Public Trustee has been so requested to act, and has accepted the trust, no trustee shall (except by an order of the court) be appointed in his place without his consent;

(iii) Any person interested in the land or the income thereof, or in the mortgage debt or in the interest thereon (as the case may be), may, at any time during the minority, apply to the court for the appointment of trustees of the trust, and the court may make such order as it thinks fit, and if thereby new trustees are appointed the legal estate (but in the case of a mortgage estate only for a term of years absolute as aforesaid) and the mortgage debt (if any) and interest shall, by virtue of this Act, vest in the trustees as joint tenants upon the trusts and subject to the equities aforesaid;

(iv) Neither a purchaser of the land nor a transferee for money or money's worth of the mortgage shall be concerned in any way with the trusts affecting the legal estate or the mortgage debt and interest thereon;

(v) The vesting in the Public Trustee of a legal estate or a mortgage debt by virtue of this Part of this Schedule shall not affect any directions previously given as to the payment of income or of interest on any mortgage money, but such instructions may, until he accepts the trust, continue to be acted on as if no such vesting had been effected.

[(3A). The county court has jurisdiction under proviso (iii) to paragraph 3 of this Part where the land which is to be dealt with in the court does not exceed [£30,000] in capital value [. . .].]

4. Where, immediately before the commencement of this Act, a legal estate in land is vested in two or more persons jointly as personal representatives, trustees, or mortgagees, and anyone of them is an infant, or where immediately after the commencement of this Act a legal estate in land would, by virtue of this Act, or otherwise have been so vested if the infant were of full age, the legal estate in the land with the mortgage debt (if any) and the interest thereon shall, by virtue of this Act, vest in the other person or persons of full age—

(a) as to the legal estate, upon the trusts and subject to the equities affecting the same (but in the case of a mortgage estate only for a term of years absolute as aforesaid); and

(b) as to the mortgage debt and interest, upon such trusts as may be requisite for giving effect to the rights (if any) of the infant or other persons beneficially interested therein;

but neither a purchaser of the land nor a transferee for money or money's worth of the mortgage shall be concerned in any way with the trusts affecting the legal estate or the mortgage debt and interest thereon:

Provided that, if, by virtue of this paragraph, the legal estate and mortgage debt, if any, become vested in a sole trustee, then, if no other person is able and willing to do so, the parents or parent, testamentary or other guardian of the infant (in the order named) may, and at the request of any person interested shall, (subject to the costs being provided for) by writing appoint a new trustee in place of the infant, and thereupon by virtue of this Act the legal estate and mortgage money shall vest in the new and continuing trustees upon the trusts and subject to the equities aforesaid.

5. This Part of this Schedule does not affect the estate or powers of an administrator durante minore ætate, nor, where there is a tenant for life or statutory owner of settled land, operate to vest the legal estate therein in the Public Trustee.

PART IV

PROVISIONS SUBJECTING LAND HELD IN UNDIVIDED SHARES TO A TRUST FOR SALE

1. Where, immediately before the commencement of this Act, land is held at law or in equity in undivided shares vested in possession, the following provisions shall have effect:—

(1) If the entirety of the land is vested in trustees or personal representatives (whether subject or not to incumbrances affecting the entirety or an undivided share) in trust for persons entitled in undivided shares, then—

(a) if the land is subject to incumbrances affecting undivided shares or to incumbrances affecting the entirety which under this Act or otherwise are not secured by legal terms of years absolute, the entirety of the land shall vest free from such incumbrances in such trustees or personal representatives and be held by them upon the statutory trusts; and

(b) in any other case, the land shall be held by such trustees or personal representatives upon the statutory trusts;

subject in the case of personal representatives, to their rights and powers for the purposes of administration.

(2) If the entirety of the land (not being settled land) is vested absolutely and beneficially in not more than four persons of full age entitled thereto in undivided shares free from incumbrances affecting undivided shares, but subject or not to incumbrances affecting the entirety, it shall, by virtue of this Act, vest in them as joint tenants upon the statutory trusts.

(3) If the entirety of the land is settled land (whether subject or not to incumbrances affecting the entirety or an undivided share) held under one and the same settlement, it shall, by virtue of this Act, vest, free from incumbrances affecting undivided shares, and from incumbrances affecting the entirety, which under this Act or otherwise are not secured by a legal [mortgage, and free from any interests, powers, and charges subsisting under the settlement, which have priority to the interests of the persons entitled to the undivided shares,] in the trustees (if any) of the settlement as joint tenants upon the statutory trusts.

Provided that if there are no such trustees, then—

(i) pending their appointment, the land shall, by virtue of this Act, vest (free as aforesaid) in the Public Trustee upon the statutory trusts;

(ii) the Public Trustee shall not be entitled to act in the trust, or charge any fee, or
be liable in any manner, unless and until requested in writing to act by or on behalf of persons interested in more than an undivided half of the land or the income thereof;

(iii) after the Public Trustee has been so requested to act, and has accepted the trust, no trustee shall (except by an order of the Court) be appointed in the place of the Public Trustee without his consent;

(iv) if, before the Public Trustee has accepted the trust, trustees of the settlement are appointed, the land shall, by virtue of this Act, vest (free as aforesaid) in them as joint tenants upon the statutory trusts;

(v) if, before the Public Trustee has accepted the trust, the persons having power to appoint new trustees are unable or unwilling to make an appointment, or if the tenant for life having power to apply to the court for the appointment of trustees of the settlement neglects to make the application for at least three months after being requested by any person interested in writing so to do, or if the tenants for life of the undivided shares are unable to agree, any person interested under the settlement may apply to the court for the appointment of such trustees.

[(3A) The county court has jurisdiction under proviso (v) to sub-paragraph (3) of this paragraph where the land to be dealt with in the court does not exceed [£30,000] in capital value [. . .].]

(4) In any case to which the foregoing provisions of this Part of this Schedule do not apply, the entirety of the land shall vest (free as aforesaid) in the Public Trustee upon the statutory trusts:

Provided that—

(i) The Public Trustee shall not be entitled to act in the trust, or charge any fee, or be liable in any manner, unless and until requested in writing to act by or on behalf of the persons interested in more than an undivided half of the land or the income thereof;

(ii) After the Public Trustee had been so requested to act, and has accepted the trust, no trustee shall (except by an order of the court) be appointed in the place of the Public Trustee without his consent;

(iii) Subject as aforesaid, any persons interested in more than an undivided half of the land or the income thereof may appoint new trustees in the place of the Public Trustee with the consent of any incumbrances of undivided shares (but so that a purchaser shall not be concerned to see whether any such consent has been given) and [thereupon the land shall by virtue of this Act vest] in the persons so appointed (free as aforesaid) upon the statutory trusts; or such persons may (without such consent as aforesaid), at any time, whether or not the Public Trustee has accepted the trust, apply to the court for the appointment of trustees of the land, and the court may make such order as it thinks fit, and if thereby trustees of the land are appointed, the same shall by virtue of this Act, vest (free as aforesaid) in the trustees as joint tenants upon the statutory trusts;

(iv) If the persons interested in more than an undivided half of the land or the income thereof do not either request the Public Trustee to act, or (whether he refuses to act or has not been requested to act) apply to the court for the appointment of trustees in his place, within three months from the time when they have been requested in writing by any person interested so to do, then and in any such case, any person interested may apply to the court for the appointment of trustees in the place of the Public Trustee, and the court may make such order as it thinks fit, and if thereby trustees of the land are appointed the same shall by virtue of this Act, vest (free as aforesaid) in the trustees upon the statutory trusts.

[(4A) The county court has jurisdiction under provisos (iii) and (iv) to sub-paragraph (4) of this paragraph where the land which is to be dealt with in the court does not exceed [£30,000] in capital value [. . .].]

(5) The vesting in the Public Trustee of land by virtue of this Part of this Schedule shall not affect any directions previously given as to the payment of income or of interest on any mortgage money, but such instructions may, until he accepts the trust, continue to be acted on as if no such vesting had been effected.

(6) The court or the Public Trustee may act on evidence given by affidavit or by statutory declaration as respects the undivided shares without investigating the title to the land.

(7) Where all the undivided shares in the land are vested in the same mortgagees for securing the same mortgage money and the rights of redemption affecting the land are the same as might have been subsisting if the entirety had been mortgaged by an owner before the undivided shares were created, the land shall, by virtue of this Act, vest in the mortgagees as joint tenants for a legal term of years absolute (in accordance with this Act) subject to cesser on redemption by the trustees for sale in whom the right of redemption is vested by this Act, and for the purposes of this Part of this Schedule the mortgage shall be deemed an incumbrance affecting the entirety.

(8) This Part of this Schedule does not (except where otherwise expressly provided) prejudice incumbrancers whose incumbrances affect the entirety of the land at the commencement of this Act, but (if the nature of the incumbrance admits) the land shall vest in them for legal terms of years absolute in accordance with this Act but not so as to affect subsisting priorities.

(9) The trust for sale and powers of management vested in persons who hold the entirety of the land on trust for sale shall, save as hereinafter mentioned, not be exercisable without the consent of any incumbrancer, being of full age, affected whose incumbrance is divested by this Part of this Schedule, but a purchaser shall not be concerned to see or inquire whether any such consent has been given, nor, where the incumbrancer is not in possession, shall any such consent be required if, independently

of this Part of this Schedule or any enactment replaced thereby the transaction would have been binding on him, had the same been effected by the mortgagor.

(10) This Part of this Schedule does not apply to land in respect of which a subsisting contract for sale (whether made under an order in a partition action or by or on behalf of all the tenants in common or coparceners) is in force at the commencement of this Act if the contract is completed in due course (in which case title may be made in like manner as if this Act, and any enactment thereby replaced, had not been passed), nor to the land in respect of which a partition action is pending at such commencement if an order for a partition or sale is subsequently made in such action [within eighteen months from the commencement of this Act.]

(11) The repeal of the enactments relating to partition shall operate without prejudice to any proceedings thereunder commenced before the commencement of this Act, and to the jurisdiction of the court to make any orders in reference thereto, and subject to the following provisions, namely:—

(i) In any such proceedings, and at any stage thereof, any person or persons interested individually or collectively in [one half or upwards] of the land to which the proceedings relate, may apply to the court for an order staying such proceedings;

(ii) The court may upon such application make an order staying the proceedings as regards the whole or any part, not being an undivided share, of the land;

(iii) As from the date of such order the said enactments shall cease to apply to the land affected by the order and the provisions of this Part of this Schedule shall apply thereto;

(iv) The court may by such order appoint trustees of the land and the same shall by virtue of this Act vest (free as aforesaid) in the trustees as joint tenants upon the statutory trusts;

(v) The court may order that the costs of the proceedings and of the application shall be raised by the trustees, by legal mortgage of the land or any part thereof, and paid either wholly or partially into court or to the trustees;

(vi) The court may act on such evidence as appears to be sufficient, without investigating the title to the land.

(12) In this Part of this Schedule 'incumbrance' does not include [a legal rentcharge affecting the entirety,] land tax, tithe rentcharge, or any similar charge on the land not created by an instrument.

2. Where undivided shares in land, created before the commencement of this Act, fall into possession after such commencement, and the land is not settled land when the shares fall into possession, the personal representatives (subject to their rights and powers for purposes of administration) or other estate owners in whom the entirety of the land is vested shall, by an assent or a conveyance, give effect to the foregoing provisions of this Part of this Schedule in like manner as if the shares had fallen into possession immediately before the commencement of this Act, and in the meantime the land shall be held on the statutory trusts.

3. This Part of this Schedule shall not save as hereinafter mentioned apply to party structures and open spaces within the meaning of the next succeeding Part of this Schedule.

[4. Where, immediately before the commencement of this Act, there are two or more tenants for life of full age entitled under the same settlement in undivided shares, and, after the cesser of all their interests in the income of the settled land, the entirety of the land is limited so as to devolve together (not in undivided shares), their interests shall, but without prejudice to any beneficial interest, be converted into a joint tenancy, and the joint tenants and the survivor of them shall, until the said cesser occurs, constitute the tenant for life for the purposes of the Settled Land Act, 1925, and this Act.]

PART V
PROVISIONS AS TO PARTY STRUCTURES AND OPEN SPACES

1. Where, immediately before the commencement of this Act, a party wall or other party structure is held in undivided shares, the ownership thereof shall be deemed to be severed vertically as between the respective owners, and the owner of each part shall have such rights to support and of user over the rest of the structure as may be requisite for conferring rights corresponding to those subsisting at the commencement of this Act.

2. Where, immediately before the commencement of this Act, an open space of land (with or without any building used in common for the purposes of any adjoining land) is held in undivided shares, in right whereof each owner has rights of access and user over the open space, the ownership thereof shall vest in the Public Trustee on the statutory trusts which shall be executed only with the leave of the court, and, subject to any order of the court to the contrary, each person who would have been a tenant in common shall, until the open space is conveyed to a purchaser, have rights of access and user over the open space corresponding to those which would have subsisted if the tenancy in common had remained subsisting.

3. Any person interested may apply to the court for an order declaring the rights and interests under this Part of this Schedule, of the persons interested in any such party structure or open space, or generally may apply in relation to the provisions of this Part of this Schedule, and the court may make such order as it thinks fit.

PART VI
CONVERSION OF TENANCIES BY ENTIRETIES INTO JOINT TENANCIES

Every tenancy by entireties existing immediately before the commencement of this Act shall, but without prejudice to any beneficial interest, as from such commencement be converted into a joint tenancy.

PART VII
CONVERSION OF EXISTING FREEHOLD MORTGAGES INTO MORTGAGES BY DEMISE

1. All land, which immediately before the commencement of this Act, was vested in a first or only mortgagee for an estate in fee simple in possession, whether legal or equitable, shall, from and after the commencement of this Act, vest in the first or only mortgagee for a term of three thousand years from such commencement, without impeachment of waste, but subject to a provision for cesser corresponding to the right of redemption which, at such commencement, was subsisting with respect to the fee simple.

2. All land, which immediately before the commencement of this Act, was vested in a second or subsequent mortgagee for an estate in fee simple in possession, whether legal or equitable, shall, from and after the commencement of this Act, vest in the second or subsequent mortgagee for a term one day longer than the term vested in the first or other mortgagee whose security ranks immediately before that of such second or subsequent mortgagee, without impeachment of waste, but subject to the term or terms vested in such first or other prior mortgagee and subject to a provision for cesser corresponding to the right of redemption which, at such commencement, was subsisting with respect to the fee simple.

3. The estate in fee simple which, immediately before the commencement of this Act, was vested in any such mortgagee shall, from and after such commencement, vest in the mortgagor or tenant for life, statutory owner, trustee for sale, personal representative, or other person of full age who, if all money owing on the security of the mortgage and all other mortgages or charges (if any) had been discharged at the

commencement of this Act, would have been entitled to have the fee simple conveyed to him, but subject to any mortgage term created by this Part of this Schedule or otherwise and to the money secured by any such mortgage or charge.

4. If a sub-mortgage by conveyance of the fee simple is subsisting immediately before the commencement of this Act, the principal mortgagee shall take the principal term created by paragraphs 1 or 2 of this Part of this Schedule (as the case may require) and the sub-mortgagee shall take a derivative term less by one day than the term so created, without impeachment of waste, subject to a provision for cesser corresponding to the right of redemption subsisting under the sub-mortgage.

5. This Part of this Schedule applies to land enfranchised by statute as well as to land which was freehold before the commencement of this Act, and (save where expressly excepted) whether or not the land is registered under the Land Registration Act, 1925, or the mortgage is made by way of trust for sale or otherwise.

6. A mortgage affecting a legal estate made before the commencement of this Act which is not protected, either by a deposit of documents of title relating to the legal estate or by registration as a land charge, shall not, as against a purchaser in good faith without notice thereof, obtain any benefit by reason of being converted into a legal mortgage by this Schedule, but shall, in favour of such purchaser, be deemed to remain an equitable interest.

This paragraph does not apply to mortgages or charges registered or protected under the Land Registration Act, 1925, or to mortgages or charges registered in a local deeds register.

7. Nothing in this Part of this Schedule shall affect priorities or the right of any mortgagee to retain possession of documents, nor affect his title to or rights over any fixtures or chattels personal comprised in the mortgage.

8. This Part of this Schedule does not apply unless a right of redemption is subsisting immediately before the commencement of this Act.

PART VIII
CONVERSION OF EXISTING LEASEHOLD MORTGAGES INTO MORTGAGES BY SUBDEMISE

1. All leasehold land, which immediately before the commencement of this Act, was vested in a first or only mortgagee by way of assignment of a term of years absolute shall, from and after the commencement of this Act, vest in the first or only mortgagee for a term equal to the term assigned by the mortgage, less the last ten days thereof, but subject to a provision for cesser corresponding to the right of redemption which at such commencement was subsisting with respect to the term assigned.

2. All leasehold land, which immediately before the commencement of this Act, was vested in a second or subsequent mortgagee by way of assignment of a term of years absolute (whether legal or equitable) shall, from and after the commencement of this Act, vest in the second or subsequent mortgagee for a term one day longer than the term vested in the first or other mortgagee whose security ranks immediately before that of such second or subsequent mortgagee if the length of the last-mentioned term permits, and in any case for a term less by one day at least than the term assigned by the mortgage, but subject to the term or terms vested in such first or other prior mortgagee, and subject to a provision for cesser corresponding to the right of redemption which, at the commencement of this Act, was subsisting with respect to the term assigned by the mortgage.

3. The term of years absolute which was assigned by any such mortgage shall from and after the commencement of this Act, vest in the mortgagor or tenant for life, statutory owner, trustee for sale, personal representative, or other person of full age who, if all the money owing on the security of the mortgage and all other mortgages or charges, if any, had been discharged at the commencement of this Act, would have been

entitled to have the term assigned or surrendered to him, but subject to any derivative mortgage term created by this Part of this Schedule or otherwise and to the money secured by any such mortgage or charge.

4. If a sub-mortgage by assignment of a term is subsisting immediately before the commencement of this Act, the principal mortgagee shall take the principal derivative term created by paragraphs 1 or 2 of this Part of this Schedule or the derivative term created by his mortgage (as the case may require), and the sub-mortgagee shall take a derivative term less by one day than the term so vested in the principal mortgagee, subject to a provision for cesser corresponding to the right of redemption subsisting under the sub-mortgage.

5. A mortgage affecting a legal estate made before the commencement of this Act which is not protected, either by a deposit of documents of title relating to the legal estate or by registration as a land charge shall not, as against a purchaser in good faith without notice thereof, obtain any benefit by reason of being converted into a legal mortgage by this Schedule, but shall, in favour of such purchaser, be deemed to remain an equitable interest.

This paragraph does not apply to mortgages or charges registered or protected under the Land Registration Act, 1925, or to mortgages or charges registered in a local deeds register.

6. This Part of this Schedule applies to perpetually renewable leaseholds, and to leaseholds for lives, which are by statute converted into long terms, with the following variations, namely:—

(a) The term to be taken by a first or only mortgagee shall be ten days less than the term created by such statute:

(b) The term to be taken by a second or subsequent mortgagee shall be one day longer than the term vested in the first or other mortgagee whose security ranks immediately before that of the second or subsequent mortgagee, if the length of the last-mentioned term permits, and in any case for a term less by one day at least than the term created by such statute:

(c) The term created by such statute shall, from and after the commencement of this Act, vest in the mortgagor or tenant for life, statutory owner, trustee for sale, personal representative, or other person of full age, who if all the money owing on the security of the mortgage and all other mortgages or charges, if any, had been discharged at the commencement of this Act, would have been entitled to have the term assigned or surrendered to him, but subject to any derivative mortgage term created by this Part of this Schedule or otherwise and to the money secured by any such mortgage or charge.

7. This Part of this Schedule applies (save where expressly excepted) whether or not the leasehold land is registered under the Land Registration Act, 1925, or the mortgage is made by way of trust for sale or otherwise.

8. Nothing in this Part of this Schedule shall affect priorities or the right of any mortgagee to retain possession of documents, nor affect his title to or rights over any fixtures or chattels personal comprised in the mortgage, but this Part of this Schedule does not apply unless a right of redemption is subsisting at the commencement of this Act.

Sections 76 and 77

SECOND SCHEDULE
IMPLIED COVENANTS
PART I
COVENANT IMPLIED IN A CONVEYANCE FOR VALUABLE CONSIDERATION, OTHER THAN A MORTGAGE, BY A PERSON WHO CONVEYS AND IS EXPRESSED TO CONVEY AS BENEFICIAL OWNER

That, notwithstanding anything by the person who so conveys or any one through whom he derives title otherwise than by purchase for value, made, done, executed, or omitted, or knowingly suffered, the person who so conveys, has, with the concurrence of every other person, if any, conveying by his direction, full power to convey the subject-matter expressed to be conveyed, subject as, if so expressed, and in the manner in which, it is expressed to be conveyed, and that, notwithstanding anything as aforesaid, that subject-matter shall remain to and be quietly entered upon, received, and held, occupied, enjoyed, and taken, by the person to whom the conveyance is expressed to be made, and any person deriving title under him, and the benefit thereof shall be received and taken accordingly, without any lawful interruption or disturbance by the person who so conveys or any person conveying by his direction, or rightfully claiming or to claim by, through, under, or in trust for the person who so conveys, or any person conveying by his direction, or by, through, or under any one (not being a person claiming in respect of an estate or interest subject whereto the conveyance is expressly made), through whom the person who so conveys derives title, otherwise than by purchase for value:

And that, freed and discharged from, or otherwise by the person who so conveys sufficiently indemnified against, all such estates, incumbrances, claims and demands, other than those subject to which the conveyance is expressly made, as, either before or after the date of the conveyance, have been or shall be made, occasioned, or suffered by that person or by any person conveying by his direction, or by any person rightfully claiming by, through, under, or in trust for the person who so conveys, or by, through or under any person conveying by his direction, by, through, or under any one through whom the person who so conveys derives title, otherwise than by purchase for value:

And further, that the person who so conveys, and any person conveying by his direction, and every other person having or rightfully claiming any estate or interest in the subject-matter of conveyance, other than an estate or interest subject whereto the conveyance is expressly made, by, through, under, or in trust for the person who so conveys, or by, through, or under any person conveying by his direction, or by, through, or under any one through whom the person who so conveys derives title, otherwise than by purchase for value, will, from time to time and at all times after the date of the conveyance, on the request and at the cost of any person to whom the conveyance is expressed to be made, or of any person deriving title under him, execute and do all such lawful assurances and things for further or more perfectly assuring the subject-matter of the conveyance to the person to whom the conveyance is made, and to those deriving title under him, subject as, if so expressed, and in the manner in which the conveyance is expressed to be made, as by him or them or any of them shall be reasonably required.

In the above covenant a purchase for value shall not be deemed to include a conveyance in consideration of marriage.

PART II
FURTHER COVENANT IMPLIED IN A CONVEYANCE OF LEASEHOLD PROPERTY FOR VALUABLE CONSIDERATION, OTHER THAN A MORTGAGE, BY A PERSON WHO CONVEYS AND IS EXPRESSED TO CONVEY AS BENEFICIAL OWNER

That, notwithstanding anything by the person who so conveys, or any one through whom he derives title, otherwise than by purchase for value, made, done, executed, or omitted, or knowingly suffered, the lease or grant creating the term or estate for which the land is conveyed is, at the time of conveyance, a good, valid, and effectual lease or grant of the property conveyed, and is in full force, unforfeited, unsurrendered, and has in nowise become void or-voidable, and that, notwithstanding anything as aforesaid, all the rents reserved by, and all the covenants, conditions, and agreements contained in, the lease or grant, and on the part of the lessee or grantee and the persons deriving title under him to be paid, observed, and performed, have been paid, observed, and performed up to the time of conveyance.

In the above covenant a purchase for value shall not be deemed to include a conveyance in consideration of marriage.

PART III
COVENANT IMPLIED IN A CONVEYANCE BY WAY OF MORTGAGE BY A PERSON WHO CONVEYS AND IS EXPRESSED TO CONVEY AS BENEFICIAL OWNER

That the person who so conveys, has, with the concurrence of every other person, if any, conveying by his direction, full power to convey the subject-matter expressed to be conveyed by him, subject as, if so expressed, and in the manner in which it is expressed to be conveyed:

And also that, if default is made in payment of the money intended to be secured by the conveyance, or any interest thereon, or any part of that money or interest, contrary to any provision in the conveyance, it shall be lawful for the person to whom the conveyance is expressed to be made, and the persons deriving title under him, to enter into and upon, or receive, and thenceforth quietly hold, occupy, and enjoy or take and have, the subject-matter expressed to be conveyed, or any part thereof, without any lawful interruption or disturbance by the person who so conveys, or any person conveying by his direction, or any other person (not being a person claiming in respect of an estate or interest subject whereto the conveyance is expressly made):

And that, freed and discharged from, or otherwise by the person who so conveys sufficiently indemnified against all estates, incumbrances, claims, and demands whatever, other than those subject whereto the conveyance is expressly made:

And further, that the person who so conveys and every person conveying by his direction, and every person deriving title under any of them, and every other person having or rightfully claiming any estate or interest in the subject-matter of conveyance, or any part thereof, other than an estate or interest subject whereto the conveyance is expressly made, will from time to time and at all times, on the request of any person to whom the conveyance is expressed to be made, or of any person deriving title under him, but, as long as any right of redemption exists under the conveyance, at the cost of the person so conveying, or of those deriving title under him, and afterwards at the cost of the person making the request, execute and do all such lawful assurances and things for further or more perfectly assuring the subject-matter of conveyance and every part thereof to the person to whom the conveyance is made, and to those deriving title under him, subject as, if so expressed, and in the manner in which the conveyance is expressed to be made, as by him or them or any of them shall be reasonably required.

The above covenant in the case of a charge shall have effect as if for references to 'conveys', 'conveyed' and 'conveyance' there were substituted respectively references to 'charges', 'charged' and 'charge.'

PART IV
COVENANT IMPLIED IN A CONVEYANCE BY WAY OF MORTGAGE OF FREEHOLD PROPERTY SUBJECT TO A RENT OR OF LEASEHOLD PROPERTY BY A PERSON WHO CONVEYS AND IS EXPRESSED TO CONVEY AS BENEFICIAL OWNER

That the lease or grant creating the term or estate for which the land is held is, at the time of conveyance, a good, valid, and effectual lease or grant of the land conveyed and is in full force, unforfeited, and unsurrendered and has in nowise become void or voidable, and that all the rents reserved by, and all the covenants, conditions, and agreements contained in, the lease or grant, and on the part of the lessee or grantee and the persons deriving title under him to be paid, observed, and performed, have been paid, observed, and performed up to the time of conveyance:

And also that the person so conveying, or the persons deriving title under him, will at all times, as long as any money remains owing on the security of the conveyance, pay, observe, and perform, or cause to be paid, observed, and performed all the rents reserved by, and all the covenants, conditions, and agreements contained in, the lease or grant, and on the part of the lessee or grantee and the persons deriving title under him to be paid, observed, and performed, and will keep the person to whom the conveyance is made, and those deriving title under him, indemnified against all actions, proceedings, costs, charges, damages, claims and demands, if any, to be incurred or sustained by him or them by reason of the non-payment of such rent or the non-observance or non-performance of such covenants, conditions, and agreements, or any of them.

The above covenant in the case of a charge shall have effect as if for references to 'conveys,' 'conveyed' and 'conveyance' there were substituted respectively references to 'charges,' 'charged' and 'charge.'

PART V
COVENANT IMPLIED IN A CONVEYANCE BY WAY OF SETTLEMENT, BY A PERSON WHO CONVEYS AND IS EXPRESSED TO CONVEY AS SETTLOR

That the person so conveying, and every person deriving title under him by deed or act or operation of law in his lifetime subsequent to that conveyance, or by testamentary disposition or devolution in law, on his death, will, from time to time, and at all times, after the date of that conveyance, at the request and cost of any person deriving title thereunder, execute and do all such lawful assurances and things for further or more perfectly assuring the subject-matter of the conveyance to the persons to whom the conveyance is made and those deriving title under them, as by them or any of them shall be reasonably required, subject as, if so expressed, and in the manner in which the conveyance is expressed to be made.

PART VI
COVENANT IMPLIED IN ANY CONVEYANCE, BY EVERY PERSON WHO CONVEYS AND IS EXPRESSED TO CONVEY AS TRUSTEE OR MORTGAGEE, OR AS PERSONAL REPRESENTATIVE OF A DECEASED PERSON, [. . .] OR UNDER AN ORDER OF THE COURT

That the person so conveying has not executed or done, or knowingly suffered, or been party or privy to, any deed or thing, whereby or by means whereof the subject-matter of the conveyance, or any part thereof, is or may be impeached, charged, affected, or incumbered in title, estate, or otherwise, or whereby or by means whereof the person who so conveys is in anywise hindered from conveying the subject-matter of the conveyance, or any part thereof, in the manner in which it is expressed to be conveyed.

The foregoing covenant may be implied in an assent in like manner as in a conveyance by deed.

PART VII
COVENANT IMPLIED IN A CONVEYANCE FOR VALUABLE CONSIDERATION, OTHER THAN A MORTGAGE, OF THE ENTIRETY OF LAND AFFECTED BY A RENTCHARGE

That the grantees or the persons deriving title under them will at all times, from the date of the conveyance or other date therein stated, duly pay the said rentcharge and observe and perform all the covenants, agreements and conditions contained in the deed or other document creating the rentcharge, and thenceforth on the part of the owner of the land to be observed and performed:

And also will at all times, from the date aforesaid, save harmless and keep indemnified the conveying parties and their respective estates and effects, from and against all proceedings, costs, claims and expenses on account of any omission to pay the said rentcharge or any part thereof, or any breach of any of the said covenants, agreements and conditions.

PART VIII
COVENANTS IMPLIED IN A CONVEYANCE FOR VALUABLE CONSIDERATION, OTHER THAN A MORTGAGE, OR PART OF LAND AFFECTED BY A RENTCHARGE, SUBJECT TO A PART (NOT LEGALLY APPORTIONED) OF THAT RENTCHARGE

(i) That the grantees, or the persons deriving title under them, will at all times, from the date of the conveyance or other date therein stated, pay the apportioned rent and observe and perform all the covenants (other than the covenant to pay the entire rent) and conditions contained in the deed or other document creating the rentcharge, so far as the same relate to the land conveyed:

And also will at all times, from the date aforesaid, save harmless and keep indemnified the conveying parties and their respective estates and effects, from and against all proceedings, costs, claims and expenses on account of any omission to pay the said apportioned rent, or any breach of any of the said covenants and conditions, so far as the same relate as aforesaid.

(ii) That the conveying parties, or the persons deriving title under them, will at all times, from the date of the conveyance or other date therein stated, pay the balance of the rentcharge (after deducting the apportioned rent aforesaid, and any other rents similarly apportioned in respect of land not retained), and observe and perform all the covenants, other than the covenant to pay the entire rent, and conditions contained in the deed or other document creating the rentcharge, so far as the same relate to the land not included in the conveyance and remaining vested in the covenantors:

And also will at all times, from the date aforesaid, save harmless and keep indemnified the grantees and their estates and effects, from and against all proceedings, costs, claims and expenses on account of any omission to pay the aforesaid balance of the rentcharge, or any breach of any of the said covenants and conditions so far as they relate as aforesaid.

PART IX
COVENANT IN A CONVEYANCE FOR VALUABLE CONSIDERATION, OTHER THAN A MORTGAGE, OF THE ENTIRETY OF THE LAND COMPRISED IN A LEASE FOR THE RESIDUE OF THE TERM OR INTEREST CREATED BY THE LEASE

That the assignees, or the persons deriving title under them, will at all times, from the date of the conveyance or other date therein stated, duly pay all rent becoming due under the lease creating the term or interest for which the land is conveyed, and observe and perform all the covenants, agreements and conditions therein contained and thenceforth on the part of the lessees to be observed and performed:

And also will at all times, from the date aforesaid, save harmless and keep indemnified the conveying parties and their estates and effects, from and against all proceedings, costs, claims and expenses on account of any omission to pay the said rent or any breach of any of the said covenants, agreements and conditions.

PART X
COVENANTS IMPLIED IN A CONVEYANCE FOR VALUABLE CONSIDERATION, OTHER THAN A MORTGAGE, OR PART OF THE LAND COMPRISED IN A LEASE, FOR THE RESIDUE OF THE TERM OR INTEREST CREATED BY THE LEASE, SUBJECT TO A PART (NOT LEGALLY APPORTIONED) OF THAT RENT

(i) That the assignees, or the persons deriving title under them, will at all times, from the date of the conveyance or other date therein stated, pay the apportioned rent and observe and perform all the covenants, other than the covenant to pay the entire rent, agreements and conditions

contained in the lease creating the term or interest for which the land is conveyed, and thenceforth on the part of the lessees to be observed and performed, so far as the same relate to the land conveyed:

And also will at all times from the date aforesaid save harmless and keep indemnified, the conveying parties and their respective estates and effects, from and against all proceedings, costs, claims and expenses on account of any omission to pay the said apportioned rent or any breach of any of the said covenants, agreements and conditions so far as the same relate as aforesaid.

(ii) That the conveying parties, or the persons deriving title under them, will at all times, from the date of the conveyance, or other date therein stated, pay the balance of the rent (after deducting the apportioned rent aforesaid and any other rents similarly apportioned in respect of land not retained) and observe and perform all the covenants, other than the covenant to pay the entire rent, agreements and conditions contained in the lease and on the part of the lessees to be observed and performed so far as the same relate to the land demised (other than the land comprised in the conveyance) and remaining vested in the convenantors:

And also will at all times, from the date aforesaid, save harmless and keep indemnified, the assignees and their estates and effects, from and against all proceedings, costs, claims and expenses on account of any omission to pay the aforesaid balance of the rent or any breach of any of the said covenants, agreements and conditions so far as they relate as aforesaid.

Note: Parts IX and X do not apply to tenancies created after the Landlord and Tenant (Covenants) Act 1995 came into force.

Sections 114 and 115

THIRD SCHEDULE
FORMS OF TRANSFER AND DISCHARGE OF MORTGAGES
FORM NO. 1
FORM OF TRANSFER OF MORTGAGE

This Transfer of Mortgage made the day of 19 , between *M.* of [&c.] of the one part and *T.* of [&c.] of the other part, supplemental to a Mortgage dated [&c.], and made between [&c.], and to a Further Charge dated [&c.], and made between [&c.] affecting &c. (*here state short particulars of the mortgaged property*).

WITNESSETH that in consideration of the sums of £ and £ (for interest) now paid by *T.* to *M.*, being the respective amounts of the mortgage money and interest owing in respect of the said mortgage and further charge (the receipt of which sums *M.* hereby acknowledges) *M.*, as mortgagee, hereby conveys and transfers to *T.* the benefit of the said mortgage and further charge.

In witness, &c.

FORM NO. 2
FORM OF RECEIPT ON DISCHARGE OF A MORTGAGE

I, *A.B.*, [&c.] hereby acknowledge that I have this day of 19 , received the sum of £ representing the [aggregate] [balance remaining owing in respect of the] principal money secured by the within [above] written [annexed] mortgage [and by a further charge dated, &c., *or otherwise as required*] together with all interest and costs, the payment having been made by *C.D.* of [&c.] and *E.F.* of [&c.].

As witness, &c.

Note.—If the persons paying are not entitled to the equity of redemption state that they are paying the money out of a fund applicable to the discharge of the mortgage.

Section 117

FOURTH SCHEDULE
FORMS RELATING TO STATUTORY CHARGES OR MORTGAGES OF FREEHOLD OR LEASEHOLD LAND
FORM NO. 1
STATUTORY CHARGE BY WAY OF LEGAL MORTGAGE

This Legal Charge made by way of Statutory Mortgage the day of 19 , between *A.* of [&c.] of the one part and *M.* of [&c.] of the other part Witnesseth that in consideration of the sum of £ now paid to *A.* by *M.* of which sum *A.* hereby acknowledges the receipt *A.* As Mortgagor and As Beneficial Owner hereby charges by way of legal mortgage All That [&c.] with the payment to *M.* on the day of 19 , of the principal sum of £ as the mortgage money with interest thereon at the rate of per centum per annum.

In witness &c.

Note.—Variations in this and the subsequent forms in this Schedule to be made, if required, for leasehold land or for giving effect to special arrangements. M. will be in the same position as if the Charge had been effected by a demise of freeholds or a subdemise of leaseholds.

Section 118 FORM NO. 2

STATUTORY TRANSFER, MORTGAGOR NOT JOINING

This Transfer of Mortgage made by way of statutory transfer the day of 19 , between *M.* of [&c.] of the one part and *T.* [of &c.] of the other part supplemental to a legal charge made by way of statutory mortgage dated [&c.] and made [&c.] Witnesseth that in consideration of the sum of £ now paid to *M.* by *T.* (being the aggregate amount of £ mortgage money and £ interest due in respect of the said legal charge of which sum M. hereby acknowledges the receipt) *M.* as Mortgagee hereby conveys and transfers to *T.* the benefit of the said legal charge.

In witness, &c.

Note.—This and the next two forms also apply to a transfer of a statutory mortgage made before the commencement of this Act, which will then be referred to as a mortgage instead of a legal charge.

Section 118 FORM NO. 3

STATUTORY TRANSFER, A COVENANTOR JOINING

This Transfer of Mortgage made by way of statutory transfer the day of 19 , between A. of [&c.] of the first part *B.* of [&c.] of the second part and *C.* of [&c.] of the third part Supplemental to a Legal Charge made by way of statutory mortgage dated [&c.] and made [&c.] Witnesseth that in consideration of the sum of £ now paid by *A.* to *C.* (being the mortgage money due in respect of the said Legal Charge no interest being now due or payable thereon of which sum *A.* hereby acknowledges the receipt) *A.* as Mortgagee with the concurrence of *B.* who joins herein as covenantor hereby conveys and transfers to C. the benefit of the said Legal Charge.

In witness, &c.

Sections 117 and 118 FORM NO. 4

STATUTORY TRANSFER AND MORTGAGE COMBINED

This Transfer and Legal Charge is made by way of statutory transfer and mortgage the day of 19 , between *A.* of [&c.] of the first part *B.* of [&c.] of the second part and *C.* of [&c] of the third part Supplemental to a Legal Charge made by way of statutory mortgage dated [&c.] and made [&c.] Whereas a principal sum of £ only remains due in respect of the said Legal Charge as the mortgage money and no interest is now due thereon And Whereas *B.* is seised in fee simple of the land comprised in the said Legal Charge subject to that Charge.

Now this Deed Witnesseth as follows:—

1. In consideration of the sum of £ now paid to *A.* by *C.* (the receipt and payment of which sum *A.* & *B.* hereby respectively acknowledge)* *A.* as mortgagee hereby conveys and transfers to *C.* the benefit of the said Legal Charge.

2. For the consideration aforesaid *B.*† as beneficial owner hereby charges by way of legal mortgage All the premises comprised in the said Legal Charge with the payment to *C.* on the day of 19 , of‡ the sum of £ as the mortgage money

with interest thereon at the rate of per centum per annum In Witness &c. [or in the case of a further advance after 'acknowledge' *at *insert* 'and of the further sum of £ now paid by *C.* to *B.* of which sum *B.* hereby acknowledges the receipt' *also at* † *before* 'as beneficial owner' *insert* 'as mortgagor and' *as well as where B. is not the original mortgagor. And after 'of' at ‡ insert* 'the sums of £ and £ making together'].

Note.—Variations to be made, as required, in case of the deed being by indorsement, or in respect of any other thing.

FORM NO. 5
RECEIPT ON DISCHARGE OF STATUTORY LEGAL CHARGE OR MORTGAGE

I *A.B.* of [&c.] hereby acknowledge that I have this day of 19 received the sum of £ representing the [aggregate] [balance remaining owing in respect of the] mortgage money secured by the [annexed] within [above] written statutory legal charge [or statutory mortgage] [and by the further statutory charge dated &c. *or otherwise as required*] together with all interest and costs the payment having been made by *C.D.* of [&c.] and *E.F.* of [&c.]

As witness &c.

Note.—If the persons paying are not entitled to the equity of redemption state that they are paying the money out of a fund applicable to the discharge of the statutory legal charge or mortgage.

LAND REGISTRATION ACT 1925
(1925, c. 21)

PRELIMINARY

[1. Registers to be continued

(1) The Chief Land Registrar shall continue to keep a register of title to freehold land and leasehold land.

(2) The register need not be kept in documentary form.]

2. What estates may be registered

(1) After the commencement of this Act, estates capable of subsisting as legal estates shall be the only interests in land in respect of which a proprietor can be registered and all other interests in registered land (except overriding interests and interests entered on the register at or before such commencement) shall take effect in equity as minor interests, but all interests (except undivided shares in land) entered on the register at such commencement which are not legal estates shall be capable of being dealt with under this Act:

Provided that, on the occasion of the first dealing with any such interest, the register shall be rectified in such manner as may be provided by rules made to secure that the entries therein shall be similar to those which would have been made if the title to the land had been registered after the commencement of this Act.

(2) Subject as aforesaid, and save as otherwise expressly provided by this Act, this Act applies to land registered under any enactment replaced by this Act in like manner as it applies to land registered under this Act.

3. Interpretation

In this Act unless the context otherwise requires, the following expressions have the meanings hereby assigned to them respectively, that is to say:—

(i) 'Charge by way of legal mortgage' means a mortgage created by charge under which, by virtue of the Law of Property Act 1925, the mortgagee is to be treated as an estate owner in like manner as if a mortgage term by demise or subdemise were vested in him, and 'legal mortgage' has the same meaning as in that Act;

[(ii) 'the court' means the High Court or, where county courts have jurisdiction by virtue of rules made under section 138(1) of this Act, the county court;]

(iii) [. . .]

(iv) 'Estate owner' means the owner of a legal estate, but an infant is not capable of being an estate owner;

(v) 'Gazette' means the London Gazette;

(vi) 'Income' includes rents and profits;

(vii) 'Instrument' does not include a statute, unless the statute creates a settlement;

(viii) 'Land' includes land of any tenure (including land, subject or not to manorial incidents, enfranchised under Part V of the Law of Property Act 1922), and mines and minerals, whether or not held with the surface, buildings or parts of buildings (whether the division is horizontal, vertical or made in any other way) and other corporeal hereditaments; also a manor [. . .], and a rent and other incorporeal hereditaments, and an easement, right, privilege, or benefit in, over, or derived from land; [. . .] and 'hereditaments' mean real property which on an intestacy might, before the commencement of this Act, have devolved on an heir;

[(ix) 'Land charge' means a land charge of any class described in section 2 of the Land Charges Act 1972 or a local land charge;]

(x) 'Lease' includes an under-lease and any tenancy or agreement for a lease, under-lease or tenancy;

(xi) 'Legal estates' mean the estates interests and charges in or over land subsisting or created at law which are by the Law of Property Act 1925, authorised to subsist or to be created at law; and 'Equitable interests' mean all the other interests and charges in or over land [. . .]; an equitable interest 'capable of subsisting at law' means such as could validly subsist at law if clothed with the legal estate;

(xii) 'Limitation Acts' mean the Real Property Limitation Acts 1833, 1837 and 1874, and any Acts amending those Acts;

(xiii) 'Manorial incidents' have the same meaning as in Part V of the Law of Property Act 1922;

(xiv) 'Mines and minerals' include any strata or seam of minerals or substances in or under any land, and powers of working and getting the same [. . .];

(xv) 'Minor interests' mean the interests not capable of being disposed of or created by registered dispositions and capable of being overridden (whether or not a purchaser has notice thereof) by the proprietors unless protected as provided by this Act, and all rights and interests which are not registered or protected on the register and are not overriding interests, and include—

(a) in the case of land [subject to a trust for sale], all interests and powers which are under the Law of Property Act 1925, capable of being overridden by the [trustees], whether or not such interests and powers are so protected; and

(b) in the case of settled land, all interests and powers which are under the settled Land Act 1925, and the Law of Property Act 1925, or either of them, capable of being overridden by the tenant for fife or statutory owner, whether or not such interests and powers are so protected as aforesaid;

(xvi) 'Overriding interests' mean all the incumbrances, interests, rights, and powers not entered on the register but subject to which registered dispositions are by this Act to take effect, and in regard to land registered at the commencement of this Act include the matters which are by any enactment repealed by this Act declared not to be incumbrances;

(xvii) 'Personal representative' means the executor, original or by representation, or administrator for the time being of a deceased person, and as regards any liability for the payment of death duties includes any person who takes possession of or intermeddles with the property of a deceased person without the authority of the personal representatives for the purposes of any settled land, it means, in relation to that land, those representatives;

(xviii) 'Possession' includes receipt of rents and profits or the right to receive the same, if any;

(xix) 'Prescribed' means prescribed by general rules made in pursuance of this Act;

(xx) 'Proprietor' means the registered proprietor for the time being of an estate in land or of a charge

(xxi) 'Purchaser' means a purchaser in good faith for valuable consideration and includes a lessee, mortgagee, or other person who for valuable consideration acquires any interest in land or in any charge on land;

(xxii) 'Registered dispositions' mean dispositions which take effect under the powers conferred on the proprietor by way of transfer, charge, lease or otherwise and to which (when required to be registered) special effect or priority is given by this Act on registration—

(xxiii) 'Registered estate,' in reference to land, means the legal estate, or other registered interest, if any, as respects which a person is for the time being registered as proprietor, but does not include a registered charge and a 'registered charge' includes a mortgage or incumbrance registered as a charge under this Act;

(xxiv) 'Registered land' means land or any estate or interest in land the title to which is registered under this Act or any enactment replaced by this Act, and includes any easement, right, privilege, or benefit which is appurtenant or appendant thereto, and any mines and minerals within or under the same and held therewith;

(xxv) 'Rent' includes a rent service or a rent-charge, or other rent, toll, duty, royalty, or annual or periodical payment, in money or money's worth, issuing out of or charged upon land, but does not include mortgage interest;

(xxvi) 'Settled land' 'settlement' 'tenant for life' 'statutory owner' 'trustees of the settlement' 'capital money' [. . .] 'trust corporation' 'trust instrument' 'vesting deed' 'vesting order' 'vesting assent' and 'vesting instrument' have the same meaning as in the Settled Land Act 1925;

(xxvii) A 'term of years absolute' means a term of years, whether at a rent or not, taking effect either in possession or in reversion, with or without impeachment for waste, subject or not to another legal estate and either certain or liable to determination by notice, re-entry, operation of law, or by a provision for cesser on redemption, or in any other event (other than the dropping of a life, or the determination of a determinable life interest), but does not include any term of years determinable with life or lives or with the cesser of a determinable life interest, nor, if created after the commencement of this Act, a term of years which is not expressed to take effect in possession within twenty-one years after the creation thereof where required by the Law of Property Act 1925, to take effect within that period; and in this definition the expression 'term of years' includes a term for less than a year, or for a year or years and a fraction of a year or from year to year;

(xxx) 'United Kingdom' means Great Britain and Northern Ireland;

(xxxi) 'Valuable consideration' includes marriage, but does not include a nominal consideration in money;

(xxxii) 'Will' includes codicil.

PART II
REGISTRATION OF LAND
Freehold Land

4. Application for registration of freehold land

Where the title to be registered is a title to a freehold estate in land—

(a) any estate owner holding an estate in fee simple (including a tenant for life, statutory owner, personal representative, or [trustee of land]) whether subject or not to incumbrances; or

(b) any other person (not being a mortgagee where there is a subsisting right of redemption or a person who has merely contracted to buy land) who is entitled to require a legal estate in fee simple whether subject or not to incumbrances, to be vested in him; may apply to the registrar to be registered in respect of such estate, or, in the case of a person not in a fiduciary position, to have registered in his stead any nominee, as proprietor with an absolute title or with a possessory title:

Provided that—

(i) Where an absolute title is required the applicant or his nominee shall not be registered as proprietor until and unless the title is approved by the registrar;

(ii) Where a possessory title is required the applicant or his nominee may be registered as proprietor on giving such evidence of title and serving such notices, if any, as may for the time being be prescribed;

(iii) If, on an application for registration with possessory title, the registrar is satisfied as to the title to the freehold estate, he may register it as absolute, whether the applicant consents to such registration or not, but in that case no higher fee shall be charged than would have been charged for registration with possessory title.[1]

Note

[1]Section 4 restricted by Land Registration Act 1966, s. 1(2).

5. Effect of first registration with absolute title

Where the registered land is a freehold estate, the registration of any person as first proprietor thereof with an absolute title shall vest in the person so registered an estate in fee simple in possession in the land, together with all rights, privileges, and appurtenances belonging or appurtenant thereto, subject to the following rights and interests, that is to say,—

(a) Subject to the incumbrances, and other entries, if any, appearing on the register; and

(b) Unless the contrary is expressed on the register, subject to such overriding interests, if any, as affect the registered land; and

(c) Where the first proprietor is not entitled for his own benefit to the registered land subject, as between himself and the persons entitled to minor interest, to any minor interests of such persons of which he has notice, but free from all other estates and interests whatsoever, including estates and interests of His Majesty.

6. Effect of first registration with possessory title

Where the registered land is a freehold estate, the registration of any person as first proprietor thereof with a possessory title only shall not affect or prejudice the enforcement of any estate, right or interest adverse to or in derogation of the title of the first proprietor, and subsisting or capable of arising at the time of registration of that proprietor; but save as aforesaid, shall have the same effect as registration of a person with an absolute title.

7. Qualified title

(1) Where an absolute title is required, and on the examination of the title it appears to the registrar that the title can be established only for a limited period, or only subject to certain reservations, the registrar may, on the application of the party applying to be registered, by an entry made in the register, except from the effect of registration any estate, right, or interest—

(a) arising before a specified date, or

(b) arising under a specified instrument or otherwise particularly described in the register, and a title registered subject to such excepted estate, right, or interest shall be called a qualified title.

(2) Where the registered land is a freehold estate, the registration of a person as first proprietor thereof with a qualified title shall have the same effect as the registration of

such person with an absolute title, save that registration with a qualified title shall not affect or prejudice the enforcement of any estate, right or interest appearing by the register to be excepted.

Leasehold Land

8. Application for registration of leasehold land

(1) Where the title to be registered is a title to a leasehold interest in land—

(a) any estate owner (including a tenant for life, statutory owner, personal representative, or [trustee of land], but not including a mortgagee where there is a subsisting right of redemption), holding under a lease for a term of years absolute of which more than twenty-one are unexpired, whether subject or not to incumbrances, or

(b) any other person (not being a mortgagee as aforesaid and not being a person who has merely contracted to buy the leasehold interest) who is entitled to require a legal leasehold estate held under such a lease as aforesaid (whether subject or not to incumbrances) to be vested in him,

may apply to the registrar to be registered in respect of such estate, or in the case of a person not being in a fiduciary position to have registered in his stead any nominee, as proprietor with an absolute title, with a good leasehold title or with a possessory title:

Provided that—

(i) Where an absolute title is required, the applicant or his nominee shall not be registered as proprietor until and unless the title both to the leasehold and to the freehold, and to any intermediate leasehold that may exist, is approved by the registrar;

(ii) Where a good leasehold title is required, the applicant or his nominee shall not be registered as proprietor until and unless the title to the leasehold interest is approved by the registrar;

(iii) Where a possessory title is required, the applicant or his nominee may be registered as proprietor on giving such evidence of title and serving such notices, if any, as may for the time being be prescribed;

(iv) If on an application for registration with a possessory title the registrar is satisfied as to the title to the leasehold interest, he may register it as good leasehold, whether the applicant consents to such registration or not, but in that case no higher fee shall be charged than would have been charged for registration with possessory title.

[(1A)[1] An application for registration in respect of leasehold land held under a lease in relation to the grant or assignment of which section 123(1) of this Act applies (whether by virtue of this Act or any later enactment) may be made within the period allowed by section 123(1), or any authorised extension of that period, notwithstanding that the lease was granted for a term of not more than twenty-one years or that the unexpired term of the lease is not more than twenty-one years.]

[(2)[2] Leasehold land held under a lease containing a prohibition or restriction on dealings therewith inter vivos shall not be registered under this Act unless and until provision is made in the prescribed manner for preventing any dealing therewith in contravention of the prohibition or restriction by an entry on the register to that effect, or otherwise.]

(3) Where on an application to register a mortgage term, wherein no right of redemption is subsisting, it appears that the applicant is entitled in equity to the superior term, if any, out of which it was created, the registrar shall register him as proprietor of the superior term without any entry to the effect that the legal interest in that term is outstanding, and on such registration the superior term shall vest in the proprietor and the mortgage term shall merge therein:

Provided that this subsection shall not apply where the mortgage term does not comprise the whole of the land included in the superior term, unless in that case the rent, if any, payable in respect of the superior term has been apportioned, or the rent is of no money value or no rent is reserved, and unless the covenants, if any, entered into for the benefit of the reversion have been apportioned (either expressly or by implication) as respects the land comprised in the mortgage term.

Notes

[1]Applies only in relation to a grant or assignment of a lease made after the commencement of the Land Registration Act 1986.

[2]Applies in relation to a lease granted before the commencement of the Land Registration Act 1986 subject to an absolute prohibition on any dealings therewith inter vivos;

(a) so as to enable an application for registration to be made, and

(b) as regards dealings therewith after that commencement, but not so as to alter the effect of any grant, assignment or other dealing before that commencement.

9. Effect of first registration with absolute title

Where the registered land is a leasehold interest, the registration under this Act of any person as first proprietor thereof with an absolute title shall be deemed to vest in such person the possession of the leasehold interest described, with all implied or expressed rights, privileges, and appurtenances attached to such interest, subject to the following obligations, rights, and interests, that is to say,—

(a) Subject to all implied and express covenants, obligations, and liabilities incident to the registered land; and

(b) Subject to the incumbrances and other entries (if any) appearing on the register; and

(c) Unless the contrary is expressed on the register, subject to such overriding interests, if any, as affect the registered land; and

(d) Where such first proprietor is not entitled for his own benefit to the registered land subject, as between himself and the persons entitled to minor interests, to any minor interests of such persons of which he has notice; but free from all other estates and interests whatsoever, including estates and interests of His Majesty.

10. Effect of first registration with good leasehold title

Where the registered land is a leasehold interest, the registration of a person as first proprietor thereof with a good leasehold title shall not affect or prejudice the enforcement of any estate, right or interest affecting or in derogation of the title of the lessor to grant the lease, but, save as aforesaid, shall have the same effect as registration with an absolute title.

11. Effect of first registration with possessory title

Where the registered land is a leasehold interest, the registration of a person as first proprietor thereof with a possessory title shall not affect or prejudice the enforcement of any estate, right, or interest (whether in respect of the lessor's title or otherwise) adverse to or in derogation of the title of such first registered proprietor, and subsisting or capable or arising at the time of the registration of such proprietor; but, save as aforesaid, shall have the same effect as registration with an absolute title.

12. Qualified title

(1) Where on examination it appears to the registrar that the title, either of the lessor to the reversion or of the lessee to the leasehold interest, can be established only for a limited period, or subject to certain reservations, the registrar may, upon the request in writing of the person applying to be registered, by an entry made in the register, except from the effect of registration any estate, right or interest—

(a) arising before a specified date, or

(b) arising under a specified instrument, or otherwise particularly described in the register,

and a title registered subject to any such exception shall be called a qualified title.

(2) Where the registered land is a leasehold interest, the registration of a person as first proprietor thereof with a qualified title shall not affect or prejudice the enforcement of any estate, right, or interest appearing by the register to be excepted, but, save as aforesaid, shall have the same effect as registration with a good leasehold title or an absolute title, as the case may be.

Preliminaries to Registration

13. Regulations as to examination of title by registrar

The examination by the registrar of any title under this Act shall be conducted in the prescribed manner:

Provided that—

(a) Due notice shall be given, where the giving of such notice is prescribed, and sufficient opportunity shall be afforded to any persons desirous of objecting to come in and state their objections to the registrar; and

(b) The registrar shall have jurisdiction to hear and determine any such objections, subject to an appeal to the court in the prescribed manner and on the prescribed conditions; and

(c) If the registrar, upon the examination of any title, is of opinion that the title is open to objection, but is nevertheless a title the holding under which will not be disturbed, he may approve of such title, or may require the applicant to apply to the court, upon a statement signed by the registrar, for its sanction to the registration.

14. Evidence required before registration

(1) Before the completion of the registration of any estate in land in respect of which an examination of title is required, the applicant for registration and his solicitor, shall each, if required by the registrar, make an affidavit or declaration that to the best of his knowledge and belief all deeds, wills, and instruments of title, and all charges and incumbrances affecting the title which is the subject of the application, and all facts material to such title, have been disclosed in the course of the investigation of title made by the registrar.

(2) The registrar may require any person making an affidavit or declaration in pursuance of this section to state in his affidavit or declaration what means he has had of becoming acquainted with the several matters referred to in this section; and if the registrar is of opinion that any further or other evidence is necessary or desirable, he may refuse to complete the registration until such further or other evidence is produced.

(3) Before the registration of any person who has not previously acquired the state intended to be registered, the registrar shall be satisfied that all ad valorem stamp duty, if any, which, if the estate had been acquired by him, would have been payable in respect of the instrument vesting that estate in him, has been discharged.

15. Production of deeds

(1) When an application has been made to the registrar for the registration of any title to land, then if any person has in his possession or custody any deeds, instruments, or evidences of title relating to or affecting such title, to the production of which the applicant or any trustee for him is entitled, the registrar may require such person to show cause, within a time limited, why he should not produce such deeds, intruments, or evidences of title to the registrar, or otherwise, as the registrar may deem fit and, unless cause is shown to the satisfaction of the registrar within the time limited, such deeds, instruments, and evidences of title may be ordered by the registrar to be produced at the expense of the applicant, at such time and place, and in such manner, and on such terms, as the registrar thinks fit.

(2) Any person aggrieved by an order of the registrar under this section may appeal in the prescribed manner to the court, which may annul or confirm the order of the registrar with or without modification.

(3) If any person disobeys any order of the registrar made in pursuance of this section, the registrar may certify such disobedience to the court, and thereupon such person, subject to such right of appeal as aforesaid, may be punished by the court in the same manner in all respects as if the order made by the registrar were the order of the court.

16. Deeds to be marked with notice of registration

A person shall not be registered as proprietor until, if required by the registrar, he has produced to him such documents of title, if any, as will, in the opinion of the registrar, when stamped or otherwise marked, give notice to any purchaser or other person dealing with the land of the fact of the registration, and the registrar shall stamp or otherwise mark the same accordingly, unless the registrar is satisfied that without such stamping or marking the fact of such registration cannot be concealed from a purchaser or other person dealing with the land:

Provided that, in the case of registration with a possessory title, the registrar may act on such reasonable evidence as may be prescribed as to the sufficiency of the documents produced, and as to dispensing with their production in special circumstances.

PART III
REGISTERED DEALINGS WITH REGISTERED LAND

Dispositions of Freehold Land

18. Powers of disposition of registered freeholds

(1) Where the registered land is a freehold estate the proprietor may, in the prescribed manner, transfer the registered estate in the land or any part thereof, and, subject to any entry in the register to the contrary, may in the prescribed manner—

(a) transfer the fee simple in possession of all or any mines or minerals apart from the surface; or of the surface without all or any of the mines and minerals

(b) grant an annuity or a rentcharge in possession (either perpetual or for a term of years absolute) in any form which sufficiently refers in the prescribed manner to the registered land charged;

(c) grant in fee simple in possession any easement, right, or privilege in, over, or derived from the registered land or any part thereof, in any form which sufficiently refers, in the prescribed manner, to the registered servient tenement and to the dominant tenement, whether being registered land or not;

(d) transfer the fee simple in possession of the registered land or any part thereof, subject to the creation thereout, by way of reservation, in favour of any person of an annuity or a rentcharge in possession (either perpetual or for a term of years absolute), or of any easement, right, or privilege in possession (either in fee simple or for a term of years absolute);

(e) grant (subject or not to the reservation of an easement, right, or privilege) a lease of the registered land or any part thereof, or of all or any mines and minerals apart from the surface, or of the surface without all or any of the mines and minerals, or of an easement, right or privilege in or over the land, or any part thereof, for any term of years absolute for any purpose (but where by way of mortgage subject to the provisions of this Act and the Law of Property Act 1925, relating thereto), and in any form which sufficiently refers, in the prescribed manner, to the registered land.

(2) A perpetual annuity or rentcharge in possession may be granted or reserved to any person with or without a power of re-entry, exercisable at any time, on default of payment thereof, or on breach of covenant, and shall have incidental thereto all the powers and remedies (as varied if at all by the disposition creating the rentcharge) for recovery thereof conferred by the Law of Property Act 1925; and where an easement, right, or privilege is reserved in a registered disposition for a legal estate, the reservation shall operate to create the same for the benefit of the land for the benefit of which the right is reserved.

(3) A lease for a term, not exceeding twenty-one years, to take effect in possession or within one year from the date thereof [. . .] may be granted and shall take effect under this section notwithstanding that a caution, notice of deposit of a certificate, restriction, or inhibition (other than a bankruptcy inhibition) may be subsisting, but subject to the interests intended to be protected by any such caution, notice, restriction, or inhibition.

(4) The foregoing powers of disposition shall (subject to the express provisions of this Act and the Law of Property Act 1925, relating to mortgages) apply to dispositions by the registered proprietor by way of charge or mortgage; but no estate, other than a legal estate, shall be capable of being disposed of, or created under this section.

(5) In this Act 'transfer' or 'disposition' when referring to registered freehold land includes any disposition authorised as aforesaid; and 'transferee' has a corresponding meaning.

19. Registration of disposition of freeholds

(1) The transfer of the registered estate in the land or part thereof shall be completed by the registrar entering on the register the transferee as the proprietor of the estate transferred, but until such entry is made the transferor shall be deemed to remain proprietor of the registered estate; and, where part only of the land is transferred, notice thereof shall also be noted on the register.

(2) All interests transferred or created by dispositions by the proprietor, other than a transfer of the registered estate in the land, or part thereof, shall, subject to the provisions relating to mortgages, be completed by registration in the same manner and with the same effect as provided by this Act with respect to transfers of registered estates and notice thereof shall also be noted on the register:

Provided that nothing in this subsection—

(a) shall authorise the registration of a lease granted for a term not exceeding twenty-one years, or require the entry of a notice of such a lease [. . .]; or

(b) shall authorise the registration of a mortgage term where there is a subsisting right of redemption; or

(c) shall render necessary the registration of any easement, right, or privilege except as appurtenant to registered land, or the entry of notice thereof except as against the registered title of the servient land.

Every such disposition shall, when registered, take effect as a registered disposition, and a lease made by the registered proprietor under the last foregoing section which is not required to be registered or noted on the register shall nevertheless take effect as if it were a registered disposition immediately on being granted.

(3) The general words implied in conveyances under the Law of Property Act 1925, shall apply, so far as applicable thereto, to dispositions of a registered estate.

20. Effect of registration of dispositions of freeholds

(1) In the case of a freehold estate registered with an absolute title, a disposition of the registered land or of a legal estate therein, including a lease thereof, for valuable consideration shall, when registered, confer on the transferee or grantee an estate in fee simple or the term of years absolute or other legal estate expressed to be created in the land dealt with, together with all rights, privileges, and appurtenances belonging or appurtenant thereto, including (subject to any entry to the contrary in the register) the appropriate rights and interests which would, under the Law of Property Act 1925, have been transferred if the land had not been registered, subject—

(a) to the incumbrances and other entries, if any, appearing on the register [and any charge for [inheritance tax] subject to which the disposition takes effect under section 73 of this Act]; and

(b) unless the contrary is expressed on the register, to the overriding interests, if any, affecting the estate transferred or created, but free from all other estates and interests whatsoever, including estates and interests of His Majesty, and the disposition shall operate in like manner as if the registered transferor or grantor were (subject to any entry to the contrary in the register) entitled to the registered land in fee simple in possession for his own benefit.

(2) In the case of a freehold estate registered with a qualified title a disposition of the registered land or of a legal estate therein, including a lease thereof, for valuable consideration shall, when registered, have the same effect as it would have had if the land had been registered with an absolute title, save that such disposition shall not affect or prejudice the enforcement of any right or interest appearing by the register to be excepted.

(3) In the case of a freehold estate registered with a possessory title, a disposition of the registered land or of a legal estate therein, including a lease thereof, for valuable consideration shall not affect or prejudice the enforcement of any right or interest adverse to or in derogation of the title of the first registered proprietor, and subsisting or capable of arising at the time of the registration of such proprietor; but, save as aforesaid, shall when registered have the same effect as it would have had if the land had been registered with an absolute title.

(4) Where any such disposition is made without valuable consideration, it shall, so far as the transferee or grantee is concerned, be subject to any minor interests subject to which the transferor or grantor held the same, but, save as aforesaid, shall, when registered, in all respects, and in particular as respects any registered dealings on the part of the transferee or grantee, have the same effect as if the disposition had been made for valuable consideration.

Dispositions of Leasehold Land

21. Powers of disposition of registered leaseholds

(1) Where the registered land is a leasehold interest the proprietor may, in the prescribed manner, transfer the registered estate in the land or any part thereof, and, subject to any entry in the register to the contrary may in the prescribed manner—

(a) transfer all or any of the leasehold mines and minerals apart from the surface; or the surface without all or any of the leasehold mines and minerals;

(b) grant (to the extent of the registered estate) any annuity or rentcharge in possession, easement, right or privilege in, over, or derived from the registered land or any part thereof, in any form which sufficiently refers, in the prescribed manner, to the registered lease, and to the dominant tenement, whether being registered land or not;

(c) transfer the registered land or any part thereof subject to a reservation to any person of any such annuity, rentcharge, easement, right, or privilege;

(d) grant (subject or not to the reservation of an easement, right or privilege) an underlease of the registered land, or any part thereof, or of all or any mines and minerals apart from the surface, or of the surface without all or any of the mines and minerals, or of an easement, right or privilege, in or over the registered land or any part thereof, for any term of years absolute of less duration than the registered estate and for any purpose (but where by way of mortgage, subject to the provisions of this Act and of the Law of Property Act 1925 relating thereto), and in any form which sufficiently refers in the prescribed manner to the registered land, and in the case of an easement right, or privilege, to the dominant tenement, whether being registered land or not.

(2) A disposition of registered leasehold land may be made subject to a rent legally apportioned in the prescribed manner, or to a rent not so apportioned.

(3) An underlease for a term, not exceeding twenty-one years, to take effect in possession or within one year from the date thereof, [. . .], may be granted and shall take effect under this section, notwithstanding that a caution, notice of deposit of a certificate, restriction, or inhibition (other than a bankruptcy inhibition) may be subsisting, but, subject to the interests intended to be protected by any such caution, notice, restriction or inhibition.

(4) The foregoing powers of disposition shall (subject to the express provisions of this Act and the Law of Property Act 1925, relating to mortgages) apply to dispositions by the registered proprietor by way of charge or mortgage, but no estate, other than a legal estate, shall be capable of being disposed of or created under this section.

(5) In this Act 'transfer' or 'disposition' when referring to registered leasehold land includes any disposition authorised as aforesaid, and 'transferee' has a corresponding meaning.

22. Registration of dispositions of leaseholds

(1) A transfer of the registered estate in the land or part thereof shall be completed by the registrar entering on the register the transferee as proprietor of the estate transferred, but until such entry is made the transferor shall be deemed to remain the proprietor of the registered estate; and where part only of the land is transferred, notice thereof shall also be noted on the register.

(2) All interests transferred or created by dispositions by the registered proprietor other than the transfer of his registered estate in the land or in part thereof shall (subject to the provisions relating to mortgages) be completed by registration in the same manner and with the same effect as provided by this Act with respect to transfers of the registered estate, and notice thereof shall also be noted on the register in accordance with this Act:

Provided that nothing in this subsection—

(a) shall authorise the registration of an underlease originally granted for a term not exceeding twenty-one years, or require the entry of a notice of such an underlease [. . .]; or

(b) shall authorise the registration of a mortgage term where there is a subsisting right of redemption, or

(c) shall render necessary the registration of any easement, right, or privilege except as appurtenant to registered land, or the entry of notice thereof except as against the registered title of the servient land.

Every such disposition shall, when registered, take effect as a registered disposition, and an underlease made by the registered proprietor which is not required to be registered or noted on the register shall nevertheless take effect as if it were a registered disposition immediately on being granted.

(3) The general words implied in conveyances under the Law of Property Act 1925, shall apply, so far as applicable thereto, to transfers of a registered leasehold estate.

23. Effect of registration of dispositions of leaseholds

(1) In the case of a leasehold estate registered with an absolute title, a disposition (including a subdemise thereof) for valuable consideration shall, when registered, be deemed to vest in the transferee or underlessee the estate transferred or created to the extent of the registered estate, or for the term created by the subdemise, as the case may require, with all implied or expressed rights, privileges, and appurtenances attached to the estate transferred or created, including (subject to any entry to the contrary on the register) the appropriate rights and interests which would under the Law of Property Act 1925, have been transferred if the land had not been registered, but subject as follows—

(a) To all implied and express covenants, obligations, and liabilities incident to the estate transferred or created; and

(b) To the incumbrances and other entries (if any) appearing on the register [and any charge for [inheritance tax] subject to which the disposition takes effect under section 73 of this Act]; and

(c) Unless the contrary is expressed on the register, to the overriding interests, if any, affecting the estate transferred or created,

but free from all other estates and interests whatsoever, including estates and interests of His Majesty; and the transfer or subdemise shall operate in like manner as if the registered transferor or sublessor were (subject to any entry to the contrary on the register) absolutely entitled to the registered lease for his own benefit.

(2) In the case of a leasehold estate registered with a good leasehold title, a disposition (including a subdemise thereof) for valuable consideration shall, when registered, have the same effect as it would have had if the land had been registered with an absolute title, save that it shall not affect or prejudice the enforcement of any right or interest affecting or in derogation of the title of the lessor to grant the lease.

(3) In the case of a leasehold estate registered with a qualified title, a disposition (including a subdemise thereof) for valuable consideration shall, when registered, have the same effect as it would have had if the land had been registered with an absolute title, save that such disposition shall not affect or prejudice the enforcement of any right or interest (whether in respect of the lessor's title or otherwise) appearing by the register to be excepted.

(4) In the case of a leasehold estate registered with a possessory title, a disposition (including a subdemise thereof) for valuable consideration shall not affect or prejudice the enforcement of any right or interest (whether in respect of the lessor's title or otherwise) adverse to or in derogation of the title of the first registered proprietor, and subsisting or capable of arising at the time of the registration of such proprietor, but save as aforesaid shall, when registered, have the same effect as it would have had if the land had been registered with an absolute title.

(5) Where any such disposition is made without valuable consideration it shall, so far as the transferee or underlessee is concerned, be subject to any minor interests subject to which the transferor or sublessor held the same; but, save as aforesaid, shall, when registered, in all respects, and in particular as respects any registered dealings on the part of the transferee or underlessee, have the same effect as if the disposition had been made for valuable consideration.

24. Implied covenants on transfers of leaseholds

(1) On the transfer, otherwise than by way of underlease, of any leasehold interest in land under this Act, unless there be an entry on the register negativing such implication, there shall be implied—

(a) on the part of the transferor, a covenant with the transferee that, notwithstanding anything by such transferor done, omitted, or knowingly suffered, the rent, covenants, and conditions reserved and contained by and in the registered lease, and on the part of the lessee to be paid, performed, and observed, have been so paid, performed, and observed up to the date of the transfer; and

Note: See section 10, Law of Property (Miscellaneous Provisions) Act 1994.

(b) on the part of the transferee, a covenant with the transferor, that during the residue of the term the transferee and the persons deriving title under him will pay, perform, and observe the rent, covenants, and conditions by and in the registered lease reserved and contained, and on the part of the lessee to be paid, performed, and observed, and will keep the transferor and the persons deriving title under him indemnified against all actions, expenses, and claims on account of the non-payment of the said rent or any part thereof, or the breach of the said covenants or conditions, or any of them.

(2) On a transfer of part of the land held under a lease, the covenant implied on the part of the transferee by this section shall be limited to the payment of the apportioned rent, if any, and the performance and observance of the covenants by the lessee and conditions in the registered lease so far only as they affect the part transferred. Where the transferor remains owner of part of the land comprised in the lease, there shall also be implied on his part, as respects the part retained, a covenant with the transferee similar to that implied on the part of the transferee under this subsection.

Note: Applies to tenancies that were created prior to the Landlord and Tenant (Covenants) Act 1995.

Charges on Freehold and Leasehold Land

25. Proprietor's power to create charges

(1) The proprietor of any registered land may by deed—

(a) charge the registered land with the payment at an appointed time of any principal sum of money either with or without interest;

(b) charge the registered land in favour of a building society [(within the meaning of the Building Societies Act 1986), in accordance with] the rules of that society.

(2) A charge may be in any form provided that—

(a) the registered land comprised in the charge is described by reference to the register or in any other manner sufficient to enable the registrar to identify the same without reference to any other document;

(b) the charge does not refer to any other interest or charge affecting the land which—

(i) would have priority over the same and is not registered or protected on the register,

(ii) is not an overriding interest.

(3) Any provision contained in a charge which purports to—

(i) take away from the proprietor thereof the power of transferring it by registered disposition or of requiring the cessation thereof to be noted on the register; or

(ii) affect any registered land or charge other than that in respect of which the charge is to be expressly registered, shall be void.

26. Registration of charges

(1) The charge shall be completed by the registrar entering on the register the person in whose favour the charge is made as the proprietor of such charge, and the particulars of the charge.

(2) A charge may be registered notwithstanding that it contains any trust, power to appoint new trustees, or other provisions for giving effect to the security.

(3) Where the land, in respect of which a charge is registered, is registered with a good leasehold, qualified or possessory title, the charge shall take effect subject to the provisions of this Act with respect to land registered with such a title.

27. Terms of years implied in or granted by charges

(1) A registered charge shall, unless made or taking effect by demise or subdemise, and subject to any provision to the contrary contained in the charge, take effect as a charge by way of legal mortgage.

(2) Subject to the provisions of the Law of Property Act 1925, a registered charge may contain in the case of freehold land, an express demise, and in the case of leasehold land an express subdemise of the land to the creditor for a term of years absolute, subject to a proviso for cesser on redemption.

(3) Any such demise or subdemise or charge by way of legal mortgage shall take effect from the date of the delivery of the deed containing the same, but subject to the estate or interest of any person (other than the proprietor of the land) whose estate or interest (whenever created) is registered or noted on the register before the date of registration of the charge.

(4) Any charge registered before the commencement of this Act shall take effect as a demise or subdemise of the land in accordance with the provisions of the Law of Property Act 1925, and the registered estate shall (without prejudice to any registered charge or any term or subterm created by a charge or by this Act) vest in the person appearing by the register to be entitled to the ultimate equity of redemption.

28. Implied covenants in charges

(1) Where a registered charge is created on any land there shall be implied on the part of the person being proprietor of such land at the time of the creation of the charge, unless there be an entry on the register negativing such implication—

(a) a covenant with the proprietor for the time being of the charge to pay the principal sum charged, and interest, if any, thereon, at the appointed time and rate; and

(b) a covenant, if the principal sum or any part thereof is unpaid at the appointed time, to pay interest half-yearly at the appointed rate as well after as before any judgment is obtained in respect of the charge on so much of the principal sum as for the time being remains unpaid.

(2) Where a registered charge is created on any leasehold land there shall (in addition to the covenants aforesaid) be implied on the part of the person being proprietor of such land at the time of the creation of the charge, unless there be an entry on the register negativing such implication, a covenant with the proprietor for the time being of the charge, that the person being proprietor of such land at the time of the creation of the charge, or the persons deriving title under him, will pay, perform, and observe the rent, covenants, and conditions, by and in the registered lease reserved and contained, and on the part of the lessee to be paid, performed, and observed, and will keep the proprietor of the charge, and the persons deriving title under him, indemnified against all proceedings, expenses, and claims, on account of the non-payment of the said rent, or any part thereof, or the breach of the said covenants or conditions, or any of them.

29. Priorities of registered charges

Subject to any entry to the contrary on the register, registered charges on the same land shall as between themselves rank according to the order in which they are entered on the register, and not according to the order in which they are created.

30. Protection of charges for securing further advances

(1) When a registered charge is made for securing further advances, the registrar shall, before making any entry on the register which would prejudicially affect the priority of any further advance thereunder, give to the proprietor of the charge at his registered address, notice by registered post of the intended entry, and the proprietor of the charge shall not, in respect of any further advance, be affected by such entry, unless the advance is made after the date when the notice ought to have been received in due course of post.

(2) If, by reason of any failure on the part of the registrar or the post office in reference to the notice, the proprietor of the charge suffers loss in relation to a further advance, he shall be entitled to be indemnified under this Act in like manner as if a mistake had occurred in the register; but if the loss arises by reason of an omission to register or amend the address for service, no indemnity shall be payable under this Act.

[(3) Where the proprietor of a charge is under an obligation, noted on the register, to make a further advance, a subsequent registered charge shall take effect subject to any further advance made pursuant to the obligation.]

31. Alteration of charges

(1) The proprietor of a charge may by deed, in the prescribed manner, alter the terms of the charge, with the consent of the proprietor of the registered land and of the proprietors of all registered charges (if any) of equal or inferior priority, affected by the alteration.

(2) A deed of alteration of a charge may contain an express demise or subdemise in like manner as an original deed of charge, and the provisions of this Act relating to a demise or subdemise contained in a deed of charge shall apply accordingly.

(3) The alteration shall be completed by the registrar entering it on the register.

32. Provisions when charge registered in names of several proprietors

Where a charge is registered in the names of two or more proprietors (whether jointly or in undivided shares) the mortgage term implied or comprised in the charge shall (but without prejudice to the beneficial interests in the mortgage money) vest in them as joint tenants, and the proprietors or the survivors or survivor of them or the personal representatives of the last survivor, shall have power to give valid receipts, notwithstanding that the mortgage money may be held in undivided shares, in like manner as if the money had been held on a joint account.

33. Transfer of charges

(1) The proprietor of any registered charge may, in the prescribed manner, transfer the charge to another person as proprietor.

(2) The transfer shall be completed by the registrar entering on the register the transferee as proprietor of the charge transferred, but the transferor shall be deemed to remain proprietor of the charge until the name of the transferee is entered on the register in respect thereof.

(3) A registered transferee for valuable consideration of a charge and his successors in title shall not be affected by any irregularity or invalidity in the original charge itself of which the transferee did not have notice when it was transferred to him.

(4) On registration of any transfer of a charge, the term or subterm (if any) granted expressly or by implication by the charge or any deed of alteration shall, without any conveyance or assignment and notwithstanding anything to the contrary in the transfer or any other instrument, vest in the proprietor for the time being of the charge.

(5) Subject to any entry to the contrary on the register, the vesting of any term or subterm in accordance with this section in the proprietor of a charge shall, subject to the right of redemption, have the same effect as if such proprietor had been registered as the transferee for valuable consideration of the term or subterm.

34. Powers of proprietor of charge

(1) Subject to any entry on the register to the contrary, the proprietor of a charge shall have and may exercise all the powers conferred by law on the owner of a legal mortgage.

(2) Subject to any entry to the contrary on the register and subject to the right of any persons appearing on the register to be prior incumbrancers, the proprietor of a charge may, after entry into possession and after having acquired a title under the Limitation Acts, execute a declaration, in the prescribed form, that the right of redemption is barred, and thereupon he shall be entitled, subject to furnishing any evidence which may be prescribed in support thereof, to be registered as proprietor of the land, with the same consequences as if he had been a purchaser for valuable consideration of the land under the power of sale.

(3) An order for foreclosure shall be completed by the registration of the proprietor of the charge (or such other person as may be named in the foreclosure order absolute for that purpose) as the proprietor of the land, and by the cancellation of the charge and of all incumbrances and entries inferior thereto; and such registration shall operate in like manner and with the same consequences as if the proprietor of the charge or other person aforesaid had been a purchaser for valuable consideration of the land under a subsisting power of sale.

(4) A sale by the court or under the power of sale shall operate and be completed by registration in the same manner, as nearly as may be (but subject to any alterations on the register affecting the priority of the charge), as a transfer for valuable consideration by the proprietor of the land at the time of the registration of the charge would have operated or been completed, and, as respects the land transferred, the charge and all incumbrances and entries inferior thereto shall be cancelled.

(5) Notwithstanding the creation of a term or subterm, expressly or by implication, under this Act, such transfer shall (subject to any prior incumbrances or other entries on the register) operate to transfer the registered estate, and the mortgage term or subterm shall become merged, and any purported disposition of or dealing with the mortgage term or subterm apart from the charge, and any process or act purporting to keep alive that term or subterm after the cessation of the charge shall be void.

(6) For the purposes of this section an incumbrance or entry on the register shall not be deemed to be inferior to the charge in right of which title is made if the incumbrance or other interest is given the requisite priority by statute or otherwise.

35. Discharge of charges

(1) The registrar shall, on the requisition of the proprietor of any charge, or on due proof of the satisfaction (whole or partial) thereof, notify on the register in the prescribed manner, by cancelling or varying the original entry or otherwise, the cessation (whole or partial) of the charge, and thereupon the charge shall be deemed to have ceased (in whole or in part) accordingly.

(2) On the notification on the register of the entire cessation of a registered charge, whether as to the whole or part only of the land affected thereby, the term or sub-term implied in or granted by the charge or by any deed of alteration, so far as it affects the land to which the discharge extends, shall merge and be extinguished in the registered estate in reversion without any surrender.

36. Rules as to subcharges

Rules shall be made for applying the provisions of the Law of Property Act, 1925, and of this Act to the case of charges by way of submortgage, whether registered before or after the commencement of this Act.

As to Dealings Generally

37. Powers of persons entitled to be registered

(1) Where a person on whom the right to be registered as proprietor of registered land or of a registered charge has devolved by reason of the death of the proprietor, or has been conferred by a disposition or charge, in accordance with this Act, desires to dispose of or charge the land or to deal with the charge before he is himself registered as proprietor, he may do so in the prescribed manner, and subject to the prescribed conditions.

(2) Subject to the provisions of this Act with regard to registered dealings for valuable consideration, a disposition or charge so made shall have the same effect as if the person making it were registered as proprietor.

(3) Rules may be made for extending the provisions of this section to the case of any person entitled to be registered as first proprietor, and to any other case for which it may be deemed expedient to prescribe.

38. Certain provisions of the Law of Property Act to apply

(1) The provisions as to execution of a conveyance on sale contained in the Law of Property Act, 1925, shall apply, so far as applicable thereto, to transfers on sale of registered land.

(2) Rules may be made for prescribing the effect of covenants implied by virtue of the Law of Property Act, 1925 [or Part I of the Law of Property (Miscellaneous Provisions) Act 1994], in dispositions of registered land.

39. Deeds off register, how far to be void

(1) Where any transaction relating exclusively to registered land or to a registered charge is capable of being effected and is effected by a registered disposition, then, subject to any prescribed exceptions, any deed or instrument, other than the registered disposition, which is executed by the proprietor for the purpose of giving effect to the transaction shall be void, but only so far as the transaction is carried out by the registered disposition.

(2) Rules may be made for providing for cases in which any additional deed or instrument may be properly executed and for enabling the registrar to certify that in any special cases an additional deed or instrument will be proper and valid.

40. Creation and discharge of restrictive covenants

(1) Subject to any entry to the contrary on the register, and without prejudice to the rights of persons entitled to overriding interests (if any) and to any incumbrances entered on the register, who may not concur therein, the proprietor may in any registered disposition or other instrument by covenant, condition or otherwise, impose or make binding, so far as the law permits, any obligation or reservation with respect to the building on or other user of the registered land or any part thereof, or with respect to mines and minerals (whether registered separately or as part of the registered land), or with respect to any other thing in like manner as if the proprietor were entitled to the registered land for his own benefit.

(2) The proprietor may (subject as aforesaid) release or waive any rights arising or which may arise by reason of any covenant or condition, or release any obligation or reservation the benefit of which is annexed or belongs to the registered land, to the same extent and in the same manner as if the rights in respect of the breach or the benefit of the covenant, condition, obligation, or reservation had been vested in him absolutely for his own benefit.

This subsection shall authorise the proprietor in reference to the registered land to give any licence, consent or approval which a tenant for life is by the Settled Land Act, 1925, authorised to give in reference to settled land.

(3) Entries shall be made on the register in the prescribed manner of all obligations and reservations imposed by the proprietor, of the release or waiver of any obligation or reservation, and of all obligations and reservations acquired by him for the benefit of the registered estate.

Transmissions of Land and Charges on Death and Bankruptcy

41. Transmissions of land and charges on death of proprietor

(1) On the death of the sole proprietor, or of the survivor of two or more joint proprietors, of any registered land or charge, the personal representative of such sole deceased proprietor, or of the survivor of such joint proprietors, shall be entitled to be registered as proprietor in his place:

Provided that, where a special or additional personal representative is appointed by the court in reference to a registered estate, then on production of the order he shall be registered as proprietor either solely or jointly with any of the other personal representatives, as the case may require, and a copy of the order shall be filed at the registry.

(2) Pending an application for the appointment of a special or additional personal representative, a caution against dealings may be lodged under this Act by any person intending to apply to the court for the appointment.

(3) Subject as aforesaid, provision shall be made by rules for the manner in which effect is to be given on the register to transmission on death.

(4) An assent by a personal representative shall, in the case of registered land, be in the prescribed form and the production of the assent in that form shall authorise the registrar to register the person named in the assent as the proprietor of the registered land.

42. Transmissions on bankruptcy of proprietor

(1) Upon the brankruptcy of the proprietor of any registered land or charge his trustee shall (on production of the prescribed evidence to be furnished by the official receiver or trustee in bankruptcy that the land or charge is [comprised in the bankrupt's estate]) be entitled to be registered as proprietor in his place.

The official receiver shall be entitled to be registered pending the appointment of a trustee.

(2) Where a trustee in bankruptcy disclaims a registered lease under [sections 315 to 319 of the Insolvency Act 1986], and an order is made by the court vesting the lease

in any person, the order shall direct the alteration of the register in favour of the person in whom the lease is so vested, and in such case the registrar shall, on being served with such order forthwith (without notice to the bankrupt or any other person and without requiring production of the land certificate) alter the register accordingly, and no right to indemnity under this Act shall arise by reason of such alteration.

43. Effect of transmissions
Any person registered in the place of a deceased or bankrupt proprietor shall hold the land or charge in respect of which he is registered upon the trusts and for the purposes upon and subject to which the same is applicable by law, and subject to any minor interests subject to which the deceased or bankrupt proprietor held the same; but, save as aforesaid, he shall in all respects, and in particular as respects any registered dealings with such land or charge, be in the same position as if he had taken such land or charge under a transfer for valuable consideration.

44. Vesting of term or subterm on transmission of charge
(1) On the registration of any transmission of a charge the term or subterm granted (expressly or by implication) by the charge or any deed of alteration shall without any conveyance or assignment vest in the proprietor for the time being of the charge.

(2) Subject to any entry to the contrary on the register, the vesting of a term or subterm in accordance with this section in the proprietor of a charge, shall, subject to the right of redemption, have the same effect as if such proprietor had been registered as the transferee for valuable consideration of the term or subterm.

45. Proof of transmission of registered proprietorship
The fact of any person having become entitled to any registered land or charge in consequence of the death or bankruptcy of any proprietor shall be proved in the prescribed manner.

Subsidiary Provisions

46. Determination or variation of leases, incumbrances, etc.
The registrar shall, on proof to his satisfaction of—

(a) the determination of any lease, rentcharge, or other estate or interest the title to which is registered under this Act; or

(b) the discharge or determination (whole or partial) or variation of any lease, incumbrance, rentcharge, easement, right or other interest in land which is noted on the register as an incumbrance, notify in the prescribed manner on the register the determination (whole or partial) or variation of such lease or other interest.

47. Vesting instruments and dispositions in name of proprietor
(1) The registrar shall give effect on the register to any vesting order or vesting declaration (express or implied) made on the appointment or discharge of a trustee or otherwise, and to dispositions made in the name and on behalf of a proprietor by a person authorised to make the disposition; and the provisions of the Trustee Act 1925, relating to the appointment and discharge of trustees and the vesting of trust property, shall apply to registered land subject to the proper entry being made on the register.

(2) The registrar shall also give effect on the register in the prescribed manner to any vesting instrument which may be made pursuant to any statutory power.

PART IV
NOTICES, CAUTIONS, INHIBITIONS AND RESTRICTIONS

Notices

48. Registration of notice of lease
(1) Any lessee or other person entitled to or interested in a lease of registered land, where the term granted is not an overriding interest, may apply to the registrar to register

notice of such lease in the prescribed manner, and when so registered, every proprietor and the persons deriving title under him shall be deemed to be affected with notice of such lease, as being an incumbrance on the registered land in respect of which the notice is entered:

Provided that a proprietor of a charge or incumbrance registered or protected on the register prior to the registration of such notice shall not be deemed to be so affected by the notice unless such proprietor is, by reason of the lease having been made under a statutory or other power or by reason of his concurrence or otherwise, bound by the terms of the lease.

(2) In order to register notice of a lease, if the proprietor of the registered land affected does not concur in registration thereof, the applicant shall obtain an order of the court authorising the registration of notice of the lease, and shall deliver the order to the registrar, accompanied with the original lease or a copy thereof, and thereupon the registrar shall make a note in the register identifying the lease or copy so deposited, and the lease or copy so deposited shall be deemed to be the instrument of which notice is given; but if the proprietor concurs in the notice being registered, notice may be entered in such manner as may be agreed upon:

Provided that, where the lease is binding on the proprietor of the land, neither the concurrence of such proprietor nor an order of the court shall be required.

49. Rules to provide for notices of other rights, interests and claims

(1) The provisions of the last foregoing section shall be extended by the rule so as to apply to the registration of notices of or of claims in respect of—

(a) The grant or reservation of any annuity or rentcharge in possesion, either perpetual or for a term of years absolute:

(b) The severance of any mines or minerals from the surface, except where the mines and minerals servered are expressly included in the registration:

(c) Land charges until the land charge is registered as a registered charge:

(d) The right of any person interested in [land subject to a trust of land] or in land subject to a settlement to require that (unless a trust corporation is acting as trustee) there shall be at least two trustees of the [trust or] settlement:

(e) The rights of any widow in respect of dower or under the Intestates' Estates Act 1890, and any right to free bench or other like right saved by any statute coming into force concurrently with this Act (which rights shall take effect in equity as minor interests):

(f) Creditors' notices and any other right, interest, or claim which it may be deemed expedient to protect by notice instead of by caution, inhibition, or restriction.

[(g) Charging orders (within the meaning of the Charging Orders Act 1979 [or the Criminal justice Act 1988] [or the Drug Trafficking Offences Act 1994]) which in the case of unregistered land may be protected by registration under the Land Charges Act 1972 and which, notwithstanding section 59 of this Act, it may be deemed expedient to protect by notice instead of by caution.]

[(h) Acquisition orders (within the meaning of Part III of the Landlord and Tenant Act 1987) which in the case of unregistered land may be protected by registration under the Land Charges Act 1972 and which, notwithstanding section 59 of this Act, it may be deemed expedient to protect by notice instead of by caution.]

[(j) Access orders under the Access to Neighbouring Land Act 1992 which, notwithstanding section 59 of this Act, it may be deemed expedient to protect by notice instead of by caution.]

[(k) Orders made under section 26(1) or 50(1) of the Leasehold Reform, Housing and Urban Development Act 1993 which in the case of unregistered land may be protected by registration under the Land Charges Act 1972 and which, notwithstanding section 59 of this Act, it may be deemed expedient to protect by notice instead of by caution.]

(2) A notice shall not be registered in respect of any estate, right, or interest which (independently of this Act) is capable of being overridden by the proprietor under a [trust of land] or the powers of the Settled Land Act 1925, or any other statute, or of a settlement, and of being protected by a restriction in the prescribed manner:

Provided that notice of such an estate right or interest may be lodged pending the appointment of trustees of [land, or trustees of] or a settlement, and if so lodged, shall be cancelled if and when the appointment is made and the proper restriction (if any) is entered.

(3) A notice when registered in respect of a right, interest, or claim shall not affect prejudicially—

(a) The powers of disposition of the personal representative of the deceased under whose will or by the operation of whose intestacy the right, interest, or claim arose; or

(b) The powers of disposition (independently of this Act) of a proprietor holding the registered [subject to a trust of land].

50. Notices of restrictive covenants

(1) Any person entitled to the benefit of a restrictive covenant or agreement (not being a covenant or agreement made between a lessor and lessee) with respect to the building on or other user of registered land may apply to the registrar to enter notice thereof on the register, and where practicable the notice shall be by reference to the instrument, if any, which contains the covenant or agreement, and a copy or abstract of such instrument shall be filed at the registry; and where any such covenant or agreement appears to exist at the time of first registration, notice thereof shall be entered on the register. In the case of registered land the notice aforesaid shall take the place of registration as a land charge.

(2) When such a notice is entered the proprietor of the land and the persons deriving title under him (except incumbrancers or other persons who at the time when the notice is entered may not be bound by the covenant or agreement) shall be deemed to be affected with notice of the covenant or agreement as being an incumbrance on the land.

(3) Where the covenant or agreement is discharged [modified or dealt with] by an order under the Law of Property Act 1925, or otherwise, or the court refuses to grant an injunction for enforcing the same, the entry shall either be cancelled or reference made to the order or other instrument and a copy of the order, judgment or instrument shall be filed at the registry.

(4) The notice shall, when practicable, refer to the land, whether registered or not, for the benefit of which the restriction was made.

51. Notice of manorial incidents

Where land is affected by manorial incidents, the registrar may enter a note of that fact on the register, and may cancel such note when extinguishment of the manorial incidents has been proved to his satisfaction.

52. Effect of notices

(1) A disposition by the proprietor shall take effect subject to all estates, rights and claims which are protected by way of notice on the register at the date of the registration or entry of notice of the disposition, but only if and so far as such estates, rights, and claims may be valid and are not (independently of this Act) overridden by the disposition.

(2) Where notice of a claim is entered on the register, such entry shall operate by way of notice only, and shall not operate to render the claim valid whether made adversely to or for the benefit of the registered land or charge.

Cautions

53. Cautions against first registration

(1) Any person having or claiming such an interest in land not already registered as entities him to object to any disposition thereof being made without his consent, may lodge a caution with the registrar to the effect that the cautioner is entitled to notice in the prescribed form, and to be served in the prescribed manner, of any application that may be made for the registration of an interest in the land affecting the right of the cautioner.

(2) The caution shall be supported by an affidavit or declaration in the prescribed form, stating the nature of the interest of the cautioner, the land and estate therein to be affected by such caution, and such other matters as may be prescribed.

(3) After a caution has been lodged in respect of any estate, which has not already been registered, registration shall not be made of such estate until notice has been served on the cautioner to appear and oppose, if he thinks fit, such registration, and the prescribed time has elapsed since the date of the service of such notice, or the cautioner has entered an appearance, whichever may first happen.

54. Cautions against dealings

(1) Any person interested under any unregistered instrument, or interested as a judgment creditor, or otherwise howsoever, in any land or charge registered in the name of any other person, may lodge a caution with the registrar to the effect that no dealing with such land or charge on the part of the proprietor is to be registered until notice has been served upon the cautioner:

Provided that a person whose estate, right, interest, or claim has been registered or protected by a notice or restriction shall not be entitled (except with the consent of the registrar) to lodge a caution in respect of such estate, right, interest, or claim, [. . .]

(2) A caution lodged under this section shall be supported by such evidence as may be prescribed.

55. Effect of cautions against dealings

(1) After any such caution against dealings has been lodged in respect of any registered land or charge, the registrar shall not, without the consent of the cautioner, register any dealing or make any entry on the register for protecting the rights acquired under a deposit of a land or charge certificate or other dealing by the proprietor with such land or charge until he has served notice on the cautioner, warning him that his caution will cease to have any effect after the expiration of the prescribed number of days next following the date at which such notice is served; and after the expiration of such time as aforesaid the caution shall cease unless an order to the contrary is made by the registrar, and upon the caution so ceasing the registered land or charge may be dealt with in the same manner as if no caution had been lodged.

(2) If before the expiration of the said period the cautioner, or some person on his behalf, appears before the registrar, and where so required by the registrar gives sufficient security to indemnify every party against any damage that may be sustained by reason of any dealing with the registered land or charge, or the making of any such entry as aforesaid, being delayed, the registrar may thereupon, if he thinks fit to do so, delay registering any dealing with the land or charge or making any such entry for such period as he thinks just.

56. General provisions as to cautions

(1) Any person aggrieved by any act done by the registrar in relation to a caution under this Act may appeal to the court in the prescribed manner.

(2) A caution lodged in pursuance of this Act shall not prejudice the claim or title of any person and shall have no effect whatever except as in this Act mentioned.

(3) If any person lodges a caution with the registrar without reasonable cause, he shall be liable to make to any person who may have sustained damage by the lodging

of the caution such compensation as may be just, and such compensation shall be recoverable as a debt by the person who has sustained damage from the person who lodged the caution.

(4) The personal representative of a deceased cautioner may consent or object to registration or a dealing in the same manner as the cautioner.

Inhibitions

57. Power for court or registrar to inhibit registered dealings

(1) The court, or, subject to an appeal to the court, the registrar, upon the application of any person interested, made in the prescribed manner, in relation to any registered land or charge, may, after directing such inquiries (if any) to be made and notices to be given and hearing such persons as the court or registrar thinks expedient, issue an order or make an entry inhibiting for a time, or until the occurrence of an event to be named in such order or entry, or generally until further order or entry, the registration or entry of any dealing with any registered land or registered charge.

(2) The court or registrar may make or refuse to make any such order or entry, and annex thereto any terms or conditions the court or registrar may think fit, and discharge such order or cancel such entry when granted, with or without costs, and generally act in the premises in such manner as the justice of the case requires.

(3) Any person aggrieved by any act done by the registrar in pursuance of this section may appeal to the court in the prescribed manner.

(4) The court or the registrar may, in lieu of an inhibition, order a notice or restriction to be placed on the register.

Restrictions

58. Power to place restrictions on register

(1) Where the proprietor of any registered land or charge desires to place restrictions on transferring or charging the land or on disposing of or dealing with the land or charge in any manner in which he is by this Act authorised to dispose of or deal with it, or on the deposit by way of security of any certificate, the proprietor may apply to the registrar to make an entry in the register that no transaction to which the application relates shall be effected, unless the following things, or such of them as the proprietor may determine, are done—

(a) unless notice of any application for the transaction is transmitted by post to such address as he may specify to the registrar,

(b) unless the consent of some person or persons, to be named by the proprietor, is given to the transaction;

(c) unless some other matter or thing is done as may be required by the applicant and approved by the registrar:

Provided that no restriction under this section shall extend or apply to dispositions of or dealings with minor interests.

(2) The registrar shall thereupon, if satisfied of the right of the applicant to give the directions, enter the requisite restriction on the register, and no transaction to which the restriction relates shall be effected except in conformity therewith; but it shall not be the duty of the registrar to enter any such restriction, except upon such terms as to payment of fees and otherwise as may be prescribed, or to enter any restriction that the registrar may deem unreasonable or calculated to cause inconvenience.

(3) In the case of joint proprietors the restriction may be to the effect that when the number of proprietors is reduced below a certain specified number no disposition shall be registered except under an order of the court, or of the registrar after inquiry into title, subject to appeal to the court, and, subject to general rules, such an entry under this subsection as may be prescribed shall be obligatory unless it is shown to the registrar's satisfaction that the joint proprietors are entitled for their own benefit, or can give valid receipts for capital money, or that one of them is a trust corporation.

(4) Any such restrictions, except such as are in this section declared to be obligatory, may at any time be withdrawn or modified at the instance of all the persons for the time being appearing by the register to be interested in such directions, and shall also be liable to be set aside by an order of the court.

(5) Rules may be made to enable applications to be made for the entry of restrictions by persons other than the proprietor.

Protection of Various Interests

59. Writs, orders, deeds of arrangement, pending actions, etc.

(1) A writ, order, deed of arrangement, pending action, or other interest which in the case of unregistered land may be protected by registration under the Land Charges Act 1925,[1] shall, where the land affected or the charge securing the debt affected is registered, be protected only by lodging a creditor's notice, a bankruptcy inhibition or a caution against dealings with the land or charge.

(2) Registration of a land charge (other than a local land charge) shall, where the land affected is registered, be effected only by registering under this Act a notice caution or other prescribed entry:

Provided that before a land charge including a local land charge affecting registered land (being a charge to secure money) is realised, it shall be registered and take effect as a registered charge under this Act in the prescribed manner, without prejudice to the priority conferred by the land charge.

(3) . . .

(4) When a land charge protected by notice has been discharged as to all or any part of the land comprised therein, the notices relating thereto and to all devolutions of and dealings therewith shall be vacated as to the registered land affected by the discharge.

(5) The foregoing provisions of this section shall apply only to writs and orders, deeds of arrangement, pending actions and land charges which if the land were unregistered would for purposes of protection be required to be registered or re-registered after the commencement of this Act under the Land Charges Act 1925;[1] and for the purposes of this section a land charge does not include a puisne mortgage [. . .]

(6) Subject to the provisions of this Act relating to fraud and to the title of a trustee in bankruptcy, a purchaser acquiring title under a registered disposition, shall not be concerned with any pending action, writ, order, deed of arrangment, or other document, matter, or claim (not being an overriding interest [or a charge for [inheritance tax] subject to which the disposition takes effect under section 73 of this Act]) which is not protected by a caution or other entry on the register, whether he has or has not notice thereof, express, implied, or constructive.

(7) In this section references to registration under the Land Charges Act 1925,[1] apply to any registration made under any other statute which, in the case of unregistered land, is by the Land Charges Act 1925,1 to have effect as if the registration had been made under that Act.

Note

[1]Now the Land Charges Act 1972.

60. Notice of incumbrances registered under the Companies Act

(1) Where a company, registered under the Companies (Consolidation) Act 1908,[1] is registered as a proprietor of any estate or charge already registered, the registrar shall not be concerned with any mortgage, charge, debenture, debenture stock, trust deed for securing the same, or other incumbrance created or issued by the company, whether or not registered under that Act, unless the same is registered or protected by caution or otherwise under this Act.

(2) No indemnity shall be payable under this Act by reason of a purchaser acquiring any interest under a registered disposition from the company free from any such incumbrance.

Note
[1]Now the Companies Act 1985.

61. Protection of creditors prior to registration of trustee in bankruptcy

(1) The registrar shall as soon as practicable after registration of a petition in bankruptcy as a pending action under the Land Charges Act 1925,[1] register a notice (in this Act called a creditors' notice) against the title of any proprietor of any registered land or charge which appears to be affected, and such notice shall protect the rights of all creditors, and unless cancelled by the registrar in the prescribed manner such notice shall remain in force until a bankruptcy inhibition is registered or the trustee in bankruptcy is registered as proprietor.

No fee shall be charged for the registration of the notice.

(2) [. . .]

(3) The registrar shall, as soon as practicable after registration of a [bankruptcy order] under the Land Charges Act 1925,[1] enter an inhibition (in this Act called a bankruptcy inhibition) against the title of any proprietor of any registered land or charge which appear to be affected.

No fee shall be charged for the registration of the inhibition.

(4) From and after the entry of a bankruptcy inhibition (but without prejudice to dealings with or in right of interests of charges having priority over the estate or charge of the bankrupt proprietor), no dealing affecting the registered land or charge of the proprietor, other than the registration of the trustee in bankruptcy, shall be entered on the register until the inhibition is vacated as to the whole or part of the land or charge dealt with.

(5) If and when a proprietor of any registered land or charge is adjudged bankrupt, his registered estate or interest, if belonging, to him beneficially, and whether acquired before or after the date of adjudication, shall vest in the trustee in bankruptcy in accordance with the statutory provisions relating to bankruptcy for the time being in force.

(6) Where under a disposition to a purchaser in good faith for money or money's worth such purchaser is registered as proprietor of an estate or a charge, then [notwithstanding that the person making the disposition is adjudged bankrupt,] the title of his trustee in bankruptcy acquired after the commencement of this Act shall, as from the date of such disposition, be void as against such purchaser unless at the date of such disposition, either a creditor's notice or a bankruptcy inhibition has been registered, but a purchaser who, at the date of the execution of the registered disposition, has notice of [the bankruptcy petition or the] adjudication, shall not be deemed to take in good faith.

Nothing in this section shall impose on a purchaser a liability to make any search under the Land Charges Act 1925.[1]

(7) Where the estate or assets of a bankrupt proprietor suffer loss by reason of the omission of the registrar to register a creditor's notice or bankruptcy inhibition, as required by this section, or on account of the execution or registration of a disposition after a petition is registered as a pending action or after [a bankruptcy order] is registered and before the registration of a creditors' notice or bankruptcy inhibition, the trustee in a bankruptcy shall be entitled to indemnity as a person suffering loss by reason of an error or omission in the register.

(8) If neither a creditors' notice nor a bankruptcy inhibition is registered against a bankrupt proprietor, nothing in this section shall prejudicially affect a registered disposition of any registered land or charge acquired by the bankrupt after adjudication [. . .]

(9) If and when a bankruptcy inhibition is wholly or partly vacated, for any cause other than by reason of the registration of the trustee in bankruptcy, any registered estate If and when a bankruptcy inhibition is wholly or partially vacated, for any cause or interest vested in the trustee in bankruptcy shall, as respects the registered land or charge to which the vacation extends, be divested and the same shall vest in the proprietor in whom it would have been vested if there had been no adjudication in bankruptcy.

(10) . . .

Note
[1]Now the Land Charges Act 1972.

62. Rules to be made as to certain details

Rules shall be made under this Act—

(a) For postponing the registration of a creditors' notice or bankruptcy inhibition, where the name, address and description of the debtor [or bankrupt] appearing in the application for the registration of the pending action or [bankruptcy order] are not identical with those stated in the register, until the registrar is satisfied as to the identity of the debtor [or bankrupt];

(b) For requiring the official receiver to notify to the registrar any mistake occurring in the [bankruptcy order] or any other fact relevant to any proposed amendment in the register; and for enabling the registrar to make any consequential amendment;

(c) For providing for the whole or partial vacation (subject to notice to the official receiver or trustee in bankruptcy and to his right to appeal to the court) of a bankruptcy inhibition, where [. . .] the bankruptcy is annulled, or the registrar is satisfied that the bankruptcy proceedings do not affect or have ceased to affect the statutory powers of the bankrupt to deal with the registered land or charge.

PART V
LAND AND CHARGE CERTIFICATES

63. Issue of land and charge certificates

(1) On the first registration of a freehold or leasehold interest in land, and on the registration of a charge, a land certificate, or charge certificate, as the case may be, shall be prepared in the prescribed form: it shall state whether the title is absolute, good leasehold, qualified or possessory, and it shall be either delivered to the proprietor or deposited in the registry as the proprietor may prefer.

(2) If so deposited in the registry it shall be officially endorsed from time to time, as in this Act provided, with notes of all subsequent entries in the register affecting the registered land or charge to which it relates.

(3) The proprietor may at any time apply for the delivery of the certificate to himself or to such person as he may direct, and may at any time again deposit it in the land registry.

(4) The preparation, issue, endorsement, and deposit in the registry of the certificate shall be effected without cost to the proprietor.

64. Certificates to be produced and noted on dealings

(1) So long as a land certificate or charge certificate is outstanding, it shall be produced to the registrar—

(a) on every entry in the register of a disposition by the proprietor of the registered land or charge to which it relates; and

(b) on every registered transmission; and

(c) in every case (except as hereinafter mentioned) where under this Act or otherwise notice of any estate right or claim or a restriction is entered or placed on the register, adversely affecting the title of the proprietor of the registered land or charge, but not in the case of the lodgment of a caution or of an inhibition or of a creditors' notice, or of the entry of a notice of a lease at a rent without taking a fine [or a notice of a charge for [inheritance tax]].

(2) A note of every such entry or transmission shall be officially entered on the certificates as are conferred on him by this Act as to the production of maps, surveys, books, and other documents.

(3) On the completion of the registration of a transferee or grantee of any registered land or charge the registrar shall deliver to him a land certificate or charge certificate, and where part only of the land is dealt with shall also deliver to the tranferor or grantor a land certificate containing a description of the land retained by him.

(4) Where a transfer of land is made by the proprietor of a registered charge in exercise of any power vested in him, it may be registered, and a new land certificate may be issued to the purchaser, without production of the former land certificate (when not deposited at the registry), but the charge certificate, if any, must be produced or accounted for in accordance with this section.

The provisions of this subsection shall be extended in the prescribed manner to the cases of—

(a) an order for foreclosure absolute;

(b) a proprietor of a charge or a mortgagee obtaining a title to the land under the Limitation Acts;

(c) title being acquired under a title paramount to the registered estate, including a title acquired pursuant to a vesting or other order of the court or other competent authority.

[(5) Subsection (1) above shall not require the production of the land certificate when a person applies for the registration of a notice by virtue of [section 31(10) of the Family Law Act 1996] (spouse's charge in respect of [matrimonial home rights]).]

[(6) Subsections (1) above shall also not require the production of the land certificate when a person applies for—

(a) the registration of a notice of any variation of a lease affected by or in pursuance of an order under section 38 of the Landlord and Tenant Act 1987 (order by the court varying leases), including any variation as modified by an order under Section 39(4) of that Act (effect of orders varying leases; applications by third parties), or

(b) the cancellation of any such notice where a variation is cancelled or modified by an order under section 39(4) of that Act.]

[(7) Subsection (1) above shall not require the production of the land certificate or of any charge certificate when a person applies for the registration of a notice in respect of an access order under the Access to Neighbouring Land Act 1992.]

65. Deposit at registry of certificate of mortgaged land

Where a charge of mortgage (otherwise than by deposit) is registered, or is protected by a caution in a specially prescribed form, the land certificate shall be deposited at the registry until the charge or mortgage is cancelled.

66. Creation of liens by deposit of certificates

The proprietor of any registered land or charge may, subject to the overriding interests, if any, to any entry to the contrary on the register, and to any estates, interests, charges, or rights registered or protected on the register at the date of the deposit, create a lien on the registered land or charge by deposit of the land certificate or charge certificate; and such lien shall, subject as aforesaid, be equivalent to a lien created in the case of unregistered land by the deposit of documents of title or of the mortgage deed by an owner entitled for his own benefit to the registered estate, or a mortgagee beneficially entitled to the mortgage, as the case may be.

68. Certificates to be evidence

Any land certificate or charge certificate shall be admissible as evidence of the several matters therein contained.

PART VI
GENERAL PROVISIONS AS TO REGISTRATION AND THE EFFECT THEREOF

69. Effect of registration on the legal estate

(1) The proprietor of land (whether he was registered before or after the commencement of this Act) shall be deemed to have vested in him without any conveyance, where the registered land is freehold, the legal estate in fee simple in possession, and where the registered land is leasehold the legal term created by the registered lease, but subject to the overriding interests, if any, including any mortgage term or charge by way of legal mortgage created by or under the Law of Property Act 1925, or this Act or otherwise which any priority to the registered estate.

(2) Where any legal estate or term left outstanding at the date of first registration (whether before or after the commencement of this Act), or disposed of or created under section 49 of the Land Transfer Act 1875, before the commencement of this Act, becomes satisfied, or the proprietor of the land becomes entitled to require the same to be vested in or surrendered to him, and the entry, if any, for protecting the same on the register has been cancelled, the same shall thereupon, without any conveyance, vest in the proprietor of the land, as if the same has been conveyed or surrendered to him as the case may be.

(3) If and when any person is registered as first proprietor of land in a compulsory area after the commencement of this Act, the provisions of the Law of Property Act 1925, for getting in legal estates shall apply to any legal estate in the land which was expressed to be conveyed or created in favour of a purchaser or lessee before the commencement of this Act but which failed to pass or to be created by reason of the omission of such purchaser or lessee to be registered as proprietor of the land under the Land Transfer Acts 1875 and 1897, and shall operate to vest that legal estate in the person so registered as proprietor on his registration, but subject to any mortgage term or charge by way of legal mortgage having priority thereto.

(4) The estate for the time being vested in the proprietor shall only be capable of being disposed of or dealt with by him in manner authorised by this Act.

(5) Nothing in this section operates to render valid a lease registered with possessory or good leasehold title.

70. Liability of registered land to overriding interests

(1) All registered land shall, unless under the provisions of this Act the contrary is expressed on the register, be deemed to be subject to such of the following overriding interests as may be for the time being subsisting in reference thereto, and such interests shall not be treated as incumbrances within the meaning of this Act, (that is to say):—

(a) Rights of common, drainage rights, customary rights (until extinguished), public rights, profits a prendre, rights of sheepwalk, rights of way, watercourses, rights of water, and other easements not being equitable easements required to be protected by notice on the register;

(b) Liability to repair highways by reason of tenure, quit-rents, crown rents, heriots and other rents and charges (until extinguished) having their origin in tenure;

(c) Liability to repair the chancel of any church;

(d) Liability in respect of embankments, and sea and river walls;

(e) [. . .] payments in lieu of tithe, and charges or annuities payable for the redemption of tithe rentcharges;

(f) Subject to the provisions of this Act, rights acquired or in course of being acquired under the Limitation Acts;

(g) The rights of every person in actual occupation of the land or in receipt of the rents and profits thereof, save where enquiry is made of such person and the rights are not disclosed;

(h) In the case of a possessory, qualified, or good leasehold title, all estates, rights, interests, and powers excepted from the effect of registration;

(i) Rights under local land charges unless and until registered or protected on the register in the prescribed manner;

(j) Rights of fishing and sporting, seignorial and manorial rights of all descriptions (until extinguished), and franchises;

[(k)[1] Leases granted for a term not exceeding twenty-one years;]

(l) In respect of land registered before the commencement of this Act, rights to mines and minerals, and rights of entry, search, and user, and other rights and reservations incidental to or required for the purpose of giving full effect to the enjoyment of rights to mines and minerals or of property in mines or minerals, being rights which, where the title was first registered before the first day of January, eighteen hundred and ninety-eight, were created before that date, and where the title was first registered after the thirty-first day of December, eighteen hundred and ninety-seven, were created before the date of first registration;

[(m) any interest or right which is an overriding interest by virtue of paragraph 1(1) of Schedule 9 of the Coal Industry Act 1994.]

Provided that, where it is proved to the satisfaction of the registrar that any land registered or about to be registered is exempt from land tax, or tithe rentcharge or payments in lieu of tithe, or from charges or annuities payable for the redemption of tithe rentcharge, the registrar may notify the fact on the register in the prescribed manner.

(2) Where at the time of first registration any easement, right, privilege, or benefit created by an instrument and appearing on the title adversely affects the land, the registrar shall enter a note thereof on the register.

(3) Where the existence of any overriding interest mentioned in this section is proved to the satisfaction of the registrar or admitted, he may (subject to any prescribed exceptions) enter notice of the same or of a claim thereto on the register, but no claim to an easement, right, or privilege not created by an instrument shall be noted against the title to the servient land if the proprietor of such land (after the prescribed notice is given to him) shows sufficient cause to the contrary.

[(4) Neither subsection (2) nor subsection (3) of this section shall apply in the case of any such interest or right as is mentioned in subsection (1)(m) of this subsection.]

Note

[1]Applies only in relation to dispositions made after the commencement of the Land Registration Act 1986. Where a lease granted before the commencement of this Act was not an overriding interest because it was not granted at a rent or without taking a fine, the amendment applies in relation to it only if the land was subject to it immediately before that commencement.

71. Dispositions by virtue of overriding interests

Where by virtue of any interest or power which is an overriding interest a mortgagee or other person disposes of any estate, charge, or right in or upon a registered estate, and the disposition is capable of being registered, the registrar shall, if so required, give effect of the disposition on the register.

72. Appurtenances

If before the registration of any freehold or leasehold interest in land with an absolute or good leasehold title any easement, right, or privilege has been acquired for the benefit thereof, then, on such registration, the easement, right, or privilege shall, subject to any entry to the contrary on the register, become appurtenant to the registered land in like manner as if it had been granted to the proprietor who is registered as aforesaid.

[73. Inland Revenue charge for inheritance tax

A disposition shall take effect subject to any subsisting Inland Revenue charge under [the Inheritance Tax Act 1984] unless—

(a) the disposition is in favour of a purchaser within the meaning of [that Act]; and

(b) the charge is not, at the time of registration of the disposition, protected by notice on the register.]

74. Notice of trust not to affect registered dealing

Subject to the provisions of this Act as to settled land, neither the registrar nor any person dealing with a registered estate or charge shall be affected with notice of a trust express implied or constructive, and references to trusts shall, so far as possible, be excluded from the register.

75. Acquisition of title by possession

(1) The Limitation Acts shall apply to registered land in the same manner and to the same extent as those Acts apply to land not registered, except that where, if the land were not registered, the estate of the person registered as proprietor would be extinguished, such estate shall not be extinguished but shall be deemed to be held by the proprietor for the time being in trust for the person who, by virtue of the said Acts, has acquired title against any proprietor, but without prejudice to the estates and interests of any other person interested in the land whose estate or interest is not extinguished by those Acts.

(2) Any person claiming to have acquired a title under the Limitation Acts to a registered estate in the land may apply to be registered as proprietor thereof.

(3) The registrar shall, on being satisfied as to the applicant's title, enter the applicant as proprietor either with absolute, good leasehold, qualified, or possessory title, as the case may require, but without prejudice to any estate or interest protected by any entry on the register which may not have been extinguished under the Limitation Acts, and such registration shall, subject as aforesaid, have the same effect as the registration of a first proprietor; but the proprietor or the applicant or any other person interested may apply to the court for the determination of any question arising under this section.

(4) [. . .]

(5) Rules may be made for applying (subject to any necessary modifications) the provisions of this section to cases where an easement, right or privilege has been acquired by prescription.

76. Description of registered land

Registered land may be described—

(a) by means of a verbal description and a filed plan or general map, based on the ordnance map; or

(b) by reference to a deed or other document, a copy or extract whereof is filed at the registry, containing a sufficient description, and a plan or map thereof; or

(c) otherwise as the applicant for registration may desire, and the registrar, or, if the applicant prefers, the court, may approve,

regard being had to ready identification of parcels, correct descriptions of boundaries, and, so far as may be, uniformity of practice; but the boundaries of all freehold land and all requisite details in relation to the same, shall whenever practicable, be entered on the register or filed plan, or general map, and the filed plan, if any, or general map shall be used for assisting the identification of the land.

[77. Conversion of title

(1) Where land is registered with a good leasehold title, or satisfies the conditions for such registration under this section, the registrar may, and on application by the proprietor shall, if he is satisfied as to the title to the freehold and the title to any intermediate leasehold, enter the title as absolute.

(2) Where land is registered with a possessory title, the registrar may, and on application by the proprietor shall—

(a) if he is satisfied as to the title, or

(b) if the land has been so registered for at least twelve years and he is satisfied that the proprietor is in possession,

enter the title in the case of freehold land as absolute and in the case of leasehold land as good leasehold.

(3) Where land is registered with a qualified title, the registrar may, and on application by the proprietor shall, if he is satisfied as to the title, enter it in the case of freehold land as good leasehold.

(4) If any claim adverse to the title of the proprietor has been made, as entry shall not be made in the register under this section unless and until the claim has been disposed of.

(5) No fee shall be charged for the making of an entry in the register under this section at the instance of the registrar or on an application by the proprietor made in connection with a transfer for valuable consideration of the land to which the application relates.

(6) Any person, other than the proprietor, who suffers loss by reason of any entry on the register made by virtue of this section shall be entitled to be indemnified under this Act as if a mistake had been made in the register.]

78. Provisions as to undivided shares in land

(1) Where in the case of land belonging to persons in undivided shares the entirety of the land is registered at the commencement of this Act, and the persons entitled to the several undivided shares are registered as proprietors, the registrar shall, on the occasion of the first dealing affecting the title after the commencement of this Act, rectify the register by entering as the proprietors of the entirety of the land the persons in whom the legal estate therein has become vested by virtue of the Law of Property Act 1925, and it shall be the duty of the persons registered as the proprietors of the undivided shares in the land to furnish to the registrar such evidence as he may require to enable him to ascertain the persons in whom such legal estate has become so vested as aforesaid.

(2) Where at the commencement of this Act the title to an undivided share in land is registered but the entirety of the land is not registered, the registrar may, at any time, after giving notice to the proprietor and to the other persons, if any, who appear by the register to be interested therein, remove from the register the title to the undivided share, and such removal shall have the like effect as it had been effected by the proprietor with the assent of such other persons as aforesaid in pursuance of the power in that behalf contained in this Act:

Provided that, if within one year from the commencement of this Act or such extended time as the registrar may allow, and before the removal of the undivided share from the register in manner aforesaid, the persons in whom the legal estate of the entirety of the land is vested by virtue of the Law of Property Act 1925, or any persons interested in more than an undivided half of the land or the income thereof, make an application in the prescribed manner for the purpose and furnish the prescribed evidence, the registrar shall, without charging any fee, register the persons in whom such legal estate is so vested as proprietors of that estate, subject to any incumbrance capable of registration affecting the entirety of the land, but free from any charge or incumbrance (whether formerly registered or not) affecting an undivided share, and when the title to the entirety of the land is so registered, the title to the undivided share shall be closed.

(3) If the person in whom the legal estate in the entirety of the land is so vested is the Public Trustee, he shall not be registered as proprietor pursuant to this section

unless and until he has been duly requested to act in accordance with the Law of Property Act 1925, and has accepted the trust.

(4) After the commencement of this Act, no entry other than a caution against dealings with the entirety shall be made in the register as respects the title to an undivided share in land [registered at the commencement of this Act].

79. Addresses for service and notices

(1) Every person whose name is entered on the register as proprietor of any registered land or charge, or as cautioner, or as entitled to receive any notice, or in any other character shall furnish to the registrar a place of address in the United Kingdom.

(2)–(4) . . .

80. Bona vacantia and forfeiture

Subject to the express provisions of this Act relating to the effect of first registration of title and the effect or registration of a disposition for valuable consideration, nothing in this Act affects any right of His Majesty to any bona vacantia or forfeiture.

81. Power to remove land from the register

(1) The proprietor of registered land not situated in an area where the registration of title is compulsory, and, in every case where the entirety of the land is not registered, the proprietor of an undivided share in land, may, with the consent of the other persons (if any) for the time being appearing by the register to be interested therein, and on delivering up the land certificate and, if the land is subject to any registered charges, the charge certificates, remove the land (including an undivided share) from the register.

(2) After land is removed from the register no further entries shall be made respecting it, and inspection of the register may be made and office copies of the entries therein may be issued, subject to such regulations as may be prescribed.

(3) . . .

PART VII
RECTIFICATION OF REGISTER AND INDEMNITY

82. Rectification of the register

(1) The register may be rectified pursuant to an order of the court or by the registrar, subject to an appeal to the court, in any of the following cases, but subject to the provisions of this section:—

(a) Subject to any express provisions of this Act to the contrary, where a court of competent jurisdiction has decided that any person is entitled to any estate right or interest in or to any registered land or charge, and as a consequence of such decision such court is of opinion that a rectification of the register is required, and makes an order to that effect;

(b) Subject to any express provision of this Act to the contrary, where the court, on the application in the prescribed manner of any person who is aggrieved by any entry made in, or by the omission of any entry from, the register, or by any default being made, or unnecessary delay taking place, in the making of any entry in the register, makes an order for the rectification of the register;

(c) In any case and at any time with the consent of all persons interested;

(d) Where the court or the registrar is satisfied that any entry in the register has been obtained by fraud;

(e) Where two or more persons are, by mistake, registered as proprietors of the same registered estate or of the same charge;

(f) Where a mortgagee has been registered as proprietor of the land instead of as proprietor of a charge and a right of redemption is subsisting;

(g) Where a legal estate has been registered in the name of a person who if the land had not been registered would not have been the estate owner; and

(h) In any other case where, by reason of any error or omission in the register, or by reason of any entry made under a mistake, it may be deemed just to rectify the register.

(2) The register may be rectified under this section, notwithstanding that the rectification may affect any estates, rights, charges, or interests acquired or protected by registration, or by any entry on the register, or otherwise.

(3) The register shall not be rectified, except for the purpose of giving effect to an overriding interest [or an order of the court], so as to affect the title of the proprietor who is in possession—

[(a) unless the proprietor has caused or substantially contributed to the error or omission by fraud or lack of proper care; or]

(b) [. . .]

(c) unless for any other reason, in any particular case, it is considered that it would be unjust not to rectify the register against him.

(4) Where a person is in possession of registered land in right of a minor interest, he shall, for the purpose of this section, be deemed to be in possession as agent for the proprietor.

(5) The registrar shall obey the order of any competent court in relation to any registered land on being served with the order or an official copy thereof.

(6) On every rectification of the register the land certificate and any charge certificate which may be affected shall be produced to the registrar unless an order to the contrary is made by him.

83. Right to indemnity in certain cases

(1) Subject to the provisions of this Act to the contrary, any persons suffering loss by reason of any rectification of the register under this Act shall be entitled to be indemnified.

(2) Where an error or omission has occurred in the register, but the register is not rectified, any person suffering loss by reason of such error or omission, shall, subject to the provisions of this Act, be entitled to be indemnified.

(3) Where any person suffers loss by reason of the loss or destruction of any document lodged at the registry for inspection or safe custody or by reason of an error in any official search, he shall be entitled to be indemnified under this Act.

(4) Subject as hereinafter provided, a proprietor of any registered land or charge claiming in good faith under a forged disposition shall, where the register is rectified, be deemed to have suffered loss by reason of such rectification and shall be entitled to be indemnified under this Act.

(5) No indemnity shall be payable under this Act in any of the following cases:—

[(a) Where the applicant or a person from whom he derives title (otherwise than under a disposition for valuable consideration which is registered or protected on the register) has caused or substantially contributed to the loss by fraud or lack of proper care;]

(b) On account of any mines or minerals or of the existence of any rights to work or get mines or minerals, unless a note is entered on the register that the mines or minerals are included in the registered title;

(c) On account of costs incurred in taking or defending any legal proceedings without the consent of the registrar.

(6) Where an indemnity is paid in respect of the loss of an estate or interest in or charge on land the amount so paid shall not exceed—

(a) Where the register is not rectified, the value of the estate, interest or charge at the time when the error or omission which caused the loss was made;

(b) Where the register is rectified, the value (if there had been no rectification) of the estate, interest or charge, immediately before the time of rectification.

(7) [. . .]

[(8) Subject to subsection (5)(c) of this section, as amended by section 2(2) of the Land Registration and Land Charges Act 1971—

(a) an indemnity under any provision of this Act shall include such amount, if any, as may be reasonable in respect of any costs or expenses properly incurred by the applicant in relation to the matter; and

(b) an applicant for an indemnity under any such provision shall be entitled to an indemnity thereunder of such amount, if any, as may be reasonable in respect of any such costs or expenses, notwithstanding that no other indemnity money is payable thereunder.]

(9) Where indemnity is paid for a loss, the registrar, on behalf of the Crown, shall be entitled to recover the amount paid from any person who has caused or substantially contributed to the loss by his fraud.

(10) The registrar shall be entitled to enforce, on behalf of the Crown, any express or implied covenant or other right which the person who is indemnified would have been entitled to enforce in relation to the matter in respect of which indemnity has been paid.

(11) A liability to pay indemnity under this Act shall be deemed a simple contract debt; and for the purposes of [the Limitation Act 1980], the cause of action shall be deemed to arise at the time when the claimant knows, or but for his own default might have known, of the existence of his claim:

Provided that, when a claim to indemnity arises in consequence of the registration of an estate in land with an absolute or good leasehold title, the claim shall be enforceable only if made within six years from the date of such registration, except in the following cases:—

(a) Where at the date of registration the person interested is an infant, the claim by him may be made within six years from the time he attains full age;

(b) In the case of settled land, or land [subject to a trust of land], a claim by a person interested in remainder or reversion, may be made within six years from the time when his interest falls into possession;

(c) Where a claim arises in respect of a restrictive covenant or agreement affecting freehold land which by reason of notice or the registration of a land charge or otherwise was binding on the first proprietor at the time of first registration, the claim shall only be enforceable within six years from the breach of the covenant or agreement;

(d) Where any person interested is entitled as a proprietor of a charge or as a mortgagee protected by a caution in the specially prescribed form, the claim by him may be made within six years from the last payment in respect of principal or interest.

(12) This section applies to the Crown in like manner as it applies to a private person.

84. Application of indemnity in case of settled land

Where any indemnity is paid in respect of settled land, and not in respect of any particular estate, remainder, or reversion therein, the money shall be paid to the trustees of the settlement and held by them as capital money for the purposes of the Settled Land Act 1925, arising from the settled land.

PART VIII
APPLICATION TO PARTICULAR CLASSES OF LAND

86. Registration of settled land

(1) Settled land shall be registered in the name of the tenant for life or statutory owner.

(2) The successive or other interests created by or arising under a settlement shall (save as regards any legal estate which cannot be overridden under the powers of the

Settled Land Act 1925, or any other statute) take effect as minor interests and not otherwise; and effect shall be given thereto by the proprietor of the settled land as provided by statute with respect to the estate owner, with such adaptations, if any, as may be prescribed in the case of registered land by rules made under this Act.

(3) There shall also be entered on the register such restrictions as may be prescribed, or may be expedient, for the protection of the rights of the persons beneficially interested in the land, and such restrictions shall (subject to the provisions of this Act relating to releases by the trustees of a settlement and to transfers by a tenant for life whose estate has ceased in his lifetime) be binding on the proprietor during his life, but shall not restrain or otherwise affect a disposition by his personal representative.

(4) Where land already registered is acquired with capital money, the same shall be transferred by a transfer in a specially prescribed form to the tenant for life or statutory owner, and such transfer shall state the names of the persons who are trustees of the settlement for the purposes of the Settled Land Act 1925, and contain an application to register the prescribed restrictions applicable to the case; a transfer made in the specially prescribed form shall be deemed to comply with the requirements of that Act, respecting vesting deeds; and where no capital money is paid but land already registered is to be made subject to a settlement, it shall not be necessary for the trustees of the settlements to concur in the transfer.

(5) References in this Act to the 'tenant for life' shall, where the context admits, be read as referring to the tenant for life, statutory owner, or personal representative who is entitled to be registered.

87. Changes of ownership of settled land

(1) On the death of a proprietor, or of the survivor of two or more joint proprietors of settled land (whether the land is settled by his will or by an instrument taking effect on or previously to his death), his personal representative shall hold the settled land subject to payment or to making provision for payment of all death duties and other liabilities affecting the land, and having priority to the settlement, upon trust to transfer the same by an assent in the prescribed manner to the tenant for life or statutory owner, and in the meantime upon trust to give effect to the minor interests under the settlement; but a transfer shall not be made to an infant.

(2) Rules may be made—

(a) for enabling a personal representative or proprietor in proper cases to create legal estates by registered dispositions for giving effect to or creating interests in priority to the settlements;

(b) to provide for the cases in which application shall be made by the personal representative or proprietor for the registration of restrictions or notices; and

(c) for discharging a personal representative or former proprietor who has complied with the requirements of this Act and rules from all liability in respect of minor interests under a settlement.

(3) Where a tenant for life or statutory owner who, if the land were not registered, would be entitled to have the settled land vested in him, is not the proprietor, the proprietor shall (notwithstanding any stipulation or provision to the contrary) be bound at the cost of the trust estate to execute such transfers as may be required for giving effect on the register to the rights of such tenant for life or statutory owner.

(4) Where the trustees of a settlement have in the prescribed manner released the land from the minor interests under such settlement, the registrar shall be entitled to assume that the settlement has determined, and the restrictions for protecting the minor interests thereunder shall be cancelled.

(5) Where an order is made under the Settled Land Act 1925, authorising the trustees of the settlement to exercise the powers on behalf of a tenant for life who is

registered as proprietor, they may in his name and on his behalf do all such acts and things under this Act as may be requisite for giving effect on the register to the powers authorised to be exercised in like manner as if they were registered as proprietors of the land, but a copy of the order shall be filed at the registry before any such powers are exercised.

(6) Where a proprietor ceases in his lifetime to be a tenant for life, he shall transfer the land to his successor in title, or, if such successor is an infant, to the statutory owner, and on the registration of such successor in title or statutory owner it shall be the duty of the trustees of the settlement, if the same be still subsisting, to apply for such alteration, if any, in the restrictions as may be required for the protection of the minor interests under the settlement.

88. Settlement may be filed in registry

(1) The settlement, or an abstract or copy thereof, may be filed in the registry for reference in the prescribed manner, but such filing shall not affect a purchaser from the proprietor with notice of its provisions, or entitle him to call for production of the settlement, or for any information or evidence as to its contents.

(2) In this section 'settlement' includes any deed stating who are the trustees of the settlement, and the vesting instrument, and any transfer or assent in the prescribed form taking the place, in the case of registered land, of a vesting instrument, as well as the trust instrument and any other instruments creating the settlement.

89. Registrar's certificate authorising proposed dealing with settled land

The registrar may, notwithstanding any restriction entered on the register, grant a certificate that an intended registered disposition is authorised by a settlement or otherwise, and will be registered, and a purchaser who obtains such a certificate shall not be concerned to see that the disposition is authorised, but where capital money is paid to the persons to whom the same is required to be paid by a restriction or into court no such certificate shall be required.

90. Charges for money actually raised

The proprietor of settled land which is registered and all other necessary parties, if any, shall, on the request, and at the expense of any person entitled to an estate, interest, or charge conveyed or created for securing money actually raised at the date of such request, charge the land in the prescribed manner with the payment of the money so raised, but so long as the estate, interest or charge is capable of being overridden under the Settled Land Act 1925, or the Law of Property Act 1925, no charge shall be created or registered under this section.

91. Minorities

The following provisions shall have effect as respects settled land (being registered land) during a minority:—

(1) The personal representatives under the will or intestacy under which the settlement is created or arises shall, during the minority, be registered as proprietors, and in reference to the settled land shall have all the powers conferred by the Settled Land Act 1925, on a tenant for life and on the trustees of the settlement; but if and when the personal representatives would, if the infant had been of full age, have been bound to transfer the registered land to him, the personal representatives shall (unless themselves the statutory owners) thenceforth during the minority give effect on the register to the directions of the statutory owner, and shall apply for the registration of any restriction which may be prescribed, but shall not be concerned with the propriety of any registered disposition so directed to be made if the same appears to be a proper disposition under the powers of the statutory owner and the capital money, if any, arising under the disposition is paid to the trustees of the settlement or into court; but a purchaser dealing with the personal representatives, who complies with the

restrictions, if any, which may be entered on the register, shall not be concerned to see or inquire whether any such directions have been given:

(2) If an infant becomes entitled in possession (or will become entitled in possession on attaining full age) to registered land otherwise than on a death, the statutory owners during the minority shall be entitled to require the settled land to be transferred to them and shall be registered as proprietors accordingly:

(3) If and when the registered land would (if not registered) have become vested in the trustees of the settlement pursuant to the Law of Property Act 1925, such trustees shall (unless they are already registered) be entitled to be registered as proprietors thereof, and shall in the prescribed manner apply for registration accordingly, and no fee shall be charged in respect of such registration or consequential alteration in the register.

92. Rights of tenants for life and statutory owners to be registered as proprietors

The foregoing provisions of this Part of this Act relating to settled land apply in every case where pursuant to the Settled Land Act 1925, settled land is to be vested in a tenant for life or statutory owner whether the estate was registered before or after the commencement of this Act, and the proprietor of settled land (not being the tenant for life or statutory owner entitled to the same) shall be bound to make such dispositions as may be required for giving effect to the rights of the tenant for life or statutory owner:

Provided that, where the registered land is not, at the commencement of this Act, registered in the name of a tenant for life or statutory owner, or personal representative who, if the land were not registered, would by virtue of the Settled Land Act 1925, or of the Law of Property Act 1925, be entitled to have the settled land vested in him, any such person shall (without any transfer) be entitled to be registered as proprietor thereof, and shall in the prescribed manner apply for registration accordingly and no fee shall be charged in respect of such registration or consequential alteration in the register.

93. As to persons in a fiduciary position

A person in a fiduciary position may apply for, or concur in, or assent to, any registration authorised by the provisions of this Act, and, if he is a proprietor, may execute a charge or other disposition in favour of any person whose registration is so authorised.

94. Land held [subject to a trust of land]

[(1) Where registered land is subject to a trust of land, the land shall be registered in the names of the trustees.]

(2) Where an order, obtained under section seven of the Settled Land Act 1884, is in force at the commencement of this Act, the person authorised by the order to exercise any of the powers conferred by the Settled Land Act 1925, may, in the names and on behalf of the proprietors, do all such acts and things under this Act as may be requisite for giving effect on the register to the powers authorised to be exercised in like manners as if such person were registered as proprietor of the land, and a copy of the order shall be filed at the registry.

(3) Where, by virtue of any statute, registered land is made subject to a [trust of land, the trustees] (unless already registered) shall be registered as proprietors thereof, and shall in the prescribed manner apply for registration accordingly, and no fee shall be charged in respect of such registration or consequential alteration of the register, but this subsection has effect subject to the provisions of this Act relating to the registration of the Public Trustee and the removal of an undivided share from the register before the title to the entirety of the land is registered.

[(4) There shall also be entered on the register such restrictions as may be prescribed, or may be expedient, for the protection of the rights of the persons beneficially interested in the land.

(5) Where a deed has been executed under section 16(4) of the Trusts of Land and Appointment of Trustees Act 1996 by trustees of land the registrar is entitled to assume that, as from the date of the deed, the land to which the deed relates is not subject to the trust unless he has actual notice that the trustees were mistaken in their belief that the land was conveyed to beneficiaries absolutely entitled to the land under the trust and of full age and capacity.]

95. Restriction on number of trustees
The statutory restrictions affecting the number of persons entitled to hold land on trust for sale and the number of trustees of a settlement apply to registered land.

98. Land subject to charitable trusts
Where an application is made to register a legal estate in land subject to charitable trusts and that estate is vested in the [official custodian for charities], he shall, notwithstanding that the powers of disposition are vested in the managing trustees or committee, be registered as proprietor thereof.

PART IX
UNREGISTERED DEALINGS WITH REGISTERED LAND

Powers of dealing with Registered Land off the Register

101. Dispositions off register creating 'minor interests'
(1) Any person, whether being the proprietor or not, having a sufficient interest or power in or over registered land, may dispose of or deal with the same, and create any interests or rights therein which are permissible in like manner and by the like modes of assurance in all respects as if the land were not registered, but subject as provided by this section.
(2) All interests and rights disposed of or created under subsection (1) of this section (whether by the proprietor or any other person) shall, subject to the provisions of this section, take effect as minor interests, and be capable of being overridden by registered dispositions for valuable consideration.
(3) Minor interests shall, subject to the express exceptions contained in this section, take effect only in equity, but may be protected by entry on the register of such notices, cautions, inhibitions and restrictions as are provided for by this Act or rules.
(4) A minor interest in registered land subsisting or capable of taking effect at the commencement of this Act, shall not fail or become invalid by reason of the same being converted into an equitable interest; but after such commencement a minor interest in registered land shall only be capable of being validly created in any case in which an equivalent equitable interest could have been validly created if the land had not been registered.
(5) Where after the commencement of this Act, the proprietor of the registered estate which is settled, disposes of or deals with his beneficial interest in possession in favour of a purchaser, and accordingly the minor interest disposed of or created would, but for the restrictions imposed by the Law of Property Act 1925, and this section, on the creation of legal estates, have been a legal estate, the purchaser (subject as provided by the next following section in regard to priorities) may exercise all such rights and remedies as he might have exercised had the minor interest been a legal estate, and the reversion (if any) on any leases or tenancies derived out of the registered estate had been vested in him.
(6) A minor interest created under this section does not operate to prevent a registered estate passing to the personal representative of a deceased proprietor, or to the survivor or survivors of two or more joint proprietors, nor does this section affect the right of any person entitled to an overriding interest, or having any power to dispose of or create an overriding interest, to dispose of or create the same.

102. Priorities as between minor interests

(1) If a minor interest subsisting or capable of taking effect at the commencement of this Act, would, if the Law of Property Acts 1922 and 1925, and this Act had not been passed have taken effect as a legal estate, then (subject and without prejudice to the estate and powers of the proprietor whose estate is affected) the conversion thereof into an equitable interest shall not affect its priority over other minor interests.

103. Obligation to give effect on the register to certain minor interests

(1) Where by the operation of any statute or statutory or other power, or by virtue of any vesting order of any court or other competent authority, or an order appointing a person to convey, or of a vesting declaration (express or implied) or of an appointment or other assurance, a minor interest in the registered land is disposed of or created which would, if registered, be capable of taking effect as a legal estate or charge by way of legal mortgage, then—

(i) if the estate owner would, had the land not been registered, have been bound to give effect thereto by conveying or creating a legal estate or charge by way of legal mortgage, the proprietor shall, subject to proper provision being made for payment of costs, be bound to give legal effect to the transaction by a registered disposition:

(ii) if the proprietor is unable or refuses to make the requisite disposition or cannot be found, or if for any other reason a disposition by him cannot be obtained within a reasonable time, or if, had the land not been registered, no conveyance by the estate owner would have been required to give legal effect to the transaction, the registrar shall give effect thereto in the prescribed manner in like manner and with the like consequences as if the transaction had been carried out by a registered disposition:

Provided that—

(a) So long as the proprietor has power under the Settled Land Act 1925, or any other statute conferring special powers on a tenant for life or statutory owner, or under the settlement, to override the minor interest so disposed of or created, no estate or charge shall be registered which would prejudicially affect any such powers:

(b) So long as the proprietor holds the land [subject to a trust of land], no estate or charge shall be registered in respect of an interest which, under the Law of Property Act 1925, or otherwise ought to remain liable to be overridden on [a sale of the land by the trustees]:

(c) Nothing in this subsection shall impose on a proprietor an obligation to make a disposition unless the person requiring the disposition to be made has a right in equity to call for the same:

(d) Nothing in this subsection shall prejudicially affect the rights of a personal representative in relation to the administration of the estate of the deceased.

(2) On every alteration in the register made pursuant to this section the land certificate and any charge certificate which may be affected shall be produced to the registrar unless an order to the contrary is made by him.

104. Protection of leases granted under statutory powers by persons other than registered proprietor and restriction on power

All leases at a rent for a term of years absolute authorised by the powers conferred by the Law of Property Act 1925, or the Settled Land Act 1925, or any other statute (whether or not as extended by any instrument) may be granted in the name and on behalf of the proprietor by any other person empowered to grant the same, and shall be valid at law or in equity (as the case may require) and shall be protected by notice on the register and registered in the same cases, in like manner and with the same effect as if the lease had been granted by the proprietor of the land, and without prejudice to any priority acquired by the exercise of the power; but nothing in this section shall authorise any person granting any lease in the name of the proprietor to impose (save in regard to the usual qualified covenant for quiet enjoyment) any personal liability on such proprietor.

105. As to minor interests in mortgage debts
Rules may be made for applying the provisions of this Part of this Act as to minor interests to the case of minor interests in a debt secured by a registered charge.

[106. Creation and protection of mortgages of registered land
(1) The proprietor of any registered land may, subject to any entry to the contrary on the register, mortgage, by deed or otherwise, the land or any part of it in any manner which would have been permissible if the land had not been registered and, subject to this section, with the like effect.
(2) Unless and until the mortgage becomes a registered charge,—
(a) it shall take effect only in equity, and
(b) it shall be capable of being overridden as a minor interest unless it is protected as provided by subsection (3) below.
(3) A mortgage which is not a registered charge may be protected on the register by—
(a) a notice under section 49 of this Act,
(b) any such other notice as may be prescribed, or
(c) a caution under section 54 of this Act.
(4) A mortgage which is not a registered charge shall devolve and may be transferred, discharged, surrendered or otherwise dealt with by the same instruments and in the same manner as if the land had not been registered.]

107. Power for proprietors to bind successors and to enforce contracts
(1) Subject to any entry to the contrary on the register, the proprietor of any registered land or charge may enter into any contract in reference thereto in like manner as if the land or charge had not been registered, and, subject to any disposition for valuable consideration which may be registered or protected on the register before the contract is completed or protected on the register, the contract may be enforced as a minor interest against any succeeding proprietor in like manner and to the same extent as if the land or charge had not been registered.
(2) A contract entered into for the benefit of any registered land or charge may (if the same would have been enforceable by the owner for the time being of the land or charge, if not registered, or by a person deriving title under the party contracting for the benefit) be enforced by the proprietor for the time being of the land or charge.

108. Acquisition of easements and other benefits
The proprietor of registered land may accept for the benefit thereof the grant of any easement, right, or privilege or the benefit of any restrictive covenant or provision (affecting other land, whether registered or not) in like manner and to the same extent as if he were legally and beneficially entitled to the fee simple in possession, or to the term created by the registered lease, for his own benefit free from incumbrances.

109. Restriction on exercise of powers off the register
Subject to the express provisions relating to leases and mortgages, nothing in this Part of this Act shall be construed as authorising any disposition of any estate, interest, or right or other dealing with land to be effected under this Part of this Act if the disposition or dealing is one which could be effected under another Part of this Act, and any such disposition or dealing shall be effected under and in the manner required by such other Part of this Act, and when so required shall be registered or protected as provided by this Act or the rules.

PART X
MISCELLANEOUS PROVISIONS

110. Provisions as between vendor and purchaser
On a sale or other disposition of registered land to a purchaser other than a lessee or chargee—

(1) The vendor shall, notwithstanding any stipulation to the contrary, at his own expense furnish the purchaser with an authority to inspect the register, and, if required, with a copy of the subsisting entries in the register and of any filed plans and copies or abstracts of any documents or any part thereof noted on the register so far as they respectively affect the land to be dealt with (except charges or incumbrances registered or protected on the register which are to be discharged or overridden at or prior to completion):

Provided that—

(a) unless the purchase money exceeds one thousand pounds the costs of the copies and abstracts of the said entries plans and documents shall, in the absence of any stipulation to the contrary, be borne by the purchaser requiring the same;

(b) nothing in this section shall give a purchaser a right to a copy or abstract of a settlement filed at the registry:

(2) The vendor shall, subject to any stipulation to the contrary, at his own expense furnish the purchaser with such copies, abstracts and evidence (if any) in respect of any subsisting rights and interests appurtenant to the registered land as to which the register is not conclusive, and of any matters excepted from the effect of registration as the purchaser would have been entitled to if the land had not been registered:

(3) Except as aforesaid, and notwithstanding any stipulation to the contrary, it shall not be necessary for the vendor to furnish the purchaser with any abstract or other written evidence of title, or any copy or abstract of the land certificate, or of any charge certificate:

(4) Where the register refers to a filed abstract or copy of or extract from a deed or other document such abstract or extract shall as between vendor and purchaser be assumed to be correct, and to contain all material portions of the original, and no person dealing with any registered land or charge shall have a right to require production of the original, or be affected in any way by any provisions of the said document other than those appearing in such abstract, copy or extract, and any person suffering loss by reason of any error or omission in such abstract, copy or extract shall be entitled to be indemnified under this Act:

(5) Where the vendor is not himself registered as proprietor of the land or the charge giving a power of sale over the land, he shall, at the request of the purchaser and at his own expense, and notwithstanding any stipulation to the contrary, either procure the registration of himself as proprietor of the land or of the charge, as the case may be, or procure a disposition from the proprietor to the purchaser:

(6) Unless the certificate is deposited at the registry the vendor shall deliver the land certificate, or the charge certificate, as the case may be, to the purchaser on completion of the purchase, or, if only a part of the land comprised in the certificate is dealt with, or only a derivative estate is created, he shall, at his own expense, produce, or procure the production of, the certificate in accordance with this Act for the completion of the purchaser's registration. Where the certificate has been lost or destroyed, the vendor shall, notwithstanding any stipulation to the contrary, pay the costs of the proceedings required to enable the registrar to proceed without it:

(7) The purchaser shall not, by reason of the registration, be affected with notice of any pending action, writ, order, deed or arrangement or land charge (other than a local land charge) to which this subsection applies, which can be protected under this Act by lodging or registering a creditors' notice, restriction, inhibition, caution or other notice, or be concerned to make any search therefor if and so far as they affect registered land.

This subsection applies only to pending actions, writs, orders, deeds of arrangement and land charges (not including local land charges) required to be registered or re-registered after the commencement of this Act, either under the Land Charges Act 1925,[1] or any other statute registration whereunder has effect as if made under that Act.

Note

[1]Now the Land Charges Act 1972.

111. Infants, defectives and lunatics

(1) A purported disposition of any registered land or charge to an infant made after the commencement of this Act, or by the will of a proprietor dying after such commencement, shall not entitle the infant to be registered as proprietor of the registered land or charge until he attains full age, but in the meantime shall operate only as a declaration binding on the proprietor or personal representative that the registered land or charge is to be held on trust to give effect to minor interests in favour of the infant corresponding, as nearly as may be, with the interests which the disposition purports to transfer or create; and the disposition or a copy thereof or extract therefrom shall be deposited at the registry, and shall, unless and until the tenants for life, statutory owners, personal representatives or [trustees of land] are registered as proprietors, be protected by means of a restriction or otherwise on the register:

Provided that—

(a) If the disposition is made to the infant jointly with another person of full age, that person shall, during the minority, be entitled to be registered as proprietor, and the infant shall not be registered until he attains full age:

(b) Where the registered land or charge is subject to any trusts or rights of redemption in favour of any person other than the infant, nothing in this section shall affect such trusts or rights of redemption;

(c) Where by reason of the minority or otherwise the land is settled land, the provisions of this Act relating to settled land shall apply thereto.

(2) Where an infant becomes entitled under a will or on an intestacy to any registered land or charge, the same shall not be transferred by the personal representative to the infant until he attains full age.

(3) Where an infant becomes entitled to the benefit or a registered charge, the charge shall during the minority be registered in the names of the personal representatives, trustees, or other persons who if the charge had affected unregistered land would have been able to dispose of the same, and they shall for the purposes of this Act have the same powers in reference thereto as the infant would have had if of full age.

(4) A caution may be lodged in the name or on behalf of an infant by his parent, trustee or guardian.

(5) Where a proprietor of any registered land or charge is incapable, by reason of mental disorder within the meaning of [the Mental Health Act 1983], of managing and administering his property and affairs, his receiver or (if no receiver is acting for him) any person authorised in that behalf shall, under an order of the authority having jurisdiction under [Part VII of the Mental Health Act 1983], or] of the court, or under any statutory power, have and may exercise in the name and behalf of [the proprietor] all the powers which under this Act [the proprietor] could have exercised if free from disability, and a copy of every such order shall be filed with the registrar and may be referred to on the register.

(6) All the provisions of the Trustee Act 1925, and of [Part VII of the Mental Health Act 1983] and of any Act amending the same, shall apply to estates and charges registered under this Act, subject to the express provisions of this Act and to the rules made thereunder.

[112. Inspection of register and other documents at land registry

(1) Subject—

(a) to [sections . . . 112AA and 112C] below;

[(aa) to paragraph 2(1) of Schedule 1 to the Diplomatic and Consular Premises Act 1987 (power of Secretary of State to inspect register in connection with exercise of power to vest in himself former diplomatic or consular premises);]

(b) to the provisions of this Act as to furnishing information to the government departments and local authorities; and

(c) to such exceptions as may be prescribed, any person registered as proprietor of any land or charge, and any person authorised—

(i) by any such proprietor; or

(ii) by an order made under subsection (2) or (3) of this section; or

(iii) by general rule,

but no other person, shall have a right, on payment of a fee and in accordance with the prescribed procedure, to inspect and make copies of the whole or any part of any register relating to such land or charge.]

[112AA. Inspection in connection with insolvency

(1) If an official receiver or the official assignee, the liquidator or administrator of a company or the trustee of a bankrupt's estate—

(a) applies to the registrar for permission to make an inspection under this section in relation to a person specified in the application or to property so specified; and

(b) gives the registrar an appropriate certificate,

the registrar shall permit him to inspect and make copies of and extracts from any register or document kept in the custody of the registrar so far as it relates to the person or property so specified.

(2) In subsection (1) above 'appropriate certificate' means a certificate that there is reason to believe that the register may contain information which would be of assistance to the person giving the certificate in the carrying out of his functions as official receiver or official assignee, as liquidator or administrator of a company or as trustee of a bankrupt's estate.

(3) In this section—

(a) references to an official receiver are references to an official receiver for the purpose of the Insolvency Act 1985 [the Insolvency Act 1986] or the Companies Act 1985 or a person acting as a deputy to such an official receiver;]

[112B. Search on behalf of mortgagee for notice or caution for statutory rights of occupation

Where registered land which consists of or includes a dwelling house is subject to a registered charge, or to a mortgage which is protected by a notice or caution in accordance with section 106(3) of this Act, the proprietor of the registered charge, or as the case may be the mortgagee, may requisition an official search of the register to ascertain whether any notice or caution affecting that land has been registered under [section 2(8) of the Matrimonial Homes Act 1983] and a certificate showing the result of that search.]

[112C. Right of residential tenant to search for landlord's name and address

(1) For the purpose of enabling him to ascertain the name and address of his landlord, the tenant of premises to which this section applies shall (subject to subsection (3)) have a right, on payment of a fee and in accordance with the prescribed procedure, to inspect and make copies of, and take extracts from, any part of any register kept in the custody of the registrar which contains the name and address of the proprietor of any registered land containing those premises.

(2) This section applies to premises which consist of or include a dwelling and are not held under a tenancy to which Part II of the Landlord and Tenant Act 1954 (business tenancies) applies.

(3) The registrar may refuse to allow a tenant to exercise his right of inspection under subsection (1) above in relation to any registered land if he has reason to believe that the proprietor of that land is not the landlord of the tenant.

(4) In this section—

'dwelling' means a building or part of a building occupied or intended to be occupied as a separate dwelling, together with any yard, garden, outhouse and appurtenances belonging to it or usually enjoyed with it;

'landlord' means the immediate landlord or, in relation to a statutory tenant, the person who, apart from the statutory tenancy, would be entitled to possession of the premises subject to the tenancy;

'statutory tenancy' and 'statutory tenant' mean a statutory tenancy or statutory tenant within the meaning of the Rent Act 1977 or the Rent (Agriculture) Act 1976; and 'tenant' includes a statutory tenant.]

113. Office copies to be evidence

Office copies of and extracts from the register and of and from documents and plans filed in the registry shall be admissible in evidence in all actions and matters, and between all persons or parties, to the same extent as the originals would be admissible, but any person suffering loss by reason of the inaccuracy of any such copy or extract shall be entitled to be indemnified under this Act, and no solicitor, trustee, personal representative, or other person in a fiduciary position shall be answerable in respect of any loss occasioned by relying on any such copy or extract.

[113A. Inspection etc. — supplementary

(1) Any duty under this Act to make a thing available for inspection is a duty to make it available for inspection in visible and legible form.

(2) Any reference in this Act to copies of and extracts from the register and of and from documents and plans filed in the registry includes a reference to reproductions of things which are kept by the registrar under this Act otherwise than in documentary form.]

114. Fraudulent dispositions how far to be void

Subject to the provisions in this Act contained with respect to indemnity and to registered dispositions for valuable consideration, any disposition of land or of a charge, which if unregistered would be fraudulent and void, shall, notwithstanding registration, be fraudulent and void in like manner.

PART XI
COMPULSORY REGISTRATION

120. Power to make orders rendering registration compulsory in certain areas

(1) His Majesty may, by Order in Council, declare, as respects any county or part of a county mentioned or defined in the Order, that, on and after a day specified in the Order, registration of title to land is to be compulsory on sale:

Provided that nothing in this Act or in any such Order shall render compulsory the registration of the title to an incorporeal hereditament or to mines and minerals apart from the surface, or to corporeal hereditaments parcel of a manor and included in the sale of a manor as such.

(2)—(5) [. . .]

(6) Any Order made under this Part of this Act or under any corresponding provision in any enactment replaced by this Act may be revoked or varied by a subsequent Order.

(7) For the purposes of this Part of this Act, 'county' means the adminstrative county [. . .]

123. Effect of Act in areas where registration is compulsory

(1) In any area in which an Order in Council declaring that registration of title to land within that area is to be compulsory on sale is for the time being in force, every conveyance on sale of freehold land and every grant of [[1]a term of years absolute of more than twenty-one years from the date of delivery of the grant,] and every assignment on sale of leasehold land held for a term of years absolute ['having more than twenty-one years to run from the date of delivery of the assignment], shall (save as herinafter

provided), on the expiration of two months from the date thereof or of any authorised extension of that period, become void so far as regards the grant or conveyance of the legal estate in the freehold or leasehold land comprised in the conveyance, grant, or assignment, or so much of such land as is situated within the area affected, unless the grantee (that is to say, the person who is entitled to be registered as proprietor of the freehold or leasehold land) or his successor in title or assign has in the meantime applied to be registered as proprietor of such land:

Provided that the registrar, or the court on appeal from the registrar, may, on the application of any persons interested in any particular case in which the registrar or the court is satisfied that the application for first registration cannot be made within the said period, or can only be made within that period by incurring unreasonable expense, or that the application has not been made within the said period by reason of some accident or other sufficient cause, make an order extending the said period; and if such order be made, then, upon the registration of the grantee or his successor or assign, a note of the order shall be endorsed on the conveyance, grant or assignment:

In the case of land in an area where, at the date of the commencement of this Act, registration of title is already compulsory on sale, this subsection shall apply to every such conveyance, grant, or assignment, executed on or after that date.

(2) Rules under this Act may provide for applying the provisions thereof to dealings with the land which may take place between the date of such conveyance, grant, or assignment and the date of application to register as if such dealings had taken place after the date of first registration, and for registration to be effected as of the date of the application to register.

(3) In this section the expressions 'conveyance on sale' and 'assignment on sale' mean an instrument made on sale by virtue whereof there is conferred or completed a title under which an application for registration as first proprietor of land may be made under this Act, and include a conveyance or assignment by way of exchange where money is paid for equality of exchange, but do not include an enfranchisement or extinguishment of manorial incidents, whether under the Law of Property Act 1922, or otherwise, or an assignment or surrender of a lease to the owner of the immediate reversion containing a declaration that the term is to merge in such reversion.

Note

[1]Substituted by Land Registration Act 1986 for grants or assignments of leases made after the commencement of the Act.

PART XII
ADMINISTRATIVE AND JUDICIAL PROVISIONS

His Majesty's Land Registry

126. His Majesty's Land Registry

(1) There shall continue to be an office in London to be called His Majesty's Land Registry, the business of which shall be conducted by a registrar to be appointed by the Lord Chancellor and known as the Chief Land Registrar, with such officers (namely, registrars, assistant registrars, clerks, messengers, and servants), as the Lord Chancellor, with the concurrence of the Treasury as to number, may appoint.

(2) [. . .]

(3)—(4) . . .

(5) The Lord Chancellor may make regulations for the land registry, and for assigning the duties to the respective officers, and determining the acts of the registrar which may be done by a registrar or assistant registrar, and for altering or adding to the official styles of the Chief Land Registrar and other officers of the land registry. Subject to such regulations, anything authorised or required by this Act to be done to or by the registrar shall be done to or by the Chief Land Registrar [. . .]

131. Indemnity to officers of registry
The Chief Land Registrar shall not, nor shall a registrar or assistant registrar nor any person acting under the authority of the Chief Land Registrar or a registrar or assistant registrar, or under any order or general rule made in pursuance of this Act, be liable to any action or proceeding for or in respect of any act or matter done or omitted to be done in good faith in the exercise or supposed exercise of the powers of this Act, or any order or general rule made in pursuance of this Act.

District Registries

132. Power to form distact registries by general orders
(1) The Lord Chancellor, with the concurrence of the Treasury, shall have power by general orders from time to time to do all or any of the following things:—

(a) To create distinct registries for the purposes of registration of titles to land within the defined districts respectively, and to alter any districts which may have been so created.

Description and Powers of the Court

[138. Jurisdiction of High Court and county courts
(1) Any jurisdiction conferred on the High Court by this Act or by the Land Registration and Land Charges Act 1971 may also be exercised, to such an extent as may be prescribed, by county courts.]

139. Powers of court in action for specific performance
(1) Where an action is instituted for the specific performance of a contract relating to registered land, or a registered charge, the court having cognizance of the action may, by summons, or by such other mode as it deems expedient, cause all or any parties who have registered interests or rights in the registered land or charge, or have entered up notices, caution, restrictions, or inhibitions against the same to appear in such action, and show cause why such contract should not be specifically performed, and the court may direct that any order made by the court in the action shall be binding on such parties or any of them.

(2) All costs incurred by any parties so appearing in an action to enforce against a vendor specific performance of his contract to sell any registered land or charge shall be taxed as between solicitor and client, and, unless the court otherwise orders, be paid by the vendor.

141. Intervention of court in case of persons under disability
Where a person under disability, or person outside the jurisdiction of the High Court, or person yet unborn, is interested in the land in respect of the title to which any question arises as aforesaid, any other person interested in such land may apply to the court for a direction that the opinion of the court shall be conclusively binding on the person under disability, person outside the jurisdiction, or unborn person.

142. Power for court to bind interests of persons under disability
(1) The court shall hear the allegations of all parties appearing.

(2) The court may disapprove altogether or may approve, either with or without modification, of the directions of the registrar respecting any case referred to the court.

(3) The court may, if necessary, appoint a guardian, next friend or other person to appear on behalf of any person under disability, person outside the jurisdiction, or unborn person.

(4) If the court is satisfied that the interest of any person under disability, outside the jurisdiction, or unborn, will be sufficiently represented in any case, it shall make an order declaring that all persons, with the exceptions, if any, named in the order, are to be conclusively bound, and thereupon all persons, with such exceptions, if any, as

aforesaid, shall be conclusively bound by any decision of the court in which any such person is concerned.

143. Appeals

(1) Any person aggrieved by any order of a judge of a county court may, within the prescribed time and in the prescribed manner, appeal to the High Court.

ADMINISTRATION OF ESTATES ACT 1925
(1925, c. 23)

PART I
DEVOLUTION OF REAL ESTATE

1. Devolution of real estate on personal representative

(1) Real estate to which a deceased person was entitled for an interest not ceasing on his death shall on his death, and notwithstanding any testamentary disposition thereof, devolve from time to time on the personal representative of the deceased, in like manner as before the commencement of this Act chattels real devolved on the personal representative from time to time of a deceased person.

(2) The personal representatives for the time being of a deceased person are deemed in law his heirs and assigns within the meaning of all trusts and powers.

(3) The personal representatives shall be the representative of the deceased in regard to his real estate to which he was entitled for an interest not ceasing on his death as well as in regard to his personal estate.

2. Application to real estate of law affecting chattels real

(1) Subject to the provisions of this Act, all enactments and rules of law, and all jurisdiction of any court with respect to the appointment of administrators or to probate or letters of administration, or to dealings before probate in the case of chattels real, and with respect to costs and other matters in the administration of personal estate, in force before the commencement of this Act, and all powers, duties, rights, equities, obligations, and liabilities of a personal representative in force at the commencement of this Act with respect to chattels real, shall apply and attach to the personal representative and shall have effect with respect to real estate vested in him, and in particular all such powers of disposition and dealing as were before the commencement of this Act exercisable as respects chattels real by the survivor or survivors of two or more personal representatives, as well as by a single personal representative, or by all the personal representatives together, shall be exercisable by the personal representatives or representative of the deceased with respect to his real estate.

(2) Where as respects real estate there are two or more personal representatives, a conveyance of real estate devolving under this Part of this Act [or contract for such a conveyance] shall not, be made without the concurrence therein of all such representatives or an order of the court, but where probate is granted to one or some of two or more persons named as executors, whether or not power is reserved to the other or others to prove, any conveyance of the real estate [or contract for such a conveyance] may be made by the proving executor or executors for the time being, without an order of the court, and shall be as effectual as if all the persons named as executors had concurred therein.

(3) Without prejudice to the rights and powers of a personal representative, the appointment of a personal representative in regard to real estate shall not, save as hereinafter provided, affect—

(a) any rule as to marshalling or as to administration of assets;

(b) the beneficial interest in real estate under any testamentary disposition;

(c) any mode of dealing with any beneficial interest in real estate, or the proceeds of sale thereof;

(d) the right of any person claiming to be interested in the real estate to take proceedings for the protection or recovery thereof against any person other than the personal representative.

3. Interpretation of Part I

(1) In this Part of this Act 'real estate' includes—

(i) Chattels real, and land in possession, remainder, or reversion, and every interest in or over land to which a deceased person was entitled at the time of his death; and

(ii) Real estate held on trust (including settled land) or by way of mortgage or security, but not [. . .] money secured or charged on land.

(2) A testator shall be deemed to have been entitled at his death to any interest in real estate passing under any gift contained in his will which operates as an appointment under a general power to appoint by will, or operates under the testamentary power conferred by statute to dispose of an entailed interest.

(3) An entailed interest of a deceased person shall (unless disposed of under the testamentary power conferred by statute) be deemed an interest ceasing on his death, but any further or other interest of the deceased in the same property in remainder or reversion which is capable of being disposed of by his will shall not be deemed to be an interest so ceasing.

(4) The interest of a deceased person under a joint tenancy where another tenant survives the deceased is an interest ceasing on his death.

(5) On the death of a corporator sole his interest in the corporation's real and personal estate shall be deemed to be an interest ceasing on his death and shall devolve to his successor.

This subsection applies on the demise of the Crown as respects all property, real and personal, vested in the Crown as a corporation sole.

PART II
EXECUTORS AND ADMINISTRATORS

General Provisions

5. Cesser of right of executor to prove

Where a person appointed executor by a will—

(i) survives the testator but dies without having taken out probate of the will; or

(ii) is cited to take out probate of the will and does not appear to the citation; or

(iii) renounces probate of the will;

his rights in respect of the executorship shall wholly cease, and the representation to the testator and the administration of his real and personal estate shall devolve and be committed in like manner as if that person had not been appointed executor.

6. Withdrawal of renunciation

(1) Where an executor who has renounced probate has been permitted, whether before or after the commencement of this Act, to withdraw the renunciation and prove the will, the probate shall take effect and be deemed always to have taken effect without prejudice to the previous acts and dealings of and notices to any other personal representative who has previously proved the will or taken out letters of administration, and a memorandum of the subsequent probate shall be endorsed on the original probate or letters of administration.

(2) This section applies whether the testator died before or after the commencement of this Act.

7. Executor of executor represents original testator

(1) An executor of a sole or last surviving executor of a testator is the executor of that testator.

This provision shall not apply to an executor who does not prove the will of his testator, and, in the case of an executor who on his death leaves surviving him some other executor of his testator who afterwards proves the will of that testator, it shall cease to apply on such probate being granted.

(2) So long as the chain of such representation is unbroken, the last executor in the chain is the executor of every preceding testator.

(3) The chain of such representation is broken by—

(a) an intestacy; or

(b) the failure of a testator to appoint an executor' or

(c) the failure to obtain probate of a will;

but is not broken by a temporary grant of administration if probate is subsequently granted.

(4) Every person in the chain of representation to a testator—

(a) has the same rights in respect of the real and personal estate of that testator as the original executor would have had if living; and

(b) is, to the extent to which the estate whether real or personal of that testator has come to his hands, answerable as if he were an original executor.

8. Right of proving executors to exercise powers

(1) Where probate is granted to one or some of two or more persons named as executors, whether or not power is reserved to the others or other to prove, all the powers which are by law conferred on the personal representative may be exercised by the proving executor or executors for the time being and shall be as effectual as if all the persons named as executors had concurred therein.

(2) This section applies whether the testator died before or after the commencement of this Act.

[9. Vesting of estate in Public Trustee where intestacy or lack of executors

(1) Where a person dies intestate, his real and personal estate shall vest in the Public Trustee until the grant of administration.

(2) Where a testator dies and—

(a) at the time of his death there is no executor with power to obtain probate of the will, or

(b) at any time before probate of the will is granted there ceases to be any executor with power to obtain probate,

the real and personal estate of which he disposes by the will shall vest in the Public Trustee until the grant of representation.

(3) The vesting of real or personal estate in the Public Trustee by virtue of this section does not confer on him any beneficial interest in, or impose on him any duty, obligation or liability in respect of, the property.

Note: by section 14 of the Law of Property (Miscellaneous Provisions) Act 1994:

(2) Any real or personal estate of a person dying before the commencement of this section shall, if it is property to which this subsection applies, vest in the Public Trustee on the commencement of this section.

(3) Subsection (2) above applies to any property—

(a) if it was vested in the Probate Judge under section 9 of the Administration of Estates Act 1925 immediately before the commencement of this section, or

(b) if it was not so vested but as at commencement there has been no grant of representation in respect of it and there is no executor with power to obtain such a grant.

(4) Any property vesting in the Public Trustee by virtue of subsection (2) above shall—

(a) if the deceased died intestate, be treated as vesting in the Public Trustee under section 9(1) of the Administration of Estates Act 1925 (as substituted by subsection (1) above); and

(b) otherwise be treated as vesting in the Public Trustee under section 9(2) of that Act (as so substituted).

(5) Anything done by or in relation to the Probate Judge with respect to property vested in him as mentioned in subsection (3)(a) above shall be treated as having been done by or in relation to the Public Trustee.

(6) So far as may be necessary in consequence of the transfer to the Public Trustee of the functions of the Probate Judge under section 9 of the Administration of Estates Act 1925, any reference in an enactment or instrument to the Probate Judge shall be construed as a reference to the Public Trustee.]

15. Executor not to act while administration is in force

Where administration has been granted in respect of any real or personal estate of a deceased person, no person shall have power to bring any action or otherwise act as executor of the deceased person in respect of the estate comprised in or affected by the grant until the grant has been recalled or revoked.

17. Continuance of legal proceedings after revocation of temporary administration

(1) If, while any legal proceeding is pending in any court by or against an administrator to whom a temporary administration has been granted, that administration is revoked, that court may order that the proceeding be continued by or against the new personal representative in like manner as if the same had been originally commenced by or against him, but subject to such conditions and variations, if any, as that court directs.

[(2) The county court has jurisdiction under this section where the proceedings are pending in that court.]

21. Rights and tiabilities of administrator

Every person to whom administration of the real and personal estate of a deceased person is granted, shall, subject to the limitations contained in the grant, have the same rights and liabilities and be accountable in like manner as if he were the executor of the deceased.

[21A. A debtor who becomes creditor's executor by representation or administration to account for debt to estate

(1) Subject to subsection (2) of this section, where a debtor becomes his deceased creditor's executor by representation or administrator—

(a) his debt shall thereupon be extinguished; but

(b) he shall be accountable for the amount of the debt, as part of the creditor's estate in any case where he would be so accountable if he had been appointed as an executor by the creditor's will.

(2) Subsection (1) of this section does not apply where the debtor's authority to act as executor or administrator is limited to part only of the creditor's estate which does not include the debt; and a debtor whose debt is extinguished by virtue of paragraph (a) shall not be accountable for its amount by virtue of paragraph (b) of that subsection in any case where the debt was barred by The Limitation Act 1939[1] before he became the creditor's executor or administrator.

(3) In this section 'debt' includes any liability, and 'debtor' and 'creditor' shall be construed accordingly.]

Note

[1]This is construed as including the Limitation Act 1980.

Special Provisions as to Settled Land

22. Special executors as respects settled land

(1) A testator may appoint, and in default of such express appointment shall be deemed to have appointed, as his special executors in regard to settled land, the persons,

if any, who are at his death the trustees of the settlement thereof, and probate may be granted to such trustees specially limited to the settled land.

In this subsection 'settled land' means land vested in the testator which was settled previously to his death and not by his will.

(2) A testator may appoint other persons either with or without such trustees as aforesaid or any of them to be his general executors in regard to his other property and assets.

23. Provisions where, as respects settled land, representation is not granted to the trustees of the settlement

(1) Where settled land becomes vested in a personal representative, not being a trustee of the settlement, upon trust to convey the land to or assent to the vesting thereof in the tenant for life or statutory owner in order to give effect to a settlement created before the death of the deceased and not by his will, or would, on the grant of representation to him, have become so vested, such representative may—

(a) before representation has been granted, renounce his office in regard only to such settled land without renouncing it in regard to other property;

(b) after representation has been granted, apply to the court for revocation of the grant in regard to the settled land without applying in regard to other property.

(2) Whether such renunciation or revocation is made or not, the trustees of the settlement, or any person beneficially interested thereunder, may apply to the High Court for an order appointing a special or additional personal representative in respect of the settled land, and a special or additional personal representative, if and when appointed under the order, shall be in the same position as if representation had originally been granted to him alone in place of the original personal representative, as the case may be, limited to the settled land, but without prejudice to the previous acts and dealings, if any, of the personal representative originally constituted or the effect of notices given to such personal representative.

(3) The court may make such order as aforesaid subject to such security, if any, being given by or on behalf of the special or additional personal representative, as the court may direct, and shall, unless the court considers that special considerations apply, appoint such persons as may be necessary to secure that the persons to act as representatives in respect of the settled land shall, if willing to act, be the same persons as are the trustees of the settlement, and an office copy of the order when made shall be furnished to the [principal registry of the Family Division of the High Court] for entry, and a memorandum of the order shall be endorsed on the probate or administration.

(4) The person applying for the appointment of a special or additional personal representative shall give notice of the application to the [principal registry of the Family Division of the High Court] in the manner prescribed.

(5) Rules of court may be made for prescribing for all matters required for giving effect to the provisions of this section, and in particular—

(a) for notice of any application being given to the proper officer;

(b) for production of orders, probates, and administration to the registry;

(c) for the endorsement on a probate or administration of a memorandum of an order, subject or not to any exceptions;

(d) for the manner in which the costs are to be borne;

(e) for protecting purchasers and trustees and other persons in a fiduciary position, dealing in good faith with or giving notices to a personal representative before notice of any order has been endorsed on the probate or administration or a pending action has been registered in respect of the proceedings.

24. Power for special personal representatives to dispose of settled land

(1) The special personal representatives may dispose of the settled land without the concurrence of the general personal representatives, who may likewise dispose of the

other property and assets of the deceased without the concurrence of the special personal representatives.

(2) In this section the expression 'special personal representatives' means the representatives appointed to act for the purposes of settled land and includes any original personal representative who is to act with an additional personal representative for those purposes.

Duties, Rights, and Obligations

[25. Duty of personal representatives

The personal representative of a deceased person shall be under a duty to—

(a) collect and get in the real and personal estate of the deceased and administer it according to law;

(b) when required to do so by the court, exhibit on oath in the court a full inventory of the estate and when so required render an account of the administration of the estate to the court;

(c) when required to do so by the High Court, deliver up the grant of probate or administration to that court.]

26. Rights of action by and against personal representative

(1)–(2) [. . .]

(3) A personal representative may distrain for arrears of a rentcharge due or accruing to the deceased in his lifetime on the land affected or charged therewith, so long as the land remains in the possession of the person liable to pay the rentcharge or of the persons deriving title under him, and in like manner as the deceased might have done had he been living.

(4) A personal representative may distrain upon land for arrears of rent due or accruing to the deceased in like manner as the deceased might have done had he been living.

Such arrears may be distrained for after the termination of the lease or tenancy as if the term or interest had not determined, if the distress is made—

(a) within six months after the termination of the lease or tenancy;

(b) during the continuance of the possession of the lessee or tenant from whom the arrears were due.

The statutory enactments relating to distress for rent apply to any distress made pursuant to this subsection.

27. Protection of persons acting on probate or administration

(1) Every person making or permitting to be made any payment or disposition in good faith under a representation shall be indemnified and protected in so doing, notwithstanding any defect or circumstance whatsoever affecting the validity of the representation.

(2) Where a representation is revoked, all payments and dispositions made in good faith to a personal representative under the representation before the revocation thereof are a valid discharge to the person making the same; and the personal representative who acted under the revoked representation may retain and reimburse himself in respect of any payments or dispositions made by him which the person to whom representation is afterwards granted might have properly made.

28. Liability of person fraudulently obtaining or retaining estate of deceased

If any person, to the defrauding of creditors or without full valuable consideration, obtains, receives or holds any real or personal estate of a deceased person or effects the release of any debt or liability due to the estate of the deceased, he shall be charged as executor in his own wrong to the extent of the real and personal estate received or coming to his hands, or the debt or liability released, after deducting—

(a) any debt for valuable consideration and without fraud due to him from the deceased person at the time of his death; and

(b) any payment made by him which might properly be made by a personal representative.

29. Liability of estate of personal representative

Where a person as personal representative of a deceased person (including an executor in his own wrong) wastes or converts to his own use any part of the real or personal estate of the deceased, and dies, his personal representative shall to the extent of the available assets of the defaulter be liable and chargeable in respect of such waste or conversion in the same manner as the defaulter would have been if living.

31. Power to make rules

Provision may be made by rules of court for giving effect to the provisions of this Part of this Act so far as relates to real estate and in particular for adapting the procedure and practice on the grant of letters of administration to the case of real estate.

PART III
ADMINISTRATION OF ASSETS

32. Real and personal estate of deceased are assets for payment of debts

(1) The real and personal estate, whether legal or equitable, of a deceased person, to the extent of his beneficial interest therein, and the real and personal estate of which a deceased person in pursuance of any general power (including the statutory power to dispose of entailed interests) disposes by his will, are assets for payment of his debts (whether by specialty or simple contract) and liabilities, and any disposition by will inconsistent with this enactment is void as against the creditors, and the court shall, if necessary, administer the property for the purpose of the payment of the debts and liabilities.

This subsection takes effect without prejudice to the rights of incumbrancers.

(2) If any person to whom any such beneficial interest devolves or is given, or in whom any such interest vests, disposes thereof in good faith before an action is brought or process is sued out against him, he shall be personally liable for the value of the interest so disposed of by him, but that interest shall not be liable to be taken in execution in the action or under the process.

33. Trust for sale

[(1) On the death of a person intestate as to any real or personal estate, that estate shall be held in trust by his personal representatives with the power to sell it.]

[(2) The personal representatives shall pay out of—

(a) the ready money of the deceased (so far as not disposed of by his will, if any); and

(b) any net money arising from disposing of any other part of his estate (after payment of costs), all] such funeral, testamentary and administration expenses, debts and other liabilities as are properly payable thereout having regard to the rules of administration contained in this Part of this Act, and out of the residue of the said money the personal representative shall set aside a fund sufficient to provide for any pecuniary legacies bequeathed by the will (if any) of the deceased.

(3) During the minority of any beneficiary or the subsistence of any life interest and pending the distribution of the whole or any part of the estate of the deceased, the personal representatives may invest the residue of the said money, or so much thereof as may not have been distributed, in any investments for the time being authorised by statute for the investment of trust money, with power, at the discretion of the personal representatives, to change such investments for others of a like nature.

(4) The residue of the said money and any investments for the time being representing the same, [and any part of the estate of the deceased which remains] unsold

and is not required for the administration purposes aforesaid, is in this Act referred to as 'the residuary estate of the intestate.'

(5) The income (including net rents and profits of real estate and chattels real after payment of rates, taxes, rent, costs of insurance, repairs and other outgoings properly attributable to income) of so much of the real and personal estate of the deceased as may not be disposed of by his will, if any, or may not be required for the administration purposes aforesaid, may, however such estate is invested, as from the death of the deceased, be treated and applied as income, and for that purpose any necessary apportionment may be made between tenant for life and remainderman.

(6) Nothing in this section affects the rights of any creditor of the deceased or the rights of the Crown in respect of death duties.

(7) Where the deceased leaves a will, this section has effect subject to the provisions contained in the will.

34. Administration of assets

(3) Where the estate of a deceased person is solvent his real and personal estate shall, subject to rules of court and the provisions hereinafter contained as to charges on property of the deceased, and to the provisions, if any, contained in his will, be applicable towards the discharge of the funeral, testamentary and administration expenses, debts and liabilities payable thereout in the order mentioned in Part II of the First Schedule to this Act.[1]

Note

[1]As to insolvent estates, see the Insolvency Act 1986, s. 421 and the Administration of Insolvent Estates of Deceased Persons Order 1986 (No. 1999).

35. Charges on property of deceased to be paid primarily out of the property charged

(1) Where a person dies possessed of, or entitled to, or, under a general power of appointment (including the statutory power to dispose of entailed interests) by his will disposes of, an interest in property, which at the time of his death is charged with the payment of money, whether by way of legal mortgage, equitable charge or otherwise (including a lien for unpaid purchase money), and the deceased has not by will deed or other document signified a contrary or other intention, the interest so charged shall, as between the different persons claiming through the deceased, be primarily liable for the payment of the charge; and every part of the said interest, according to its value, shall bear a proportionate part of the charge on the whole thereof.

(2) Such contrary or other intention shall not be deemed to be signified—

(a) by a general direction for the payment of debts or of all the debts of the testator out of his personal estate, or his residuary real and personal estate, or his residuary real estate; or

(b) by a charge of debts upon any such estate; unless such intention is further signified by words expressly or by necessary implication referring to all or some part of the charge.

(3) Nothing in this section affects the right of a person entitled to the charge to obtain payment or satisfaction thereof either out of the other assets of the deceased or otherwise.

36. Effect of assent or conveyance by personal representative

(1) A personal representative may assent to the vesting, in any person who (whether by devise, bequest, devolution, appropriation or otherwise) may be entitled thereto, either beneficially or as a trustee or personal representative, of any estate or interest in real estate to which the testator or intestate was entitled or over which he exercised a general power of appointment by his will, including the statutory power to dispose of entailed interests, and which devolved upon the personal representative.

(2) The assent shall operate to vest in that person the estate or interest to which the assent relates, and, unless a contrary intention appears, the assent shall relate back to the death of the deceased.

(4) An assent to the vesting of a legal estate shall be in writing, signed by the personal representative, and shall name the person in whose favour it is given and shall operate to vest in that person the legal estate to which it relates; and an assent not in writing or not in favour of a named person shall not be effectual to pass a legal estate.

(5) Any person in whose favour an assent or conveyance of a legal estate is made by a personal representative may require that notice of the assent or conveyance be written or endorsed on or permanently annexed to the probate or letters of administration, at the cost of the estate of the deceased, and that the probate or letter of administration be produced, at the like cost, to prove that the notice has been placed thereon or annexed thereto.

(6) A statement in writing by a personal representative that he has not given or made an assent or conveyance in respect of a legal estate, shall, in favour of a purchaser, but without prejudice to any previous disposition made in favour of another purchaser deriving title mediately or immediately under the personal representative, be sufficient evidence that an assent or conveyance has not been given or made in respect of the legal estate to which the statement relates, unless notice of a previous assent or conveyance affecting that estate has been placed on or annexed to the probate or administration.

A conveyance by a personal representative of a legal estate to a purchaser accepted on the faith of such a statement shall (without prejudice as aforesaid and unless notice of a previous assent or conveyance affecting that estate has been placed on or annexed to the probate or administration) operate to transfer or create the legal estate expressed to be conveyed in like manner as if no previous assent or conveyance had been made by the personal representative.

A personal representative making a false statement, in regard to any such matter, shall be liable in like manner as if the statement had been contained in a statutory declaration.

(7) An assent or conveyance by a personal representative in respect of a legal estate shall, in favour of a purchaser, unless notice of a previous assent or conveyance affecting that legal estate has been placed on or annexed to the probate or administration, be taken as sufficient evidence that the person in whose favour the assent or conveyance is given or made is the person entitled to have the legal estate conveyed to him, and upon the proper trusts, if any, but shall not otherwise prejudicially affect the claim of any person rightfully entitled to the estate vested or conveyed or any charge thereon.

(8) A conveyance of a legal estate by a personal representative to a purchaser shall not be invalidated by reason only that the purchaser may have notice that all the debts, liabilities, funeral, and testamentary or administration expenses, duties, and legacies of the deceased have been discharged or provided for.

(9) An assent or conveyance given or made by a personal representative shall not, except in favour of a purchaser of a legal estate, prejudice the right of the personal representative or any other person to recover the estate or interest to which the assent or conveyance relates, or to be indemnified out of such estate or interest against any duties, debt, or liability to which such estate or interest would have been subject if there had not been any assent or conveyance.

(10) A personal representative may, as a condition of giving an assent or making a conveyance, require security for the discharge of any such duties, debt, or liability, but shall not be entitled to postpone the giving of an assent merely by reason of the subsistence of any such duties, debt or liability if reasonable arrangements have been made for discharging the same; and an assent may be given subject to any legal estate or charge by way of legal mortgage.

(11) This section shall not operate to impose any stamp duty in respect of an assent, and in this section 'purchaser' means a purchaser for money or money's worth.

(12) This section applies to assents and conveyances made after the commencement of this Act, whether the testator or intestate died before or after such commencement.

37. Validity of conveyance not affected by revocation of representation

(1) All conveyances of any interest in real or personal estate made to a purchaser either before or after the commencement of this Act by a person to whom probate or letters of administration have been granted are valid, notwithstanding any subsequent revocation or variation, either before or after the commencement of this Act, of the probate or administration.

(2) This section takes effect without prejudice to any order of the court made before the commencement of this Act, and applies whether the testator or intestate died before or after such commencement.

38. Right to follow property and powers of the court in relation thereto

(1) An assent or conveyance by a personal representative to a person other than a purchaser does not prejudice the rights of any person to follow the property to which the assent or conveyance relates, or any property representing the same, into the hands of the person in whom it is vested by the assent or conveyance, or of any other person (not being a purchaser) who may have received the same or in whom it may be vested.

(2) Notwithstanding any such assent or conveyance the court may, on the application of any creditor or other person interested—

(a) order a sale, exchange, mortgage, charge, lease, payment, transfer or other transaction to be carried out which the court considers requisite for the purpose of giving effect to the rights of the persons interested;

(b) declare that the person, not being a purchaser, in whom the property is vested is a trustee for those purposes;

(c) give directions respecting the preparation and execution of any conveyance or other instrument or as to any other matter required for giving effect to the order;

(d) make any vesting order, or appoint a person to convey in accordance with the provisions of the Trustee Act, 1925.

(3) This section does not prejudice the rights of a purchaser or a person deriving title under him, but applies whether the testator or intestate died before or after the commencement of this Act.

[(4) The County Court has jurisdiction under this section where the estate in respect of which the application is made does not exceed in amount or value the County Court limit.]

39. Powers of management

(1) In dealing with the real and personal estate of the deceased his personal representatives shall, for purposes of administration, or during a minority of any beneficiary or the subsistence of any life interest, or until the period of distribution arrives, have—

(i) [as respects the personal estate,] the same powers and discretions, including power to raise money by mortgage or charge (whether or not by deposit of documents), as a personal representative had before the commencement of this Act, with respect to personal estate vested in him [. . .]; and

[(ii) as respects the real estate, all the functions conferred on them by Part I of the Trusts of Land and Appointment of Trustees Act 1996;]

(iii) all the powers [necessary] and so that every contract entered into by a personal representative shall be binding on and be enforceable against and by the personal representative for the time being of the deceased, and may be carried into effect, or be varied or rescinded by him, and, in the case of a contract entered into by a predecessor, as if it had been entered into by himself.

(2) Nothing in this section shall affect the right of any person to require an assent or conveyance to be made.

(3) This section applies whether the testator or intestate died before or after the commencement of this Act.

40. Powers of personal representative for raising money, etc.

(1) For giving effect to beneficial interests the personal representative may limit or demise land for a term of years absolute, with or without impeachment for waste, to trustees on usual trusts for raising or securing any principal sum and the interest thereon for which the land, or any part thereof, is liable, and may limit or grant a rentcharge for giving effect to any annual or periodical sum for which the land or the income thereof or any part thereof is liable.

(2) This section applies whether the testator or intestate died before or after the commencement of this Act.

41. Powers of personal representative as to appropriation

(1) The personal representative may appropriate any part of the real or personal estate, including things in action, of the deceased in the actual condition or state of investment thereof at the time of appropriation in or towards satisfaction of any legacy bequeathed by the deceased, or of any other interest or share in his property, whether settled or not, as to the personal representative may seem just and reasonable, according to the respective rights of the persons interested in the property of the deceased:

Provided that—

(i) an appropriation shall not be made under this section so as to affect prejudicially any specific devise or bequest;

(ii) an appropriation of property, whether or not being an investment authorised by law or by the will, if any, of the deceased for the investment of money subject to the trust, shall not (save as hereinafter mentioned) be made under this section except with the following consents:—

(a) when made for the benefit of a person absolutely and beneficially entitled in possession, the consent of that person;

(b) when made in respect of any settled legacy share or interest, the consent of either the trustee thereof, if any (not being also the personal representative), or the person who may for the time being be entitled to the income:

If the person whose consent is so required as aforesaid is an infant or [is incapable, by reason of mental disorder within the meaning of [the Mental Health Act, 1983] of managing and administering his property and affairs], the consent shall be given on his behalf by his parents or parent, testamentary or other guardian, [. . .] or receiver, or if, in the case of an infant, there is no such parent or guardian, by the court on the application of his next friend;

(iii) no consent (save of such trustee as aforesaid) shall be required on behalf of a person who may come into existence after the time of appropriation, or who cannot be found or ascertained at that time,

(iv) if no [receiver is acting for a person suffering from mental disorder], then, if the appropriation is of an investment authorised by law or by the will, if any, of the deceased for the investment of money subject to the trust, no consent shall be required on behalf of the [said person],

(v) if, independently of the personal representative, there is no trustee of a settled legacy share or interest, and no person of full age and capacity entitled to the income thereof, no consent shall be required to an appropriation in respect of such legacy share or interest, provided that the appropriation is of an investment authorised as aforesaid.

[(1A) The County Court has jurisdiction under proviso (ii) to subsection (1) of this section where the estate in respect of which the application is made does not exceed in amount or value the County Court limit.]

(2) Any property duly appropriated under the powers conferred by this section shall thereafter be treated as an authorised investment, and may be retained or dealt with accordingly.

(3) For the purposes of such appropriation, the personal representative may ascertain and fix the value of the respective parts of the real and personal estate and the liabilities of the deceased as he may think fit, and shall for that purpose employ a duly qualified valuer in any case where such employment may be necessary; and may make any conveyance (including an assent) which may be requisite for giving effect to the appropriation.

(4) An appropriation made pursuant to this section shall bind all persons interested in the property of the deceased whose consent is not hereby made requisite.

(5) The personal representative shall, in making the appropriation, have regard to the rights of any person who may thereafter come into existence, or who cannot be found or ascertained at the time of appropriation, and of any other person whose consent is not required by this section.

(6) This section does not prejudice any other power of appropriation conferred by law or by the will (if any) of the deceased, and takes effect with any extended powers conferred by the will (if any) of the deceased, and where an appropriation is made under this section, in respect of a settled legacy, share or interest, the property appropriated shall remain subject to all [trusts] and powers of leasing, disposition, and management or varying investments which would have been applicable thereto or to the legacy, share or interest in respect of which the appropriation is made, if no such appropriation had been made.

(7) If after any real estate has been appropriated in purported exercise of the powers conferred by this section, the person to whom it was conveyed disposes of it or any interest therein, then, in favour of a purchaser, the appropriation shall be deemed to have been made in accordance with the requirements of this section and after all requisite consents, if any, had been given.

(8) In this section, a settled legacy, share or interest includes any legacy, share or interest to which a person is not absolutely entitled in possession at that date of the appropriation, also an annuity, and 'purchaser' means a purchaser for money or money's worth.

(9) This section applies whether the deceased died intestate or not, and whether before or after the commencement of this Act, and extends to property over which a testator exercises a general power of appointment, including the statutory power to dispose of entailed interests, and authorise the setting apart of a fund to answer an annuity by means of the income of that fund or otherwise.

42. Power to appoint trustees of infants' property

(1) Where an infant is absolutely entitled under the will or on the intestacy of a person dying before or after the commencement of this Act (in this subsection called 'the deceased') to a devise or legacy, or to the residue of the estate of the deceased, or any share therein, and such devise, legacy, residue or share is not under the will, if any, of the deceased, devised or bequeathed to trustees for the infant, the personal representatives of the deceased may appoint a trust corporation or two or more individuals not exceeding four (whether or not including the personal representatives or one or more of the personal representatives), to be the trustee or trustees of such devise, legacy, residue or share for the infant, and to be trustees of any land devised or any land being or forming part of such residue or share for the purposes of the Settled Land Act, 1925, and of the statutory provisions relating to the management of land during a minority, and may execute or do any assurance or thing requisite for vesting such devise, legacy, residue or share in the trustee or trustees so appointed.

On such appointment the personal representatives, as such, shall be discharged from all further liability in respect of such devise, legacy, residue, or share, and the same may be retained in its existing condition or state of investment, or may be converted into money, and such money may be invested in any authorised investment.

(2) Where a personal representative has before the commencement of this Act retained or sold any such devise, legacy, residue or share, and invested the same or the proceeds thereof in any investments in which he was authorised to invest money subject to the trust, then, subject to any order of the court made before such commencement, he shall not be deemed to have incurred any liability on that account, or by reason of not having paid or transferred the money or property into court.

43. Obligations of personal representative as to giving possession of land and powers of the court

(1) A personal representative, before giving an assent or making a conveyance in favour of any person entitled, may permit that person to take possession of the land, and such possession shall not prejudicially affect the right of the personal representative to take or resume possession nor his power to convey the land as if he were in possession thereof, but subject to the interest of any lessee, tenant or occupier in possession or in actual occupation of the land.

(2) Any person who as against the personal representative claims possession of real estate, or the appointment of a receiver thereof, or a conveyance thereof, or an assent to the vesting thereof, or to be registered as proprietor thereof under the Land Registration Act, 1925, may apply to the court for directions with reference thereto, and the court may make such vesting or other order as may be deemed proper, and the provisions of the Trustee Act, 1925, relating to vesting orders and to the appointment of a person to convey, shall apply.

(3) This section applies whether the testator or intestate died before or after the commencement of this Act.

[(4) The county court has jurisdiction under this section where the estate in respect of which the application is made does not exceed in amount or value the county court limit.]

44. Power to postpone distribution

Subject to the foregoing provisions of this Act, a personal representative is not bound to distribute the estate of the deceased before the expiration of one year from the death.

PART IV
DISTRIBUTION OF RESIDUARY ESTATE

45. Abolition of descent to heir, curtesy, dower and escheat

(1) With regard to the real estate and personal inheritance of every person dying after the commencement of this Act, there shall be abolished—

(a) All existing modes rules and canons of descent, and of devolution by special occupancy or otherwise, of real estate, or of a personal inheritance, whether operating by the general law or by the custom of gavelkind or borough english or by any other custom of any county, locality, or manor, or otherwise howsoever; and

(b) Tenancy by the curtesy and every other estate and interest of a husband in real estate as to which his wife dies intestate, whether arising under the general law or by custom or otherwise; and

(c) Dower and freebench and every other estate and interest of a wife in real estate as to which her husband dies intestate, whether arising under the general law or by custom or otherwise: Provided that where a right (if any) to freebench or other like right has attached before the commencement of this Act which cannot be barred by a testamentary or other disposition made by the husband, such right shall, unless released, remain in force as an equitable interest; and

(d) Escheat to the Crown or the Duchy of Lancaster or the Duke of Cornwall or to a mesne lord for want of heirs.

(2) Nothing in this section affects the descent or devolution of an entailed interest.

46. Succession to real and personal estate on intestacy

(1) The residuary estate of an intestate shall be distributed in the manner or be held on the trusts mentioned in this section, namely:—

[(i) If the intestate leaves a husband or wife, then in accordance with the following table:

TABLE

If the intestate—	
(1) leaves— (a) no issue, and (b) no parent, or brother or sister of the whole blood, or issue of a brother or sister of the whole blood.	the residuary estate shall be held in trust for the surviving husband or wife absolutely.
(2) leaves issue (whether or not persons mentioned in sub-paragraph (b) above also survive)	the surviving husband or wife shall take the personal chattels absolutely and, in addition the residuary estate of the intestate (other than the personal chattels) shall stand charged with the payment of a [fixed net sum], free of death duties and costs, to the surviving husband or wife with interest thereon from the date of the death [at such rate as the Lord Chancellor may specify by order] until paid or appropriated, and, subject to providing for that sum and the interest thereon, the residuary estate (other than the personal chattels) shall be held— (a) as to one half upon trust for the surviving husband or wife during his or her life, and, subject to such life interest, on the statutory trusts for the issue of the intestate, and (b) as to the other half, on the statutory trusts for the issue of the intestate.
[2A) Where the intestate's husband or wife survived the intestate but died before the end of the period of 28 days beginning with the day on which the intestate died, this section shall have effect as respects the intestate as if the husband or wife had not survived the intestate.]	
(3) leaves one or more of the following, that is to say, a parent, a brother or sister of the whole blood, or issue of a brother or sister of the whole blood, but leaves no issue.	the surviving husband or wife shall take the personal chattels absolutely and, in addition, the residuary estate of the intestate (other than the personal chattels) shall stand charged with the payment of a [fixed net sum], free of death duties and costs, to the surviving husband or wife with interest thereon from the date of the death [at such rate as the Lord Chancellor may specify by

order] until paid or appropriated, and, subject to providing for that sum and the interest thereon, the residuary estate (other than the personal chattels) shall be held—

(a) as to one half in trust for the surviving husband or wife absolutely, and

(b) as to the other half—

(i) where the intestate leaves one parent or both parents (whether or not brothers or sisters of the intestate or their issue also survive) in trust for the parent absolutely or, as the case may be, for the two parents in equal shares absolutely,

(ii) where the intestate leaves no parent, on the statutory trusts for the brothers and sisters of the whole blood of the intestate.]

[The fixed net sums referred to in paragraphs (2) and (3) of this Table shall be of the amounts provided by or under section 1 of the Family Provision Act 1966.]

(ii) If the intestate leaves issue but no husband or wife, the residuary estate of the intestate shall be held on the statutory trusts for the issue of the intestate;

(iii) If the intestate leaves [no husband or wife and] no issue but both parents, then [. . .] the residuary estate of the intestate shall be held in trust for the father and mother in equal share absolutely

(iv) If the intestate leaves [no husband or wife and] no issue but one parent, then, [. . .] the residuary estate of the intestate shall be held in trust for the surviving father or mother absolutely;

(v) If the intestate leaves no [husband or wife and no issue and no] parent, then, [. . .] the residuary estate of the intestate shall be held in trust for the following persons living at the death of the intestate, and in the following order and manner, namely:—

First, on the statutory trusts for the brothers and sisters of the whole blood of the intestate; but if no person takes an absolutely vested interest under such trusts, then

Secondly, on the statutory trusts for the brothers and sisters of the half blood of the intestate; but if no person takes an absolutely vested interest under such trusts; then

Thirdly, for the grandparents of the intestate and, if more than one survive the intestate, in equal shares; but if there is no member of this class; then

Fourthly, on the statutory trusts for the uncles and aunts of the intestate (being brothers or sisters of the whole blood of a parent of the intestate); but if no person takes an absolutely vested interest under such trusts; then

Fifthly, on the statutory trusts for the uncles and aunts of the intestate (being brothers or sisters of the half blood of a parent of the intestate); [. . .]

(vi) In default of any person taking an absolute interest under the foregoing provisions, the residuary estate of the intestate shall belong to the Crown or to the Duchy of Lancaster or to the Duke of Cornwall for the time being, as the case may be, as bona vacantia, and in lieu of any right to escheat.

The Crown or the said Duchy or the said Duke may (without prejudice to the powers reserved by section nine of the Civil List Act, 1910, or any other powers), out of the whole or any part of the property devolving on them respectively, provide, in accordance with the existing practice, for dependants, whether kindred or not, of the intestate, and other persons for whom the intestate might reasonably have been expected to make provision.

[(1A) The power to make orders under subsection (1) above shall be exercisable by statutory instrument subject to annulment in pursuance of a resolution of either House of Parliament; and any such order may be varied or revoked by a subsequent order made under the power.]

(2) A husband and wife shall for all purposes of distribution or division under the foregoing provisions of this section be treated as two persons.

[(3) Where the intestate and the intestate's husband or wife have died in circumstances rendering it uncertain which of them survived the other and the intestate's husband or wife is by virtue of section 184 of the Law of Property Act 1925, deemed to have survived the intestate, this section shall, nevertheless, have effect as respects the intestate as if the husband or wife has not survived the intestate.]

[(4) The interest payable on [the fixed net sum] payable to a surviving husband or wife shall be primarily payable out of income.]

Note: Section 46(2A) was inserted by section 1 Law Reform (Succession) Act 1995.

47. Statutory trusts in favour of issue and other classes of relatives of intestate

(1) Where under this Part of this Act the residuary estate of an intestate, or any part thereof, is directed to be held on the statutory trusts for the issue of the intestate, the same shall be held upon the following trusts, namely:—

(i) In trust, in equal shares if more than one, for all or any children or child of the intestate, living at the death of the intestate, who attain the age of [eighteen years] or marry under that age, and for all or any of the issue living at the death of the intestate who attain the age of [eighteen years] or marry under that age of any child of the intestate who predeceases the intestate, such issue to take through all degrees, according to their stocks, in equal shares if more than one, the share which their parent would have taken if living at the death of the intestate, and so that no issue shall take whose parent is living at the death of the intestate and so capable of taking;

(ii) The statutory power of advancement, and the statutory provisions which relate to maintenance and accumulation of surplus income, shall apply, but when an infant marries such infant shall be entitled to give valid receipts for the income of the infant's share or interest;

(iv) The personal representatives may permit any infant contingently interested to have the use and enjoyment of any personal chattels in such manner and subject to such conditions (if any) as the personal representatives may consider reasonable, and without being liable to account for any consequential loss.

(2) If the trusts in favour of the issue of the intestate fail by reason of no child or other issue attaining an absolutely vested interest—

(a) the residuary estate of the intestate and the income thereof and all statutory accumulations, if any, of the income thereof, or so much thereof as may not have been paid or applied under any power affecting the same, shall go, devolve and be held under the provisions of this Part of this Act as if the intestate had died without leaving issue living at the death of the intestate;

(b) references in this Part of this Act to the intestate 'leaving no issue' shall be construed as 'leaving no issue who attain an absolutely vested interest';

(c) references in this Part of this Act to the intestate 'leaving issue' or 'leaving a child or other issue' shall be construed as 'leaving issue who attain an absolutely vested interest.

(3) Where under this Part of this Act the residuary estate of an intestate or any part thereof is directed to be held on the statutory trusts for any class of relatives of the intestate, other than issue of the intestate, the same shall be held on trusts corresponding to the statutory trusts for the issue of the intestate (other than the provision for bringing any money or property into account) as if such trusts (other than as aforesaid) were repeated with the substitution of references to the members or member of that class for references to the children or child of the intestate.

[(4) References in paragraph (i) of subsection (1) of the last foregoing section to the intestate leaving, or not leaving, a member of the class consisting of brothers or sisters of the whole blood of the intestate and issue of brothers or sisters of the whole blood of the intestate shall be construed as references to the intestate leaving, or not leaving, a member of that class who attains an absolutely vested interest.]

(5) [. . .]

[47A. Right of surviving spouse to have own life interest redeemed

(1) Where a surviving husband or wife is entitled to a life interest in part of the residuary estate, and so elects, the personal representative shall purchase or redeem the life interest by paying the capital value thereof to the tenant for life, or the persons deriving title under the tenant for life, and the costs of the transaction; and thereupon the residuary estate of the intestate may be dealt with and distributed free from the life interest.

(2) [. . .]

(3) An election under this section shall only be exercisable if at the time of the election the whole of the said part of the residuary estate consists of property in possession, but, for the purposes of this section, a life interest in property partly in possession and partly not in possession may be treated as consisting of two separate life interests in those respective parts of the property.

[(3A) The capital value shall be reckoned in such manner as the Lord Chancellor may by order direct, and an order under this subsection may include transitional provisions.

(3B) The power to make orders under subsection (3A) above shall be exercisable by statutory instrument subject to annulment in pursuance of a resolution of either House of Parliament; and any such order may be varied or revoked by a subsequent order made under the power.]

(5) An election under this section shall be exercisable only within the period of twelve months from the date on which representation with respect to the estate of the intestate is first taken out:

Provided that if the surviving husband or wife satisfies the court that the limitation to the said period of twelve months will operate unfairly—

(a) in consequence of the representation first taken out being probate of a will subsequently revoked on the ground that the will was invalid or,

(b) in consequence of a question whether a person had an interest in the estate, or as to the nature of an interest in the estate, not having been determined at the time when representation was first taken out, or

(c) in consequence of some other circumstances affecting the administration or distribution of the estate,

the court may extend the said period.

(6) An election under this section shall be exercisable, except where the tenant for life is the sole personal representative, by notifying the personal representative (or, where there are two or more personal representatives of whom one is the tenant for life all of them except the tenant for life) in writing; and a notification in writing under this subsection shall not be revocable except with the consent of the personal representative.

(7) Where the tenant for life is the sole personal representative an election under this section shall not be effective unless written notice thereof is given to the [[Senior Registrar] of the Family Division of the High Court] within the period within which it must be made; and provision may be made by probate rules for keeping a record of such notices and making that record available to the public.

In this subsection the expression 'probate rules' means rules [of court made under section 127 of the Supreme Court Act 1981].

(8) An election under this section by a tenant for life who is an infant shall be as valid and binding as it would be if the tenant for life were of age; but the personal representative shall, instead of paying the capital value of the life interest to the tenant for life, deal with it in the same manner as with any other part of the residuary estate to which the tenant for life is absolutely entitled.

(9) In considering for the purposes of the foregoing provisions of this section the question when representation was first taken out, a grant limited to settled land or to trust property shall be left out of account and a grant limited to real estate or to personal estate shall be left out of account unless a grant limited to the remainder of the estate has previously been made or is made at the same time.]

48. Powers of personal representative in respect of interests of surviving spouse

(2) The personal representatives may raise—

(a) [the fixed net sum] or any part thereof and the interest thereon payable to the surviving husband or wife of the intestate on the security of the whole or any part of the residuary estate of the intestate (other than the personal chattels), so far as that estate may be sufficient for the purpose or the said sum and interest may not have been satisfied by an appropriation under the statutory power available in that behalf; and

(b) in like manner the capital sum, if any, required for the purchase or redemption of the life interest of the surviving husband or wife of the intestate, or any part thereof not satisfied by the application for that purpose of any part of the residuary estate of the intestate;

and in either case the amount, if any, properly required for the payment of the costs of the transaction.

49. Application to cases of partial intestacy

(1) Where any person dies leaving a will effectively disposing of part of his property, this Part of this Act shall have effect as respects the part of his property not so disposed of subject to the provisions contained in the will and subject to the following modifications:

[. . .]

(b) The personal representative shall, subject to his rights and powers for the purposes of administration, be a trustee for the persons entitled under this Part of this Act in respect of the part of the estate not expressly disposed of unless it appears by the will that the personal representative is intended to take such part beneficially.

(2)–(3) [. . .]

(4) The references in subsection (3) of section 47 A of this Act to property are references to property comprised in the residuary estate and, accordingly, where a will of the deceased creates a life interest in property in possession, and the remaining interest in that property forms part of the residuary estate, the said references are references to that remaining interest (which, until the life interest determines, is property not in possession).]

50. Construction of documents

(1) References to any Statutes of Distribution in an instrument inter vivos made or in a will coming into operation after the commencement of this Act, shall be construed as references to this Part of this Act; and references in such an instrument or will to statutory next of kin shall be construed, unless the context otherwise requires, as referring to the persons who would take beneficially on an intestacy under the foregoing provisions of this Part of this Act.

(2) Trusts declared in an instrument inter vivos made, or in a will coming into operation, before the commencement of this Act by reference to the Statutes of Distribution, shall, unless the contrary thereby appears, be construed as referring to the

enactments (other than the Intestates' Estates Act, 1890) relating to the distribution of effects of intestates which were in force immediately before the commencement of this Act.

[(3) In subsection (1) of this section the reference to this Part of this Act, or the foregoing provisions of this Part of this Act shall in relation to an instrument inter vivos made, or a will or codicil coming into operation after the coming into force of s. 18 of the Family Reform Act 1987 (but not in relation to instruments inter vivos made or wills or codicils coming into operation earlier) be construed as including references to that section.]

51. Savings

(1) Nothing in this Part of this Act affects the right of any person to take beneficially, by purchase, as heir either general or special.

(2) The foregoing provisions of this Part of this Act do not apply to any beneficial interest in real estate (not including chattels real) to which a [person of unsound mind] or defective living and of full age at the commencement of this Act, and unable, by reason of his incapacity, to make a will, who thereafter dies intestate in respect of such interest without having recovered his testamentary capacity, was entitled at his death, and any such beneficial interest (not being an interest ceasing on his death), shall, without prejudice to any will of the deceased, devolve in accordance with the general law in force before the commencement of this Act applicable to freehold land, and that law shall, notwithstanding any repeal, apply to the case.

For the purposes of this subsection, [a person of unsound mind] or defective who dies intestate as respects any beneficial interest in real estate shall not be deemed to have recovered his testamentary capacity unless his [. . .] receiver has been discharged.

(3) Where an infant dies after the commencement of this Act without having been married [and without issue], and independently of this subsection he would, at his death, have been equitably entitled under a [trust or] settlement (including a will) to a vested estate in fee simple or absolute interest in freehold land, or in any property [. . .] to devolve therewith or as freehold land, such infant shall be deemed to have had [a life interest], and the settlement shall be construed accordingly.

52. Interpretation of Part IV

In this Part of this Act 'real and personal estate' means every beneficial interest (including rights of entry and reverter) of the intestate in real and personal estate which (otherwise than in right of a power of appointment or of the testamentary power conferred by statute to dispose of entailed interests) he could, if of full age and capacity, have disposed of by his will [and references (however expressed) to any relationship between two persons shall be construed in accordance with section 1 of the Family Reform Act 1987.]

PART V
SUPPLEMENTAL

54. Application of Act

Save as otherwise expressly provided, this Act does not apply in any case where the death occurred before the commencement of this Act.

55. Definitions

In this Act, unless the context otherwise requires, the following expressions have the meanings hereby assigned to them respectively, that is to say:—

(1)(i) 'Administration' means, with reference to the real and personal estate of a deceased person, letters of administration, whether general or limited, or with the will annexed or otherwise:

(ii) 'Administrator' means a person to whom administration is granted:

(iii) 'Conveyance' includes a mortgage, charge by way of legal mortgage, lease, assent, vesting, declaration, vesting instrument, disclaimer, release and every other assurance of property or of an interest therein by any instrument, except a will, and 'convey' has a corresponding meaning, and 'disposition' includes a 'conveyance' also a devise bequest and an appointment of property contained in a will, and 'dispose of' has a corresponding meaning:

[(iiiA) 'the County Court limit', in relation to any enactment contained in this Act, means the amount for the time being specified by an Order in Council under section 145 of the County Courts Act 1984 as the county court limit for the purposes of that enactment (or, where no such Order in Council has been made, the corresponding limit specified by Order in Council under section 192 of the County Courts Act 1959);]

(iv) 'the Court' means the High Court, and also the county court, where that court has jurisdiction, [. . .]

(v) 'Income' includes rents and profits:

(vi) 'Intestate' includes a person who leaves a will but dies intestate as to some beneficial interest in his real or personal estate:

[(via) 'Land' has the same meaning as in the Law of Property Act 1925;]

(vii) 'Legal estates' mean the estates charges and interests in or over land (subsisting or created at law) which are by statute authorised to subsist or to be created at law; and 'equitable interests' mean all other interests and charges in or over land [. . .]:

(viii) ['Person of unsound mind'] includes a [person of unsound mind] whether so found or not, and in relation to a [person of unsound mind] not so found; [. . .], and 'defective' includes every person affected by the provisions of section one hundred and sixteen of the Lunacy Act, 1890, as extended by section sixty-four of the Mental Deficiency Act, 1913, and for whose benefit a receiver has been appointed:

(ix) 'Pecuniary legacy' includes an annuity, a general legacy, a demonstrative legacy so far as it is not discharged out of the designated property, and any other general direction by a testator for the payment of money, including all death duties free from which any devise, bequest, or payment is made to take effect:

(x) 'Personal chattels' mean carriages, horses, stable furniture and effects (not used for business purposes), motor cars and accessories (not used for business purposes), garden effects, domestic animals, plate, plated articles, linen, china, glass, books, pictures, prints, furniture, jewellery, articles of household or personal use or ornament, musical and scientific instruments and apparatus, wines, liquors and consumable stores, but do not include any chattels used at the death of the intestate for business purposes nor money or securities for money:

(xi) 'Personal representative' means the executor, original or by representation, or administrator for the time being of a deceased person, and as regards any liability for the payment of death duties includes any person who takes possession of or intermeddles with the property of a deceased person without the authority of the personal representatives or the court, and 'executor' includes a person deemed to be appointed executor as respects settled land:

(xii) 'Possession' includes the receipt of rents and profits or the right to receive the same, if any:

(xiii) 'Prescribed' means prescribed by rules of court [. . .]

(xiv) 'Probate' means the probate of a will:

(xvii) 'Property' includes a thing in action and any interest in real or personal property:

(xviii) 'Purchaser' means a lessee, mortgagee or other person who in good faith acquires an interest in property for valuable consideration, also an intending purchaser and 'valuable consideration' includes marriage, but does not include a nominal consideration in money:

(xix) 'Real estate', save as provided in Part IV of this Act means real estate, including chattels real, which by virtue of Part I of this Act devolves on the personal representative of a deceased person:

(xx) 'Representation' means the probate of a will and administration, and the expression 'taking out representation' refers to the obtaining of the probate of a will or of the grant of administration:

(xxi) 'Rent' includes a rent service or a rentcharge, or other rent, toll, duty, or annual or periodical payment in money or money's worth, issuing out of or charged upon land, but does not include mortgage interest, and 'rentcharge' includes a fee farm rent:

(xxiii) 'Securities' include stocks, funds, or shares:

(xxiv) 'Tenant for life,' 'statutory owner,' [. . .] 'settled land,' 'settlement,' 'trustees of the settlement,' 'term of years absolute,' 'death duties,' and 'legal mortgage,' have the same meanings as in the Settled Land Act, 1925, and 'entailed interest' and 'charge by way of legal mortgage' have the same meanings as in the Law of Property Act, 1925.

(xxv) 'Treasury solicitor' means the solicitor for the affairs of His Majesty's Treasury, and includes the solicitor for the affairs of the Duchy of Lancaster:

(xxvi) 'Trust corporation' means the public trustee or a corporation either appointed by the court in any particular case to be a trustee or entitled by rules made under subsection (3) of section four of the Public Trustee Act, 1906, to act as custodian trustee:

(xxvii) [. . .]

(xxviii) 'Will' includes codicil.

(2) References to a child or issue living at the death of any person include a child or issue enventre sa mere at the death.

(3) References to the estate of a deceased person include property over which the deceased exercises a general power of appointment (including the statutory power to dispose of entailed interests) by his will.

SCHEDULES

Section 34

FIRST SCHEDULE

PART I

RULES AS TO PAYMENT OF DEBTS WHERE THE ESTATE IS INSOLVENT[1]

Note

[1]See Insolvency Act 1986, s. 42 1, post and also the Administration of Insolvent Estates of Deceased Persons Order 1986 (SI 1986 No. 1999).

PART II

ORDER OF APPLICATION OF ASSETS WHERE THE ESTATE IS SOLVENT

1. Property of the deceased undisposed of by will, subject to the retention thereout of a fund sufficient to meet any pecuniary legacies.

2. Property of the deceased not specifically devised or bequeathed but included (either by a specific or general description) in a residuary gift, subject to the retention out of such property of a fund sufficient to meet any pecuniary legacies, so far as not provided for as aforesaid.

3. Property of the deceased specifically appropriated or devised or bequeathed (either by a specific or general description) for the payment of debts.

4. Property of the deceased charged with, or devised or bequeathed (either by a specific or general description) subject to a charge for the payment of debts.

5. The fund, if any, retained to meet pecuniary legacies.

6. Property specifically devised or bequeathed, rateably according to value.

7. Property appointed by will under a general power, including the statutory power to dispose of entailed interests, rateably according to value.

8. The following provisions shall also apply—

(a) The order of application may be varied by the will of the deceased.

Note: Sections 22(1A), (1B), (1C), (1D) and (1E) were added by section 22 Landlord & Tenant (Covenants) Act 1995.

LAW OF PROPERTY (AMENDMENT) ACT 1926
(1926, c. 11)

1. Conveyances of legal estates subject to certain interests

(1) Nothing in the Settled Land Act, 1925, shall prevent a person on whom the powers of a tenant for life are conferred by paragraph (ix) of subsection (1) of section twenty of that Act from conveying or creating a legal estate subject to a prior interest as if the land had not been settled land.

(2) In any of the following cases, namely—

(a) where a legal estate has been conveyed or created under subsection one of this section, or under section sixteen of the Settled Land Act, 1925, subject to any prior interest, or

(b) where before the first day of January, nineteen hundred and twenty-six, land has been conveyed to a purchaser for money or money's worth subject to any prior interest whether or not on the purchase the land was expressed to be exonerated from, or the grantor agreed to indemnify the purchaser against, such prior interest, the estate owner for the time being of the land subject to such prior interest may, notwithstanding any provision contained in the Settled Land Act, 1925, but without prejudice to any power whereby such prior interest is capable of being overreached, convey or create a legal estate subject to such prior interest as if the instrument creating the prior interest was not an instrument or one of the instruments constituting a settlement of the land.

(3) In this section 'interest' means an estate, interest, charge or power of charging subsisting, or capable of arising or of being exercised, under a settlement, and, where a prior interest arises under the exercise of a power, 'instrument' includes both the instrument conferring the power and the instrument exercising it.

3. Meaning of 'trust corporation'

(1) For the purposes of the Law of Property Act, 1925, the Settled Land Act, 1925, the Trustee Act, 1925, the Administration of Estates Act, 1925, and the [Supreme Court Act 1981], the expression 'Trust Corporation' includes the Treasury Solicitor, the Official Solicitor and any person holding any other official position prescribed by the Lord Chancellor, and, in relation to the property of a bankrupt and property subject to a deed of arrangement, includes the trustee in bankruptcy and the trustee under the deed respectively, and, in relation to charitable ecclesiastical and public trusts, also includes any local or public authority so prescribed, and any other corporation constituted under the laws of the United Kingdom or any part thereof which satisfies the Lord Chancellor that it undertakes the administration of any such trusts without remuneration, or that by its constitution it is required to apply the whole of its net income after payment of outgoings for charitable, ecclesiastical or public purposes, and is prohibited from distributing, directly or indirectly, any part thereof by way of profits amongst any of its members, and is authorised by him to act in relation to such trusts as a trust corporation.

(2) For the purposes of this provision, the expression 'Treasury Solicitor' means the solicitor for the affairs of His Majesty's Treasury, and includes the solicitor for the affairs of the Duchy of Lancaster.

LANDLORD AND TENANT ACT 1927
(1927, c. 36)

18. Provisions as to covenants to repair

(1) Damages for a breach of a covenant or agreement to keep or put premises in repair during the currency of a lease, or to leave or put premises in repair at the termination of a lease, whether such covenant or agreement is expressed or implied, and whether general or specific, shall in no case exceed the amount (if any) by which the value of the reversion (whether immediate or not) in the premises is diminished owing to the breach of such covenant or agreement as aforesaid; and in particular no damage shall be recovered for a breach of any such covenant or agreement to leave or put premises in repair at the termination of a lease, if it is shown that the premises, in whatever state of repair they might be, would at or shortly after the termination of the tenancy have been or be pulled down, or such structural alterations made therein as would render valueless the repairs covered by the covenant or agreement.

(2) A right of re-entry or forfeiture for a breach of any such covenant or agreement as aforesaid shall not be enforceable, by action or otherwise, unless the lessor proves that the fact that such a notice as is required by section one hundred and forty-six of the Law of Property Act, 1925, had been served on the lessee was known either—

(a) to the lessee; or

(b) to an under-lessee holding under an under-lease which reserved a nominal reversion only to the lessee; or

(c) to the person who last paid the rent due under the lease either on his own behalf or as agent for the lessee or under-lessee;

and that a time reasonably sufficient to enable the repairs to be executed had elapsed since the time when the fact of the service of the notice came to the knowledge of any such person.

Where a notice has been sent by registered post addressed to a person at his last known place of abode in the United Kingdom, then, for the purposes of this subsection, that person shall be deemed, unless the contrary is proved, to have had knowledge of the fact that the notice had been served as from the time at which the letter would have been delivered in the ordinary course of post.

This subsection shall be construed as one with section one hundred and forty-six of the Law of Property Act, 1925.

(3) This section applies whether the lease was created before or after the commencement of this Act.

19. Provisions as to covenants not to assign, etc. without licence or consent

(1) In all leases whether made before or after the commencement of this Act containing a covenant condition or agreement against assigning, underletting, charging or parting with the possession of demised premises or any part thereof without licence or consent, such covenant condition or agreement shall, notwithstanding any express provision to the contrary, be deemed to be subject—

(a) to a proviso to the effect that such licence or consent is not to be unreasonably withheld, but this proviso does not preclude the right of the landlord to require payment of a reasonable sum in respect of any legal or other expenses incurred in connection with such licence or consent; and

(b) (if the lease is for more than forty years, and is made in consideration wholly or partially of the erection, or the substantial improvement, addition or alteration of buildings, and the lessor is not a Government department or local or public authority, or a statutory or public utility company) to a proviso to the effect that in the case of any assignment, under-letting, charging or parting with the possession (whether by the holders of the lease or any under-tenant whether immediate or not) effected more than seven years before the end of the term no consent or licence shall be required, if notice in writing of the transaction is given to the lessor within six months after the transaction is effected.

[(1A) Where the landlord and the tenant under a qualifying lease have entered into an agreement specifying for the purposes of this subsection—

(a) any circumstances in which the landlord may withhold his licence or consent to an assignment of the demised premises or any part of them, or

(b) any conditions subject to which any such licence or consent may be granted, then the landlord—

(i) shall not be regarded as unreasonably withholding his licence or consent to any such assignment if he withholds it on the ground (and it is the case) that any such circumstances exist, and

(ii) if he gives any such licence or consent subject to any such conditions, shall not be regarded as giving it subject to unreasonable conditions;

and section 1 of the Landlord and Tenant Act 1988 (qualified duty to consent to assignment etc.) shall have effect subject to the provisions of this subsection.

(1B) Subsection (1A) of this section applies to such an agreement as is mentioned in that subsection—

(a) whether it is contained in the lease or not, and

(b) whether it is made at the time when the lease is granted or at any other time falling before the application for the landlord's licence or consent is made.

(1C) Subsection (1A) shall not, however, apply to any such agreement to the extent that any circumstances or conditions specified in it are framed by reference to any matter falling to be determined by the landlord or by any other person for the purposes of the agreement, unless under the terms of the agreement—

(a) that person's power to determine that matter is required to be exercised reasonably, or

(b) the tenant is given an unrestricted right to have any such determination reviewed by a person independent of both landlord and tenant whose identity is ascertainable by reference to the agreement,

and in the latter case the agreement provides for the determination made by any such independent person on the review to be conclusive as to the matter in question.

(1D) In its application to a qualifying lease, subsection (1)(b) of this section shall not have effect in relation to any assignment of the lease.

(1E) In subsections (1A) and (1D) of this section—

(a) 'qualifying lease' means any lease which is a new tenancy for the purposes of section 1 of the Landlord and Tenant (Covenants) Act 1995 other than a residential lease, namely a lease by which a building or part of a building is let wholly or mainly as a single private residence; and

(b) references to assignment include parting with possession on assignment.]

(2) In all leases whether made before or after the commencement of this Act containing a covenant condition or agreement against the making of improvements without a licence or consent, such covenant condition or agreement shall be deemed, notwithstanding any express provision to the contrary, to be subject to a proviso that such licence or consent is not to be unreasonably withheld; but this proviso does not preclude the right to require as a condition of such licence or consent the payment of a reasonable sum in respect of any damage to or diminution in the value of the premises or any neighbouring premises belonging to the landlord, and of any legal or other expenses properly incurred in connection with such licence or consent nor, in the case of an improvement which does not add to the letting value of the holding, does it preclude the right to require as a condition of such licence or consent, where such a requirement would be reasonable, an undertaking on the part of the tenant to reinstate the premises in the condition in which they were before the improvement was executed.

(3) In all leases whether made before or after the commencement of this Act containing a covenant condition or agreement against the alteration of the user of the demised premises, without licence or consent, such covenant condition or agreement shall, if the alteration does not involve any structural alteration of the premises, be deemed, notwithstanding any express provision to the contrary, to be subject to a proviso that no fine or sum of money in the nature of a fine, whether by way of increase of rent or otherwise, shall be payable for or in respect of such licence or consent; but this proviso does not preclude the right of the landlord to require payment of a reasonable sum in respect of any damage to or diminution in the value of the premises or any neighbouring premises belonging to him and of legal or other expenses incurred in connection with such licence or consent.

Where a dispute as to the reasonableness of any such sum has been determined by a court of competent jurisdiction, the landlord shall be bound to grant the licence or consent on payment of the sum so determined to be reasonable.

(4) This section shall not apply to leases of agricultural holdings within the meaning of the [Agricultural Holdings Act, 1986], [which are leases in relation to which the Act applies, or to farm business tenancies within the meaning of the Agricultural Tenancies Act 1995] and paragraph (b) of subsection (1), subsection (2) and subsection (3) of this section shall not apply to mining leases.

Note: Sections 19(1A), (1B), (1C), D, and (1E) were added by section 22 Landord and Tenant (Covenants) Act 1995.

LAW OF PROPERTY (ENTAILED INTERESTS) ACT 1932
(1932, c. 27)

2. Definition of rent charge

For removing doubt it is hereby declared that a rent charge (not being a rent charge limited to take effect in remainder after or expectant on the failure or determination of some other interest) is a rent charge in possession within the meaning of paragraph (b) of subsection (2) of section one of the Law of Property Act, 1925, notwithstanding that the payments in respect thereof are limited to commence or accrue at some time subsequent to its creation.

LEASEHOLD PROPERTY (REPAIRS) ACT 1938
(1938, c. 34)

1. Restriction on enforcement of repairing covenants in long leases of small houses

(1) Where a lessor serves on a lessee under subsection (1) of section one hundred and forty-six of the Law of Property Act, 1925, a notice that relates to a breach of a covenant or agreement to keep or put in repair during the currency of the lease [all or any of the property comprised in the lease], and at the date of the service of the notice [three] years or more of the term of the lease remain unexpired, the lessee may within twenty-eight days from that date serve on the lessor a counter-notice to the effect that he claims the benefit of this Act.

(2) A right to damages for a breach of such a covenant as aforesaid shall not be enforceable by action commenced at any time at which [three] years or more of the term of the lease remain unexpired unless the lessor has served on the lessee not less than one month before the commencement of the action such a notice as is specified in subsection (1) of section one hundred and forty-six of the Law of Property Act, 1925, and where a notice is served under this subsection, the lessee may, within twenty-eight days from the date of the service thereof, serve on the lessor a counter-notice to the effect that he claims the benefit of this Act.

(3) Where a counter-notice is served by a lessee under this section, then, notwithstanding anything in any enactment or rule of law, no proceedings, by action or otherwise, shall be taken by the lessor for the enforcement of any right of re-entry or forfeiture under any proviso or stipulation in the lease for breach of the covenant or agreement in question, or for damages for breach thereof, otherwise than with the leave of the court.

(4) A notice served under subsection (1) of section one hundred and forty-six of the Law of Property Act, 1925, in the circumstances specified in subsection (1) of this section, and a notice served under subsection (2) of this section shall not be valid unless it contains a statement, in characters not less conspicuous than those used in any other part of the notice, to the effect that the lessee is entitled under this Act to serve on the lessor a counter-notice claiming the benefit of this Act, and a statement in the like characters specifying the time within which, and the manner in which, under this Act a counter-notice may be served and specifying the name and address for service of the lessor.

(5) Leave for the purposes of this section shall not be given unless the lessor proves—

(a) that the immediate remedying of the breach in question is requisite for preventing substantial diminution in the value of his reversion, or that the value thereof has been substantially diminished by the breach;

(b) that the immediate remedying of the breach is required for giving effect in relation to the [premises] to the purposes of any enactment, or of any byelaw or other provision having effect under an enactment, [or for giving effect to any order of a court or requirement of any authority under any enactment or any such byelaw or other provision as aforesaid];

(c) in a case in which the lessee is not in occupation of the whole of the [premises as respects which the covenant or agreement is proposed to be enforced], that the immediate remedying of the breach is required in the interests of the occupier of [those premises] or of part thereof;

(d) that the breach can be immediately remedied at an expense that is relatively small in comparison with the much greater expense that would probably be occasioned by postponement of the necessary work; or

(e) special circumstances which in the opinion of the court, render it just and equitable that leave should be given.

(6) The court may, in granting or in refusing leave for the purposes of this section, impose such terms and conditions on the lessor or on the lessee as it may think fit.

3. Saving for obligation to repair on taking possession

This Act shall not apply to a breach of a covenant or agreement in so far as it imposes on the lessee an obligation to put [premises] in repair that is to be performed upon the lessee taking possession of the premises or within a reasonable time thereafter.

7. Application of certain provisions of 15 & 16 Geo. 5 c. 20

(1) In this Act the expressions 'lessor,' 'lessee' and 'lease' have the meanings assigned to them respectively by sections one hundred and forty-six and one hundred and fifty-four of the Law of Property Act, 1925, except that they do not include any reference to such a grant as is mentioned in the said section one hundred and forty-six, or to the person making, or to the grantee under such a grant, or to persons deriving title under such a person; and 'lease' means a lease for a term of [seven years or more, not being a lease of an agricultural holding within the meaning of the [Agricultural Holdings Act, 1986]].

(2) The provisions of section one hundred and ninety-six of the said Act (which relate to the service of notices) shall extend to notices and counter-notices required or authorised by this Act.

INTESTATES' ESTATES ACT 1952
(1952, c. 64)

AMENDMENTS OF LAW OF INTESTATE SUCCESSION

5. Rights of surviving spouse as respects the matrimonial home

The Second Schedule to this Act shall have effect for enabling the surviving husband or wife of a person dying intestate after the commencement of this Act to acquire the matrimonial home.

SECOND SCHEDULE
RIGHTS OF SURVIVING SPOUSE AS RESPECTS THE MATRIMONIAL HOME

1.—(1) Subject to the provisions of this Schedule, where the residuary estate of the intestate comprises an interest in a dwelling-house in which the surviving husband or wife was resident at the time of the intestate's death, the surviving husband or wife may require the personal representative, in exercise of the power conferred by section forty-one of the principal Act (and with due regard to the requirements of that section as to valuation) to appropriate the said interest in the dwelling-house in or towards satisfaction of any absolute interest of the surviving husband or wife in the real and personal estate of the intestate.

(2) The right conferred by this paragraph shall not be exercisable where the interest is—

(a) a tenancy which at the date of the death of the intestate was a tenancy which would determine within the period of two years from that date; or

(b) a tenancy which the landlord by notice given after that date could determine within the remainder of that period.

(3) Nothing in subsection (5) of section forty-one of the principal Act (which requires the personal representative, in making an appropriation to any person under that section, to have regard to the rights of others) shall prevent the personal representative from giving effect to the right conferred by this paragraph.

(4) The reference in this paragraph to an absolute interest in the real and personal estate of the intestate includes a reference to the capital value of a life interest which the surviving husband or wife has under this Act elected to have redeemed.

(5) Where part of a building was, at the date of the death of the intestate, occupied as a separate dwelling, that dwelling shall for the purposes of this Schedule be treated as a dwelling-house.

2.—where—

(a) the dwelling-house forms part of a building and an interest in the whole of the building is comprised in the residuary estate; or

(b) the dwelling-house is held with agricultural land and an interest in the agricultural land is comprised in the residuary estate; or

(c) the whole or a part of the dwelling-house was at the time of the intestate's death used as a hotel or lodging house; or

(d) a part of the dwelling-house was at the time of the intestate's death used for purposes other than domestic purposes,

the right conferred by paragraph 1 of this Schedule shall not be exercisable unless the court, on being satisfied that the exercise of that right is not likely to diminish the value of assets in the residuary estate (other than the said interest in the dwelling-house) or make them more difficult to dispose of, so orders.

3.—(1) The right conferred by paragraph 1 of this Schedule—

(a) shall not be exercisable after the expiration of twelve months from the first taking out of representation with respect to the intestate's estate;

(b) shall not be exercisable after the death of the surviving husband or wife;

(c) shall be exercisable, except where the surviving husband or wife is the sole personal representative, by notifying the personal representative (or, where there are two or more personal representatives of whom one is the surviving husband or wife, all of them except the surviving husband or wife) in writing.

(2) A notification in writing under paragraph (c) of the foregoing subparagraph shall not be revocable except with the consent of the personal representative; but the surviving husband or wife may require the personal representative to have the said interest in the dwelling-house valued in accordance with section forty-one of the principal Act and to inform him or her of the result of that valuation before he or she decides whether to exercise the right.

(3) Subsection (9) of the section forty-seven A added to the principal Act by section two of this Act shall apply for the purposes of the construction of the reference in this paragraph to the first taking out of representation, and the proviso to subsection (5) of that section shall apply for the purpose of enabling the surviving husband or wife to apply for an extension of the period of twelve months mentioned in this paragraph.

4.—(1) During the period of twelve months mentioned in paragraph 3 of this Schedule the personal representative shall not without the written consent of the surviving husband or wife sell or otherwise dispose of the said interest in the dwelling-house except in the course of administration owing to want of other assets.

(2) An application to the court under paragraph 2 of this Schedule may be made by the personal representative as well as by the surviving husband or wife, and if, on an application under that paragraph, the court does not order that the right conferred by paragraph 1 of this Schedule shall be exercisable by the surviving husband or wife, the court may authorise the personal representative to dispose of the said interest in the dwelling-house within the said period of twelve months.

(3) Where the court under sub-paragraph (3) of paragraph 3 of this Schedule extends the said period of twelve months, the court may direct that this paragraph shall apply in relation to the extended period as it applied in relation to the original period of twelve months.

(4) This paragraph shall not apply where the surviving husband or wife is the sole personal representative or one of two or more personal representatives.

(5) Nothing in this paragraph shall confer any right on the surviving husband or wife as against a purchaser from the personal representative.

5.—(1) Where the surviving husband or wife is one of two or more personal representatives, the rule that a trustee may not be a purchaser of trust property shall not prevent the surviving husband or wife from purchasing out of the estate of the intestate an interest in a dwelling-house in which the surviving husband or wife was resident at the time of the intestate's death.

(2) The power of appropriation under section forty-one of the principal Act shall include power to appropriate an interest in a dwelling-house in which the surviving husband or wife was resident at the time of the intestate's death partly in satisfaction of an interest of the surviving husband or wife in the real and personal estate of the intestate and partly in return for a payment of money by the surviving husband or wife to the personal representative.

6.—(1) Where the surviving husband or wife is a person of unsound mind or a defective, a requirement or consent under this Schedule may be made or given on his or her behalf by the committee or receiver, if any, or, where there is no committee or receiver, by the court.

(2) A requirement or consent made or given under this Schedule by a surviving husband or wife who is an infant shall be as valid and binding as it would be if he or she were of age and, as respects an appropriation in pursuance of paragraph 1 of this Schedule, the provisions of section forty-one of the principal Act as to obtaining the

consent of the infant's parent or guardian, or of the court on behalf of the infant, shall not apply.

7.—(1) Except where the context otherwise requires, references in this Schedule to a dwelling-house include references to any garden or portion of ground attached to and usually occupied with the dwelling-house or otherwise required for the amenity or convenience of the dwelling-house.

(2) . . .

CHARITABLE TRUSTS (VALIDATION) ACT 1954
(1954, c. 58)

1. Validation and modification of imperfect trust instruments

(1) In this Act, 'imperfect trust provision' means any provision declaring the objects for which property is to be held or applied, and so describing those objects that, consistently with the terms of the provision, the property could be used exclusively for charitable purposes, but could nevertheless be used for purposes which are not charitable.

(2) Subject to the following provisions of this Act, any imperfect trust provision contained in an instrument taking effect before the sixteenth day of December, nineteen hundred and fifty-two, shall have, and be deemed to have had, effect in relation to any disposition or covenant to which this Act applies—

(a) as respects the period before the commencement of this Act, as if the whole of the declared objects were charitable; and

(b) as respects the period after that commencement as if the provision had required the property to be held or applied for the declared objects in so far only as they authorise use for charitable purposes.

(3) A document inviting gifts of property to be held or applied for objects declared by the document shall be treated for the purposes of this section as an instrument taking effect when it is first issued.

(4) In this Act, 'covenant' includes any agreement, whether under seal or not, and 'covenantor' is to be construed accordingly.

2. Dispositions and covenants to which the Act applies

(1) Subject to the next following subsection, this Act applies to any disposition of property to be held or applied for objects declared by an imperfect trust provision, and to any covenant to make such a disposition, where apart from this Act the disposition or covenant is invalid under the law of England and Wales, but would be valid if the objects were exclusively charitable.

(2) This Act does not apply to a disposition if before the sixteenth day of December, nineteen hundred and fifty-two, property comprised in, or representing that comprised in, the disposition in question or another disposition made for the objects declared by the same imperfect trust provision, or income arising from any such property, has been paid or conveyed to, or applied for the benefit of, the persons entitled by reason of the invalidity of the disposition in question or of such other disposition as aforesaid, as the case may be.

(3) A disposition in settlement or other disposition creating more than one interest in the same property shall be treated for the purposes of this Act as a separate disposition in relation to each of the interests created.

3. Savings for adverse claims, etc.

(1) Subject to the next following subsection, where a disposition to which this Act applies was made before, and is not confirmed after, the commencement of this Act, the foregoing sections shall not prejudice a person's right, by reason of the invalidity of the disposition, to property comprised in, or representing that comprised in, the disposition as against the persons administering the imperfect trust provision or the

persons on whose behalf they do so, unless the right accrued to him or some person through whom he claims more than six years before the sixteenth day of December, nineteen hundred and fifty-two; but the persons administering the imperfect trust provision, and any trustee for them or for the persons on whose behalf they do so, shall be entitled, as against a person whose right to the property is saved by this subsection, to deal with the property as if this subsection had not been passed, unless they have express notice of a claim by him to enforce his right to the property.

(2) No proceedings shall be begun by any person to enforce his right to any property by virtue of the foregoing subsection after the expiration of one year beginning with the date of the passing of this Act or the date when the right first accrues to him or to some person through whom he claims, whichever is the later, unless the right (before of after its accrual) either—

(a) has been concealed by the fraud of some person administering the imperfect trust provision or his agent, or

(b) has been acknowledged by some such person or his agent by means of a written acknowledgement given to the person having the right or his agent and signed by the person making it, or by means of a payment or transfer of property in respect of the right; and if the period prescribed by this subsection for any person to bring proceedings to recover any property expires without his having recovered the property or begun proceedings to do so, his title to the property shall be extinguished.

This subsection shall not be taken as extending the time for bringing any proceedings beyond the period of limitation prescribed by any other enactment.

(3) For the purposes of the foregoing subsections, a right by reason of the invalidity of a disposition to property comprised in, or representing that comprised in, the disposition shall not be deemed to accrue to anyone so long as he is under a disability or has a future interest only, or so long as the disposition is subject to another disposition made by the same person, and the whole of the property or the income arising from it is held or applied for the purposes of that other disposition.

(4) [Subsections (2) to (6) of section thirty-eight of the Limitation Act 1980] (which define the circumstances in which, for the purposes of that Act, a person is to be deemed to be under a disability or to claim through another person), shall apply for the purposes of the foregoing subsections as they apply for the purposes of that Act.

(5) Where subsection (1) of this section applies to save a person's right to property comprised in, or representing that comprised in, a disposition, or would have so applied but for some dealing with the property by persons administering the imperfect trust provision, or by any trustee for them or for the persons on whose behalf they do so, the foregoing sections shall not prejudice the first-mentioned person's right by virtue of his interest in the property to damages or other relief in respect of any dealing with the property by any person administering the imperfect trust provision or by any such trustee as aforesaid, if the person dealing with the property had at the time express notice of a claim by him to enforce his right to the property.

(6) A covenant entered into before the commencement of this Act shall not be enforceable by virtue of this Act unless confirmed by the covenantor after that commencement, but a disposition made in accordance with such a covenant shall be treated for the purposes of this Act as confirming the covenant and any previous disposition made in accordance with it.

RECREATIONAL CHARITIES ACT 1958
(1958, c. 17)

1. General provision as to recreational and similar trusts, etc.

(1) Subject to the provisions of this Act, it shall be and be deemed always to have been charitable to provide, or assist in the provision of, facilities for recreation or other leisure-time occupation, if the facilities are provided in the interests of social welfare:

Provided that nothing in this section shall be taken to derogate from the principle that a trust or institution to be charitable must be for the public benefit.

(2) The requirement of the foregoing subsection that the facilities are provided in the interests of social welfare shall not be treated as satisfied unless—

(a) the facilities are provided with the object of improving the conditions of life for the persons for whom the facilities are primarily intended; and

(b) either—

(i) those persons have need of such facilities as aforesaid by reason of their youth, age, infirmity or disablement, poverty or social and economic circumstances; or

(ii) the facilities are to be available to the members or female members of the public at large.

(3) Subject to the said requirement, subsection (1) of this section applies in particular to the provision of facilities at village halls, community centres and women's institutes, and to the provision and maintenance of grounds and buildings to be used for purposes of recreation or leisure-time occupation, and extends to the provision of facilities for those purposes by the organising of any activity.

2. Miners' welfare trust

(1) Where trusts declared before the seventeenth day of December, nineteen hundred and fifty-seven, required or purported to require property to be held for the purpose of activities which are social welfare activities within the meaning of the Miners' Welfare Act 1952 and at that date the whole or part of the property held on those trusts or of any property held with that property represented an application of moneys standing to the credit of the miners' welfare fund or moneys provided by the Coal Industry Social Welfare Organisation, those trusts shall be treated as if they were and always had been charitable.

(2) For the purposes of this section property held on the same trusts as other property shall be deemed to be held with it, though vested in different trustees.

3. Savings and other provisions as to past transactions

(1) Nothing in this Act shall be taken to restrict the purposes which are to be regarded as charitable independently of this Act.

(2)–(5) . . .

VARIATION OF TRUSTS ACT 1958
(1958, c. 53)

1. Jurisdiction of courts to vary trusts

(1) Where property, whether real or personal, is held on trusts arising, whether before or after the passing of this Act, under any will, settlement or other disposition, the court may if it thinks fit by order approve on behalf of—

(a) any person having, directly or indirectly, an interest, whether vested or contingent, under the trusts who by reason of infancy or other incapacity is incapable of assenting, or

(b) any person (whether ascertained or not) who may become entitled, directly or indirectly, to an interest under the trusts as being at a future date or on the happening of a future event a person of any specified description or a member of any specified class of persons, so however that this paragraph shall not include any person who would be of that description, or a member of that class, as the case may be, if the said date had fallen or the said event had happened at the date of the application to the court, or

(c) any person unborn, or

(d) any person in respect of any discretionary interest of his under protective trusts where the interest of the principal beneficiary has not failed or determined,

any arrangement (by whomsoever proposed, and whether or not there is any other person beneficially interested who is capable of assenting thereto) varying or revoking all or any of the trusts, or enlarging the powers of the trustees of managing or administering any of the property subject to the trusts:

Provided that except by virtue of paragraph (d) of this subsection the court shall not approve an arrangement on behalf of any person unless the carrying out thereof would be for the benefit of that person.

(2) In the foregoing subsection 'protective trusts' means the trusts specified in paragraphs (i) and (ii) of subsection (1) of section thirty-three of the Trustee Act, 1925, or any like trusts, 'the principal beneficiary' has the same meaning as in the said subsection (1) and 'discretionary interest' means an interest arising under the trust specified in paragraph (ii) of the said subsection (1) or any like trust.

(3) [. . .] the jurisdiction conferred by subsection (1) of this section shall be exercisable by the High Court, except that the question whether the carrying out of any arrangement would be for the benefit of a person falling within paragraph (a) of the said subsection (1) shall be determined by order of [the authority having jurisdiction under [Part VII of the Mental Health Act, 1983], if that person is a patient within the meaning of the said Part VII].

(4) [. . .]

(5) Nothing in the foregoing provisions of this section shall apply to trusts affecting property settled by Act of Parliament.

(6) Nothing in this section shall be taken to limit the powers conferred by section sixty-four of the Settled Land Act, 1925, section fifty-seven of the Trustee Act, 1925, or [the powers of the authority having jurisdiction under Part VII of the Mental Health Act, 1983].

RIGHTS OF LIGHT ACT 1959
(1959, c. 56)

2. Registration of notice in lieu of obstruction of access of light

(1) For the purpose of preventing the access and use of light from being taken to be enjoyed without interruption, any person who is an owner of land (in this and the next following section referred to as 'the servient land') over which light passes to a dwelling-house, workshop or other building (in this and the next following section referred to as 'the dominant building') may apply to the local authority in whose area the dominant building is situated for the registration of a notice under this section.

(2) An application for the registration of a notice under this section shall be in the prescribed form and shall—

(a) identify the servient land and the dominant building in the prescribed manner, and

(b) state that the registration of a notice in pursuance of the application is intended to be equivalent to the obstruction of the access of light to the dominant building across the servient land which would be caused by the erection, in such position on the servient land as may be specified in the application, of an opaque structure of such dimensions (including, if the application so states, unlimited height) as may be so specified.

(3) Any such application shall be accompanied by one or other of the following certificates issued by the Lands Tribunal, that is to say,—

(a) a certificate certifying that adequate notice of the proposed application has been given to all persons who, in the circumstances existing at the time when the certificate is issued, appear to the Lands Tribunal to be persons likely to be affected by the registration of a notice in pursuance of the application;

(b) a certificate certifying that, in the opinion of the Lands Tribunal, the case is one of exceptional urgency, and that accordingly a notice should be registered forthwith as a temporary notice for such period as may be specified in the certificate.

(4) Where application is duly made to a local authority for the registration of a notice under this section, it shall be the duty of [that authority to register the notice in the appropriate local land charges register, and—

(a) any notice so registered under this section shall be a local land charge; but

(b) section 5(1) and (2) and section 10 of the Local Land Charges Act 1975 shall not apply in relation thereto.]

3. Effect of registered notice and proceedings relating thereto

(1) Where, in pursuance of an application made in accordance with the last preceding section, a notice is registered thereunder, then, for the purpose of determining whether any person is entitled (by virtue of the Prescription Act, 1832, or otherwise) to a right to the access of light to the dominant building across the servient land, the access of light to that building across that land shall be treated as obstructed to the same extent, and with the like consequences, as if an opaque structure, of the dimensions specified in the application,—

(a) had, on the date of registration of the notice, been erected in the position on the servient land specified in the application, and had been so erected by the person who made the application, and

(b) had remained in that position during the period for which the notice has effect and had been removed at the end of that period.

(2) For the purposes of this section a notice registered under the last preceding section shall be taken to have effect until either—

(a) the registration is cancelled, or

(b) the period of one year beginning with the date of registration of the notice expires, or

(c) in the case of a notice registered in pursuance of an application accompanied by a certificate issued under paragraph (b) of subsection (3) of the last preceding section, the period specified in the certificate expires without such a further certificate as is mentioned in paragraph (c) of subsection (5) of that section having before the end of that period been lodged with the local authority,

and shall cease to have effect on the occurrence of any one of those events.

(3) Subject to the following provisions of this section, any person who, if such a structure as is mentioned in subsection (1) of this section had been erected as therein mentioned, would have had a right of action in any court in respect of that structure, on the grounds that he was entitled to a right to the access of light to the dominant building across the servient land, and that the said right was infringed by that structure, shall have the like right of action in that court in respect of the registration of a notice under the last preceding section:

Provided that an action shall not be begun by virtue of this subsection after the notice in question has ceased to have effect.

(4) Where, at any time during the period for which a notice registered under the last preceding section has effect, the circumstances are such that, if the access of light to the dominant building had been enjoyed continuously from a date one year earlier than the date on which the enjoyment thereof in fact began, a person would have had a right of action in any court by virtue of the last preceding subsection in respect of the registration of the notice, that person shall have the like right of action in that court by virtue of this subsection in respect of the registration of the notice.

(5) The remedies available to the plaintiff in an action brought by virtue of subsection (3) or subsection (4) of this section (apart from any order as to costs) shall be such declaration as the court may consider appropriate in the circumstances, and an order directing the registration of the notice to be cancelled or varied, as the court may determine.

(6) For the purposes of section four of the Prescriptions Act, 1832 (under which a period of enjoyment of any of the rights to which that Act applies is not to be treated

as interrupted except by a matter submitted to or acquiesced in for one year after notice thereof)—

(a) as from the date of registration of a notice under the last preceding section, all persons interested in the dominant building or any part thereof shall be deemed to have notice of the registration thereof and of the person on whose application it was registered;

(b) until such time as an action is brought by virtue of subsection (3) or subsection (4) of this section in respect of the registration of a notice under the last preceding section, all persons interested in the dominant building or any part thereof shall be deemed to acquiesce in the obstruction which, in accordance with subsection (1) of this section, is to be treated as resulting from the registration of the notice;

(c) as from the date on which such an action is brought, no person shall be treated as submitting to or acquiescing in that obstruction.

Provided that if, in any such action, the court decides against the claim of the plaintiff, the court may direct that the preceding provisions of this subsection shall apply in relation to the notice as if that action had not been brought.

7. Interpretation

(1) In this Act, except in so far as the context otherwise requires, the following expressions have the meanings hereby assigned to them respectively, that is to say:—

'action' includes a counterclaim, and any reference to the plaintiff in an action shall be construed accordingly;

['local authority', in relation to land in a district or London Borough, means the council of the borough or district, and, in relation to land in the City of London, means the Common Council of the City;]

'owner', in relation to any land, means a person who is the estate owner in respect of the fee simple thereof, or is entitled to a tenancy thereof (within the meaning of the Landlord and Tenant Act, 1954) for a term of years certain of which, at the time in question, not less than seven years remain unexpired, or is a mortgagee in possession (within the meaning of the Law of Property Act, 1925) where the interest mortgaged is either the fee simple of the land or such a tenancy thereof;

'prescribed' means prescribed by rules made by virtue of subsection (6) of section fifteen of the Land Charges Act, 1925;[1] as applied by section five of this Act.

(2) References in this Act to any enactment shall, except where the context otherwise requires, be construed as references to that enactment as amended by or under any other enactment.

Note

[1]Now the Local Land Charges Act 1975, s. 14.

TRUSTEE INVESTMENTS ACT 1961
(1961, c. 62)

1. New powers of investment of trustees

(1) A trustee may invest any property in his hands, whether at the time in a state of investment or not, in any manner specified in Part I or II of the First Schedule to this Act or, subject to the next following section, in any manner specified in Part III of that Schedule, and may also from time to time vary any such investments.

(2) The supplemental provisions contained in Part IV of that Schedule shall have effect for the interpretation and for restricting the operation of the said Parts I to III.

(3) No provision relating to the powers of the trustee contained in any instrument (not being an enactment or an instrument made under an enactment) made before the passing of this Act shall limit the powers conferred by this section, but those powers are exercisable only in so far as a contrary intention is not expressed in any Act or

instrument made under an enactment, whenever passed or made, and so relating or in any other instrument so relating which is made after the passing of this Act.

(4) In this Act 'narrower-range investment' means an investment falling with Part I or II of the First Schedule to this Act and 'wider-range investment' means an investment falling within Part III of that Schedule.

2. Restrictions on wider-range investment

(1) A trustee shall not have power by virtue of the foregoing section to make or retain any wider-range investment unless the trust fund has been divided into two parts (hereinafter referred to as the narrower-range part and the wider-range part), the parts being, subject to the provisions of this Act, equal in value at the time of the division; and where such a division has been made no subsequent division of the same fund shall be made for the purposes of this section, and no property shall be transferred from one part of the fund to the other unless either—

(a) the transfer is authorised or required by the following provisions of this Act, or

(b) a compensating transfer is made at the same time.

In this section 'compensating transfer', in relation to any transferred property, means a transfer in the opposite direction of property of equal value.

(2) Property belonging to the narrower-range part of a trust fund shall not by virtue of the foregoing section be invested except in narrower-range investments, and any property invested in any other manner which is or becomes comprised in that part of the trust fund shall either be transferred to the wider-range part of the fund, with a compensating transfer, or be reinvested in narrower-range investments as soon as may be.

(3) Where any property accrues to a trust fund after the fund has been divided in pursuance of subsection (1) of this section, then—

(a) if the property accrues to the trustee as owner or former owner of property comprised in either part of the fund, it shall be treated as belonging to that part of the fund;

(b) in any other case, the trustee shall secure, by apportioniment of the accruing property or the transfer of property from one part of the fund to the other, or both, that the value of [the wider-range part of the fund is increased by the amount which bears the specified proportion to the amount by which the fund is increased.]

Where a trustee acquires property in consideration of a money payment the acquisition of the property shall be treated for the purposes of this section as investment and not as the accrual of property to the trust fund, notwithstanding that the amount of the consideration is less than the value of the property acquired; and paragraph (a) of this subsection shall not include the case of a dividend or interest becoming part of a trust fund.

(4) Where in the exercise of any power or duty of a trustee property falls to be taken out of the trust fund, nothing in this section shall restrict his discretion as to the choice of property to be taken out.

Note: The Trustee Investments (Division of Trust Fund) Order 1996 (SI 1996 No. 845) has prescribed that the division of the fund pursuant to s. 2(1) shall be made so that the value of the wider-range part of the fund at the time of the division to the value of the narrower-range part of the fund is in the proportion of three to one.

3. Relationship between Act and other powers of investment

(1) The powers conferred by section one of this Act are in addition to and not in derogation from any power conferred otherwise than by this Act of investment or postponing conversion exercisable by a trustee (hereinafter referred to as a 'special power').

(2) Any special power (however expressed) to invest property in any investment for the time being authorised by law for the investment of trust property, being a power

conferred on a trustee before the passing of this Act or conferred on him under any enactment passed before the passing of this Act, shall have effect as a power to invest property in like manner and subject to the like provisions as under the foregoing provisions of this Act.

(3) In relation to property, including wider-range but not including narrower-range investments,—

(a) which a trustee is authorised to hold apart from—

(i) the provisions of section one of this Act or any of the provisions of Part I of the Trustee Act, 1925, . . . or

(ii) any such power to invest in authorised investments as is mentioned in the foregoing subsection, or

(b) which became part of a trust fund in consequence of the exercise by the trustee, as owner of property falling within this subsection, of any power conferred by subsection (3) or (4) of section ten of the Trustee Act, 1925, . . . the foregoing section shall have effect subject to the modifications set out in the Second Schedule to this Act.

(4) The foregoing subsection shall not apply where the powers of the trustee to invest or postpone conversion have been conferred or varied—

(a) by an order of any court made within the period of ten years ending with the passing of this Act, or

(b) by any enactment passed, or instrument having effect under an enactment made, within that period, being an enactment or instrument relating specifically to the trusts in question; or

(c) by an enactment contained in a local Act of the present Session;

but the provisions of the Third Schedule to this Act shall have effect in a case falling within this subsection.

4. Interpretation of references to trust property and trust funds

(1) In this Act 'property' includes real or personal property of any description, including money and things in action;

Provided that it does not include an interest in expectancy, but the falling into possession of such an interest, or the receipt of proceeds of the sale thereof, shall be treated for the purposes of this Act as an accrual of property to the trust fund.

(2) So much of the property in the hands of a trustee shall for the purposes of this Act constitute one trust fund as is held on trusts which (as respects the beneficiaries or their respective interests or the purposes of the trust or as respects the powers of the trustee) are not identical with those on which any other property in his hands is held.

(3) Where property is taken out of a trust fund by way of appropriation so as to form a separate fund, and at the time of the appropriation the trust fund had (as to the whole or a part thereof) been divided in pursuance of subsection (1) of section two of this Act, or that subsection as modified by the Second Schedule to this Act, then if the separate fund is so divided the narrower-range and wider-range parts of the separate fund may be constituted [so as to bear to each other either the specified proportion or] the same proportion as the two corresponding parts of the fund out of which it was so appropriated (the values of those parts of those funds being ascertained as at the time of appropriation), or some intermediate proportion.

(4) . . .

5. Certain valuations to be conclusive for purposes of division of trust fund

(1) If for the purposes of section two or four of this Act or the Second Schedule thereto a trustee obtains, from a person reasonably believed by the trustee to be qualified to make it, a valuation in writing of any property, the valuation shall be conclusive in determining whether the division of the trust fund in pursuance of subsection (1) of the said section two, or any transfer or apportionment of property under that section or the said Second Schedule, has been duly made.

(2) The foregoing subsection applies to any such valuation notwithstanding that it is made by a person in the course of his employment as an officer or servant.

6. Duty of trustees in choosing investments

(1) In the exercise of his powers of investment a trustee shall have regard—

(a) to the need for diversification of investments of the trust, in so far as is appropriate to the circumstances of the trust;

(b) to the suitability to the trust of investments of the description of investment proposed and of the investment proposed as an investment of that description.

(2) Before exercising any power conferred by section one of this Act to invest in a manner specified in Part II or III of the First Schedule to this Act, or before investing in any such manner in the exercise of a power failing within subsection (2) of section three of this Act, a trustee shall obtain and consider proper advice on the question whether the investment is satisfactory having regard to the matters mentioned in paragraphs (a) and (b) of the foregoing subsection.

(3) A trustee retaining any investment made in the exercise of such a power and in such a manner as aforesaid shall determine at what intervals the circumstances, and in particular the nature of the investment, make it desirable to obtain such advice as aforesaid, and shall obtain and consider such advice accordingly.

(4) For the purposes of the two foregoing subsections, proper advice is the advice of a person who is reasonably believed by the trustee to be qualified by his ability in and practical experience of financial matters; and such advice may be given by a person notwithstanding that he gives it in the course of his employment as an officer or servant.

(5) A trustee shall not be treated as having complied with subsection (2) or (3) of this section unless the advice was given or has been subsequently confirmed in writing.

(6) Subsections (2) and (3) of this section shall not apply to one of two or more trustees where he is the person giving the advice required by this section to his co-trustee or co-trustees, and shall not apply where powers of a trustee are lawfully exercised by an officer or servant competent under subsection (4) of this section to give proper advice.

(7) Without prejudice to section eight of the Trustee Act, 1925, . . . the advice required by this section shall not include, in the case of a loan on the security of freehold or leasehold property in England and Wales or Northern Ireland . . . advice on the suitability of the particular loan.

13. Power to modify provisions as to division of trust fund

(1) The Treasury may by order made by statutory instrument direct that, subject to subsection (3) of section four of this Act, any division of a trust fund made in pursuance of subsection (1) of section two of this Act during the continuance in force of the order shall be made so that the value of the wider-range part at the time of the division bears to the then value of the narrower-range part such proportion, greater than one but not greater than three to one, as may be prescribed by the order; and in this Act 'the prescribed proportion' means the proportion for the time being prescribed under this subsection.

(2) A fund which has been divided in pursuance of subsection (1) of section two of this Act before the coming into operation of an order under the foregoing subsection may notwithstanding anything in that subsection be again divided (once only) in pursuance of the said subsection (1) during the continuance in force of the order.

(3) If an order is made under subsection (1) of this section, then as from the coming into operation of the order—

(a) paragraph (b) of subsection (3) of section two of this Act and sub-paragraph (b) of paragraph 3 of the Second Schedule thereto shall have effect with the substitution, for the words from 'each' to the end, of the words 'the wider-range part of the fund is increased by an amount which bears the prescribed proportion to the amount by which the value of the narrower-range part of the fund is increased';

(b) subsection (3) of section four of this Act shall have effect as if for the words 'so as either' to 'each other' there were substituted the words 'so as to bear to each other either the prescribed proportion or'.

(4) An order under this section may be revoked by a subsequent order thereunder prescribing a greater proportion.

(5) An order under this section shall not have effect unless approved by a resolution of each House of Parliament.

15. Saving for powers of court

The enlargement of the investment powers of trustees by this Act shall not lessen any power of a court to confer wider powers of investment on trustees, or affect the extent to which any such power is to be exercised.

SCHEDULES

Section 1

FIRST SCHEDULE
MANNER OF INVESTMENT

PART I
NARROWER-RANGE INVESTMENTS NOT REQUIRING ADVICE

1. In Defence Bonds, National Savings Certificates and Ulster Savings Certificates [Ulster Development Bonds] [National Development Bonds] [British Savings Bonds] [National Savings Income Bonds] [National Savings Deposit Bonds] [National Savings Indexed-Income Bonds.] [National Savings Pensioners Guaranteed Income Bonds.]

2. In deposits in [the National Savings Bank] and deposits in a bank or department thereof certified under subsection (3) of section nine of the Finance Act, 1956.

PART II
NARROWER-RANGE INVESTMENTS REQUIRING ADVICE

1. In securities issued by Her Majesty's Government in the United Kingdom, the Government of Northern Ireland or the Government of the Isle of Man, not being securities failing within Part I of this Schedule and being fixed-interest securities registered in the United Kingdom or the Isle of Man, Treasury Bills or Tax Reserve Certificates [or any variable interest securities issued by Her Majesty's Government in the United Kingdom and registered in the United Kingdom.]

2. In any securities the payment of interest on which is guaranteed by Her Majesty's Government in the United Kingdom or the Government of Northern Ireland.

3. In fixed-interest securities issued in the United Kingdom by any public authority or nationalised industry or undertaking in the United Kingdom.

4. In fixed-interest securities issued in the United Kingdom by the government of any overseas territory within the Commonwealth or by any public or local authority within such a territory, being securities registered in the United Kingdom.

References in this paragraph to an overseas territory or to the government of such a territory shall be construed as if they occurred in the Overseas Service Act 1958.

[4A. In securities issued in the United Kingdom by the government of an overseas territory within the Commonwealth or by an public or local authority within such a territory, being securities registered in the United Kingdom and in respect of which the rate of interest is variable by reference to one or more of the following:

(a) the Bank of England's minimum lending rate;
(b) the average rate of discount on allotment on 91-day Treasury Bills;
(c) a yield on 91-day Treasury Bills;
(d) a London sterling inter-bank offered rate;
(e) a London sterling certificate of deposit rate.

References in this paragraph to an overseas territory or to the government of such a territory shall be construed as if they occurred in the Overseas Service Act 1958.]

5. In fixed-interest securities issued in the United Kingdom by [the African Development Bank, the Asian Development Bank, the Caribbean Development Bank, [The European Bank for Reconstruction and Development] the International Finance Corporation, the International Monetary Fund or by] the International Bank for Reconstruction and Development, being securities registered in the United Kingdom.

[In fixed-interest securities issued in the United Kingdom by the Inter-American Development Bank.]

[In fixed-interest securities issued in the United Kingdom by [the European Atomic Energy Community, the European Economic Community,] the European Investment Bank or by the European Coal and Steel Community, being securities registered in the United Kingdom.]

[5A. In securities issued in the United Kingdom by

(i) the International Bank for Reconstruction and Development or by the European Investment Bank or by the European Coal and Steel Community, being securities registered in the United Kingdom; or

(ii) the Inter-American Development Bank; being securities in respect of which the rate of interest is variable by reference to one or more of the following:

(a) the Bank of England's minimum lending rate,
(b) the average rate of discount on allotment on 91-day Treasury Bills;
(c) a yield on 91-day Treasury Bills;
(d) a London sterling inter-bank offered rate;
(e) a London sterling certificate of deposit rate.]

[5B. In securities issued in the United Kingdom by the African Development Bank, the Asian Development Bank, the Caribbean Development Bank, the European Atomic Energy Community, [The European Bank for Reconstruction and Development] the European Economic Community, the International Finance Corporation or by the International Monetary Fund, being securities registered in the United Kingdom and in respect of which the rate of interest is variable by reference to one or more of the following:—

(a) The average rate of discount on allotment on 91-day Treasury Bills:
(b) a yield on 91-day Treasury Bills;
(c) a London sterling inter-bank offered rate;
(d) a London sterling certificate of deposit rate.]

6. In debentures issued in the United Kingdom by a company incorporated in the United Kingdom, being debentures registered in the United Kingdom.

7. In stock of the Bank of Ireland.

[In Bank of Ireland 7 per cent Loan Stock 1986/91.]

8. . . .

9. In loans to any authority to which this paragraph applies charged on all or any of the revenues of the authority or on a fund into which all or any of those revenues are payable, in any fixed-interest securities issued in the United Kingdom by any such authority for the purpose of borrowing money so charged, and in deposits with any such authority by way of temporary loan made on the giving of a receipt for the loan by the treasurer or other similar officer of the authority and on the giving of an undertaking by the authority that, if requested to charge the loan as aforesaid, it will either comply with the request or repay the loan.

This paragraph applies to the following authorities, that is to say—

(a) any local authority in the United Kingdom;

(b) any authority all the members of which are appointed or elected by one or more local authorities in the United Kingdom;

(c) any authority the majority of the members of which are appointed or elected by one or more local authorities in the United Kingdom, being an authority which by virtue of any enactment has power to issue a precept to a local authority in England and Wales, or a requisition to a local authority in Scotland, or to the expenses of which, by virtue of any enactment, a local authority in the United Kingdom is or can be required to contribute;

(d) the Receiver for the Metropolitan Police District or [any police authority established under section 3 of the Police Act 1964];

(e) the Belfast City and District Water Commissioners;

[(f) the Great Ouse Water Authority.]

[(g) any district council in Northern Ireland.]

[(h) the Inner London Education Authority;]

[(i) any residuary body established by section 57 of the Local Government Act 1985.]

[9A. In any securities issued in the United Kingdom by any authority to which paragraph 9 applies for the purpose of borrowing money charged on all or any of the revenues of the authority or on a fund into which all or any of these revenues are payable and being securities in respect of which the rate of interest is variable by reference to one or more of the following:

(a) the Bank of England's minimum lending rate;

(b) the average rate of discount on allotment on 91-day Treasury Bills;

(c) a yield on 91-day Treasury Bills;

(d) a London sterling inter-bank offered rate;

(e) a London sterling certificate of deposit rate.]

[10A. In any units of a gilt unit trust scheme.

References in this Schedule to a gilt unit trust scheme are references to a collective investment scheme—

(a) which is an authorised unit trust scheme within the meaning of the Financial Services Act 1986, a recognised scheme within the meaning of that Act or a UCITS; and

(b) whose objective is to invest not less than 90% of the property of the scheme in loan stock, bonds and other instruments creating or acknowledging indebtedness which are transferable and which are issued or guaranteed by—

(i) the government of the United Kingdom [or of any other country or territory],

(ii) by a local authority in the United Kingdom or in a relevant state, or

(iii) by an international organisation the members of which include the United Kingdom or relevant state;

and, in respect of the remainder of the property of the scheme, whose objective is to invest in any instrument falling within any of paragraphs 1 to 3, 5 or 6 of Schedule 1 to the Financial Services Act 1986.]

[12. In deposits with a building society within the meaning of the Building Societies Act 1986.]

13. In mortgages of freehold property in England and Wales or Northern Ireland and of leasehold property in those countries of which the unexpired term at the time of investment is not less than sixty years, and in loans on heritable security in Scotland.

14. In perpetual rent charges charged on land in England and Wales or Northern Ireland and fee-farm rents (not being rentcharges) issuing out of such land, and in feu-duties or ground annuals in Scotland.

[15. In Certificates of Tax Deposit.]

[16. In a fixed-interest or variable interest securities issued by the government of a relevant state.

17. In any securities the payment of interest on which is guaranteed by the government of a relevant state.

18. In fixed-interest securities issued in any relevant state by any public authority or nationalised industry or undertaking in that state.

19. In fixed-interest or variable interest securities issued in a relevant state by the government of any overseas territory within the Commonwealth or by any public or local authority within such a territory.

References in this paragraph to an overseas territory or to the government of such a territory shall be construed as if they occured in the Overseas Development and Co-operation Act 1980.

20. In fixed-interest or variable interest securities issued in a relevant state by—

(a) the African Development Bank;
(b) the Asian Development Bank;
(c) the Caribbean Development Bank;
(d) the International Finance Corporation;
(e) the International Monetary Fund;
(f) the International Bank for Reconstruction and Development;
(g) the Inter-American Development Bank;
(h) the European Atomic Energy Community;
(i) the European Bank for Reconstruction and Development;
(j) the European Economic Community;
(k) the European Investment Bank; or
(l) the European Coal and Steel Community.

21. In debentures issued in any relevant state by a company incorporated in that state.

22. In loans to any authority to which this paragraph applies secured on all or any of the revenues of the authority or on a fund into which all or any of those revenues are payable, in fixed-interest or variable interest securities issued in a relevant state by any such authority in that state for the purpose of borrowing money so secured, and in deposits with any authority to which this paragraph applies by way of temporary loan made on the giving of a receipt for the loan by the treasurer or other similar officer of the authority and on the giving of an undertaking by the authority that, if requested to charge the loan as aforesaid, it will either comply with the request or repay the loan.

This paragraph applies to the following authorities, that is to say—

(a) any local authority in a relevant state; or

(b) any authority all the members of which are appointed or elected by one or more local authorities in any such state.

23. In deposits with a mutual investment society whose head office is located in a relevant state.

24. In loans secured on any interest in property in a relevant state which corresponds to an interest in property falling within paragraph 13 of this Part of this Schedule.]

PART III
WIDER-RANGE INVESTMENTS

1. In any securities issued in the United Kingdom by a company incorporated in the United Kingdom, being securities registered in the United Kingdom and not being securities failing within Part II of this Schedule.

[2. In shares in a building society within the meaning of the Building Societies Act 1986.]

[3. In any units of an authorised unit trust scheme within the meaning of the Financial Services Act 1986.]

[4. In any securities issued in any relevant state by a company incorporated in that state or by any unincorporated body constituted under the law of that state, not being (in either case) securities falling within Part II of this Schedule or paragraph 6 of this Part of this Schedule.

5. In shares in a mutual investment society whose head office is located in a relevant state.

6. In any units of a collective investment scheme which is—

(a) a recognised scheme within the meaning of the Financial Services Act 1986(a) which is constituted in a relevant state; or

(b) a UCITS;

and which does not fall within Part II of this Schedule.]

PART IV
SUPPLEMENTAL

1. The securities mentioned in Parts I to III of this Schedule do not include any securities where the holder can be required to accept repayment of the principal, or the payment of any interest, otherwise than in sterling, [in the currency of a relevant state or in the European currency unit (as defined in article 1 in Council Regulations No 3180/78/EEC(b)].

2. The securities mentioned in paragraphs 1 to 8 of Part II, other than Treasury Bills or Tax Reserve Certificates, securities issued before the passing of this Act by the Government of the Isle of Man, securities falling within paragraph 4 of the said Part II issued before the passing of this Act or securities falling within paragraph 9 of that Part, and the securities mentioned in paragraph 1 of Part Ill of this Schedule, do not include—

(a) securities the price of which is not quoted on [a recognised investment exchange within the meaning of the Financial Services Act 1986] [or on an investment exchange which constitutes the principal or only market established in a relevant state on which securities admitted to official listing are dealt in or traded.]

(b) shares or debenture stock not fully paid up (except shares or debenture stock which by the terms of issue are required to be fully paid up within nine months of the date of issue).

[2A. The securities mentioned in paragraphs 16 to 21 of Part II of this Schedule, other than securities traded on a relevant money market or securities falling within paragraph 22 of Part II of this Schedule, and the securities mentioned in paragraph 4 of Part III of this Schedule do not include—

(a) securities the price for which is not quoted on a recognised investment exchange within the meaning of the Financial Services Act 1986 or on an investment exchange which constitutes the principal or only market established in a relevant state on which securities admitted to official listing are dealt in or traded;

(b) shares or debenture stock not fully paid up (except shares or debenture stock which by the terms of issue are required to be fully paid up within nine months of the date of issue or shares issued with no nominal value).]

3. The securities mentioned in paragraph 6 [and 21] of Part II and paragraph 1 [or 4] of Part III of this Schedule do not include—

(a) shares or debentures of an incorporated company of which the total issued and paid up share capital is less than one million pounds;

[(ab) shares or debentures of an incorporated company of which the total issued and paid up share capital at any time on the business day before the investment is made is less than the equivalent of one million pounds in the currency of a relevant state (at the exchange rate prevailing in the United Kingdom at the close of business on the day before the investment is made);]

(b) shares or debentures of an incorporated company which has not in each of the five years immediately preceding the calendar year in which the investment is made paid a dividend on all the shares issued by the company, excluding any shares issued after the dividend was declared and any shares which by their terms of issue did not rank for the dividend for that year.

For the purposes of sub-paragraph (b) of this paragraph a company formed—

(i) to take over the business of another company or other companies, or

(ii) to acquire the securities of, or control of, another company or other companies,

or for either of those purposes and for other purposes shall be deemed to have paid a dividend as mentioned in that sub-paragraph in any year in which such a dividend has been paid by the other company or all the other companies, as the case may be.

. . .

4. In this Schedule, unless the context otherwise requires, the following expressions have the meanings hereby respectively assigned to them, that is to say—

'debenture' includes debenture stock and bonds, whether constituting a charge on assets or not, and loan stock or notes;

'enactment' includes an enactment of the Parliament of Northern Ireland;

'fixed-interest securities' means securities which under their terms of issue bear a fixed rate of interest;

'local authority' in relation to the United Kingdom, means any of the following authorities—

(a) in England and Wales, the council of a county, a borough an urban or rural district or a parish, the Common Council of the City of London [the Greater London Council] and the Council of the Isles of Scilly;

(b) . . .

(c) [. . .]

['mutual investment society' means a credit institution which operates on mutual principles and which is authorised by the appropriate supervisory authority of a relevant state;

'relevant money market' means a money market which is supervised by the central bank, or a government agency, of a relevant state;

'relevant state' means Austria, Finland, Iceland, [Liechtenstein], Norway, Sweden or a member state other than the United Kingdom,]

'securities' include shares, debentures [units within paragraph 3 [or 6] of Part III of this Schedule], Treasury Bills and Tax Reserve Certificates;

'share' includes stock;

'Treasury Bills' includes bills issued by Her Majesty's Government in the United Kingdom and Northern Ireland Treasury Bills.

5. It is hereby declared that in this Schedule 'mortgage', in relation to freehold or leasehold property in Northern Ireland, includes a registered charge which, by virtue of subsection (4) of section forty of the Local Registration of Title (Ireland) Act 1891, or any other enactment, operates as a mortgage by deed.

6. [In relation to the United Kingdom] references in this Schedule to an incorporated company are references to a company incorporated by or under any enactment and include references to a body of persons established for the purpose of trading for profit and incorporated by Royal Charter.

[6A. References in this Schedule to a UCITS are references to a collective investment scheme which is constituted in a relevant state and which complies with the conditions necessary for it to enjoy the rights conferred by Council Directive 85/611/EEC co-ordinating the laws, regulations and administrative provisions relating to undertakings for collective investment in transferable securities (a); and section 86(8) of the Financial Services Act 1986 (meaning of 'constituted in a member state') shall apply for the purposes of this paragraph as it applies for the purposes of that section but as if for references in that section to a member state there were substituted references to a relevant state.]

Section 3 SECOND SCHEDULE

MODIFICATION OF S. 2 IN RELATION TO PROPERTY FALLING WITHIN S. 3(3)

1. In this Schedule 'special-range property' means property falling within subsection (3) of section three of this Act.

2.—(1) Where a trust fund includes special-range property, subsection (1) of section two of this Act shall have effect as if references to the trust fund were references to so much thereof as does not consist of special-range property, and the special-range property shall be carried to a separate part of the fund.

(2) Any property which—

(a) being property belonging to the narrower-range or wider-range part of a trust fund, is converted into special-range property, or

(b) being special-range property, accrues to a trust fund after the division of the fund or part thereof in pursuance of subsection (1) of section two of this Act or of that subsection as modified by sub-paragraph (1) of this paragraph, shall be carried to such a separate part of the fund as aforesaid; and subsections (2) and (3) of the said section two shall have effect subject to this sub-paragraph.

3. Where property carried to such a separate part as aforesaid is converted into property other than special-range property—

(a) it shall be transferred to the narrower-range part of the fund or the wider-range part of the fund or apportioned between them, and

(b) any transfer of property from one of those parts to the other shall be made which is necessary to secure that the value of [the wider-range part of the fund is increased by an amount which bears the specified proportion to the amount by which the value of the narrower-range part of the fund is increased].

Section 3 THIRD SCHEDULE

PROVISIONS SUPPLEMENTARY TO S. 3(4)

1. Where in a case falling within subsection (4) of section three of this Act, property belonging to the narrower-range part of a trust fund—

(a) is invested otherwise than in a narrower-range investment, or

(b) being so invested, is retained and not transferred or as soon as may be reinvested as mentioned in subsection (2) of section two of this Act,

then, so long as the property continues so invested and comprised in the narrower-range part of the fund, section one of this Act shall not authorise the making or retention of any wider-range investment.

2. Section four of the Trustee Act, 1925. . . . shall not apply where an investment ceases to be authorised in consequence of the foregoing paragraph.

PERPETUITIES AND ACCUMULATIONS ACT 1964
(1964, c. 55)

Perpetuities

1. Power to specify perpetuity period

(1) Subject to section 9(2) of this Act and subsection (2) below, where the instrument by which any disposition is made so provides, the perpetuity period applicable to the disposition under the rule against perpetuities, instead of being of any other duration, shall be of a duration equal to such number of years not exceeding eighty as is specified in that behalf in the instrument.

(2) Subsection (1) above shall not have effect where the disposition is made in exercise of a special power of appointment, but where a period is specified under that

subsection in the instrument creating such a power the period shall apply in relation to any disposition under the power as it applies in relation to the power itself.

2. Presumptions and evidence as to future parenthood

(1) Where in any proceedings there arises on the rule against perpetuities a question which turns on the ability of a person to have a child at some future time, then—

(a) subject to paragraph (b) below, it shall be presumed that a male can have a child at the age of fourteen years or over, but not under that age, and that a female can have a child at the age of twelve years or over, but not under that age or over the age of fifty-five years; but

(b) in the case of a living person evidence may be given to show that he or she will or will not be able to have a child at the time in question.

(2) Where any such question is decided by treating a person as unable to have a child at a particular time, and he or she does so, the High Court may make such order as it thinks fit for placing the persons interested in the property comprised in the disposition, so far as may be just, in the position they would have held if the question had not been so decided.

(3) Subject to subsection (2) above, where any such question is decided in relation to a disposition by treating a person as able or unable to have a child at a particular time, then he or she shall be so treated for the purpose of any question which may arise on the rule against perpetuities in relation to the same disposition in any subsequent proceedings.

(4) In the foregoing provisions of this section references to having a child are references to begetting or giving birth to a child, but those provisions (except subsection (1)(b) shall apply in relation to the possibility that a person will at any time have a child by adoption, legitimation or other means as they apply to his or her ability at that time to beget or give birth to a child.

3. Uncertainty as to remoteness

(1) Where, apart from the provisions of this section and section 4 and 5 of this Act, a disposition would be void on the ground that the interest disposed of might not become vested until too remote a time, the disposition shall be treated, until such time (if any) as it becomes established that the vesting must occur, if at all, after the end of the perpetuity period, as if the disposition were not subject to the rule against perpetuities; and its becoming so established shall not affect the validity of anything previously done in relation to the interest disposed of by way of advancement, application of intermediate income or otherwise.

(2) Where, apart from the said provisions, a disposition consisting of the conferring of a general power of appointment would be void on the ground that the power might not become exercisable until too remote a time, the disposition shall be treated, until such time (if any) as it becomes established that the power will not be exercisable within the perpetuity period, as if the disposition were not subject to the rule against perpetuities.

(3) Where, apart from the said provisions, a disposition consisting of the conferring of any power, option or other right would be void on the ground that the right might be exercised at too remote a time, the disposition shall be treated as regards any exercise of the right within the perpetuity period as if it were not subject to the rule against perpetuities and, subject to the said provisions, shall be treated as void for remoteness only if, and so far as, the right is not fully exercised within that period.

(4) Where this section applies to a disposition and the duration of the perpetuity period is not determined by virtue of section 1 or 9(2) of this Act, it shall be determined as follows:—

(a) where any persons failing within subsection (5) below are individuals in being and ascertainable at the commencement of the perpetuity period the duration of the period shall be determined by reference to their lives and no others, but so that the lives of any description of persons falling within paragraph (b) or (c) of that subsection shall be disregarded if the number of persons of that description is such as to render it impracticable to ascertain the date of death of the survivor;

(b) where there are no lives under paragraph (a) above the period shall be twenty-one years.

(5) The said persons are as follows:—

(a) the person by whom the disposition was made;

(b) a person to whom or in whose favour the disposition was made, that is to say—

(i) in the case of a disposition to a class of persons, any member or potential member of the class;

(ii) in the case of an individual disposition to a person taking only on certain conditions being satisfied, any person as to whom some of the conditions are satisfied and the remainder may in time be satisfied;

(iii) in the case of a special power of appointment exercisable in favour of members of a class, any member or potential member of the class;

(iv) in the case of a special power of appointment exercisable in favour of one person only, that person or, where the object of the power is ascertainable only on certain conditions being satisfied, any person as to whom some of the conditions are satisfied and the remainder may in time be satisfied;

(v) in the case of any power, option or other right, the person on whom the right is conferred;

(c) a person having a child or grandchild within sub-paragraphs (i) to (iv) of paragraph (b) above, or any of those children or grandchildren, if subsequently born, would by virtue of his or her descent fall within those sub-paragraphs;

(d) any person on the failure or determination of whose prior interest the disposition is limited to take effect.

4. Reduction of age and exclusion of class members to avoid remoteness

(1) Where a disposition is limited by reference to the attainment by any person or persons of a specified age exceeding twenty-one years, and it is apparent at the time the disposition is made or becomes apparent at a subsequent time—

(a) that the disposition would, apart from this section, be void for remoteness, but

(b) that it would not be so void if the specified age had been twenty-one years,

the disposition shall be treated for all purposes as if, instead of being limited by reference to the age in fact specified, it had been limited by reference to the age nearest to that age which would, if specified instead, have prevented the disposition from being so void.

(2) Where in the case of any disposition different ages exceeding twenty-one years are specified in relation to different persons—

(a) the reference in paragraph (b) of subsection (1) above to the specified age shall be construed as a reference to all the specified ages, and

(b) that subsection shall operate to reduce each such age so far as is necessary to save the disposition from being void for remoteness.

(3) Where the inclusion of any persons, being potential members of a class of unborn persons who at birth would become members or potential members of the class, prevents the foregoing provisions of this section from operating to save a disposition from being void for remoteness, those persons shall thenceforth be deemed for all the purposes of the disposition to be excluded from the class, and the said provisions shall thereupon have effect accordingly.

(4) Where, in the case of a disposition to which subsection (3) above does not apply, it is apparent at the time the disposition is made or becomes apparent at a subsequent time that, apart from this subsection, the inclusion of any persons, being potential

members of a class or unborn persons who at birth would become members or potential members of the class, would cause the disposition to be treated as void for remoteness, those persons shall, unless their exclusion would exhaust the class, thenceforth be deemed for all the purposes of the disposition to be excluded from the class.

(5) Where this section has effect in relation to a disposition to which section 3 above applies, the operation of this section shall not affect the validity of anything previously done in relation to the interest disposed of by way of advancement, application or intermediate income or otherwise.

(6) . . .

[(7) For the avoidance of doubt it is hereby declared that a question arising under section 3 of this Act or subsection (1)(a) above of whether a disposition would be void apart from this section is to be determined as if subsection (6) above had been a separate section of this Act.]

5. Condition relating to death of surviving spouse

Where a disposition is limited by reference to the time of death of the survivor of a person in being at the commencement of the perpetuity period and any spouse of that person, and that time has not arrived at the end of the perpetuity period, the disposition shall be treated for all purposes, where to do so would save it from being void for remoteness, as if it had been limited by reference to the time immediately before the end of that period.

6. Saving and acceleration of expectant interests

A disposition shall not be treated as void for remoteness by reason only that the interest disposed of is ulterior to and dependant upon an interest under a disposition which is so void, and the vesting of an interest shall not be prevented from being accelerated on the failure of a prior interest by reason only that the failure arises because of remoteness.

7. Powers of appointment

For the purposes of the rule against perpetuities, a power of appointment shall be treated as a special power unless—

(a) in the instrument creating the power it is expressed to be exercisable by one person only, and

(b) it could, at all times during its currency when that person is of full age and capacity, be exercised by him so as immediately to transfer to himself the whole of the interest governed by the power without the consent of any other person or compliance with any other condition, not being a formal condition relating only to the mode of exercise of the power:

Provided that for the purpose of determining whether a disposition made under a power of appointment exercisable by will only is void for remoteness, the power shall be treated as a general power where it would have fallen to be so treated if exercisable by deed.

8. Administrative powers of trustees

(1) The rule against perpetuities shall not operate to invalidate a power conferred on trustees or other persons to sell, lease, exchange or otherwise dispose of any property for full consideration, or to do any other act in the administration (as opposed to the distribution) of any property, and shall not prevent the payment to trustees or other persons or reasonable remuneration for their services.

(2) Subsection (1) above shall apply for the purpose of enabling a power to be exercised at any time after the commencement of this Act notwithstanding that the power is conferred by an instrument which took effect before that commencement.

9. Options relating to land

(1) The rule against perpetuities shall not apply to a disposition consisting of the conferring of an option to acquire for valuable consideration an interest reversionary (whether directly or indirectly) on the term of a lease if—

(a) the option is exercisable only by the lessee or his successors in title, and

(b) it ceases to be exercisable at or before the expiration of one year following the determination of the lease.

This subsection shall apply in relation to an agreement for a lease as it applies in relation to a lease, and 'lessee' shall be construed accordingly.

(2) In the case of a disposition consisting of the conferring of an option to acquire for valuable consideration any interest in land, the perpetuity period under the rule against perpetuities shall be twenty-one years, and section 1 of this Act shall not apply: provided that this subsection shall not apply to a right of preemption conferred on a public or local authority in respect of land used or to be used for religious purposes where the right becomes exercisable only if the land ceases to be used for such purposes.

10. Avoidance of contractual and other rights in cases of remoteness

Where a disposition inter vivos would fall to be treated as void for remoteness if the rights and duties thereunder were capable of transmission to persons other than the original parties and had been so transmitted, it shall be treated as void as between the person by whom it was made and the person to whom or in whose favour it was made or any successor of his, and no remedy shall lie in contract or otherwise for giving effect to it or making restitution for its lack of effect.

11. Rights for enforcement of rentcharges 1925 c. 20

(1) The rule against perpetuities shall not apply to any powers or remedies for recovering or compelling the payment of an annual sum to which section 121 or 122 of the Law of Property Act 1925 applies, or otherwise becoming exercisable or enforceable on the breach of any condition or other requirement relating to that sum.

(2) [. . .]

12. Possibilities of reverter, conditions subsequent, exceptions and reservations

(1) In the case of—

(a) a possibility of reverter on the determination of a determinable fee simple, or

(b) a possibility of a resulting trust on the determination of any other determinable interest in property,

the rule against perpetuities shall apply in relation to the provision causing the interest to be determinable as it would apply if that provision were expressed in the form of a condition subsequent giving rise, on breach thereof, to a right of re-entry or an equivalent right in the case of property other than land, and where the provision falls to be treated as void for remoteness the determinable interest shall become an absolute interest.

(2) Where a disposition is subject to any such provision, or to any such condition subsequent, or to any exception or reservation, the disposition shall be treated for the purposes of this Act as including a separate disposition of any rights arising by virtue of the provision, condition subsequent, exception or reservation.

Accumulations

13. Amendment of s. 164 of Law of Property Act 1925

(1) The periods for which accumulations of income under a settlement or other disposition are permitted by section 164 of the Law of Property Act 1925 shall include—

(a) a term of twenty-one years from the date of the making of the disposition, and

(b) the duration of the minority or respective minorities of any person or persons in being at that date.

(2) It is hereby declared that the restrictions imposed by the said section 164 apply in relation to a power to accumulate income whether or not there is a duty to exercise that power, and that they apply whether or not the power to accumulate extends to income produced by the investment of income previously accumulated.

14. Right to stop accumulations
Section 2 above shall apply to any question as to the right of beneficiaries to put an end to accumulations of income under any disposition as it applies to questions arising on the rule against perpetuities.

Supplemental

15. Short title, interpretation and extent
(1) This Act may be cited as the Perpetuities and Accumulations Act 1964.
(2) In this Act—
'disposition' includes the conferring of a power of appointment and any other disposition of an interest in or right over property, and references to the interest disposed of shall be construed accordingly;
'in being' means living or en ventre sa mere;
'power of appointment' includes any discretionary power to transfer a beneficial interest in property without the furnishing of valuable consideration;
'will' includes a codicil;
and for the purposes of this Act a disposition contained in a will shall be deemed to be made at the death of the testator.
(3) For the purposes of this Act a person shall be treated as a member of a class if in his case all the conditions identifying a member of the class are satisfied, and shall be treated as a potential member if in his case some only of those conditions are satisfied but there is a possibility that the remainder will in time be satisfied.
(4) Nothing in this Act shall affect the operation of the rule of law rendering void for remoteness certain dispositions under which property is limited to be applied for purposes other than the benefit of any person or class of persons in cases where the property may be so applied after the end of the perpetuity period.
(5) The foregoing sections of this Act shall apply (except as provided in section 8(2) above) only in relation to instruments taking effect after the commencement of this Act, and in the case of an instrument made in the exercise of a special power of appointment shall apply only where the instrument creating the power takes effect after that commencement:
Provided that section 7 above shall apply in all cases for construing the foregoing reference to a special power of appointment.
(6) This Act shall apply in relation to a disposition made otherwise than by an instrument as if the disposition had been contained in an instrument taking effect when the disposition was made.
(7) This Act binds the Crown.
(8) Except in so far as the contrary intention appears, any enactment of the Parliament of Northern Ireland passed for purposes similar to the purposes of this Act shall bind the Crown.

LAW OF PROPERTY (JOINT TENANTS) ACT 1964
(1964, c. 63)

1. Assumptions on sale of land by survivor of joint tenants
(1) For the purposes of section 36(2) of the Law of Property Act 1925, as amended by section 7 of and the Schedule to the Law of Property (Amendment) Act 1926, the survivor of two or more joint tenants shall, in favour of a purchaser of the legal estate, be deemed to be solely and beneficially interested if the conveyance includes a statement that he is so interested.
Provided that the foregoing provisions of this subsection shall not apply if, at any time before the date of the conveyance by the survivor—
(a) a memorandum of severance (that is to say a note or memorandum signed by the joint tenants or one of them and recording that the joint tenancy was severed in

equity on a date therein specified) had been endorsed on or annexed to the conveyance by virtue of which the legal estate was vested in the joint tenants; or

(b) a [bankruptcy order] made against any of the joint tenants, or a petition for such an order, had been registered under the Land Charges Act 1925,[1] being an order or petition of which the purchaser has notice, by virtue of the registration, on the date of the conveyance by the survivor.

(2) The foregoing provisions of this section shall apply with the necessary modifications in relation to a conveyance by the personal representatives of the survivor of joint tenants as they apply in relation to a conveyance by such a survivor.

Note

[1]Now the Land Charges Act 1972.

2. Retrospective and transitional provisions

Section 1 of this Act shall be deemed to have come into force on 1st January 1926, and for the purposes of that section in its application to a conveyance executed before the passing of this Act a statement signed by the vendor or by his personal representatives that he was solely and beneficially interested shall be treated as if it had been included in the conveyance.

3. Exclusion of registered land

This Act shall not apply to any land the title of which has been registered under the provisions of the Land Registration Acts 1925 and 1936.

WILLS ACT 1968
(1968, c. 28)

1. Restriction of operation of Wills Act 1837, s. 15

(1) For the purposes of section 15 of the Wills Act 1837 (avoidance of gifts to attesting witnesses and their spouses) the attestation of a will by a person to whom or to whose spouse there is given or made any such disposition as is described in that section shall be disregarded if the will is duly executed without his attestation and without that of any other such person.

(2) This section applies to the will of any person dying after the passing of this Act, whether executed before or after the passing of this Act.

LAW OF PROPERTY ACT 1969
(1969, c. 59)

PART III
AMENDMENT OF LAW RELATING TO DISPOSITIONS OF ESTATES AND INTERESTS IN LAND AND TO LAND CHARGES

23. Reduction of statutory period of title

Section 44(1) of the Law of Property Act 1925 (under which the period of commencement of title which may be required under a contract expressing no contrary intention is thirty years except in certain cases) shall have effect, in its application to contracts made after the commencement of this Act, as if it specified fifteen years instead of thirty years as the period of commencement of title which may be so required.

24. Contracts for purchase of land affected by land charge, etc.

(1) Where under a contract for the sale or other disposition of any estate or interest in land the title to which is not registered under the Land Registration Act 1925 or any enactment replaced by it any question arises whether the purchaser had knowledge, at the time of entering into the contract, of a registered land charge, that question shall be determined by reference to his actual knowledge and without regard to the provisions

of section 198 of the Law of Property Act 1925 (under which registration under the Land Charges Act 1925[1] or any enactment replaced by it is deemed to constitute actual notice).

(2) Where any estate or interest with which such a contract is concerned is affected by a registered land charge and the purchaser, at the time of entering into the contract, had not received notice and did not otherwise actually know that the estate or interest was affected by the charge, any provision of the contract shall be void so far as it purports to exclude the operation of subsection (1) above or to exclude or restrict any right or remedy that might otherwise be exercisable by the purchaser on the ground that the estate or interest is affected by the charge.

(3) In this section—

'purchaser' includes a lessee, mortgagee or other person acquiring or intending to acquire an estate or interest in land; and

'registered land charge' means any instrument or matter registered, otherwise than in a register of local land charges, under the Land Charges Act 1925[1] or any Act replaced by it.

(4) For the purposes of this section any knowledge acquired in the course of a transaction by a person who is acting therein as counsel, or as solicitor or other agent, for another shall be treated as the knowledge of that other.

(5) This section does not apply to contracts made before the commencement of this Act.

Note
[1]Now the Land Charges Act 1972.

25. Compensation in certain cases for loss due to undisclosed land charges

(1) Where a purchaser of any estate or interest in land under a disposition to which this section applies has suffered loss by reason that the estate or interest is affected by a registered land charge, then if—

(a) the date of completion was after the commencement of this Act; and

(b) on that date the purchaser had no actual knowledge of the charge, and

(c) the charge was registered against the name of an owner of an estate in the land who was not as owner of any such estate a party to any transaction, or concerned in any event, comprised in the relevant title;

the purchaser shall be entitled to compensation for the loss.

(2) For the purposes of subsection (1)(b) above, the question whether any person had actual knowledge of a charge shall be determined without regard to the provisions of section 198 of the Law of Property Act 1925 (under which registration under the Land Charges Act 1925[1] or any enactment replaced by it is deemed to constitute actual notice).

(3) Where a transaction comprised in the relevant title was effected or evidenced by a document which expressly provided that it should take effect subject to an interest or obligation capable of registration in any of the relevant registers, the transaction which created that interest or obligation shall be treated for the purposes of subsection (1)(c) above as comprised in the relevant title.

(4) Any compensation for loss under this section shall be paid by the Chief Land Registrar, and where the purchaser of the estate or interest in question has incurred expenditure for the purpose—

(a) of securing that the estate or interest is no longer affected by the registered land charge or is so affected to a less extent; or

(b) of obtaining compensation under this section;

the amount of the compensation shall include the amount of the expenditure (so far as it would not otherwise fall to be treated as compensation for loss) reasonably incurred by the purchaser for that purpose.

(5) In the case of an action to recover compensation under this section, the cause of action shall be deemed for the purposes of the [Limitation Act 1980] to accrue at

the time when the registered land charge affecting the estate or interest in question comes to the notice of the purchaser.

(9) This section applies to the following dispositions, that is to say—

(a) any sale or exchange and, subject to the following provisions of this subsection, any mortgage of an estate or interest in land;

(b) any grant of a lease for a term of years derived out of a leasehold interest;

(c) any compulsory purchase, by whatever procedure, of land; and

(d) any conveyance of a fee simple in land under Part I of the Leasehold Reform Act 1967;

but does not apply to the grant of a term of years derived out of the freehold or the mortgage of such a term by the lessee; and references in this section to a purchaser shall be construed accordingly.

(10) In this section—

'date of completion', in relation to land which vests in the Land Commission or another acquiring authority by virtue of a general vesting declaration under the Land Commission Act 1967 or the Town and County Planning Act 1968, means the date on which it so vests;

'mortgage' includes any charge;

'registered land charge' means any instrument or matter registered, otherwise than in a register of local land charges, under the Land Charges Act 19251 or any Act replaced by it, except that—

(a) in relation to an assignment of a lease or underlease or a mortgage by an assignee under such an assignment, it does not include any instrument or matter affecting the title to the freehold or to any relevant leasehold reversion; and

(b) in relation to the grant of an underlease or the mortgage by the underlessee of the term of years created by an underlease, it does not include any instrument or matter affecting the title to the freehold or to any leasehold reversion superior to the leasehold interest out of which the term of years is derived—

'relevant registers' means the registers kept under section 1 of the Land Charges Act 1925;[1]

'relevant title' means—

(a) in relation to a disposition made under a contract, the title which the purchaser was, apart from any acceptance by him (by agreement or otherwise) of a shorter or an imperfect title, entitled to require; or

(b) in relation to any other disposition, the title which he would have been entitled to require if the disposition had been made under a contract to which section 44(1) of the Law of Property Act 1925 applied and that contract had been made on the date of completion.

(11) For the purposes of this section any knowledge acquired in the course of a transaction by a person who is acting therein as counsel, or as solicitor or other agent, for another shall be treated as the knowledge of that other.

Note

[1]Now the Land Charges Act 1972.

ADMINISTRATION OF JUSTICE ACT 1970
(1970, c. 31)

PART IV

36. Additional powers of court in action by mortgagee for possession of dwelling-house

(1) Where the mortgagee under a mortgage of land which consists of or includes a dwelling-house brings an action in which he claims possession of the mortgaged

property, not being an action for foreclosure in which a claim for possession of the mortgaged property is also made, the court may exercise any of the powers conferred on it by subsection (2) below if it appears to the court that in the event of its exercising the power the mortgagor is likely to be able within a reasonable period to pay any sums due under the mortgage or to remedy a default consisting of a breach of any other obligation arising under or by virtue of the mortgage.

(2) The court—

(a) may adjourn the proceedings, or

(b) on giving judgment, or making an order, for delivery of possession of the mortgaged property, or at any time before the execution of such judgment or order, may—

(i) stay or suspend execution of the judgment or order, or

(ii) postpone the date for delivery of possession,

for such period or periods as the court thinks reasonable.

(3) Any such adjournment, stay, suspension or postponement as is referred to in subsection (2) above may be made subject to such conditions with regard to payment by the mortgagor of any sum secured by the mortgage or the remedying of any default as the court thinks fit.

(4) The court may from time to time vary or revoke any condition imposed by virtue of this section.

(5) This section shall have effect in relation to such an action as is referred to in subsection (1) above begun before the date on which this section comes into force unless in that action judgment has been given, or an order made, for delivery of possession of the mortgaged property and that judgment or order was executed before that date.

(6) . . .

[38A. This Part of this Act shall not apply to a mortgage securing an agreement which is a regulated agreement within the meaning of the Consumer Credit Act 1974.]

39. Interpretation of Part IV

(1) In this Part of this Act—

'dwelling house' includes any building or part thereof which is used as a dwelling;

'mortgage' includes a charge and 'mortgagor' and 'mortgagee' shall be construed accordingly;

'mortgagor' and 'mortgagee' includes any person deriving title under the original mortgagor or mortgagee.

(2) The fact that part of the premises comprised in a dwelling-house is used as a shop or office or for business, trade or professional purposes shall not prevent the dwelling-house from being a dwelling-house for the purposes of this Part of this Act.

MATRIMONIAL PROCEEDINGS AND PROPERTY ACT 1970
(1970, c. 45)

Provisions relating to property of married persons

37. Contributions by spouse in money or money's worth to the improvement of property

It is hereby declared that where a husband or wife contributes in money or money's worth to the improvement of real or personal property in which or in the proceeds of sale of which either or both of them has or have a beneficial interest, the husband or wife so contributing shall, if the contribution is of a substantial nature and subject to any agreement between them to the contrary express or implied, be treated as having then acquired by virtue of his or her contribution a share or an enlarged share, as the case may be, in that beneficial interest of such an extent as may have been then agreed or, in default of such agreement, as may seem in all the circumstances just to any court before which the question of the existence or extent of the beneficial interest of the husband or wife arises (whether in proceedings between them or in any other proceedings).

LAND REGISTRATION AND LAND CHARGES ACT 1971
(1971, c. 54)

PART I
AMENDMENT OF LAND REGISTRATION ACTS 1925 TO 1966

1. Payment of indemnity

(1) Any indemnity payable after the commencement of this section under any provision of the Land Registration Act 1925, including so much of any indemnity which has become so payable at any time before then as has not then been paid, shall, instead of being paid out of the insurance fund, be paid by the registrar out of moneys provided by Parliament; and no other person shall thereafter be under any liability to pay any such indemnity.

(2) Any money which at the commencement of this section stands to the credit of the insurance fund shall be paid into the Consolidated Fund, and any other assets then comprised in the insurance fund shall be realised forthwith, and the proceeds thereof shall be paid into the Consolidated Fund; and as soon as its assets have been so dealt with, the insurance fund shall cease to exist.

(3) In this section 'the insurance fund' means the insurance fund established under the Land Transfer Act 1897.

2. Determination of questions as to right to or amount of indemnity

(1) If any question arises as to whether a person is entitled to an indemnity under any provision of the Land Registration Act 1925 or as to the amount of any such indemnity, he may apply to the court to have that question determined.

(2) Section 83(5)(c) of the Land Registration Act 1925 (by virtue of which no indemnity is payable under that Act on account of costs incurred in taking or defending any legal proceedings without the consent of the registrar) shall not apply to the costs of an application to the court under subsection (1) above or of any legal proceedings arising out of such an application; and as regards any such application or proceedings section 131 of that Act (which provides that the registrar, among others, shall not be liable to any action or proceeding for or in respect of anything done or omitted as there mentioned) shall not apply to the registrar.

(3) On an application under subsection (1) above the court shall not order the applicant, even if unsuccessful, to pay any costs except his own unless it considers that the application was unreasonable.

(4) [. . .]

(5) Nothing in this section shall be taken to preclude the registrar from settling by agreement claims for indemnity under the Land Registration Act 1925.

(6) [. . .]

3. Right to indemnify not to be excluded by reason of act etc. not amounting to fraud or lack of proper care

(1) [. . .]

(2) Subsection (1) above shall have effect in relation to any claim for indemnity made before the time of the commencement of this section and not settled by agreement or finally determined before that time, as well as to all such claims made after that time.

LAND CHARGES ACT 1972
(1972, c. 61)

Preliminary

1. The registers and the index

(1) The registrar shall continue to keep at the registry in the prescribed manner the following registers, namely—

(a) a register of land charges;
(b) a register of pending actions;
(c) a register of writs and orders affecting land;
(d) a register of deeds of arrangement affecting land;
(e) a register of annuities,

and shall also continue to keep there an index whereby all entries made in any of those registers can readily be traced.

(2) Every application to register shall be in the prescribed form and shall contain the prescribed particulars.

[(3) Where any charge or other matter is registrable in more than one of the registers kept under this Act it shall be sufficient if it is registered in one register, and if it is so registered the person entitled to the benefit of it shall not be prejudicially affected by the provision of this Act as to the effect of non-registration in any other such register.]

[(3A) Where any charge or other matter is registrable in a register kept under this Act and was also, before the commencement of the Local Land Charges Act 1975, registrable in a local land charges register, then, if before the commencement of the said Act it was registered in the appropriate local land charges register it shall be treated for the purposes of the provisions of this Act as to the effect of non-registration as if it had been registered in the appropriate register under this Act, and any certificate setting out the result of an official search of the appropriate local land charges register shall, in relation to it, have effect as if it were a certificate setting out the result of an official search under this Act.]

(4) Schedule 1 to this Act shall have effect in relation to the register of annuities.

(5) An office copy of an entry in any register kept under this section shall be admissible in evidence in all proceedings and between all parties to the same extent as the original would be admissible.

(6) Subject to the provisions of this Act, registration may be vacated pursuant to an order of the court.

[(6A) The county court has jurisdiction under subsection (6) above—

(a) in the case of a land charge of Class C(i), C(ii) or D(i) if the amount does not exceed the county court limit;

(b) in the case of a land charge of Class C(iii), if it is for a specified capital sum of money, not exceeding the county court limit or, where it is not for a specified capital sum, if the land affected does not exceed the county court limit in capital value or in net annual value for rating;

(c) in the case of a land charge of Class A, Class B, Class C(iv), Class D(ii), Class D(iii) or Class E, if the land affected does not exceed the county court limit in capital value or in net annual value for rating;

(d) in the case of a land charge of Class F, if the land affected by it is the subject of an order made by the court under section 1 of the Matrimonial Homes Act 1983 [or section 33 of the Family Law Act 1996] or an application for an order under [either of those sections] relating to that land has been made to the court.

(e) in a case where an application under section 23 of the Deeds of Arrangement Act 1914 could be entertained by the court.

(6B) . . .

(7) In this section 'index' includes any device or combination of devices serving the purpose of an index.

Registration in register of land charges

2. The register of land charges

(1) If a charge on or obligation affecting land falls into one of the classes described in this section, it may be registered in the register of land charges as a land charge of that class.

(2) A Class A land charge is—

(a) a rent or annuity or principal money payable by instalments or otherwise, with or without interest, which is not a charge created by deed but is a charge upon land (other than a rate) created pursuant to the application of some person under the provisions of any Act of Parliament, for securing to any person either the money spent by him or the costs, charges and expenses incurred by him under such Act, or the money advanced by him for repaying the money spent or the costs, charges and expenses incurred by another person under the authority of an Act of Parliament; or

(b) a rent or annuity or principal money payable as mentioned in paragraph (a) above which is not a charge created by deed but is a charge upon land (other than a rate) created pursuant to the application of some person under any of the enactments mentioned in Schedule 2 to this Act.

(3) A Class B land charge is a charge on land (not being a local land charge) of any of the kinds described in paragraph (a) of subsection (2) above, created otherwise than pursuant to the application of any person.

(4) A Class C land charge is any of the following, [(not being a local land charge)], namely—

(i) a puisne mortgage;
(ii) a limited owner's charge;
(iii) a general equitable charge;
(iv) an estate contract;

and for this purpose—

(i) a puisne mortgage is a legal mortgage which is not protected by a deposit of documents relating to the legal estate affected;

(ii) a limited owner's charge is an equitable charge acquired by a tenant for life or statutory owner under [[the Inheritance Tax Act 1984] or under] any other statute by reason of the discharge by him of any [inheritance tax] or other liabilities and to which special priority is given by the statute;

(iii) a general equitable charge is any equitable charge which—

(a) is not secured by a deposit of documents relating to the legal estate affected; and

(b) does not arise or affect an interest arising under a [trust of land] or a settlement; and

(c) is not a charge given by way of indemnity against rents equitably apportioned or charged exclusively on land in exoneration of other land and against the breach or non-observance of covenants or conditions; and

(d) is not included in any other class of land charge;

(iv) an estate contract is a contract by an estate owner or by a person entitled at the date of the contract to have a legal estate conveyed to him to convey or create a legal estate, including a contract conferring either expressly or by statutory implication a valid option to purchase, a right of preemption or any other like right.

(5) A Class D land charge is any of the following, [(not being a local land charge)], namely—

(i) an Inland Revenue charge;
(ii) a restrictive covenant;

(iii) an equitable easement;

and for this purpose—

(i) an Inland Revenue charge is a charge on land, being a charge acquired by the Board under [the Inheritance Tax Act 1984];

(ii) a restrictive covenant is a covenant or agreement (other than a covenant or agreement between a lessor and a lessee) restrictive of the user of land and entered into on or after 1st January 1926,

(iii) an equitable easement is an easement, right or privilege over or affecting land created or arising on or after 1st January 1926, and being merely an equitable interest.

(6) A Class E land charge is an annuity created before 1st January 1926 and not registered in the register of annuities.

(7) A Class F land charge is a charge affecting any land by virtue of the [Part IV of the Family Law Act 1996].

(8) A charge or obligation created before 1st January 1926 can only be registered as a Class B land charge or a Class C land charge if it is acquired under a conveyance made on or after that date.

(9) [. . .]

3. Registration of land charges

(1) A land charge shall be registered in the name of the estate owner whose estate is intended to be affected.

[(1A) Where a person has died and a land charge created before his death would apart from his death have been registered in his name, it shall be so registered notwithstanding his death.]

(2) A land charge registered before lst January l926 under any enactment replaced by the Land Charges Act 1925 in the name of a person other than the estate owner may remain so registered until it is registered in the name of the estate owner in the prescribed manner.

(3) A puisne mortgage created before 1st January 1926 may be registered as a land charge before any transfer of the mortgage is made.

(4) The expenses incurred by the person entitled to the charge in registering a land charge of Class A, Class B or Class C (other than an estate contract) or by the Board in registering an Inland Revenue charge shall be deemed to form part of the land charge, and shall be recoverable accordingly on the day for payment of any part of the land charge next after such expenses are incurred.

(5) Where a land charge is not created by an instrument, short particulars of the effect of the charge shall be furnished with the application to register the charge.

(6) An application to register an Inland Revenue charge shall state the [tax] in respect of which the charge is claimed and, so far as possible, shall define the land affected, and such particulars shall be entered or referred to in the register.

(7) In the case of a land charge for securing money created by a company before 1st January 1970 or so created at any time as a floating charge, registration under any of the enactments mentioned in subsection (8) below shall be sufficient in place of registration under this Act, and shall have effect as if the land charge had been registered under this Act.

(8) The enactments referred to in subsection (7) above are section 93 of the Companies (Consolidation) Act 1908, section 79 of the Companies Act 1929 [and sections 395–398 of the Companies Act 1985].

4. Effect of land charges and protection of purchasers

(1) A land charge of Class A (other than a land improvement charge registered after 31st December 1969) or of Class B shall, when registered, take effect as if it had been created by a deed of charge by way of legal mortgage, but without prejudice to the priority of the charge.

(2) A land charge of Class A created after 31st December 1888 shall be void as against a purchaser of the land charged with it or of any interest in such land, unless the land charge is registered in the register of land charges before the completion of the purchase.

(3) After the expiration of one year from the first conveyance occurring on or after 1st January 1889 of a land charge of Class A created before that date the person entitled to the land charge shall not be able to recover the land charge or any part of it as against a purchaser of the land charged with it or of any interest in the land, unless the land charge is registered in the register of land charges before the completion of the purchase.

(4) If a land improvement charge was registered as a land charge of Class A before 1st January 1970, any body corporate which, but for the charge, would have power to advance money on the security of the estate or interest affected by it shall have that power notwithstanding the charge.

(5) A land charge of Class B and a land charge of Class C (other than an estate contract) created or arising on or after 1st January 1926 shall be void as against a purchaser of the land charged with it, or of any interest in such land, unless the land charge is registered in the appropriate register before the completion of the purchase.

(6) An estate contract and a land charge of Class D created or entered into on or after 1st January 1926 shall be void as against a purchaser for money or money's worth [(or in the case of an Inland Revenue charge, a purchaser within the meaning of [the Inheritance Tax Act 1984])] of a legal estate in the land charged with it, unless the land charge is registered in the appropriate register before the completion of the purchase.

(7) After the expiration of one year from the first conveyance occurring on or after 1st January 1926 of a land charge of Class B or Class C created before that date the person entitled to the land charge shall not be able to enforce or recover the land charge or any part of it as against a purchaser of the land charged with it, or of any interest in the land, unless the land charge is registered in the appropriate register before the completion of the purchase.

(8) A land charge of Class F shall be void as against a purchaser of the land charged with it, or of any interest in such land, unless the land charge is registered in the appropriate register before the completion of the purchase.

Registration in registers of pending actions, writs and orders and deeds of arrangement

5. The register of pending actions

(1) There may be registered in the register of pending actions—

(a) a pending land action;

(b) a petition in bankruptcy filed on or after 1st January 1926.

(2) Subject to general rules under section 16 of this Act, every application for registration under this section shall contain particulars of the title of the proceedings and the name, address and description of the estate owner or other person whose estate or interest is intended to be affected.

(3) An application for registration shall also state—

(a) if it relates to a pending land action, the court in which and the day on which the action was commenced; and

(b) if it relates to a petition in bankruptcy, the court in which and the day on which the petition was filed.

(4) The registrar shall forthwith enter the particulars in the register, in the name of the estate owner or other person whose estate or interest is intended to be affected.

[(4A) Where a person has died and a pending land action would apart from his death have been registered in his name, it shall be so registered notwithstanding his death.]

(5) An application to register a petition in bankruptcy against a firm shall state the names and addresses of the partners, and the registration shall be effected against each partner as well as against the firm.

(6) No fee shall be charged for the registration of a petition in bankruptcy if the application for registration is made by the registrar of the court in which the petition is filed.

(7) A pending land action shall not bind a purchaser without express notice of it unless it is for the time being registered under this section.

(8) A petition in bankruptcy shall not bind a purchaser of a legal estate in good faith, for money or money's worth, [. . .] unless it is for the time being registered under this section.

(9) . . .

(10) The court, if it thinks fit, may, upon the determination of the proceedings, or during the pendency of the proceedings if satisfied that they are not prosecuted in good faith, make an order vacating a registration under this section, and direct the party on whose behalf it was made to pay all or any of the costs and expenses occasioned by the registration and by its vacation.

[(11) The county court has jurisdiction under subsection (10) of this section where the action was brought or the petition in bankruptcy was filed by the court.]

6. The register of writs and orders affecting land

(1) There may be registered in the register of writs and orders affecting land—

(a) any writ or order affecting land issued or made by any court for the purpose of enforcing a judgment or recognisance—

(b) any order appointing a receiver or sequestrator of land;

[(c) any bankruptcy order whether or not the bankrupt's estate is known to include land]

(c) any receiving order in bankruptcy made on or after 1st January 1926, whether or not it is known to affect land.

[(d) any access order under the Access to Neighbouring Land Act 1992.]

[(1A) No writ or order affecting an interest under a trust of land may be registered under subsection (1) above.]

(2) Every entry made pursuant to this section shall be made in the name of the estate owner or other person whose land, if any, is affected by the writ or order registered.

[2A) Where a person has died and any such writ or order as is mentioned in subsection (1)(a) or (b) above would apart from his death have been registered in his name, it shall be so registered notwithstanding his death.]

(3) No fee shall be charged for the registration of a receiving order in bankruptcy if the application for registration is made by an official receiver.

(4) Except as provided by subsection (5) below and by [section 37(5) of the Supreme Court Act 198 1] and [section 107(3) of the County Courts Act 1984] (which make special provision as to receiving orders in respect of land of judgment debtors) every such writ and order as is mentioned in subsection (1) above, and every delivery in execution or other proceeding taken pursuant to any such writ or order, or in obedience to any such writ or order, shall be void as against a purchaser of the land unless the writ or order is for the time being registered under this section.

[(5) Subject to subsection (6) below, the title of a trustee in bankruptcy shall be void as against a purchaser of a legal estate in good faith for money or money's worth unless the bankruptcy order is for the time being registered under this section.]

(6) Where a petition in bankruptcy has been registered under section 5 above, the title of the trustee in bankruptcy shall be void as against a purchaser of a legal estate in good faith for money or money's worth [. . .] claiming under a conveyance made after the date of registration, unless at the date of the conveyance either the registration of the petition is in force or a receiving order on the petition is registered under this section.

7. The register of deeds of arrangement affecting land

(1) A deed of arrangement affecting land may be registered in the register of deeds of arrangement affecting land, in the name of the debtor, on the application of a trustee of the deed or a creditor assenting to or taking the benefit of the deed.

(2) Every deed of arrangement shall be void as against a purchaser of any land comprised in it or affected by it unless it is for the time being registered under this section.

8. Expiry and renewal of registrations

A registration under section 5, section 6 or section 7 of this Act shall cease to have effect at the end of the period of five years from the date on which it is made, but may be renewed from time to time and, if so renewed, shall have effect for five years from the date of renewal.

Searches and official searches

9. Searches

(1) Any person may search in any register kept under this Act on paying the prescribed fee.

(2) Without prejudice to subsection (1) above, the registrar may provide facilities for enabling persons entitled to search in any such register to see photographic or other images or copies of any portion of the register which they may wish to examine.

10. Official searches

(1) Where any person requires search to be made at the registry for entries of any matters or documents, entries of which are required or allowed to be made in the registry by this Act, he may make a requisition in that behalf to the registrar, which may be either—

(a) a written requisition delivered at or sent by post to the registry, or

(b) a requisition communicated by teleprinter, telephone or other means in such manner as may be prescribed in relation to the means in question, in which case it shall be treated as made to the registrar if, but only if, he accepts it and the registrar shall not accept a requisition made in accordance with paragraph (b) above unless it is made by a person maintaining a credit account at the registry, and may at his discretion refuse to accept it notwithstanding that it is made by such a person.

(2) The prescribed fee shall be payable in respect of every requisition made under this section; and that fee—

(a) in the case of a requisition made in accordance with subsection (1)(a) above, shall be paid in such manner as may be prescribed for the purposes of this paragraph unless the requisition is made by a person maintaining a credit account at the registry and the fee is debited to that account;

(b) in the case of a requisition made in accordance with subsection (1)(b) above, shall be debited to the credit account of the person by whom the requisition is made.

(3) Where a requisition is made under subsection (1) above and the fee payable in respect of it is paid or debited in accordance with subsection (2) above, the registrar shall thereupon make the search required and—

(a) shall issue a certificate setting out the result of the search; and

(b) without prejudice to paragraph (a) above, may take such other steps as he considers appropriate to communicate that result to the person by whom the requisition was made.

(4) In favour of a purchaser or an intending purchaser, as against persons interested under or in respect of matters or documents entries of which are required or allowed as aforesaid, the certificate, according to its tenor, shall be conclusive, affirmatively or negatively, as the case may be.

(5) If any officer, clerk or person employed in the registry commits, or is party or privy to, any act of fraud or collusion, or is wilfully negligent, in the making of or

otherwise in relation to any certificate under this section, he shall be guilty of an offence and shall be liable on conviction on indictment to imprisonment for a term not exceeding two years, or on summary conviction to imprisonment for a term not exceeding three months or to a fine not exceeding [the prescribed sum], or to both such imprisonment and fine.

(6) Without prejudice to subsection (5) above, no officer, clerk or person employed in the registry shall, in the absence of fraud on his part, be liable for any loss which may be suffered—

(a) by reason of any discrepancy between—

(i) the particulars which are shown in a certificate under this section as being the particulars in respect of which the search for entries was made, and

(ii) the particulars in respect of which a search for entries was required by the person who made the requisition; or

(b) by reason of any communication of the result of a search under this section made otherwise than by issuing a certificate under this section.

Miscellaneous and supplementary

11. Date of effective registration and priority notices

(1) Any person intending to make an application for the registration of any contemplated charge, instrument or other matter in pursuance of this Act or any rule made under this Act may give a priority notice in the prescribed form at least the relevant number of days before the registration is to take effect.

(2) Where a notice is given under subsection (1) above, it shall be entered in the register to which the intended application when made will relate.

(3) If the application is presented within the relevant number of days thereafter and refers in the prescribed manner to the notice, the registration shall take effect as if the registration had been made at the time when the charge, instrument or matter was created, entered into, made or arose, and the date at which the registration so takes effect shall be deemed to be the date of registration.

(4) Where—

(a) any two charges, instruments or matters are contemporaneous; and

(b) one of them (whether or not protected by a priority notice) is subject to or dependent on the other; and

(c) the latter is protected by a priority notice,

the subsequent or dependent charge, instrument or matter shall be deemed to have been created, entered into or made, or to have arisen, after the registration of the other.

(5) Where a purchaser has obtained a certificate under section 10 above, any entry which is made in the register after the date of the certificate and before the completion of the purchase, and is not made pursuant to a priority notice entered on the register on or before the date of the certificate, shall not affect the purchaser if the purchase is completed before the expiration of the relevant number of days after the date of the certificate.

(6) The relevant number of days is—

(a) for the purposes of subsection (1) and (5) above, fifteen;

(b) for the purposes of subsection (3) above, thirty,

or such other number as may be prescribed; but in reckoning the relevant number of days for any of the purposes of this section any days when the registry is not open to the public shall be excluded.

12. Protection of solicitors, trustees, etc.

A solicitor, or a trustee, personal representative, agent or other person in a fiduciary position, shall not be answerable—

(a) in respect of any loss occasioned by reliance on an office copy of an entry in any register kept under this Act;

(b) for any loss that may arise from error in a certificate under section 10 above obtained by him.

13. Saving for overreaching powers

(1) The registration of any charge, annuity or other interest under this Act shall not prevent the charge, annuity or interest being overreached under any other Act, except where otherwise provided by that other Act.

(2) The registration as a land charge of a puisne mortgage or charge shall not operate to prevent that mortgage or charge being overreached in favour of a prior mortgagee or a person deriving title under him where, by reason of a sale or foreclosure, or otherwise, the right of the puisne mortgagee or subsequent chargee to redeem is barred.

14. Exclusion of matters affecting registered land or created by instruments necessitating registration of land

(1) This Act shall not apply to instruments or matters required to be registered or re-registered on or after 1st January 1926, if and so far as they affect registered land, and can be protected under the Land Registration Act 1925 by lodging or registering a creditor's notice, restriction, caution, inhibition or other notice.

(2) Nothing in this Act imposes on the registrar any obligation to ascertain whether or not an instrument or matter affects registered land.

(3) Where an instrument executed on or after 27th July 1971 conveys, grants or assigns an estate in land and creates a land charge affecting that estate, this Act shall not apply to the land charge, so far as it affects that estate, if under section 123 of the Land Registration Act 1925 (effect of that Act in areas where registration is compulsory) the instrument will, unless the necessary application for registration under that Act is made within the time allowed by or under that section, become void so far as respects the conveyance, grant or assignment of that estate.

17. Interpretation

(1) In this Act, unless the context otherwise requires:—

'annuity' means a rentcharge or an annuity for a life or lives or for any term of years or greater estate determinable on a life or on lives and created after 25th April 1855 and before 1st January 1926, but does not include an annuity created by a marriage settlement or will;

'the Board' means the Commissioners of Inland Revenue;

'conveyance' includes a mortgage, charge, lease, assent, vesting declaration, vesting instrument, release and every other assurance of property, or of an interest in property, by any instrument except a will, and 'convey' has a corresponding meaning;

'court' means the High Court, or the county court in a case where that court has jurisdiction;

'deed of arrangement' has the same meaning as in the Deeds of Arrangement Act 1914;

'estate owner', 'legal estate', 'equitable interest', 'trust for sale', 'charge by way of legal mortgage', [and 'will'] have the same meanings as in the Law of Property Act 1925;

'judgment' includes any order or decree having the effect of a judgment;

'land' includes land of any tenure and mines and minerals, whether or not severed from the surface, buildings or parts of buildings (whether the division is horizontal, vertical or made in any other way) and other corporeal hereditaments, also a manor, an advowson and a rent and other incorporeal hereditaments, and an easement, right, privilege or benefit in, over or derived from land, but not an undivided share in land, and 'hereditament' means real property which, on an intestacy occurring before 1st January 1926, might have devolved on an heir;

'land improvement charge' means any charge under the Improvement of Land Act 1864 or under any special improvement Act within the meaning of the Improvement of Land Act 1899;

'pending land action' means any action or proceeding pending in court relating to land or any interest in or charge on land;

'prescribed' means prescribed by rules made pursuant to this Act;

'purchaser' means any person (including a mortgagee or lessee) who, for valuable consideration, takes any interest in land or in a charge on land, and 'purchase' has a corresponding meaning;

'registrar' means the Chief Land Registrar, 'registry' means Her Majesty's Land Registry, and 'registered land' has the same meaning as in the Land Registration Act 1925;

'tenant for life', 'statutory owner', 'vesting instrument' and 'settlement' have the same meanings as in the Settled Land Act 1925.

(2) [. . .]

(3) Any reference in this Act to any enactment is a reference to it as amended by or under any other enactment, including this Act.

Section 1

SCHEDULES

SCHEDULE 1
ANNUITIES

1. No further entries shall be made in the register of annuities.

2. An entry of anannuity made in the register of annuities before 1st January 1926 may be vacated in the prescribed manner on the prescribed evidence as to satisfaction, cesser or discharge being furnished.

3. The register shall be closed when all the entries in it have been vacated or the prescribed evidence of the satisfaction, cesser or discharge of all the annuities has been furnished.

4. An annuity which before 1st January 1926 was capable of being registered in the register of annuities shall be void as against a creditor or a purchaser of any interest in the land charged with the annuity unless the annuity is for the time being registered in the register of annuities or in the register of land charges.

Section 2

SCHEDULE 2
CLASS A LAND CHARGES

1. Charges created pursuant to applications under the enactments mentioned in this Schedule may be registered as land charges of Class A by virtue of paragraph (b) of section 2(2) of this Act:—

(a) The Tithe Act 1918 (8 & 9 Geo. 5. c. 54) — Sections 4(2) and 6(1) (charge of consideration money for redemption of tithe rentcharge).

(b) The Tithe Annuities Apportionment Act 1921 (11 & 12 Geo. 5 c. 20) — Section 1 (charge of apportioned part of tithe redemption annuity).

(c) The Landlord and Tenant Act 1927 (17 & 18 Geo. 5 c. 36) — Paragraph (7) of Schedule 1 (charge in respect of improvements to business premises).

(d) [The Land Drainage Act 1976] — [Section 34(2)] (charge in respect of sum paid in commutation of certain obligations to repair banks, watercourses etc.).

(e) The Tithe Act 1936 (26 Geo. 5 & 1 Edw. 8. c. 43) — Section 30(1) (charge for redemption of corn rents etc.).

(f) The Civil Defence Act 1939 (2 & 3 Geo. 6. c. 31)	Sections 18(4) and 19(1) (charges in respect of civil defence works).
(g) The Agricultural Holdings Act 1948 (11 & 12 Geo. 6. c. 63)	[Section 74 charges in respect of sums due to occupier of agricultural holding.]
(h) The Corn Rents Act 1963 (1963 c. 14)	Section 1(5) (charge under a scheme for the apportionment or redemption of corn rents or other payments in lieu of tithes).
[(i) The Agricultural Holdings Act	Section 85 (charges in respect of sums due to tenant of agricultural holdings). Section 86 (charges in favour of landlord of agricultural holding in respect of compensation for or cost of certain improvements).]

2. The following provisions of paragraph 1 above shall cease to have effect upon the coming into operation of the first scheme under the Corn Rents Act 1963, that is to say:—

(a) in sub-paragraph (a), the words 'and 6(1)'; and

(b) sub-paragraph (e).

3. [The references in paragraph 1(g) above to section 74 of the Agricultural Holdings Act 1948 and the references in paragraph 1(i) above to sections 85 and 86 of the Agricultural Holdings Act 1986] include references to any previous similar enactment.

ADMINISTRATION OF JUSTICE ACT 1973
(1973, c. 15)

8. Extension of powers by court in action by mortgagee of dwelling-house

(1) Where by a mortgage of land which consists of or includes a dwelling-house, or by any agreement between the mortgagee under such a mortgage and the mortgagor, the mortgagor is entitled or is to be permitted to pay the principal sum secured by instalments or otherwise to defer payment of it in whole or in part, but provision is also made for earlier payment in the event of any default by the mortgagor or of a demand by the mortgagee or otherwise, then for purposes of section 36 of the Administration of Justice Act 1970 (under which a court has power to delay giving a mortgagee possession of the mortgaged property so as to allow the mortgagor a reasonable time to pay any sums due under the mortgage) a court may treat as due under the mortgage on account of the principal sum secured and of interest on it only such amounts as the mortgagor would have expected to be required to pay if there had been no such provision for earlier payment.

(2) A court shall not exercise by virtue of subsection (1) above the powers conferred by section 36 of the Administration of Justice Act 1970 unless it appears to the court not only that the mortgagor is likely to be able within a reasonable period to pay any amounts regarded (in accordance with subsection (1) above) as due on account of the principal sum secured, together with the interest on those amounts, but also that he is likely to be able by the end of that period to pay any further amounts that he would have expected to be required to pay by then on account of that sum and of interest on it if there had been no such provision as is referred to in subsection (1) above for earlier payment.

(3) Where subsection (1) above would apply to an action in which a mortgagee only claimed possession of the mortgaged property, and the mortgagee brings an action for foreclosure (with or without also claiming possession of the property), then section 36 of the Administration of Justice Act 1970 together with subsections (1) and (2) above shall apply as they would apply if it were an action in which the mortgagee only claimed possession of the mortgaged property, except that—

(a) section 36(2)(b) shall apply only in relation to any claim for possession; and

(b) section 36(5) shall not apply.

(4) For purposes of this section the expressions 'dwelling-house', 'mortgage', mortgagee' and 'mortgagor' shall be construed in the same way as for the purposes of Part IV of the Administration of Justice Act 1970.

(5) This section shall have effect in relation to an action begun before the date on which this section comes into force if before that date judgment has not been given, nor an order made, in that action for delivery of possession of the mortgaged property and, where it is a question of subsection (3) above, an order nisi for foreclosure has not been made in that action.

(6) . . .

INHERITANCE (PROVISION FOR FAMILY AND DEPENDANTS) ACT 1975 (1975, c. 63)

1. Application for financial provision from deceased's estate

(1) Where after the commencement of this Act a person dies domiciled in England and Wales and is survived by any of the following persons:—

(a) the wife or husband of the deceased;

(b) a former wife or former husband of the deceased who has not remarried;

[(ba) any person (not being a person included in paragraph (a) or (b) above) to whom subsection (1A) below applies]

(c) a child of the deceased;

(d) any person (not being a child of the deceased) who, in the case of any marriage to which the deceased was at any time a party, was treated by the deceased as a child of the family in relation to that marriage;

(e) any person (not being a person included in the foregoing paragraphs of this subsection) who immediately before the death of the deceased was being maintained, either wholly or partly, by the deceased;

that person may apply to the court for an order under section 2 of this Act on the ground that the disposition of the deceased's estate effected by his will or the law relating to intestacy, or the combination of his will and that law, is not such as to make reasonable financial provision for the applicant.

[(1A) This section applies to a person if the deceased died on or after 1st January 1996 and, during the whole of the period of two years ending immediately before the date when the deceased died, the person was living—

(a) in the same household as the deceased, and

(b) as the husband or wife of the deceased.]

(2) In this Act 'reasonable financial provision'—

(a) in the case of an application made by virtue of subsection (1)(a) above by the husband or wife of the deceased (except where [at the date of death, a separation order under the Family Law Act 1996 was in force in relation to the marriage] and the separation was continuing), means such financial provision as it would be reasonable in all the circumstances of the case for a husband or wife to receive, whether or not that provision is required for his or her maintenance;

(b) in the case of any other application made by virtue of subsection (1) above, means such financial provision as it would be reasonable in all the circumstances of the case for the applicant to receive for his maintenance.

(3) For the purposes of subsection (1)(e) above, a person shall be treated as being maintained by the deceased, either wholly or partly, as the case may be, if the deceased, otherwise than for full valuable consideration, was making a substantial contribution in money or money's worth towards the reasonable needs of that person.

Note: Section 1(1)(ba) and section 1(1A) were inserted by the Law Reform (Succession) Act 1995.

2. Powers of court to make orders

(1) Subject to the provisions of this Act, where an application is made for an order under this section, the court may, if it is satisfied that the disposition of the deceased's estate effected by his will or the law relating to intestacy, or the combination of his will and that law, is not such as to make reasonable financial provision for the applicant, make any one or more of the following orders:—

(a) an order for the making to the applicant out of the net estate of the deceased of such periodical payments and for such term as may be specified in the order;

(b) an order for the payment to the applicant out of that estate of a lump sum of such amount as may be so specified;

(c) an order for the transfer to the applicant of such property comprised in that estate as may be so specified;

(d) an order for the settlement for the benefit of the applicant of such property comprised in that estate as may be so specified;

(e) an order for the acquisition out of property comprised in that estate of such property as may be so specified and for the transfer of the property so acquired to the applicant or for the settlement thereof for his benefit;

(f) an order varying any ante-nuptial or post-nuptial settlement (including such a settlement made by will) made on the parties to a marriage to which the deceased was one of the parties, the variation being for the benefit of the surviving party to that marriage, or any child of that marriage, or any person who was treated by the deceased as a child of the family in relation to that marriage.

(2) An order under subsection (1)(a) above providing for the making out of the net estate of the deceased of periodical payments may provide for—

(a) payments of such amount as may be specified in the order,

(b) payments equal to the whole of the income of the net estate or of such portion thereof as may be so specified.

(c) payments equal to the whole of the income of such part of the net estate as the court may direct to be set aside or appropriated for the making out of the income thereof of payments under this section,

or may provide for the amount of the payments or any of them to be determined in any other way the court thinks fit.

(3) Where an order under subsection (1)(a) above provides for the making of payments of an amount specified in the order, the order may direct that such part of the net estate as may be so specified shall be set aside or appropriated for the making out of the income thereof of those payments; but no larger part of the net estate shall be so set aside or appropriated than is sufficient, at the date of the order, to produce by the income thereof the amount required for the making of those payments.

(4) An order under this section may contain such consequential and supplemental provisions as the court thinks necessary or expedient for the purpose of giving effect to the order or for the purpose of securing that the order operates fairly as between one beneficiary of the estate of the deceased and another and may, in particular, but without prejudice to the generality of this subsection—

(a) order any person who holds any property which forms part of the net estate of the deceased to make such payment or transfer such property as may be specified in the order;

(b) vary the disposition of the deceased's estate effected by the will or the law relating to intestacy, or by both the will and the law relating to intestacy, in such manner as the court thinks fair and reasonable having regard to the provisions of the order and all the circumstances of the case;

(c) confer on the trustees of any property which is the subject of an order under this section such powers as appear to the court to be necessary or expedient.

3. Matters to which court is to have regard in exercising powers under s. 2

(1) Where an application is made for an order under section 2 of this Act, the court shall, in determining whether the disposition of the deceased's estate effected by his will or the law relating to intestacy, or the combination of his will and that law, is such as to make reasonable financial provision for the applicant and, if the court considers that reasonable financial provision has not been made, in determining whether and in what manner it shall exercise its powers under that section, have regard to the following matters, that is to say—

(a) the financial resources and financial needs which the applicant has or is likely to have in the foreseeable future;

(b) the financial resources and financial needs which any other applicant for an order under section 2 of this Act has or is likely to have in the foreseeable future;

(c) the financial resources and financial needs which any beneficiary of the estate of the deceased has or is likely to have in the foreseeable future;

(d) any obligations and responsibilities which the deceased had towards any applicant for an order under the said section 2 or towards any beneficiary of the estate of the deceased;

(e) the size and nature of the net estate of the deceased;

(f) any physical or mental disability of any applicant for an order under the said section 2 or any beneficiary of the estate of the deceased;

(g) any other matter, including the conduct of the applicant or any other person, which in the circumstances of the case the court may consider relevant.

(2) Without prejudice to the generality of paragraph (g) of subsection (1) above, where an application for an order under section 2 of this Act is made by virtue of section 1(1)(a) or 1(1)(b) of this Act, the court shall, in addition to the matters specifically mentioned in paragraphs (a) to (f) of that subsection, have regard to—

(a) the age of the applicant and the duration of the marriage;

(b) the contribution made by the applicant to the welfare of the family of the deceased, including any contribution made by looking after the home or caring for the family;

and, in the case of an application by the wife or husband of the deceased, the court shall also, unless at the date of death a [separation order under the Family Law Act 1996] was in force and the separation was continuing, have regard to the provision which the applicant might reasonably have expected to receive if on the day on which the deceased died the marriage, instead of being terminated by death, had been terminated by a [divorce order].

[(2A) Without prejudice to the generality of paragraph (g) of subsection (1) above, where an application for an order under section 2 of this Act is made by virtue of section 1(1)(ba) of this Act, the court shall, in that subsection have regard to—

(a) the age of the applicant and the length of the period during which the applicant lived as the husband or wife of the deceased and in the same household as the deceased;

(b) the contribution made by the applicant to the welfare of the family of the deceased, including any contribution made by looking after the home or caring for the family.]

(3) Without prejudice to the generality of paragraph (g) of subsection (1) above, where an application for an order under section 2 of this Act is made by virtue of section 1(1)(c) or 1(1)(d) of this Act, the court shall, in addition to the matters specifically mentioned in paragraphs (a) to (f) of that subsection, have regard to the manner in which the applicant was being or in which he might expect to be educated or trained, and where the application is made by virtue of section 1(1)(d) the court shall also have regard—

(a) to whether the deceased had assumed any responsibility for the applicant's maintenance and, if so, to the extent to which and the basis upon which the deceased assumed that responsibility and to the length of time for which the deceased discharged that responsibility;

(b) to whether in assuming and discharging that responsibility the deceased did so knowing that the applicant was not his own child;

(c) to the liability of any other person to maintain the applicant.

(4) Without prejudice to the generality of paragraph (g) of subsection (1) above, where an application for an order under section 2 of this Act is made by virtue of section 1(1)(e) of this Act, the court shall, in addition to the matters specifically mentioned in paragraphs (a) to (f) of that subsection, have regard to the extent to which and the basis upon which the deceased assumed responsibility for the maintenance of the applicant and to the length of time for which the deceased discharged that responsibility.

(5) In considering the matters to which the court is required to have regard under this section, the court shall take into account the facts as known to the court at the date of the hearing.

(6) In considering the financial resources of any person for the purposes of this section the court shall take into account his earning capacity and in considering the financial needs of any person for the purposes of this section the court shall take into account his financial obligations and responsibilities.

Note: Section 3(2A) was inserted by the Law Reform (Succession) Act 1995.

4. Time-limit for applications

An application for an order under section 2 of this Act shall not, except with the permission of the court, be made after the end of the period of six months from the date on which representation with respect to the estate of the deceased is first taken out.

5. Interim orders

Where on an application for an order under section 2 of this Act it appears to the court—

(a) that the applicant is in immediate need of financial assistance, but it is not yet possible to determine what order (if any) should be made under that section; and

(b) that property forming part of the net estate of the deceased is or can be made available to meet the need of the applicant;

the court may order that, subject to such conditions or restrictions, if any, as the court may impose and to any further order of the court, there shall be paid to the applicant out of the net estate of the deceased such sum or sums and (if more than one) at such intervals as the court thinks reasonable; and the court may order that, subject to the provisions of this Act, such payments are to be made until such date as the court may specify, not being later than the date on which the court either makes an order under the said section 2 or decides not to exercise its powers under that section.

(2) Subsections (2), (3) and (4) of section 2 of this Act shall apply in relation to an order under this section as they apply in relation to an order under that section.

(3) In determining what order, if any, should be made under this section the court shall, so far as the urgency of the case admits, have regard to the same matters as those to which the court is required to have regard under section 3 of this Act.

(4) An order made under section 2 of this Act may provide that any sum paid to the applicant by virtue of this section shall be treated to such an extent and in such manner as may be provided by that order as having been paid on account of any payment provided for by that order.

6. Variation, discharge etc. of orders for periodical payments

(1) Subject to the provisions of this Act, where the court has made an order under section 2(1)(a) of this Act (in this section referred to as 'the original order') for the making of periodical payments to any person (in this section referred to as 'the original

recipient'), the court, on an application under this section, shall have power by order to vary or discharge the original order or to suspend any provision of it temporarily and to revive the operation of any provision so suspended.

(2) Without prejudice to the generality of subsection (1) above, an order made on an application for the variation of the original order may—

(a) provide for the making out of any relevant property of such periodical payments and for such term as may be specified in the order to any person who has applied, or would but for section 4 of this Act be entitled to apply, for an order under section 2 of this Act (whether or not, in the case of any application, an order was made in favour of the applicant);

(b) provide for the payment out of any relevant property of a lump sum of such amount as may be so specified to the original recipient or to any such person as is mentioned in paragraph (a) above;

(c) provide for the transfer of the relevant property, or such part thereof as may be so specified, to the original recipient or to any such person as is so mentioned.

(3) Where the original order provides that any periodical payments payable thereunder to the original recipient are to cease on the occurrence of an event specified in the order (other than the remarriage of a former wife or former husband) or on the expiration of a period so specified, then, if, before the end of the period of six months from the date of the occurrence of that event or of the expiration of that period, an application is made for an order under this section, the court shall have power to make any order which it would have had power to make if the application had been made before that date (whether in favour of the original recipient or any such person as is mentioned in subsection (2)(a) above and whether having effect from that date or from such later date as the court may specify).

(4) Any reference in this section to the original order shall include a reference to an order made under this section and any reference in this section to the original recipient shall include a reference to any person to whom periodical payments are required to be made by virtue of an order under this section.

(5) An application under this section may be made by any of the following persons, that is to say—

(a) any person who by virtue of section 1(1) of this Act has applied, or would but for section 4 of this Act be entitled to apply, for an order under section 2 of this Act,

(b) the personal representatives of the deceased,

(c) the trustees of any relevant property, and

(d) any beneficiary of the estate of the deceased.

(6) An order under this section may only affect—

(a) property the income of which is at the date of the order applicable wholly or in part for the making of periodical payments to any person who has applied for an order under this Act, or

(b) in the case of an application under subsection (3) above in respect of payments which have ceased to be payable on the occurrence of an event or the expiration of a period, property the income of which was so applicable immediately before the occurrence of that event or the expiration of that period, as the case may be,

and any such property as is mentioned in paragraph (a) or (b) above is in subsections (2) and (5) above referred to as 'relevant property'.

(7) In exercising the powers conferred by this section the court shall have regard to all the circumstances of the case, including any change in any of the matters to which the court was required to have regard when making the order to which the application relates.

(8) Where the court makes an order under this section, it may give such consequential directions as it thinks necessary or expedient having regard to the provisions of the order.

(9) No such order as is mentioned in sections 2(1)(d), (e) or (f), 9, 10 or 11 of this Act shall be made on an application under this section.

(10) For the avoidance of doubt it is hereby declared that, in relation to an order which provides for the making of periodical payments which are to cease on the occurrence of an event specified in the order (other than the remarriage of a former wife or former husband) or on the expiration of a period so specified, the power to vary an order includes power to provide for the making of periodical payments after the expiration of that period or the occurrence of that event.

7. Payment of lump sums by instalments

(1) An order under section 2(1)(b) or 6(2)(b) of this Act for the payment of a lump sum may provide for the payment of that sum by instalments of such amount as may be specified in the order.

(2) Where an order is made by virtue of subsection (1) above, the court shall have power, on an application made by the person to whom the lump sum is payable, by the personal representatives of the deceased or by the trustees of the property out of which the lump sum is payable, to vary that order by varying the number of instalments payable, the amount of any instalment and the date on which any instalment becomes payable.

Property available for financial provision

8. Property treated as part of 'net estate'

(1) Where a deceased person has in accordance with the provisions of any enactment nominated any person to receive any sum of money or other property on his death and that nomination is in force at the time of his death, that sum of money, after deducting therefrom any [inheritance tax] payable in respect thereof, or that other property, to the extent of the value thereof at the date of the death of the deceased after deducting therefrom any [inheritance tax] so payable, shall be treated for the purposes of this Act as part of the net estate of the deceased; but this subsection shall not render any person liable for having paid that sum or transferred that other property to the person named in the nomination in accordance with the directions given in the nomination.

(2) Where any sum of money or other property is received by any person as a donatio mortis causa made by a deceased person, that sum of money, after deducting therefrom any [inheritance tax] payable thereon, or that other property, to the extent of the value thereof at the date of the death of the deceased after deducting therefrom any [inheritance tax] so payable, shall be treated for the purposes of this Act as part of the net estate of the deceased; but this subsection shall not render any person liable for having paid that sum or transferred that other property in order to give effect to that donatio mortis causa.

(3) The amount of [inheritance tax] to be deducted for the purposes of this section shall not exceed the amount of that tax which has been borne by the person nominated by the deceased or, as the case may be, the person who has received a sum of money or other property as a donatio mortis causa.

9. Property held on a joint tenancy

(1) Where a deceased person was immediately before his death beneficially entitled to a joint tenancy of any property, then, if, before the end of the period of six months from the date on which representation with respect to the estate of the deceased was first taken out, an application is made for an order under section 2 of this Act, the court for the purpose of facilitating the making of financial provision for the applicant under this Act may order that the deceased's severable share of that property, at the value thereof immediately before his death, shall, to such extent as appears to the court to be

just in all the circumstances of the case, be treated for the purposes of this Act as part of the net estate of the deceased.

(2) In determining the extent to which any severable share is to be treated as part of the net estate of the deceased by virtue of an order under subsection (1) above, the court shall have regard to any [inheritance tax] payable in respect of that severable share.

(3) Where an order is made under subsection (1) above, the provisions of this section shall not render any person liable for anything done by him before the order was made.

(4) For the avoidance of doubt it is hereby declared that for the purposes of this section there may be a joint tenancy of a chose in action.

Powers of court in relation to transactions intended to defeat applications for financial provision

10. Dispositions intended to defeat applications for financial provisions

(1) Where an application is made to the court for an order under section 2 of this Act, the applicant may, in the proceedings on that application, apply to the court for an order under subsection (2) below.

(2) Where on an application under subsection (1) above the court is satisfied—

(a) that, less than six years before the date of the death of the deceased, the deceased with the intention of defeating an application for financial provision under this Act made a disposition, and

(b) that full valuable consideration for that disposition was not given by the person to whom or for the benefit of whom the disposition was made (in this section referred to as the donee') or by any other person, and

(c) that the exercise of the powers conferred by this section would facilitate the making of financial provision for the applicant under this Act, then, subject to the provisions of this section and of sections 12 and 13 of this Act, the court may order the donee (whether or not at the date of the order he holds any interest in the property disposed of to him or for his benefit by the deceased) to provide, for the purpose of the making of that financial provision, such sum of money or other property as may be specified in the order.

(3) Where an order is made under subsection (2) above as respects any disposition made by the deceased which consisted of the payment of money to or for the benefit of the donee, the amount of any sum of money or the value of any property ordered to be provided under that subsection shall not exceed the amount of the payment made by the deceased after deducting therefrom any [inheritance tax] borne by the donee in respect of that payment.

(4) Where an order is made under subsection (2) above as respects any disposition made by the deceased which consisted of the transfer of property (other than a sum of money) to or for the benefit of the donee, the amount of any sum of money or the value of any property ordered to be provided under that subsection shall not exceed the value at the date of the death of the deceased of the property disposed of by him to or for the benefit of the donee (or if that property has been disposed of by the person to whom it was transferred by the deceased, the value at the date of that disposal thereof) after deducting therefrom any [inheritance tax] borne by the donee in respect of the transfer of that property by the deceased.

(5) Where an application (in this subsection referred to as 'the original application') is made for an order under subsection (2) above in relation to any disposition, then, if on an application under this subsection by the donee or by any applicant for an order under section 2 of this Act the court is satisfied—

(a) that, less than six years before the date of the death of the deceased, the deceased with the intention of defeating an application for financial provision under this Act made a disposition other than the disposition which is the subject of the original application, and

(b) that full valuable consideration for that other disposition was not given by the person to whom or for the benefit of whom that other disposition was made or by any other person,

the court may exercise in relation to the person to whom or for the benefit of whom that other disposition was made the powers which the court would have had under subsection (2) above if the original application had been made in respect of that other disposition and the court had been satisfied as to the matters set out in paragraphs (a), (b) and (c) of that subsection; and where any application is made under this subsection, any reference in this section (except in subsection (2)(b)) to the donee shall include a reference to the person to whom or for the benefit of whom that other disposition was made.

(6) In determining whether and in what manner to exercise its powers under this section, the court shall have regard to the circumstances in which any disposition was made and any valuable consideration which was given therefor, the relationship, if any, of the donee to the deceased, the conduct and financial resources of the donee and all the other circumstances of the case.

(7) In this section 'disposition' does not include—

(a) any provision in a will, any such nomination as is mentioned in section 8(1) of this Act or any donatio mortis causa, or

(b) any appointment of property made, otherwise than by will, in the exercise of a special power of appointment,

but, subject to these exceptions, includes any payment of money (including the payment of a premium under a policy of assurance) and any conveyance, assurance, appointment or gift of property of any description, whether made by an instrument or otherwise.

(8) The provisions of this section do not apply to any disposition made before the commencement of this Act.

11. Contracts to leave property by will

(1) Where an application is made to a court for an order under section 2 of this Act, the applicant may, in the proceedings on that application, apply to the court for an order under this section.

(2) Where on an application under subsection (1) above the court is satisfied—

(a) that the deceased made a contract by which he agreed to leave by his will a sum of money or other property to any person or by which he agreed that a sum of money or other property would be paid or transferred to any person out of his estate, and

(b) that the deceased made that contract with the intention of defeating an application for financial provision under this Act, and

(c) that when the contract was made full valuable consideration for that contract was not given or promised by the person with whom or for the benefit of whom the contract was made (in this section referred to as 'the donee') or by any other person, and

(d) that the exercise of the powers conferred by this section would facilitate the making of financial provision for the applicant under this Act, then, subject to the provisions of this section and of sections 12 and 13 of this Act, the court may make any one or more of the following orders, that is to say—

(i) if any money has been paid or any other property has been transferred to or for the benefit of the donee in accordance with the contract, an order directing the donee to provide, for the purpose of the making of that financial provision, such sum of money or other property as may be specified in the order;

(ii) if the money or all the money has not been paid or the property or all the property has not been transferred in accordance with the contract, an order directing the personal representatives not to make any payment or transfer any property, or not to make any further payment or transfer any further property, as the case may be, in accordance therewith or directing the personal representatives only to make such payment or transfer such property as may be specified in the order.

(3) Notwithstanding anything in subsection (2) above, the court may exercise its powers thereunder in relation to any contract made by the deceased only to the extent that the court considers that the amount of any sum of money paid or to be paid or the value of any property transferred or to be transferred in accordance with the contract exceeds the value of any valuable consideration given or to be given for that contract, and for this purpose the court shall have regard to the value of property at the date of the hearing.

(4) In determining whether and in what manner to exercise its powers under this section, the court shall have regard to the circumstances in which the contract was made, the relationship, if any, of the donee to the deceased, the conduct and financial resources of the donee and all the other circumstances of the case.

(5) Where an order has been made under subsection (2) above in relation to any contract, the rights of any person to enforce that contract or to recover damages or to obtain other relief for the breach thereof shall be subject to any adjustment made by the court under section 12(3) of this Act and shall survive to such extent only as is consistent with giving effect to the terms of that order.

(6) The provisions of this section do not apply to a contract made before the commencement of this Act.

12. Provisions supplementary to ss. 10 and 11

(1) Where the exercise of any of the powers conferred by section 10 or 11 of this Act is conditional on the court being satisfied that a disposition or contract was made by a deceased person with the intention of defeating an application for financial provision under this Act, that condition shall be fulfilled if the court is of the opinion that, on a balance of probabilities, the intention of the deceased (though not necessarily his sole intention) in making the disposition or contract was to prevent an order for financial provision being made under this Act or to reduce the amount of the provision which might otherwise be granted by an order thereunder.

(2) Where an application is made under section 11 of this Act with respect to any contract made by the deceased and no valuable consideration was given or promised by any person for that contract then, notwithstanding anything in subsection (1) above, it shall be presumed, unless the contrary is shown, that the deceased made that contract with the intention of defeating an application for financial provision under this Act.

(3) Where the court makes an order under section 10 or 11 of this Act it may give such consequential directions as it thinks fit (including directions requiring the making of any payment or the transfer of any property) for giving effect to the order or for securing a fair adjustment of the rights of the persons affected thereby.

(4) Any power conferred on the court by the said section 10 or 11 to order the donee, in relation to any disposition or contract, to provide any sum of money or other property shall be exercisable in like manner in relation to the personal representative of the donee, and

(a) any reference in section 10(4) to the disposal of property by the donee shall include a reference to disposal by the personal representative of the donee, and

(b) any reference in section 10(5) to an application by the donee under that subsection shall include a reference to an application by the personal representative of a donee; but the court shall not have power under the said section 10 or 11 to make an order in respect of any property forming part of the estate of the donee which has been distributed by the personal representative; and the personal representative shall not be liable for having distributed any such property before he has notice of the making of an application under the said section 10 or 11 on the ground that he ought to have taken into account the possibility that such an application would be made.

13. Provisions as to trustees in relation to ss. 10 and 11

(1) Where an application is made for—

(a) an order under section 10 of this Act in respect of a disposition made by the deceased to any person as a trustee, or

(b) an order under section 11 of this Act in respect of any payment made or property transferred, in accordance with a contract made by the deceased, to any person as a trustee, the powers of the court under the said section 10 or 11 to order that trustee to provide a sum of money or other property shall be subject to the following limitation (in addition, in a case of an application under section 10, to any provision regarding the deduction of [inheritance tax]) namely, that the amount of any sum of money or the value of any property ordered to be provided—

(i) in the case of an application in respect of a disposition which consisted of the payment of money or an application in respect of the payment of money in accordance with a contract, shall not exceed the aggregate of so much of that money as is at the date of the order in the hands of the trustee and the value at that date of any property which represents that money or is derived therefrom and is at that date in the hands of the trustee;

(ii) in the case of an application in respect of a disposition which consisted of the transfer of property (other than a sum of money) or an application in respect of the transfer of property (other than a sum of money) in accordance with a contract, shall not exceed the aggregate of the value at the date of the order of so much of that property as is at that date in the hands of the trustee and the value at that date of any property which represents the first-mentioned property or is derived therefrom and is at that date in the hands of the trustee.

(2) Where any such application is made in respect of a disposition made to any person as a trustee or in respect of any payment made or property transferred in pursuance of a contract to any person as a trustee, the trustee shall not be liable for having distributed any money or other property on the ground that he ought to have taken into account the possibility that such an application would be made.

(3) Where any such application is made in respect of a disposition made to any person as a trustee or in respect of any payment made or property transferred in accordance with a contract to any person as a trustee, any reference in the said section 10 or 11 to the donee shall be construed as including a reference to the trustee or trustees for the time being of the trust in question and any reference in subsection (1) or (2) above to a trustee shall be construed in the same way.

Special provisions relating to cases of divorce, separation etc.

14. Provision as to cases where no financial relief was granted in divorce proceedings etc.

(1) Where, within twelve months from the date on which a [divorce order or separation order has been made under the Family Law Act 1996 in relation to a marrige or a decree of nullity of marriage has been made absolute], a party to the marriage dies and—

(a) an application for a financial provision order under [section 22A or 23] of the Matrimonial Causes Act 1973 or a property adjustment order under [section 23A or 24] of that Act has not been made by the other party to that marriage, or

(b) such an application has been made but the proceedings thereon have not been determined at the time of the death of the deceased, then, if an application for an order under section 2 of this Act is made by that other party, the court shall, notwithstanding anything in section 1 or section 3 of this Act, have power, if it thinks it just to do so, to treat that party for the purposes of that application as if, [as the case may be, the divorce order or separation order had not been made or the decree of nullity had not been made absolute.]

(2) This section shall not apply in relation to a [separation order] unless at the date of the death of the deceased [the order] was in force and the separation was continuing.

15. Restriction imposed in divorce proceedings etc. on application under this Act

[(1) At any time when the court—

(a) has jurisdiction under section 23A or 24 of the Matrimonial Causes Act 1973 to make a property adjustment order in relation to a marriage; or

(b) would have such jurisdiction if either the jurisdiction had not already been exercised or an application for such an order were made with the leave of the court,]

the court, if it considers it just to do so, may, on the application of either party to the marriage order that either party to the marriage shall not on the death of the applicant be entitled to apply for an order under section 2 of this Act.

In this subsection 'the court' means the High Court or, where a county court has jurisdiction by virtue of Part V of the Matrimonial and Family Proceedings Act 1984, a county court.]

[(2) An order made under subsection (1) above with respect to any party to a marriage has effect in accordance with subsection (3) below at any time—

(a) after the marriage has been dissolved;

(b) after a degree of nullity has been made absolute in relation to the marriage; and

(c) while a separation order under the Family Law Act 1996 is in force in relation to the marriage and the separation is continuing.

(3) If at any time when an order made under subsection (1) above with respect to any party to a marriage has effect the other party to the marriage dies, the court shall not entertain any application made by the surviving party to the marriage for an order under section 2 of this Act.]

[15A. Restriction imposed in proceedings under the Matrimonial and Family Proceedings Act 1984 on application under this Act

(1) On making an order under section 17 of the Matrimonial and Family Proceedings Act 1984 (orders for financial provision and property adjustment following overseas divorces etc.) the court, if it considers it just to do so, may, on the application of either party to the marriage order that the other party to the marriage shall not on the death of the applicant be entitled to apply for an order under section 2 of this Act.

In this subsection 'the court' means the High Court or, where a county court has jurisdiction by virtue of Part V of the Matrimonial and Family Proceedings Act 1984, a county court.

(2) Where an order under subsection (1) above has been made with respect to a party to a marriage which has been dissolved or annulled then, on the death of the other party to that marriage, the court shall not entertain an application under section 2 of this Act by the first-mentioned party.

(3) Where an order under subsection (1) above has been made with respect to a party to a marriage the parties to which have been legally separated, then, if the other party to the marriage dies while the legal separation is in force, the court shall not entertain an application under section 2 of this Act made by the first-mentioned party.]

16. Variation and discharge of secured periodical payments orders made under Matrimonial Causes Act 1973

(1) Where an application for an order under section 2 of this Act is made to the court by any person who was at the time of the death of the deceased entitled to payments from the deceased under a secured periodical payments order made under the Matrimonial Causes Act 1973, then, in the proceedings on that application, the court shall have power, if an application is made under this section by that person or by the personal representative of the deceased, to vary or discharge that periodical payments order or to revive the operation of any provision thereof which has been suspended under section 31 of that Act.

(2) In exercising the powers conferred by this section the court shall have regard to all the circumstances of the case, including any order which the court proposes to make under section 2 or section 5 of this Act and any change (whether resulting from the death of the deceased or otherwise) in any of the matters to which the court was required to have regard when making the secured periodical payments order.

(3) The power exercisable by the court under this section in relation to an order shall be exercisable also in relation to any instrument executed in pursuance of the order.

17. Variation and revocation of maintenance agreements

(1) Where an application for an order under section 2 of this Act is made to the court by any person who was at the time of the death of the deceased entitled to payments from the deceased under a maintenance agreement which provided for the continuation of payments under the agreement after the death of the deceased, then, in the proceedings on that application, the court shall have power, if an application is made under this section by that person or by the personal representative of the deceased, to vary or revoke that agreement.

(2) In exercising the powers conferred by this section the court shall have regard to all the circumstances of the case, including any order which the court proposes to make under section 2 or section 5 of this Act and any change (whether resulting from the death of the deceased or otherwise) in any of the circumstances in the light of which the agreement was made.

(3) If a maintenance agreement is varied by the court under this section the like consequences shall ensue as if the variation had been made immediately before the death of the deceased by agreement between the parties and for valuable consideration.

(4) In this section 'maintenance agreement', in relation to a deceased person, means any agreement made, whether in writing or not and whether before or after the commencement of this Act, by the deceased with any person with whom he entered into a marriage, being an agreement which contained provisions governing the rights and liabilities towards one another when living separately of the parties to that marriage (whether or not the marriage has been dissolved or annulled) in respect of the making or securing of payments or the disposition or use of any property, including such rights and liabilities with respect to the maintenance or education of any child, whether or not a child of the deceased or a person who was treated by the deceased as a child of the family in relation to that marriage.

18. Availability of court's powers under this Act in applications under ss. 31 and 36 of the Matrimonial Causes Act 1973

(1) Where—

(a) a person against whom a secured periodical payments order was made under the Matrimonial Causes Act 1973 has died and an application is made under section 31(6) of that Act for the variation or discharge of that order or for the revival of the operation of any provision thereof which has been suspended, or

(b) a party to a maintenance agreement within the meaning of section 34 of that Act has died, the agreement being one which provides for the continuation of payments thereunder after the death of one of the parties, and an application is made under section 36(1) of that Act for the alteration of the agreement under section 35 thereof, the court shall have power to direct that the application made under the said section 31(6) or 36(1) shall be deemed to have been accompanied by an application for an order under section 2 of this Act.

(2) Where the court gives a direction under subsection (1) above it shall have power, in the proceedings on the application under the said section 31(6) or 36(1), to make any order which the court would have had power to make under the provisions of this Act if the application under the said section 31(6) or 36(1), as the case may be, had

been made jointly with an application for an order under the said section 2; and the court shall have power to give such consequential directions as may be necessary for enabling the court to exercise any of the powers available to the court under this Act in the case of an application for an order under section 2.

(3) Where an order made under section 15(1) of this Act is in force with respect to a party to a marriage, the court shall not give a direction under subsection (1) above with respect to any application made under the said section 31(6) or 36(1) by that party on the death of the other party.

Miscellaneous and supplementary provisions

19. Effect, duration and form of orders

(1) Where an order is made under section 2 of this Act then for all purposes, including the purposes of the enactments relating to [inheritance tax] the will or the law relating to intestacy, or both the will and the law relating to intestacy, as the case may be, shall have effect and be deemed to have had effect as from the deceased's death subject to the provisions of the order.

(2) Any order made under section 2 or 5 of this Act in favour of—

(a) an applicant who was the former husband or former wife of the deceased, or

(b) an applicant who was the husband or wife of the deceased in a case where, [at the date of death, a separation order under the Family Law Act 1996 was in force in relation to the marriage with the deceased] and the separation was continuing,

shall, in so far as it provides for the making of periodical payments, cease to have effect on the remarriage of the applicant, except in relation to any arrears due under the order on the date of the remarriage.

(3) A copy of every order made under this Act [other than an order made under section 15(1) of this Act] shall be sent to the principal registry of the Family Division for entry and filing, and a memorandum of the order shall be endorsed on, or permanently annexed to, the probate or letters of administration under which the estate is being administered.

20. Provisions as to personal representatives

(1) The provisions of this Act shall not render the personal representative of a deceased person liable for having distributed any part of the estate of the deceased, after the end of the period of six months from the date on which representation with respect to the estate of the deceased is first taken out, on the ground that he ought to have taken into account the possibility—

(a) that the court might permit the making of an application for an order under section 2 of this Act after the end of that period, or

(b) that, where an order has been made under the said section 2, the court might exercise in relation thereto the powers conferred on it by section 6 of this Act, but this subsection shall not prejudice any power to recover, by reason of the making of an order under this Act, any part of the estate so distributed.

(2) Where the personal representative of a deceased person pays any sum directed by an order under section 5 of this Act to be paid out of the deceased's net estate, he shall not be under any liability by reason of that estate not being sufficient to make the payment, unless at the time of making the payment he has reasonable cause to believe that the estate is not sufficient.

(3) Where a deceased person entered into a contract by which he agreed to leave by his will any sum of money or other property to any person or by which he agreed that a sum of money or other property would be paid or transferred to any person out of his estate, then, if the personal representative of the deceased has reason to believe that the deceased entered into the contract with the intention of defeating an application for financial provision under this Act, he may, notwithstanding anything in that

contract, postpone the payment of that sum of money or the transfer of that property until the expiration of the period of six months from the date on which representation with respect to the estate of the deceased is first taken out or, if during that period an application is made for an order under section 2 of this Act, until the determination of the proceedings on that application.

23. Determination of date on which representation was first taken out
In considering for the purposes of this Act when representation with respect to the estate of a deceased person was first taken out, a grant limited to settled land or to trust property shall be left out of account, and a grant limited to real estate or to personal estate shall be left out of account unless a grant limited to the remainder of the estate has previously been made or is made at the same time.

24. Effect of this Act on s. 46(1)(vi) of Administration of Estates Act 1925
Section 46(1)(vi) of the Administration of Estates Act 1925, in so far as it provides for the devolution of property on the Crown, the Duchy of Lancaster or the Duke of Cornwall as bona vacantia, shall have effect subject to the provisions of this Act.

25. Interpretation

(1) In this Act—

'beneficiary', in relation to the estate of a deceased person, means—

(a) a person who under the will of the deceased or under the law relating to intestacy is beneficially interested in the estate or would be so interested if an order had not been made under this Act, and

(b) a person who has received any sum of money or other property which by virtue of section 8(1) or 8(2) of this Act is treated as part of the net estate of the deceased or would have received that sum or other property if an order had not been made under this Act;

'child' includes an illegitimate child and a child en ventre sa mere at the death of the deceased;

'the court' means [unless the context otherwise requires] the High Court, or where a county court has jurisdiction by virtue of section 22 of this Act, a county court;

['former wife' or 'former husband' means a person whose marriage with the deceased was during the lifetime of the deceased either—

(a) dissolved or annulled by [an order or decree] of divorce or a decree of nullity of marriage granted under the law of any part of the British Islands; or

(b) dissolved or annulled in any country or territory outside the British Islands by a divorce or annulment which is entitled to be recognised as valid by the law of England and Wales;]

'net estate', in relation to a deceased person, means—

(a) all property of which the deceased had power to dispose by his will (otherwise than by virtue of a special power of appointment) less the amount of his funeral, testamentary and administration expenses, debts and liabilities, including any [inheritance tax] payable out of his estate on his death;

(b) any property in respect of which the deceased held a general power of appointment (not being a power exercisable by will) which has not been exercised,

(c) any sum of money or other property which is treated for the purposes of this Act as part of the net estate of the deceased by virtue of section 8(1) or (2) of this Act;

(d) any property which is treated for the purposes of this Act as part of the net estate of the deceased by virtue of an order made under section 9 of the Act;

(e) any sum of money or other property which is, by reason of a disposition or contract made by the deceased, ordered under section 10 or 11 of this Act to be provided for the purpose of the making of financial provision under this Act;

'property' includes any chose in action;

'reasonable financial provision' has the meaning assigned to it by section 1 of this Act;

'valuable consideration' does not include a marriage or a promise of marriage;

'will' includes codicil.

(2) For the purposes of paragraph (a) of the definition of 'net estate' in subsection (1) above a person who is not of full age and capacity shall be treated as having power to dispose by will of all property of which he would have had power to dispose by will if he had been of full age and capacity.

(3) Any reference in this Act to provision out of the net estate of a deceased person includes a reference to provision extending to the whole of that estate.

(4) For the purposes of this Act any reference to a wife or husband shall be treated as including a reference to a person who in good faith entered into a void marriage with the deceased unless either—

(a) the marriage of the deceased and that person was dissolved or annulled during the lifetime of the deceased and the dissolution or annulment is recognised by the law of England and Wales, or

(b) that person has during the lifetime of the deceased entered into a later marriage.

(5) Any reference in this Act to remarriage or to a person who has remarried includes a reference to a marriage which is by law void or voidable or to a person who has entered into such a marriage, as the case may be, and a marriage shall be treated for the purposes of this Act as a remarriage, in relation to any party thereto, notwithstanding that the previous marriage of that party was void or voidable.

(6) Any reference in this Act to an order or decree made under the Matrimonial Causes Act 1973 or under any section of that Act shall be construed as including a reference to an order or decree which is deemed to have been made under that Act or under that section thereof, as the case may be.

(7) Any reference in this Act to any enactment is a reference to that enactment as amended by or under any subsequent enactment.

LOCAL LAND CHARGES ACT 1975
(1975, c. 76)

Definition of local land charges

1. Local land charges

(1) A charge or other matter affecting land is a local land charge if it falls within any of the following descriptions and is not one of the matters set out in section 2 below:—

(a) any charge acquired either before of after the commencement of this Act by a local authority [or National Park authority], water authority, [sewerage undertaker] or new town development corporation under the Public Health Acts 1936 and 1937, [. . .] the Public Health Act 1961 or the [Highways Act 1980 (or any Act repealed by that Act)] [or the Building Act 1984] or any similar charge acquired by a local authority [or National Park authority] under any other Act, whether passed before or after this Act, being a charge that is binding on successive owners of the land affected;

(b) any prohibition of or restriction on the use of land—

(i) imposed by a local authority [or National Park authority] on or after 1st January 1926 (including any prohibition or restriction embodied in any condition attached to a consent, approval or licence granted by a local authority on or after that date), or

(ii) enforceable by a local authority [or National Park Authority] under any covenant or agreement made with them on or after that date,

being a prohibition or restriction binding on successive owners of the land affected;

(c) any prohibition of or restriction on the use of land—

(i) imposed by a Minister of the Crown or government department on or after the date of the commencement of this Act (including any prohibition or restriction embodied in any condition attached to a consent, approval or licence granted by such a Minister or department on or after that date), or

(ii) enforceable by such a Minister or department under any covenant or agreement made with him or them on or after that date,

being a prohibition or restriction binding on successive owners of the land affected,

(d) any positive obligation affecting land enforceable by a Minister of the Crown, government department or local authority [or National Park authority] under any covenant or agreement made with him or them on or after the date of the commencement of this Act and binding on successive owners of the land affected;

(e) any charge or other matter which is expressly made a local land charge by any statutory provision not contained in this section.

(2) For the purposes of subsection (1)(a) above, any sum which is recoverable from successive owners or occupiers of the land in respect of which the sum is recoverable shall be treated as a charge, whether the sum is expressed to be a charge on the land or not.

2. Matters which are not local land charges

The following matters are not local land charges:—

(a) a prohibition or restriction enforceable under a covenant or agreement made between a lessor and a lessee;

(b) a positive obligation enforceable under a covenant or agreement made between a lessor and a lessee;

(c) a prohibition or restriction enforceable by a Minister of the Crown, government department or local authority [or National Park authority] under any covenant or agreement, being a prohibition or restriction binding on successive owners of the land affected by reason of the fact that the covenant or agreement is made for the benefit of land of the Minister, government department or local authority;

(d) a prohibition or restriction embodied in any bye-laws;

(e) a condition or limitation subject to which planning permission was granted at any time before the commencement of this Act or was or is (at any time) deemed to be granted under any statutory provision relating to town and country planning, whether by a Minister of the Crown, government department or local authority [or National Park authority];

(f) a prohibition or restriction embodied in a scheme under the Town and Country Planning Act 1932 or any enactment repealed by that Act;

(g) a prohibition or restriction enforceable under a forestry dedication covenant entered into pursuant to section 5 of the Forestry Act 1967;

(h) a prohibition or restriction affecting the whole of any of the following areas:—

(i) England, Wales or England and Wales;

(ii) England, or England and Wales, with the exception of, or any part of, Greater London;

(iii) Greater London.

7. Effect of registering certain financial charges

A local land charge falling within section 1(1)(a) above shall, when registered, take effect as if it had been created by a deed of charge by way of legal mortgage within the meaning of the Law of Property Act 1925, but without prejudice to the priority of the charge.

Searches

8. Personal searches

(1) Any person may search in any local land charges register on paying the prescribed fee.

RENTCHARGES ACT 1977
(1977, c. 30)

PROHIBITION AND EXTINGUISHMENT

1. Meaning of 'rentcharge'

For the purposes of this Act 'rentcharge' means any annual or other periodic sum charged on or issuing out of land, except—

(a) rent reserved by a lease or tenancy, or

(b) any sum payable by way of interest.

2. Creation of rentcharges prohibited

(1) Subject to this section, no rentcharge may be created whether at law or in equity after the coming into force of this section.

(2) Any instrument made after the coming into force of this section shall, to the extent that it purports to create a rentcharge the creation of which is prohibited by this section, be void.

(3) This section does not prohibit the creation of a rentcharge—

[(a) in the case of which paragraph 3 of Schedule 1 to the Trusts of Land and Appointment of Trustees Act 1996 (trust in case of family charge) applies to the land on which the rent is charged;

(b) in the case of which paragraph (a) above would effect but for the fact that the land on which the rent is charged is settled land or subject to a trust of land;]

(c) which is an estate rentcharge;

(d) under any Act of Parliament providing for the creation of rentcharges in connection with the execution of works on land (whether by way of improvements, repairs or otherwise) or the commutation of any obligation to do any such work; or

(e) by, or in accordance with the requirements of, any order of a court.

(4) For the purposes of this section 'estate rentcharge' means (subject to subsection (5) below) a rentcharge created for the purpose—

(a) of making covenants to be performed by the owner of the land affected by the rentcharge enforceable by the rent owner against the owner for the time being of the land; or

(b) of meeting, or contributing towards, the cost of the performance by the rent owner of covenants for the provision of services, the carrying out of maintenance or repairs, the effecting of insurance or the making of any payment by him for the benefit of the land affected by the rentcharge or for the benefit of that and other land.

(5) A rentcharge of more than a nominal amount shall not be treated as an estate rentcharge for the purposes of this section unless it represents a payment for the performance by the rent owner of any such covenant as is mentioned in subsection (4)(b) above which is reasonable in relation to that covenant.

3. Extinguishment of rentcharges

(1) Subject to this section, every rentcharge shall (if it has not then ceased to have effect) be extinguished at the expiry of the period of 60 years beginning—

(a) with the passing of this Act, or

(b) with the date on which the rentcharge first became payable,

whichever is the later; and accordingly the land on which it was charged or out of which it issued shall, at the expiration of that period, be discharged and freed from the rentcharge.

(2) The extinguishment of a rentcharge under this section shall not affect the exercise by any person of any right or remedy for the recovery of any rent which accrues before the rentcharge is so extinguished.

(3) This section shall not have the effect of extinguishing any rentcharge—

(a) which is, by virtue of any enactment or agreement or by custom, charged on or otherwise payable in relation to land wholly or partly in lieu of tithes; or

(b) which is of a kind referred to in subsection (3) of section 2 above (disregarding subsection (5) of that section).

(4) Subsection (1) above shall not apply to a variable rentcharge; but where such a rentcharge ceases to be variable, subsection (1) above shall apply as if the date on which the rentcharge first became payable were the date on which it ceased to be variable.

(5) For the purposes of subsection (4) above, a rentcharge shall (at any time) be treated as variable if at any time thereafter the amount of the rentcharge will, or may, vary in accordance with the provisions of the instrument under which it is payable.

MISCELLANEOUS AND GENERAL

11. Implied covenants

(1) Where any land affected by a rentcharge created after the passing of this Act by virtue of section 2(3)(a) or (b) above—

(a) is conveyed for consideration in money or money's worth, and

(b) remains affected by the rentcharge or by any part of it,

the following provisions of this section shall have effect in place of those of section 77 of the Law of Property Act 1925, in respect of the covenants deemed to be included and implied in the conveyance.

(2) In addition to the covenants implied under [Part I of the Law of Property (Miscellaneous Provisions) Act 1994], there shall be deemed to be included and implied in the conveyance covenants by the conveying party or joint and several covenants by the conveying parties (if more than one) with the grantee (or with each of the grantees) in the following terms:—

(a) that the conveying party will at all times from the date of the conveyance duly pay the rentcharge (or part of the rentcharge) and keep the grantee and those deriving title under him and their respective estates and effects indemnified against all claims and demands whatsoever in respect of the rentcharge; and

(b) that the conveying party will (at his expense), in the event of the rentcharge (or part of the rentcharge) ceasing to affect the land conveyed, furnish evidence of that fact to the grantee and those deriving title under him.

(3) The benefit of the covenants deemed to be included and implied in a conveyance, by virtue of subsection (2) above, shall be annexed and incident to and shall go with the estate or interest of the implied covenantee and shall be capable of being enforced by every person in whom the estate or interest is from time to time vested.

(4) Any stipulation which is contained in an agreement and which is inconsistent with, or designed to prevent the operation of, the said covenants (or any part of them) shall be void.

PROTECTION FROM EVICTION ACT 1977
(1977, c. 43)

2. Restriction on re-entry without due process of law

Where any premises are let as a dwelling on a lease which is subject to a right of re-entry or forfeiture it shall not be lawful to enforce that right otherwise than by proceedings in the court while any person is lawfully residing in the premises or part of them.

CHARGING ORDERS ACT 1979
(1979, c. 53)

Charging orders

1. Charging orders

(1) Where, under a judgment or order of the High Court or a county court, a person (the 'debtor') is required to pay a sum of money to another person (the 'creditor') then,

for the purpose of enforcing that judgment or order, the appropriate court may make an order in accordance with the provisions of this Act imposing on any such property of the debtor as may be specified in the order a charge for securing the payment of any money due or to become due under the judgment or order.

(2) The appropriate court is—

(a) in a case where the property to be charged is a fund in court, the court in which that fund is lodged;

(b) in a case where paragraph (a) above does not apply and the order to be enforced is a maintenance order of the High Court, the High Court or a county court;

(c) in a case where neither paragraph (a) nor paragraph (b) above applies and the judgment or order to be enforced is a judgment or order of the High Court for a sum exceeding [the county court limit], the High Court [or a county court]; and

(d) in any other case, a county court.

In this section ['county court limit' means the county court limit for the time being specified in an Order in Council under [section 145 of the County Courts Act 1984], as the county court limit for the purposes of this section and] 'maintenance order' has the same meaning as in section 2(a) of the Attachment of Earnings Act 1971.

(3) An order under subsection (1) above is referred to in this Act as a 'charging order'.

(4) Where a person applies to the High Court for a charging order to enforce more than one judgment or order, that court shall be the appropriate court in relation to the application if it would be the appropriate court, apart from this subsection, on an application relating to one or more of the judgments or orders concerned.

(5) In deciding whether to make a charging order the court shall consider all the circumstances of the case and, in particular, any evidence before it as to—

(a) the personal circumstances of the debtor, and

(b) whether any other creditor of the debt or would be likely to be unduly prejudiced by the making of the order.

2. Property which may be charged

(1) Subject to subsection (3) below, a charge may be imposed by a charging order only on—

(a) any interest held by the debtor beneficially—

(i) in any asset of a kind mentioned in subsection (2) below, or

(ii) under any trust, or

(b) any interest held by a person as trustee of a trust ('the trust'), if the interest is in such an asset or is an interest under another trust and—

(i) the judgment or order in respect of which a charge is to be imposed was made against that person as trustee of the trust, or

(ii) the whole beneficial interest under the trust is held by the debtor unencumbered and for his own benefit, or

(iii) in a case where there are two or more debtors all of whom are liable to the creditor for the same debt, they together hold the whole beneficial interest under the trust unencumbered and for their own benefit.

(2) The assets referred to in subsection (1) above are—

(a) land,

(b) securities of any of the following kinds—

(i) government stock,

(ii) stock of any body (other than a building society) incorporated within England and Wales,

(iii) stock of any body incorporated outside England and Wales or of any state or territory outside the United Kingdom, being stock registered in a register kept at any place within England and Wales,

(iv) units of any unit trust in respect of which a register of the unit holders is kept at any place within England and Wales, or

(c) funds in court.

(3) In any case where a charge is imposed by a charging order on any interest in an asset of a kind mentioned in paragraph (b) or (c) of subsection (2) above, the court making the order may provide for the charge to extend to any interest or dividend payable in respect of the asset.

3. Provisions supplementing sections 1 and 2

(1) A charging order may be made either absolutely or subject to conditions as to notifying the debtor or as to the time when the charge is to become enforceable, or as to other matters.

(2) The Land Charges Act 1972 and the Land Registration Act 1925 shall apply in relation to charging orders as they apply in relation to other orders or writs issued or made for the purpose of enforcing judgments.

(3) . . .

(4) Subject to the provisions of this Act, a charge imposed by a charging order shall have the like effect and shall be enforceable in the same courts and in the same manner as an equitable charge created by the debtor by writing under his hand.

(5) The court by which a charging order was made may at any time, on the application of the debtor or of any person interested in any property to which the order relates, make an order discharging or varying the charging order.

(6) Where a charging order has been protected by an entry registered under the Land Charges Act 1972 or the Land Registration Act 1925, an order under subsection (5) above discharging the charging order may direct that the entry be cancelled.

(7) The Lord Chancellor may by order made by statutory instrument amend section 2(2) of this Act by adding to, or removing from, the kinds of asset for the time being referred to there, any asset of a kind which in his opinion ought to be so added or removed.

(8) Any order under subsection (7) above shall be subject to annulment in pursuance of a resolution of either House of Parliament.

Supplemental

6. Interpretation

(1) In this Act—

'building society' has the same meaning as in the Building Societies Act [1986];

'charging order' means an order made under section 1(1) of this Act;

'debtor' and 'creditor' have the meanings given by section 1(1) of this Act;

'dividend' includes any distribution in respect of any unit of a unit trust;

'government stock' means any stock issued by Her Majesty's government in the United Kingdom or any funds of, or annuity granted by, that government;

'stock' includes shares, debentures and any securities of the body concerned, whether or not constituting a charge on the assets of that body;

'unit trust' means any trust established for the purpose, or having the effect, of providing, for persons having funds available for investment, facilities for the participation by them, as beneficiaries under the trust, in any profits or income arising from the acquisition, holding, management or disposal of any property whatsoever.

(2) For the purposes of section 1 of this Act references to a judgment or order of the High Court or a county court shall be taken to include references to a judgment, order, decree or award (however called) of any court or arbitrator (including any foreign court of arbitrator) which is or has become enforceable (whether wholly or to a limited extent) as if it were a judgment or order of the High Court or a county court.

(3) References in section 2 of this Act to any securities include references to any such securities standing in the name of the Accountant General.

LIMITATION ACT 1980
(1980, c. 58)

Actions to recover land and rent

15. Time limit for actions to recover land

(1) No action shall be brought by any person to recover any land after the expiration of twelve years from the date on which the right of action accrued to him or, if it first accrued to some person through whom he claims, to that person.

(2) Subject to the following provisions of this section, where—

(a) the estate or interest claimed was an estate or interest in reversion or remainder or any other future estate or interest and the right of action to recover the land accrued on the date on which the estate or interest fell into possession by the determination of the preceding estate or interest; and

(b) the person entitled to the preceding estate or interest (not being a term of years absolute) was not in possession of the land on that date; no action shall be brought by the person entitled to the succeeding estate or interest after the expiration of twelve years from the date on which the right of action accrued to the person entitled to the preceding estate or interest or six years from the date on which the right of action accrued to the person entitled to the succeeding estate or interest, whichever period last expires.

(3) Subsection (2) above shall not apply to any estate or interest which falls into possession on the determination of an entailed interest and which might have been barred by the person entitled to the entailed interest.

(4) No person shall bring an action to recover any estate or interest in land under an assurance taking effect after the right of action to recover the land had accrued to the person by whom the assurance was made or some person through whom he claimed or some person entitled to a preceding estate or interest, unless the action is brought within the period during which the person by whom the assurance was made could have brought such an action.

(5) Where any person is entitled to any estate or interest in land in possession and, while so entitled, is also entitled to any future estate or interest in that land, and his right to recover the estate or interest in possession is barred under this Act, no action shall be brought by that person, or by any person claiming through him, in respect of the future estate or interest, unless in the meantime possession of the land has been recovered by a person entitled to an intermediate estate or interest.

(6) Part I of Schedule 1 to this Act contains provisions for determining the date of accrual of rights of action to recover land in the cases there mentioned.

(7) Part II of that Schedule contains provisions modifying the provisions of this section in their application to actions brought by, or by a person claiming through, the Crown or any spiritual or eleemosynary corporation sole.

16. Time limit for redemption actions

When a mortgagee of land has been in possession of any of the mortgaged land for a period of twelve years, no action to redeem the land of which the mortgagee has been so in possession shall be brought after the end of that period by the mortgagor or any person claiming through him.

17. Extinction of title to land after expiration of time limit

Subject to—

(a) section 18 of this Act, and

(b) section 75 of the Land Registration Act 1925;
at the expiration of the period prescribed by this Act for any person to bring an action to recover land (including a redemption action) the title of that person to the land shall be extinguished.

18. Settled land and land held on trust

(1) Subject to section 21(1) and (2) of this Act, the provisions of this Act shall apply to equitable interests in land, including interests in the proceeds of the sale of land held upon trust for sale, as they apply to legal estates.

Accordingly a right of action to recover the land shall, for the purposes of this Act but not otherwise, be treated as accruing to a person entitled in possession to such an equitable interest in the like manner and circumstances, and on the same date, as it would accrue if his interest were a legal estate in the land (and any relevant provision of Part I of Schedule 1 to this Act shall apply in any such case accordingly).

(2) Where the period prescribed by this Act has expired for the bringing of an action to recover land by a tenant for life or a statutory owner of settled land—

(a) his legal estate shall not be extinguished if and so long as the right of action to recover the land of any person entitled to a beneficial interest in the land either has not accrued or has not been barred by this Act; and

(b) the legal estate shall accordingly remain vested in the tenant for life or statutory owner and shall devolve in accordance with the Settled Land Act 1925; but if and when every such right of action has been barred by this Act, his legal estate shall be extinguished.

(3) Where any land is held upon trust (including a trust for sale) and the period prescribed by this Act has expired for the bringing of an action to recover the land by the trustees, the estate of the trustees shall not be extinguished if and so long as the right of action to recover the land of any person entitled to a beneficial interest in the land or in the proceeds of sale either has not accrued or has not been barred by this Act; but if and when every such right of action has been so barred the estate of the trustees shall be extinguished.

(4) Where—

(a) any settled land is vested in a statutory owner; or

(b) any land is held upon trust (including a trust for sale);

an action to recover the land may be brought by the statutory owner or trustees on behalf of any person entitled to a beneficial interest in possession in the land or in the proceeds of sale whose right of action has not been barred by this Act, notwithstanding that the right of action of the statutory owner or trustees would apart from this provision have been barred by this Act.

19. Time limit for actions to recover rent

No action shall be brought, or distress made, to recover arrears of rent, or damages in respect of arrears of rent, after the expiration of six years from the date on which the arrears became due.

Actions to recover money secured by a mortgage or charge or to recover proceeds of the sale of land

20. Time limit for actions to recover money secured by a mortgage or charge or to recover proceeds of the sale of land

(1) No action shall be brought to recover—

(a) any principal sum of money secured by a mortgage or other charge on property (whether real or personal); or

(b) proceeds of the sale of land;

after the expiration of twelve years from the date on which the right to receive the money accrued.

(2) No foreclosure action in respect of mortgaged personal property shall be brought after the expiration of twelve years from the date on which the right to foreclose accrued.

But if the mortgagee was in possession of the mortgaged property after that date, the right to foreclose on the property which was in his possession shall not be treated as having accrued for the purposes of this subsection until the date on which his possession discontinued.

(3) The right to receive any principal sum of money secured by a mortgage or other charge and the right to foreclose on the property subject to the mortgage or charge shall not be treated as accruing so long as that property comprises any future interest or any life insurance policy which has not matured or been determined.

(4) Nothing in this section shall apply to a foreclosure action in respect of mortgaged land, but the provisions of this Act relating to actions to recover land shall apply to such an action.

(5) Subject to subsections (6) and (7) below, no action to recover arrears of interest payable in respect of any sum of money secured by a mortgage or other charge or payable in respect of proceeds of the sale of land, or to recover damages in respect of such arrears shall be brought after the expiration of six years from the date on which the interest became due.

(6) Where—

(a) a prior mortgagee or other incumbrancer has been in possession of the property charged; and

(b) an action is brought within one year of the discontinuance of that possession by the subsequent incumbrancer;

the subsequent incumbrancer may recover by that action all the arrears of interest which fell due during the period of possession by the prior incumbrancer or damages in respect of those arrears, notwithstanding that the period exceeded six years.

(7) Where—

(a) the property subject to the mortgage or charge comprises any future interest or fife insurance policy; and

(b) it is a term of the mortgage or charge that arrears of interest shall be treated as part of the principal sum of money secured by the mortgage or charge; interest shall not be treated as becoming due before the right to recover the principal sum of money has accrued or is treated as having accrued.

Actions in respect of trust property or the personal estate of deceased persons

21. Time limit for actions in respect of trust property

(1) No period of limitation prescribed by this Act shall apply to an action by a beneficiary under a trust, being an action—

(a) in respect of any fraud or fraudulent breach of trust to which the trustee was a party or privy; or

(b) to recover from the trustee trust property or the proceeds of trust property in the possession of the trustee, or previously received by the trustee and converted to his use.

(2) Where a trustee who is also a beneficiary under the trust receives or retains trust property or its proceeds as his share on a distribution of trust property under the trust, his liability in any action brought by virtue of subsection (1)(b) above to recover that property or its proceeds after the expiration of the period of limitation prescribed by this Act for bringing an action to recover trust property shall be limited to the excess over his proper share.

This subsection only applies if the trustee acted honestly and reasonably in making the distribution.

(3) Subject to the preceding provisions of this section, an action by a beneficiary to recover trust property or in respect of any breach of trust, not being an action for which a period of limitation is prescribed by any other provision of this Act, shall not be brought after the expiration of six years from the date on which the right of action accrued.

For the purposes of this subsection, the right of action shall not be treated as having accrued to any beneficiary entitled to a future interest in the trust property until the interest fell into possession.

(4) No beneficiary as against whom there would be a good defence under this Act shall derive any greater or other benefit from a judgment or order obtained by any other beneficiary that he could have obtained if he had brought the action and this Act had been pleaded in defence.

22. Time limit for actions claiming personal estate of a deceased person

Subject to section 21(1) and (2) of this Act—

(a) no action in respect of any claim to the personal estate of a deceased person or to any share or interest in any such estate (whether under a will or on intestacy) shall be brought after the expiration of twelve years from the date on which the right to receive the share or interest accrued; and

(b) no action to recover arrears of interest in respect of any legacy, or damages in respect of such arrears, shall be brought after the expiration of six years from the date on which the interest became due.

Actions for an account

23. Time limit in respect of actions for an account

An action for an account shall not be brought after the expiration of any time limit under this Act which is applicable to the claim which is the basis of the duty to account.

26. Administration to date back to death

For the purposes of the provisions of this Act relating to actions for the recovery of land . . . an administrator of the estate of a deceased person shall be treated as claiming as if there had been no interval of time between the death of the deceased person and the grant of the letters of administration.

27. Cure of defective disentailing assurance

(1) This section applies where—

(a) a person entitled in remainder to an entailed interest in any land makes an assurance of his interest which fails to bar the issue in tail or the estates and interests taking effect on the determination of the entailed interest, or fails to bar those estates and interests only; and

(b) any person takes possession of the land by virtue of the assurance.

(2) If the person taking possession of the land by virtue of the assurance, or any other person whatsoever (other than a person entitled to possession by virtue of the settlement) is in possession of the land for a period of twelve years from the commencement of the time when the assurance could have operated as an effective bar, the assurance shall thereupon operate, and be treated as having always operated, to bar the issue in tail and the estates and interests taking effect on the determination of the entailed interest.

(3) The reference in subsection (2) above to the time when the assurance could have operated as an effective bar is a reference to the time at which the assurance, as it had then been executed by the person entitled to the entailed interest, would have operated, without the consent of any other person, to bar the issue in tail and the estates and interests taking effect on the determination of the entailed interest.

PART II
EXTENSION OR EXCLUSION OF ORDINARY TIME LIMITS

Disability

28. Extension of limitation period in case of disability

(1) Subject to the following provisions of this section, if on the date when any right of action accrued for which a period of limitation is prescribed by this Act, the person to whom it accrued was under a disability, the action may be brought at any time before the expiration of six years from the date when he ceased to be under a disability or died (whichever first occurred) notwithstanding that the period of limitation has expired.

(2) This section shall not affect any case where the right of action first accrued to some person (not under a disability) through whom the person under a disability claims.

(3) When a right of action which has accrued to a person under a disability accrues, on the death of that person while still under a disability, to another person under a disability, no further extension of time shall be allowed by reason of the disability of the second person.

(4) No action to recover land or money charged on land shall be brought by virtue of this section by any person after the expiration of thirty years from the date on which the right of action accrued to that person or some person through whom he claims.

Acknowledgment and part payment

29. Fresh accrual of action on acknowledgment or part payment

(1) Subsections (2) and (3) below apply where any right of action (including a foreclosure action) to recover land . . . or any right of a mortgagee of personal property to bring a foreclosure action in respect of the property has accrued.

(2) If the person in possession of the land, benefice or personal property in question acknowledges the title of the person to whom the right of action has accrued—

(a) the right shall be treated as having accrued on and not before the date of the acknowledgment; and

(b) in the case of a right of action to recover land which has accrued to a person entitled to an estate or interest taking effect on the determination of an entailed interest against whom time is running under section 27 of this Act, section 27 shall thereupon cease to apply to the land.

(3) In the case of a foreclosure or other action by a mortgagee, if the person in possession of the land, benefice or personal property in question or the person liable for the mortgage debt makes any payment in respect of the debt (whether of principal or interest) the right shall be treated as having accrued on and not before the date of the payment.

(4) Where a mortgagee is by virtue of the mortgage in possession of any mortgaged land and either—

(a) receives any sum in respect of the principal or interest of the mortgage debt; or

(b) acknowledges the title of the mortgagor, or his equity of redemption;

an action to redeem the land in his possession may be brought at any time before the expiration of twelve years from the date of the payment or acknowledgment.

(5) Subject to subsection (6) below, where any right of action has accrued to recover—

(a) any debt or other liquidated pecuniary claim; or

(b) any claim to the personal estate of a deceased person or to any share or interest in any such estate;

and the person liable or accountable for the claim acknowledges the claim or makes any payment in respect of it the right shall be treated as having accrued on and not before the date of the acknowledgment or payment.

(6) A payment of a part of the rent or interest due at any time shall not extend the period for claiming the remainder then due, but any payment of interest shall be treated as a payment in respect of the principal debt.

(7) Subject to subsection (6) above, a current period of limitation may be repeatedly extended under this section by further acknowledgments or payments, but a right of action, once barred by this Act, shall not be revived by any subsequent acknowledgment or payment.

30. Formal provisions as to acknowledgments and part payments

(1) To be effective for the purposes of section 29 of this Act, an acknowledgment must be in writing and signed by the person making it.

(2) For the purposes of section 29, any acknowledgment or payment—

(a) may be sent by the agent of the person by whom it is required to be made under that section; and

(b) shall be made to the person, or to an agent of the person, whose title or claim is being acknowledged or, as the case may be, in respect of whose claim the payment is being made.

31. Effect of acknowledgment or part payment on persons other than the maker or recipient

(1) An acknowledgment of the title to any land, benefice, or mortgaged personalty by any person in possession of it shall bind all other persons in possession during the ensuing period of limitation.

(2) A payment in respect of a mortgage debt by the mortgagor or any other person liable for the debt, or by any person in possession of the mortgaged property, shall, so far as any right of the mortgagee to foreclose or otherwise to recover the property is concerned, bind all other persons in possession of the mortgaged property during the ensuing period of limitation.

(3) Where two or more mortgagees are by virtue of the mortgage in possession of the mortgaged land, an acknowledgment of the mortgagor's title or of his equity of redemption by one of the mortgagees shall only bind him and his successors and shall not bind any other mortgagee or his successors.

(4) Where in a case within subsection (3) above the mortgagee by whom the acknowledgment is given is entitled to a part of the mortgaged land and not to any ascertained part of the mortgage debt the mortgagor shall be entitled to redeem that part of the land on payment, with interest, of the part of the mortgage debt which bears the same proportion to the whole of the debt as the value of the part of the land bears to the whole of the mortgaged land.

(5) Where there are two or more mortgagors, and the title or equity of redemption of one of the mortgagors is acknowledged as mentioned above in this section, the acknowledgment shall be treated as having been made to all the mortgagors.

(6) An acknowledgment of any debt or other liquidated pecuniary claim shall bind the acknowledgor and his successors but not any other person.

(7) A payment made in respect of any debt or other liquidated pecuniary claim shall bind all persons liable in respect of the debt or claim.

(8) An acknowledgment by one of several personal representatives of any claim to the personal estate of the deceased person or to any share or interest in any such estate, or a payment by one of several personal representatives in respect of any such claim, shall bind the estate of the deceased person.

(9) In this section 'successor', in relation to any mortgagee or person liable in respect of any debt or claim, means his personal representatives and any other person on whom the rights under the mortgage or, as the case may be, the liability in respect of the debt or claim devolve (whether on death or bankruptcy or the disposition of property or the determination of a limited estate or interest in settled property or otherwise).

Fraud, concealment and mistake

32. Postponement of limitation period in casc of fraud, concealment or mistake

(1)Subject to [subsection (3)] below, where in the case of any action for which a period of limitation is prescribed by this Act, either—

(a) the action is based upon the fraud of the defendant; or

(b) any fact relevant to the plaintiff s right of action has been deliberately concealed from him by the defendant; or

(c) the action is for relief from the consequences of a mistake;

the period of limitation shall not begin to run until the plaintiff has discovered the fraud, concealment or mistake (as the case may be) or could with reasonable diligence have discovered it.

References in this subsection to the defendant include references to the defendant's agent and to any person through whom the defendant claims and his agent.

(2) For the purposes of subsection (1) above, deliberate commission of a breach of duty in circumstances in which it is unlikely to be discovered for some time amounts to deliberate concealment of the facts involved in that breach of duty.

(3) Nothing in this section shall enable any action—

(a) to recover, or recover the value of, any property; or

(b) to enforce any charge against, or set aside any transaction affecting, any property;

to be brought against the purchaser of the property or any person claiming through him in any case where the property has been purchased for valuable consideration by an innocent third party since the fraud or concealment or (as the case may be) the transaction in which the mistake was made took place.

(4) A purchaser is an innocent third party for the purposes of this section—

(a) in the case of fraud or concealment of any fact relevant to the plaintiff's right of action, if he was not a party to the fraud or (as the case may be) to the concealment of that fact and did not at the time of the purchase know or have reason to believe that the fraud or concealment had taken place; and

(b) in the case of mistake, if he did not at that time of the purchase know or have reason to believe that the mistake had been made.

38. Interpretation

(1) In this Act, unless the context otherwise requires—

'action' includes any proceeding in a court of law, including an ecclesiastical court;

'land' includes corporeal hereditaments, tithes and rentcharges and any legal or equitable estate or interest therein, including an interest in the proceeds of the sale of land held upon trust for sale, but except as provided above in this definition does not include any incorporeal hereditament;

'personal estate' and 'personal property' do not include chattels real; 'rent' includes a rentcharge and a rentservice;

'rentcharge' means any annuity or periodical sum of money charged upon or payable out of land, except a rent service or interest on a mortgage on land;

'settled land', 'statutory owner' and 'tenant for life' have the same meanings respectively as in the Settled Land Act 1925;

'trust' and 'trustee' have the same meanings respectively as in the Trustee Act 1925; and

'trust for sale' has the same meaning as in the Law of Property Act 1925.

(2) For the purposes of this Act a person shall be treated as under a disability while he is an infant, or of unsound mind.

(3) For the purposes of subsection (2) above a person is of unsound mind if he is a person who, by reason of mental disorder within the meaning of the [Mental Health Act 1983] is incapable of managing and administering his property and affairs.

(4) Without prejudice to the generality of subsection (3) above, a person shall be conclusively presumed for the purposes of subsection (2) above to be of unsound mind—

(a) while he is liable to be detained or subject to guardianship under the [Mental Health Act 1983 (otherwise than by virtue of section 35 or 89)] or

[(b) while he is receiving treatment as an in-patient in any hospital within the meaning of the Mental Health Act 1983 or mental nursing home within the meaning of the Nursing Homes Act 1975 without being liable to be detained under the said Act of 1983 (otherwise than by virtue of section 35 or 89), being treatment which follows without any interval a period during which he was liable to be detained or subject to guardianship under the Mental Health Act 1959, or the said Act of 1983 (otherwise than by virtue of section 35 or 89) or by virtue of any enactment repealed or excluded by the Mental Health Act 1959.]

(5) Subject to subsection (6) below, a person shall be treated as claiming through another person if he became entitled by, through, under, or by the act of that other person to the right claimed, and any person whose estate or interest might have been barred by a person entitled to an entailed interest in possession shall be treated as claiming through the person so entitled.

(6) A person becoming entitled to any estate or interest by virtue of a special power of appointment shall not be treated as claiming through the appointor.

(7) References in this Act to a right of action to recover land shall include references to a right to enter into possession of the land or, in the case of rentcharges and tithes, to distrain for arrears of rent or tithe, and references to the bringing of such an action shall include references to the making of such an entry or distress.

(8) References in this Act to the possession of land shall, in the case of tithes and rentcharges, be construed as references to the receipt of the tithe or rent, and references to the date of dispossession or discontinuance of possession of land shall, in the case of rentcharges, be construed as references to the date of the last receipt of rent.

(9) References in Part II of this Act to a right of action shall include references to—

(a) a cause of action;
(b) a right to receive money secured by a mortgage or charge on any property,
(c) a right to recover proceeds of the sale of land; and
(d) a right to receive a share of interest in the personal estate of a deceased person.

SCHEDULES

Section 15(6), (7)

SCHEDULE I
PROVISIONS WITH RESPECT TO ACTIONS TO RECOVER LAND
PART I
ACCRUAL OF RIGHTS OF ACTION TO RECOVER LAND

Accrual of right of action in case of present interests in land

1. Where the person bringing an action to recover land, or some person through whom he claims, has been in possession of the land, and has while entitled to the land been dispossessed or discontinued his possession, the right of action shall be treated as having accrued on the date of the dispossession or discontinuance.

2. Where any person brings an action to recover any land of a deceased person (whether under a will or on intestacy) and the deceased person—

(a) was on the date of his death in possession of the land or, in the case of a rent charge created by will or taking effect upon his death, in possession of the land charged; and

(b) was the last person entitled to the land to be in possession of it;

the right of action shall be treated as having accrued on the date of his death.

3. Where any person brings an action to recover land, being an estate or interest in possession assured otherwise than by will to him, or to some person through whom he claims, and—

(a) the person making the assurance was on the date when the assurance took effect in possession of the land or, in the case of a rentcharge created by the assurance, in possession of the land charged; and

(b) no person has been in possession of the land by virtue of the assurance; the right of action shall be treated as having accrued on the date when the assurance took effect.

Accrual of right of action in case of future interests

4. The right of action to recover any land shall, in a case where—

(a) the estate or interest claimed was an estate or interest in reversion or remainder or any other future estate or interest, and

(b) no person has taken possession of the land by virtue of the estate or interest claimed;

be treated as having accrued on the date on which the estate or interest fell into possession by the determination of the preceding estate or interest.

5.—(1) Subject to sub-paragraph (2) below, a tenancy from year to year or other period, without a lease in writing, shall for the purposes of this Act be treated as being determined at the expiration of the first year or other period; and accordingly the right of action of the person entitled to the land subject to the tenancy shall be treated as having accrued at the date on which in accordance with this sub-paragraph the tenancy is determined.

(2) Where any rent has subsequently been received in respect of the tenancy, the right of action shall be treated as having accrued on the date of the last receipt of rent.

6.—(1) Where—

(a) any person is in possession of land by virtue of a lease in writing by which a rent of not less than ten pounds a year is reserved; and

(b) the rent is received by some person wrongfully claiming to be entitled to the land in reversion immediately expectant on the determination of the lease; and

(c) no rent is subsequently received by the person rightfully so entitled; the right of action to recover the land of the person rightfully so entitled shall be treated as having accrued on the date when the rent was first received by the person wrongfully claiming to be so entitled and not on the date of the determination of the lease.

(2) Sub-paragraph (1) above shall not apply to any lease granted by the Crown.

Accrual of right of action in case of forfeiture or breach of condition

7.—(1) Subject to sub-paragraph (2) below, a right of action to recover land by virtue of a forfeiture or breach of condition shall be treated as having accrued on the date on which the forfeiture was incurred or the condition broken.

(2) If any such right has accrued to a person entitled to an estate or interest in reversion or remainder and the land was not recovered by virtue of that right, the right of action to recover the land shall not be treated as having accrued to that person until his estate or interest fell into possession, as if no such forfeiture or breach of condition had occurred.

Right of action not to accrue or continue unless there is adverse possession

8.—(1) No right of action to recover land shall be treated as accruing unless the land is in the possession of some person in whose favour the period of limitation can run (referred to below in this paragraph as 'adverse possession'); and where under the preceding provisions of this Schedule any such right of action is treated as accruing on a certain date and no person is in adverse possession on that date, the right of action shall not be treated as accruing unless and until adverse possession is taken of the land.

(2) Where a right of action to recover land has accrued and after its accrual, before the right is barred, the land ceases to be in adverse possession, the right of action shall no longer be treated as having accrued and no fresh right of action shall be treated as accruing unless and until the land is again taken into adverse possession.

(3) For the purposes of this paragraph—

(a) possession of any land subject to a rentcharge by a person (other than the person entitled to the rentcharge) who does not pay the rent shall be treated as adverse possession of the rentcharge; and

(b) receipt of rent under a lease by a person wrongfully claiming to be entitled to the land in reversion immediately expectant on the determination of the lease shall be treated as adverse possession of the land.

(4) For the purpose of determining whether a person occupying any land is in adverse possession of the land it shall not be assumed by implication of law that his occupation is by permission of the person entitled to the land merely by virtue of the fact that his occupation is not inconsistent with the latter's present or future enjoyment of the land.

This provision shall not be taken as prejudicing a finding to the effect that a person's occupation of any land is by implied permission of the person entitled to the land in any case where such a finding is justified on the actual facts of the case.

Possession of beneficiary not adverse to others interested in settled land or land [subject to a trust of land]

9. Where any settled land or any land [subject to a trust of land] is in the possession of a person entitled to a beneficial interest in the land or in the proceeds of sale (not being a person solely or absolutely entitled to the land or the proceeds), no right of action to recover the land shall be treated for the purposes of this Act as accruing during that possession to any person in whom the land is vested as tenant for life, statutory owner or trustee, or to any other person entitled to a beneficial interest in the land or the proceeds of sale.

SUPREME COURT ACT 1981
(1981, c. 54)

49. Concurrent administration of law and equity

(1) Subject to the provisions of this or any other Act, every court exercising jurisdiction in England or Wales in any civil cause or matter shall continue to administer law and equity on the basis that, wherever there is any conflict or variance between the rules of equity and the rules of the common law with reference to the same matter, the rules of equity shall prevail.

(2) Every such court shall give the same effect as hitherto—

(a) to all equitable estates, titles, rights, reliefs, defences and counterclaims, and to all equitable duties and liabilities; and

(b) subject thereto, to all legal claims and demands and all estates, titles, rights, duties, obligations and liabilities existing by the common law or by any custom or created by any statute,

and, subject to the provisions of this or any other Act, shall so exercise its jurisdiction in every cause or matter before it as to secure that, as far as possible, all matters in dispute between the parties are completely and finally determined, and all multiplicity of legal proceedings with respect to any of those matters is avoided.

(3) Nothing in this Act shall affect the power of the Court of Appeal or the High Court to stay any proceedings before it, where it thinks fit to do so, either of its own motion or on the application of any person, whether or not a party to the proceedings.

50. Power to award damages as well as, or in substitution for, injunction or specific performance

Where the Court of Appeal or the High Court has jurisdiction to entertain an application for an injunction or specific performance, it may award damages in addition to, or in substitution for, an injunction or specific performance.

Powers of court in relation to personal representatives

112. Summons to executor to prove or renounce

The High Court may summon any person named as executor in a will to prove, or renounce probate of, the will, and to do such other things concerning the will as the court had power to order such a person to do immediately before the commencement of this Act.

113. Power of court to sever grant

(1) Subject to subsection (2), the High Court may grant probate or administration in respect of any part of the estate of a deceased person, limited in any way the court thinks fit.

(2) Where the estate of a deceased person is known to be insolvent, the grant of representation to it shall not be severed under subsection (1) except as regards a trust estate in which he had no beneficial interest.

114. Number of personal representatives

(1) Probate or administration shall not be granted by the High Court to more than four persons in respect of the same part of the estate of a deceased person.

(2) Where under a will or intestacy any beneficiary is a minor or a life interest arises, any grant of administration by the High Court shall be made either to a trust corporation (with or without an individual) or to not less than two individuals, unless it appears to the court to be expedient in all the circumstances to appoint an individual as sole administrator.

(3) For the purpose of determining whether a minority or life interest arises in any particular case, the court may act on such evidence as may be prescribed.

(4) If at any time during the minority of a beneficiary or the subsistence of a life interest under a will or intestacy there is only one personal representative (not being a trust corporation), the High Court may, on the application of any person interested or the guardian or receiver of any such person, and in accordance with probate rules, appoint one or more additional personal representatives to act while the minority or life interest subsists and until the estate is fully administered.

(5) An appointment of an additional personal representative under subsection (4) to act with an executor shall not have the effect of including him in any chain of representation.

116. Power of court to pass over prior claims to grant

(1) If by reason of any special circumstances it appears to the High Court to be necessary or expedient to appoint as administrator some person other than the person who, but for this section, would in accordance with probate rules have been entitled to the grant, the court may in its discretion appoint as administrator such person as it thinks expedient.

(2) Any grant of administration under this section may be limited in any way the court thinks fit.

117. Administration pending suit

(1) Where any legal proceedings concerning the validity of the will of a deceased person, or for obtaining, recalling or revoking any grant, are pending, the High Court may grant administration of the estate of the deceased person in question to an administrator pending suit, who shall, subject to subsection (2), have all the rights, duties and powers of a general administrator.

(2) An administrator pending suit shall be subject to the immediate control of the court and act under its direction; and, except in such circumstances as may be prescribed, no distribution of the estate, or any part of the estate, of the deceased person in question shall be made by such an administrator without the leave of the court.

(3) The court may, out of the estate of the deceased, assign an administrator pending suit such reasonable remuneration as it thinks fit.

118. Effect of appointment of minor as executor

Where a testator by his will appoints a minor to be an executor, the appointment shall not operate to vest in the minor the estate, or any part of the estate, of the testator, or to constitute him a personal representative for any purpose, unless and until probate is granted to him in accordance with probate rules.

119. Administration with will annexed

(1) Administration with the will annexed shall be granted, subject to and in accordance with probate rules, in every class of case in which the High Court had power to make such a grant immediately before the commencement of this Act.

(2) Where administration with the will annexed is granted, the will of the deceased shall be performed and observed in the same manner as if probate of it had been granted to an executor.

120. Power to require administrators to produce sureties

(1) As a condition of granting administration to any person the High Court may, subject to the following provisions of this section and subject to and in accordance with probate rules, require one or more sureties to guarantee that they will make good, within any limit imposed by the court on the total liability of the surety or sureties, any loss which any person interested in the administration of the estate of the deceased may suffer in consequence of a breach by the administrator of his duties as such.

(2) A guarantee given in pursuance of any such requirement shall enure for the benefit of every person interested in the administration of the estate of the deceased as if contained in a contract under seal made by the surety or sureties with every such person and, where there are two or more sureties, as if they had bound themselves jointly and severally.

(3) No action shall be brought on any such guarantee without the leave of the High Court.

(4) Stamp duty shall not be chargeable on any such guarantee.

(5) This section does not apply where administration is granted to the Treasury Solicitor, the Official Solicitor, the Public Trustee, the Solicitor for the affairs of the Duchy of Lancaster, or the Duchy of Cornwall or the Crown Solicitor for Northern Ireland, or to the consular officer of a foreign state to which section 1 of the Consular Conventions Act 1949 applies, or in such other cases as may be prescribed.

Revocation of grants and cancellation of resealing at instance of court

121. Revocation of grants and cancellation of resealing at instance of court

(1) Where it appears to the High Court that a grant either ought not to have been made or contains an error, the court may call in the grant and, if satisfied that it would be revoked at the instance of a party interested, may revoke it.

(2) A grant may be revoked under subsection (1) without being called in, if it cannot be called in.

(3) Where it appears to the High Court that a grant resealed under the Colonial Probates Acts 1892 and 1927 ought not to have been resealed, the court may call in the relevant document and, if satisfied that the reseating would be cancelled at the instance of a party interested, may cancel the resealing.

In this and the following subsection 'the relevant document' means the original grant or, where some other document was sealed by the court under those Acts, that document.

(4) A resealing may be cancelled under subsection (3) without the relevant document being called in, if it cannot be called in.

Ancillary powers of court

122. Examination of person with knowledge of testamentary document

(1) Where it appears that there are reasonable grounds for believing that any person has knowledge of any document which is or purports to be a testamentary document, the High Court may, whether or not any legal proceedings are pending, order him to attend for the purpose of being examined in open court.

(2) The court may—

(a) require any person who is before it in compliance with an order under subsection (1) to answer any question relating to the document concerned; and

(b) if appropriate, order him to bring in the document in such manner as the court may direct.

(3) Any person who, having been required by the court to do so under this section, fails to attend for examination, answer any question or bring in any document shall be guilty of contempt of court.

123. Subpoena to bring in testamentary document

Where it appears that any person has in his possession, custody or power any document which is or purports to be a testamentary document, the High Court may, whether or not any legal prodeedings are pending, issue a subpoena requiring him to bring in the document in such manner as the court may in the subpoena direct.

Provisions as to documents

124. Place for deposit of original wills and other documents

All original wills and other documents which are under the control of the High Court in the Principal Registry or in any district probate registry shall be deposited and preserved in such places as the Lord Chancellor may direct; and any wills or other documents so deposited shall, subject to the control of the High Court and to probate rules, be open to inspection.

125. Copies of wills and grants

An office copy, or a sealed and certified copy, of any will or part of a will open to inspection under section 124 or of any grant may, on payment of the prescribed fee, be obtained—

(a) from the registry in which in accordance with section 124 the will or documents relating to the grant are preserved; or

(b) where in accordance with that section the will or such documents are preserved in some place other than a registry, from the Principal Registry; or

(c) subject to the approval of the Senior Registrar of the Family Division, from the Principal Registry in any case where the will was proved in or the grant was issued from a district probate registry.

Probate rules

127. Probate rules

(1) The President of the Family Division may, with the concurrence of the Lord Chancellor, make rules of court (in this Part referred to as 'probate rules') for regulating and prescribing the practice and procedure of the High Court with respect to non-contentious or common form probate business.

(2) Without prejudice to the generality of subsection (1), probate rules may make provision for regulating the classes of persons entitled to grants of probate or administration in particular circumstances and the relative priorities of their claims thereto.

(3) Probate rules shall be made by statutory instrument subject to annulment in pursuance of a resolution of either House of Parliament; and the Statutory Instruments Act 1946 shall apply to a statutory instrument containing probate rules in like manner as if they had been made by a Minister of the Crown.

FORFEITURE ACT 1982
(1982, c. 34)

1. The 'forfeiture rule'

(1) In this Act, the 'forfeiture rule' means the rule of public policy which in certain circumstances precludes a person who has unlawfully killed another from acquiring a benefit in consequence of the killing.

(2) References in this Act to a person who has unlawfully killed another include a reference to a person who has unlawfully aided, abetted, counselled or procured the death of that other and references in this Act to unlawful killing shall be interpreted accordingly.

2. Power to modify the rule

(1) Where a court determines that the forfeiture rule has precluded a person (in this section referred to as 'the offender') who has unlawfully killed another from acquiring any interest in property mentioned in subsection (4) below, the court may make an order under this section modifying the effect of that rule.

(2) The court shall not make an order under this section modifying the effect of the forfeiture rule in any case unless it is satisfied that, having regard to the conduct of the offender and of the deceased and to such other circumstances as appear to the court to be material, the justice of the case requires the effect of the rule to be so modified in that case.

(3) In any case where a person stands convicted of an offence of which unlawful killing is an element, the court shall not make an order under this section modifying the effect of the forfeiture rule in that case unless proceedings for the purpose are brought before the expiry of the period of three months beginning with his conviction.

(4) The interests in property referred to in subsection (1) above are—

(a) any beneficial interest in property which (apart from the forfeiture rule) the offender would have acquired—

(i) under the deceased's will . . . or the law relating to intestacy or by way of ius relicti, ius relictae or legitim;

(ii) on the nomination of the deceased in accordance with the provisions of any enactment,

(iii) as a donatio mortis causa made by the deceased;

(iv) under a special destination (whether relating to heritable or moveable property); or

(b) any beneficial interest in property which (apart from the forfeiture rule) the offender would have acquired in consequence of the death of the deceased, being property which, before the death, was held on trust for any person.

(5) An order under this section may modify the effect of the for feiture rule in respect of any interest in property to which the determination referred to in subsection (1) above relates and may do so in either or both of the following ways, that is—

(a) where there is more than one such interest, by excluding the application of the rule in respect of any (but not all) of those interests; and

(b) in the case of any such interest in property, by excluding the application of the rule in respect of part of the property.

(6) On the making of an order under this section, the forfeiture rule shall have effect for all purposes (including purposes relating to anything done before the order is made) subject to the modifications made by the order.

(7) The court shall not make an order under this section modifying the effect of the forfeiture rule in respect of any interest in property which, in consequence of the rule, has been acquired before the coming into force of this section by a person other than the offender or a person claiming through him.

(8) In this section—

'property' includes any chose in action or incorporeal moveable property; and
'will' includes codicil.

3. Application for financial provision not affected by the rule

(1) The forfeiture rule shall not be taken to preclude any person from making any application under a provision mentioned in subsection (2) below or the making of any order on the application.

(2) The provisions referred to in subsection (1) above are—

(a) any provision of the Inheritance (Provision for Family and Dependants) Act 1975; and

(b) sections 31(6) (variation etc. of periodical payments orders) and 36(1) (variation of maintenance agreements) of the Matrimonial Causes Act 1973 . . .

5. Exclusion of murderers

Nothing in this Act or in any order made under section 2 or referred to in section 3(1) of this Act . . . shall affect the application of the forfeiture rule in the case of a person who stands convicted of murder.

ADMINISTRATION OF JUSTICE ACT 1982
(1982, c. 53)

Rectification and interpretation of wills

20. Rectification

(1) If a court is satisfied that a will is so expressed that it fails to carry out the testator's intentions, in consequence—

(a) of a clerical error; or

(b) of a failure to understand his instructions,

it may order that the will shall be rectified so as to carry out his intentions.

(2) An application for an order under this section shall not, except with the permission of the court, be made after the end of the period of six months from the date on which representation with respect to the estate of the deceased is first taken out.

(3) The provisions of this section shall not render the personal representatives of a deceased person liable for having distributed any part of the estate of the deceased, after the end of the period of six months from the date on which representation with respect to the estate of the deceased is first taken out, on the ground that they ought to have taken into account the possibility that the court might permit the making of an application for an order under this section after the end of that period; but this subsection shall not prejudice any power to recover, by reason of the making of an order under this section, any part of the estate so distributed.

(4) In considering for the purposes of this section when representation with respect to the estate of a deceased person was first taken out, a grant limited to settled land or to trust property shall be left out of account, and a grant limited to real estate or to personal estate shall be left out of account unless a grant limited to the remainder of the estate has previously been made or is made at the same time.

21. Interpretation of wills — general rules as to evidence
(1) This section applies to a will—
(a) insofar as any part of it is meaningless—
(b) in so far as the language used in any part of it is ambiguous on the face of it;
(c) in so far as evidence, other than evidence of the testator's intention, shows that the language used in any part of it is ambiguous in the light of surrounding circumstances.
(2) Insofar as this section applies to a will extrinsic evidence, including evidence of the testator's intention, may be admitted to assist in its interpretation.

22. Presumption as to effect of gifts to spouses
Except where a contrary intention is shown it shall be presumed that if a testator devises or bequeaths property to his spouse in terms which in themselves would give an absolute interest to the spouse, but by the same instrument purports to give his issue an interest in the same property, the gift to the spouse is absolute notwithstanding the purported gift to the issue.

Registration of wills

23. Deposit and registration of wills of living persons
(1) The following, namely—
(a) the Principal Registry of the Family Division of the High Court of Justice;
(b)-(c) . . .
shall be registering authority for the purposes of this section.
(2) . . . (It) shall provide and maintain safe and convenient depositories for the custody of the wills of living persons.

LANDLORD AND TENANT ACT 1985
(1985, c. 70)

Information to be given to tenant

1. Disclosure of landlord's identity
(1) If the tenant of premises occupied as a dwelling makes a written request for the landlord's name and address to—
(a) any person who demands, or the last person who received, rent payable under the tenancy, or
(b) any other person for the time being acting as agent for the landlord, in relation to the tenancy.
that person shall supply the tenant with a written statement of the landlord's name and address within the period of 21 days beginning with the day on which he receives the request.
(2) . . .
(3) In this section and section 2—
(a) 'tenant' includes a statutory tenant;
and
(b) 'landlord' means the immediate landlord.

Provision of rent books

4. Provision of rent books
(1) Where a tenant has a right to occupy premises as a residence in consideration of a rent payable weekly, the landlord shall provide a rent book or other similar document for use in respect of the premises.
(2) Subsection (1) does not apply to premises if the rent includes a payment in respect of board and the value of that board to the tenant forms a substantial proportion of the whole rent.

(3) In this section and sections 5 . . .

(a) 'tenant' includes a statutory tenant and a person having a contractual right to occupy the premises; and

(b) 'landlord', in relation to a person having such a contractual right, means the person who granted the right or any successor in title of his, as the case may require.

5. Information to be contained in rent books

(1) A rent book or other similar document provided in pursuance of section 4 shall contain notice of the name and address of the landlord of the premises and—

(a) if the premises are occupied by virtue of a restricted contract, particulars of the rent and of the other terms and conditions of the contract and notice of such other matters as may be prescribed;

(b) if the premises are let on or subject to a protected or statutory tenancy, [or let on an assured tenancy within the meaning of Part I of the Housing Act 1988], notice of such matters as may be prescribed.

(2) If the premises are occupied by virtue of a restricted contractor let on or subject to a protected or statutory tenancy, [or let on an assured tenancy within the meaning of Part I of the Housing Act 1988] the notice and particulars required by this section shall be in the prescribed form.

(3) In this section 'prescribed' means prescribed by regulations made by the Secretary of State, which—

(a) may make different provision for different cases, and

(b) shall be made by statutory instrument which shall be subject to annulment in pursuance of a resolution of either House of Parliament.

Implied terms as to fitness for human habitation

8. Implied terms as to fitness for human habitation

(1) In a contract to which this section applies for the letting of a house for human habitation there is implied, notwithstanding any stipulation to the contrary—

(a) a condition that the house is fit for human habitation at the commencement of the tenancy, and

(b) an undertaking that the house will be kept by the landlord fit for human habitation during the tenancy.

(2) The landlord, or a person authorised by him in writing, may at reasonable times of the day, on giving 24 hours' notice in writing to the tenant or occupier, enter premises to which this section applies for the purpose of viewing their state and condition.

(3)–(4) . . .

10. Fitness for human habitation

In determining for the purposes of this Act whether a house is unfit for human habitation, regard shall be had to its condition in respect of the following matters—

repair,
stability,
freedom from damp,
internal arrangement,
natural lighting,
ventilation,
water supply,
drainage and sanitary conveniences,
facilities for preparation and cooking of food and for the disposal of waste water; and the house shall be regarded as unfit for human habitation if, and only if, it is so far defective in one or more of those matters that it is not reasonably suitable for occupation in that condition.

Repairing obligations

11. Repairing obligations in short leases

(1) In a lease to which this section applies (as to which, see sections 13 and 14) there is implied a covenant by the lessor—

(a) to keep in repair the structure and exterior of the dwelling-house (including drains, gutters and external pipes),

(b) to keep in repair and proper working order the installations in the dwelling-house for the supply of water, gas and electricity and for sanitation (including basins, sinks, baths and sanitary conveniences, but not other fixtures, fittings and appliances for making use of the supply of water, gas or electricity), and

(c) to keep in repair and proper working order the installations in the dwelling-house for space heating and heating water.

[(1A) If a lease to which this section applies is a lease of a dwelling-house which forms part only of a building, then, subject to subsection (1B), the covenant implied by subsection (1) shall have effect as if—

(a) the reference in paragraph (a) of that subsection to the dwelling-house included a reference to any part of the building in which the lessor has an estate or interest; and

(b) any reference in paragraph (b) and (c) of that subsection to an installation in the dwelling-house includes a reference to an installation which, directly or indirectly, serves the dwelling-house and which either—

(i) forms part of any part of a building in which the lessor has an estate or interest; or

(ii) is owned by the lessor or under his control.

(1B) Nothing in subsection (1A) shall be construed as requiring the lessor to carry out any works or repairs unless the disrepair (or failure to maintainin working order) is such as to affect the lessee's enjoyment of the dwelling-house or of any common parts, as defined in section 60(1) of the Landlord and Tenant Act 1987, which the lessee, as such, is entitled to use.]

(2) The covenant implied by subsection (1) ('the lessor's repairing covenant') shall not be construed as requiring the lessor—

(a) to carry out works or repairs for which the lessee is liable by virtue of his duty to use the premises in a tenant-like manner, or would be so liable but for an express covenant on his part,

(b) to rebuild or reinstate the premises in the case of destruction or damage by fire, or by tempest, flood or other inevitable accident, or

(c) to keep in repair or maintain anything which the lessee is entitled to remove from the dwelling-house.

(3) In determining the standard of repair required by the lessor's repairing covenant, regard shall be had to the age, character and prospective life of the dwelling-house and the locality in which it is situated.

[(3A) In any case where—

(a) the lessor's repairing covenant has effect as mentioned in subsection (1A), and

(b) in order to comply with the covenant the lessor needs to carry out works or repairs otherwise than in, or to an installation in the dwelling-house, and

(c) the lessor does not have a sufficient right in the part of the building or the installation concerned to enable him to carry out the required works or repairs, then, in any proceedings relating to a failure to comply with the lessor's repairing covenant, so far as it requires the lessor to carry out the works or repairs in question, it shall be a defence for the lessor to prove that he used all reasonable endeavours to obtain, but was unable to obtain, such rights as would be adequate to enable him to carry out the works or repairs.]

(4) A covenant by the lessee for the repair of the premises is of no effect so far as it relates to the matters mentioned in subsection (1)(a) to (c), except so far as it imposes on the lessee any of the requirements mentioned in subsection (2)(a) or (c).

(5) The reference in subsection (4) to a covenant by the lessee for the repair of the premises includes a covenant—

(a) to put in repair or deliver up in repair,
(b) to paint, point or render,
(c) to pay money in lieu of repairs by the lessee, or
(d) to pay money on account of repairs by the lessor.

(6) In a lease in which the lessor's repairing covenant is implied there is also implied a covenant by the lessee that the lessor, or any person authorised by him in writing, may at reasonable times of the day and on giving 24 hours' notice in writing to the occupier, enter the premises comprised in the lease for the purpose of viewing their condition and state of repair.

13. Leases to which s. 11 applies: general rule

(1) Section 11 (repairing obligations) applies to a lease of a dwelling-house granted on or after 24th October 1961 for a term of less than seven years.

(2) In determining whether a lease is one to which section 11 applies—

(a) any part of the term which falls before the grant shall be left out of account and the lease shall be treated as a lease for a term commencing with the grant,

(b) a lease which is determinable at the option of the lessor before the expiration of seven years from the commencement of the term shall be treated as a lease for a term of less than seven years, and

(c) a lease (other than a lease to which paragraph (b) applies) shall not be treated as a lease for a term of less than seven years if it confers on the lessee an option for renewal for a term which, together with the original term, amounts to seven years or more.

(3) This section has effect subject to—

section 14 (leases to which section 11 applies: exceptions), and

section 32(2) (provisions not applying to tenancies within Part II of the Landlord and Tenant Act 1954).

14. Leases to which s. 11 applies: exceptions

(1) Section 11 (repairing obligations) does not apply to a new lease granted to an existing tenant, or to a former tenant still in possession, if the previous lease was not a lease to which section 11 applied (and, in the case of a lease granted before 24th October 1961, would not have been if it had been granted on or after that date).

(2) 'In subsection (1)—

'existing tenant' means a person who is when, or immediately before the new lease is granted, the lessee under another lease of the dwelling-house;

'former tenant still in possession' means a person who—

(a) was the lessee under another lease of the dwelling-house which terminated at some time before the new lease was granted, and

(b) between the termination of that other lease and the grant of the new lease was continuously in possession of the dwelling-house or of the rents and profits of the dwelling-house; and

'the previous lease' means the other lease referred to in the above definitions.

(3) Section 11 does not apply to a lease of a dwelling-house which is a tenancy of an agricultural holding within the meaning of the [Agricultural Holdings Act 1986] [and in relation to which that Act applies or to a farm business tenancy within the meaning of the Agricultural Tenancies Act 1995].

(4) Section 11 does not apply to a lease granted on or after 3rd October 1980 to—

a local authority,

[a National Park authority]
a new town corporation,
an urban development corporation,
the Development Board for Rural Wales,
a registered housing association,
a cooperative housing association, or
an educational institution or other body specified, or of a class specified, by regulations under section 8 of the Rent Act 1977 [or paragraph 8 of Schedule 1 to the Housing Act 1988] (bodies making student lettings)
[a housing action trust established under Part III of the Housing Act 1988.]

(5) Section 11 does not apply to a lease granted on or after 3rd October 1980 to—

(a) Her Majesty in right of the Crown (unless the lease is under the management of the Crown Estate Commissioners), or

(b) a government department or a person holding in trust for Her Majesty for the purposes of a government department.

LAND REGISTRATION ACT 1986
(1986, c. 26)

5. Abolition of Minor Interests Index

(1) In section 102 of the 1925 Act, subsection (2) (under which priorities between certain dealings with equitable interests are regulated by the order of lodging of priority cautions and inhibitions) is repealed, and accordingly—

(a) the index maintained for the purposes of that subsection and known as the Minor Interests Index shall cease to be kept, and

(b) any question of priority which would have fallen to be determined in accordance with that subsection shall be determined in accordance with the rule of law referred to in section 137(1) of the Law of Property Act 1925 (which applies to dealings with equitable interests in land the rule commonly known as the rule in *Dearle* v *Hall*).

(2) The following provisions have effect for the purposes of the application of the rule in *Dearle* v *Hall*, and of sections 137 and 138 of the Law of Property Act 1925, to dealings in respect of which a priority caution or inhibition was entered in the Minor Interests Index—

(a) the notice of the making of the entry which was given under the Land Registration Rules 1925 before the commencement of this Act to the proprietor or, in the case of settled land, to the trustees of the settlement, shall be treated for those purposes as a notice of the dealing to which the entry relates given (at the time it was issued by the registrar) by the person on whose behalf the entry was made to the trustees or other persons appropriate to receive it for the purposes of establishing priority under the rule in *Dearle* v *Hall*;

(b) where a trust corporation has been nominated to receive notices of dealings in accordance with section 138, subsection (4) of that section (under which the notice does not affect priority until received by the corporation) does not apply but the trustees shall, if the notice has not already been transmitted to the corporation, deliver it or send it by post to the corporation as soon as practicable after the commencement of this Act.

(3) A person who suffers loss as a result of the operation of this section is entitled to be indemnified in the same way as a person suffering loss by reason of an error or omission in the register, except that in relation to a claim under this subsection the reference in section 83(6)(a) of the 1925 Act (restriction on amount of indemnity in certain cases) to the value of the relevant estate, interest or charge at the time when the error or omission was made shall be construed as a reference to its value immediately before the commencement of this Act.

(4) For the purposes of subsection (3) above, a loss resulting from trustees failing to comply with their duty under subsection (2)(b) above shall be treated as a loss

resulting from the operation of this section; but this is without prejudice to the liability of the trustees for breach of that duty or to the registrar's right of recourse against them under section 83(10) of the 1925 Act (under which the registrar may enforce a right which a person indemnified would have been entitled to enforce in relation to a matter in respect of which an indemnity has been paid).

(5) . . .

INSOLVENCY ACT 1986
(1986, c. 45)

CHAPTER V
EFFECT OF BANKRUPTCY ON CERTAIN RIGHTS, TRANSACTIONS, ETC.

[*Rights under trusts of land*

335A. Rights under trusts of land

(1) Any application by a trustee of a bankrupt's estate under section 14 of the Trusts of Land and Appointment of Trustees Act 1996 (powers of court in relation to trusts of land) for an order under that section for the sale of land shall be made to the court having jurisdiction in relation to the bankruptcy.

(2) On such an application the court shall make such order as it thinks just and reasonable having regard to—

(a) the interests of the bankrupt's creditors;

(b) where the application is made in respect of land which includes a dwelling house which is or has been the home of the bankrupt or the bankrupt's spouse or former spouse—

(i) the conduct of the spouse or former spouse, so far as contributing to the bankruptcy,

(ii) the needs and financial resources of the spouse or former spouse, and

(iii) the needs of any children; and

(c) all the circumstances of the case other than the needs of the bankrupt.

(3) Where such an application is made after the end of the period of one year beginning with the first vesting under Chapter IV of this Part of the bankrupt's estate in a trustee, the court shall assume, unless the circumstances of the case are exceptional, that the interests of the bankrupt's creditors outweigh all other considerations.

(4) The powers conferred on the court by this section are exercisable on an application whether it is made before or after the commencement of this section.]

Rights of occupation

336. Rights of occupation etc. of bankrupt's spouse

(1) Nothing occurring in the initial period of the bankruptcy (that is to say, the period beginning with the day of the presentation of the petition for the bankruptcy order and ending with the vesting of the bankrupt's estate in a trustee) is to be taken as having given rise to any [matrimonial home rights under Part IV of the Family Law Act 1996] in relation to a dwelling house comprised in the bankrupt's estate.

(2) Where a spouse's [matrimonial home rights under the Act of 1996] are a charge on the estate or interest of the other spouse, or of trustees for the other spouse, and the other spouse is adjudged bankrupt—

(a) the charge continues to subsist notwithstanding the bankruptcy and, subject to the provisions of that Act, binds the trustee of the bankrupt's estate and persons deriving title under that trustee, and

(b) any application for an order under [section 33 of that Act] shall be made to the court having jurisdiction in relation to the bankruptcy.

(3) [. . .]

(4) On such an application as is mentioned in subsection (2) [. . .] the court shall make such order under [section 33 of the Act of 1996] [. . .] as it thinks just and reasonable having regard to—

(a) the interests of the bankrupt's creditors,

(b) the conduct of the spouse or former spouse, so far as contributing to the bankruptcy,

(c) the needs and financial resources of the spouse or former spouse,

(d) the needs of any children, and

(e) all the circumstances of the case other than the needs of the bankrupt.

(5) Where such an application is made after the end of the period of one year beginning with the first vesting under Chapter IV of this Part of the bankrupt's estate in a trustee, the court shall assume, unless the circumstances of the case are exceptional, that the interests of the bankrupt's creditors outweigh all other considerations.

337. Rights of occupation of bankrupt

(1) This section applies where—

(a) a person who is entitled to occupy a dwelling house by virtue of a beneficial estate or interest is adjudged bankrupt, and

(b) any persons under the age of 18 with whom that person had at some time occupied that dwelling house had their home with that person at the time when the bankruptcy petition was presented and at the commencement of the bankruptcy.

(2) Whether or not the bankrupt's spouse (if any) has rights of occupation under [matrimonial home rights under Part IV of the Family Law Act 1996]—

(a) the bankrupt has the following rights as against the trustee of his estate—

(i) if in occupation, a right not to be evicted or excluded from the dwelling house or any part of it, except with the leave of the court,

(ii) if not in occupation, a right with the leave of the court to enter into and occupy the dwelling house, and

(b) the bankrupt's rights are a charge, having the like priority as an equitable interest created immediately before the commencement of the bankruptcy, on so much of his estate or interest in the dwelling house as vests in the trustee.

[(3) The Act of 1996 has effect, with the necessary modifications, as if—

(a) the rights conferred by paragraph (a) of subsection (2) were matrimonial home rights under that Act,

(b) any application for such leave as is mentioned in that paragraph were an application for an order under section 33 of that Act, and

(c) any charge under paragraph (b) of that subsection on the estate or interest of the trustee were a charge under that Act on the estate or interest of a spouse.]

(4) Any application for leave such as is mentioned in subsection (2)(a) or otherwise by virtue of this section for an order under [section 33 of the Act of 1996] shall be made to the court having jurisdiction in relation to the bankruptcy.

(5) On such an application the court shall make such order under [section 33 of the Act of 1996] as it thinks just and reasonable having regard to the interests of the creditors, to the bankrupt's financial resources, to the needs of the children and to all the circumstances of the case other than the needs of the bankrupt.

(6) Where such an application is made after the end of the period of one year beginning with the first vesting . . . of the bankrupt's estate in a trustee, the court shall asume, unless the circumstances of the case are exceptional, that the interests of the bankrupt's creditors outweight all other considerations.

338. Payments in respect of premises occupied by bankrupt

Where any premises comprised in a bankrupt's estate are occupied by him (whether by virtue of the preceding section or otherwise) on condition that he makes payments towards satisfying any liability arising under a mortgage of the premises or otherwise towards the outgoings of the premises, the bankrupt does not, by virtue of those payments, acquire any interest in the premises.

Adjustment of prior transactions, etc.

339. Transactions at an undervalue

(1) Subject as follows in this section and sections 341 and 342, where an individual is adjudged bankrupt and he has at a relevant time (defined in section 341) entered into a transaction with any person at an undervalue, the trustee of the bankrupt's estate may apply to the court for an order under this section.

(2) The court shall, on such an application, make such order as it thinks fit for restoring the position to what it would have been if that individual had not entered into that transaction.

(3) For the purposes of this section and sections 341 and 342, an individual enters into a transaction with a person at an undervalue if—

(a) he makes a gift to that person or he otherwise enters into a transaction with that person on terms that provide for him to receive no consideration,

(b) he enters into a transaction with that person in consideration of marriage, or

(c) he enters into a transaction with that person for a consideration the value of which, in money or money's worth, is significantly less than the value, in money or money's worth, of the consideration provided by the individual.

340. Preferences

(1) Subject as follows in this and the next two sections, where an individual is adjudged bankrupt and he has at a relevant time (defined in section 341) given a preference to any person, the trustee of the bankrupt's estate may apply to the court for an order under this section.

(2) The court shall, on such an application, make such order as it thinks fit for restoring the position to what it would have been if that individual had not given that preference.

(3) For the purposes of this and the next two sections, an individual gives a preference to a person if—

(a) that person is one of the individual's creditors or a surety or guarantor for any of his debts or other liabilities, and

(b) the individual does anything or suffers anything to be done which (in either case) has the effect of putting that person into a position which, in the event of the individual's bankruptcy, will be better than the position he would have been in if that thing had not been done.

(4) The court shall not make an order under this section in respect of a preference given to any person unless the individual who gave the preference was influenced in deciding to give it by a desire to produce in relation to that person the effect mentioned in subsection (3)(b) above.

(5) An individual who has given a preference to a person who, at the time the preference was given, was an associate of his (otherwise than by reason only of being his employee) is presumed, unless the contrary is shown, to have been influenced in deciding to give it by such a desire as is mentioned in subsection (4).

(6) The fact that something has been done in pursuance of the order of a court does not, without more, prevent the doing or suffering of that thing from constituting the giving of a preference.

341. 'Relevant time' under ss. 339, 340

(1) Subject as follows, the time at which an individual enters into a transaction at an undervalue or gives a preference is a relevant time if the transaction is entered into or the preference given—

(a) in the case of a transaction at an undervalue, at a time in the period of 5 years ending with the day of the presentation of the bankruptcy petition on which the individual is adjudged bankrupt,

(b) in the case of a preference which is not a transaction at an undervalue and is given to a person who is an associate of the individual (otherwise than by reason only of being his employee), at a time in the period of 2 years ending with that day, and

(c) in any other case of a preference which is not a transaction at an undervalue, at a time in the period of 6 months ending with that day.

(2) Where an individual enters into a transaction at an undervalue or gives a preference at a time mentioned in paragraph (a), (b) or (c) of subsection (1) (not being, in the case of a transaction at an undervalue, a time less than 2 years before the end of the period mentioned in paragraph (a)), that time is not a relevant time for the purposes of sections 339 and 340 unless the individual—

(a) is insolvent at that time, or

(b) becomes insolvent in consequence of the transaction or preference;

but the requirements of this subsection are presumed to be satisfied, unless the contrary is shown, in relation to any transaction at an undervalue which is entered into by an individual with a person who is an associate of his (otherwise than by reason only of being his employee).

(3) For the purposes of subsection (2), an individual is insolvent if—

(a) he is unable to pay his debts as they fall due, or

(b) the value of his assets is less than the amount of his liabilities, taking into account his contingent and prospective liabilities.

(4) . . .

(5) No order shall be made under section 339 or 340 by virtue of subsection (4) of this section where an appeal is pending (within the meaning of section 277) against the individual's conviction of any offence by virtue of which the criminal bankruptcy order was made.

342. Orders under ss. 339, 340

(1) Without prejudice to the generality of section 339(2) or 340(2), an order under either of those sections with respect to a transaction or preference entered into or given by an individual who is subsequently adjudged bankrupt may (subject as follows)—

(a) require any property transferred as part of the transaction, or in connection with the giving of the preference, to be vested in the trustee of the bankrupt's estate as part of that estate;

(b) require any property to be so vested if it represents in any person's hands the application either of the proceeds of sale of property so transferred or of money so transferred;

(c) release or discharge (in whole or in part) any security given by the individual;

(d) require any person to pay, in respect of benefits received by him from the individual, such sums to the trustee of his estate as the court may direct,

(e) provide for any surety or guarantor whose obligations to any person were released or discharged (in whole or in part) under the transaction or by the giving of the preference to be under such new or revived obligations to that person as the court thinks appropriate;

(f) provide for security to be provided for the discharge of any obligation imposed by or arising under the order, for such an obligation to be charged on any property and for the security or charge to have the same priority as a security or charge released or discharged (in whole or in part) under the transaction or by the giving of the preference; and

(g) provide for the extent to which any person whose property is vested by the order in the trustee of the bankrupt's estate, or on whom obligations are imposed by the order, is to be able to prove in the bankruptcy for debts or other liabilities which arose from, or were released or discharged (in whole or in part) under or by, the transaction or the giving of the preference.

(2) An order under section 339 or 340 may affect the property of, or impose any obligation on, any person whether or not he is the person with whom the individual in question entered into the transaction or, as the case may be, the person to whom the preference was given; but such an order—

(a) shall not prejudice any interest in property which was acquired from a person other than that individual and was acquired [in good faith and for value], or prejudice any interest deriving from such an interest, and

(b) shall not require a person who received a benefit from the transaction or preference [in good faith and for value] to pay a sum to the trustee of the bankrupt's estate, except where he was a party to the transaction or the payment is to be in respect of a preference given to that person at a time when he was a creditor of that individual.

[(2A) Where a person has acquired an interest in property from a person other than the individual in question, or has received a benefit from the transaction or preference, and at the time of that acquisition a receipt—

(a) he had notice of the relevant surrounding circumstances and of the relevant proceedings, or

(b) he was an associate of, or was connected with, either the individual in question or the person with whom that individual gave the preference,

then, unless the contrary is shown, it shall be presumed for the purposes of paragraph (a) or (as the case may be) paragraph (b) of subsection (2) that the interest was acquired or the benefit was received otherwise than in good faith.]

(3) Any sums required to be paid to the trustee in accordance with an order under section 339 or 340 shall be comprised in the bankrupt's estate.

[(4) For the purposes of subsection (2A)(a), the relevant surrounding circumstances are (as the case may require)—

(a) the fact that the individual in question entered into the transaction at an undervalue; or

(b) the circumstances which amounted to the giving of the preference by the individual in question.]

[(5) For the purposes of subsection (2A)(a), a person has notice of the relevant proceedings if he has notice—

(a) of the fact that the petition on which the individual in question is adjudged bankrupt has been presented; or

(b) of the fact that the individual in question has been adjudged bankrupt.]

PART XVI
PROVISIONS AGAINST DEBT AVOIDANCE (ENGLAND AND WALES ONLY)

423. Transactions defrauding creditors

(1) This section relates to transactions entered into at an undervalue, and a person enters into such a transaction with another person if—

(a) he makes a gift to the other person or he otherwise enters into a transaction with the other on terms that provide for him to receive no consideration;

(b) he enters into a transaction with the other in consideration of marriage; or

(c) he enters into a transaction with the other for a consideration the value of which, in money or money's worth, is significantly less than the value, in money or money's worth, of the consideration provided by himself.

(2) Where a person has entered into such a transaction, the court may, if satisfied under the next subsection, make such order as it thinks fit for—

(a) restoring the position to what it would have been if the transaction had not been entered into, and

(b) protecting the interests of persons who are victims of the transaction.

(3) In the case of a person entering into such a transaction, an order shall only be made if the court is satisfied that it was entered into by him for the purpose—

(a) of putting assets beyond the reach of a person who is making, or may at some time make, a claim against him, or

(b) of otherwise prejudicing the interests of such a person in relation to the claim which he is making or may make.

(4) In this section 'the court' means the High Court or—

(a) if the person entering into the transaction is an individual, any other court which would have jurisdiction in relation to a bankruptcy petition relating to him;

(b) if that person is a body capable of being wound up . . . any other court having jurisdiction to wind it up.

(5) In relation to a transaction at an undervalue, references here and below to a victim of the transaction are to a person who is, or is capable of being, prejudiced by it; and in the following two sections the person entering into the transaction is referred to as 'the debtor'.

424. Those who may apply for an order under s. 423

(1) An application for an order under section 423 shall not be made in relation to a transaction except—

(a) in a case where the debtor has been adjudged bankrupt or is a body corporate which is being wound up or in relation to which an administration order is in force, by the official receiver, by the trustee of the bankrupt's estate or the liquidator or administrator of the body corporate or (with the leave of the court) by a victim of the transaction;

(b) in a case where a victim of the transaction is bound by a voluntary arrangement approved under Part I or Part VIII of this Act, by the supervisor of the voluntary arrangement or by any person who (whether or not so bound) is such a victim; or

(c) in any other case, by a victim of the transaction.

(2) An application made under any of the paragraphs of subsection (1) is to be treated as made on behalf of every victim of the transaction.

425. Provision which may be made by order under s. 423

(1) Without prejudice to the generality of section 423, an order made under that section with respect to a transaction may (subject as follows)—

(a) require any property transferred as part of the transaction to be vested in any person, either absolutely or for the benefit of all the persons on whose behalf the application for the order is treated as made;

(b) require any property to be so vested if it represents, in any person's hands, the application either of the proceeds of sale of property so transferred or of money so tranferred;

(c) release or discharge (in whole or in part) any security given by the debtor;

(d) require any person to pay to any other person in respect of benefits received from the debtor such sums as the court may direct;

(e) provide for any surety or guarantor whose obligations to any person were released or discharged (in whole or in part) under the transaction to be under such new or revived obligations as the court thinks appropriate;

(f) provide for security to be provided for the discharge of any obligation imposed by or arising under the order, for such an obligation to be charged on any property and for such security or charge to have the same priority as a security or charge released or discharged (in whole are in part) under the transaction.

(2) An order under section 423 may affect the property of, or impose any obligation on, any person whether or not he is the person with whom the debtor entered into the transaction; but such an order—

(a) shall not prejudice any interest in property which was acquired from a person other than the debtor and was acquired in good faith, for value and without notice of the relevant circumstances, or prejudice any interest deriving from such an interest, and

(b) shall not require a person who received a benefit from the transaction in good faith, for value and without notice of the relevant circumstances to pay any sum unless he was a party to the transaction.

(3) For the purposes of this section the relevant circumstances in relation to a transaction are the circumstances by virtue of which an order under section 423 may be made in respect of the transaction.

(4) In this section 'security' means any mortgage, charge, lien or other security.

FAMILY LAW REFORM ACT 1987
(1987, c. 42)

1. General principle

(1) In this Act and enactments passed and instruments made after the coming into force of this section, references (however expressed) to any relationship between two persons shall, unless the contrary intention appears, be construed without regard to whether or not the father and mother of either of them, or the father and mother of any person through whom the relationship is deduced, have or had been married to each other at any time.

(2) In this Act and enactments passed after the coming into force of this section, unless the contrary intention appears—

(a) references to a person whose father and mother were married to each other at the time of his birth include; and

(b) references to a person whose father and mother were not married to each other at the time of his birth do not include,

references to any person to whom subsection (3) below applies, and cognate references shall be construed accordingly.

(3) This subsection applies to any person who—

(a) is treated as legitimate by virtue of section 1 of the Legitimacy Act 1976;

(b) is a legitimated person within the meaning of section 10 of that Act;

(c) is an adopted child within the meaning of Part IV of the Adoption Act 1976; or

(d) is otherwise treated in law as legitimate.

(4) For the purpose of construing references falling within subsection (2) above, the time of a person's birth shall be taken to include any time during the period beginning with—

(a) the insemination resulting in his birth, or

(b) where there was no such insemination, his conception, and (in either case) ending with his birth.

PART III
PROPERTY RIGHTS

18. Succession on intestacy

(1) In Part IV of the Administration of Estates Act 1925 (which deals with the distribution of the estate of an intestate), references (however expressed) to any relationship between two persons shall be construed in accordance with section 1 above.

(2) For the purposes of subsection (1) above and that Part of that Act, a person whose father and mother were not married to each other at the time of his birth shall be presumed not to have been survived by his father, or by any person related to him only through his father, unless the contrary is shown.

(3) In section 50(1) of that Act (which relates to the construction of documents), the reference to Part IV of that Act, or to the foregoing provisions of that Part, shall in

relation to an instrument inter vivos made, or a will or codicil coming into operation, after the coming into force of this section (but not in relation to instruments inter vivos made or wills or codicils coming into operation earlier) be construed as including references to this section.

(4) This section does not affect any rights under the intestacy of a person dying before the coming into force of this section.

19. Dispositions of property

(1) In the following dispositions, namely—

(a) dispositions inter vivos made on or after the date on which this section comes into force; and

(b) dispositions by will or codicil where the will or codicil is made on or after that date,

references (whether express or implied) to any relationship between two persons shall be construed in accordance with section 1 above.

(2) It is hereby declared that the use, without more, of the word 'heir' or 'heirs' or any expression which is used to create an entailed interest in real or personal property does not show a contrary intention for the purposes of section 1 as applied by subsection (1) above.

(3) In relation to the dispositions mentioned in subsection (1) above, section 33 of the Trustee Act 1925 (which specifies the trust implied by a direction that income is to be held on protective trusts for the benefit of any person) shall have effect as if any reference (however expressed) to any relationship between two persons were construed in accordance with section 1 above.

(4) Where under any disposition of real or personal property, any interest in such property is limited (whether subject to any preceding limitation or charge or not) in such a way that it would, apart from this section, devolve (as nearly as the law permits) along with a dignity or title of honour, then—

(a) whether or not the disposition contains an express reference to the dignity or title of honour; and

(b) whether or not the property or some interest in the property may in some event become severed from it,

nothing in this section shall operate to sever the property or any interest in it from the dignity or title, but the property or interest shall devolve in all respects as if this section had not been enacted.

(5) This section is without prejudice to section 42 of the Adoption Act 1976 (construction of dispositions in cases of adoption).

(6) In this section 'disposition' means a disposition, including an oral disposition, of real or personal property whether inter vivos or by will or codicil.

(7) Notwithstanding any rule of law, a disposition made by will or codicil executed before the date on which this section comes into force shall not be treated for the purposes of this section as made on or after that date by reason only that the will or codicil is confirmed by a codicil executed on or after that date.

21. Entitlement to grant of probate etc.

(1) For the purpose of determining the person or persons who would in accordance with probate rules be entitled to a grant of probate or administration in respect of the estate of a deceased person, the deceased shall be presumed, unless the contrary is shown, not to have been survived—

(a) by any person related to him whose father and mother were not married to each other at the time of his birth; or

(b) by any person whose relationship with him is deduced through such a person as is mentioned in paragraph (a) above.

(2) In this section 'probate rules' means rules of court made under section 127 of the Supreme Court Act 1981.

(3) This section does not apply in relation to the estate of a person dying before the coming into force of this section.

HOUSING ACT 1988
(1988, c. 50)

17. Succession to assured periodic tenancy by spouse

(1) In any case where—

(a) the sole tenant under an assured periodic tenancy dies, and

(b) immediately before the death, the tenant's spouse was occupying the dwelling-house as his or her only or principal home, and

(c) the tenant was not himself a successor, as defined in subsection (2) or subsection (3) below,

then, on the death, the tenancy vests by virtue of this section in the spouse (and, accordingly, does not devolve under the tenant's will or intestacy).

(2) For the purposes of this section, a tenant is a successor in relation to a tenancy if—

(a) the tenancy became vested in him either by virtue of this section or under the will or intestacy of a previous tenant; or

(b) at some time before the tenant's death the tenancy was a joint tenancy held by himself and one or more other persons and, prior to his death, he became the sole tenant by survivorship; or

(c) he became entitled to the tenancy as mentioned in section 39(5) below.

(3) For the purposes of this section, a tenant is also a successor in relation to a tenancy (in this subsection referred to as 'the new tenancy') which was granted to him (alone or jointly with others) if—

(a) at some time before the grant of the new tenancy, he was, by virtue of subsection (2) above, a successor in relation to an earlier tenancy of the same or substantially the same dwelling-house as is let under the new tenancy; and

(b) at all times since he became such a successor he has been a tenant (alone or jointly with others) of the dwelling-house which is let under the new tenancy or of a dwelling-house which is substantially the same as that dwelling-house.

(4) For the purposes of this section, a person who was living with the tenant as his or her wife or husband shall be treated as the tenant's spouse.

(5) If, on the death of the tenant, there is, by virtue of subsection (4) above, more than one person who fulfils the condition in subsection (1)(b) above, such one of them as may be decided by agreement or, in default of agreement, by the county court shall be treated as the tenant's spouse for the purposes of this section.

LAW OF PROPERTY (MISCELLANEOUS PROVISIONS) ACT 1989
(1989, c. 34)

1. Deeds and their execution

(1) Any rule of law which—

(a) restricts the substances on which a deed may be written;

(b) requires a seal for the valid execution of an instrument as a deed by an individual; or

(c) requires authority by one person to another to deliver an instrument as a deed on his behalf to be given by deed,

is abolished.

(2) An instrument shall not be a deed unless—

(a) it makes it clear on its face that it is intended to be a deed by the person making it or, as the case may be, by the parties to it (whether describing itself as a deed or expressing itself to be executed or signed as a deed or otherwise); and

(b) it is validly executed as a deed by that person or, as the case may be, one or more of those parties,

(3) An instrument is validly executed as a deed by an individual if, and only if—

(a) it is signed—

(i) by him in the presence of a witness who attests the signature; or

(ii) at his direction and in his presence and the presence of two witnesses who each attest the signature; and

(b) it is delivered as a deed by him or a person authorised to do so on his behalf.

(4) In subsection (2) and (3) above 'sign', in relation to an instrument, includes making one's mark on the instrument and 'signature' is to be construed accordingly.

(5) Where a solicitor, [duly certified notary public] or licensed conveyancer, or an agent or employee of a solicitor, [duly certified notary public] or licensed conveyancer, in the course of or in connection with a transaction involving the disposition or creation of an interest in land, purports to deliver an instrument as a deed on behalf of a party to the instrument, it shall be conclusively presumed in favour of a purchaser that he is authorised so to deliver the instrument.

(6) In subsection (5) above—

'disposition' and 'purchaser' have the same meaning as in the Law of Property Act 1925; and

['duly certified notary public' has the same meaning as it has in the Solicitors Act 1974 by virtue of section 87 of that Act,]

'interest in land' means any estate, interest or charge in or over land [. . .].

(7) Where an instrument under seal that constitutes a deed is required for the purposes of an Act passed before this section comes into force, this section shall have effect as to signing, sealing or delivery of an instrument by an individual in place of any provision of that Act as to signing, sealing or delivery.

(8) . . .

(9) Nothing in subsection (1)(b), (2), (3), or (7) . . . above applies in relation to deeds required or authorised to be made under—

(a) the seal of the country palantine of Lancaster;

(b) the seal of the Duchy of Lancaster; or

(c) the seal of the Duchy of Cornwall.

(10) The references in this section to the execution of a deed by an individual do not include execution by a corporation sole and the reference in subsection (7) above to signing, sealing or delivery by an individual does not include signing, sealing or delivery by such a corporation.

(11) Nothing in this section applies in relation to instruments delivered as deeds before this section comes into force.

2. Contracts for sale etc. of land to be made by signed writing

(1) A contract for the sale or other disposition of an interest in land can only be made in writing and only by incorporating all the terms which the parties have expressly agreed in one document or, where contracts are exchanged, in each.

(2) The terms may be incorporated in a document either by being set out in it or by reference to some other document.

(3) The document incorporating the terms or, where contracts are exchanged, one of the documents incorporating them (but not necessarily the same one) must be signed by or on behalf of each party to the contract.

(4) Where a contract for the sale or other disposition of an interest in land satisfies the conditions of this section by reason only of the rectification of one or more documents in pursuance of an order of a court, the contract shall come into being, or be deemed to have come into being, at such time as may be specified in the order.

(5) This section does not apply in relation to—

(a) a contract to grant such a lease as is mentioned in section 54(2) of the Law of Property Act 1926 (short leases);

(b) a contract made in the course of a public auction; or

(c) a contract regulated under the Financial Services Act 1986;

and nothing in this section affects the creation or operation of resulting, implied or constructive trusts.

(6) In this section—

'disposition' has the same meaning as in the Law of Property Act 1925;

'interest in land' means any estate, interest or charge in or over land [. . .].

(7) Nothing in this section shall apply in relation to contracts made before this section comes into force.

(8) Section 40 of the Law of Property Act 1925 (which is superseded by this section) shall cease to have effect.

3. Abolition of rule in *Bain* v *Fothergill*

The rule of law known as the rule in *Bain* v *Fothergill* is abolished in relation to contracts made after this section comes into force.

5. Commencement

(1) The provisions of this Act to which this subsection applies shall come into force on such day as the Lord Chancellor may by order made by statutory instrument appoint.

(2) The provisions to which subsection (1) above applies are—

(a) section 1 above; and

(b) section 4 above, except so far as it relates to section 40 of the Law of Property Act 1925.

(3) The provisions of this Act to which this subsection applies shall come into force at the end of the period of two months beginning with the day on which this Act is passed.

(4) The provisions of this Act to which subsection (3) above applies are—

(a) sections 2 and 3 above; and

(b) section 4 above, so far as it relates to section 40 of the Law of Property Act 1925.

ACCESS TO NEIGHBOURING LAND ACT 1992
(1992, c. 23)

1. Access orders

(1) A person—

(a) who, for the purpose of carrying out works to any land (the 'dominant land'), desires to enter upon any adjoining or adjacent land (the 'servient land'), and

(b) who needs, but does not have, the consent of some other person to that entry, may make an application to the court for an order under this section ('an access order') against that other person.

(2) On application under this section, the court shall make an access order if, and only if, it is satisfied—

(a) that the works are reasonably necessary for the preservation of the whole or any part of the dominant land; and

(b) that they cannot be carried out, or would be substantially more difficult to carry out, without entry upon the servient land;

but this subsection is subject to subsection (3) below.

(3) The court shall not make an access order in any case where it is satisfied that, were it to make such an order—

(a) the respondent or any other person would suffer interference with, or disturbance of, his use or enjoyment of the servient land, or

(b) the respondent, or any other person (whether of full age or capacity or not) in occupation of the whole or any part of the servient land, would suffer hardship, to such a degree by reason of the entry (notwithstanding any requirement of this Act or any term or condition that may be imposed under it) that it would be unreasonable to make the order.

(4) Where the court is satisfied on an application under this section that it is reasonably necessary to carry out any basic preservation works to the dominant land, those works shall be taken for the purposes of this Act to be reasonably necessary for the preservation of the land; and in this subsection 'basic preservation works' means any of the following, that is to say—

(a) the maintenance, repair or renewal of any part of a building or other structure comprised in, or situate on, the dominant land;

(b) the clearance, repair or renewal of any drain, sewer, pipe or cable so comprised or situate;

(c) the treatment, cutting back, felling, removal or replacement of any hedge, tree, shrub or other growing thing which is so comprised and which is, or is in danger of becoming, damaged, diseased, dangerous, insecurely rooted or dead;

(d) the filling in, or clearance, of any ditch so comprised;

but this subsection is without prejudice to the generality of the works which may, apart from it, be regarded by the court as reasonably necessary for the preservation of any land.

(5) If the court considers it fair and reasonable in all the circumstances of the case, works may be regarded for the purposes of this Act as being reasonably necessary for the preservation of any land (or, for the purposes of subsection (4) above, as being basic preservation works which it is reasonably necessary to carry out to any land) notwithstanding that the works incidentally involve—

(a) the making of some alteration, adjustment or improvement to the land, or

(b) the demolition of the whole or any part of a building or structure comprised in or situate upon the land.

(6) Where any works are reasonably necessary for the preservation of the whole or any part of the dominant land, the doing to the dominant land of anything which is requisite for, incidental to, or consequential on, the carrying out of those works shall be treated for the purposes of this Act as the carrying out of works which are reasonably necessary for the preservation of that land; and references in this Act to works, or to the carrying out of works, shall be construed accordingly.

(7) Without prejudice to the generality of subsection (6) above, if it is reasonably necessary for a person to inspect the dominant land—

(a) for the purpose of ascertaining whether any works may be reasonably necessary for the preservation of the whole or any part of that land,

(b) for the purpose of making any map or plan, or ascertaining the course of any drain, sewer, pipe or cable, in preparation for, or otherwise in connection with, the carrying out of works which are so reasonably necessary, or

(c) otherwise in connection with the carrying out of any such works,

the making of such an inspection shall be taken for the purposes of this Act to be the carrying out to the dominant land of works which are reasonably necessary for the preservation of that land; and references in this Act to works, or to the carrying out of works, shall be construed accordingly.

2. Terms and conditions of access orders

(1) An access order shall specify—

(a) the works to the dominant land that may be carried out by entering upon the servient land in pursuance of the order;

(b) the particuar area of servient land that may be entered upon by virtue of the order for the purpose of carrying out those works to the dominant land; and

(c) the date on which, or the period during which, the land may be so entered upon;

and in the following provisions of this Act any reference to the servient land is a reference to the area specified in the order in pursuance of paragraph (b) above.

(2) An access order may impose upon the applicant or the respondent such terms and conditions as appear to the court to be reasonably necessary for the purpose of avoiding or restricting—

(a) any loss, damage, or injury which might otherwise be caused to the respondent or any other person by reason of the entry authorised by the order; or

(b) any inconvenience or loss of privacy that might otherwise be so caused to the respondent or any other person.

(3) Without prejudice to the generality of subsection (2) above, the terms and conditions which may be imposed under that subsection include provisions with respect to—

(a) the manner in which the specified works are to be carried out;

(b) the days on which, and the hours between which, the work involved may be executed;

(c) the persons who may undertake the carrying out of the specified works or enter upon the servient land under or by virtue of the order;

(d) the taking of any such precautions by the applicant as may be spcified in the order.

(4) An access order may also impose terms and conditions—

(a) requiring the applicant to pay, or to secure that such person connected with him as may be specified in the order pays, compensation for—

(i) any loss, damage or injury, or

(ii) any substantial loss of privacy or other substantial inconvenience,

which will, or might, be caused to the respondent or any other person by reason of the entry authorised by the order;

(b) requiring the applicant to secure that he, or such person connected with him as may be specified in the order, is insured against any such risks as may be so specified; or

(c) requiring such a record to be made of the condition of the servient land, or of such part of it as may be so specified, as the court may consider expedient with a view to facilitating the determination of any question that may arise concerning damage to that land.

(5) An access order may include provision requiring the applicant to pay the respondent such sum by way of consideration for the privilege of entering the servient land in pursuance of the order as appears to the court to be fair and reasonable having regard to all the circumstances of the case, including, in particular—

(a) the likely financial advantage of the order to the applicant and any persons connected with him; and

(b) the degree of inconvenience likely to be caused to the respondent or any other person by the entry;

but no payment shall be ordered under this subsection if and to the extent that the works which the applicant desires to carry out by means of the entry are works to residential land.

(6) For the purposes of subsection (5)(a) above, the likely financial advantage of an access order to the applicant and any persons connected with him shall in all cases be taken to be a sum of money equal to the greater of the following amounts, that is to say—

(a) the amount (if any) by which so much of any likely increase in the value of any land—

(i) which consists of or includes the dominant land, and

(ii) which is owned or occupied by the same person as the dominant land, as may reasonably be regarded as attributable to the carrying out of the specified works exceeds the likely cost of carrying out those works with the benefit of the access order; and

(b) the difference (if it would have been possible to carry out the specified works without entering upon the servient land) between—

(i) the likely cost of carrying out those works without entering upon the servient land; and

(ii) the likely cost of carrying them out with the benefit of the access order.

(7) For the purpses of subsection (5) above, 'residential land' means so much of any land as consists of—

(a) a dwelling or part of a dwelling;

(b) a garden, yard, private garage or outbuilding which is used and enjoyed wholly or mainly with a dwelling; or

(c) in the case of a building which includes one or more dwellings, any part of the building which is used and enjoyed wholly or mainly with those dwellings or any of them.

(8) The persons who are to be regarded for the purposes of this section as 'connected with' the applicants are—

(a) the owner of any estate or interest in, or right over, the whole or any part of the dominant land;

(b) the occupier of the whole or any part of the dominant land; and

(c) any person whom the applicant may authorise under section 3(7) below to exercise the power of entry conferred by the access order.

(9) The court may make provision—

(a) for the reimbursement by the applicant of any expenses reasonably incurred by the respondent in connection with the application which are not otherwise recoverable as costs;

(b) for the giving of security by the applicant for any sum that might become payable to the respondent or any other person by virtue of this section or section 3 below.

3. Effect of access order

(1) An access order requires the respondent, so far as he has power to do so, to permit the applicant or any of his associates to do anything which the applicant or associate is authorised or required to do under or by virtue of the order or this section.

(2) Except as otherwise provided by or under this Act, an access order authorises the applicant or any of his associates, without the consent of the respondent,—

(a) to enter upon the servient land for the purpose of carrying out the specified works;

(b) to bring on to that land, leave there during the period permitted by the order and, before the end of that period, remove, such materials, plant and equipment as are reasonably necessary for the carrying out of those works; and

(c) to bring on to that land any waste arising from the carrying out of those works, if it is reasonably necessary to do so in the course of removing it from the dominant land;

but nothing in this Act or in any access order shall authorise the applicant or any of his associates to leave anything in, on or over the servient land (otherwise than in discharge of their duty to make good that land) after their entry for the purpose of carrying out works to the dominant land ceases to be authorised under or by virtue of the order.

(3) An access order requires the applicant—

(a) to secure that any waste arising from the carrying out of the specified works is removed from the servient land forthwith;

(b) to secure that, before the entry ceases to be authorised under or by virtue of the order, the servient land is, so far as reasonably prqcticable, made good; and

(c) to indemnify the respondent against any damage which may be caused to the servient land or any goods by the applicant or any of his associates which would not have been so caused had the order not been made;

but this subsection is subject to subsections (4) and (5) below.

(4) In making an access order, the court may vary or exclude, in whole or in part,—

(a) any authorisation that would otherwise by conferred by subsection (2)(b) or (c) above; or

(b) any requirement that would otherwise by imposed by subsection (3) above.

(5) Without prejudice to the generality of subsection (4) above, if the court is satisfied that it is reasonably necessary for any such waste as may arise from the carrying out of the specified works to be left on the servient land for some period before removal, the access order may, in place of subsection (3)(a) above, include provision—

(a) authorising the waste to be left on that land for such period as may be permitted by the order; and

(b) requiring the applicant to secure that the waste is removed before the end of that period.

(6) Where the applicant or any of his associates is authorised or required under or by virtue of an access order or this section to enter, or do any other thing, upon the servient land, he shall not (as respects that access order) be taken to be a trespasser from the beginning on account of his, or any other person's, subsequent conduct.

(7) For the purposes of this section, the applicant's 'associates' are such number of persons (whether or not servants or agents of his) whom he may reasonably authorise under this subsection to exercise the power of entry conferred by the access order as may be reasonably necessary for carrying out the specified works.

4. Persons bound by access order, unidentified persons and bar on contracting out

(1) In addition to the respondent, an access order shall, subject to the provisions of the Land Charges Act 1972 and the Land Registration Act 1925, be binding on—

(a) any of his successors in title to the servient land; and

(b) any person who has an estate or interest in, or right over, the whole or any part of the servient land which was created after the making of the order and who derives his title to that estate, interest or right under the respondent;

and references to the respondent shall be construed accordingly.

(2) If and to the extent that the court considers it just and equitable to allow him to do so, a person on whom an access order becomes binding by virtue of subsection (1)(a) or (b) above shall be entitled, as respects anything falling to be done after the order becomes binding on him, to enforce the order or any of its terms or conditions as if he were the respondent, and references to the respondent shall be construed accordingly.

(3) Rules of court may—

(a) provide a procedure which may be followed where the applicant does not know, and cannot reasonably ascertain, the name of any person whom he desires to make respondent to the application; and

(b) make provision enabling such an applicant to make such a person respondent by description instead of by name;

and in this subsection 'applicant' includes a person who proposes to make an application for an access order.

(4) Any agreement, whenever made, shall be void if and to the extent that it would, apart from this subsection, prevent a person from applying for an access order or restrict his right to do so.

5. Registration of access orders and of applications for such orders

(4) In any case where—

(a) an access order is discharged under section 6(1)(a) below, and

(b) the order has been protected by an entry registered under the Land Charges Act 1972 or by a notice or caution under the Land Registration Act 1925,

the court may by order direct that the entry, notice or caution shall be cancelled.

(5) The rights conferred on a person by or under an access order are not capable of constituting an overriding interest within the meaning of the Land Registration Act 1925, notwithstanding that he or any other person is in actual occupation of the whole or any part of the servient land in question.

(6) An application for an access order shall be regarded as a pending land action for the purposes of the Land Charges Act 1972 and the Land Registration Act 1925.

6. Variation of orders and damages for breach

(1) Where an access order or an order under this subsection has been made, the court may, on the application of any party to the proceedings in which the order was made or of any other person on whom the order is binding—

(a) discharge or vary the order or any of its terms or conditions;

(b) suspend any of its terms or conditions; or

(c) revive any term or condition suspended under paragraph (b) above;

and in the application of subsections (1) and (2) of section 4 above in relation to an access order, any order under this subsection which relates to the access order shall be treated for the purposes of those subsections as included in the access order.

(2) If any person contravenes or fails to comply with any requirement, term or condition imposed upon him by or under this Act, the court may, without prejudice to any other remedy available, make an order for the payment of damages by him to any other person affected by the contravention or failure who makes an application for relief under this subsection.

7. Jurisdiction over, and allocation of, proceedings

(1) The High Court and the county courts shall both have jurisdiction under this Act.

8. Interpretation and application

(1) Any reference in this Act to an 'entry' upon any servient land includes a reference to the doing on that land of anything necessary for carrying out the works to the dominant land which are reasonably necessary for its preservation; and 'enter' shall be construed accordingly.

(2) This Act applies in relation to any obstruction of, or other interference with, a right over, or interest in, any land as it applies in relation to an entry upon that land; and 'enter' and 'entry' shall be construed accordingly.

(3) In this Act—

'access order' has the meaning given by section 1(1) above;

'applicant' means a person making an applicatiaon for an access order and, subject to section 4 above, 'the respondent' means the respondent, or any of the respondents, to such an application;

'the court' means the High Court or a county court;

'the dominant land' and 'the servient land' respectively have the meanings given by section 1(1) above, but subject, in the case of servient land, to section 2(1) above;

'land' does not include a highway;

'the specified works' means the works specified in the access order in pursuance of section 2(1)(a) above.

CHARITIES ACT 1993
(1993, c. 10)

PART I
THE CHARITY COMMISSIONERS AND THE OFFICIAL CUSTODIAN FOR CHARITIES

1. The Charity Commissioners

(1) There shall continue to be a body of Charity Commissioners for England and Wales, and they shall have such functions as are conferred on them by this Act in addition to any functions under any other enactment for the time being in force.

(2) The provisions of Schedule 1 to this Act shall have effect with respect to the constitution and proceedings of the Commissioners and other matters relating to the Commissioners and their officers and employees.

(3) The Commissioners shall (without prejudice to their specific powers and duties under other enactments) have the general function of promoting the effective use of charitable resources by encouraging the development of better methods of administration, by giving charity trustees information or advice on any matter affecting the charity and by investigating and checking abuses.

(4) It shall be the general object of the Commissioners so to act in the case of any charity (unless it is a matter of altering its purposes) as best to promote and make effective the work of the charity in meeting the needs designated by its trusts; but the Commissioners shall not themselves have power to act in the administration of a charity.

(5) The Commissioners shall, as soon as possible after the end of every year, make to the Secretary of State a report on their operations during that year, and he shall lay a copy of the report before each House of Parliament.

2. The official custodian for charities

(1) There shall continue to be an officer known as the official custodian for charities (in this Act referred to as 'the official custodian') whose function it shall be to act as trustee for charities in the cases provided for by this Act; and the official custodian shall be by that name a corporation sole having perpetual succession and using an official seal which shall be officially and judicially noticed.

(2) Such officer of the Commissioners as they may from time to time designate shall be the official custodian.

(3) The official custodian shall perform his duties in accordance with such general or special directions as may be given him by the Commissioners, and his expenses (except those re-imbursed to him or recovered by him as trustee for any charity) shall be defrayed by the Commissioners.

(4) Anything which is required to or may be done by, to or before the official custodian may be done by, to or before any officer of the Commissioners generally or specially authorised by them to act for him during a vacancy in his office or otherwise.

(5) The official custodian shall not be liable as trustee for any charity in respect of any loss or of the mis-application of any property unless it is occasioned by or through the wilful neglect or default of the custodian or of any person acting for him; but the Consolidated Fund shall be liable to make good to a charity any sums for which the custodian may be liable by reason of any such neglect or default.

(6) The official custodian shall keep such books of account and such records in relation thereto as may be directed by the Treasury and shall prepare accounts in such form, in such manner and at such times as may be so directed.

(7) The accounts so prepared shall be examined and certified by the Comptroller and Auditor General, and the report to be made by the Commissioners to the Secretary of State for any year shall include a copy of the accounts so prepared for any period ending in or with the year and of the certificate and report of the Comptroller and Auditor General with respect to those accounts.

PART II
REGISTRATION AND NAMES OF CHARITIES
Registration of charities

3. The register of charities

(1) The Commissioners shall continue to keep a register of charities, which shall be kept by them in such manner as they think fit.

(2) There shall be entered in the register every charity not excepted by subsection (5) below; and a charity so excepted (other than one excepted by paragraph (a) of that subsection) may be entered in the register at the request of the charity, but (whether or not it was excepted at the time of registration) may at any time, and shall at the request of the charity, be removed from the register.

(3) The register shall contain—

(a) the name of every registered charity; and

(b) such other particulars of, and such other information relating to, every such charity as the Commissioners think fit.

(4) Any institution which no longer appears to the Commissioners to be a charity shall be removed from the register, with effect, where the removal is due to any change in its purposes or trusts, from the date of that change; and there shall also be removed from the register any charity which ceases to exist or does not operate.

(5) The following charities are not required to be registered—

(a) any charity comprised in Schedule 2 to this Act (in this Act referred to as an 'exempt charity');

(b) any charity which is excepted by order or regulations;

(c) any charity which has neither—

(i) any permanent endowment, nor

(ii) the use or occupation of any land,

and whose income from all sources does not in aggregate amount to more than £1,000 a year;

and no charity is required to be registered in respect of any registered place of worship.

(6) With any application for a charity to be registered there shall be supplied to the Commissioners copies of its trusts (or, if they are not set out in any extant document, particulars of them), and such other documents or information as may be prescribed by regulations made by the Secretary of State or as the Commissioners may require for the purpose of the application.

(7) It shall be the duty—

(a) of the charity trustees of any charity which is not registered nor excepted from registration to apply for it to be registered, and to supply the documents and information required by subsection (6) above; and

(b) of the charity trustees (or last charity trustees) of any institution which is for the time being registered to notify the Commissioners if it ceases to exist, or if there is any change in its trusts or in the particulars of it entered in the register, and to supply to the Commissioners particulars of any such change and copies of any new trusts or alterations of the trusts.

(8) The register (including the entries cancelled when institutions are removed from the register) shall be open to public inspection at all reasonable times; and copies (or particulars) of the trusts of any registered charity as supplied to the Commissioners under this section shall, so long as it remains on the register, be kept by them and be open to public inspection at all reasonable times, except in so far as regulations made by the Secretary of State otherwise provide.

(9) Where any information contained in the register is not in documentary form, subsection (8) above shall be construed as requiring the information to be available for public inspection in legible form at all reasonable times.

(10) If the Commissioners so determine, subsection (8) above shall not apply to any particular information contained in the register and specified in their determination.

(11) Nothing in the foregoing subsections shall require any person to supply the Commissioners with copies of schemes for the administration of a charity made otherwise than by the court, or to notify the Commissioners of any change made with respect to a registered charity by such a scheme, or require a person, if he refers the Commissioners to a document or copy already in the possession of the Commissioners, to supply a further copy of the document; but where by virtue of this subsection a copy of any document need not be supplied to the Commissioners, a copy of it, if it relates to a registered charity, shall be open to inspection under subsection (8) above as if supplied to the Commissioners under this section.

(12) If the Secretary of State thinks it expedient to do so—

(a) in consequence of changes in the value of money, or

(b) with a view to extending the scope of the exception provided for by subsection (5)(c) above,

he may by order amend subsection (5)(c) by substituting a different sum for the sum for the time being specified there.

(13) The reference in subsection (5)(b) above to a charity which is excepted by order or regulations is to a charity which—

(a) is for the time being permanently or temporarily excepted by order of the Commissioners; or

(b) is of a description permanently or temporarily excepted by regulations made by the Secretary of State,

and which complies with any conditions of the exception.

(14) In this section 'registered place of worship' means any land or building falling within section 9 of the Places of Worship Registration Act 1855 (that is to say, the land and buildings which if the Charities Act 1960 had not been passed, would by virtue of that section as amended by subsequent enactments be partially exempted from the operation of the Charitable Trusts Act 1853), and for the purposes of this subsection 'building' includes part of a building.

4. Effect of, and claims and objections to, registration

(1) An institution shall for all purposes other than rectification of the register be conclusively presumed to be or to have been a charity at any time when it is or was on the register of charities.

(2) Any person who is or may be affected by the registration of an institution as a charity may, on the ground that it is not a charity, object to its being entered by the Commissioners in the register, or apply to them for it to be removed from the register; and provision may be made by regulations made by the Secretary of State as to the manner in which any such objection or application is to be made, prosecuted or dealt with.

(3) An appeal against any decision of the Commissioners to enter or not to enter an institution in the register of charities, or to remove or not to remove an institution from the register, may be brought in the High Court by the Attorney General, or by the persons who are or claim to be the charity trustees of the institution, or by any person whose objection or application under subsection (2) above is disallowed by the decision.

(4) If there is an appeal to the High Court against any decision of the Commissioners to enter an institution in the register, or not to remove an institution from the register, then until the Commissioners are satisfied whether the decision of the Commissioners is or is not to stand, the entry in the register shall be maintained, but shall be in suspense and marked to indicate that it is in suspense; and for the purposes

of subsection (1) above an institution shall be deemed not to be on the register during any period when the entry relating to it is in suspense under this subsection.

(5) Any question affecting the registration or removal from the register of an institution may, notwithstanding that it has been determined by a decision on appeal under subsection (3) above, be considered afresh by the Commissioners and shall not be concluded by that decision, if it appears to the Commissioners that there has been a change of circumstances or that the decision is inconsistent with a later judicial decision, whether given on such an appeal or not.

PART III
COMMISSIONERS' INFORMATION POWERS

8. General power to institute inquiries

(1) The Commissioners may from time to time institute inquiries with regard to charities or a particular charity or class of charities, either generally or for particular purposes, but no such inquiry shall extend to any exempt charity.

(2) The Commissioners may either conduct such an inquiry themselves or appoint a person to conduct it and make a report to them.

(3) For the purposes of any such inquiry the Commissioners, or a person appointed by them to conduct it, may direct any person (subject to the provisions of this section)—

(a) to furnish accounts and statements in writing with respect to any matter in question at the inquiry, being a matter on which he has or can reasonably obtain information, or to return answers in writing to any questions or inquiries addressed to him on any such matter, and to verify any such accounts, statements or answers by statutory declaration;

(b) to furnish copies of documents in his custody or under his control which relate to any matter in question at the inquiry, and to verify any such copies by statutory declaration;

(c) to attend at a specified time and place and give evidence or produce any such documents.

(4) For the purposes of any such inquiry evidence may be taken on oath, and the person conducting the inquiry may for that purpose administer oaths, or may instead of administering an oath require the person examined to make and subscribe a declaration of the truth of the matters about which he is examined.

(5) The Commissioners may pay to any person the necessary expenses of his attendance to give evidence or produce documents for the purpose of an inquiry under this section, and a person shall not be required in obedience to a direction under paragraph (c) of subsection (3) above to go more than ten miles from his place of residence unless those expenses are paid or tendered to him.

(6) Where an inquiry has been held under this section, the Commissioners may either—

(a) cause the report of the person conducting the inquiry, or such other statement of the results of the inquiry as they think fit, to be printed and published, or

(b) publish any such report or statement in some other way which is calculated in their opinion to bring it to the attention of persons who may wish to make representations to them about the action to be taken.

(7) The council of a county or district, the Common Council of the City of London and the council of a London borough may contribute to the expenses of the Commissioners in connection with inquiries under this section into local charities in the council's area.

PART IV
APPLICATION OF PROPERTY CY-PRÈS AND ASSISTANCE AND SUPERVISION OF CHARITIES BY COURT AND COMMISSIONERS

Extended powers of court and variation of charters

13. Occasions for applying property cy-près

(1) Subject to subsection (2) below, the circumstances in which the original purposes of a charitable gift can be altered to allow the property given or part of it to be applied cy-près shall be as follows—

(a) where the original purposes, in whole or in part—

(i) have been as far as may be fulfilled; or

(ii) cannot be carried out, or not according to the directions given and to the spirit of the gift; or

(b) where the original purposes provide a use for part only of the property available by virtue of the gift; or

(c) where the property available by virtue of the gift and other property applicable for similar purposes can be more effectively used in conjunction, and to that end can suitably, regard being had to the spirit of the gift, be made applicable to common purposes; or

(d) where the original purposes were laid down by reference to an area which then was but has since ceased to be a unit for some other purpose, or by reference to a class of persons or to an area which has for any reason since ceased to be suitable, regard being had to the spirit of the gift, or to be practical in administering the gift; or

(e) where the original purposes, in whole or in part, have, since they were laid down,—

(i) been adequately provided for by other means; or

(ii) ceased, as being useless or harmful to the community or for other reasons, to be in law charitable; or

(iii) ceased in any other way to provide a suitable and effective method of using the property available by virtue of the gift, regard being had to the spirit of the gift.

(2) Subsection (1) above shall not affect the conditions which must be satisfied in order that property given for charitable purposes may be applied cy-près except in so far as those conditions require a failure of the original purposes.

(3) References in the foregoing subsections to the original purposes of a gift shall be construed, where the application of the property given has been altered or regulated by a scheme or otherwise, as referring to the purposes for which the property is for the time being applicable.

(4) Without prejudice to the power to make schemes in circumstances falling within subsection (1) above, the court may by scheme made under the court's jurisdiction with respect to charities, in any case where the purposes for which the property is held are laid down by reference to any such area as is mentioned in the first column in Schedule 3 to this Act, provide for enlarging the area to any such area as is mentioned in the second column in the same entry in that Schedule.

(5) It is hereby declared that a trust for charitable purposes places a trustee under a duty, where the case permits and requires the property or some part of it to be applied cy-près, to secure its effective use for charity by taking steps to enable it to be so applied.

14. Application cy-près of gifts of donors unknown or disclaiming

(1) Property given for specific charitable purposes which fail shall be applicable cy-près as if given for charitable purposes generally, where it belongs—

(a) to a donor who after—

(i) the prescribed advertisements and inquiries have been published and made, and

(ii) the prescribed period beginning with the publication of those advertisements has expired,

cannot be identified or cannot be found; or

(b) to a donor who has executed a disclaimer in the prescribed form of his right to have the property returned.

(2) Where the prescribed advertisements and inquiries have been published and made by or on behalf of trustees with respect to any such property, the trustees shall not be liable to any person in respect of the property if no claim by him to be interested in it is received by them before the expiry of the period mentioned in subsection (1)(a)(ii) above.

(3) For the purposes of this section property shall be conclusively presumed (without any advertisement or inquiry) to belong to donors who cannot be identified, in so far as it consists—

(a) of the proceeds of cash collections made by means of collecting boxes or by other means not adapted for distinguishing one gift from another; or

(b) of the proceeds of any lottery, competition, entertainment, sale or similar money-raising activity, after allowing for property given to provide prizes or articles for sale or otherwise to enable the activity to be undertaken.

(4) The court may by order direct that property not falling within subsection (3) above shall for the purposes of this section be treated (without any advertisement or inquiry) as belonging to donors who cannot be identified where it appears to the court either—

(a) that it would be unreasonable, having regard to the amounts likely to be returned to the donors, to incur expense with a view to returning the property; or

(b) that it would be unreasonable, having regard to the nature, circumstances and amounts of the gifts, and to the lapse of time since the gifts were made, for the donors to expect the property to be returned.

(5) Where property is applied cy-près by virtue of this section, the donor shall be deemed to have parted with all his interest at the time when the gift was made; but where property is so applied as belonging to donors who cannot be identified or cannot be found, and is not so applied by virtue of subsection (3) or (4) above—

(a) the scheme shall specify the total amount of that property; and

(b) the donor of any part of that amount shall be entitled, if he makes a claim not later than six months after the date on which the scheme is made, to recover from the charity for which the property is applied a sum equal to that part, less any expenses properly incurred by the charity trustees after that date in connection with claims relating to his gift; and

(c) the scheme may include directions as to the provision to be made for meeting any such claim.

(6) Where—

(a) any sum is, in accordance with any such directions, set aside for meeting any such claims, but

(b) the aggregate amount of any such claims actually made exceeds the relevant amount,

then, if the Commissioners so direct, each of the donors in question shall be entitled only to such proportion of the relevant amount as the amount of his claim bears to the aggregate amount referred to in paragraph (b) above; and for this purpose 'the relevant amount' means the amount of the sum so set aside after deduction of any expenses properly incurred by the charity trustees in connection with claims relating to the donors' gifts.

(7) For the purposes of this section, charitable purposes shall be deemed to 'fail' where any difficulty in applying property to those purposes makes that property or the part not applicable cy-près available to be returned to the donors.

(8) In this section 'prescribed' means prescribed by regulations made by the Commissioners; and such regulations may, as respects the advertisements which are to be published for the purposes of subsection (1)(a) above, make provision as to the form and content of such advertisements as well as the manner in which they are to be published.

(9) Any regulations made by the Commissioners under this section shall be published by the Commissioners in such manner as they think fit.

(10) In this section, except in so far as the context otherwise requires, references to a donor include persons claiming through or under the original donor, and references to property given include the property for the time being representing the property originally given or property derived from it.

(11) This section shall apply to property given for charitable purposes, notwithstanding that it was so given before the commencement of this Act.

Powers of Commissioners to make schemes and act for protection of charities etc.

16. Concurrent jurisdiction with High Court for certain purposes

(1) Subject to the provisions of this Act, the Commissioners may by order exercise the same jurisdiction and powers as are exercisable by the High Court in charity proceedings for the following purposes—

(a) establishing a scheme for the administration of a charity;

(b) appointing, discharging or removing a charity trustee or trustee for a charity, or removing an officer or employee;

(c) vesting or transferring property, or requiring or entitling any person to call for or make any transfer of property or any payment.

(2) Where the court directs a scheme for the administration of a charity to be established, the court may by order refer the matter to the Commissioners for them to prepare or settle a scheme in accordance with such directions (if any) as the court sees fit to give, and any such order may provide for the scheme to be put into effect by order of the Commissioners as if prepared under subsection (1) above and without any further order of the court.

(3) The Commissioners shall not have jurisdiction under this section to try or determine the title at law or in equity to any property as between a charity or trustee for a charity and a person holding or claiming the property or an interest in it adversely to the charity, or to try or determine any question as to the existence or extent of any charge or trust.

(4) Subject to the following subsections, the Commissioners shall not exercise their jurisdiction under this section as respects any charity, except—

(a) on the application of the charity; or

(b) on an order of the court under subsection (2) above; or

(c) in the case of a charity other than an exempt charity, on the application of the Attorney General.

(5) In the case of a charity which is not an exempt charity and whose income from all sources does not in aggregate exceed £500 a year, the Commissioners may exercise their jurisdiction under this section on the application—

(a) of any one or more of the charity trustees; or

(b) of any person interested in the charity; or

(c) of any two or more inhabitants of the area of the charity if it is a local charity.

(6) Where in the case of a charity, other than an exempt charity, the Commissioners are satisfied that the charity trustees ought in the interests of the charity to apply for a scheme, but have unreasonably refused or neglected to do so and the Commissioners have given the charity trustees an opportunity to make representations to them, the Commissioners may proceed as if an application for a scheme had been made by the charity but the Commissioners shall not have power in a case where they act by virtue

of this subsection to alter the purposes of a charity, unless forty years have elapsed from the date of its foundation.

(7) Where—

(a) a charity cannot apply to the Commissioners for a scheme by reason of any vacancy among the charity trustees or the absence or incapacity of any of them, but

(b) such an application is made by such number of the charity trustees as the Commissioners consider appropriate in the circumstances of the case,

the Commissioners may nevertheless proceed as if the application were an application made by the charity.

(8) The Commissioners may on the application of any charity trustee or trustee for a charity exercise their jurisdiction under this section for the purpose of discharging him from his trusteeship.

(9) Before exercising any jurisdiction under this section otherwise than on an order of the court, the Commissioners shall give notice of their intention to do so to each of the charity trustees, except any that cannot be found or has no known address in the United Kingdom or who is party or privy to an application for the exercise of the jurisdiction; and any such notice may be given by post, and, if given by post, may be addressed to the recipient's last known address in the United Kingdom.

(10) The Commissioners shall not exercise their jurisdiction under this section in any case (not referred to them by order of the court) which, by reason of its contentious character, or of any special question of law or of fact which it may involve, or for other reasons, the Commissioners may consider more fit to be adjudicated on by the court.

(11) An appeal against any order of the Commissioners under this section may be brought in the High Court by the Attorney General.

(12) An appeal against any order of the Commissioners under this section may also, at any time within the three months beginning with the day following that on which the order is published, be brought in the High Court by the charity or any of the charity trustees, or by any person removed from any office or employment by the order (unless he is removed with the concurrence of the charity trustees or with the approval of the special visitor, if any, of the charity).

(13) No appeal shall be brought under subsection (12) above except with a certificate of the Commissioners that it is a proper case for an appeal or with the leave of one of the judges of the High Court attached to the Chancery Division.

(14) Where an order of the Commissioners under this section establishes a scheme for the administration of a charity, any person interested in the charity shall have the like right of appeal under subsection (12) above as a charity trustee, and so also, in the case of a charity which is a local charity in any area, shall any two or more inhabitants of the area and the council of any parish or (in Wales) any community comprising the area or any part of it.

(15) If the Secretary of State thinks it expedient to do so—

(a) in consequence of changes in the value of money, or

(b) with a view to increasing the number of charities in respect of which the Commissioners may exercise their jurisdiction under this section in accordance with subsection (5) above,

he may by order amend that subsection by substituting a different sum for the sum for the time being specified there.

17. Further powers to make schemes or alter application of charitable property

(1) Where it appears to the Commissioners that a scheme should be established for the administration of a charity, but also that it is necessary or desirable for the scheme to alter the provision made by an Act of Parliament establishing or regulating the charity or to make any other provision which goes or might go beyond the powers exercisable

by them apart from this section, or that it is for any reason proper for the scheme to be subject to parliamentary review, then (subject to subsection (6) below) the Commissioners may settle a scheme accordingly with a view to its being given effect under this section.

(2) A scheme settled by the Commissioners under this section may be given effect by order of the Secretary of State, and a draft of the order shall be laid before Parliament.

(3) Without prejudice to the operation of section 6 of the Statutory Instruments Act 1946 in other cases, in the case of a scheme which goes beyond the powers exercisable apart from this section in altering a statutory provision contained in or having effect under any public general Act of Parliament, the order shall not be made unless the draft has been approved by resolution of each House of Parliament.

(4) Subject to subsection (5) below, any provision of a scheme brought into effect under this section may be modified or superseded by the court or the Commissioners as if it were a scheme brought into effect by order of the Commissioners under section 16 above.

(5) Where subsection (3) above applies to a scheme, the order giving effect to it may direct that the scheme shall not he modified or superseded by a scheme brought into effect otherwise than under this section, and may also direct that that subsection shall apply to any scheme modifying or superseding the scheme to which the order gives effect.

(6) The Commissioners shall not proceed under this section without the like application and the like notice to the charity trustees, as would be required if they were proceeding (without an order of the court) under section 16 above; but on any application for a scheme, or in a case where they act by virtue of subsection (6) or (7) of that section, the Commissioners may proceed under this section or that section as appears to them appropriate.

(7) Notwithstanding anything in the trusts of a charity, no expenditure incurred in preparing or promoting a Bill in Parliament shall without the consent of the court or the Commissioners be defrayed out of any moneys applicable for the purposes of a charity but this subsection shall not apply in the case of an exempt charity.

(8) Where the Commissioners are satisfied—

(a) that the whole of the income of a charity cannot in existing circumstances be effectively applied for the purposes of the charity; and

(b) that, if those circumstances continue, a scheme might be made for applying the surplus cy-près; and

(c) that it is for any reason not yet desirable to make such a scheme;

then the Commissioners may by order authorise the charity trustees at their discretion (but subject to any conditions imposed by the order) to apply any accrued or accruing income for any purposes for which it might be made applicable by such a scheme, and any application authorised by the order shall be deemed to be within the purposes of the charity.

(9) An order under subsection (8) above shall not extend to more than £300 out of income accrued before the date of the order, nor to income accruing more than three years after that date, nor to more than £100 out of the income accruing in any of those three years.

Property vested in official custodian

21. Entrusting charity property to official custodian, and termination of trust

(1) The court may by order—

(a) vest in the official custodian any land held by or in trust for a charity;

(b) authorise or require the persons in whom any such land is vested to transfer it to him; or

(c) appoint any person to transfer any such land to him;

but this subsection does not apply to any interest in land by way of mortgage or other security.

(2) Where property is vested in the official custodian in trust for a charity, the court may make an order discharging him from the trusteeship as respects all or any of that property.

(3) Where the official custodian is discharged from his trusteeship of any property, or the trusts on which he holds any property come to an end, the court may make such vesting orders and give such directions as may seem to the court to be necessary or expedient in consequence.

(4) No person shall be liable for any loss occasioned by his acting in conformity with an order under this section or by his giving effect to anything done in pursuance of such an order, or be excused from so doing by reason of the order having been in any respect improperly obtained.

22. Supplementary provisions as to property vested in official custodian

(1) Subject to the provisions of this Act, where property is vested in the official custodian in trust for a charity, he shall not exercise any powers of management, but he shall as trustee of any property have all the same powers, duties and liabilities, and be entitled to the same rights and immunities, and be subject to the control and orders of the court, as a corporation appointed custodian trustee under section 4 of the Public Trustee Act 1906 except that he shall have no power to charge fees.

(2) Subject to subsection (3) below, where any land is vested in the official custodian in trust for a charity, the charity trustees shall have power in his name and on his behalf to execute and do all assurances and things which they could properly execute or do in their own name and on their own behalf if the land were vested in them.

(3) If any land is so vested in the official custodian by virtue of an order under section 18 above, the power conferred on the charity trustees by subsection (2) above shall not be exercisable by them in relation to any transaction affecting the land, unless the transaction is authorised by order of the court or of the Commissioners.

(4) Where any land is vested in the official custodian in trust for a charity, the charity trustees shall have the like power to make obligations entered into by them binding on the land as if it were vested in them; and any covenant, agreement or condition which is enforceable by or against the custodian by reason of the land being vested in him shall be enforceable by or against the charity trustees as if the land were vested in them.

(5) In relation to a corporate charity, subsections (2), (3) and (4) above shall apply with the substitution of references to the charity for references to the charity trustees.

(6) Subsections (2), (3) and (4) above shall not authorise any charity trustees or charity to impose any personal liability on the official custodian.

(7) Where the official custodian is entitled as trustee for a charity to the custody of securities or documents of title relating to the trust property, he may permit them to be in the possession or under the control of the charity trustees without thereby incurring any liability.

Establishment of common investment or deposit funds

24. Schemes to establish common investment funds

(1) The court or the Commissioners may by order make and bring into effect schemes (in this section referred to as 'common investment schemes') for the establishment of common investment funds under trusts which provide—

(a) for property transferred to the fund by or on behalf of a charity participating in the scheme to be invested under the control of trustees appointed to manage the fund; and

(b) for the participating charities to be entitled (subject to the provisions of the scheme) to the capital and income of the fund in shares determined by reference to the amount or value of the property transferred to it by or on behalf of each of them and to the value of the fund at the time of the transfers.

(2) The court or the Commissioners may make a common investment scheme on the application of any two or more charities.

(3) A common investment scheme may be made in terms admitting any charity to participate, or the scheme may restrict the right to participate in any manner.

(4) A common investment scheme may make provision for, and for all matters connected with, the establishment, investment, management and winding up of the common investment fund, and may in particular include provision—

(a) for remunerating persons appointed trustees to hold or manage the fund or any part of it, with or without provision authorising a person to receive the remuneration notwithstanding that he is also a charity trustee of or trustee for a participating charity;

(b) for restricting the size of the fund, and for regulating as to time, amount or otherwise the right to transfer property to or withdraw it from the fund, and for enabling sums to be advanced out of the fund by way of loan to a participating charity pending the withdrawal of property from the fund by the charity;

(c) for enabling income to be withheld from distribution with a view to avoiding fluctuations in the amounts distributed, and generally for regulating distributions of income;

(d) for enabling money to be borrowed temporarily for the purpose of meeting payments to be made out of the funds;

(e) for enabling questions arising under the scheme as to the right of a charity to participate, or as to the rights of participating charities, or as to any other matter, to be conclusively determined by the decision of the trustees managing the fund or in any other manner;

(f) for regulating the accounts and information to be supplied to participating charities.

(5) A common investment scheme, in addition to the provision for property to be transferred to the fund on the basis that the charity shall be entitled to a share in the capital and income of the fund, may include provision for enabling sums to be deposited by or on behalf of a charity on the basis that (subject to the provisions of the scheme) the charity shall be entitled to repayment of the sums deposited and to interest thereon at a rate determined by or under the scheme; and where a scheme makes any such provision it shall also provide for excluding from the amount of capital and income to be shared between charities participating otherwise than by way of deposit such amounts (not exceeding the amounts properly attributable to the making of deposits) as are from time to time reasonably required in respect of the liabilities of the fund for the repayment of deposits and for the interest on deposits, including amounts required by way of reserve.

(6) Except in so far as a common investment scheme provides to the contrary, the rights under it of a participating charity shall not be capable of being assigned or charged, nor shall any trustee or other person concerned in the management of the common investment fund be required or entitled to take account of any trust or other equity affecting a participating charity or its property or rights.

(7) The powers of investment of every charity shall include power to participate in common investment schemes unless the power is excluded by a provision specifically referring to common investment schemes in the trusts of the charity.

(8) A common investment fund shall be deemed for all purposes to be a charity; and if the scheme admits only exempt charities, the fund shall be an exempt charity for the purposes of this Act.

(9) Subsection (8) above shall apply not only to common investment funds established under the powers of this section, but also to any similar fund established for the exclusive benefit of charities by or under any enactment relating to any particular charities or class of charity.

25. Schemes to establish common deposit funds

(1) The court or the Commissioners may by order make and bring into effect schemes (in this section referred to as 'common deposit schemes') for the establishment of common deposit funds under trusts which provide—

(a) for sums to be deposited by or on behalf of a charity participating in the scheme and invested under the control of trustees appointed to manage the fund; and

(b) for any such charity to be entitled (subject to the provisions of the scheme) to repayment of any sums so deposited and to interest thereon at a rate determined under the scheme.

(2) Subject to subsection (3) below, the following provisions of section 24 above, namely—

(a) subsections (2) to (4), and

(b) subsections (6) to (9),

shall have effect in relation to common deposit schemes and common deposit funds as they have effect in relation to common investment schemes and common investment funds.

(3) In its application in accordance with subsection (2) above, subsection (4) of that section shall have effect with the substitution for paragraphs (b) and (c) of the following paragraphs—

'(b) for regulating as to time, amount or otherwise the right to repayment of sums deposited in the fund;

(c) for authorising a part of the income for any year to be credited to a reserve account maintained for the purpose of counteracting any losses accruing to the fund, and generally for regulating the manner in which the rate of interest on deposits is to be determined from time to time;'.

Additional powers of Commissioners

26. Power to authorise dealings with charity property etc.

(1) Subject to the provisions of this section, where it appears to the Commissioners that any action proposed or contemplated in the administration of a charity is expedient in the interests of the charity, they may by order sanction that action, whether or not it would otherwise be within the powers exercisable by the charity trustees in the administration of the charity; and anything done under the authority of such an order shall be deemed to be properly done in the exercise of those powers.

29. Power to advise charity trustees

(1) The Commissioners may on the written application of any charity trustee give him their opinion or advice on any matter affecting the performance of his duties as such.

(2) A charity trustee or trustee for a charity acting in accordance with the opinion or advice of the Commissioners given under this section with respect to the charity shall be deemed, as regards his responsibility for so acting, to have acted in accordance with his trust, unless, when he does so, either—

(a) he knows or has reasonable cause to suspect that the opinion or advice was given in ignorance of material facts; or

(b) the decision of the court has been obtained on the matter or proceedings are pending to obtain one.

PART IX
MISCELLANEOUS

Powers of investment

70. Relaxation of restrictions on wider-range investments

(1) The Secretary of State may by order made with the consent of the Treasury—

(a) direct that, in the case of a trust fund consisting of propery held by or in trust for a charity, any division of the fund in pursuance of section 2(1) of the Trustee Investments Act 1961 (trust funds to be divided so that wider-range and narrower-range investments are equal in value) shall be made so that the value of the wider-range part at the time of the division bears to the then value of the narrower-range part such proportion as is specified in the order;

(b) provide that, in its application in relation to such a trust fund, that Act shall have effect subject to such modifications so specified as the Secretary of State considers appropriate in consequence of, or in connection with, any such direction.

(2) Where, before the coming into force of an order under this section, a trust fund consisting of property held by or in trust for a charity has already been divided in pursuance of section 2(1) of that Act, the fund may, notwithstanding anything in that provision, be again divided (once only) in pursuance of that provision during the continuance in force of the order.

(3) No order shall be made under this section unless a draft of the order has been laid before and approved by a resolution of each House of Parliament.

(4) Expressions used in this section which are also used in the Trustee Investments Act 1961 have the same meaning as in that Act.

(5) In the application of this section to Scotland, 'charity' means a recognised body within the meaning of section 1(7) of the Law Reform (Miscellaneous Provisions) (Scotland) Act 1990.

Note: The Charities (Trustee Investments Act 1961) Order 1995 (SI 1995 No. 1092) directs that in the case of a trust fund comprising of property held by or in trust for a charity, any division of the fund in pursuance of section 2(1) Trustee Investments Act 1961 shall be made so that the value of the wider-range part at the time of the division bears to the then value of the narrower-range part the properties of three to one.

71. Extension of powers of investment

(1) The Secretary of State may by regulations made with the consent of the Treasury make, with respect to property held by or in trust for a charity, provision authorising a trustee to invest such property in any manner specified in the regulations, being a manner of investment not for the time being included in any Part of Schedule 1 to the Trustee Investments Act 1961.

(2) Regulations under this section may make such provision—

(a) regulating the investment of property in any manner authorised by virtue of subsection (1) above, and

(b) with respect to the variation and retention of investments so made,

as the Secretary of State considers appropriate.

(3) Such regulations may, in particular, make provision—

(a) imposing restrictions with respect to the proportion of the property held by or in trust for a charity which may be invested in any manner authorised by virtue of subsection (1) above, being either restrictions applying to investment in any such manner generally or restrictions applying to investment in any particular such manner;

(b) imposing the like requirements with respect to the obtaining and consideration of advice as are imposed by any of the provisions of section 6 of the Trustee Investments Act 1961 (duty of trustees in choosing investments).

(4) Any power of investment conferred by any regulations under this section—

(a) shall be in addition to, and not in derogation from, any power conferred otherwise than by such regulations; and

(b) shall not be limited by the trusts of a charity (in so far as they are not contained in any Act or instrument made under an enactment) unless it is excluded by those trusts in express terms;

but any such power shall only be exercisable by a trustee in so far as a contrary intention is not expressed in any Act or in any instrument made under an enactment and relating to the powers of the trustee.

(5) No regulations shall be made under this section unless a draft of the regulations has been laid before and approved by a resolution of each House of Parliament.

(6) In this section 'property'—

(a) in England and Wales, means real or personal property of any description, including money and things in action, but does not include an interest in expectancy; and

(b) in Scotland, means property of any description (whether heritable. or moveable, corporeal or incorporeal) which is presently enjoyable, but does not include a future interest, whether vested or contingent;

and any reference to property held by or in trust for a charity is a reference to property so held, whether it is for the time being in a state of investment or not.

Disqualification for acting as charity trustee

72. Persons disqualified for being trustees of a charity

(1) Subject to the following provisions of this section a person shall be disqualified for being a charity trustee or trustee for a charity if—

(a) he has been convicted of any offence involving dishonesty or deception;

(b) he has been adjudged bankrupt or sequestration of his estate has been awarded and (in either case) he has not been discharged;

(c) he has made a composition or arrangement with, or granted a trust deed for, his creditors and has not been discharged in respect of it;

(d) he has been removed from the office of charity trustee or trustee for a charity by an order made—

(i) by the Commissioners under section 18(2)(i) above, or

(ii) by the Commissioners under section 20(1A)(i) of the Charities Act 1960 (power to act for protection of charities) or under section 20(1)(i) of that Act (as in force before the commencement of section 8 of the Charities Act 1992), or

(iii) by the High Court,

on the grounds of any misconduct or mismanagement in the administration of the charity for which he was responsible or to which he was privy, or which he by his conduct contributed to or facilitated;

(e) he has been removed, under section 7 of the Law Reform (Miscellaneous Provisions) (Scotland) Act 1990 (powers of Court of Session to deal with management of charities), from being concerned in the management or control of any body;

(f) he is subject to a disqualification order under the Company Directors Disqualification Act 1986 or to an order made under section 429(2)(b) of the Insolvency Act 1986 (failure to pay under county court administration order).

(2) In subsection (1) above—

(a) paragraph (a) applies whether the conviction occurred before or after the commencement of that subsection, but does not apply in relation to any conviction which is a spent conviction for the purposes of the Rehabilitation of Offenders Act 1974;

(b) paragraph (b) applies whether the adjudication of bankruptcy or the sequestration occurred before or after the commencement of that subsection;

(c) paragraph (c) applies whether the composition or arrangement was made, or the trust deed was granted, before or after the commencement of that subsection; and

(d) paragraphs (d) to (f) apply in relation to orders made and removals effected before or after the commencement of that subsection.

(3) Where (apart from this subsection) a person is disqualified under subsection (1)(b) above for being a charity trustee or trustee for any charity which is a company, he shall not be so disqualified if leave has been granted under section 11 of the Company Directors Disqualification Act 1986 (undischarged bankrupts) for him to act as director

of the charity; and similarly a person shall not be disqualified under subsection (1)(f) above for being a charity trustee or trustee for such a charity if—

(a) in the case of a person subject to a disqualification order, leave under the order has been granted for him to act as director of the charity, or

(b) in the case of a person subject to an order under section 429(2)(b) of the Insolvency Act 1986, leave has been granted by the court which made the order for him to so act.

(4) The Commissioners may, on the application of any person disqualified under subsection (1) above, waive his disqualification either generally or in relation to a particular charity or a particular class of charities; but no such waiver may be granted in relation to any charity which is a company if—

(a) the person concerned is for the time being prohibited, by virtue of—

(i) a disqualification order under the Company Directors Disqualification Act 1986, or

(ii) section 11(1) or 12(2) of that Act (undischarged bankrupts; failure to pay under county court administration order),

from acting as director of the charity; and

(b) leave has not been granted for him to act as director of any other company.

(5) Any waiver under subsection (4) above shall be notified in writing to the person concerned.

(6) For the purposes of this section the Commissioners shall keep, in such manner as they think fit, a register of all persons who have been removed from office as mentioned in subsection (1)(d) above either—

(a) by an order of the Commissioners made before or after the commencement of subsection (1) above, or

(b) by an order of the High Court made after the commencement of section 45(1) of the Charities Act 1992;

and, where any person is so removed from office by an order of the High Court, the court shall notify the Commissioners of his removal.

(7) The entries in the register kept under subsection (6) above shall be available for public inspection in legible form at all reasonable times.

73. Person acting as charity trustee while disqualified

(1) Subject to subsection (2) below, any person who acts as a charity trustee or trustee for a charity while he is disqualified for being such a trustee by virtue of section 72 above shall be guilty of an offence and liable—

(a) on summary conviction, to imprisonment for a term not exceeding six months or to a fine not exceeding the statutory maximum, or both;

(b) on conviction on indictment, to imprisonment for a term not exceeding two years or to a fine, or both.

(2) Subsection (1) above shall not apply where—

(a) the charity concerned is a company; and

(b) the disqualified person is disqualified by virtue only of paragraph (b) or (f) of section 72(1) above.

(3) Any acts done as charity trustee or trustee for a charity by a person disqualified for being such a trustee by virtue of section 72 above shall not be invalid by reason only of that disqualification.

(4) Where the Commissioners are satisfied—

(a) that any person has acted as charity trustee or trustee for a charity (other than an exempt charity) while disqualified for being such a trustee by virtue of section 72 above, and

(b) that, while so acting, he has received from the charity any sums by way of remuneration or expenses, or any benefit in kind, in connection with his acting as charity trustee or trustee for the charity, they may by order direct him to repay to the charity the whole or part of any such sums, or (as the case may be) to pay to the charity the whole or part of the monetary value (as determined by them) of any such benefit.

(5) Subsection (4) above does not apply to any sums received by way of remuneration or expenses in respect of any time when the person concerned was not disqualified for being a charity trustee or trustee for the charity.

Small charities

74. Power to transfer all property, modify objects etc.

(1) This section applies to a charity if—

(a) its gross income in its last financial year did not exceed £5,000, and

(b) it does not hold any land on trusts which stipulate that the land is to be used for the purposes, or any particular purposes, of the charity,

and it is neither an exempt charity nor a charitable company.

(2) Subject to the following provisions of this section, the charity trustees of a charity to which this section applies may resolve for the purposes of this section—

(a) that all the property of the charity should be transferred to such other charity as is specified in the resolution, being either a registered charity or a charity which is not required to be registered;

(b) that all the property of the charity should be divided, in such manner as is specified in the resolution, between such two or more other charities as are so specified, being in each case either a registered charity or a charity which is not required to be registered;

(c) that the trusts of the charity should be modified by replacing all or any of the purposes of the charity with such other purposes, being in law charitable, as are specified in the resolution;

(d) that any provision of the trusts of the charity—

(i) relating to any of the powers exercisable by the charity trustees in the administration of the charity, or

(ii) regulating the procedure to be followed in any respect in connection with its administration,

should be modified in such manner as is specified in the resolution.

(3) Any resolution passed under subsection (2) above must be passed by a majority of not less than two-thirds of such charity trustees as vote on the resolution.

(4) The charity trustees of a charity to which this section applies ('the transferor charity') shall not have power to pass a resolution under sub-section (2)(a) or (b) above unless they are satisfied—

(a) that the existing purposes of the transferor charity have ceased to be conducive to a suitable and effective application of the charity's resources; and

(b) that the purposes of the charity or charities specified in the resolution are as similar in character to the purposes of the transferor charity as is reasonably practicable;

and before passing the resolution they must have received from the charity trustees of the charity, or (as the case may be) of each of the charities, specified in the resolution written confirmation that those trustees are willing to accept a transfer of property under this section.

(5) The charity trustees of any such charity shall not have power to pass a resolution under subsection (2)(c) above unless they are satisfied—

(a) that the existing purposes of the charity (or, as the case may be, such of them as it is proposed to replace) have ceased to be conducive to a suitable and effective application of the charity's resources; and

(b) that the purposes specified in the resolution are as similar in character to those existing purposes as is practical in the circumstances.

(6) Where charity trustees have passed a resolution under subsection (2) above, they shall—

(a) give public notice of the resolution in such manner as they think reasonable in the circumstances; and

(b) send a copy of the resolution to the Commissioners, together with a statement of their reasons for passing it.

(7) The Commissioners may, when considering the resolution, require the charity trustees to provide additional information or explanation—

(a) as to the circumstances in and by reference to which they have determined to act under this section, or

(b) relating to their compliance with this section in connection with the resolution;

and the Commissioners shall take into account any representations made to them by persons appearing to them to be interested in the charity where those representations are made within the period of six weeks beginning with the date when the Commissioners receive a copy of the resolution by virtue of subsection (6)(b) above.

(8) Where the Commissioners have so received a copy of a resolution from any charity trustees and it appears to them that the trustees have complied with this section in connection with the resolution, the Commissioners shall, within the period of three months beginning with the date when they receive the copy of the resolution, notify the trustees in writing either—

(a) that the Commissioners concur with the resolution; or

(b) that they do not concur with it.

(9) Where the Commissioners so notify their concurrence with the resolution, then—

(a) if the resolution was passed under subsection (2)(a) or (b) above, the charity trustees shall arrange for all the property of the transferor charity to be transferred in accordance with the resolution and on terms that any property so transferred—

(i) shall be held and applied by the charity to which it is transferred ('the transferee charity') for the purposes of that charity, but

(ii) shall, as property of the transferee charity, nevertheless by subject to any restrictions on expenditure to which it is subject as property of the transferor charity,

and those trustees shall arrange for it to be so transferred by such date as may be specified in the notification; and

(b) if the resolution was passed under subsection (2)(c) or (d) above, the trusts of the charity shall be deemed, as from such date as may be specified in the notification, to have been modified in accordance with the terms of the resolution.

(10) For the purpose of enabling any property to be transferred to a charity under this section, the Commissioners shall have power, at the request of the charity trustees of that charity, to make orders vesting any property of the transferor charity—

(a) in the charity trustees of the first-mentioned charity or in any trustee for that charity, or

(b) in any other person nominated by those charity trustees to hold the property in trusts for that charity.

(11) The Secretary of State may by order amend subsection (1) above by substituting a different sum for the sum for the time being specified there.

(12) In this section—

(a) 'charitable company' means a charity which is a company or other body corporate; and

(b) references to the transfer of property to a charity are references to its transfer—

(i) to the charity trustees, or

(ii) to any trustee for the charity, or

(iii) to a person nominated by the charity trustees to hold it in trust for the charity,

as the charity trustees may determine.

Administrative provisions about charities

83. Transfer and evidence of title to property vested in trustees

(1) Where, under the trusts of a charity, trustees of property held for the purposes of the charity may be appointed or discharged by resolution of a meeting of the charity trustees, members or other persons, a memorandum declaring a trustee to have been so appointed or discharged shall be sufficient evidence of that fact if the memorandum is signed either at the meeting by the person presiding or in some other manner directed by the meeting and is attested by two persons present at the meeting.

(2) A memorandum evidencing the appointment or discharge of a trustee under subsection (1) above, if executed as a deed, shall have the like operation under section 40 of the Trustee Act 1925 (which relates to vesting declarations as respects trust property in deeds appointing or discharging trustees) as if the appointment or discharge were effected by the deed.

(3) For the purposes of this section, where a document purports to have been signed and attested as mentioned in subsection (1) above, then on proof (whether by evidence or as a matter of presumption) of the signature the document shall be presumed to have been so signed and attested, unless the contrary is shown.

(4) This section shall apply to a memorandum made at any time, except that subsection (2) shall apply only to those made after the commencement of the Charities Act 1960.

(5) This section shall apply in relation to any institution to which the Literary and Scientific Institutions Act 1854 applies as it applies in relation to a charity.

96. Construction of references to a charity or to particular classes of charity

(1) In this Act, except in so far as the context otherwise requires—

'charity' means any institution, corporate or not, which is established for charitable purposes and is subject to the control of the High Court in the exercise of the court's jurisdiction with respect to charities;

'ecclesiastical charity' has the same meaning as in the Local Government Act 1894;

'exempt charity' means (subject to section 24(8) above) a charity comprised in Schedule 2 to this Act;

'local charity' means, in relation to any area, a charity established for purposes which are by their nature or by the trusts of the charity directed wholly or mainly to the benefit of that area or of part of it;

'parochial charity' means, in relation to any parish or (in Wales) community, a charity the benefits of which are, or the separate distribution of the benefits of which is, confined to inhabitants of the parish or community, or of a single ancient ecclesiastical parish which included that parish or community or part of it, or of an area consisting of that parish or community with not more than four neighbouring parishes or communities.

(2) The expression 'charity' is not in this Act applicable—

(a) to any ecclesiastical corporation (that is to say, any corporation in the Church of England, whether sole or aggregate, which is established for spiritual purposes) in respect of the corporate property of the corporation, except to a corporation aggregate having some purposes which are not ecclesiastical in respect of its corporate property held for those purposes; or

(b) to any Diocesan Board of Finance within the meaning of the Endowments and Glebe Measure 1976 for any diocese in respect of the diocesan glebe land of that diocese within the meaning of that Measure; or

(c) to any trust of property for purposes for which the property has been consecrated.

(3) . . .

(4) References in this Act to a charity whose income from all sources does not in aggregate amount to more than a specified amount shall be construed—

(a) by reference to the gross revenues of the charity, or

(b) if the Commissioners so determine, by reference to the amount which they estimate to be the likely amount of those revenues,

but without (in either case) bringing into account anything for the yearly value of land occupied by the charity apart from the pecuniary income (if any) received from that land; and any question as to the application of any such reference to a charity shall be determined by the Commissioners, whose decision shall be final.

(5) The Commissioners may direct that for all or any of the purposes of this Act an institution established for any special purposes of or in connection with a charity (being charitable purposes) shall be treated as forming part of that charity or as forming a distinct charity.

97. General interpretation

(1) In this Act, except in so far as the context otherwise requires—

'charitable purposes' means purposes which are exclusively charitable according to the law of England and Wales;

'charity trustees' means the persons having the general control and management of the administration of a charity;

'the Commissioners' means the Charity Commissioners for England and Wales;

'company' means a company formed and registered under the Companies Act 1985 or to which the provisions of that Act apply as they apply to such a company;

'the court' means the High Court and, within the limits of its jurisdiction, any other court in England and Wales having a jurisdiction in respect of charities concurrent (within any limit of area or amount) with that of the High Court, and includes any judge or officer of the court exercising the jurisdiction of the court;

'financial year'—

(a) in relation to a charity which is a company, shall be construed in accordance with section 223 of the Companies Act 1985; and

(b) in relation to any other charity, shall be construed in accordance with regulations made by virtue of section 42(2) above;

but this definition is subject to the transitional provisions in section 99(4) below and Part II of Schedule 8 to this Act;

'gross income', in relation to charity, means its gross recorded income from all sources including special trusts;

'independent examiner', in relation to a charity, means such a person as is mentioned in section 43(3)(a) above;

'institution' includes any trust or undertaking;

'the official custodian' means the official custodian for charities;

'permanent endowment' shall be construed in accordance with section 96(3) above;

'the register' means the register of charities kept under section 3 above and 'registered' shall be construed accordingly;

'special trust' means property which is held and administered by or on behalf of a charity for any special purposes of the charity, and is so held and administered on separate trusts relating only to that property but a special trust shall not, by itself, constitute a charity for the purposes of Part VI of this Act;

'trusts' in relation to a charity, means the provisions establishing it as a charity and regulating its purposes and administration, whether those provisions take effect by way of trust or not, and in relation to other institutions has a corresponding meaning.

(2) In this Act, except in so far as the context otherwise requires, 'document' includes information recorded in any form, and, in relation to information recorded otherwise than in legible form—

(a) any reference to its production shall be construed as a reference to the furnishing of a copy of it in legible form; and

(b) any reference to the furnishing of a copy of, or extract from, it shall accordingly be construed as a reference to the furnishing of a copy of, or extract from, it in legible form.

(3) No vesting or transfer of any property in pursuance of any provision of Part IV or IX of this Act shall operate as a breach of a covenant or condition against alienation or give rise to a forfeiture.

SCHEDULES

Section 1

SCHEDULE 1
CONSTITUTION ETC. OF CHARITY COMMISSIONERS

1.—(1) There shall be a Chief Charity Commissioner and two other commissioners.

(2) Two at least of the commissioners shall be persons who have a seven year general qualification within the meaning of section 71 of the Courts and Legal Services Act 1990.

(3) The chief commissioner and the other commissioners shall be appointed by the Secretary of State, and shall be deemed for all purposes to be employed in the civil service of the Crown.

(4) There may be paid to each of the commissioners such salary and allowances as the Secretary of State may with the approval of the Treasury determine.

(5) If at any time it appears to the Secretary of State that there should be more than three commissioners, he may with the approval of the Treasury appoint not more than two additional commissioners.

2.—(1) The chief commissioner may, with the approval of the Treasury as to number and conditions of service, appoint such assistant commissioners and other officers and such employees as he thinks necessary for the proper discharge of the functions of the Commissioners and of the official custodian.

(2) There may be paid to officers and employees so appointed such salaries or remuneration as the Treasury may determine.

3.—(1) The Commissioners may use an official seal for the authentication of documents, and their seal shall be officially and judicially noticed.

(2) The Documentary Evidence Act 1868, as amended by the Documentary Evidence Act 1882, shall have effect as if in the Schedule to the Act of 1868 the Commissioners were included in the first column and any commissioner or assistant commissioner and any officer authorised to act on behalf of the Commissioners were mentioned in the second column.

(3) The Commissioners shall have power to regulate their own procedure and, subject to any such regulations and to any directions of the chief commissioner, any one commissioner or any assistant commissioner may act for and in the name of the Commissioners.

(4) Where the Commissioners act as a board, then—

(a) if not more than four commissioners hold office for the time being, the quorum shall be two commissioners (of whom at least one must be a person having a qualification such as is mentioned in paragraph 1(2) above); and

(b) if five commissioners so hold office, the quorum shall be three commissioners (of whom at least one must be a person having such a qualification);

and in the case of an equality of votes the chief commissioner or in his absence the commissioner presiding shall have a second or casting vote.

(5) The Commissioners shall have power to act notwithstanding any vacancy in their number.

(6) It is hereby declared that the power of a commissioner or assistant commissioner to act for and in the name of the Commissioners in accordance with sub-paragraph (3) above may, in particular, be exercised in relation to functions of the Commissioners under sections 8, 18, 19 and 63 of this Act, including functions under sections 8, 18 and 19 as applied by section 80(1).

4. Legal proceedings may be instituted by or against the Commissioners by the name of the Charity Commissioners for England and Wales, and shall not abate or be affected by any change in the persons who are the commissioners.

Sections 3 and 96

SCHEDULE 2
EXEMPT CHARITIES

The following institutions, so far as they are charities, are exempt charities within the meaning of this Act, that is to say—

(a) any institution which, if the Charities Act 1960 had not been passed, would be exempted from the powers and jurisdiction, under the Charitable Trusts Acts 1853 to 1939, of the Commissioners or Minister of Education (apart from any power of the Commissioners or Minister to apply those Acts in whole or in part to charities otherwise exempt) by the terms of any enactment not contained in those Acts other than section 9 of the Places of Worship Registration Act 1855;

(b) the universities of Oxford, Cambridge, London, Durham and Newcastle, the colleges and halls in the universities of Oxford, Cambridge, Durham and Newcastle, Queen Mary and Westfield College in the University of London and the colleges of Winchester and Eton;

(c) any university, university college, or institution connected with a university or university college, which Her Majesty declares by Order in Council to be an exempt charity for the purposes of this Act;

(d) a grant-maintained school;

[(da) the School Curriculum and Assessment authority;]

(f) [the Curriculum and Assessment authority for Wales;]

(h) a higher education corporation;

(i) a successor company to a higher education corporation (within the meaning of section 129(5) of the Education Reform Act 1988) at a time when an institution conducted by the company is for the time being designated under that section;

(j) a further education corporation;

(k) the Board of Trustees of the Victoria and Albert Museum;

(l) the Board of Trustees of the Science Museum;

(m) the Board of Trustees of the Armouries;

(n) the Board of Trustees of the Royal Botanic Gardens, Kew;

(o) the Board of Trustees of the National Museums and Galleries on Merseyside;

(p) the trustees of the British Museum and the trustees of the Natural History Museum;

(q) the Board of Trustees of the National Gallery;

(r) the Board of Trustees of the Tate Gallery ;

(s) the Board of Trustees of the National Portrait Gallery;

(t) the Board of Trustees of the Wallace Collection;

(u) the Trustees of the Imperial War Museum;

(v) the Trustees of the National Maritime Museum;

(w) any institution which is administered by or on behalf of an institution included above and is established for the general purposes of, or for any special purpose of or in connection with, the last-mentioned institution;

(x) the Church Commissioners and any institution which is administered by them;
(y) any registered society within the meaning of the Industrial and Provident Societies Act 1965 and any registered society or branch within the meaning of the Friendly Societies Act 1974;
(z) the Board of Governors of the Museum of London;
(za) the British Library Board.

Section 13

SCHEDULE 3
ENLARGEMENT OF AREAS OF LOCAL CHARITIES

Existing area	*Permissible enlargement*
1. Greater London	Any area comprising Greater London.
2. Any area in Greater London and not in, or partly in, the City of London.	(i) Any area in Greater London and not in, or partly in, the City of London; (ii) the area of Greater London exclusive of the City of London; (iii) any area comprising the area of Greater London, exclusive of the City of London; (iv) any area partly in Greater London and partly in any adjacent parish or parishes (civil or ecclesiastical), and not partly in the City of London.
3. A district	Any area comprising the district
[3A. A Welsh county or county borough	(i) Any area comprising that county or county borough.]
4. Any area in a district	(i) any area in the district; (ii) the district; (iii) any area comprising the district; (iv) any area partly in the district and partly in any adjacent district.
4A. Any area in a Welsh county or county borough.	(i) Any area in the county or county borough; (ii) the county or county borough; (iii) any area comprising the county or county borough; (iv) any area partly in the county or county borough and partly in any adjacent Welsh county or county borough or in any adjacent district.]
5. A parish (civil or ecclesiastical), or two or more parishes, or an area in a parish, or partly in each of two or more parishes.	Any area not extending beyond the parish or parishes comprising or adjacent to-the area in column 1.
6. In Wales, a community, or two or more communities, or an area in a community, or partly in ĕach of two or more communities.	Any area not extending beyond the community or communities comprising or adjacent to the area in column 1.

LAW OF PROPERTY (MISCELLANEOUS PROVISIONS) ACT 1994

PART I
IMPLIED COVENANTS FOR TITLE

The covenants

1. Covenants to be implied on a disposition of property

(1) In an instrument effecting or purporting to effect a disposition of property there shall be implied on the part of the person making the disposition, whether or not the disposition is for valuable consideration, such of the covenants specified in sections 2 to 5 as are applicable to the disposition.

(2) Of those sections—

(a) sections 2, 3(1), 4 and 5 apply where dispositions are expressed to be made with full guarantee; and

(b) sections 2, 3(2), 4 and 5 apply where dispositions are expressed to be made with limited guarantee.

(3) In this Part—

'disposition' includes the creation of a term of years;

'instrument' includes an instrument which is not a deed; and

'property' includes a thing in action, and any interest in real or personal property.

2. Right to dispose and further assurance

(1) If the disposition is expressed to be made with full guarantee or with limited guarantee there shall be implied the following covenants—

(a) that the person making the disposition has the right (with the concurrence of any other person conveying the property) to dispose of the property as he purports to, and

(b) that that person will at his own cost do all that he reasonably can to give the person to whom he disposes of the property the title he purports to give.

(2) The latter obligation includes—

(a) in relation to a disposition of an interest in land the title to which is registered, doing all that he reasonably can to ensure that the person to whom the disposition is made is entitled to be registered as proprietor with at least the class of title registered immediately before the disposition; and

(b) in relation to a disposition of an interest in land the title to which is required to be registered by virtue of the disposition, giving all reasonable assistance fully to establish to the satisfaction of the registrar the right of the person to whom the disposition is made to registration as proprietor.

(3) In the case of a disposition of an existing legal interest in land, the following presumptions apply, subject to the terms of the instrument, in ascertaining for the purposes of the covenants implied by this section what the person making the disposition purports to dispose of—

(a) where the title to the interest is registered, it shall be presumed that the disposition is of the whole of that interest;

(b) where the title to the interest is not registered, then—

(i) if it appears from the instrument that the interest is a leasehold interest, it shall be presumed that the disposition is of the property for the unexpired portion of the term of years created by the lease; and

(ii) in any other case, it shall be presumed that what is disposed of is the fee simple.

3. Charges, incumbrances and third party rights

(1) If the disposition is expressed to be made with full guarantee there shall be implied a covenant that the person making the disposition is disposing of the property

free from all charges and incumbrances (whether monetary or not) and from all other rights exercisable by third parties.

(2) If the disposition is expressed to be made with limited guarantee there shall be implied a covenant that the person making the disposition has not since the date of the last disposition for value—

(a) charged or incumbered the property or granted third party rights in relation to it, or

(b) suffered the property to be charged, incumbered or subjected to any such rights,

and that he is not aware that anyone else has done so since that date.

4. Validity of lease

(1) Where the disposition is of leasehold land and is expressed to be made with full guarantee or with limited guarantee, the following covenants shall also be implied—

(a) that the lease is subsisting at the date of the disposition, and

(b) that there is no subsisting breach of a condition or tenant's obligation, and nothing which at the date of the disposition would render the lease liable to forfeiture.

(2) In subsection (1) 'the lease' means—

(a) if the disposition is an assignment of a lease, that lease;

(b) if the disposition is an underlease, the lease out of which the underlease is derived (or, as the case may be, immediately derived); and

(c) in any other case, the lease having effect subject to the disposition.

5. Discharge of obligations where property subject to rentcharge or leasehold land

(1) Where the disposition is a mortgage of property subject to a rentcharge, or of leasehold land, and is expressed to be made with full guarantee or with limited guarantee, the following covenants shall also be implied.

(2) If the property is subject to a rentcharge, there shall be implied a covenant that the mortgagor will fully and promptly observe and perform all the obligations under the instrument creating the rentcharge that are for the time being enforceable with respect to the property by the owner of the rentcharge in his capacity as such.

(3) If the property is leasehold land, there shall be implied a covenant that the mortgagor will fully and promptly observe and perform all the obligations under the lease subject to the mortgage that are for the time being imposed on the tenant under the lease.

(4) In this section 'mortgage' includes charge, and 'mortgagor' shall be construed accordingly.

Supplementary provisions as to effect of covenants

6. Matters within knowledge of person to whom disposition is made

(1) The person making the disposition is not liable under the covenants implied by virtue of—

(a) section 2(1)(a) (right to dispose),

(b) section 3 (charges, incumbrances and third party rights), or

(c) section 4 (validity of lease),

for anything that is the result of facts which at the date of the disposition are within the actual knowledge of the person to whom the disposition is made.

(2) For this purpose section 198 of the Law of Property Act 1925 (deemed notice by virtue of registration) shall be disregarded.

7. Passing of benefit of implied covenant

(1) The benefit of a covenant implied by virtue of this Part shall not be annexed and incident to the interest of the person to whom the disposition is made so as to pass generally to his successors in title.

(2) The benefit shall, however, pass to a person without express assignment so far as it relates to property which passes to him—

(a) by operation of law, or

(b) on an assent to him by personal representatives.

(3) Any power by court order, or other instrument not involving a disposition by the owner of the property, to transfer property from one person to another includes power to provide that there is also transferred, so far as it relates to that property, the benefit of a covenant implied by virtue of this Part.

(4) Except as mentioned above, the benefit of a covenant implied by virtue of this Part passes only by assignment.

(5) Nothing in this section affects the enforcement of a covenant by the registrar under section 83(10) of the Land Registration Act 1925 (enforcement of covenants and other rights for benefit of Crown where indemnity has been paid).

8. Other supplementary provisions

(1) The operation of any covenant implied in an instrument by virtue of this Part may be limited or extended by that instrument.

(2) Sections 81 and 83 of the Law of Property Act 1925 (effect of covenant with two or more jointly; construction of implied covenants) apply to a covenant implied by virtue of this Part as they apply to a covenant implied by virtue of that Act.

. . .

9. Modifications of statutory forms

(1) Where a form set out in an enactment, or in an instrument made under an enactment, includes words which (in an appropriate case) would have resulted in the implication of a covenant by virtue of section 76 of the Law of Property Act 1925, the form shall be taken to authorise instead the use of the words 'with full guarantee' or 'with limited guarantee' . . .

. . .

Transitional provisions

10. General saving for covenants in old form

(1) Except as provided by section 11 below (cases in which covenants in old form implied on disposition after commencement), the following provisions, namely—

(a) section 76 of the Law of Property Act 1925, and

(b) section 24(1)(a) of the Land Registration Act 1925,

are repealed as regards dispositions of property made after the commencement of this Part.

(2) The repeal of those provisions by this Act accordingly does not affect the enforcement of a covenant implied by virtue of either of them on a disposition before the commencement of this Part.

(3) But section 7 (passing of benefit of implied covenant) applies as regards the passing of the benefit of such a covenant after the commencement of this Part as in relation to the benefit of a covenant implied by virtue of this Part.

11. Covenants in old form implied in certain cases

(1) Section 76 of the Law of Property Act 1925 applies in relation to a disposition of property made after the commencement of this Part in pursuance of a contract entered into before commencement where—

(a) the contract contains a term providing for a disposition to which that section would have applied if the disposition had been made before commencement, and

(b) the existence of the contract and of that term is apparent on the face of the instrument effecting the disposition,

unless there has been an intervening disposition of the property expressed, in accordance with this Part, to be made with full guarantee.

(2) Section 24(1)(a) of the Land Registration Act 1925 applies in relation to a disposition of a leasehold interest in land made after the commencement of this Part in pursuance of a contract entered into before commencement where—

(a) the covenant specified in that provision would have been implied on the disposition if it had been made before commencement, and

(b) the existence of the contract is apparent on the face of the instrument effecting the disposition,

unless there has been an intervening disposition of the leasehold interest expressed, in accordance with this Part, to be made with full guarantee.

(3) In subsections (1) and (2) an 'intervening disposition' means a disposition after the commencement of this Part to, or to a predecessor in title of, the person by whom the disposition in question is made.

(4) Where one of the following provisions, namely—

(a) section 76 of the Law of Property Act 1925, or

(b) section 24(1)(a) of the Land Registration Act 1925,

applies in relation to a disposition in accordance with subsection (1) or (2), section 7 (passing of benefit of implied covenant) applies as regards the passing of the benefit of a covenant implied by virtue of that provision as in relation to the benefit of a covenant implied by virtue of this Part.

(5) Where in order for subsection (1) or (2) to apply it is necessary for certain matters to be apparent on the face of the instrument effecting the disposition, the contract shall be deemed to contain an implied term that they should so appear.

12. Covenants in new form to be implied in other cases

(1) This section applies to a contract for the disposition of property entered into before the commencement of this Part where the disposition is made after commencement and section 11 (cases in which covenants in old form to be implied) does not apply because there has been an intervening disposition expressed, in accordance with this Part, to be with full guarantee.

(2) A contract which contains a term that the person making the disposition shall do so as beneficial owner shall be construed as requiring that person to do so by an instrument expressed to be made with full guarantee.

(3) A contract which contains a term that the person making the disposition shall do so—

(a) as settlor, or

(b) as trustee or mortgagee or personal representative,

shall be construed as requiring that person to do so by an instrument expressed to be made with limited guarantee.

(4) A contract for the disposition of a leasehold interest in land entered into at a date when the title to the leasehold interest was registered shall be construed as requiring the person making the disposition for which it provides to do so by an instrument expressed to be made with full guarantee.

(5) Where this section applies and the contract provides that any of the covenants to be implied by virtue of section 76 of the Law of Property Act 1925 or section 24(1)(a) of the Land Registration Act 1925 shall be implied in a modified form, the contract shall be construed as requiring a corresponding modification of the covenants implied by virtue of this Part.

13. Application of transitional provisions in relation to options

For the purposes of sections 11 and 12 (transitional provisions: implication of covenants in old form in certain cases and new form in others) as they apply in relation to a disposition of property in accordance with an option granted before the commencement of this Part and exercised after commencement, the contract for the disposition shall be deemed to have been entered into on the grant of the option.

PART II
MATTERS ARISING IN CONNECTION WITH DEATH

17. Notices affecting land: absence of knowledge of intended recipient's death

(1) Service of a notice affecting land which would be effective but for the death of the intended recipient is effective despite his death if the person serving the notice has no reason to believe that he has died.

(2) Where the person serving a notice affecting land has no reason to believe that the intended recipient has died, the proper address for the purposes of section 7 of the Interpretation Act 1978 (service of documents by post) shall be what would be the proper address apart from his death.

(3) The above provisions do not apply to a notice authorised or required to be served for the purposes of proceedings before—

(a) any court,

(b) any tribunal specified in Schedule 1 to the Tribunals and Inquiries Act 1992 (tribunals within general supervision of Council on Tribunals), or

(c) the Chief Land Registrar or any district registrar or assistant district registrar;

but this is without prejudice to the power to make provision in relation to such proceedings by rules of court, procedural rules within the meaning of section 8 of the Tribunals and Inquiries Act 1992 or rules under section 144 of the Land Registration Act 1925.

18. Notices affecting land: service on personal representatives before filing of grant

(1) A notice affecting land which would have been authorised or required to be served on a person but for his death shall be sufficiently served before a grant of representation has been filed if—

(a) it is addressed to 'The Personal Representatives of' the deceased (naming him) and left at or sent by post to his last known place of residence or business in the United Kingdom, and

(b) a copy of it, similarly addressed, is served on the Public Trustee.

(2) The reference in subsection (1) to the filing of a grant of representation is to the filing at the Principal Registry of the Family Division of the High Court of a copy of a grant of representation in respect of the deceased's estate or, as the case may be, the part of his estate which includes the land in question.

(3) The method of service provided for by this section is not available where provision is made—

(a) by or under any enactment, or

(b) by an agreement in writing,

requiring a different method of service, or expressly prohibiting the method of service provided for by this section, in the circumstances.

19. Functions of Public Trustee in relation to notices, etc.

(1) The Public Trustee may give directions as to the office or offices at which documents may be served on him—

(a) by virtue of section 9 of the Administration of Estates Act 1925 (as substituted by section 14(1) above), or

(b) in pursuance of section 18(1)(b) above (service on Public Trustee of copy of certain notices affecting land);

and he shall publish such directions in such manner as he considers appropriate.

(2) The Lord Chancellor may by regulations make provision with respect to the functions of the Public Trustee in relation to such documents; and the regulations may make different provision in relation to different descriptions of document or different circumstances.

(3) The regulations may, in particular, make provision requiring the Public Trustee—

(a) to keep such documents for a specified period and thereafter to keep a copy or record of their contents in such form as may be specified;

(b) to keep such documents, copies and records available for inspection at such reasonable hours as may be specified; and

(c) to supply copies to any person on request.

In this subsection 'specified' means specified by or under the regulations.

(4) Regulations under this section shall be made by statutory instrument which shall be subject to annulment in pursuance of a resolution of either House of Parliament.

(5) The following provisions of the Public Trustee Act 1906, namely—

(a) section 8(5) (payment of expenses out of money provided by Parliament), and

(b) section 9(1), (3) and (4) (provisions as to fees),

apply in relation to the functions of the Public Trustee in relation to documents to which this section applies as in relation to his functions under that Act.

LANDLORD AND TENANT (COVENANTS) ACT 1995

Preliminary

1. Tenancies to which the Act applies

(1) Sections 3 to 16 and 21 apply only to new tenancies.

(2) Sections 17 to 20 apply to both new and other tenancies.

(3) For the purposes of this section a tenancy is a new tenancy if it is granted on or after the date on which this Act comes into force otherwise than in pursuance of—

(a) an agreement entered into before that date, or

(b) an order of a court made before that date.

(4) Subsection (3) has effect subject to section 20(1) in the case of overriding leases granted under section 19.

(5) Without prejudice to the generality of subsection (3), that subsection applies to the grant of a tenancy where by virtue of any variation of a tenancy there is a deemed surrender and regrant as it applies to any other grant of a tenancy.

(6) Where a tenancy granted on or after the date on which this Act comes into force is so granted in pursuance of an option granted before that date, the tenancy shall be regarded for the purposes of subsection (3) as granted in pursuance of an agreement entered into before that date (and accordingly is not a new tenancy), whether or not the option was exercised before that date.

(7) In subsection (6) 'option' includes right of first refusal.

2. Covenants to which the Act applies

(1) This Act applies to a landlord covenant or a tenant covenant of a tenancy—

(a) whether or not the covenant has reference to the subject matter of tenancy, and

(b) whether the covenant is express, implied or imposed by law,

but does not apply to a covenant falling within subsection (2).

(2) Nothing in this Act affects any covenant imposed in pursuance of—

(a) section 35 or 155 of the Housing Act 1985 (covenants for repayment of discount on early disposals);

(b) paragraph 1 of Schedule 6A to that Act (covenants requiring redemption of landlord's share); or

(c) paragraph 1 or 3 of Schedule 2 to the Housing Associations Act 1985 covenants for repaying of discount on early disposals or for restricting disposals).

Transmission of covenants

3. Transmission of benefit and burden of covenants

(1) The benefit and burden of all landlord and tenant covenants of a tenancy—

(a) shall be annexed and incident to the whole, and to each and every part, of the premises demised by the tenancy and of the reversion in them, and

(b) shall in accordance with this section pass on an assignment of the whole or any part of those premises or of the reversion in them.

(2) Where the assignment is by the tenant under the tenancy, then as from the assignment the assignee—

(a) becomes bound by the tenant covenants of the tenancy except to the extent that—

(i) immediately before the assignment they did not bind the assignor, or

(ii) they fall to be complied with in relation to any demised premises not comprised in the assignment; and

(b) becomes entitled to the benefit of the landlord covenants of the tenancy except to the extent that they fall to be complied with in relation to any such premises.

(3) Where the assignment is by the landlord under the tenancy, then as from the assignment the assignee—

(a) becomes bound by the landlord covenants of the tenancy except to the extent that—

(i) immediately before the assignment they did not bind the assignor, or

(ii) they fall to be complied with in relation to any demised premises not comprised in the assignment; and

(b) becomes entitled to the benefit of the tenant covenants of the tenancy except to the extent that they fall to be complied with in relation to any such premises.

(4) In determining for the purposes of subsection (2) or (3) whether any covenant bound the assignor immediately before the assignment, any waiver or release of the covenant (in whatever terms) is expressed to be personal to the assignor shall be disregarded.

(5) Any landlord or tenant covenant of a tenancy which is restrictive of the user of land shall, as well as being capable of enforcement against an assignee, be capable of being enforced against any other person who is the owner or occupier of any demised premises to which the covenant relates even though there is no express provision in the tenancy to that effect.

(6) Nothing in this section shall operate—

(a) in the case of a covenant which (in whatever terms) is expressed to be personal to any person, to make the covenant enforceable by or (as the case may be) against any other person; or

(b) to make a covenant enforceable against any person if, apart from this section, it would not be enforceable against him by reason of its not having been registered under the Land Registration Act 1925 or the Land Charges Act 1972.

(7) To the extent that there remains in force any rule of law by virtue of which the burden of a covenant whose subject matter is not in existence at the time when it is made does not run with the land affected unless the covenantor covenants on behalf of himself and his assigns, that rule of law is hereby abolished in relation to tenancies.

4. Transmission of rights of re-entry

The benefit of a landlord's right of re-entry under a tenancy—

(a) shall be annexed and incident to the whole, and to each and every part, of the reversion in the premises demised by the tenancy, and

(b) shall pass on an assignment of the whole or any part of the reversion in those premises.

Release of covenants on assignment

5. Tenant released from covenants on assignment of tenancy

(1) This section applies where a tenant assigns premises demised to him under a tenancy.

(2) If the tenant assigns the whole of the premises demised to him, he—

(a) is released from the tenant covenants of the tenancy, and

(b) ceases to be entitled to the benefit of the landlord covenants of the tenancy as from the assignment.

(3) If the tenant assigns part only of the premises demised to him, then as from the assignment he—

(a) is released from the tenant covenants of the tenancy, and

(b) ceases to be entitled to the benefit of the landlord covenants of the tenancy, only to the extent that those covenants fall to be complied with in relation to that part of the demised premises.

(4) This section applies as mentioned in subsection (1) whether or not the tenant is tenant of the whole of the premises comprised in the tenancy.

6. Landlord may be released from covenants on assignment of reversion

(1) This section applies where a landlord assigns the reversion in premises of which he is the landlord under a tenancy.

(2) If the landlord assigns the reversion in the whole of the premises of which he is the landlord—

(a) he may apply to be released from the landlord covenants of the tenancy in accordance with section 8; and

(b) if he is so released from all of those covenants, he ceases to be entitled to the benefit of the tenant covenants of the tenancy as from the assignment.

(3) If the landlord assigns the reversion in part only of the premises of which he is the landlord—

(a) he may apply to be so released from the landlord covenants of the tenancy to the extent that they fall to be complied with in relation to that part of those premises; and

(b) if he is, to that extent, so released from all of those covenants, then as from the assignment he ceases to be entitled to the benefit of the tenant covenants only to the extent that they fall to be complied with in relation to that part of those premises.

(4) This section applies as mentioned in subsection (1) whether or not the landlord is landlord of the whole of the premises comprised in the tenancy.

7. Former landlord may be released from covenants on assignment of reversion

(1) This section applies where—

(a) a landlord assigns the reversion in premises of which he is the landlord under a tenancy, and

(b) immediately before the assignment a former landlord of the premises remains bound by a landlord covenant of the tenancy ('the relevant covenant').

(2) If immediately before the assignment the former landlord does not remain the landlord of any other premises demised by the tenancy, he may apply to be released from the relevant covenant in accordance with section 8.

(3) In any other case the former landlord may apply to be so released from the relevant covenant to the extent that it falls to be complied with in relation to any premises comprised in the assignment.

(4) If the former landlord is so released from every landlord covenant by which he remained bound immediately before the assignment, he ceases to be entitled to the benefit of the tenant covenants of the tenancy.

(5) If the former landlord is so released from every such landlord covenant to the extent that it falls to be complied with in relation to any premises comprised in the

assignment, he ceases to be entitled to the benefit of the tenant covenants of the tenancy to the extent that they fall to be so complied with.

(6) This section applies as mentioned in subsection (1)—

(a) whether or not the landlord making the assignment is landlord of the whole of the premises comprised in the tenancy; and

(b) whether or not the former landlord has previously applied (whether under section 6 or this section) to be released from the relevant covenant.

8. Procedure for seeking release from a covenant under section 6 or 7

(1) For the purposes of section 6 or 7 an application for the release of a covenant to any extent is made by serving on the tenant, either before or within the period of four weeks beginning with the date of the assignment in question, a notice informing him of—

(a) the proposed assignment or (as the case may be) the fact that the assignment has taken place, and

(b) the request for the covenant to be released to that extent.

(2) Where an application for the release of a covenant is made in accordance with subsection (1), the covenant is released to the extent mentioned in the notice if—

(a) the tenant does not, within the period of four weeks beginning with the day on which the notice is served, serve on the landlord or former landlord a notice in writing objecting to the release, or

(b) the tenant does so serve such a notice but the court, on the application of the landlord or former landlord, makes a declaration that it is reasonable for the covenant to be so released, or

(c) the tenant serves on the landlord or former landlord a notice in writing consenting to the release and, if he has previously served a notice objecting to it, stating that that notice is withdrawn.

(3) Any release from a covenant in accordance with this section shall be regarded as occurring at the time when the assignment in question takes place.

(4) In this section—

(a) 'the tenant' means the tenant of the premises comprised in the assignment in question (or, if different parts of those premises are held under the tenancy by different tenants, each of those tenants);

(b) any reference to the landlord or the former landlord is a reference to the landlord referred to in section 6 or the former landlord referred to in section 7, as the case may be; and

(c) 'the court' means a county court.

Apportionment of liability between assignor and assignee

9. Apportionment of liability under covenants binding both assignor and assignee of tenancy or reversion

(1) This section applies where—

(a) a tenant assigns part only of the premises demised to him by a tenancy;

(b) after the assignment both the tenant and his assignee are to be bound by a non-attributable tenant covenant of the tenancy, and

(c) the tenant and his assignee agree that as from the assignment liability under the covenant is to be apportioned between them in such manner as is specified in the agreement.

(2) This section also applies where—

(a) a landlord assigns the reversion in part only of the premises of which he is the landlord under a tenancy;

(b) after the assignment both the landlord and his assignee are to be bound by a non-attributable landlord covenant of the tenancy, and

(c) the landlord and his assignee agree that as from the assignment liability under the covenant is to be apportioned between them in such manner as is specified in the agreement.

(3) Any such agreement as is mentioned in subsection (1) or (2) may apportion liability in such a way that a party to the agreement is exonerated from all liability under a covenant.

(4) In any case falling within subsection (1) or (2) the parties to the agreement may apply for the apportionment to become binding on the appropriate person in accordance with section 10.

(5) In any such case the parties to the agreement may also apply for the apportionment to become binding on any person (other than the appropriate person) who is for the time being entitled to enforce the covenant in question, and section 10 shall apply in relation to such an application as it applies in relation to an application made with respect to the appropriate person.

(6) For the purposes of this section a covenant is, in relation to an assignment, a 'non-attributable' covenant if it does not fall to be complied with in relation to any premises comprised in the assignment.

(7) In this section 'the appropriate person' means either—

(a) the landlord of the entire premises referred to in subsection (1)(a) (or, if different parts of those premises are held under the tenancy by different landlords, each of those landlords), or

(b) the tenant of the entire premises referred to in subsection (2)(a) (or, if different parts of those premises are held under the tenancy by different tenants, each of those tenants),

depending on whether the agreement in question falls within subsection (1) or subsection (2).

10. Procedure for making apportionment bind other party to lease

(1) For the purposes of section 9 the parties to an agreement falling within subsection (1) or (2) of that section apply for an apportionment to become binding on the appropriate person if, either before or within the period of four weeks beginning with the date of the assignment in question, they serve on that person a notice informing him of—

(a) the proposed assignment or (as the case may be) the fact that the assignment has taken place;

(b) the prescribed particulars of the agreement; and

(c) their request that the apportionment should become binding on him.

(2) Where an application for an apportionment to become binding has been made in accordance with subsection (1), the apportionment becomes binding on the appropriate person if—

(a) he does not, within the period of four weeks beginning with the day on which the notice is served under subsection (1), serve on the parties to the agreement a notice in writing objecting to the apportionment becoming binding on him, or

(b) he does so serve such a notice but the court, on the application of the parties to the agreement, makes a declaration that it is reasonable for the apportionment to become binding on him, or

(c) he serves on the parties to the agreement a notice in writing consenting to the apportionment becoming binding on him and, if he has previously served a notice objecting thereto, stating that the notice is withdrawn.

(3) Where any apportionment becomes binding in accordance with this section, this shall be regarded as occurring at the time when the assignment in question takes place.

(4) In this section—

'the appropriate persons' has the same meaning as in section 9;
'the court' means a county court;
'prescribed' means prescribed by virtue of section 27.

Excluded assignments

11. Assignments in breach of covenant or by operation of law

(1) This section provides for the operation of sections 5 to 10 in relation to assignments in breach of a covenant of a tenancy or assignments by operation of law ('excluded assignments').

(2) In the case of an excluded assignment subsection (2) or (3) of section 5—

(a) shall not have the effect mentioned in that subsection in relation to the tenant as from that assignment, but

(b) shall have that effect as from the next assignment (if any) of the premises assigned by him which is not an excluded assignment.

(3) In the case of an excluded assignment subsection (2) or (3) of section 6 or 7—

(a) shall not enable the landlord or former landlord to apply for such a release as is mentioned in that subsection as from that assignment, but

(b) shall apply on the next assignment (if any) of the reversion assigned by the landlord which is not an excluded assignment so as to enable the landlord or former landlord to apply for any such release as from that subsequent assignment.

(4) Where subsection (2) or (3) of section 6 or 7 does so apply—

(a) any reference in that section to the assignment (except where it relates to the time as from which the release takes effect) is a reference to the excluded assignment; but

(b) in that excepted case and in section 8 as it applies in relation to any application under that section made by virtue of subsection (3) above, any reference to the assignment or proposed assignment is a reference to any such subsequent assignment as is mentioned in that subsection.

(5) In the case of an excluded assignment section 9—

(a) shall not enable the tenant or landlord and his assignee to apply for an agreed apportionment to become binding in accordance with section 10 as from that assignment, but

(b) shall apply on the next assignment (if any) of the premises or reversion assigned by the tenant or landlord which is not an excluded assignment so as to enable him and his assignee to apply for such an apportionment to become binding in accordance with section 10 as from that subsequent assignment.

(6) Where section 9 does so apply—

(a) any reference in that section to the assignment or the assignee under it is a reference to the excluded assignment and the assignee under that assignment; but

(b) in section 10 as it applies in relation to any application under section 9 made by virtue of subsection (5) above, any reference to the assignment or proposed assignment is a reference to any such subsequent assignment as is mentioned in that subsection.

(7) If any such subsequent assignment as is mentioned in subsection (2), (3) or (5) above comprises only part of the premises assigned by the tenant or (as the case may be) only part of the premises the reversion in which was assigned by the landlord on the excluded assignment—

(a) the relevant provision or provisions of section 5, 6, 7 or 9 shall only have the effect mentioned in that subsection to the extent that the covenants or covenant in question fall or falls to be complied with in relation to that part of those premises; and

(b) that subsection may accordingly apply on different occasions in relation to different parts of those premises.

Third party covenants

12. Covenants with management companies etc.

(1) This section applies where—

(a) a person other than the landlord or tenant ('the third party') is under a covenant of a tenancy liable (as principal) to discharge any function with respect to all or any of the demised premises ('the relevant function'); and

(b) that liability is not the liability of a guarantor or any other financial liability referable to the performance or otherwise of a covenant of the tenancy by another party to it.

(2) To the extent that any covenant of the tenancy confers any rights against the third party with respect to the relevant function, then for the purposes of the transmission of the benefit of the covenant in accordance with this Act it shall be treated as if it were—

(a) a tenant covenant of the tenancy to the extent that those rights are exercisable by the landlord; and

(b) a landlord covenant of the tenancy to the extent that those rights are exercisable by the tenant.

(3) To the extent that any covenant of the tenancy confers any rights exercisable by the third party with respect to the relevant functions, then for the purposes mentioned in subsection (4), it shall be treated as if it were—

(a) a tenant covenant of the tenancy to the extent that those rights are exercisable against the tenant; and

(b) a landlord covenant of the tenancy to the extent that those rights are exercisable against the landlord.

(4) The purposes mentioned in subsection (3) are—

(a) the transmission of the burden of the covenant in accordance with this Act; and

(b) any release from, or apportionment of liability in respect of, the covenant in accordance with this Act.

(5) In relation to the release of the landlord from any covenant which is to be treated as a landlord covenant by virtue of subsection (3), section 8 shall apply as if any reference to the tenant were a reference to the third party.

Joint liability under covenants

13. Covenants binding two or more persons

(1) Where in consequence of this Act two or more persons are bound by the same covenant, they are so bound both jointly and severally.

(2) Subject to section 24(2), where by virtue of this Act—

(a) two or more persons are bound jointly and severally by the same covenant, and

(b) any of the persons so bound is released from the covenant, the release does not extend to any other of those persons.

(3) For the purpose of providing for contribution between persons who, by virtue of this Act, are bound jointly and severally by a covenant, the Civil Liability (Contribution) Act 1978 shall have effect as if—

(a) liability to a person under a covenant were liability in respect of damage suffered by that person;

(b) references to damage accordingly included a breach of a covenant of a tenancy, and

(c) section 7(2) of that Act were omitted.

14. Abolition of indemnity covenants implied by statute

The following provisions (by virtue of which indemnity covenants are implied on the assignment of a tenancy) shall cease to have effect—

(a) subsections (1)(C) and (D) of section 77 of the Law of Property Act 1925; and
(b) subsections (1)(b) and (2) of section 24 of the Land Registration Act 1925.

Enforcement of covenants

15. Enforcement of covenants

(1) Where any tenant covenant of a tenancy, or any right of re-entry contained in a tenancy, is enforceable by the reversioner in respect of any premises demised by the tenancy, it shall also be so enforceable by—

(a) any person (other that the reversioner) who, as the holder of the immediate reversion in those premises, is for the time being entitled to the rents and profits under the tenancy in respect of those premises, or

(b) any mortgagee in possession of the reversion in those premises who is so entitled.

(2) Where any landlord covenant of a tenancy is enforceable against the reversioner in respect of any premise demised by the tenancy, it shall also be enforceable against any person falling within subsection (1)(a) or (b).

(3) Where any landlord covenant of a tenancy is enforceable by the tenant in respect of any premises demised by the tenancy, it shall also be so enforceable by any mortgagee in possession of those premises under a mortgage granted by the tenant.

(4) Where any tenant covenant of a tenancy, or any right of re-entry contained in a tenancy, is enforceable against the tenant in respect of any premises demised by the tenancy, it shall also be so enforceable against any such mortgagee.

(5) Nothing in this section shall operate—

(a) in the case of a covenant which (in whatever terms) is expressed to be personal to any person to make the covenant enforceable by or (as the case may be) against any other person; or

(b) to make a covenant enforceable against any person if, apart from this section, it would not be enforceable against him by reason of its not having been registered under the Land Registration Act 1925 or the Land Charges Act 1972.

(6) In this section—

'mortgagee' and 'mortgage' include 'chargee' and 'charge' respectively;

'the reversioner', in relation to a tenancy, means the holder for the time being of the interest of the landlord under the tenancy.

Liability of former tenant etc. in respect of covenants

16. Tenant guaranteeing performance of covenant by assignee

(1) Where on an assignment a tenant is to any extent released from a tenant covenant of a tenancy by virtue of this Act ('the relevant covenant'), nothing in this Act (and in particular section 25) shall preclude him from entering into an authorised guarantee agreement with respect to the performance of that covenant by the assignee.

(2) For the purposes of this section an agreement is an authorised guarantee agreement if—

(a) under it the tenant guarantees the performance of the relevant covenant to any extent by the assignee; and

(b) it is entered into in the circumstances set out in subsection (3); and

(c) its provisions conform with subsections (4) and (5).

(3) those circumstances are as follows—

(a) by virtue of a covenant against assignment (whether absolute or qualified) the assignment cannot be effected without the consent of the landlord under the tenancy or some other person;

(b) any such consent is given subject to a condition (lawfully imposed) that the tenant is to enter into an agreement guaranteeing the performance of the covenant by the assignee; and

(c) the agreement is entered into by the tenant in pursuance of that condition.

(4) An agreement is not an authorised guarantee agreement to the extent that it purports—

(a) to impose on the tenant any requirement to guarantee in any way the performance of the relevant covenant by any person other than the assignee; or

(b) to impose on the tenant any liability, restriction or other requirement (of whatever nature) in relation to any time after the assignee is released from that covenant by virtue of this Act.

(5) Subject to subsection (4), an authorised guarantee agreement may—

(a) impose on the tenant any liability as sole or principal debtor in respect of any obligation owed by the assignee under the relevant covenant;

(b) impose on the tenant liabilities as guarantor in respect of the assignee's performance of that covenant which are no more onerous than those to which he would be subject in the event of his being liable as sole or principal debtor in respect of any obligation owed by the assignee under that covenant;

(c) require the tenant, in the event of the tenancy assigned by him being disclaimed, to enter into a new tenancy of the premises comprised in the assignment—

(i) whose term expires not later than the term of the tenancy assigned by the tenant, and

(ii) whose tenant covenants are no more onerous than those of that tenancy;

(d) make provision incidental or supplementary to any provision made by virtue of any of paragraphs (a) to (c).

(6) Where a person ('the former tenant') is to any extent released from a covenant of a tenancy by virtue of section 11(2) as from an assignment and the assignor under the assignment enters into an authorised guarantee agreement with the landlord with respect to the performance of that covenant by the assignee under the assignment—

(a) the landlord may require the former tenant to enter into an agreement under which he guarantees, on terms corresponding to those of that authorised guarantee agreement, the performance of that covenant by the assignee under the assignment; and

(b) if its provisions conform with subsections (4) and (5), any such agreement shall be an authorised guarantee agreement for the purposes of this section; and

(c) in the application of this section in relation to any such agreement—

(i) subsections (2)(b) and (c) and (3) shall be omitted, and

(ii) any reference to the tenant or to the assignee shall be read as a reference to the former tenant or to the assignee under the assignment.

(7) For the purposes of subsection (1) it is immaterial that—

(a) the tenant has already made an authorised guarantee agreement in respect of a previous assignment by him of the tenancy referred to in that subsection, it having been subsequently revested in him following a disclaimer on behalf of the previous assignee, or

(b) the tenancy referred to in that subsection is a new tenancy entered into by the tenant in pursuance of an authorised guarantee agreement;

and in any such case subsections (2) to (5) shall apply accordingly

(8) It is hereby declared that the rules of law relating to guarantees (and in particular those relating to the release of sureties) are, subject to its terms, applicable in relation to any authorised guarantee agreement as in relation to any other guarantee agreement.

17. Restriction on liability of former tenant or his guarantor for rent or service charge etc.

(1) This section applies where a person ('the former tenant') is as a result of an assignment no longer a tenant under a tenancy but—

(a) (in the case of a tenancy which is a new tenancy) he has under an authorised guarantee agreement guaranteed the performance by his assignee of a tenant covenant of the tenancy under which any fixed charge is payable; or

(b) (in the case of any tenancy) he remains bound by such a covenant.

(2) The former tenant shall not be liable under that agreement or (as the case may be) the covenant to pay any amount in respect of any fixed charge payable under the covenant unless, within the period of six months beginning with the date when the charge becomes due, the landlord serves on the former tenant a notice informing him—

(a) that the charge is now due; and

(b) that in respect of the charge the landlord intends to recover from the former tenant such amount as is specified in the notice and (where payable) interest calculated on such basis as is so specified.

(3) Where a person ('the guarantor') has agreed to guarantee the performance by the former tenant of such a covenant as is mentioned in subsection (1), the guarantor shall not be liable under the agreement to pay any amount in respect of any fixed charge payable under the covenant unless, within the period of six months beginning with the date when the charge becomes due, the landlord serves on the guarantor a notice informing him—

(a) that the charge is now due; and

(b) that in respect of the charge the landlord intends to recover from the guarantor such amount as is specified in the notice and (where payable) interest calculated on such basis as is so specified.

(4) Where the landlord has duly served a notice under subsection (2) or (3), the amount (exclusive of interest) which the former tenant or (as the case may be) the guarantor is liable to pay in respect of the fixed charge in question shall not exceed the amount specified in the notice unless—

(a) his liability in respect of the charge is subsequently determined to be for a greater amount,

(b) the notice informed him of the possibility that that liability would be so determined, and

(c) within the period of three months beginning with the date of the determination, the landlord serves on him a further notice informing him that the landlord intends to recover that greater amount from him (plus interest, where payable).

(5) For the purposes of subsection (2) or (3) any fixed charge which has become due before the date on which this Act comes into force shall be treated as becoming due on that date; but neither of those subsections applies to any such charge if before that date proceedings have been instituted by the landlord for the recovery from the former tenant of any amount in respect of it.

(6) In this section—

'fixed charge', in relation to a tenancy, means—

(a) rent,

(b) any service charge as defined by section 18 of the Landlord and Tenant Act 1985 (the words 'of a dwelling' being disregarded for this purpose), and

(c) any amount payable under a tenant covenant of the tenancy providing for the payment of a liquidated sum in the event of a failure to comply with any such covenant;

'landlord', in relation to a fixed charge, includes any person who has a right to enforce payment of the charge.

18. Restriction of liability of former tenant or his guarantor where tenancy subsequently varied

(1) This section applies where a person ('the former tenant') is as a result of an assignment no longer a tenant under a tenancy but—

(a) (in the case of a new tenancy) he has under an authorised guarantee agreement guaranteed the performance by his assignee of any tenant covenant of the tenancy; or

(b) (in the case of any tenancy) he remains bound by such a covenant.

(2) The former tenant shall not be liable under the agreement or (as the case may be) the covenant to pay any amount in respect of the covenant to the extent that the amount is referable to any relevant variation of the tenant covenants of the tenancy effected after the assignment.

(3) Where a person ('the guarantor') has agreed to guarantee the performance by the former tenant of a tenant covenant of the tenancy, the guarantor (where his liability to do so is not wholly discharged by any such variation of the tenant covenants of the tenancy) shall not be liable under the agreement to pay any amount in respect of the covenant to the extent that the amount is referable to any such variation.

(4) For the purposes of this section a variation of the tenant covenants of a tenancy is a 'relevant variation' if either—

(a) the landlord has, at the time of the variation, an absolute right to refuse to allow it; or

(b) the landlord would have had such a right if the variation had been sought by the former tenant immediately before the assignment by him but, between the time of that assignment and the time of the variation, the tenant covenants of the tenancy have been so varied as to deprive the landlord of such a right.

(5) In determining whether the landlord has or would have had such a right at any particular time regard shall be had to all the circumstances (including the effect of any provision made by or under any enactment).

(6) Nothing in this section applies to any variation of the tenant covenants of a tenancy effected before the date on which this Act comes into force.

(7) In this section 'variation' means a variation whether effected by deed or otherwise.

Overriding leases

19. Right of former tenant or his guarantor to overriding lease

(1) Where in respect of any tenancy ('the relevant tenancy') any person ('the claimant') makes full payment of an amount which he has been duly required to pay in accordance with section 17 together with any interest payable, he shall be entitled (subject to and in accordance with this section) to have the landlord under that tenancy grant him an overriding lease of the premises demised by the tenancy.

(2) For the purposes of this section 'overriding lease' means a tenancy of the reversion expectant on the relevant tenancy which—

(a) is granted for a term equal to the remainder of the term of the relevant tenancy plus three days or the longest period (less than three days) that will not wholly displace the landlord's reversionary interest expectant on the relevant tenancy as the case may require and

(b) (subject to subsections (3) and (4) and to any modifications agreed to by the claimant and the landlord) otherwise contains the same covenants as the relevant tenancy, as they have effect immediately before the grant of the lease.

(3) An overriding lease shall not be required to reproduce any covenant of the relevant tenancy to the extent that the covenant is (in whatever terms) expressed to be a personal covenant between the landlord and the tenant under that tenancy.

(4) If any right, liability or other matter arising under a covenant of the relevant tenancy falls to be determined or otherwise operates (whether expressly or otherwise) by reference to the commencement of that tenancy—

(a) the corresponding covenant of the overriding lease shall be so framed that that right, liability or matter falls to be determined or otherwise operates by reference to the commencement of that tenancy; but

(b) the overriding lease shall not be required to reproduce any covenant of that tenancy to the extent that it has become spent by the time that that lease is granted.

(5) A claim to exercise the right to an overriding lease under this section is made by the claimant making a request for such a lease to the landlord; and any such request—

(a) must be made to the landlord in writing and specify the payment by virtue of which the claimant claims to be entitled to the lease ('the qualifying payment'); and

(b) must be so made at the time of making the qualifying payment or within the period of 12 months beginning with the date of that payment.

(6) Where the claimant duly makes such a request—

(a) the landlord shall (subject to subsection (7)) grant and deliver to the claimant an overriding lease of the demised premises within a reasonable time of the request being received by the landlord; and

(b) the claimant—

(i) shall thereupon deliver to the landlord a counterpart of the lease duly executed by the claimant, and

(ii) shall be liable for the landlord's reasonable costs of and incidental to the grant of the lease.

(7) The landlord shall not be under any obligation to grant an overriding lease of the demised premises under this section at a time when the relevant tenancy has been determined; and a claimant shall not be entitled to the grant of such a lease if at the time when he makes his request—

(a) the landlord has already granted such a lease and that lease remains in force; or

(b) another person has already duly made a request for such a lease to the landlord and that request has been neither withdrawn nor abandoned by that person.

(8) Where two or more requests are duly made on the same day, then for the purposes of subsection (7)—

(a) a request made by a person who was liable for the qualifying payment as a former tenant shall be treated as made before a request made by a person who was so liable as a guarantor; and

(b) a request made by a person whose liability in respect of the covenant in question commenced earlier than any such liability of another person shall be treated as made before a request made by that other person.

(9) Where a claimant who has duly made a request for an overriding lease under this section subsequently withdraws or abandons the request before he is granted such a lease by the landlord, the claimant shall be liable for the landlord's reasonable costs incurred in pursuance of the request down to the time of its withdrawal or abandonment; and for the purposes of this section—

(a) a claimant's request is withdrawn by the claimant notifying the landlord in writing that he is withdrawing his request; and

(b) a claimant is to be regarded as having abandoned his request if—

(i) the landlord has requested the claimant in writing to take within such reasonable period as is specified in the landlord's request, all or any of the remaining steps required to be taken by the claimant before the lease can be granted, and

(ii) the claimant fails to comply with the landlord's request,

and is accordingly to be regarded as having abandoned it at the time when that period expires.

(10) Any request or notification under this section may be sent by post.

(11) The preceding provisions of this section shall apply where the landlord is the tenant under an overriding lease granted under this section as they apply where no such lease has been granted; and accordingly there may be two or more such leases interposed between the first such lease and the relevant tenancy.

20. Overriding leases: supplementary provisions

(1) For the purposes of section 1 an overriding lease shall be a new tenancy only if the relevant tenancy is a new tenancy.

(2) Every overriding lease shall state—

(a) that it is a lease granted under section 19, and

(b) whether it is or is not a new tenancy for the purposes of section 1;

and any such statement shall comply with such requirements as may be prescribed by rules made in pursuance of section 144 of the Land Registration Act 1925 (power to make general rules).

(3) A claim that the landlord has failed to comply with subsection (6)(a) of section 19 may be made the subject of civil proceedings in like manner as any other claim in tort for breach of statutory duty; and if the claimant under that section fails to comply with subsection (6)(b)(i) of that section he shall not be entitled to exercise any of the rights otherwise exercisable by him under the overriding lease.

(4) An overriding lease—

(a) shall be deemed to be authorised as against the persons interested in any mortgage of the landlord's interest (however created or arising); and

(b) shall be binding on any such persons;

and if any such person is by virtue of such a mortgage entitled to possession of the documents of title relating to the landlord's interest—

(i) the landlord shall within one month of the execution of the lease deliver to that person the counterpart executed in pursuance of section 19(6)(b)(i); and

(ii) if he fails to do so, the instrument creating or evidencing the mortgage shall apply as if the obligation to deliver a counterpart were included in the terms of the mortgage as set out in that instrument.

(5) It is hereby declared—

(a) that the fact that an overriding lease takes effect subject to the relevant tenancy shall not constitute a breach of any covenant of the lease against subletting or parting with possession of the premises demised by the lease or any part of them, and

(b) that each of sections 16,17 and 18 applies where the tenancy referred to in subsection (1) of that section is an overriding lease as it applies in other cases falling within that subsection.

(6) No tenancy shall be registrable under the Land Charges Act 1972 or be taken to be an estate contract within the meaning of that Act by reason of any right or obligation that may arise under section 19, and any right arising from a request made under that section shall not be an overriding interest within the meaning of the Land Registration Act 1925; but any such request shall be registrable under the Land Charges Act 1972, or may be the subject of a notice or caution under the Land Registration Act 1925, as if it were an estate contract.

(7) In this section—

(a) 'mortgage' includes 'charge'; and

(b) any expression which is also used in section 19 has the same meaning as in that section.

Forfeiture and disclaimer

21. Forfeiture or disclaimer limited to part only of demised premises

(1) Where—

(a) as a result of one or more assignments a person is the tenant of part only of the premises demised by a tenancy, and

(b) under a proviso or stipulation in the tenancy there is a right of re-entry or forfeiture for a breach of a tenant covenant of the tenancy, and

(c) the right is (apart from this subsection) exercisable in relation to that part and other land demised by the tenancy,

the right shall nevertheless, in connection with a breach of any such covenant by that person, be taken to be a right exercisable only in relation to that part.

(2) Where—

(a) a company which is being wound up, or a trustee in bankruptcy, is as a result of one or more assignments the tenant of part only of the premises demised by a tenancy, and

(b) the liquidator of the company exercises his power under section 178 of the Insolvency Act 1986, or the trustee in bankruptcy exercises his power under section 315 of that Act, to disclaim property demised by the tenancy,

the power is exercisable only in relation to the part of the premises referred to in paragraph (a).

Supplemental

23. Effects of becoming subject to liability under, or entitled to benefit of, covenant etc.

(1) Where as a result of an assignment a person becomes by virtue of this Act, bound by or entitled to the benefit of a covenant, he shall not by virtue of this Act have any liability or rights under the covenant in relation to any time falling before the assignment.

(2) Subsection (1) does not preclude any such rights being expressly assigned to the person in question.

(3) Where as a result of an assignment a person becomes, by virtue of this Act, entitled to a right of re-entry contained in a tenancy, that right shall be exercisable in relation to any breach of a covenant of the tenancy occurring before the assignment as in relation to one occurring thereafter, unless by reason of any waiver or release it was not so exercisable immediately before the assignment.

24. Effects of release from liability under, or loss of benefit of, covenant

(1) Any release of a person from a covenant by virtue of this Act does not affect any liability of his arising from a breach of the covenant occurring before the release.

(2) Where—

(a) by virtue of this Act a tenant is released from a tenant covenant of a tenancy, and

(b) immediately before the release another person is bound by a covenant of the tenancy imposing any liability or penalty in the event of a failure to comply with that tenant covenant,

then, as from the release of the tenant, that other person is released from the covenant mentioned in paragraph (b) to the same extent as the tenant is released from that tenant covenant.

(3) Where a person bound by a landlord or tenant covenant of a tenancy—

(a) assigns the whole or part of his interest in the premises demised by the tenancy, but

(b) is not released by virtue of this Act from the covenant (with the result that subsection (1) does not apply),

the assignment does not affect any liability of his arising from a breach of the covenant occurring before the assignment.

(4) Where by virtue of this Act a person ceases to be entitled to the benefit of a covenant, this does not affect any rights of his arising from a breach of the covenant occurring before he ceases to be so entitled.

25. Agreement void if it restricts operation of the Act

(1) Any agreement relating to a tenancy is void to the extent that—

(a) it would apart from this section have effect to exclude, modify or otherwise frustrate the operation of any provision of this Act, or

(b) it provides for—

(i) the termination or surrender of the tenancy, or

(ii) the imposition on the tenant of any penalty, disability or liability,

in the event of the operation of any provision of this Act, or

(c) it provides for any of the matters referred to in paragraph (b)(i) or (ii) and does so (whether expressly or otherwise) in connection with, or in consequence of, the operation of any provision of this Act.

(2) To the extent that an agreement relating to a tenancy constitutes a covenant (whether absolute or qualified) against the assignment, or parting with the possession, of the premises demised by the tenancy or any part of them—

(a) the agreement is not void by virtue of subsection (1) by reason only of the fact that as such the covenant prohibits or restricts any such assignment or parting with possession; but

(b) paragraph (a) above does not otherwise affect the operation of that subsection in relation to the agreement (and in particular does not preclude its application to the agreement to the extent that it purports to regulate the giving of, or the making of any application for, consent to any such assignment or parting with possession).

(3) In accordance with section 16(1) nothing in this section applies to any agreement to the extent that it is an authorised guarantee agreement; but (without prejudice to the generality of subsection (1) above) an agreement is void to the extent that it is one falling within section 16(4)(a) or (b).

(4) This section applies to an agreement relating to a tenancy whether or not the agreement is—

(a) contained in the instrument creating the tenancy; or

(b) made before the creation of the tenancy.

26. Miscellaneous savings etc.

(1) Nothing in this Act is to be read as preventing—

(a) a party to a tenancy from releasing a person from a landlord covenant or a tenant covenant of the tenancy; or

(b) the parties to a tenancy from agreeing to an apportionment of liability under such a covenant.

(2) Nothing in this Act affects the operation of section 3(3A) of the Landlord and Tenant Act 1985 (preservation of former landlord's liability until tenant notified of new landlord).

(3) No apportionment which has become binding in accordance with section 10 shall be affected by any order or decision made under or by virtue of any enactment not contained in this Act which relates to apportionment.

28. Interpretation

(1) In this Act (unless the context otherwise requires)—

'assignment' includes equitable assignment and in addition (subject to section 11) assignment in breach of a covenant of a tenancy or by operation of law;

'authorised guarantee agreement' means an agreement which is an authorised guarantee agreement for the purposes of section 16;

'collateral agreement', in relation to a tenancy, means any agreement collateral to the tenancy, whether made before or after its creation;

'consent' includes licence;

'covenant' includes term, condition and obligation, and references to a covenant (or any description of covenant) of a tenancy include a covenant (or a covenant of that description) contained in a collateral agreement;

'landlord' and 'tenant', in relation to a tenancy, mean the person for the time being entitled to the reversion expectant on the term of the tenancy and the person so entitled to that term respectively;

'landlord covenant', in relation to a tenancy, means that a covenant falling to be complied with the landlord of premises demised by the tenancy;

'new tenancy' means a tenancy which is a new tenancy for the purposes of section 1;

'reversion' means the interest expectant on the termination of a tenancy;

'tenancy' means any lease or other tenancy and includes—

(a) a sub-tenancy, and

(b) and agreement for a tenancy,

but does not include a mortgage term;

'tenant covenant', in relation to a tenancy, means a covenant falling to be complied with by the tenant of premises demised by the tenancy.

(2) For the purposes of any reference in this Act to a covenant falling to be complied with in relation to a particular part of the premises demised by a tenancy, a covenant falls to be so complied with if—

(a) it in terms applies to that part of the premises, or

(b) in its practical application it can be attributed to that part of the premises (whether or not it can also be so attributed to other individual parts of those premises).

(3) Subsection (2) does not apply in relation to covenants to pay money; and, for the purposes of any reference in this Act to a covenant falling to be complied with in relation to a particular part of the premises demised by a tenancy, a covenant of a tenancy which is a covenant to pay money falls to be so complied with if—

(a) the covenant in terms applies to that part; or

(b) the amount of the payment is determinable specifically by reference—

(i) to that part, or

(ii) to anything falling to be done by or for a person as tenant or occupier of that part (if it is a tenant covenant), or

(iii) to anything falling to be done by or for a person as landlord of that part (if it is a landlord covenant).

(4) Where two or more persons jointly constitute either the landlord or the tenant in relation to a tenancy, any reference in this Act to the landlord or the tenant is a reference to both or all of the persons who jointly constitute the landlord or the tenant, as the case may be (and accordingly nothing in section 13 applies in relation to the rights and liabilities of such persons between themselves).

(5) References in this Act to the assignment by a landlord of the reversion in the whole or part of the premises demised by a tenancy are to the assignment by him of the whole of his interest (as owner of the reversion) in the whole or part of those premises.

(6) For the purposes of this Act—

(a) any assignment (however effected) consisting in the transfer of the whole of the landlord's interest (as owner of the reversion) in any premises demised by a tenancy shall be treated as an assignment by the landlord of the reversion in those premises even if it is not effected by him; and

(b) any assignment (however effected) consisting in the transfer of the whole of the tenant's interest in any premises demised by a tenancy shall be treated as an assignment by the tenant of those premises even if it is not effected by him.

30. Consequential amendments and repeals

(4) In consequence of this Act nothing in the following provisions, namely—

(a) Sections 78 and 79 of the Law of Property Act 1925 (benefit and burden of covenants relating to land), and

(b) section 141 and 142 of that Act (running of benefit and burden of covenants with reversion),

shall apply in relation to new tenancies.

FAMILY LAW ACT 1996

PART II
DIVORCE AND SEPARATION

Intestacy

21. Intestacy: effect of separation

Where—

(a) a separation order is in force, and

(b) while the parties to the marriage remain separated, one of them dies intestate as respects any real or personal property

that property devolves as if the other had died before the intestacy occurred.

PART IV
FAMILY HOMES AND DOMESTIC VIOLENCE

Rights to occupy matrimonial home

30. Rights concerning matrimonial home where one spouse has no estate, etc.

(1) This section applies if—

(a) one spouse is entitled to occupy a dwelling-house by virtue of—

(i) a beneficial estate or interest or contract; or

(ii) any enactment giving that spouse the right to remain in occupation; and

(b) the other spouse is not so entitled.

(2) Subject to the provisions of this Part, the spouse not so entitled has the following rights ('matrimonial home rights')—

(a) if in occupation, a right not to be evicted or excluded from the dwelling-house or any part of it by the other spouse except with the leave of the court given by an order under section 33;

(b) if not in occupation, a right with the leave of the court so given to enter into and occupy the dwelling-house.

(3) If a spouse is entitled under this section to occupy a dwelling-house or any part of a dwelling-house, any payment or tender made or other thing done by that spouse in or towards satisfaction of any liability of the other spouse in respect of rent, mortgage payments or other outgoings affecting the dwelling-house is, whether or not it is made or done in pursuance of an order under section 40, as good as if made or done by the other spouse.

(4) A spouse's occupation by virtue of this section—

(a) is to be treated, for the purposes of the Rent (Agriculture) Act 1976 and the Rent Act 1977 (other than Part V and sections 103 to 106 of that Act), as occupation by the other spouse as the other spouse's residence, and

(b) if the spouse occupies the dwelling-house as that spouse's only or principal home, is to be treated, for the purposes of the Housing Act 1985 and Part I of the Housing Act 1988, as occupation by the other spouse as the other spouse's only or principal home.

(5) If a spouse ('the first spouse')—

(a) is entitled under this section to occupy a dwelling-house or any part of a dwelling-house, and

(b) makes any payment in or towards satisfaction of any liability of the other spouse ('the second spouse') in respect of mortgage payments affecting the dwelling-house,

the person to whom the payment is made may treat it as having been made by the second spouse, but the fact that that person has treated any such payment as having been so made does not affect any claim of the first spouse against the second spouse to an interest in the dwelling-house by virtue of the payment.

(6) If a spouse is entitled under this section to occupy a dwelling-house or part of a dwelling-house by reason of an interest of the other spouse under a trust, all the provisions of subsections (3) to (5) apply in relation to the trustees as they apply in relation to the other spouse.

(7) This section does not apply to a dwelling-house which has at no time been, and which was at no time intended by the spouses to be, a matrimonial home of theirs.

(8) A spouse's matrimonial home rights continue—

(a) only so long as the marriage subsists, except to the extent that an order under section 33(5) otherwise provides; and

(b) only so long as the other spouse is entitled as mentioned in subsection (1) to occupy the dwelling-house, except where provision is made by section 31 for those rights to be a charge on an estate or interest in the dwelling-house.

(9) It is hereby declared that a spouse—

(a) who has an equitable interest in a dwelling-house or in its proceeds of sale, but

(b) is not a spouse in whom there is vested (whether solely or as joint tenant) a legal estate in fee simple or a legal term of years absolute in the dwelling-house,

is to be treated, only for the purpose of determining whether he has matrimonial home rights, as not being entitled to occupy the dwelling-house by virtue of that interest.

31. Effect of matrimonial home rights as charge on dwelling-house

(1) Subsections (2) and (3) apply if, at any time during a marriage, one spouse is entitled to occupy a dwelling-house by virtue of a beneficial estate or interest.

(2) The other spouse's matrimonial home rights are a charge on the estate or interest.

(3) The charge created by subsection (2) has the same priority as if it were an equitable interest created at whichever is the latest of the following dates—

(a) the date on which the spouse so entitled acquires the estate or interest;

(b) the date of the marriage; and

(c) 1st January 1968 (the commencement date of the Matrimonial Homes Act 1967).

(4) Subsections (5) and (6) apply if, at any time when a spouse's matrimonial home rights are a charge on an interest of the other spouse under a trust, there are, apart from either of the spouses, no persons, living or unborn, who are or could become beneficiaries under the trust.

(5) The rights are a charge also on the estate or interest of the trustees for the other spouse.

(6) The charge created by subsection (5) has the same priority as if it were an equitable interest created (under powers overriding the trusts) on the date when it arises.

(7) In determining for the purposes of subsection (4) whether there are any persons who are not, but could become, beneficiaries under the trust, there is to be disregarded any potential exercise of a general power of appointment exercisable by either or both of the spouses alone (whether or not the exercise of it requires the consent of another person).

(8) Even though a spouse's matrimonial home rights are a charge on an estate or interest in the dwelling-house, those rights are brought to an end by—

(a) the death of the other spouse, or

(b) the termination (otherwise than by death) of the marriage,

unless the court directs otherwise by an order made under section 33(5).

(9) If—

(a) a spouse's matrimonial home rights are a charge on an estate or interest in the dwelling-house, and

(b) that estate or interest is surrendered to merge in some other estate or interest expectant on it in such circumstances that, but for the merger, the person taking the estate or interest would be bound by the charge, the surrender has effect subject to the charge and the persons thereafter entitled to the other estate or interest are, for so long as the estate or interest surrendered would have endured if not so surrendered, to be treated for all purposes of this Part as deriving title to the other estate or interest under the other spouse or, as the case may be, under the trustees for the other spouse, by virtue of the surrender.

(10) If the title to the legal estate by virtue of which a spouse is entitled to occupy a dwelling-house (including any legal estate held by trustees for that spouse) is registered under the Land Registration Act 1925 or any enactment replaced by that Act—

(a) registration of a land charge affecting the dwelling-house by virtue of this Part is to be effected by registering a notice under that Act; and

(b) a spouse's matrimonial home rights are not an overriding interest within the meaning of that Act affecting the dwelling-house even though the spouse is in actual occupation of the dwelling-house.

(11) A spouse's matrimonial home rights (whether or not constituting a charge) do not entitle that spouse to lodge a caution under section 54 of the Land Registration Act 1925.

(12) If—

(a) a spouse's matrimonial home rights are a charge on the estate of the other spouse or of trustees of the other spouse, and

(b) that estate is the subject of a mortgage,

then if, after the date of the creation of the mortgage ('the first mortgage'), the charge is registered under section 2 of the Land Charges Act 1972, the charge is, for the purposes of section 94 of the Law of Property Act 1925 (which regulates the rights of mortgagees to make further advances ranking in priority to subsequent mortgages), to be deemed to be a mortgage subsequent in date to the first mortgage.

(13) It is hereby declared that a charge under subsection (2) or (5) is not registrable under subsection (10) or under section 2 of the Land Charges Act 1972 unless it is a charge on a legal estate.

32. Further provisions relating to matrimonial home rights

Schedule 4 re-enacts with consequential amendments and minor modifications provisions of the Matrimonial Homes Act 1983.

Occupation orders

33. Occupation orders where applicant has estate or interest etc. or has matrimonial home rights

(1) If—

(a) a person ('the person entitled')—

(i) is entitled to occupy a dwelling-house by virtue of a beneficial estate or interest or contract or by virtue of any enactment giving him the right to remain in occupation, or

(ii) has matrimonial home rights in relation to a dwelling-house, and

(b) the dwelling-house—

(i) is or at any time has been the home of the person entitled and of another person with whom he is associated, or

(ii) was at any time intended by the person entitled and any such other person to be their home,

the person entitled may apply to the court for an order containing any of the provisions specified in subsections (3), (4) and (5).

(2) If an agreement to marry is terminated, no application under this section may be made by virtue of section 62(3)(e) by reference to that agreement after the end of the period of three years beginning with the day on which it is terminated.

(3) An order under this section may—

(a) enforce the applicant's entitlement to remain in occupation as against the other person ('the respondent');

(b) require the respondent to permit the applicant to enter and remain in the dwelling-house or part of the dwelling-house;

(c) regulate the occupation of the dwelling-house by either or both parties;

(d) if the respondent is entitled as mentioned in subsection (1)(a)(i), prohibit, suspend or restrict the exercise by him of his right to occupy the dwelling-house;

(e) if the respondent has matrimonial home rights in relation to the dwelling-house and the applicant is the other spouse, restrict or terminate those rights;

(f) require the respondent to leave the dwelling-house or part of the dwelling-house; or

(g) exclude the respondent from a defined area in which the dwelling-house is included.

(4) An order under this section may declare that the applicant is entitled as mentioned in subsection (1)(a)(i) or has matrimonial home rights.

(5) If the applicant has matrimonial home rights and the respondent is the other spouse, an order under this section made during the marriage may provide that those rights are not brought to an end by—

(a) the death of the other spouse; or

(b) the termination (otherwise than by death) of the marriage.

(6) In deciding whether to exercise its powers under subsection (3) and (if so) in what manner, the court shall have regard to all the circumstances including—

(a) the housing needs and housing resources of each of the parties and of any relevant child;

(b) the financial resources of each of the parties;

(c) the likely effect of any order, or of any decision by the court not to exercise its powers under subsection (3), on the health, safety or well-being of the parties and of any relevant child; and

(d) the conduct of the parties in relation to each other and otherwise.

(7) If it appears to the court that the applicant or any relevant child is likely to suffer significant harm attributable to conduct of the respondent if an order under this section containing one or more of the provisions mentioned in subsection (3) is not made, the court shall make the order unless it appears to it that—

(a) the respondent or any relevant child is likely to suffer significant harm if the order is made; and

(b) the harm likely to be suffered by the respondent or child in that event is as great as, or greater than, the harm attributable to conduct of the respondent which is likely to be suffered by the applicant or child if the order is not made.

(8) The court may exercise its powers under subsection (5) in any case where it considers that in all the circumstances it is just and reasonable to do so.

(9) An order under this section—

(a) may not be made after the death of either of the parties mentioned in subsection (1); and

(b) except in the case of an order made by virtue of subsection (5)(a), ceases to have effect on the death of either party.

(10) An order under this section may, in so far as it has continuing effect, be made for a specified period, until the occurrence of a specified event or until further order.

34. Effect of order under s. 33 where rights are charge on dwelling-house

(1) If a spouse's matrimonial home rights are a charge on the the estate or interest of the other spouse or of trustees for the other spouse—

(a) an order under section 33 against the other spouse has, except so far as a contrary intention appears, the same effect against persons deriving title under the other spouse or under the trustees and affected by the charge, and

(b) sections 33(1), (3), (4) and (10) and 30(3) to (6) apply in relation to any person deriving title under the other spouse or under the trustees and affected by the charge as they apply in relation to the other spouse.

(2) The court may make an order under section 33 by virtue of subsection (1)(b) if it considers that in all the circumstances it is just and reasonable to do so.

35. One former spouse with no existing right to occupy

(1) This section applies if—

(a) one former spouse is entitled to occupy a dwelling-house by virtue of a beneficial estate or interest or contract, or by virtue of any enactment giving him the right to remain in occupation;

(b) the other former spouse is not so entitled; and

(c) the dwelling-house was at any time their matrimonial home or was at any time intended by them to be their matrimonial home.

(2) The former spouse not so entitled may apply to the court for an order under this section against the other former spouse ('the respondent').

(3) If the applicant is in occupation, an order under this section must contain provision—

(a) giving the applicant the right not to be evicted or excluded from the dwelling-house or any part of it by the respondent for the period specified in the order; and

(b) prohibiting the respondent from evicting or excluding the applicant during that period.

(4) If the applicant is not in occupation, an order under this section must contain provision—

(a) giving the applicant the right to enter into and occupy the dwelling-house for the period specified in the order; and

(b) requiring the respondent to permit the exercise of that right.

(5) An order under this section may also—

(a) regulate the occupation of the dwelling-house by either or both of the parties;

(b) prohibit, suspend or restrict the exercise by the respondent of his right to occupy the dwelling-house;

(c) require the respondent to leave the dwelling-house or part of the dwelling-house; or

(d) exclude the respondent from a defined area in which the dwelling-house is included.

(6) In deciding whether to make an order under this section containing provision of the kind mentioned in subsection (3) or (4) and (if so) in what manner, the court shall have regard to all the circumstances including—

(a) the housing needs and housing resources of each of the parties and of any relevant child;

(b) the financial resources of each of the parties;

(c) the likely effect of any order, or of any decision by the court not to exercise its powers under subsection (3) or (4), on the health, safety or well-being of the parties and of any relevant child;

(d) the conduct of the parties in relation to each other and otherwise;

(e) the length of time that has elapsed since the parties ceased to live together;

(f) the length of time that has elapsed since the marriage was dissolved or annulled; and

(g) the existence of any pending proceedings between the parties—

(i) for an order under section 23A or 24 of the Matrimonial Causes Act 1973 (property adjustment orders in connection with divorce proceedings etc.);

(ii) for an order under paragraph 1(2)(d) or (e) of Schedule 1 to the Children Act 1989 (orders for financial relief against parents); or

(iii) relating to the legal or beneficial ownership of the dwelling-house.

(7) In deciding whether to exercise its power to include one or more of the provisions referred to in subsection (5) ('a subsection (5) provision') and (if so) in what manner, the court shall have regard to all the circumstances including the matters mentioned in subsection (6)(a) to (e).

(8) If the court decides to make an order under this section and it appears to it that, if the order does not include a subsection (5) provision, the applicant or any relevant child is likely to suffer significant harm attributable to conduct of the respondent, the court shall include the subsection (5) provision in the order unless it appears to the court that—

(a) the respondent or any relevant child is likely to suffer significant harm if the provision is included in the order; and

(b) the harm likely to be suffered by the respondent or child in that event is as great as or greater than the harm attributable to conduct of the respondent which is likely to be suffered by the applicant or child if the provision is not included.

(9) An order under this section—

(a) may not be made after the death of either of the former spouses; and

(b) ceases to have effect on the death of either of them.

(10) An order under this section must be limited so as to have effect for a specified period not exceeding six months, but may be extended on one or more occasions for a further specified period not exceeding six months.

(11) A former spouse who has an equitable interest in the dwelling-house or in the proceeds of sale of the dwelling-house but in whom there is not vested (whether solely or as joint tenant) a legal estate in fee simple or a legal term of years absolute in the dwelling-house is to be treated (but only for the purpose of determining whether he is eligible to apply under this section) as not being entitled to occupy the dwelling-house by virtue of that interest.

(12) Subsection (11) does not prejudice any right of such a former spouse to apply for an order under section 33.

(13) So long as an order under this section remains in force, subsections (3) to (6) of section 30 apply in relation to the applicant—

(a) as if he were the spouse entitled to occupy the dwelling-house by virtue of that section; and

(b) as if the respondent were the other spouse.

36. One cohabitant or former cohabitant with no existing right to occupy

(1) This section applies if—

(a) one cohabitant or former cohabitant is entitled to occupy a dwelling-house by virtue of a beneficial estate or interest or contract or by virtue of any enactment giving him the right to remain in occupation;

(b) the other cohabitant or former cohabitant is not so entitled; and

(c) that dwelling-house is the home in which they live together as husband and wife or a home in which they at any time so lived together or intended so to live together.

(2) The cohabitant or former cohabitant not so entitled may apply to the court for an order under this section against the other cohabitant or former cohabitant ('the respondent').

(3) If the applicant is in occupation, an order under this section must contain provision—

(a) giving the applicant the right not to be evicted or excluded from the dwelling-house or any part of it by the respondent for the period specified in the order; and

(b) prohibiting the respondent from evicting or excluding the applicant during that period.

(4) If the applicant is not in occupation, an order under this section must contain provision—

(a) giving the applicant the right to enter into and occupy the dwelling-house for the period specified in the order; and

(b) requiring the respondent to permit the exercise of that right.

(5) An order under this section may also—

(a) regulate the occupation of the dwelling-house by either or both of the parties;

(b) prohibit, suspend or restrict the exercise by the respondent of his right to occupy the dwelling-house;

(c) require the respondent to leave the dwelling-house or part of the dwelling-house; or

(d) exclude the respondent from a defined area in which the dwelling-house is included.

(6) In deciding whether to make an order under this section containing provision of the kind mentioned in subsection (3) or (4) and (if so) in what manner, the court shall have regard to all the circumstances including—

(a) the housing needs and housing resources of each of the parties and of any relevant child;

(b) the financial resources of each of the parties;

(c) the likely effect of any order, or of any decision by the court not to exercise its powers under subsection (3) or (4), on the health, safety or well-being of the parties and of any relevant child;

(d) the conduct of the parties in relation to each other and otherwise;

(e) the nature of the parties' relationship;

(f) the length of time during which they have lived together as husband and wife;

(g) whether there are or have been any children who are children of both parties or for whom both parties have or have had parental responsibility;

(h) the length of time that has elapsed since the parties ceased to live together; and

(i) the existence of any pending proceedings between the parties—

(i) for an order under paragraph 1(2)(d) or (e) of Schedule 1 to the Children Act 1989 (orders for financial relief against parents); or

(ii) relating to the legal or beneficial ownership of the dwelling-house.

(7) In deciding whether to exercise its powers to include one or more of the provisions referred to in subsection (5) ('a subsection (5) provision') and (if so) in what manner, the court shall have regard to all the circumstances including—

(a) the matters mentioned in subsection (6)(a) to (d); and

(b) the questions mentioned in subsection (8).

(8) The questions are—

(a) whether the applicant or any relevant child is likely to suffer significant harm attributable to conduct of the respondent if the subsection (5) provision is not included in the order; and

(b) whether the harm likely to be suffered by the respondent or child if the provision is included is as great as or greater than the harm attributable to conduct of the respondent which is likely to be suffered by the applicant or child if the provision is not included.

(9) An order under this section—

(a) may not be made after the death of either of the parties; and

(b) ceases to have effect on the death of either of them.

(10) An order under this section must be limited so as to have effect for a specified period not exceeding six months, but may be extended on one occasion for a further specified period not exceeding six months.

(11) A person who has an equitable interest in the dwelling-house or in the proceeds of sale of the dwelling-house but in whom there is not vested (whether solely or as joint tenant) a legal estate in fee simple or a legal term of years absolute in the dwelling-house is to be treated (but only for the purpose of determining whether he is eligible to apply under this section) as not being entitled to occupy the dwelling-house by virtue of that interest.

(12) Subsection (11) does not prejudice any right of such a person to apply for an order under section 33.

(13) So long as the order remains in force, subsections (3) to (6) of section 30 apply in relation to the applicant—

(a) as if he were a spouse entitled to occupy the dwelling-house by virtue of that section; and

(b) as if the respondent were the other spouse.

37. Neither spouse entitled to occupy

(1) This section applies if—

(a) one spouse or former spouse and the other spouse or former spouse occupy a dwelling-house which is or was the matrimonial home; but

(b) neither of them is entitled to remain in occupation—

(i) by virtue of a beneficial estate or interest or contract; or

(ii) by virtue of any enactment giving him the right to remain in occupation.

(2) Either of the parties may apply to the court for an order against the other under this section.

(3) An order under this section may—

(a) require the respondent to permit the applicant to enter and remain in the dwelling-house or part of the dwelling-house;

(b) regulate the occupation of the dwelling-house by either or both of the spouses;

(c) require the respondent to leave the dwelling-house or part of the dwelling-house; or

(d) exclude the respondent from a defined area in which the dwelling-house is included.

(4) Subsections (6) and (7) of section 33 apply to the exercise by the court of its powers under this section as they apply to the exercise by the court of its powers under subsection (3) of that section.

(5) An order under this section must be limited so as to have effect for a specified period not exceeding six months, but may be extended on one or more occasions for a further specified period not exceeding six months.

38. Neither cohabitant or former cohabitant entitled to occupy

(1) This section applies if—

(a) one cohabitant or former cohabitant and the other cohabitant or former cohabitant occupy a dwelling-house which is the home in which they live or lived together as husband and wife; but

(b) neither of them is entitled to remain in occupation—

(i) by virtue of a beneficial estate or interest or contract; or

(ii) by virtue of any enactment giving him the right to remain in occupation.

(2) Either of the parties may apply to the court for an order against the other under this section.

(3) An order under this section may—

(a) require the respondent to permit the applicant to enter and remain in the dwelling-house or part of the dwelling-house;

(b) regulate the occupation of the dwelling-house by either or both of the parties;

(c) require the respondent to leave the dwelling-house or part of the dwelling-house; or

(d) exclude the respondent from a defined area in which the dwelling-house is included.

(4) In deciding whether to exercise its powers to include one or more of the provisions referred to in subsection (3) ('a subsection (3) provision') and (if so) in what manner, the court shall have regard to all the circumstances including—

(a) the housing needs and housing resources of each of the parties and of any relevant child;

(b) the financial resources of each of the parties;

(c) the likely effect of any order, or of any decision by the court not to exercise its powers under subsection (3), on the health, safety or well-being of the parties and of any relevant child;

(d) the conduct of the parties in relation to each other and otherwise; and

(e) the questions mentioned in subsection (5).

(5) The questions are—

(a) whether the applicant or any relevant child is likely to suffer significant harm attributable to conduct of the respondent if the subsection (3) provision is not included in the order; and

(b) whether the harm likely to be suffered by the respondent or child if the provision is included is as great as or greater than the harm attributable to conduct of the respondent which is likely to be suffered by the applicant or child if the provision is not included.

(6) An order under this section shall be limited so as to have effect for a specified period not exceeding six months, but may be extended on one occasion for a further specified period not exceeding six months.

39. Supplementary provisions

(1) In this Part an 'occupation order' means an order under section 33, 35, 36, 37 or 38.

(2) An application for an occupation order may be made in other family proceedings or without any other family proceedings being instituted.

(3) If—

(a) an application for an occupation order is made under section 33, 35, 36, 37 or 38, and

(b) the court considers that it has no power to make the order under the section concerned, but that it has power to make an order under one of the other sections, the court may make an order under that other section.

(4) The fact that a person has applied for an occupation order under sections 35 to 38, or that an occupation order has been made, does not affect the right of any person to claim a legal or equitable interest in any property in any subsequent proceedings (including subsequent proceedings under this Part).

40. Additional provisions that may be included in certain occupation orders

(1) The court may on, or at any time after, making an occupation order under section 33, 35 or 36—

(a) impose on either party obligations as to—

(i) the repair and maintenance of the dwelling-house; or

(ii) the discharge of rent, mortgage payments or other outgoings affecting the dwelling-house;

(b) order a party occupying the dwelling-house or any part of it (including a party who is entitled to do so by virtue of a beneficial estate or interest or contract or by virtue of any enactment giving him the right to remain in occupation) to make periodical payments to the other party in respect of the accommodation, if the other party would (but for the order) be entitled to occupy the dwelling-house by virtue of a beneficial estate or interest or contract or by virtue of any such enactment;

(c) grant either party possession or use of furniture or other contents of the dwelling-house;

(d) order either party to take reasonable care of any furniture or other contents of the dwelling-house;

(e) order either party to take reasonable steps to keep the dwelling-house and any furniture or other contents secure.

(2) In deciding whether and, if so, how to exercise its powers under this section, the court shall have regard to all the circumstances of the case including—

(a) the financial needs and financial resources of the parties; and

(b) the financial obligations which they have, or are likely to have in the foreseeable future, including financial obligations to each other and to any relevant child.

(3) An order under this section ceases to have effect when the occupation order to which it relates ceases to have effect.

41. Additional considerations if parties are cohabitants or former cohabitants

(1) This section applies if the parties are cohabitants or former cohabitants.

(2) Where the court is required to consider the nature of the parties' relationship, it is to have regard to the fact that they have not given each other the commitment involved in marriage.

Dwelling-house subject to mortgage

54. Dwelling-house subject to mortgage

(1) In determining for the purposes of this Part whether a person is entitled to occupy a dwelling-house by virtue of an estate or interest, any right to possession of the dwelling-house conferred on a mortgagee of the dwelling-house under or by virtue of his mortgage is to be disregarded.

(2) Subsection (1) applies whether or not the mortgagee is in possession.

(3) Where a person ('A') is entitled to occupy a dwelling-house by virtue of an estate or interest, a connected person does not by virtue of—

(a) any matrimonial home rights conferred by section 30, or

(b) any rights conferred by an order under section 35 or 36,

have any larger right against the mortgagee to occupy the dwelling-house than A has by virtue of his estate or interest and of any contract with the mortgagee.

(4) Subsection (3) does not apply, in the case of matrimonial home rights, if under section 31 those rights are a charge, affecting the mortgagee, on the estate or interest mortgaged.

(5) In this section 'connected person', in relation to any person, means that person's spouse, former spouse, cohabitant or former cohabitant.

55. Actions by mortgagees: joining connected persons as parties

(1) This section applies if a mortgagee of land which consists of or includes a dwelling-house brings an action in any court for the enforcement of his security.

(2) A connected person who is not already a party to the action is entitled to be made a party in the circumstances mentioned in subsection (3).

(3) The circumstances are that—

(a) the connected person is enabled by section 30(3) or (6) (or by section 30(3) or (6) as applied by section 35(13) or 36(13)), to meet the mortgagor's liabilities under the mortgage;

(b) he has applied to the court before the action is finally disposed of in that court; and

(c) the court sees no special reason against his being made a party to the action and is satisfied—

(i) that he may be expected to make such payments or do such other things in or towards satisfaction of the mortgagor's liabilities or obligations as might affect the outcome of the proceedings; or

(ii) that the expectation of it should be considered under section 36 of the Administration of Justice Act 1970.

(4) In this section 'connected person' has the same meaning as in section 54.

56. Actions by mortgagees: service of notice on certain persons

(1) This section applies if a mortgagee of land which consists, or substantially consists, of a dwelling-house brings an action for the enforcement of his security, and at the relevant time there is—

(a) in the case of unregistered land, a land charge of Class F registered against the person who is the estate owner at the relevant time or any person who, where the estate owner is a trustee, preceded him as trustee during the subsistence of the mortgage; or

(b) in the case of registered land, a subsisting registration of—

(i) a notice under section 31(10);

(ii) a notice under section 2(8) of the Matrimonial Homes Act 1983; or

(iii) a notice or caution under section 2(7) of the Matrimonial Homes Act 1967.

(2) If the person on whose behalf—

(a) the land charge is registered, or

(b) the notice or caution is entered,

is not a party to the action, the mortgagee must serve notice of the action on him.

(3) If—

(a) an official search has been made on behalf of the mortgagee which would disclose any land charge of Class F, notice or caution within subsection (1)(a) or (b),

(b) a certificate of the result of the search has been issued, and

(c) the action is commenced within the priority period,

the relevant time is the date of the certificate.

(4) In any other case the relevant time is the time when the action is commenced.

(5) The priority period is, for both registered and unregistered land the period for which, in accordance with section 11(5) and (6) of the Land Charges Act 1972, a certificate on an official search operates in favour of a purchaser.

SCHEDULE 4
PROVISIONS SUPPLEMENTARY TO SECTIONS 30 AND 31

Restriction on registration where spouse entitled to more than one charge

2. Where one spouse is entitled by virtue of section 31 to a registrable charge in respect of each of two or more dwelling-houses, only one of the charges to which that spouse is so entitled shall be registered under section 31(10) or under section 2 of the Land Charges Act 1972 at any one time, and if any of those charges is registered under either of those provisions the Chief Land Registrar, on being satisfied that any other of them is so registered, shall cancel the registration of the charge first registered.

Contract for sale of house affected by registered charge to include term requiring cancellation of registration before completion

3. (1) Where one spouse is entitled by virtue of section 31 to a charge on an estate in a dwelling-house and the charge is registered under section 31(10) or section 2 of the Land Charges Act 1972, it shall be a term of any contract for the sale of that estate whereby the vendor agrees to give vacant possession of the dwelling-house on completion of the contract that the vendor will before such completion procure the cancellation of the registration of the charge at his expense.

(2) Sub-paragraph (1) shall not apply to any such contract made by a vendor who is entitled to sell the estate in the dwelling-house freed from any such charge.

(3) If, on the completion of such a contract as is referred to in sub-paragraph (1), there is delivered to the purchaser or his solicitor an application by the spouse entitled to the charge for the cancellation of the registration of that charge, the term of the contract for which sub-paragraph (1) provides shall be deemed to have been performed.

(4) This paragraph applies only if and so far as a contrary intention is not expressed in the contract.

(5) This paragraph shall apply to a contract for exchange as it applies to a contract for sale.

(6) This paragraph shall, with the necessary modifications, apply to a contract for the grant of a lease or underlease of a dwelling-house as it applies to a contract for the sale of an estate in a dwelling-house.

Cancellation of registration after termination of marriage, etc.

4.—(1) Where a spouse's matrimonial home rights are a charge on an estate in the dwelling-house and the charge is registered under section 31(10) or under section 2 of the Land Charges Act 1972, the Chief Land Registrar shall, subject to sub-paragraph (2), cancel the registration of the charge if he is satisfied—

(a) by the production of a certificate or other sufficient evidence, that either spouse is dead, or

(b) by the production of an official copy of a decree or order of a court, that the marriage in question has been terminated otherwise than by death, or

(c) by the production of an order of the court, that the spouse's matrimonial home rights constituting the charge have been terminated by the order.

(2) Where—

(a) the marriage in question has been terminated by the death of the spouse entitled to an estate in the dwelling-house or otherwise than by death, and

(b) an order affecting the charge of the spouse not so entitled had been made under section 33(5),

then if, after the making of the order, registration of the charge was renewed or the charge registered in pursuance of sub-paragraph (3), the Chief Land Registrar shall not cancel the registration of the charge in accordance with sub-paragraph (1) unless he is also satisfied that the order has ceased to have effect.

(3) Where such an order has been made, then, for the purposes of sub-paragraph (2), the spouse entitled to the charge affected by the order may—

(a) if before the date of the order the charge was registered under section 31(10) or under section 2 of the Land Charges Act 1972, renew the registration of the charge, and

(b) if before the said date the charge was not so registered, register the charge under section 31(10) or under section 2 of the Land Charges Act 1972.

(4) Renewal of the registration of a charge in pursuance of sub-paragraph (3) shall be effected in such manner as may be prescribed, and an application for such renewal or for registration of a charge in pursuance of that sub-paragraph shall contain such particulars of any order affecting the charge made under section 33(5) as may be prescribed.

(5) The renewal in pursuance of sub-paragraph (3) of the registration of a charge shall not affect the priority of the charge.

(6) In this paragraph 'prescribed' means prescribed by rules made under section 16 of the Land Charges Act 1972 or section 144 of the Land Registration Act 1925, as the circumstances of the case require.

Release of matrimonial home rights

5.—(1) A spouse entitled to matrimonial home rights may by a release in writing release those rights or release them as respects part only of the dwelling-house affected by them.

(2) Where a contract is made for the sale of an estate or interest in a dwelling-house, or for the grant of a lease or underlease of a dwelling-house, being (in either case) a dwelling-house affected by a charge registered under section 31(10) or under section 2 of the Land Charges Act 1972, then, without prejudice to sub-paragraph (1), the matrimonial home rights constituting the charge shall be deemed to have been released on the happening of whichever of the following events first occurs—

(a) the delivery to the purchaser or lessee, as the case may be, or his solicitor on completion of the contract of an application by the spouse entitled to the charge for the cancellation of the registration of the charge; or

(b) the lodging of such an application at Her Majesty's Land Registry.

Postponement of priority of charge

6. A spouse entitled by virtue of section 31 to a charge on an estate or interest may agree in writing that any other charge on, or interest in, that estate or interest shall rank in priority to the charge to which that spouse is so entitled.

SCHEDULE 9

Matrimonial home rights

11.—(1) Any reference (however expressed) in any enactment, instrument or document (whether passed or made before or after the passing of this Act) to rights of occupation under, or within the meaning of, the 1983 Act shall be construed, so far as is required for continuing the effect of the instrument or document, as being or as the case requires including a reference to matrimonial home rights under, or within the meaning of, Part IV.

(2) Any reference (however expressed) in this Act or in any other enactment, instrument or document (including any enactment amended by Schedule 8) to matrimonial home rights under, or within the meaning of, Part IV shall be construed as including, in relation to times, circumstances and purposes before the commencement of sections 30 to 32, a reference to rights of occupation under, or within the meaning of, the 1983 Act.

12.—(1) Any reference (however expressed) in any enactment, instrument or document (whether passed or made before or after the passing of this Act) to registration under section 2(8) of the 1983 Act shall, in relation to any time after the commencement of sections 30 to 32, be construed as being or as the case requires including a reference to registration under section 31(10).

(2) Any reference (however expressed) in this Act or in any other enactment, instrument or document (including any enactment amended by Schedule 8) to registration under section 31(10) shall be construed as including a reference to—

(a) registration under section 2(7) of the Matrimonial Homes Act 1967 or section 2(8) of the 1983 Act, and

(b) registration by caution duly lodged under section 2(7) of the Matrimonial Homes Act 1967 before 14th February 1983 (the date of the commencement of section 4(2) of the Matrimonial Homes and Property Act 1981).

13. In sections 30 and 31 and Schedule 4—

(a) any reference to an order made under section 33 shall be construed as including a reference to an order made under section 1 of the 1983 Act, and

(b) any reference to an order made under section 33(5) shall be construed as including a reference to an order made under section 1 of the 1983 Act by virtue of section 2(4) of that Act.

14. Neither section 31(11) nor the repeal by the Matrimonial Homes and Property Act 1981 of the words 'or caution' in section 2(7) of the Matrimonial Homes Act 1967, affects any caution duly lodged as respects any estate or interest before 14th February 1983.

15. Nothing in this Schedule is to be taken to prejudice the operation of sections 16 and 17 of the Interpretation Act 1978 (which relate to the effect of repeals).

TRUSTS OF LAND AND APPOINTMENT OF TRUSTEES ACT 1996

PART I
TRUSTS OF LAND

Introductory

1. Meaning of 'trust of land'

(1) In this Act—

(a) 'trust of land' means (subject to subsection (3)) any trust of property which consists of or includes land, and

(b) 'trustees of land' means trustees of a trust of land.

(2) The reference in subsection (1)(a) to a trust—

(a) is to any description of trust (whether express, implied, resulting or constructive), including a trust for sale and a bare trust, and

(b) includes a trust created, or arising, before the commencement of this Act.

(3) The reference to land in subsection (1)(a) does not include land which (despite section 2) is settled land or which is land to which the Universities and College Estates Act 1925 applies.

Settlements and trusts for sale as trusts of land

2. Trusts in place of settlements

(1) No settlement created after the commencement of this Act is a settlement for the purposes of the Settled Land Act 1925; and no settlement shall be deemed to be made under that Act after that commencement.

(2) Subsection (1) does not apply to a settlement created on the occasion of an alteration in any interest in, or of a person becoming entitled under, a settlement which—

(a) is in existence at the commencement of this Act, or

(b) derives from a settlement within paragraph (a) or this paragraph.

(3) But a settlement created as mentioned in subsection (2) is not a settlement for the purposes of the Settled Land Act 1925 if provision to the effect that it is not is made in the instrument, or any of the instruments, by which it is created.

(4) Where at any time after the commencement of this Act there is in the case of any settlement which is a settlement for the purposes of the Settled Land Act 1925 no relevant property which is, or is deemed to be, subject to the settlement, the settlement permanently ceases at that time to be a settlement for the purposes of that Act.

In this subsection 'relevant property' means land and personal chattels to which section 67(1) of the Settled Land Act 1925 (heirlooms) applies.

(5) No land held on charitable, ecclesiastical or public trusts shall be or be deemed to be settled land after the commencement of this Act, even if it was or was deemed to be settled land before that commencement.

(6) Schedule 1 has effect to make provision consequential on this section (including provision to impose a trust in circumstances in which, apart from this section, there would be a settlement for the purposes of the Settled Land Act 1925 (and there would not otherwise be a trust)).

3. Abolition of doctrine of conversion

(1) Where land is held by trustees subject to a trust for sale, the land is not to be regarded as personal property; and where personal property is subject to a trust for sale in order that the trustees may acquire land, the personal property is not to be regarded as land.

(2) Subsection (1) does not apply to a trust created by a will if the testator died before the commencement of this Act.

(3) Subject to that, subsection (1) applies to a trust whether it is created, or arises, before or after that commencement.

4. Express trusts for sale as trusts of land

(1) In the case of every trust for sale of land created by a disposition there is to be implied, despite any provision to the contrary made by the disposition, a power for the trustees to postpone sale of the land; and the trustees are not liable in any way for postponing sale of the land, in the exercise of their discretion, for an indefinite period.

(2) Subsection (1) applies to a trust whether it is created, or arises, before or after the commencement of this Act.

(3) Subsection (1) does not affect any liability incurred by trustees before that commencement.

5. Implied trusts for sale as trusts of land

(1) Schedule 2 has effect in relation to statutory provisions which impose a trust for sale of land in certain circumstances so that in those circumstances there is instead a trust of the land (without a duty to sell).

(2) Section 1 of the Settled Land Act 1925 does not apply to land held on any trust arising by virtue of that Schedule (so that any such land is subject to a trust of land).

Functions of trustees of land

6. General powers of trustees

(1) For the purpose of exercising their functions as trustees, the trustees of land have in relation to the land subject to the trust all the powers of an absolute owner.

(2) Where in the case of any land subject to a trust of land each of the beneficiaries interested in the land is a person of full age and capacity who is absolutely entitled to the land, the powers conferred on the trustees by subsection (1) include the power to convey the land to the beneficiaries even though they have not required the trustees to do so; and where land is conveyed by virtue of this subsection—

(a) the beneficiaries shall do whatever is necessary to secure that it vests in them, and

(b) if they fail to do so, the court may make an order requiring them to do so.

(3) The trustees of land have power to purchase a legal estate in any land in England or Wales.

(4) The power conferred by subsection (3) may be exercised by trustees to purchase land—

(a) by way of investment,
(b) for occupation by any beneficiary, or
(c) for any other reason.

(5) In exercising the powers conferred by this section trustees shall have regard to the rights of the beneficiaries.

(6) The powers conferred by this section shall not be exercised in contravention of, or of any order made in pursuance of, any other enactment or any rule of law or equity.

(7) The reference in subsection (6) to an order includes an order of any court or of the Charity Commissioners.

(8) Where any enactment other than this section confers on trustees authority to act subject to any restriction, limitation or condition, trustees of land may not exercise

the powers conferred by this section to do any act which they are prevented from doing under the other enactment by reason of the restriction, limitation or condition.

7. Partition by trustees

(1) The trustees of land may, where beneficiaries of full age are absolutely entitled in undivided shares to land subject to the trust, partition the land, or any part of it, and provide (by way of mortgage or otherwise) for the payment of any equality money.

(2) The trustees shall give effect to any such partition by conveying the partitioned land in severalty (whether or not subject to any legal mortgage created for raising equality money), either absolutely or in trust, in accordance with the rights of those beneficiaries.

(3) Before exercising their powers under subsection (2) the trustees shall obtain the consent of each of those beneficiaries.

(4) Where a share in the land is affected by an incumbrance, the trustees may either give effect to it or provide for its discharge from the property allotted to that share as they think fit.

(5) If a share in the land is absolutely vested in a minor, subsections (1) to (4) apply as if he were of full age, except that the trustees may act on his behalf and retain land or other property representing his share in trust for him.

8. Exclusion and restriction of powers

(1) Sections 6 and 7 do not apply in the case of a trust of land created by a disposition in so far as provision to the effect that they do not apply is made by the disposition.

(2) If the disposition creating such a trust makes provision requiring any consent to be obtained to the exercise of any power conferred by section 6 or 7, the power may not be exercised without that consent.

(3) Subsection (1) does not apply in the case of charitable, ecclesiastical or public trusts.

(4) Subsections (1) and (2) have effect subject to any enactment which prohibits or restricts the effect of provision of the description mentioned in them.

9. Delegation by trustees

(1) The trustees of land may, by power of attorney, delegate to any beneficiary or beneficiaries of full age and beneficially entitled to an interest in possession in land subject to the trust any of their functions as trustees which relate to the land.

(2) Where trustees purport to delegate to a person by a power of attorney under subsection (1) functions relating to any land and another person in good faith deals with him in relation to the land, he shall be presumed in favour of that other person to have been a person to whom the functions could be delegated unless that other person has knowledge at the time of the transaction that he was not such a person.

And it shall be conclusively presumed in favour of any purchaser whose interest depends on the validity of that transaction that that other person dealt in good faith and did not have such knowledge if that other person makes a statutory declaration to that effect before or within three months after the completion of the purchase.

(3) A power of attorney under subsection (1) shall be given by all the trustees jointly and (unless expressed to be irrevocable and to be given by way of security) may be revoked by any one or more of them; and such a power is revoked by the appointment as a trustee of a person other than those by whom it is given (though not by any of those persons dying or otherwise ceasing to be a trustee).

(4) Where a beneficiary to whom functions are delegated by a power of attorney under subsection (1) ceases to be a person beneficially entitled to an interest in possession in land subject to the trust—

(a) if the functions are delegated to him alone, the power is revoked,

(b) if the functions are delegated to him and to other beneficiaries to be exercised by them jointly (but not separately), the power is revoked if each of the other beneficiaries ceases to be so entitled (but otherwise functions exercisable in accordance with the power are so exercisable by the remaining beneficiary or beneficiaries), and

(c) if the functions are delegated to him and to other beneficiaries to be exercised by them separately (or either separately or jointly), the power is revoked in so far as it relates to him.

(5) A delegation under subsection (1) may be for any period or indefinite.

(6) A power of attorney under subsection (1) cannot be an enduring power within the meaning of the Enduring Powers of Attorney Act 1985.

(7) Beneficiaries to whom functions have been delegated under subsection (1) are, in relation to the exercise of the functions, in the same position as trustees (with the same duties and liabilities); but such beneficiaries shall not be regarded as trustees for any other purposes (including, in particular, the purposes of any enactment permitting the delegation of functions by trustees or imposing requirements relating to the payment of capital money).

(8) Where any function has been delegated to a beneficiary or beneficiaries under subsection (1), the trustees are jointly and severally liable for any act or default of the beneficiary, or any of the beneficiaries, in the exercise of the function if, and only if, the trustees did not exercise reasonable care in deciding to delegate the function to the beneficiary or beneficiaries.

(9) Neither this section nor the repeal by this Act of section 29 of the Law of Property Act 1925 (which is superseded by this section) affects the operation after the commencement of this Act of any delegation effected before that commencement.

Consents and consultation

10. Consents

(1) If a disposition creating a trust of land requires the consent of more than two persons to the exercise by the trustees of any function relating to the land, the consent of any two of them to the exercise of the function is sufficient in favour of a purchaser.

(2) Subsection (1) does not apply to the exercise of a function by trustees of land held on charitable, ecclesiastical or public trusts.

(3) Where at any time a person whose consent is expressed by a disposition creating a trust of land to be required to the exercise by the trustees of any function relating to the land is not of full age—

(a) his consent is not, in favour of a purchaser, required to the exercise of the function, but

(b) the trustees shall obtain the consent of a parent who has parental responsibility for him (within the meaning of the Children Act 1989) or of a guardian of his.

11. Consultation with beneficiaries

(1) The trustees of land shall in the exercise of any function relating to land subject to the trust—

(a) so far as practicable, consult the beneficiaries of full age and beneficially entitled to an interest in possession in the land, and

(b) so far as consistent with the general interest of the trust, give effect to the wishes of those beneficiaries, or (in case of dispute) of the majority (according to the value of their combined interests).

(2) Subsection (1) does not apply—

(a) in relation to a trust created by a disposition in so far as provision that it does not apply is made by the disposition,

(b) in relation to a trust created or arising under a will made before the commencement of this Act, or

(c) in relation to the exercise of the power mentioned in section 6(2).

(3) Subsection (1) does not apply to a trust created before the commencement of this Act by a disposition, or a trust created after that commencement by reference to such a trust, unless provision to the effect that it is to apply is made by a deed executed—

(a) in a case in which the trust was created by one person and he is of full capacity, by that person, or

(b) in a case in which the trust was created by more than one person, by such of the persons who created the trust as are alive and of full capacity.

(4) A deed executed for the purposes of subsection (3) is irrevocable.

Right of beneficiaries to occupy trust land

12. The right to occupy

(1) A beneficiary who is beneficially entitled to an interest in possession in land subject to a trust of land is entitled by reason of his interest to occupy the land at any time if at that time—

(a) the purposes of the trust include making the land available for his occupation (or for the occupation of beneficiaries of a class of which he is a member or of beneficiaries in general), or

(b) the land is held by the trustees so as to be so available.

(2) Subsection (1) does not confer on a beneficiary a right to occupy land if it is either unavailable or unsuitable for occupation by him.

(3) This section is subject to section 13.

13. Exclusion and restriction of right to occupy

(1) Where two or more beneficiaries are (or apart from this subsection would be) entitled under section 12 to occupy land, the trustees of land may exclude or restrict the entitlement of any one or more (but not all) of them.

(2) Trustees may not under subsection (1)—

(a) unreasonably exclude any beneficiary's entitlement to occupy land, or

(b) restrict any such entitlement to an unreasonable extent.

(3) The trustees of land may from time to time impose reasonable conditions on any beneficiary in relation to his occupation of land by reason of his entitlement under section 12.

(4) The matters to which trustees are to have regard in exercising the powers conferred by this section include—

(a) the intentions of the person or persons (if any) who created the trust,

(b) the purposes for which the land is held, and

(c) the circumstances and wishes of each of the beneficiaries who is (or apart from any previous exercise by the trustees of those powers would be) entitled to occupy the land under section 12.

(5) The conditions which may be imposed on a beneficiary under subsection (3) include, in particular, conditions requiring him—

(a) to pay any outgoings or expenses in respect of the land, or

(b) to assume any other obligation in relation to the land or to any activity which is or is proposed to be conducted there.

(6) Where the entitlement of any beneficiary to occupy land under section 12 has been excluded or restricted, the conditions which may be imposed on any other beneficiary under subsection (3) include, in particular, conditions requiring him to—

(a) make payments by way of compensation to the beneficiary whose entitlement has been excluded or restricted, or

(b) forgo any payment or other benefit to which he would otherwise be entitled under the trust so as to benefit that beneficiary.

(7) The powers conferred on trustees by this section may not be exercised—

(a) so as prevent any person who is in occupationt of land (whether or not by reason of an entitlement under section 12) from continuing to occupy the land, or

(b) in a manner likely to result in any such person ceasing to occupy the land, unless he consents or the court has given approval.

(8) The matters to which the court is to have regard in determining whether to give approval under subsection (7) include the matters mentioned in subsection (4)(a) to (c).

Powers of court

14. Applications for order

(1) Any person who is a trustee of land or has an interest in property subject to a trust of land may make an application to the court for an order under this section.

(2) On an application for an order under this section the court may make any such order—

(a) relating to the exercise by the trustees of any of their functions (including an order relieving them of any obligation to obtain the consent of, or to consult, any person in connection with the exercise of any of their functions), or

(b) declaring the nature or extent of a person's interest in property subject to the trust,

as the court thinks fit.

(3) The court may not under this section make any order as to the appointment or removal of trustees.

(4) The powers conferred on the court by this section are exercisable on an application whether it is made before or after the commencement of this Act.

15. Matters relevant in determining applications

(1) The matters to which the court is to have regard in determining an application for an order under section 14 include—

(a) the intentions of the person or persons (if any) who created the trust,

(b) the purposes for which the property subject to the trust is held,

(c) the welfare of any minor who occupies or might reasonably be expected to occupy any land subject to the trust as his home, and

(d) the interests of any secured creditor of any beneficiary.

(2) In the case of an application relating to the exercise in relation to any land of the powers conferred on the trustees by section 13, the matters to which the court is to have regard also include the circumstances and wishes of each of the beneficiaries who is (or apart from any previous exercise by the trustees of those powers would be) entitled to occupy the land under section 12.

(3) In the case of any other application, other than one relating to the exercise of the power mentioned in section 6(2), the matters to which the court is to have regard also include the circumstances and wishes of any beneficiaries of full age and entitled to an interest in possession in property subject to the trust or (in case of dispute) of the majority (according to the value of their combined interests).

(4) This section does not apply to an application if section 335A of the Insolvency Act 1986 [. . .] applies to it.

Purchaser protection

16. Protection of purchasers

(1) A purchaser of land which is or has been subject to a trust need not be concerned to see that any requirement imposed on the trustees by section 6(5), 7(3) or 11(1) has been complied with.

(2) Where—

(a) trustees of land who convey land which (immediately before it is conveyed) is subject to the trust contravene section 6(6) or (8), but

(b) the purchaser of the land from the trustees has no actual notice of the contravention,

the contravention does not invalidate the conveyance.

(3) Where the powers of trustees of land are limited by virtue of section 8—

(a) the trustees shall take all reasonable steps to bring the limitation to the notice of any purchaser of the land from them, but

(b) the limitation does not invalidate any conveyance by the trustees to a purchaser who has no actual notice of the limitation.

(4) Where trustees of land convey land which (immediately before it is conveyed) is subject to the trust to persons believed by them to be beneficiaries absolutely entitled to the land under the trust and of full age and capacity—

(a) the trustees shall execute a deed declaring that they are discharged from the trust in relation to that land, and

(b) if they fail to do so, the court may make an order requiring them to do so.

(5) A purchaser of land to which a deed under subsection (4) relates is entitled to assume that, as from the date of the deed, the land is not subject to the trust unless he has actual notice that the trustees were mistaken in their belief that the land was conveyed to beneficiaries absolutely entitled to the land under the trust and of full age and capacity.

(6) Subsections (2) and (3) do not apply to land held on charitable, ecclesiastical or public trusts.

(7) This section does not apply to registered land.

Supplementary

17. Applications of provisions to trusts of proceeds of sale

(1) Section 6(3) applies in relation to trustees of a trust of proceeds of sale of land as in relation to trustees of land.

(2) Section 14 applies in relation to a trust of proceeds of sale of land and trustees of such a trust as in relation to a trust of land and trustees of land.

(3) In this section 'trust of proceeds of sale of land' means (subject to subsection (5)) any trust of property (other than a trust of land) which consists of or includes—

(a) any proceeds of a disposition of land held in trust (including settled land), or

(b) any property representing any such proceeds.

(4) The references in subsection (3) to a trust—

(a) are to any description of trust (whether express, implied, resulting or constructive), including a trust for sale and a bare trust, and

(b) include a trust created, or arising, before the commencement of this Act.

(5) A trust which (despite section 2) is a settlement for the purposes of the Settled Land Act 1925 cannot be a trust of proceeds of sale of land.

(6) In subsection (3)—

(a) 'disposition' includes any disposition made, or coming into operation, before the commencement of this Act, and

(b) the reference to settled land includes personal chattels to which section 67(1) of the Settled Land Act 1925 (heirlooms) applies.

18. Application of Part to personal representatives

(1) The provisions of this Part relating to trustees, other than sections 10, 11 and 14, apply to personal representatives, but with appropriate modifications and without prejudice to the functions of personal representatives for the purposes of administration.

(2) The appropriate modifications include—

(a) the substitution of references to persons interested in the due administration of the estate for references to beneficiaries, and

(b) the substitution of references to the will for references to the disposition creating the trust.

(3) Section 3(1) does not apply to personal representatives if the death occurs before the commencement of this Act.

PART II
APPOINTMENT AND RETIREMENT OF TRUSTEES

19. Appointment and retirement of trustee at instance of beneficiaries

(1) This section applies in the case of a trust where—

(a) there is no person nominated for the purpose of appointing new trustees by the instrument, if any, creating the trust, and

(b) the beneficiaries under the trust are of full age and capacity and (taken together) are absolutely entitled to the property subject to the trust.

(2) The beneficiaries may give a direction or directions of either or both of the following descriptions—

(a) a written direction to a trustee or trustees to retire from the trust, and

(b) a written direction to the trustees or trustee for the time being (or, if there are none, to the personal representative of the last person who was a trustee) to appoint by writing to be a trustee or trustees the person or persons specified in the direction.

(3) Where—

(a) a trustee has been given a direction under subsection (2)(a),

(b) reasonable arrangements have been made for the protection of any rights of his in connection with the trust,

(c) after he has retired there will be either a trust corporation or at least two persons to act as trustees to perform the trust, and

(d) either another person is to be appointed to be a new trustee on his retirement (whether in compliance with a direction under subsection (2)(b) or otherwise) or the continuing trustees by deed consent to his retirement,

he shall make a deed declaring his retirement and shall be deemed to have retired and be discharged from the trust.

(4) Where a trustee retires under subsection (3) he and the continuing trustees (together with any new trustee) shall (subject to any arrangements for the protection of his rights) do anything necessary to vest the trust property in the continuing trustees (or the continuing and new trustees).

(5) This section has effect subject to the restrictions imposed by the Trustee Act 1925 on the number of trustees.

20. Appointment of substitute for incapable trustee

(1) This section applies where—

(a) a trustee is incapable by reason of mental disorder of exercising his functions as trustee,

(b) there is no person who is both entitled and willing and able to appoint a trustee in place of him under section 36(1) of the Trustee Act 1925, and

(c) the beneficiaries under the trust are of full age and capacity and (taken together) are absolutely entitled to the property subject to the trust.

(2) The beneficiaries may give to—

(a) a receiver of the trustee,

(b) an attorney acting for him under the authority of a power of attorney created by an instrument which is registered under section 6 of the Enduring Powers of Attorney Act 1985, or

(c) a person authorised for the purpose by the authority having jurisdiction under Part VII of the Mental Health Act 1983,
a written direction to appoint by writing the person or persons specified in the direction to be a trustee or trustees in place of the incapable trustee.

21. Supplementary

(1) For the purposes of section 19 or 20 a direction is given by beneficiaries if—

(a) a single direction is jointly given by all of them, or

(b) (subject to subsection (2)) a direction is given by each of them (whether solely or jointly with one or more, but not all, of the others),

and none of them by writing withdraws the direction given by him before it has been complied with.

(2) Where more than one direction is given each must specify for appointment or retirement the same person or persons.

(3) Subsection (7) of section 36 of the Trustee Act 1925 (powers of trustees appointed under that section) applies to a trustee appointed under section 19 or 20 as if he were appointed under that section.

(4) A direction under section 19 or 20 must not specify a person or persons for appointment if the appointment of that person or those persons would be in contravention of section 35(1) of the Trustee Act 1925 or section 24(1) of the Law of Property Act 1925 (requirements as to identity of trustees).

(5) Sections 19 and 20 do not apply in relation to a trust created by a disposition in so far as provision that they do not apply is made by the disposition.

(6) Sections 19 and 20 do not apply in relation to a trust created before the commencement of this Act by a disposition in so far as provision to the effect that they do not apply is made by a deed executed—

(a) in a case in which the trust was created by one person and he is of full capacity, by that person, or

(b) in a case in which the trust was created by more than one person, by such of the persons who created the trust as are alive and of full capacity.

(7) A deed executed for the purposes of subsection (6) is irrevocable.

(8) Where a deed is executed for the purposes of subsection (6)—

(a) it does not affect anything done before its execution to comply with a direction under section 19 or 20, but

(b) a direction under section 19 or 20 which has been given but not complied with before its execution shall cease to have effect.

PART III
SUPPLEMENTARY

22. Meaning of 'beneficiary'

(1) In this Act 'beneficiary', in relation to a trust, means any person who under the trust has an interest in property subject to the trust (including a person who has such an interest as a trustee or a personal representative).

(2) In this Act references to a beneficiary who is beneficially entitled do not include a beneficiary who has an interest in property subject to the trust only by reason of being a trustee or personal representative.

(3) For the purposes of this Act a person who is a beneficiary only by reason of being an annuitant is not to be regarded as entitled to an interest in possession in land subject to the trust.

23. Other interpretation provisions

(1) In this Act 'purchaser' has the same meaning as in Part I of the Law of Property Act 1925.

(2) Subject to that, where an expression used in this Act is given a meaning by the Law of Property Act 1925 it has the same meaning as in that Act unless the context otherwise requires.

(3) In this Act 'the court' means—

(a) the High Court, or

(b) a county court.

SCHEDULES

Section 2

SCHEDULE 1
PROVISIONS CONSEQUENTIAL ON SECTION 2

Minors

1.—(1) Where after the commencement of this Act a person purports to convey a legal estate in land to a minor, or two or more minors, alone, the conveyance—

(a) is not effective to pass the legal estate, but

(b) operates as a declaration that the land is held in trust for the minor or minors (or if he purports to convey it to the minor or minors in trust for any persons, for those persons).

(2) Where after the commencement of this Act a person purports to convey a legal estate in land to—

(a) a minor or two or more minors, and

(b) another person who is, or other persons who are, of full age,

the conveyance operates to vest the land in the other person or persons in trust for the minor or minors and the other person or persons (or if he purports to convey it to them in trust for any persons, for those persons).

(3) Where immediately before the commencement of this Act a conveyance is operating (by virtue of section 27 of the Settled Land Act 1925) as an agreement to execute a settlement in favour of a minor or minors—

(a) the agreement ceases to have effect on the commencement of this Act, and

(b) the conveyance subsequently operates instead as a declaration that the land is held in trust for the minor or minors.

2. Where after the commencement of this Act a legal estate in land would, by reason of intestacy or in any other circumstances not dealt with in paragraph 1, vest in a person who is a minor if he were a person of full age, the land is held in trust for the minor.

Family charges

3. Where, by virtue of an instrument coming into operation after the commencement of this Act, land becomes charged voluntarily (or in consideration of marriage) or by way of family arrangement, whether immediately or after an interval, with the payment of—

(a) a rentcharge for the life of a person or a shorter period, or

(b) capital, annual or periodical sums for the benefit of a person,

the instrument operates as a declaration that the land is held in trust for giving effect to the charge.

Charitable, ecclesiastical and public trusts

4.—(1) This paragraph applies in the case of land held on charitable, ecclesiastical or public trusts (other than land to which the Universities and College Estates Act 1925 applies).

(2) Where there is a conveyance of such land—

(a) if neither section 37(1) nor section 39(1) of the Charities Act 1993 applies to the conveyance, it shall state that the land is held on such trusts, and

(b) if neither section 37(2) nor section 39(2) of that Act has been complied with in relation to the conveyance and a purchaser has notice that the land is held on such trusts, he must see that any consents or orders necessary to authorise the transaction have been obtained.

(3) Where any trustees or the majority of any set of trustees have power to transfer or create any legal estate in the land, the estate shall be transferred or created by them in the names and on behalf of the persons in whom it is vested.

Entailed interests

5.—(1) Where a person purports by an instrument coming into operation after the commencement of this Act to grant to another person an entailed interest in real or personal property, the instrument—

(a) is not effective to grant an entailed interest, but

(b) operates instead as a declaration that the property is held in trust absolutely for the person to whom an entailed interest in the property was purportedly granted.

(2) Where a person purports by an instrument coming into operation after the commencement of this Act to declare himself a tenant in tail of real or personal property, the instrument is not effective to create an entailed interest.

Property held on settlement ceasing to exist

6. Where a settlement ceases to be a settlement for the purposes of the Settled Land Act 1925 because no relevant property (within the meaning of section 2(4)) is, or is deemed to be, subject to the settlement, any property which is or later becomes subject to the settlement is held in trust for the persons interested under the settlement.

INDEX

BLACKSTONE'S STATUTES

TITLES IN THE SERIES

Contract, Tort and Restitution Statutes
Public Law Statutes
Employment Law Statutes
Criminal Law Statutes
Evidence Statutes
Family Law Statutes
Property Law Statutes
Commercial and Consumer Law Statutes
English Legal System Statutes
EC Legislation
International Law Documents
Landlord and Tenant Statutes
Medical Law Statutes
Planning Law Statutes
Intellectual Property Statutes
Environmental Law Statutes
International Human Rights Documents